GUIDE TO
SUMMER
Programs

GUIDE TO
SUMMER programs

An objective, comparative reference source
for Residential summer programs

2014/2015
34th Edition

WINTERGREEN ORCHARD HOUSE
A Division of Carnegie Communications
2 LAN Drive, Suite 100
Westford, Massachusetts 01886
Tel: 978-692-9708   Fax: 978-692-2304
info@wintergreenorchardhouse.com
www.wintergreenorchardhouse.com

PRINTED IN THE UNITED STATES OF AMERICA

ISBN: 978-1-9360356-61-8
ISSN: 0072-8705

In Appreciation
We are indebted to the many people who helped develop and produce the *Guide to Summer Programs*, 2014/2015 edition. We appreciate the assistance and counsel of summer program personnel during the development of this resource. Special thanks go to editors Megan Gibbs, Meaghan Heffernan, and Leslie A. Weston for their hard work and devotion in the production of this book.

Joseph F. Moore
CEO & President

Colene Glennon
Project Manager

Meghan Dalesandro
Vice President, Operations

Cover art and design: Erik Ledder
Additional layout work: Matt Bradshaw

TABLE OF CONTENTS

MUSIC AND ARTS PROGRAMS
INDEX BY FOCUS

TRAVEL PROGRAMS
INDEX BY DESTINATION

SPECIAL-NEEDS PROGRAMS
INDEX BY CONDITION ACCEPTED

HOW TO READ THE PROGRAM DESCRIPTIONS

Listing arrangement varies by chapter; consult Table of Contents or chapter introductions for details.

1.   **CARNEGIE SUMMER PROGRAM**
Res — Boys Ages 14-18; Day — Coed 12-18

2. **Higganum, CT 06441. 1400 W. Shore Dr. Tel: 123-523-0945.**
Contact (Sept-May): 2 LAN Dr., Ste. 100, Westford, MA 01886.
Tel: 978-692-9708.
Year-round Toll-free: 800-123-4567, Fax: 978-692-2304.
www.carnegiecomm.com E-mail: info@carnegiecomm.com

3. **Jack Curtin, Lew Bryson & Mary Nestle, Dirs. Student Contact: Bryan Antonio, E-mail: bam@carnegiecomm.com.**

4. **Gr 7-PG (younger if qualified). Adm:** Selective. Admitted: 40%. Priority: URM. Prereqs: IQ 100. **Appl**—Fee $20. Due: Rolling. Transcript, rec.

5. **Enr: 50. Enr cap: 50.** Intl: 5%. Non-White 10%. **Fac 17.** Profs 12. Col/grad students 3. K-12 staff 1. Specialists 1. **Staff:** Admin 2. Res 5.

6. **Type of instruction:** Enrich SAT/ACT_Prep Study_Skills Undergrad. **Courses:** Eng Comp_Sci Hist Sci Dance Music Painting. **Avg class size:** 10. **Daily hours for:** Classes 4. Study 1. Rec 3. Homework. Tests. **Col Credit:** 3/crse, total 6.

7. **Conditions accepted:** ADD ED LD. **Therapy:** Psych Speech.

8. **Intl program focus:** Lang Culture. Home stays avail. **Travel:** Europe.

9. **Features:** Eng ESL Expository_Writing Govt Creative_Writing Media Aquatics Farm Riding Rock_Climb Sail Basketball Equestrian Soccer Tennis Track Watersports.

10. **Fees 2014: Res $9500 (+$650), 5 wks. Day $7950 (+$475), 5 wks.** Aid 2009 (Merit & Need): $57,500.

11. **Housing:** Dorms. Avg per room/unit: 2. **Swimming:** Lake Pool. Campus facilities avail.

12. **Est 1914.** Nonprofit. Roman Catholic. **Spons:** GABF Foundation. **Ses:** 1. **Wks/ses:** 5. Operates June-Aug. ACA.

13. CSP provides a selection of review and credit courses six days per week. Pupils, who attend four courses per class day, have options in the disciplines of English, math, science, foreign languages and computer science. Special programs are available in SAT preparation, study skills, American history, computer science and public speaking. A well-balanced recreational schedule supplements academics.

1. PROGRAM NAME and TYPE. Following the program name is participant gender and age range information.

2. CITY or TOWN, STATE, ZIP CODE, STREET ADDRESS, TELEPHONE, TTY (teletypewriter) and FAX NUMBERS, and WEB SITE and E-MAIL ADDRESSES. Program location and contact information is listed. In many cases, programs have both summer and winter coordinates. If so, summer information appears first, followed by winter data. Whenever possible, the winter address is prefaced parenthetically by the months for which it is in effect; if this information was not furnished by the program, "Winter" appears instead. If only one address, phone or fax number, or E-mail address is present, said contact point is valid year-round. Where available, toll-free phone numbers are listed; they begin with area codes 800, 866, 877 and 888. Be advised that, although toll-free numbers often work throughout the US and Canada, the valid calling area may vary. For this reason, a toll number is listed whenever possible.

3. DIRECTOR. The name of the program head, who often serves as a contact person, is followed by the administrator's job title. Many programs, particularly family-run camps, will list more than one director. When programs have provided a contact for applicants aside from the director, this person's name and E-mail address follow.

4. GRADE RANGE, ADMISSIONS and APPLICATIONS. When applicant grade level is considered, this information follows. Note that grade listings refer to the applicant's grade level in the coming fall. Programs that accept qualified students in lower grades are so indicated. An appraisal of the program's admissions selectivity follows, with programs categorized as "Very selective," "Selective," "Somewhat selective" or "FCFS [first-come, first-served]." Following are the percentage of applicants admitted, priority admissions policies (with "URM" used to designate enrollment priority for underrepresented minority groups) and prerequisites for admission. Listed next are application particulars: fee, deadline month (or "Rolling" if the application process continues until the session fills) and accompanying materials (e.g., transcript, recommendation).

5. ENROLLMENT, FACULTY and STAFF. The total number of participants enrolled in each session appears here, as does the capacity per session. When available, the percentages of international and non-White participants appear next. Teaching faculty (where appropriate) are listed as a total, then broken down into college professors, college/graduate school students, K-12 teachers and other specialists. Numbers of administrative staff, counselors, residential and special-needs staff follow.

6. TYPE OF INSTRUCTION and COURSES. For academic programs, the focus is indicated and primary courses are listed. If the program offers instruction for students with learning disabilities, either as its main focus or in addition to regular instruction, the services offered are detailed. Average class size and average daily hours devoted to classes, study and recreation may also appear. Programs featuring homework, tests, grades or some combination are so noted.

When credit is available, the number of college credits per course and the maximum available credits per session are shown; high school credit availability is also indicated, but the number of transferable credits granted depends upon the policies of the student's home school. Program accreditation by an outside institution is noted next.

7. CONDITIONS ACCEPTED and THERAPY. Listings of programs described in the chapters devoted to children with learning disabilities and other special needs indicate which conditions the program accommodates. (See Key to Conditions Accepted prior to the Special-Needs Programs chapter.) If the school or camp offers therapy, types of therapy are listed.

8. INTERNATIONAL PROGRAM FOCUS and TRAVEL. For programs that offer travel opportunities or study abroad, an emphasis on academics, language instruction or culture is noted, as is the availability of home stays. The program's destinations, both domestic and abroad, are listed next.

9. CENTRAL FOCUS and FEATURES. Specialized academic and music and arts programs have a focus listed. For all programs, offerings are listed alphabetically.

10. FEES. Residential and day fees are provided, with grouped fee figures (for example, $1500-5000) generally indicating the fee span from the shortest to the longest session. The program's estimate of extra expenses incurred by the average participant follows in parentheses. Corresponding length of session appears next. Note that a reference year for listed tuition figure(s) precedes this data. Free sessions may be available to all or to state residents only. Programs that furnish data concerning need- or merit-based financial aid will often include a reference to total aid money provided over the course of a summer.

11. HOUSING and AMENITIES. This section provides information on the lodging option(s) that a program provides. Areas for swimming are listed next. School programs that make all of their campus facilities available to enrolled students are so indicated.

12. ESTABLISHMENT and CALENDAR. The establishment date, religious affiliation, sponsor, number of sessions and weeks per session (often expressed as a range) are cited. The program's months of operation follow.

13. PARAGRAPH DESCRIPTION. Significant aspects of the programs are objectively summarized at the end of the listing. Descriptions, which are written by staff editors, are based upon questionnaires and supplementary literature submitted by program officials.

KEY TO ABBREVIATIONS

Commonly accepted abbreviations do not appear on this list. For further clarification, refer to How to Read the Program Descriptions.

ACA	American Camp Association
Accred	Accreditation
Actg	Acting
Adm	Admission(s)
Admin	Administration, Administrator
Adv	Advanced
Amer	American
Anat	Anatomy
Anthro	Anthropology
Appl	Applications
ASL	American Sign Language
Architect	Architecture
Avail	Available
Bio	Biology
Bus	Business
Canoe	Canoeing
Cap	Capacity
Climb	Climbing
Comp	Computer(s)
Coord	Coordinate
Couns	Counselors
Crse	Course
Dev	Development, Developmental
Ed, Educ	Education
Enr	Enrollment
Enrich	Enrichment
Environ	Environmental
ESL	English as a Second Language
FCFS	First-Come, First-Served
Fin	Finance
Geog	Geography
Gr	Grade(s)

Head	Head of Program, Headmaster, Headmistress
Impair	Impairments
Japan	Japanese
Journ	Journalism
JROTC	Junior Reserve Officers' Training Corps
Kayak	Kayaking
PG	Postgraduate
Philos	Philosophy
Phys	Physical
Pol	Political, Politics
Prgm	Program
Profs	Professors
PS	Preschool
Rec	Recreation, Recommendation
Rem	Remedial
Res	Residential, Residents
Sail	Sailing
SAT	Scholastic Aptitude Test
Sculpt	Sculpture
Sem	Semester
Ses	Session(s)
Sociol	Sociology
Speak	Speaking
Spons	Sponsor
Stud	Studies
Swim	Swimming
Tech	Technical, Technology
Theol	Theology
TOEFL	Test of English as a Foreign Language
Trng	Training
Tut	Tutorial, Tutoring
Undergrad	Undergraduates
URM	Underrepresented Minority

INDEXES BY FEATURE
FOR ACADEMIC CHAPTERS

Programs offering a family session are indicated by "FAM" at the end of the age range in the index, and programs granting high school credit [H], college credit [C] or both [CH] are denoted.

VERY SELECTIVE ADMISSIONS

SCIENCE RESEARCH PROGRAMS

PROGRAMS FREE FOR IN-STATE RESIDENTS ONLY

PROGRAMS FREE FOR ALL PARTICIPANTS

PROGRAMS OFFERING ADVANCED CURRICULA FOR MIDDLE SCHOOL STUDENTS

DEVELOPMENTAL READING

REMEDIAL INSTRUCTION

REMEDIAL INSTRUCTION (CONT.)

SAT PREPARATION

SAT PREPARATION (CONT.)

ACADEMIC PROGRAMS

Academic programs are arranged alphabetically by state and then alphabetically by program name within each state. An index beginning on page 15 lists programs by features, as shown in the Table of Contents.

Academic Programs

ARIZONA

FENSTER SCHOOL SUMMER SESSION
Res — Coed Ages 14-18

Tucson, AZ 85750. 8505 E Ocotillo Dr. Tel: 520-749-3340. Fax: 520-749-3349.
www.fensterschool.org E-mail: admissions@fensterschool.org
Tony Tsang, Admin.
Grades 9-12. **Adm:** FCFS. **Appl**—Due: Rolling.
Enr: 85. **Fac 10. Staff:** Admin 5.
Type of instruction: Dev_Read Enrich Rem_Eng Rem_Math Rem_Read Tut. **Courses:** Span Econ Eng ESL Govt Hist Sci Anat & Physiol. **Daily hours for:** Classes 6. **College credit.**
Features: Hiking Mtn_Biking Mtn_Trips Ropes_Crse Equestrian Golf Swim.
Fees 2013: Res $6000 (+$500), 6 wks. Day $4950 (+$500), 6 wks.
Housing: Dorms. **Swimming:** Pool.
Est 1944. Nonprofit. **Ses:** 1. **Wks/ses:** 6. Operates June-July.

Fenster offers makeup, remedial and advanced work in most academic areas: English, math, Spanish, science and social studies. Courses in developmental reading and English as a Second Language are also available, and capable underachievers may enroll. Fenster's daily structure includes regular monitoring of grades, attendance and homework. Recreation includes swimming and horseback riding, in addition to a variety of off-campus weekend activities.

SOUTHWESTERN SUMMER ADVENTURES
Res — Coed Ages 14-18

Rimrock, AZ. Tel: 520-567-4581. Fax: 520-567-5036.
c/o Southwestern Academy Admissions Office, 2800 Monterey Rd, San Marino, CA 91108. Tel: 626-799-5010. Fax: 626-799-0407.
www.southwesternacademy.edu E-mail: admissions@southwesternacademy.edu
Jack Leyden, Head.
Student contact: Joseph M. Blake, E-mail: jblake@southwesternacademy.edu.
Grades 9-12. **Adm:** FCFS. **Appl**—Fee $100. Due: Rolling.
Fac 5. Staff: Admin 3.
Type of instruction: Enrich Preview Rem_Eng Rem_Math Rem_Read Rev SAT/ACT_Prep. **Courses:** Eng ESL Hist Math Sci Crafts Creative_Writing Fashion Fine_Arts Media Music. **Daily hours for:** Classes 6. Study 2. Rec 3. **High school credit.**
Features: Conservation Exploration Fishing Hiking Mtn_Biking Ranch Riding Wilderness_Camp Basketball Soccer Softball Swim.
Fees 2013: Res $5500-13,920, 4-8½ wks.
Housing: Dorms. **Swimming:** Pool Stream.
Est 1963. Nonprofit. **Spons:** Southwestern Academy. **Ses:** 3. **Wks/ses:** 4-8½. Operates June-Aug.

The program offers high school credit for makeup or new courses in English, math, science and social studies, as well as remedial and enrichment work. Intensive, individualized morning classes are combined with informal, camp-style activities in the afternoon and evening. Various outdoor activities—as well as field trips to the Grand Canyon, Meteor Crater, the Petrified Forest and nearby Native American sites—round out the program.

UNIVERSITY OF ARIZONA
A SUMMER OF EXCELLENCE
Res — Coed Ages 16-18

Tucson, AZ 85716. PO Box 210006. Tel: 520-621-6901. Fax: 520-621-8655.
http://admissions.arizona.edu/counselors/newsletter/content/all/96
E-mail: soe@email.arizona.edu
Ashley McClung, Dir.
Grades 11-PG. Adm: Selective. Prereqs: GPA 3.5. Appl—Fee $30. Due: Rolling.
Transcript, 1-2 recs, essay.
Enr: 50-75.
Type of instruction: Adv Undergrad. Courses: Fr Ger Greek Ital Lat Russ Span Bus/Fin
Comp_Sci Econ Eng Math Psych Sci Philos Sociol Dance Music Studio_Art Theater.
Homework. Grades. College credit: 6.
Housing: Dorms.
Nonprofit. Ses: 2. Wks/ses: 5. Operates June-Aug.

High school students earn three to six units of transferable college credit during the five-week SOE session. Boys and girls take regular University of Arizona courses that are taught by university faculty. Pupils also learn strategies for a successful transition to college life, and peer advisors and counselors are on hand to offer support.

CALIFORNIA

ACADEMY BY THE SEA ACADEMIC PROGRAM
Res — Coed Ages 12-16

Carlsbad, CA 92008. 2605 Carlsbad Blvd. Tel: 760-434-7564. Fax: 760-729-1574.
www.abts.com   E-mail: summer@abts.com
Ken Weeks, Dir.
Grades 7-12. Adm: FCFS. Appl—Fee $500. Due: Rolling.
Enr cap: 180. Fac 35. Staff: Admin 13. Couns 18.
Type of instruction: Adv Enrich Preview Rem_Eng Rem_Math Rem_Read Rev Study_
Skills Tut. Courses: Span ESL Hist Math Sci Writing/Journ Acting Crafts Dance Drama
Filmmaking Music Studio_Art. Avg class size: 11. Daily hours for: Classes 4. Study 2.
Rec 4. High school credit: 2.
Features: Aquatics Kayak Riflery Baseball Basketball Cricket Field_Hockey Football
Lacrosse Rugby Soccer Softball Surfing Swim Tennis Ultimate_Frisbee Volleyball
Watersports Weight_Trng Ping-Pong.
Fees 2014: Res $4200.
Housing: Cabins Dorms. Avg per room/unit: 2. Swimming: Ocean Pool.
Est 1943. Nonprofit. Spons: Army and Navy Academy. Ses: 2. Wks/ses: 4-5. Operates
June-July.

Balancing academics and recreation, ABTS helps students prepare for the upcoming school year and for future educational endeavors. Pupils select four courses and learn in a small-class setting that enables faculty to address different learning styles and provide individual attention. Students choose either a four-week enrichment option or a five-week credit-bearing program that offers remediation only. Course work includes offerings in the traditional disciplines, ESL and various elective areas. A mandatory evening study hall operates five nights weekly. Afternoon activities and weekend excursions round out the program.

EDUCATION PROGRAM FOR GIFTED YOUTH
SUMMER INSTITUTES
Res — Coed Ages 11-17

Stanford, CA 94305. Stanford Univ, 220 Panama St. Fax: 866-835-3312.
https://summerinstitutes.stanford.edu   E-mail: summerinstitutes@stanford.edu
Grades 7-12. Adm: Selective. **Appl**—Fee $40. Due: Rolling. Transcript, teacher rec, standardized test results.
Type of instruction: Enrich. **Courses:** Bus/Fin Comp_Sci Econ Engineering Expository_Writing Law Math Sci Humanities Philos Robotics Creative_Writing Playwriting.
Fees 2014: Res $3880-7250, 2-4 wks.
Housing: Dorms. Campus facilities avail.
Nonprofit. **Spons:** Stanford University. **Ses:** 6. **Wks/ses:** 2-3. Operates June-Aug.

Held at Stanford University, these residential programs serve motivated and academically talented middle school and high school pupils. Students enroll in intensive courses, taught by Stanford professors, on topics that are not typically available at the participant's grade level. Children in the Middle School Program (entering grades 7 and 8) study several related topics within a single subject area while getting an early exposure to college life. The more focused High School Program involves the intensive study of a single course.

EDUCATION UNLIMITED SUMMER FOCUS AT BERKELEY
Res — Coed Ages 16-18

Berkeley, CA. Univ of California.
Contact (Year-round): 1700 Shattuck Ave, Ste 305, Berkeley, CA 94709. Tel: 510-548-6612. Fax: 510-548-0212.
www.educationunlimited.com   E-mail: campinfo@educationunlimited.com
Matthew Fraser, Exec Dir.
Grades 11-12. Adm: Selective. Prereqs: GPA 3.0. **Appl**—Fee $0. Due: Rolling. Rec.
Enr cap: 15-35. **Fac 3. Staff:** Admin 8. Couns 2.
Type of instruction: Adv Enrich SAT/ACT_Prep Study_Skills Tut. **Courses:** Archaeol Astron Environ_Sci Expository_Writing Geol Govt Hist Pol_Sci Speech Writing/Journ Creative_Writing Fine_Arts Music. **Avg class size:** 30. **Daily hours for:** Classes 3. Study 4. Rec 5. **College credit:** 3-4/crse, total 4.
Features: Climbing_Wall Kayak Mtn_Trips White-water_Raft Badminton Baseball Basketball Martial_Arts Swim Tennis Volleyball Weight_Trng.
Fees 2013: Res $10,800-11,680, 6 wks. Aid avail.
Housing: Dorms. **Swimming:** Ocean Pool.
Est 1998. Inc. **Ses:** 4. **Wks/ses:** 6. Operates July-Aug.

Summer Focus enables rising high school juniors and seniors to take UC-Berkeley courses for university credit, while also previewing college life. Pupils attend class with continuing Berkeley students, visitors from other schools and countries, and members of the Bay Area community. In addition to taking core courses, program participants receive tutoring most evenings and have exclusive access to electives taught by Education Unlimited faculty. The program includes weekend excursions to San Francisco, Santa Cruz, nearby amusement parks, theatrical and musical productions, and professional baseball games.

POMONA COLLEGE
ACADEMY FOR YOUTH SUCCESS
Res — Coed Ages 15-18

Claremont, CA 91711. Office of Community & Multicultural Prgms, 170 E 6th St, Ste 231. Tel: 909-607-1810.
www.pomona.edu/administration/draper-center/pays/index.aspx
E-mail: pays@pomona.edu
Maria Tucker, Dir.

Grades 10-12. Adm: Selective. Priority: Low-income. URM. **Appl**—Fee $0. Transcript, 2 recs, 2 essays.
Enr: 90. **Enr cap:** 90.
Type of instruction: Enrich. **Courses:** Japan Econ Math Sci. **Avg class size:** 15.
Features: Basketball Soccer.
Fees 2014: Free. Res 4 wks.
Housing: Dorms.
Nonprofit. **Ses:** 1. **Wks/ses:** 4.

This intensive academic program serves high schoolers from groups that are traditionally underrepresented in higher education, particularly those who are African-American or Latino or who come from low-income families. Students enroll in two faculty-taught core courses, math/problem solving and critical inquiry, as well as in two electives that are taught by Pomona College undergraduates. Rising seniors may apply for the program only if they attended PAYS during a previous summer. Boys and girls return home each weekend.

ROBERT LOUIS STEVENSON SCHOOL SUMMER CAMP
Res and Day — Coed Ages 9-15

Pebble Beach, CA 93953. 3152 Forest Lake Rd. Tel: 831-625-8349. **Fax:** 831-625-5208.
www.stevensonschool.org/summer   E-mail: summercamp@stevensonschool.org
Tony Klevan, Dir. **Student contact:** Katie Klevan.
Grades 4-10. Adm: FCFS. Admitted: 100%. **Appl**—Fee $0. Due: May.
Enr: 144. **Enr cap:** 150. Intl: 30%. Non-White: 10%. **Fac 6.** K-12 staff 4. Specialists 2.
Staff: Admin 6. Couns 24.
Type of instruction: Enrich Preview Rev Study_Skills. **Courses:** Span Eng Marine_Bio/Stud Math Acting Ceramics Creative_Writing Dance Filmmaking Music Photog Studio_Art. **Avg class size:** 9. **Daily hours for:** Classes 3. Rec 7.
Features: Aquatics Archery Hiking Mtn_Biking Mtn_Trips Wilderness_Camp Baseball Basketball Fencing Golf In-line_Skating Lacrosse Soccer Softball Swim Tennis Ultimate_Frisbee Volleyball Watersports Weight_Trng.
Fees 2013: Res $5000, 5 wks. Day $2400, 5 wks. Aid 2009 (Merit & Need): $120,000.
Housing: Dorms. Avg per room/unit: 2. **Swimming:** Pool. Campus facilities avail.
Est 1972. Nonprofit. **Ses:** 1. **Wks/ses:** 5. Operates June-Aug.

Stevenson offers workshops in language skills, the sciences, math and the arts. Pupils attend morning workshops, then have time for socializing and relaxation after lunch. Each day concludes with afternoon sports. Resident campers participate in various evening activities and embark on weekend trips in the area.

ST. CATHERINE'S ACADEMY
SUMMER ENRICHMENT PROGRAM
Res and Day — Boys Ages 5-14

Anaheim, CA 92805. 215 N Harbor Blvd. Tel: 714-772-1363. **Fax:** 714-772-3004.
www.stcatherinesacademy.org/summer
E-mail: admissions@stcatherinesacademy.org
Sr. Johnellen Turner, OP, Prin. **Student contact:** Graciela Salvador.
Grades K-8. Adm: FCFS. **Appl**—Fee $50. Due: Rolling. Transcript, standardized tests, rec.
Enr: 120. **Fac 10. Staff:** Admin 3. Couns 10.
Type of instruction: Adv Preview Rem_Eng Rem_Math Rem_Read Rev Study_Skills Tut. **Courses:** Environ_Sci ESL Expository_Writing Math Sci Creative_Writing Drawing Fine_Arts Music. **Avg class size:** 8. **Daily hours for:** Classes 4.
Features: Basketball Football Soccer Swim Volleyball.
Fees 2013: Res $1400-3300, 4 wks. Day $700-1250, 4 wks.
Housing: Dorms. **Swimming:** Pool.

Nonprofit. Roman Catholic. **Ses:** 1. **Wks/ses:** 4. Operates July.

St. Catherine's summer program includes new and review work in English, math, social studies and science. ESL and study skills courses are available, as are tutoring sessions. Students may register for beginning or intermediate instrumental music training. Recreational activities include sports and weekend trips.

SOUTHWESTERN SUMMER ADVENTURES
Res and Day — Coed Ages 12-18

San Marino, CA 91108. c/o Southwestern Academy, 2800 Monterey Rd. Tel: 626-799-5010. Fax: 626-799-0407.
www.southwesternacademy.edu/academics/summer.html
E-mail: admissions@southwesternacademy.edu
Kenneth R. Veronda, Head. Student contact: Maia Moore.
Grades 6-12. **Adm:** Selective. **Appl**—Fee $100. Due: Rolling. Transcript.
Enr: 39. **Enr cap:** 160. Intl: 90%. Non-White: 8%. **Fac 11.** K-12 staff 11. **Staff:** Admin 15. Res 6.
Type of instruction: Adv Enrich Rem_Eng Rem_Math Rev ESL/TOEFL_Prep SAT/ACT_Prep. **Courses:** Span ESL Hist Marine_Bio/Stud Math Sci Creative_Writing Filmmaking Media. **Avg class size:** 5. **Daily hours for:** Classes 6. Study 3. Rec 4. Homework. Tests. Grades. **High school credit.**
Features: Exploration Mtn_Biking Baseball Basketball Soccer Swim Tennis Volleyball Ping-Pong.
Fees 2013: Res $5500-19,250 (+$500), 4-14 wks. **Day** $2640-9240, 4-14 wks. Aid 2010 (Need): $138,000.
Housing: Dorms Houses. **Swimming:** Ocean Pool. Campus facilities avail.
Est 1924. Nonprofit. **Spons:** Southwestern Academy. **Ses:** 3. **Wks/ses:** 4-14. Operates June-Sept.

Summer Adventures features morning academic class work in all subjects for enrichment, credit or review. English as a Second Language programming is available for international students seeking to prepare for American schools and colleges. Programs run for four or 14 weeks, depending upon the student's needs. On afternoons and weekends, boys and girls go on excursions to Los Angeles-area cultural sites, landmarks and beaches.

STANFORD UNIVERSITY
HIGH SCHOOL SUMMER COLLEGE
Res and Day — Coed Ages 16-19

Stanford, CA 94305. Summer Session Office, 482 Galvez St. Tel: 650-723-3109. Fax: 650-725-6080.
https://summercollege.stanford.edu   E-mail: summercollege@stanford.edu
Grades 12-PG (younger if qualified). **Adm:** Selective. **Appl**—Fee $50. Due: Rolling. Transcript, rec, standardized test scores, essay.
Type of instruction: Adv Tut Undergrad. **Courses:** Arabic Chin Fr Ger Japan Lat Span Astron Bus/Fin Col_Prep Comp_Sci Econ Eng Engineering Expository_Writing Hist Math Psych Relig_Stud Sci Anthro Genetics Philos Physiol Sociol Stats Drama Film Media Music Painting Photog Studio_Art. **College credit.**
Features: Yoga Basketball Golf Swim Tennis Ultimate_Frisbee.
Fees 2014: Res $11,599-12,583 (+$1019), 8 wks. **Day** $8859. Aid (Need).
Housing: Dorms. **Swimming:** Pool. Campus facilities avail.
Nonprofit. **Ses:** 1. **Wks/ses:** 8. Operates June-Aug.

This precollege program allows accomplished boys and girls who have completed grades 11 or 12 (or, in the case of particularly mature students, grade 10) to sample college life while taking undergraduate courses and earning Stanford University credit. Residential pupils register for at least eight units of course work during the eight-week session, commuters at least three units. In addition to the varied selection of college courses, boys and girls may participate in voluntary classes and seminars designed to prepare them for a successful transition to college; options address the college admission process, study skills and time management, and expository writing, among others. Field trips, intramural athletics, outreach projects, coastal excursions and informal discussions with Stanford faculty complement class work.

SUMMER DISCOVERY
Res — Coed Ages 14-18

Santa Barbara, CA. Univ of California-Santa Barbara.
Contact (Year-round): 1326 Old Northern Blvd, Roslyn, NY 11576. Tel: 516-621-3939. Fax: 516-625-3438.
www.summerdiscovery.com   E-mail: discovery@summerdiscovery.com
Bob Musiker, Exec Dir.
Grades 9-12. **Adm:** Somewhat_selective. **Appl**—Fee $95. **Due:** Rolling.
Enr cap: 200.
Type of instruction: Enrich SAT/ACT_Prep Study_Skills Undergrad. **Courses:** Archaeol Bus/Fin Debate ESL Expository_Writing Govt Speech Writing/Journ Crafts Creative_Writing Dance Filmmaking Fine_Arts Music Photog Theater. Homework. Tests. **College credit:** 8.
Features: Adventure_Travel Aquatics Canoe Community_Serv Hiking Kayak Mountaineering White-water_Raft Basketball Golf Lacrosse Soccer Swim Tennis Volleyball Watersports.
Fees 2014: Res $6899-8399 (+$75), 4-6 wks. Aid (Need).
Housing: Dorms. **Swimming:** Ocean Pool. Campus facilities avail.
Inc. **Ses:** 2. **Wks/ses:** 4-6. Operates June-July.

See program description under Los Angeles, CA.

SUMMER DISCOVERY
Res — Coed Ages 14-18

Los Angeles, CA. Univ of California-Los Angeles.
Contact (Year-round): 1326 Old Northern Blvd, Roslyn, NY 11576. Tel: 516-621-3939. Fax: 516-625-3438.
www.summerdiscovery.com   E-mail: discovery@summerdiscovery.com
Bob Musiker, Exec Dir.
Grades 9-12. **Adm:** FCFS. **Appl**—**Due:** Rolling.
Enr cap: 525.
Type of instruction: Enrich SAT/ACT_Prep Study_Skills. **Courses:** Archaeol Bus/Fin Debate ESL Expository_Writing Govt Speech Writing/Journ Crafts Creative_Writing Dance Filmmaking Fine_Arts Music Photog Theater. Tests. **College credit:** 8.
Features: Adventure_Travel Aquatics Canoe Community_Serv Hiking Kayak Mountaineering White-water_Raft Basketball Golf Lacrosse Soccer Swim Tennis Volleyball Watersports.
Fees 2014: Res $5999-8999, 3-6 wks.
Housing: Dorms. **Swimming:** Pool. Campus facilities avail.
Inc. **Ses:** 3. **Wks/ses:** 3-6. Operates June-Aug.

Precollege programs for high school students are held on university campuses throughout the US and abroad. Boys and girls take a college-credit course and an enrichment course during their stay. Other aspects of the program include community service, excursions, travel, sports and recreational activities. See other Summer Discovery listings under Santa Barbara; San Diego; Ann Arbor, MI; Washington, DC; Florence, Italy; and Valencia, Spain.

THOMAS AQUINAS COLLEGE
SUMMER GREAT BOOKS PROGRAM
Res — Coed Ages 17-18

Santa Paula, CA 93060. 10000 N Ojai Rd. Tel: 805-525-4417, 800-634-9797. Fax: 805-525-9342.
www.thomasaquinas.edu/admission/high-school-summer-program
E-mail: summerprogram@thomasaquinas.edu
Grades 12-PG. Adm: Selective. **Appl**—Fee $0. Due: Rolling. Transcript, rec, essay.
Type of instruction: Enrich. **Courses:** Eng Philos.
Fees 2014: Res $975, 2 wks.
Housing: Dorms.
Est 1997. Nonprofit. Roman Catholic. **Ses: 1. Wks/ses: 2.** Operates July-Aug.

Exceptionally talented students from around the country spend two weeks at Thomas Aquinas College reading and discussing works from such figures as Plato, Euclid, Sophocles, Pascal, Boethius and St. Thomas Aquinas with college faculty. During the first week of the program, boys and girls ponder questions of moral, political and religious authority, then consider the relationship between faith and reason. The second and final week begins with a Shakespearean examination of the imperfection and corruption of man, progresses to a discussion of Euclidean geometry and concludes with readings designed to spur further consideration of key issues of the session. Organized recreation and off-campus excursions balance academics.

UNIVERSITY OF CALIFORNIA-SAN DIEGO
ACADEMIC CONNECTIONS
Res and Day — Coed Ages 14-18

La Jolla, CA 92093. MC 0176-S, 9500 Gilman Dr. Tel: 858-534-0804. Fax: 858-534-7385.
www.academicconnections.ucsd.edu   E-mail: academicconnections@ucsd.edu
Edward Abeyta, Dir. Student contact: Robin Wittman, E-mail: rwittman@ucsd.edu.
Grades 10-12 (younger if qualified). Adm: Selective. Admitted: 80%. Prereqs: GPA 3.3.
Appl—Fee $100. Due: June. Transcript, rec.
Enr: 309. **Enr cap:** 350. Intl: 5%. Non-White: 50%. **Fac 30.** Col/grad students 30. **Staff:** Admin 4. Res 25.
Type of instruction: Adv SAT/ACT_Prep Undergrad. **Courses:** Astron Comp_Sci Econ Engineering Environ_Sci Law Marine_Bio/Stud Oceanog Sci Writing/Journ Crafts Filmmaking Theater. **Avg class size:** 20. **Daily hours for:** Classes 5. Study 2. Rec 4. Homework. Tests. Grades. **High school & college credit:** 6/crse, total 6.
Travel: HI.
Features: Aquatics Exploration Hiking Rock_Climb Swim.
Fees 2014: Res $3700, 1-3 wks. Day $2700, 3 wks.
Housing: Dorms. **Swimming:** Ocean Pool.
Est 2001. Nonprofit. **Ses: 3. Wks/ses:** 1-3. Operates July-Aug.

Academic Connections' curriculum consists of college-level course work in the physical and social sciences, engineering, and the arts and humanities. UCSD doctoral candidates generally teach the courses, which meet in five-hour blocks every weekday. Small classes (limited to 22 students each) emphasize active learning. An optional SAT test-taking workshop operates two nights per week, and students may meet with campus admissions representatives one evening a week. Offered for a slightly higher cost than the traditional three-week program, a weeklong, strictly residential session in Hawaii focuses on global environmental leadership and sustainability.

COLORADO

HIGH MOUNTAIN INSTITUTE SUMMER TERM
Res — Coed Ages 16-17

Leadville, CO 80461. 531 Country Rd 5A. Tel: 719-486-8200, 888-464-9991. Fax: 719-486-8201.
www.hminet.org/semester-and-summer-term/about
E-mail: admissions@hminet.org
Christina Reiff, Dir.
Grades 11-12. Adm: Selective. Appl—Fee $35. Due: Feb. Transcript, essays, 2 recs.
Enr: 17. Enr cap: 24. Fac 3.
Courses: Environ_Sci Leadership Humanities. Avg class size: 10. Daily hours for: Classes 4½. High school credit.
Features: Climbing_Wall Exploration Fishing Outdoor_Ed Rock_Climb White-water_Raft Wilderness_Camp.
Fees 2013: Res $8950, 6 wks. Aid 2011 (Need): $30,000.
Housing: Cabins. Avg per room/unit: 10.
Est 2011. Nonprofit. Ses: 1. Wks/ses: 6. Operates June-Aug.

Rising high school juniors and seniors engage in a variety of academic, wilderness and community pursuits during a six-week session that represents a condensed version of HMI Semester. Students supplement a compulsory wilderness and leadership course with either an environmental science class or a multidisciplinary humanities offering that examines the manner in which Americans have viewed and interacted with the natural world. Seven- and nine-day backcountry expeditions develop wilderness skills and employ the mountains as an extended classroom.

SUMMER STUDY IN COLORADO
Res — Coed Ages 15-18

Boulder, CO. Univ of Colorado.
Contact (Year-round): 900 Walt Whitman Rd, Melville, NY 11747. Tel: 631-424-1000, 800-666-2556. Fax: 631-424-0567.
www.summerstudy.com   E-mail: info@summerstudy.com
William Cooperman, Exec Dir.
Grades 9-11. Adm: Selective. Appl—Fee $75. Due: Rolling. Transcript, standardized test scores.
Enr: 250. Fac 25. Staff: Admin 7. Couns 20.
Type of instruction: Adv Enrich Preview Rev ESL/TOEFL_Prep SAT/ACT_Prep Study_Skills Tut. Courses: Fr Architect Astron Bus/Fin Debate Econ Expository_Writing Hist Law Math Pol_Sci Relig_Stud Anthro Mythology Philos Sociol Women's_Stud Art Creative_Writing Dance Filmmaking Music Painting Photog Theater Pottery. Daily hours for: Classes 2½. Study 1. Rec 4. College credit: 3.
Features: Adventure_Travel Aquatics Bicycle_Tours Boating Caving Climbing_Wall Community_Serv Exploration Hiking Mountaineering Mtn_Biking Mtn_Trips Riding Rock_Climb White-water_Raft Wilderness_Camp Yoga Basketball Cross-country Football Ice_Hockey Lacrosse Roller_Hockey Soccer Softball Swim Tennis Track Ultimate_Frisbee Volleyball Watersports Weight_Trng Wrestling.
Fees 2013: Res $2899-9299, 2-5 wks. Aid (Need).
Housing: Dorms. Swimming: Pool.
Inc. Spons: Summer Study Programs. Ses: 2. Wks/ses: 3-5. Operates July-Aug.

High schoolers who have completed at least grade 10 and recent graduates earn two or three college credits over five weeks while taking freshman-level courses and previewing college life. Each student takes one or two courses for credit and one for enrichment. Pupils who have completed grades 9-11 may enroll in a three-week, noncredit enrichment session. The program's location lends itself to such outdoor pursuits as rock climbing, hiking, biking and white-water rafting; sports clinics and community service opportunities are among Summer Study's other activities. Weekends provide opportunities for travel to Vail, Breckenridge, Colorado Springs and Rocky Mountain National Park.

UNITED STATES AIR FORCE ACADEMY
SUMMER SEMINAR
Res — Coed Ages 17-18

USAF Academy, CO 80840. 2304 Cadet Dr, Ste 200. Tel: 719-333-2236.
www.academyadmissions.com E-mail: usafa_summer_seminar@usafa.edu
Grade 12. Adm: Selective. Prereqs: GPA 2.5. **Appl**—Due: Jan. Transcript, standardized test scores, resume.
Type of instruction: Enrich.
Features: Milit_Trng.
Fees 2014: Res $300, 1 wk.
Housing: Dorms. Campus facilities avail.
Nonprofit. **Ses: 2. Wks/ses: 1.**

Rising high school seniors enroll in this competitive program to sample college life at this service academy. Students choose from more than 30 course options in an array of subject areas.

CONNECTICUT

ACCESS CHESHIRE AT THE ACADEMY
Res and Day — Coed Ages 12-16

Cheshire, CT 06410. 10 Main St. Tel: 203-272-5396. Fax: 203-250-7209.
www.cheshireacademy.org/summer E-mail: summer@cheshireacademy.org
Rich Ferraro, Dir.
Grades 7-12. Adm: Selective. Admitted: 85%. **Appl**—Fee $65. Due: Rolling. Transcript, rec.
Enr: 100. Enr cap: 100. Intl: 33%. Non-White: 35%.
Type of instruction: Adv Enrich Rem_Eng Rem_Math Rem_Read ESL/TOEFL_Prep SAT/ACT_Prep. **Courses:** Chin Span Architect Econ Eng ESL Forensic_Sci Sci Anat & Physiol Ceramics Film Media Photog. **Avg class size:** 8. **Daily hours for:** Classes 4. Study 3. Rec 3. Homework. Tests. Grades.
Features: Canoe Caving Climbing_Wall Community_Serv Conservation Exploration Fishing Hiking Kayak Mtn_Biking Mtn_Trips Outdoor_Ed Rappelling Rock_Climb Ropes_Crse White-water_Raft Wilderness_Camp Wilderness_Canoe Yoga Basketball Football Golf Swim.
Fees 2012: Res $5295 (+$500), 4 wks. Day $3995 (+$500), 4 wks. Aid 2011 (Merit & Need): $30,000.
Housing: Dorms. Avg per room/unit: 2. **Swimming:** Ocean Pool. Campus facilities avail.
Est 2010. Nonprofit. **Spons:** Cheshire Academy. **Ses: 1. Wks/ses: 4.** Operates July-Aug.

Designed for students entering grades 7-12, ACCESS CHESHIRE provides a comprehensive summer experience of academic enrichment and exciting extracurricular activities.

CHOATE ROSEMARY HALL
ACADEMIC ENRICHMENT PROGRAM
Res and Day — Coed Ages 12-18

Wallingford, CT 06492. 333 Christian St. Tel: 203-697-2365. Fax: 203-697-2519.
www.choate.edu/summerprograms E-mail: choatesummer@choate.edu

Eera Sharma, Dir.
Grades 7-12. Adm: Selective. Admitted: 90%. **Appl**—Fee $60. Due: Rolling. Transcript, 3 recs.
Enr: 250. Intl: 25%. Non-White: 30%.
Type of instruction: Enrich SAT/ACT_Prep Study_Skills. **Courses:** Chin Fr Span Architect Bus/Fin Ecol Econ Expository_Writing Hist Math Pol_Sci Psych Public_Speak Sci Writing/Journ Ethics Forensic_Sci Robotics Dance Drama Fine_Arts Music. **Avg class size:** 12. **Daily hours for:** Classes 5½. Study 2. Rec 2. Homework. Tests. **High school credit.**
Features: Baseball Basketball Football Swim Volleyball.
Fees 2011: Res $6700 (+$500), 5 wks. Day $1040-2180/crse (+$500), 5 wks. Aid 2011 (Need): $300,000.
Housing: Dorms. Avg per room/unit: 2. **Swimming:** Pool. Campus facilities avail.
Est 1916. Nonprofit. **Ses:** 1. **Wks/ses:** 5. Operates June-July.

The Academic Enrichment Program allows students to develop skills and explore new subjects beyond the normal high school curriculum. Students select courses from offerings in the arts, English, history and social sciences, languages, math, science and interdisciplinary courses. Classes meet Monday through Saturday. Students engage in sports on weekday afternoons, with evening hours devoted to study. Choate schedules recreational trips on Wednesday and Saturday afternoons.

THE LOOMIS CHAFFEE SUMMER PROGRAM
Res and Day — Coed Ages 12-17

Windsor, CT 06095. 4 Batchelder Rd. Tel: 860-687-6355. Fax: 860-687-6859.
www.loomischaffee.org/summerprogram   E-mail: summer_program@loomis.org
Jeffrey Scanlon, Dir.
Grades 7-12. Adm: Selective. **Appl**—Fee $60. Due: Rolling. Transcript, 3 recs, essay, personal statement.
Enr cap: 100. **Fac** 15. Prof 1. K-12 staff 13. Specialists 1. **Staff:** Admin 2. Couns 20.
Type of instruction: Enrich SAT/ACT_Prep. **Courses:** Chin Environ_Sci Expository_ Writing Hist Math Public_Speak Sci Robotics Creative_Writing Dance Drawing Painting Photog Studio_Art Theater Pottery. **Avg class size:** 10. **Daily hours for:** Classes 4. Study 2. Rec 2. Homework. **High school credit.**
Features: Aquatics Canoe Climbing_Wall Community_Serv Exploration Hiking Kayak Outdoor_Ed Ropes_Crse White-water_Raft Yoga Aerobics Basketball Soccer Swim Volleyball Weight_Trng.
Fees 2014: Res $6950 (+$350), 5 wks. Day $4950, 5 wks. Aid (Need).
Housing: Dorms. Avg per room/unit: 2. **Swimming:** Pool. Campus facilities avail.
Est 2011. Inc. **Ses:** 1. **Wks/ses:** 5. Operates June-Aug.

The cornerstone of the summer program at Loomis Chaffee is its emphasis on writing. Middle and upper school students choose from writing courses covering poetry, drama, fiction, nonfiction and public speaking. General studies course offerings are drawn from the areas of the humanities, mathematics, and the arts and sciences. SSAT and SAT exam preparation is also available.

MARIANAPOLIS PREPARATORY SCHOOL
ONLINE SUMMER SESSION
Res and Day — Coed Ages 14-18

Thompson, CT 06277. 26 Chase Rd, PO Box 304. Tel: 860-923-9565. Fax: 860-923-3730.
www.marianapolis.org/page.cfm?p=401   E-mail: esembor@marianapolis.org
Ed Sembor, Dir.
Grades 9-PG. Adm: Selective. **Appl**—Fee $0. Due: Mar.

Type of instruction: Enrich SAT/ACT_Prep. **Courses:** Chin Comp_Sci Environ_Sci ESL Hist Marine_Bio/Stud Math Sci Film Photog Studio_Art. Homework. Tests. Grades. **Fees 2009:** Res $6000, 6 wks. Day $2000, 6 wks. **Housing:** Dorms. Campus facilities avail. Nonprofit. **Ses:** 1. **Wks/ses:** 6. Operates June-July.

Marianapolis enables boys and girls to choose two or three enrichment courses from a selection of offerings drawn from every major discipline.

THE MARVELWOOD SCHOOL SUMMER PROGRAMS
Res and Day — Coed Ages 13-17

Kent, CT 06757. 476 Skiff Mountain Rd, PO Box 3001. Tel: 860-927-0047. Fax: 860-927-0021.
www.marvelwood.org   E-mail: kane.szydolowski@marvelwood.org
Kane Szydlowski, Dir.
Grades 8-11. Adm: Selective. **Appl**—Fee $50. Due: Rolling. Transcript, 3 recs.
Enr: 50. Enr cap: 60. Fac 13.
Type of instruction: Dev_Read Enrich Preview Rem_Eng Rem_Math Rev SAT/ACT_Prep Study_Skills. **Courses:** Eng ESL Hist Math Sci Creative_Writing Drama Music Photog Studio_Art. **Avg class size:** 6. **Daily hours for:** Classes 4. Study 3. Rec 2. **High school credit.**
Features: Canoe Hiking Leadership Mtn_Biking Riding Rock_Climb Sail Woodcraft Basketball Swim Tennis.
Fees 2011: Res $2700-5600 (+$600), 2-4 wks. Day $2000 (+$300), 4 wks.
Housing: Dorms. **Swimming:** Pond.
Est 1964. Nonprofit. **Ses:** 2. **Wks/ses:** 2-4. Operates July-Aug.

Marvelwood's four-week Academic and Leadership Program features core academic enrichment classes, electives and study skills instruction, supplemented by afternoon leadership seminars and art activities. Students are assigned an advisor and attend structured study hall sessions six days each week. Afternoon leadership activities make use of nearby natural resources and include whitewater canoeing, rock climbing and team-building challenges. The two-week English Language Learners' Program immerses international students in American culture and beginning or intermediate English.

THE RECTORY SCHOOL
SUMMER@RECTORY
Res and Day — Coed Ages 10-14

Pomfret, CT 06258. 528 Pomfret St, PO Box 68. Tel: 860-963-6740. Fax: 860-963-2355.
www.rectoryschool.org   E-mail: summer@rectoryschool.org
Glenn Ames, Hdmstr.
Grades 5-9. Adm: FCFS. **Appl**—Fee $0. Due: Rolling.
Enr: 85. Fac 15. Staff: Admin 3.
Type of instruction: Dev_Read Enrich Preview Rem_Eng Rem_Math Rem_Read Rev Study_Skills Tut. **LD Services:** Acad_Instruction Tut. **Courses:** Lat Span Environ_Sci ESL Expository_Writing Leadership Math SSAT_Prep Drama Media Music Photog. **Avg class size:** 8. **Daily hours for:** Classes 4. Study 1. Rec 3.
Conditions accepted: Dx LD.
Features: Canoe Chess Exploration Hiking Ropes_Crse Baseball Basketball Cross-country Golf Lacrosse Soccer Softball Swim Tennis Weight_Trng.
Fees 2011: Res $5725 (+$600), 4 wks. Day $1295 (+$300), 4 wks. Aid (Need).
Housing: Dorms. **Swimming:** Ocean Pool. Campus facilities avail.
Est 1950. Nonprofit. Episcopal. **Ses:** 1. **Wks/ses:** 4. Operates June-July.

Rectory's academic program stresses English, developmental and remedial reading, math and study skills. Each student receives tutoring for one period per day to address study skills or problems in a specific academic area. A supervised recreational program includes clubs, swimming and instructional sports clinics.

RUMSEY HALL SCHOOL SUMMER SESSION
Res and Day — Coed Ages 8-15

Washington Depot, CT 06794. 201 Romford Rd. Tel: 860-868-0535. Fax: 860-868-7907.
www.rumseyhall.org   E-mail: admiss@rumseyhall.org
Doug Kolpak, Dir.
Grades 3-9. Adm: FCFS. **Appl**—Fee $50-100. Due: Rolling. Transcript, standardized test scores, 1-2 recs.
Enr: 65. **Enr cap:** 65. **Fac 12. Staff:** Admin 1. Couns 2.
Type of instruction: Dev_Read Enrich Rev Study_Skills. **Courses:** Computers ESL Math Creative_Writing. **Avg class size:** 8. **Daily hours for:** Classes 4. Study 1. Rec 4.
Features: Canoe Fishing Hiking Riding Baseball Basketball Lacrosse Soccer Swim Tennis.
Fees 2014: Res $7385 (+$750), 5 wks. Day $1750-2640 (+$200), 5 wks. Aid (Need).
Housing: Dorms. Avg per room/unit: 2. **Swimming:** Lake. Campus facilities avail.
Est 1966. Nonprofit. **Ses:** 1. **Wks/ses:** 5. Operates June-Aug.

Rumsey Hall's summer program provides intensive academic review in English, mathematics, study skills and computers. Individual tutoring can be arranged, and instruction by trained reading specialists is available. Recreational and enrichment options include swimming, sports, daily hiking and horseback riding, and occasional off-campus trips.

SAINT THOMAS MORE SCHOOL SUMMER ACADEMIC CAMP
Res and Day — Boys Ages 12-17

Oakdale, CT 06370. 45 Cottage Rd. Tel: 860-823-3861. Fax: 860-823-3863.
www.stmct.org/pages/St_Thomas_More_Oakdale/Admission/Summer_Program
E-mail: triordan@stmct.org
Todd Holt, Dir.
Grades 7-12. Adm: FCFS. **Appl**—Fee $50. Due: Rolling.
Enr cap: 90.
Type of instruction: Dev_Read Enrich Rem_Eng Rem_Math Rem_Read Rev ESL/TOEFL_Prep SAT/ACT_Prep Study_Skills. **Courses:** Span Comp_Sci Eng ESL Hist Math Sci Crafts Creative_Writing. **Avg class size:** 5. **Daily hours for:** Classes 4. Study 2. Rec 4. **High school credit:** 3.
Features: Boating Canoe Fishing Kayak Sail Baseball Basketball Cross-country Lacrosse Soccer Softball Swim Tennis Volleyball Watersports.
Fees 2012: Res $5495 (+$50-75), 5 wks. Day $2748 (+$50-75), 5 wks.
Housing: Dorms. **Swimming:** Lake. Campus facilities avail.
Est 1970. Nonprofit. Roman Catholic. **Ses:** 1. **Wks/ses:** 5. Operates July-Aug.

In addition to remedial and developmental reading, Saint Thomas More offers courses for makeup credit, enrichment or preview in various disciplines. A comprehensive English as a Second Language curriculum is available for international students. Recreational activities include a full waterfront program, water-skiing, sports and off-campus trips.

THE SUMMER ACADEMY AT SUFFIELD
Res and Day — Coed Ages 12-18

Suffield, CT 06078. 185 N Main St, PO Box 999. Tel: 860-386-4444. Fax: 860-668-2966.
www.suffieldacademy.org   E-mail: tony_oshaughnessy@suffieldacademy.org
Gregory Lynch, Dir.
Grades 7-12. Adm: Selective. **Appl**—Fee $50. Due: Rolling. Rec, essay.

Enr: 130. **Fac 20. Staff:** Admin 2. Couns 35.
Type of instruction: Enrich SAT/ACT_Prep Study_Skills. **Courses:** Span ESL Expository_ Writing Math Sci Creative_Writing Fine_Arts Music Photog Theater. **Avg class size:** 10. **Daily hours for:** Classes 6. Study 2. Rec 2. **High school credit.**
Features: Basketball Soccer Swim Tennis Ultimate_Frisbee Volleyball.
Fees 2013: Res $6500 (+$400), 5 wks. Day $3750 (+$200), 5 wks. Aid (Need).
Housing: Dorms. **Swimming:** Pool.
Est 1995. Nonprofit. **Spons:** Suffield Academy. **Ses:** 1. **Wks/ses:** 5. Operates June-July.

Drawing its students from across the US and from other countries, Suffield provides a liberal arts curriculum that features intensive, 100-minute-long class and project periods. Course work is available in the arts, English, ESL, foreign language, science, math and the humanities. Pupils may also take part in a skills program that focuses on computer skills, study and research techniques, standardized test-taking strategies and planning for the college admission process. Recreational activities and trips supplement academics.

TAFT SUMMER SCHOOL
Res and Day — Coed Ages 12-18

Watertown, CT 06795. 110 Woodbury Rd. Tel: 860-945-7961. Fax: 860-945-7859.
www.taftschool.org/summer   E-mail: summerschool@taftschool.org
Thomas W. Antonucci, Dir.
Grades 7-12. Adm: Selective. **Appl**—Fee $50. Due: Rolling. Transcript, 2 teacher recs, guidance counselor rec.
Enr: 165. **Intl:** 45%. **Fac 35. Staff:** Admin 6. Res 41.
Type of instruction: Adv Enrich Preview Rev SAT/ACT_Prep Study_Skills. **Courses:** Fr Span Eng ESL Hist Math Public_Speak Sci Speech Ceramics Creative_Writing Drama Fine_Arts Photog Studio_Art. **Avg class size:** 10. **Daily hours for:** Classes 4½. Study 2. Rec 1½. Homework. Tests. Grades.
Features: Basketball Soccer Squash Tennis Track Ultimate_Frisbee Volleyball Weight_ Trng.
Fees 2014: Res $6700 (+$450), 5 wks. Day $3850 (+$300), 5 wks. Aid 2010 (Merit & Need): $55,000.
Housing: Dorms. Avg per room/unit: 2. Campus facilities avail.
Est 1982. Nonprofit. **Ses:** 1. **Wks/ses:** 5. Operates June-Aug.

Taft's summer session, which comprises the Young Scholars Program (grades 7-9) and the Liberal Studies Program (grades 9-12), is designed for students who wish to improve their academic standing through a concentrated and rigorous program. Course work provides them with the opportunity to enrich their school experiences by taking classes not otherwise available to them or by concentrating on fundamental skills development. All pupils enroll in two major courses and two minor electives. Taft also conducts a full sports program, various on-campus activities and cultural weekend day trips.

UNIVERSITY OF CONNECTICUT
UCONN MENTOR CONNECTION
Res — Coed Ages 15-17

Storrs, CT 06269. 2131 Hillside Rd, Unit 3007. Tel: 860-486-0283. Fax: 860-486-2900.
www.gifted.uconn.edu   E-mail: mentorconnection@uconn.edu
Joseph S. Renzulli, Dir. Student contact: Heather L. Spottiswoode.
Grades 11-12. Adm: Selective. Prereqs: GPA 3.0. **Appl**—Due: Mar. Transcript, 3 essays, 2 teacher recs.
Enr: 81. **Enr cap:** 85. **Non-White:** 50%. **Fac 30. Staff:** Admin 4. Couns 8.
Type of instruction: Adv. **Courses:** Archaeol Astron Engineering Expository_Writing Math Med/Healthcare Sci Web_Design Creative_Writing Fine_Arts Painting. **Avg class size:** 4. **Daily hours for:** Classes 7. Study 2. Rec 5. Grades. **College credit:** 3.
Features: Conservation Hiking Basketball Swim Volleyball.

Fees 2014: Res $3800, 3 wks.
Housing: Dorms. Avg per room/unit: 2-4. **Swimming:** Pool.
Est 1996. Ses: 1. **Wks/ses:** 3. Operates July.

This program for rising high school sophomores and juniors who are in the top quarter of their class allows students to participate in creative projects and research investigations in the arts and sciences under the supervision of university mentors. Research topics include archaeology, biology, chemistry, materials science, engineering, physics, psychology, Web design, education, nursing, pharmacy, arts and humanities. Special presentations address SAT preparation, college admissions and financial aid, and career planning. Recreation and weekend trips balance academic work.

YALE UNIVERSITY SUMMER SESSION
Res and Day — Coed Ages 16-21

New Haven, CT 06520. PO Box 208355. Tel: 203-432-2430. Fax: 203-432-2434.
http://summer.yale.edu   **E-mail: summer.session@yale.edu**
Kathryn Young, Dir.
Grades 12-Col. Adm: Very_selective. **Appl**—Fee $55. Due: Rolling. Transcript, standardized test scores, 2 recs.
Enr: 1000. Intl: 20%. **Fac 200.** Prof 100. Col/grad students 20. Specialists 80. **Staff:** Admin 10. Couns 40.
Type of instruction: Adv Undergrad. **Courses:** Fr Ger Greek Ital Lat Russ Span Czech Nahuatl Portuguese Swahili Archaeol Astron Ecol Environ_Sci Writing/Journ Creative_ Writing Drama Filmmaking Fine_Arts. **Avg class size:** 10. **Daily hours for:** Classes 2. Study 2. **College credit.**
Features: Swim.
Fees 2013: Res $2168-5420, 5-10 wks. Aid (Merit).
Housing: Dorms. Avg per room/unit: 2. **Swimming:** Pool. Campus facilities avail.
Est 1975. Nonprofit. **Ses:** 2. **Wks/ses:** 5. Operates June-Aug.

Qualified college students and high schoolers who have completed junior year may earn up to 12 credit hours of college credit in such areas as humanities, the social and natural sciences, languages and drama. Instructors cover the same amount of material in five weeks as they do in a 13-week term during the academic year. Residential counselors (chosen from current Yale students) organize an array of social and athletic events for boarding pupils.

DELAWARE

UNIVERSITY OF DELAWARE EDGE PRE-COLLEGE PROGRAM
Res — Coed Ages 16-18

Newark, DE 19716. Honors Program, 186 S College Ave. Tel: 302-831-6560. Fax: 302-831-4194.
www.udel.edu/edge   **E-mail: edge@udel.edu**
Kevin Liedel, Prgm Coord.
Grades 11-12. Adm: Somewhat selective. **Appl**—Fee $60. Due: May. Transcript, essays, test scores, 2-3 recs.
Enr cap: 90. **Fac 10.** Prof 10. **Staff:** Admin 1.
Type of instruction: Enrich Undergrad. **Courses:** Comm Econ Eng Intl_Relations Relig_ Stud Sci Dance Music Studio_Art. **Avg class size:** 25. **Daily hours for:** Classes 3. Study 6. Homework. Tests. Grades. **College credit:** 3-4/crse, total 7.
Features: Swim.
Fees 2013: Res $4500-6950, 5 wks. Aid (Merit & Need).
Housing: Dorms. Avg per room/unit: 4. **Swimming:** Pool. Campus facilities avail.
Est 1983. Nonprofit. **Ses:** 1. **Wks/ses:** 5. Operates July-Aug.

Academically talented students entering grades 11 and 12 sample courses and earn up to seven college credits through this University of Delaware program. Core courses, composed entirely of Summer College students, vary by year. Qualified pupils may also enroll in Second Summer Session courses, introductory level classes offered to both Summer College students and current undergraduates.

DISTRICT OF COLUMBIA

GEORGETOWN UNIVERSITY
SUMMER COLLEGE FOR HIGH SCHOOL STUDENTS
Res and Day — Coed Ages 15-18

Washington, DC 20007. School of Continuing Studies, 3307 M St NW, Ste 202. Tel: 202-687-8600. Fax: 202-687-8954.
http://scs.georgetown.edu/hoyas   E-mail: highschool@georgetown.edu
Robert L. Manuel, Dir.
Grades 10-12. Adm: Selective. Prereqs: GPA 2.0. **Appl**—Fee $50. Due: Rolling. Transcript, essay, rec, standardized test results.
Enr: 41-87. **Staff:** Couns 12.
Type of instruction: Adv Undergrad. **Courses:** Arabic Fr Ger Span Bus/Fin Comp_Sci Econ Expository_Writing Forensic_Sci Hist Intl_Relations Law Math Pol_Sci Psych Public_Speak Sci Sociol Music Studio_Art Theater. **Daily hours for:** Classes 3. Study 3. **College credit:** 3-6/crse, total 12.
Features: Basketball Cross-country Soccer Swim Tennis.
Fees 2014: Res $5200-6575, 5 wks. Day $4123-5500, 5 wks. Aid (Need).
Housing: Dorms. **Swimming:** Pool.
Nonprofit. **Ses:** 2. **Wks/ses:** 5. Operates June-Aug.

Boys and girls who have completed at least one year of high school enroll in one or two undergraduate courses suited to their interests, background and previous academic achievement. Alongside current Georgetown students, pupils choose from more than 100 offerings in the arts, foreign language, business, math, science, computers and the social sciences. Participants benefit from the services available through the university, take part in programs designed by the counseling staff, and learn the importance of time management. Activities include recreational options, trips to nearby theatrical performances and sporting events, and community service opportunities. Students may enroll in two sessions with the director's approval.

SUMMER DISCOVERY
Res — Coed Ages 15-18

Washington, DC. Georgetown Univ.
Contact (Year-round): 1326 Old Northern Blvd, Roslyn, NY 11576. Tel: 516-621-3939. Fax: 516-625-3438.
www.summerdiscovery.com   E-mail: discovery@summerdiscovery.com
Bob Musiker, Exec Dir.
Grades 10-PG. Adm: FCFS. **Appl**—Fee $95. Due: Rolling.
Enr: 195. **Enr cap:** 225.
Type of instruction: Enrich SAT/ACT_Prep Study_Skills. **Courses:** Bus/Fin Debate ESL Govt Speech Writing/Journ Crafts Creative_Writing Dance Drama Filmmaking Fine_ Arts Media Music Photog. Homework. Tests.
Features: Adventure_Travel Canoe Community_Serv Hiking Kayak Aerobics Basketball Soccer Swim Tennis Weight_Trng.
Fees 2014: Res $5699-7899, 4 wks. Aid (Need).
Housing: Dorms. **Swimming:** Pool River.
Inc. **Ses:** 1. **Wks/ses:** 4. Operates July.

See program description under Los Angeles, CA.

FLORIDA

FLORIDA AIR ACADEMY SUMMER SESSION
Res and Day — Coed Ages 11-18

Melbourne, FL 32901. 1950 S Academy Dr. **Tel:** 321-723-3211, 877-422-2338. **Fax:** 321-676-0422.
www.flair.com   E-mail: admissions@flair.com
Col. James Dwight, Pres.
Grades 6-12. Adm: Selective. **Appl**—Due: Rolling.
Enr: 150. **Fac 22.**
Type of instruction: Adv Dev_Read Enrich Preview Rem_Eng Rem_Math Rem_Read Rev SAT/ACT_Prep Study_Skills Tut. **Courses:** Comp_Sci ESL Math. **Avg class size:** 8. **Daily hours for:** Classes 4. Study 2. Rec 5. **High school credit:** 1.
Features: Aviation/Aero Climbing_Wall Milit_Trng Rock_Climb Scuba Baseball Basketball Cross-country Football Golf Martial_Arts Skateboarding Soccer Surfing Swim Tennis Track Watersports.
Fees 2014: Res $6500 (+$1200), 6 wks. Day $2800 (+$600), 6 wks.
Housing: Dorms. **Swimming:** Ocean Pool. Campus facilities avail.
Est 1961. Inc. Ses: 1. Wks/ses: 5. Operates June-July.

Florida Air's summer session offers advanced, review and remedial courses. Instructional courses include ESL, SAT Prep and tutoring and study skills sessions. The academy conducts all levels of flight instruction, including Junior Wings for boys and girls in grades 6-8.

MONTVERDE ACADEMY SUMMER SCHOOL
Res and Day — Coed Ages 12-18

Montverde, FL 34756. 17235 7th St. **Tel:** 407-469-2561. **Fax:** 407-469-3711.
http://montverde.org/summer-programs/summer-school
E-mail: admissions@montverde.org
Sue Tortora, Dir.
Grades 7-12. Adm: Selective. **Appl**—Due: Rolling.
Enr: 60. **Fac 10. Staff:** Admin 7.
Type of instruction: Enrich Rem_Read Rev SAT/ACT_Prep. **Courses:** Span Comp_Sci Econ Eng ESL Govt Hist Math Sci Anat & Physiol. **Daily hours for:** Classes 5. Study 2. Rec 4. **High school credit:** 1½.
Features: Aquatics Boating Canoe Weight_Loss Baseball Soccer Swim Tennis Track Watersports.
Fees 2014: Res $3100-6100, 2-4 wks. Day $1300-2550, 2-4 wks.
Housing: Dorms. **Swimming:** Lake Pool. Campus facilities avail.
Nonprofit. **Ses: 2. Wks/ses:** 2-4. Operates June-July.

This summer session offers courses for review, preview and enrichment in English, math, civics, history, science and government. Activities include swimming, sports, and excursions to nearby theme parks and other local attractions.

GEORGIA

EMORY UNIVERSITY PRE-COLLEGE PROGRAM
Res — Coed Ages 15-18

Atlanta, GA 30322. Candler Library, Ste 200, MS 1580-002-2AA, 550 Asbury Cir. Tel: 404-727-0671. Fax: 404-727-6724.
www.precollege.emory.edu   E-mail: precollege@emory.edu
Philip Wainwright, Dir. Student contact: Mollie Korski.
Grades 11-12. Adm: Selective. Prereqs: GPA 3.0. SAT M/CR 1100. **Appl**—Fee $60. Due: Rolling. Transcript, standardized test scores, rec.
Enr: 100. **Enr cap:** 100. Intl: 5%. Non-White: 15%. **Fac 10.** Prof 10. **Staff:** Admin 6. Couns 9.
Type of instruction: Adv Undergrad. **Courses:** Arabic Fr Ital Span Comp_Sci Econ Hist Math Med/Healthcare Psych Philos Sociol Acting Drawing Film Photog Theater Poetry. **Avg class size:** 10. **Daily hours for:** Classes 3. Study 3. Rec 3. Homework. Tests. College credit: 4/crse, total 4.
Features: Swim.
Fees 2014: Res $3630-9689. Day $2560-5879. Aid (Need).
Housing: Dorms. **Swimming:** Pool. Campus facilities avail.
Est 2009. Nonprofit. Methodist. **Ses:** 5. **Wks/ses:** 2-6. Operates June-Aug.

Rising high school juniors and seniors preview college life while enrolling in university-level courses along current Emory undergraduates in this program. Participants choose between two-week noncredit courses and six-week for-credit classes. Credit-bearing courses lead to transferable college credit. Boarding students live together in a campus dorm and participate in various programs, activities and excursions, many of which are designed to prepare boys and girls for college life.

HAWAII

HAWAII PREPARATORY ACADEMY SUMMER SESSION
Res and Day — Coed Ages 11-17

Kamuela, HI 96743. 65-1692 Kohala Mountain Rd. Tel: 808-881-4088. Fax: 808-881-4071.
www.hpa.edu/summer   E-mail: summer@hpa.edu
Shirley Ann Fukumoto, Dir.
Grades 6-12. Adm: Selective. **Appl**—Fee $25. Due: Apr. Transcript, one rec, standardized testing.
Enr: 100. **Enr cap:** 100. **Fac 18.** K-12 staff 18. **Staff:** Admin 3.
Type of instruction: Adv Enrich Preview SAT/ACT_Prep Study_Skills. **Courses:** Japan Span Ecol Econ Environ_Sci ESL Marine_Bio/Stud Math Sci Writing/Journ Robotics Ceramics Crafts Creative_Writing Dance Filmmaking Fine_Arts Music Photog. **Avg class size:** 10. **Daily hours for:** Classes 6. Study 1. Rec 2. **High school credit.**
Features: Aquatics Cooking Exploration Hiking Kayak Scuba Equestrian Swim Tennis Weight_Trng.
Fees 2013: Res $4800, 4 wks. Day $1100, 4 wks.
Housing: Dorms. Avg per room/unit: 2. **Swimming:** Ocean Pool.
Est 1974. Nonprofit. **Ses:** 1. **Wks/ses:** 4. Operates June-July.

HPA offers academic enrichment opportunities in science, math, English and other disciplines. Afternoon activities include intramural sports, an equestrian program, scuba certification, swimming, tennis lessons and driver education. In addition, students learn about the big island through excursions to Volcanoes National Park, ocean kayaking, snorkeling and hiking.

ILLINOIS

AMERICAN COLLEGIATE ADVENTURES
Res — Coed Ages 14-18

Chicago, IL 60622. 1811 W North Ave, Ste 201. Tel: 773-342-0200, 800-509-7867. Fax: 773-342-0246.
www.acasummer.com   E-mail: info@acasummer.com
Jason Lubar, Founder & Exec Dir.
Grades 9-12. Adm: Selective. Appl—Fee $95. Due: Rolling.
Intl: 15%. Staff: Admin 4.
Type of instruction: Enrich Rem_Eng Rem_Math Rem_Read ESL/TOEFL_Prep SAT/ACT_Prep Study_Skills Tut Undergrad. Avg class size: 10. Daily hours for: Classes 5. Rec 6. Tests. Grades. College credit: 3/crse, total 6.
Intl program focus: Acad Lang Culture. Travel: CA MA WI Europe.
Features: Adventure_Travel Bicycle_Tours Boating Canoe Caving Community_Serv Cooking Hiking Kayak Outdoor_Ed Ropes_Crse Yoga Cricket Football Golf Soccer Swim Tennis Ultimate_Frisbee Volleyball Weight_Trng.
Fees 2014: Res $4995-8495, 3-5 wks.
Housing: Dorms Hotels. Avg per room/unit: 2. Swimming: Lake Ocean Pool.
Est 1993. Inc. Ses: 8. Wks/ses: 3-5. Operates June-Aug.

American Collegiate Adventures' pre-college summer programs send students in grades 9-12 to travel to Boston, California, Wisconsin, Seville, Florence, London, Barcelona or Milan for cultural and academic experiences. Students may earn college credit in programs from film and fashion to business and law, and engage in various sports and cultural activities in their free time.

NORTHWESTERN UNIVERSITY
COLLEGE PREPARATION PROGRAM
Res and Day — Coed Ages 17-18

Evanston, IL 60208. 405 Church St. Tel: 847-467-6703. Fax: 847-491-3660.
www.northwestern.edu/collegeprep   E-mail: cpp@northwestern.edu
Stephanie Teterycz, Dir.
Grade 12 (younger if qualified). Adm: Selective. Prereqs: GPA 3.0. Appl—Fee $50. Due: Apr. Transcript, rec, personal statement.
Enr: 95. Fac 100. Staff: Admin 3. Couns 6.
Type of instruction: Adv Preview Undergrad. Courses: Arabic Chin Fr Ger Ital Japan Span Archaeol Astron Bus/Fin Ecol Environ_Sci Expository_Writing Govt Speech Writing/Journ Creative_Writing Fine_Arts Media Music Photog Theater. Avg class size: 15. Daily hours for: Classes 3. College credit: 9.
Features: Swim.
Fees 2013: Res $4560 (+$440), 3-8 wks. Aid (Need).
Housing: Dorms. Swimming: Lake Pool.
Nonprofit. Spons: Northwestern University. Ses: 1. Wks/ses: 3-8. Operates June-Aug.

CPP offers more than 350 college-level courses to rising high school seniors with at least a 3.0 grade point average; highly qualified rising juniors may also apply. Classes range in length from three to eight weeks. Participants may earn a full year of college credit in biology, chemistry, physics or a foreign language through an intensive, three-course sequence. The intensive session, for which pupils must receive prior CPP approval, covers a year's worth of material in an eight-week program that meets for approximately three hours each weekday (plus lab time). Two-week noncredit IN FOCUS seminars cover such topics as the legal profession, global justice and environmental sustainability.

INDIANA

EARLHAM COLLEGE
EXPLORE-A-COLLEGE
Res — Coed Ages 15-17

Richmond, IN 47374. 801 National Rd W. Tel: 765-983-1330, 800-327-5426. Fax: 765-983-1560.
www.earlham.edu/~eac E-mail: exploreacollege@earlham.edu
Susan Hillmann de Castaneda, Dir.
Grades 10-12. **Adm:** Somewhat_selective. Admitted: 98%. Prereqs: GPA 3.0. **Appl**—Fee $50. Due: Apr. Transcript, 2 recs, essay.
Enr: 72. **Enr cap:** 100. Intl: 1%. Non-White: 45%. **Fac 10.** Prof 10. **Staff:** Admin 2. Couns 18.
Type of instruction: Adv Enrich Study_Skills. **Courses:** Japan Econ Expository_Writing Psych Sci Creative_Writing Photog Studio_Art. **Avg class size:** 10. **Daily hours for:** Classes 5. Study 4. Rec 5. Homework. Tests. Grades. **College credit:** 2/crse, total 2.
Features: Climbing_Wall Community_Serv Peace/Cross-cultural Rock_Climb Swim.
Fees 2012: Res $1700 (+$150), 2 wks. Aid 2011 (Need): $28,000.
Housing: Dorms. Avg per room/unit: 2. **Swimming:** Pool. Campus facilities avail.
Est 1981. Nonprofit. Religious Society of Friends. **Ses:** 1. **Wks/ses:** 2. Operates June-July.

Conducted on its campus by Earlham College, the program provides high-ability high schoolers with the opportunity to develop college-level skills while sampling college life. College faculty teach courses in art, biology, English, philosophy, Japanese, psychology and Spanish. Students earn two semester hours of transferable college credit for each course completed. Current Earlham students serve as counselors and teaching assistants.

HOWE MILITARY ACADEMY SUMMER CAMP
Res — Boys Ages 9-15

Howe, IN 46746. 5755 N State Road 9. Tel: 260-562-2131, 888-462-4693. Fax: 260-562-3678.
www.thehoweschool.org E-mail: admissions@howemilitary.org
George Douglass, Supt.
Grades 4-10. **Adm:** FCFS. **Appl**—Due: Rolling.
Enr: 122. **Fac 10. Staff:** Admin 4. Couns 18.
Courses: Crafts Theater.
Features: Aquatics Archery Canoe Hiking Milit_Trng Riding Ropes_Crse Sail Scuba Baseball Basketball Golf Swim Tennis Volleyball.
Fees 2013: Res $2200-3500 (+$50), 3-6 wks.
Housing: Cabins Houses. **Swimming:** Lake.
Est 1932. Nonprofit. **Ses:** 3. **Wks/ses:** 3-6. Operates June-July.

Howe combines academic work with a range of outdoor recreational activities and leadership training. Campers at all grade levels receive review instruction in science, mathematics, and English, while boys entering grades 9 and 10 take English or math courses for high school credit. In addition to traditional camping activities, boys may take part in less common pursuits, such as scuba, sailing, horsemanship and a ropes course, and instructors place emphasis on a different sport each week. Military training, designed to develop orderliness, self-discipline and social skills, is part of the daily program.

INDIANA STATE UNIVERSITY SUMMER HONORS PROGRAM
Res — Coed Ages 15-17

Terre Haute, IN 47809. Office of Adm, 218 N 6th St. Tel: 812-237-2121, 800-468-6478. Fax: 812-237-8023.

www.indstate.edu/experience   E-mail: admissions@indstate.edu
Grades 10-12. Adm: Selective. **Prereqs:** GPA 3.0. **Appl**—Due: Rolling. Transcript, rec.
Enr cap: 180. **Fac** 23. **Staff:** Admin 1. Couns 6.
Type of instruction: Adv Undergrad. **Courses:** Astron Bus/Fin Education Engineering Med/Healthcare Fine_Arts Photog. **Daily hours for:** Classes 7. Homework. **College credit:** 2.
Features: Aviation/Aero Swim.
Fees 2013: Res $375.
Housing: Dorms. **Swimming:** Pool.
Est 1969. Nonprofit. **Spons:** Indiana State University. **Ses:** 1. **Wks/ses:** 1. Operates July.

High schoolers who have completed junior year may earn two college credits through a demanding weeklong seminar that covers a variety of liberal arts, science and business topics. Experienced ISU faculty guide all of the seminars. Recreational and cultural activities supplement academics.

PURDUE UNIVERSITY
GIFTED EDUCATION RESOURCE INSTITUTE
SUMMER YOUTH PROGRAMS
Res — Coed Ages 11-18; Day — Coed 4-10

West Lafayette, IN 47907. Beering Hall, Rm 5178, 100 N University St. **Tel:** 765-494-7243. **Fax:** 765-496-2706.
www.purdue.edu/geri   E-mail: geri@purdue.edu
Matt Fugate, Coord. Student contact: Stacey L. Folyer, E-mail: sfolyer@purdue.edu.
Grades 5-12. Adm: Selective. Admitted: 98%. **Prereqs:** GPA 3.5. IQ 120. **Appl**—Due: Rolling. Transcript, standardized test results, rec, essay.
Enr: 600. **Intl:** 10%. **Fac** 25. **Staff:** Admin 5. Res 15.
Type of instruction: Adv Enrich. **Courses:** Span Archaeol Bus/Fin Comp_Sci Debate Ecol Engineering Environ_Sci Expository_Writing Forensic_Sci Govt Marine_Bio/Stud Med/Healthcare Speech Writing/Journ Crafts Creative_Writing Filmmaking Fine_Arts Media Painting Photog Studio_Art Theater. **Avg class size:** 15. **Daily hours for:** Classes 6. Study 1½. Rec 3.
Features: Adventure_Travel Aquatics Canoe Cooking Leadership Basketball Football Swim Tennis Volleyball.
Fees 2012: Res $975-1950 (+$50), 1-2 wks. **Day** $625, 1 wk. Aid 2010 (Need): $26,675.
Housing: Dorms. **Swimming:** Pool. Campus facilities avail.
Est 1977. Nonprofit. **Ses:** 4. **Wks/ses:** 1-2. Operates June-July.

GERI Super Summer day program provides enrichment opportunities for gifted young children. In GERI Summer Camps, students entering grades 5-12 pursue individual interests as they choose from course work in an array of subjects. Participants reside on campus and thus have access to the university's computers, labs, art studios, and athletic and recreational facilities.

UNIVERSITY OF NOTRE DAME SUMMER SCHOLARS
Res — Coed Ages 15-17

Notre Dame, IN 46556. Office of Pre-College Prgms, 307 Brownson Hall. **Tel:** 574-631-0990. **Fax:** 574-631-8964.
www.precollege.nd.edu/summer-scholars   E-mail: precoll@nd.edu
Alyssia J. Coates, Dir.
Grades 10-11. Adm: Selective. **Appl**—Fee $50. Due: Jan. Transcript, test scores, counselor report, rec.
Enr: 280. **Enr cap:** 280.
Type of instruction: Enrich. **Courses:** Bus/Fin Eng Law Psych Public_Speak Relig_Stud Sci Acting Film Music. **Avg class size:** 20. **College credit:** 1.
Features: Community_Serv.

Fees 2014: Res $3100, 2 wks.
Housing: Dorms. Campus facilities avail.
Roman Catholic. **Ses:** 1. **Wks/ses:** 2. Operates June-July.

Summer Scholars preview college life and pursue intensive study in one of 14 academic tracks. Notre Dame faculty conduct all courses. The program schedule incorporates time for spiritual and personal development activities, and scholars have the opportunity to work with various service organizations. Among the available social and recreational activities are a talent show, sports, film screenings and campus lectures.

IOWA

IOWA STATE UNIVERSITY
OFFICE OF PRECOLLEGIATE PROGRAMS
FOR TALENTED AND GIFTED SUMMER PROGRAMS
Res — Coed Ages 13-17; Day — Coed 8-17

Ames, IA 50011. 357 Carver Hall. Tel: 515-294-1772, 800-262-3810. Fax: 515-294-3505.
www.opptag.iastate.edu E-mail: opptag@iastate.edu
Carmen P. Flagge, Coord.
Grades 3-12 (younger if qualified). Adm: Somewhat_selective. Admitted: 97%. Prereqs: GPA 3.5. SAT M/CR 950; ACT 20. **Appl**—Fee $35-50. Due: May.
Enr: 100. **Enr cap:** 100. Intl: 5%. Non-White: 20%. **Fac 45.** Prof 5. Col/grad students 20. K-12 staff 20. **Staff:** Admin 4. Couns 9.
Type of instruction: Adv Enrich. **Courses:** Comp_Sci Math Sci Engineering Neurosci Robotics Web_Design Creative_Writing Drama Studio_Art. **Avg class size:** 15. **Daily hours for:** Classes 6. Study 1. Rec 3. Homework. Tests. **High school credit.**
Features: Canoe Swim Tennis.
Fees 2014: Res $750-2150 (+$50-600), 1-3 wks. Day $650-1850 (+$60-360), 1-3 wks. Aid 2011 (Need): $7000.
Housing: Dorms. **Swimming:** Pool.
Est 1986. Nonprofit. **Ses:** 3. **Wks/ses:** 1-3. Operates June-July.

OPPTAG conducts several precollege programs for gifted students. Adventures! allows day students who have completed grades 2-6 to choose from enrichment courses in various subjects. CY-TAG, enrolling pupils entering grades 8-11, combines three-week high school enrichment classes with social, recreational and cultural activities. A third program, Explorations!, provides rising eighth through tenth graders with one week of intensive instruction in a chosen subject. In lieu of a letter grade, students receive a written evaluation from the instructor upon completion of the course.

KANSAS

DUKE UNIVERSITY TALENT IDENTIFICATION PROGRAM
SUMMER STUDIES PROGRAMS
Res — Coed Ages 12-16

Lawrence, KS. Univ of Kansas.
Contact (Year-round): 1121 W Main St, Durham, NC 27701. Tel: 919-668-9100. Fax: 919-681-7921.
www.tip.duke.edu E-mail: information@tip.duke.edu
Brian Cooper, Dir.

Grades 8-11. Adm: Selective. **Appl**—Fee $25. Due: Rolling. SAT/ACT requirement, personal statement.
Type of instruction: Adv Enrich. **Courses:** Architect Comp_Sci Engineering Expository_ Writing Med/Healthcare Writing/Journ Creative_Writing Filmmaking. **Avg class size:** 16. **Daily hours for:** Classes 7. Rec 3.
Fees 2014: Res $3675-3925, 3 wks.
Housing: Dorms.
Est 1980. Nonprofit. **Ses:** 2. **Wks/ses:** 3. Operates June-Aug.

Conducted on several college campuses, the Duke TIP Summer Studies Programs allow advanced students to intensively study a single subject. While previewing college life, boys and girls attend class for seven hours per day from Monday through Friday, then another three hours each Saturday morning. A residential staff supervises students during meals, recreational periods and free time. See other TIP listings under Boone, NC; Durham, NC; College Station, TX; and Davidson, NC.

KENTUCKY

KENTUCKY GOVERNOR'S SCHOLARS PROGRAM
Res — Coed Ages 16-17

Frankfort, KY 40601. 1024 Capital Center Dr, Ste 210. Tel: 502-573-1618. Fax: 502-573-1641.
www.kygsp.org   E-mail: gsp@ky.gov
Aristofanes Cedeno, Exec Dir.
Grades 11-12. Adm: Very selective. **Appl**—Due: Jan.
Enr: 1000.
Type of instruction: Enrich. Chin Span
Fees 2014: Free (in-state residents). Res 5 wks.
Housing: Dorms. Avg per room/unit: 2.
Est 1983. Nonprofit. **Ses:** 3. **Wks/ses:** 5. Operates June-July.

Conducted on three Kentucky college campuses, GSP encourages academic and personal growth by means of a strong liberal arts program. Rising high school juniors from Kentucky choose one major course from roughly two dozen subjects. Instruction follows a nontraditional, interdisciplinary approach. Guest speakers, student productions, publications, experiments and field trips enhance the curriculum. Faculty come from Kentucky colleges, universities and high schools. Interested pupils must be nominated by their schools.

MURRAY STATE UNIVERSITY
THE CENTER FOR GIFTED STUDIES
SUMMER CHALLENGE
Res and Day — Coed Ages 11-14

Murray, KY 42071. Office of Non-Credit & Youth Prgms, 211 Industry & Technology Ctr. Tel: 270-809-2539.
www.murraystate.edu/centerforgiftedstudies.aspx   E-mail: tatiana.adams@coe.murraystate.edu
Toddie Adams, Dir.
Grades 6-9. Adm: Very selective. Prereqs: IQ 125. **Appl**—Fee $0. Due: Mar. Rec.
Enr: 60. **Enr cap:** 75. **Fac** 7. **Staff:** Admin 3. Couns 6.
Type of instruction: Adv Enrich. **Courses:** Span Architect Comp_Sci Photog. **Avg class size:** 10. **Daily hours for:** Classes 6. Rec 3.
Intl program focus: Acad Lang Culture.
Features: Cooking Martial_Arts Swim.
Fees 2013: Res $450 (+$20), 1 wk. Day $370 (+$10), 1 wk. Aid (Need).

Housing: Dorms. Avg per room/unit: 2. **Swimming:** Pool.
Est 1980. Ses: 2. **Wks/ses:** 1. Operates June-July.

Gifted students enrolled in Summer Challenge choose one class from a curriculum that includes such subjects as Chinese, computer science, architecture, photography and Spanish. Boarders reside in Murray State dormitories. Applicants should have an IQ of at least 125.

LOUISIANA

THE GOVERNOR'S PROGRAM FOR GIFTED CHILDREN
Res — Coed Ages 12-16

Lake Charles, LA 70609. McNeese State Univ, MSU Box 91490. Tel: 337-475-5446, 800-291-7840. Fax: 337-475-5447.
www.gpgc.org   E-mail: office@gpgc.org
Joshua Brown, Dir.
Grades 7-11. Adm: Selective. **Appl**—Fee $20. Due: Apr. Standardized test results, transcript.
Enr: 85. Non-White: 20%. **Fac 13.** Prof 3. K-12 staff 10. **Staff:** Admin 3. Couns 10.
Type of instruction: Adv Enrich. **Courses:** Debate Expository_Writing Creative_Writing Fine_Arts Music Theater. **Avg class size:** 10. **Daily hours for:** Classes 7. Study 2. Rec 2. **College credit:** 6.
Features: Basketball Soccer Softball Swim Tennis Track.
Fees 2012: Res $2550-3550, 7 wks. Aid 2009 (Need): $35,000.
Housing: Dorms. **Swimming:** Pool.
Est 1959. Nonprofit. **Ses:** 1. **Wks/ses:** 7. Operates June-July.

Conducted on the McNeese State University campus for boys and girls whose score on an acceptable aptitude test is in the 96th percentile or higher, GPGC employs a project-based method in which students engage in independent individual and group projects. This approach enables pupils to maintain and stimulate their interest levels in areas ranging from the humanities to the fine arts to the social sciences. Information acquisition is secondary to the development of thinking and problem-solving skills. GPGC operates two divisions: Junior Division students follow the prescribed curriculum in science, humanities and composition, while Senior Division students (generally 15- and 16-year-olds) take college courses taught by McNeese State faculty. The program is not limited to Louisiana residents, although out-of-state students pay a higher tuition rate.

NORTHWESTERN STATE UNIVERSITY
ADVANCE PROGRAM FOR YOUNG SCHOLARS
Res — Coed Ages 13-17

Natchitoches, LA 71497. NSU Box 5671. Tel: 318-357-4500. Fax: 318-357-4547.
http://advance.nsula.edu   E-mail: palmerh@nsula.edu
David Wood, Dir. Student contact: Harriette Palmer.
Grades 8-12. Adm: Somewhat selective. Admitted: 85%. **Appl**—Fee $50. Due: Apr. Test scores or teacher rec & 2 schoolwork examples, transcript.
Enr: 175-200. Non-White: 41%. **Fac 17. Staff:** Admin 6. Res 26.
Type of instruction: Adv. **Courses:** Comp_Sci Math Psych Sci Humanities Shakespeare Crafts Creative_Writing Film Fine_Arts. **Avg class size:** 15. **Daily hours for:** Classes 6. Study 1. Rec 3. **High school credit:** 1/crse, total 1.
Features: Chess Hiking Basketball Golf Soccer Swim Tennis Volleyball.
Fees 2013: Res $2250 (+$75-150), 3 wks. Aid 2006 (Need): $10,000.
Housing: Dorms. **Swimming:** Pool Stream.
Est 1989. Nonprofit. **Ses:** 1. **Wks/ses:** 3. Operates June.

Affiliated with and patterned after Duke University's Talent Identification Program,

ADVANCE is an intensive educational summer program designed for academically gifted youth. Students enroll in one academic class and receive six hours of daily instruction in the chosen course of study. Evening study periods and recreational activities take place in the evening. Weekend activities include dances, movies, sports, arts and crafts, and a talent show.

MARYLAND

JOHNS HOPKINS UNIVERSITY
CENTER FOR TALENTED YOUTH SUMMER PROGRAMS
Res — Coed Ages 11-18; Day — Coed 7-12

Baltimore, MD 21209. McAuley Hall, 5801 Smith Ave, Ste 400. Tel: 410-735-4100.
Fax: 410-735-6200.
www.cty.jhu.edu   E-mail: ctyinfo@jhu.edu
Elizabeth Albert, Dir.
Grades 2-PG (younger if qualified). Adm: Selective. Admitted: 90%. Appl—Fee $50.
Due: Rolling. Standardized test results.
Intl: 7%.
Type of instruction: Adv Enrich. Courses: Chin Fr Greek Span Astron Comp_Sci Ecol Engineering Environ_Sci Expository_Writing Forensic_Sci Hist Intl_Relations Law Marine_Bio/Stud Math Oceanog Pol_Sci Sci Creative_Writing Drama Music. Avg class size: 15. Daily hours for: Classes 5. Study 2. Rec 3. High school credit.
Locations: CA MA MD PA VA.
Features: Swim.
Fees 2014: Res $4065-5145 (+$75), 3 wks. Day $2255-3500, 3 wks.
Housing: Dorms. Swimming: Pool.
Est 1979. Nonprofit. Ses: 2. Wks/ses: 3. Operates June-Aug.

CTY conducts advanced programs in a range of disciplines for academically talented youth at colleges and preparatory schools in five states. Programs for young students include day-only courses for boys and girls who have completed grades 2-4 and residential programs for those who have completed grades 5 and 6; eligibility is based on School and College Abilities Test (SCAT) scores. CTY courses for students who have completed grade 7 or above require SAT, ACT or SCAT scores above the mean for college-bound high school seniors; the Academic Expressions program features courses with less selective eligibility requirements. A global issues program at Princeton University serves pupils who have completed grades 10-12.

UNITED STATES NAVAL ACADEMY
SUMMER SEMINAR PROGRAM
Res — Coed Ages 17-18

Annapolis, MD 21402. 52 King George St. Tel: 410-293-4361.
www.usna.edu/admissions/nass.htm
Grade 12. Adm: Selective. Appl—Due: Mar. Transcript, standardized test scores.
Enr: 850. Enr cap: 850.
Type of instruction: Enrich. Courses: Architect Econ Eng Engineering Hist Math Pol_Sci Sci Ethics Meteorology.
Features: Seamanship Martial_Arts.
Fees 2014: Res $400, 1 wk.
Housing: Dorms. Campus facilities avail.
Nonprofit. Ses: 3. Wks/ses: 1. Operates May-June.

High-achieving students who have just completed their junior year of high school take part in a six-day program that balances academics, athletics and professional training. The Summer Seminar is designed especially for those boys and girls who are considering seeking an appointment the one of the US service academies. Each pupils attends eight 90-minute academic workshops during the session; while some course options have a nautical orientation, many others are in traditional subject areas.

MASSACHUSETTS

BOSTON COLLEGE EXPERIENCE
Res and Day — Coed Ages 17-18

Chestnut Hill, MA 02467. McGuinn Hall, Rm 100. Tel: 617-552-3800. Fax: 617-552-8404.
www.bc.edu/schools/summer/bce   E-mail: bce@bc.edu
Grade 12. Adm: Somewhat_selective. Admitted: 90%. **Appl**—Fee $25. Due: Rolling. Transcript, standardized test scores, principal/counselor rec.
Type of instruction: Adv Undergrad. **Courses:** Fr Span Comp_Sci Econ Eng Geol Hist Math Psych Public_Speak Relig_Stud Sci Anat & Physiol Philos Sociol Film. **College credit.**
Features: Swim.
Fees 2014: Res $5692, 6 wks. Day $2767, 6 wks.
Housing: Dorms. Avg per room/unit: 1-2. **Swimming:** Pool. Nonprofit. Roman Catholic. **Ses:** 1. **Wks/ses:** 6. Operates June-Aug.

This precollege program enrolls talented and motivated rising high school seniors who are interested in sampling college life. Alongside Boston College undergraduates, each student enrolls in two freshman-level courses for full college credit. Program participation leads to improved time-management skills and allows boys and girls to take classes not available in traditional high school settings. College visits and recreational and shopping excursions round out the program.

BOSTON UNIVERSITY HIGH SCHOOL HONORS PROGRAM
Res and Day — Coed Ages 16-18

Boston, MA 02215. 755 Commonwealth Ave, Rm 105. Tel: 617-353-1378. Fax: 617-353-5532.
www.bu.edu/summer/high-school-programs/honors   E-mail: summerhs@bu.edu
Donna Shea, Dir. Student contact: Matthew Cobb, E-mail: mcobb@bu.edu.
Grades 11-12. Adm: Selective. Prereqs: GPA 3.69. 1252. **Appl**—Due: May. Transcript, personal statement, standardized test scores, 2 recs.
Enr: 100. Intl: 19%. Non-White: 36%. **Staff:** Admin 2. Couns 9.
Type of instruction: Adv Undergrad. **Courses:** Arabic Chin Fr Ger Greek Ital Japan Lat Span Korean Turkish African-Amer_Stud Archaeol Astron Bus/Fin Comm Comp_Sci Econ Environ_Sci Expository_Writing Govt Hist Math Pol_Sci Sci Speech Writing/Journ Accounting Creative_Writing Filmmaking Fine_Arts Media Music Painting Photog Studio_Art Theater. **Avg class size:** 35. **Daily hours for:** Classes 3-5. Homework. Tests. Grades. **College credit:** 2-4/crse, total 8.
Features: Swim.
Fees 2013: Res $5270 (+$2274), 6 wks. Day $5270, 6 wks. Aid (Merit & Need).
Housing: Dorms. Avg per room/unit: 2. **Swimming:** Pool. Campus facilities avail.
Est 1980. Ses: 1. **Wks/ses:** 6. Operates June-Aug.

Rising high school seniors and exceptional rising juniors enroll in two courses for credit alongside Boston University undergraduates. Course options vary each year and include more than 100 offerings in dozens of subject areas. Students participate in planned social and recreational activities, as well as workshops on the college application process.

BOSTON UNIVERSITY SUMMER CHALLENGE PROGRAM
Res — Coed Ages 15-17

Boston, MA 02215. 755 Commonwealth Ave, Rm 105. Tel: 617-353-1378. Fax: 617-353-5532.
www.bu.edu/summer/high-school-programs/summer-challenge
E-mail: summerhs@bu.edu
Donna Shea, Dir. Student contact: **Matthew Cobb, E-mail: mcobb@bu.edu.**
Grades 10-12. Adm: Selective. **Appl**—Fee $50. Due: Rolling. Transcript, personal statement.
Intl: 19%. **Fac 11. Staff:** Admin 2. Couns 14.
Type of instruction: Adv Enrich Preview. **Courses:** Chin Bus/Fin Engineering Expository_ Writing Hist Law Pol_Sci Psych Writing/Journ Ethics Creative_Writing Visual_Arts. **Avg class size:** 20. **Daily hours for:** Classes 4. Study 2. Rec 3. Homework.
Features: Swim.
Fees 2013: Res $3630 (+$25), 2 wks.
Housing: Dorms. **Swimming:** Pool.
Est 2002. Nonprofit. **Ses:** 3. **Wks/ses:** 2. Operates June-Aug.

Summer Challenge exposes high school students to the standards of college-level work. Participants enroll in two seminars during the two-week session, one that addresses an existing interest and another that leads to the exploration of a new subject. Seminars combine lectures, individual and group work, project-based assignments and field trips. Summer Challenge schedules various social activities for afternoons, evenings and weekends.

CUSHING ACADEMY SUMMER SESSION
Res and Day — Coed Ages 12-18

Ashburnham, MA 01430. 39 School St, PO Box 8000. Tel: 978-827-7700. Fax: 978-827-6927.
www.cushing.org/summer   E-mail: **summersession@cushing.org**
Margaret H. Lee, Dir.
Grades 7-12. Adm: Selective. **Appl**—Fee $60. Due: Rolling. Transcript, essay, recs.
Enr: 365.
Type of instruction: Adv Enrich Rev ESL/TOEFL_Prep SAT/ACT_Prep Study_Skills. **Courses:** Col_Prep ESL Creative_Writing Dance Filmmaking Painting Photog Studio_ Art Theater. **Avg class size:** 10. **Daily hours for:** Classes 4. Study 2. Rec 2. Homework. Tests. Grades. **High school credit:** 1.
Features: Chess Community_Serv Aerobics Basketball Martial_Arts Soccer Tennis Ultimate_Frisbee Volleyball Weight_Trng Zumba.
Fees 2013: Res $7250, 5 wks. Day $3400, 5 wks.
Housing: Dorms Houses.
Nonprofit. **Ses:** 1. **Wks/ses:** 5. Operates July-Aug.

Students from throughout the US and around the world enroll in one of five core programs. Prep for Success explores literature, writing, and math for students ages 12 and 13. Studio Art (ages 13-18) provides instruction in a variety of media. The ESL program places students ages 14-18 into appropriately leveled classes that increase proficiency in reading, writing, speaking and listening. College Prep courses offer Cushing Academy credit, and a college advising workshop admits rising juniors and seniors. Pupils choose from various performing/visual arts and athletic electives. Cushing schedules campus events and trips throughout New England.

EAGLEBROOK SUMMER SEMESTER
Res — Coed Ages 11-13

Deerfield, MA 01342. 271 Pine Nook Rd, PO Box 7. Tel: 413-774-7411. Fax: 413-774-9136.
www.eaglebrook.org   E-mail: **kjk@eaglebrook.org**
Karl J. Koenigsbauer, Dir.

Adm: Selective. **Appl**—Fee $40. **Due:** Rolling. Transcript, standardized test results, 2 recs. **Enr cap:** 65. **Fac 26. Staff:** Admin 5.
Type of instruction: Adv Dev_Read Enrich Preview Rem_Eng Rem_Math Rem_Read Rev Study_Skills Tut. **Courses:** Fr Span Computers Eng ESL Expository_Writing Math Sci Drama Studio_Art. **Avg class size:** 7. **Daily hours for:** Classes 4. Homework. **Features:** Canoe Fishing Hiking Wilderness_Camp Baseball Basketball Field_Hockey Golf Lacrosse Soccer Softball Swim Tennis Ultimate_Frisbee.
Fees 2013: Res $6500 (+$400), 4 wks. Aid 2006 (Need): $5000.
Housing: Dorms. **Swimming:** Pool.
Est 1996. Nonprofit. **Spons:** Eaglebrook School. **Ses:** 1. **Wks/ses:** 4. Operates July.

Conducted by Eaglebrook School, Summer Semester enables young students to take four courses per day, two academic and two elective. Mornings and early afternoons consist of four hour-long learning blocks, while afternoons provide time for sports and leisure pursuits. Following an early evening activity period, pupils take part in a closely supervised study period five nights a week.

EXCEL AT AMHERST COLLEGE
Res — Coed Ages 15-18

Amherst, MA. Amherst College.
Contact (Year-round): c/o Putney Student Travel, 345 Hickory Ridge Rd, Putney, VT 05346. Tel: 802-387-5000. Fax: 802-387-4276.
https://goputney.com/programs/amherst-college   **E-mail: info@goputney.com**
Maggie Strassman, Dir.
Grades 9-12. Adm: FCFS. **Appl**—Due: Rolling.
Enr: 80-120. **Staff:** Admin 20.
Type of instruction: Adv Enrich Rem_Eng SAT/ACT_Prep Study_Skills Undergrad.
Courses: Fr Span Architect Bus/Fin Debate ESL Expository_Writing Hist Intl_Relations Law Public_Speak Relig_Stud Writing/Journ Philos Creative_Writing Dance Drawing Fashion Film Music Photog Theater Video_Production. **Avg class size:** 10. **Daily hours for:** Classes 4.
Features: Canoe Community_Serv Hiking Mountaineering Wilderness_Camp Soccer Tennis.
Fees 2013: Res $5090, 3 wks.
Housing: Dorms. Campus facilities avail.
Est 1950. Spons: Putney Student Travel. **Ses:** 3. **Wks/ses:** 3-6. Operates June-Aug.

Excel participants choose from courses in the arts, the humanities and contemporary issues, languages and SAT preparation in a collegiate learning environment. Each student enrolls in one major and one enrichment course. Community service opportunities; instructional sports clinics in tennis, soccer and golf; and evening activities supplement academics. See the other domestic Excel listing under Williamstown, MA.

HARVARD UNIVERSITY SUMMER SCHOOL
SECONDARY SCHOOL PROGRAM
Res — Coed Ages 16-18

Cambridge, MA 02138. 51 Brattle St. Tel: 617-495-3192. Fax: 617-496-4525.
www.ssp.harvard.edu   E-mail: ssp@dcemail.harvard.edu
William J. Holinger, Dir.
Grades 11-PG. Adm: Selective. **Appl**—Fee $50. Due: Rolling. Transcript, teacher & administrator recs, PSAT/SAT/ACT scores.
Enr: 1000. **Staff:** Admin 6.
Type of instruction: Adv Preview ESL/TOEFL_Prep Study_Skills Tut Undergrad.
Courses: Arabic Chin Fr Ger Greek Ital Japan Lat Russ Span Hindi Korean Portuguese Sanskrit Archaeol Astron Comp_Sci Econ Education Engineering Environ_Sci ESL Expository_Writing Govt Math Psych Relig_Stud Writing/Journ Sociol Stats Creative_

Writing Dance Drama Music Photog Studio_Art. **Daily hours for:** Classes 2. Homework. Tests. Grades. **College credit:** 4-8/crse, total 8. **Features:** Boating Community_Serv Basketball Soccer Softball Swim Tennis Volleyball. **Fees 2013: Res $2850-5700 (+$5100), 7 wks.** **Housing:** Dorms. **Swimming:** Pool. Campus facilities avail. **Est 1966.** Nonprofit. **Ses:** 1. **Wks/ses:** 7. Operates June-Aug.

Highly qualified high schoolers who have completed their sophomore, junior or senior year may enroll for college credit in the full range of Harvard summer undergraduate courses. The college preparatory program includes study skills workshops, a college fair and trips to other colleges. Summer seminars, based on Harvard's freshman seminars, are limited to 15 students and allow for classroom discussions, close attention to writing and opportunities for independent research under a faculty member. Dances, trivia bowl, a talent show, musical groups, sports, and sightseeing excursions around Boston and New England are among the SSP's activities. SSP also offers distance-learning courses featuring online course materials, discussions and video lectures.

LIFE-TECH VENTURES
Res and Day — Coed Ages 8-16

Charlton, MA 01507. c/o Nature's Classroom, 19 Harrington Rd. Tel: 508-248-2741, 800-433-8375. **www.naturesclassroom.org** **E-mail: info@naturesclassroom.org** John G. Santos, Dir. **Grades 3-10. Adm:** FCFS. **Enr:** 180. **Fac 12. Staff:** Admin 3. **Type of instruction:** Enrich. **Courses:** Astron Ecol Environ_Sci Geol Fine_Arts Theater. **Avg class size:** 9. **Features:** Aquatics Exploration Hiking Ropes_Crse Baseball Basketball Football Soccer Swim Volleyball. **Fees 2013: Res $680, 1-3 wks. Day $225, 1-3 wks.** **Housing:** Dorms. **Swimming:** Pond Pool. **Est 1972.** Nonprofit. **Spons:** Nature's Classroom. **Ses:** 10. **Wks/ses:** 1-2. Operates July-Aug.

LTV offers specific core subjects to which children devote two and a half hours per day. Areas of study include natural science, physical science, computers, robotics, sports, the fine arts and the performing arts. In addition to core classes, each student participates in daily enrichment activities. Traditional recreational activities are also incorporated into the program.

NORTHFIELD MOUNT HERMON SUMMER SESSION
Res and Day — Coed Ages 12-18

Northfield, MA 01354. 1 Lamplighter Way. Tel: 413-498-3290. Fax: 413-498-3112. **www.nmhschool.org/summer-program** **E-mail: summer_school@nmhschool.org** Gregory T. Leeds, Dir. **Grades 7-12. Adm:** FCFS. **Appl**—Fee $50. Due: Rolling. Transcript,2 recs. **Enr:** 250. **Enr cap:** 250. **Fac 75.** Col/grad students 35. K-12 staff 40. **Type of instruction:** Enrich SAT/ACT_Prep Study_Skills. **Courses:** Chin Fr Span Econ ESL Expository_Writing Hist Math Psych Public_Speak Sci Writing/Journ Creative_ Writing Dance Drama Drawing Music Photog Studio_Art. **Avg class size:** 10. **Daily hours for:** Classes 4. Study 2½. Rec 1½. **Features:** Community_Serv Hiking Mtn_Biking Badminton Basketball Soccer Swim Tennis Ultimate_Frisbee Volleyball Weight_Trng. **Fees 2013: Res $7300 (+$50-200), 5 wks. Day $2200 (+$50-200), 5 wks.** **Housing:** Dorms. Avg per room/unit: 2. **Swimming:** Pool. Campus facilities avail. **Est 1961.** Nonprofit. **Ses:** 1. **Wks/ses:** 5. Operates June-Aug.

NMH's Middle School Program (entering grades 7-9) provides a small-class environment in which motivated children take two major courses in the morning, along with a minor afternoon class. Boys and girls play sports in the afternoon. Students entering grades 10-12 may enroll in the College Prep Program, during which they pursue one intensive course three hours each morning (Monday through Saturday). In addition, a sport and an afternoon lab or a minor course convene four afternoons per week. College Prep pupils also spend a few days of the session participating in a community work program. Extracurricular activities typically include both on-campus events and optional trips to beaches, summer theater, an amusement park, classical music concerts, museums and professional baseball games.

PHILLIPS ACADEMY SUMMER SESSION
Res and Day — Coed Ages 13-18

Andover, MA 01810. 180 Main St. Tel: 978-749-4400. Fax: 978-749-4414.
www.andover.edu/summer   E-mail: summer@andover.edu
Fernando Alonso, Dir.
Grades 8-12. Adm: Selective. **Appl**—Fee $60. Due: Rolling. Transcript, essay, 2 recs.
Enr: 659. **Intl:** 47%. **Fac 150. Staff:** Admin 16.
Type of instruction: Adv Enrich Preview Rev SAT/ACT_Prep Study_Skills Undergrad.
  Courses: Chin Fr Lat Span Archaeol Astron Comp_Sci Debate Ecol Econ Engineering ESL Expository_Writing Intl_Relations Math Sci Speech Writing/Journ Acting Animation Ceramics Creative_Writing Dance Filmmaking Fine_Arts Media Music Painting Photog Theater Graphic_Design. **Avg class size:** 14. **Daily hours for:** Classes 3½. Study 4. Rec 2. Homework. Tests. Grades.
Features: Ropes_Crse Yoga Badminton Basketball Soccer Squash Swim Tennis Ultimate_ Frisbee Volleyball Weight_Trng Kickboxing.
Fees 2014: Res $8300-8600 (+$700), 5 wks. Day $4200 (+$700), 5 wks. Aid 2010 (Need): $425,000.
Housing: Dorms. Avg per room/unit: 1-2. **Swimming:** Pool. Campus facilities avail.
Est 1942. Nonprofit. **Ses:** 1. **Wks/ses:** 5. Operates June-Aug.

Enrolling a diverse student body drawn from around the world, Andover maintains a selection of approximately 60 courses in all major disciplines. The individualized program features a low student-faculty ratio and small classes. As the Summer Session provides in-depth study of the material, pupils may take only two courses. In addition to class work, the program includes afternoon recreation, college counseling workshops and trips to nearby colleges, social and cultural opportunities, and a dormitory setting that approximates collegiate living. Rising eighth graders take part in the Lower School Institutes, in which boys and girls pursue an integrated curriculum in two areas of study: math/biology and literature/performance/film.

SUMMERFUEL
THE COLLEGE EXPERIENCE
Res — Coed Ages 15-18

Amherst, MA. Univ of Massachusetts.
Contact (Year-round): c/o Academic Study Associates, 375 W Broadway, Ste 200, New York, NY 10012. **Tel:** 212-796-8340, 800-752-2250. **Fax:** 212-334-4934.
www.summerfuel.com/pre_college/umass_amherst   E-mail: info@summerfuel.com
Grades 10-PG. Adm: FCFS. **Appl**—Fee $0. Due: Rolling. Transcript, rec.
Type of instruction: Enrich Preview SAT/ACT_Prep. **Courses:** Bus/Fin Econ ESL Expository_Writing Intl_Relations Psych Public_Speak Creative_Writing Film Fine_Arts Media Photog Theater Design.
Fees 2014: Res $3695-6695, 2-4 wks.
Housing: Dorms. Avg per room/unit: 4.
Est 1987. Inc. **Spons:** Academic Study Associates. **Ses:** 2. **Wks/ses:** 2-4. Operates June-July.

See program description under Berkeley, CA.

TUFTS SUMMER SESSION
Res and Day — Coed Ages 16-18

Medford, MA 02155. 419 Boston Ave. Tel: 617-627-2000. Fax: 617-627-4691.
www.ase.tufts.edu/summer   E-mail: summer@tufts.edu
Sean Recroft, Dir.
Adm: Selective. **Appl**—Fee $25. Due: May. Transcript, 2 recs, essay, SAT/PSAT scores.
Grades. **College credit.**
Fees 2014: Res $2275-2450. Day $2275.
Housing: Dorms.
Est 1983. Ses: 1. Operates July-Aug.

TuftsStudy gives talented high school students the opportunity to take introductory college courses at Tufts University during the summer before senior year. Students are encouraged to participate in a series of tours and talks introducing them to a variety of career choices and have the opportunity to participate in workshops designed to help them make college decisions.

MICHIGAN

CALVIN COLLEGE
ENTRADA SCHOLARS PROGRAM
Res — Coed Ages 16-18

Grand Rapids, MI 49546. Office of Pre-College Prgms, 3201 Burton St SE. Tel: 616-526-6749, 800-688-0122.
www.calvin.edu/pre-college/programs/entrada   E-mail: entrada@calvin.edu
Grades 11-12. Adm: Selective. Priority: URM. Prereqs: GPA 3.0. **Appl**—Fee $0. Due: Mar.
Transcript, essay, test scores, 2 recs.
Type of instruction: Undergrad. Homework. Tests. Grades. **College credit:** 3-4/crse, total 4.
Features: Community_Serv.
Fees 2014: Res $500, 4 wks. Aid (Merit).
Housing: Dorms. Campus facilities avail.
Ses: 1. **Wks/ses:** 4. Operates June-July.

Entrada Scholars enroll in summer-term classes alongside current Calvin students. Participants are assigned an academic coach, a trained teacher who attends classes with them in the morning and leads a study period after class. Worship services at local churches, Bible studies and daily devotions are also part of the program. Entrada primarily serves African-American, Latino, Asian-American and Native American students entering grades 11 and 12.

MICHIGAN STATE UNIVERSITY
HIGH ACHIEVERS
Res and Day — Coed Ages 15-18

East Lansing, MI 48824. 219 S Harrison Rd, Rm 8. Tel: 517-432-2129. Fax: 517-353-6464.
www.gifted.msu.edu   E-mail: gifted@msu.edu
Stephen Esquith, Dir.
Grades 10-PG. Adm: Somewhat_selective. Admitted: 98%. Prereqs: SAT CR 530, CR/M 1040; PSAT CR 53, CR/M 104; ACT Eng 21, Comp 22; PLAN Eng 21, Comp 22. **Appl**—Fee $70. Due: Apr. Transcript, test scores, essay, rec.
Enr: 20. **Enr cap:** 20. **Staff:** Admin 3.
Type of instruction: Enrich Undergrad. **Courses:** Econ Global_Stud Sci Philos. **Daily**

hours for: Classes 3. Study 2-3. Rec 3. Homework. Tests. Grades. **College credit:** 3½/ crse, total 3.
Features: Swim.
Fees 2012: Res $3620-4688 (+$100-200), 4 wks. Day $1220-2288 (+$100-200), 4 wks.
Housing: Dorms. **Swimming:** Pool. Campus facilities avail.
Est 1986. Nonprofit. **Ses:** 2. **Wks/ses:** 4. Operates June-Aug.

High Achievers participants enroll in an honors-level college course and earn transferable credit. Courses are taught by MSU faculty on topics that vary by year. Boys and girls study a range of subjects through lectures or a combination of lectures and laboratory work.

MICHIGAN TECHNOLOGICAL UNIVERSITY
SUMMER YOUTH PROGRAMS
Res and Day — Coed Ages 11-18

Houghton, MI 49931. 1400 Townsend Dr, 310 Administration Bldg. **Tel:** 906-487-2219, 888-773-2655. **Fax:** 906-487-1136.
www.syp.mtu.edu **E-mail:** yp@mtu.edu
Steve Patchin, Dir.
Grades 6-12 (younger if qualified). Adm: FCFS. **Appl**—Fee $0. Due: Rolling.
Enr: 250. **Enr cap:** 250. Intl: 5%. Non-White: 40%. **Fac 150.** Prof 37. Col/grad students 90. K-12 staff 8. Specialists 15. **Staff:** Admin 7. Couns 75.
Type of instruction: Adv Enrich Preview. **Courses:** Bus/Fin Comp_Sci Engineering Forensic_Sci Web_Design Crafts Media Music Photog. **Avg class size:** 16. **Daily hours for:** Classes 7. Rec 3½. Homework. Tests. Grades.
Features: Adventure_Travel Aquatics Aviation/Aero Climbing_Wall Exploration Fishing Hiking Mountaineering Mtn_Biking Rappelling Rock_Climb Ropes_Crse Wilderness_ Camp Basketball Soccer Swim Tennis Ultimate_Frisbee Volleyball.
Fees 2013: Res $895-920 (+$85-250), 1 wk. Day $450-500 (+$85-250), 1 wk. Aid (Merit & Need).
Housing: Dorms. Avg per room/unit: 2. **Swimming:** Lake Pool. Campus facilities avail.
Est 1973. Nonprofit. **Ses:** 6. **Wks/ses:** 1. Operates June-Aug.

SYP enables students to explore careers and develop skills through hands-on laboratory, classroom and field experiences. Conducted by faculty members, graduate students and other specialists, each session explores one of six areas of study: engineering, science and technology, computers, business, environmental studies, or the arts and the human sciences. Evening and weekend activities facilitate student interaction.

SUMMER DISCOVERY
Res — Coed Ages 15-18

Ann Arbor, MI. Univ of Michigan.
Contact (Year-round): 1326 Old Northern Blvd, Roslyn, NY 11576. **Tel:** 516-621-3939. **Fax:** 516-625-3438.
www.summerdiscovery.com **E-mail:** discovery@summerdiscovery.com
Bob Musiker, Exec Dir.
Grades 10-PG. Adm: FCFS. **Appl**—Fee $95. Due: Rolling.
Type of instruction: Enrich SAT/ACT_Prep Study_Skills. **Courses:** Architect Bus/Fin Comm ESL Govt Law Med/Healthcare Speech Writing/Journ Sports_Management Creative_Writing Filmmaking Fine_Arts Music Photog Theater. Homework.
Features: Adventure_Travel Aquatics Canoe Community_Serv Hiking Kayak Aerobics Basketball Golf Lacrosse Soccer Softball Swim Tennis Track Weight_Trng.
Fees 2014: Res $3499-7199, 2-5 wks. Aid (Need).
Housing: Dorms. **Swimming:** Lake Pool.
Inc. **Ses:** 3. **Wks/ses:** 2-5. Operates June-July.

See program description under Los Angeles, CA.

TELLURIDE ASSOCIATION SUMMER PROGRAM
Res — Coed Ages 17-18

Ann Arbor, MI. Univ of Michigan.
Contact (Year-round): 217 West Ave, Ithaca, NY 14850. **Tel:** 607-273-5011. **Fax:** 607-272-2667.
http://tasp.tellurideassociation.org   **E-mail:** telluride@tellurideassociation.org
Ellen Baer, Admin Dir.
Grade 11. Adm: Very selective. **Appl**—Fee $0. **Due:** Jan. Essays, transcript, standardized test scores.
Enr: 16-18.
Type of instruction: Adv Enrich. **Courses:** Eng Sci Philos.
Fees 2014: Free. Res 6 wks.
Housing: Dorms.
Nonprofit. **Ses:** 2. **Wks/ses:** 6. Operates June-Aug.

This free program for high school juniors operates at two college sites around the country. At each location, TASP students attend an academic seminar that meets each weekday morning for about three hours. Two professors lead each seminar, which is organized around group discussions rather than lectures. Professors meet individually with pupils to discuss writing assignments; instructors do not grade these assignments, instead issuing written comments. Students also attend guest lectures and deliver speeches on topics that interest them.

MINNESOTA

CARLETON LIBERAL ARTS EXPERIENCE
Res — Coed Ages 15-16

Northfield, MN 55057. Carleton College, 100 S College St. **Tel:** 507-222-4190, 800-995-2275. **Fax:** 507-222-4526.
www.carleton.edu/summer/clae   **E-mail:** clae@carleton.edu
Brian Swann, Dir.
Grade 10. Adm: Very selective. **Priority:** URM. **Appl**—Fee $0. **Due:** Apr. Transcript, short essays, teacher recs.
Enr: 50. **Enr cap:** 50. **Fac 4. Staff:** Admin 2. Res 8.
Type of instruction: Enrich SAT/ACT_Prep Undergrad. **Courses:** Col_Prep Econ Expository_Writing Forensic_Sci Sci. **Daily hours for:** Classes 4. Study 2. Rec 1. Homework. Tests.
Features: Basketball Soccer Tennis Track Ultimate_Frisbee.
Fees 2013: Free. Res 1 wk.
Housing: Dorms. Avg per room/unit: 2. Campus facilities avail.
Est 2000. Nonprofit. **Spons:** Carleton College. **Ses:** 1. **Wks/ses:** 1. Operates July.

Current high school sophomores who are of African-American decent or who have an interest in African-American culture may apply to this free, weeklong program. CLAE introduces students to a college liberal arts setting through a varied curriculum that features courses in science, art, the social sciences and technology. In addition to academics, Carleton offers workshops designed to assist boys and girls with their high school and college careers; workshops address such topics as ACT/SAT preparation and the college application process. Various group activities, such as trips to sites of interest in Metropolitan Minneapolis-St. Paul, round out the program.

MINNESOTA INSTITUTE FOR TALENTED YOUTH
EXPAND YOUR MIND
Res and Day — Coed Ages 12-17

St Paul, MN 55105. c/o Macalester College, 1600 Grand Ave. Tel: 651-696-6590. Fax: 651-696-6592.
www.mity.org E-mail: mity@macalester.edu
Roberta Seum, Dir.
Grades 7-11. Adm: Selective. **Appl**—Fee $0. Due: Apr. Transcript, teacher rec, essay.
Type of instruction: Adv Enrich. **Courses:** Architect Math Psych Sci Speech Writing/ Journ Creative_Writing Studio_Art Theater Jazz. **Avg class size:** 16.
Features: Chess Soccer Ultimate_Frisbee.
Fees 2013: Res $1500, 2 wks. Day $580, 2 wks. Aid (Need).
Housing: Dorms. Campus facilities avail.
Est 1967. Nonprofit. **Ses:** 2. Wks/ses: 2. Operates June-July.

Held on the Macalester College campus, this two-week program allows able, intellectually curious teenagers to take a course in one of a variety of subject areas. EYM's enrichment classes employ a hands-on approach. Another program of the Minnesota Institute for Talented Youth, ExplorSchool, serves day pupils entering grades 4-6.

MISSISSIPPI

UNIVERSITY OF MISSISSIPPI
SUMMER COLLEGE FOR HIGH SCHOOL STUDENTS
Res — Coed Ages 16-17

University, MS 38677. PO Box 9. Tel: 662-915-7621. Fax: 662-915-1535.
www.outreach.olemiss.edu/schs E-mail: summercollege@olemiss.edu
Jason E. Wilkins, Dir.
Grades 11-12. Adm: Selective. **Prereqs:** GPA 2.75. **Appl**—Fee $50. Due: May. Transcript, 2 recs.
Enr: 200. **Enr cap:** 200.
Type of instruction: ESL/TOEFL_Prep Undergrad. **Courses:** Span Bus/Fin Comp_Sci Engineering Law Med/Healthcare Writing/Journ Studio_Art. **Daily hours for:** Classes 4. Tests. Grades. **College credit:** 6.
Fees 2014: Res $2050-2400 (+$400), 4 wks. Aid (Merit & Need).
Housing: Dorms. Campus facilities avail.
Est 1980. Nonprofit. **Ses:** 2. Wks/ses: 4. Operates May-July.

Academically gifted high school upperclassmen get a head start on their college careers by choosing two courses from a full complement of University of Mississippi offerings. In most cases, these courses, which are taught by university faculty and which result in an average of six hours of transferable college credit, also include current Ole Miss underclassmen. An accompanying noncredit class helps students explore their academic and career interests while also learning about the college selection process. Boys and girls devote some afternoon time to creative, academic and athletic activities, and weekends provide opportunities for various excursions and entertainment options.

MISSOURI

MISSOURI MILITARY ACADEMY
SUMMER SCHOOL
Res — Boys Ages 12-17; Day — Coed 12-17

Mexico, MO 65265. 204 N Grand St. Tel: 573-581-1776, 888-564-6662. Fax: 573-581-0081.
www.missourimilitaryacademy.org   E-mail: info@missourimilitaryacademy.org
Maj. Mark Vaughan, Dir.
Grades 7-12. Adm: FCFS. **Appl**—Fee $100. **Due:** Rolling.
Staff: Admin 3. Couns 15.
Courses: Span Eng ESL Hist Math Sci.
Features: Aquatics Archery Boating Canoe Exploration Fishing Hiking Leadership Milit_ Trng Paintball Rappelling Riding Riflery Ropes_Crse Wilderness_Camp Wilderness_ Canoe Basketball Equestrian Soccer Swim Tennis Watersports Weight_Trng.
Fees 2013: Res $3750, 4 wks. Day $2500, 4 wks.
Housing: Dorms. **Swimming:** Pool.
Est 1999. Nonprofit. Ses: 1. **Wks/ses:** 4. Operates July.

This recovery and enrichment program allows students to repair poor past performances, expand scope of knowledge and sharpen study skills. Students may participate in a variety of recreational activities, and a sports camp is included in the cost of the boarding program. The academy also runs a two-week leadership camp for boys, ages 13-17.

NEW HAMPSHIRE

BREWSTER ACADEMY SUMMER SESSION
Res and Day — Coed Ages 13-17

Wolfeboro, NH 03894. 80 Academy Dr. Tel: 603-569-7155. Fax: 603-569-7050.
www.brewsteracademy.org   E-mail: summer@brewsteracademy.org
Raylene Davis, Dir.
Adm: Selective. **Appl**—Fee $35. **Due:** Rolling. Transcript, standardized test results, 2 teacher recs, writing samples (Eng/ESL core crses).
Enr cap: 55. **Fac** 10. **K-12 staff** 10. **Staff:** Admin 8. Couns 10.
Type of instruction: Adv Enrich Study_Skills. **Courses:** Comp_Sci ESL Math Sci Comp_ Graphics Video_Production. **Daily hours for:** Classes 4. Study 1½. Rec 3. Homework. Tests. Grades. **High school credit:** 1.
Features: Canoe Climbing_Wall Hiking Kayak Rock_Climb Basketball Soccer Softball Swim Volleyball.
Fees 2013: Res $6400-7025 (+$850), 6 wks. Day $3600 (+$850), 6 wks.
Housing: Dorms. **Swimming:** Lake. Campus facilities avail.
Est 1994. Nonprofit. Ses: 1. **Wks/ses:** 6. Operates June-Aug.

Brewster Summer Session offers a combination of classroom academics and outdoor education. Students take one core course in English, math or ESL, and choose two electives from computer graphics and design, experiential science, video production and instructional support. Afternoon outdoor activities include survival training, rock climbing, canoeing and kayaking. Recreational sports, games and social activities are popular evening pursuits.

CARDIGAN MOUNTAIN SCHOOL SUMMER SESSION
Res and Day — Coed Ages 8-15

Canaan, NH 03741. 62 Alumni Dr. Tel: 603-523-3526. Fax: 603-523-3565.

www.cardigan.org/summer   E-mail: summer@cardigan.org
Devin Clifford, Dir.
Grades 3-9 (younger if qualified). Adm: Selective. Admitted: 90%. **Appl**—Fee $50. Due: Rolling. Transcript, teacher rec, parent & student statements.
Enr: 146. **Enr cap:** 150. Intl: 40%. Non-White: 35%. **Fac 40.** Col/grad students 7. K-12 staff 33. **Staff:** Admin 7. Couns 40.
Type of instruction: Adv Dev_Read Enrich Rem_Eng Rem_Math Rem_Read Rev ESL/TOEFL_Prep SAT/ACT_Prep Study_Skills Tut. **Courses:** Fr Lat Span Ecol Environ_Sci ESL Expository_Writing Math Writing/Journ Crafts Creative_Writing Fine_Arts Music Photog Studio_Art Theater. **Avg class size:** 6. **Daily hours for:** Classes 4. Study 1. Rec 4. Homework. Grades.
Features: Canoe Hiking Riding Riflery Sail Wilderness_Camp Wilderness_Canoe Woodcraft Basketball Lacrosse Soccer Swim Tennis.
Fees 2013: Res $5045-8400, 3-6 wks. Day $2570-4300, 3-6 wks. Aid 2011 (Need): $115,000.
Housing: Dorms Houses. Avg per room/unit: 2. **Swimming:** Lake. Campus facilities avail.
Est 1951. Nonprofit. **Ses:** 3. **Wks/ses:** 3-6. Operates June-Aug.

Cardigan Mountain offers individualized and intensive developmental, enrichment and remedial work in English, math, Spanish, Latin, French, environmental science, reading and study skills, computers and ESL. A language learning lab serves students who require significant remediation in reading or writing. Afternoons are devoted to such traditional camp activities as tennis, swimming and soccer.

OLIVERIAN SCHOOL SUMMER SESSION
Res — Coed Ages 14-17

Haverhill, NH 03765. Mt Moosilauke Hwy, PO Box 98. Tel: 603-989-5368. Fax: 603-989-3055.
www.oliverianschool.org/summer_program
E-mail: bmackinnon@oliverianschool.org
Barclay Mackinnon, Head Emeritus, Dir of Adm.
Grades 9-12. Adm: FCFS. **Appl**—Due: Rolling.
Type of instruction: Enrich. **Courses:** Eng Math Dance Studio_Art Theater Pottery. **High school credit.**
Features: Hiking Kayak Paintball Riding Rock_Climb Martial_Arts Gardening.
Fees 2007: Res $8000, 7 wks. Aid (Need).
Housing: Dorms.
Ses: 1. **Wks/ses:** 7. Operates June-Aug.

Oliverian combines academics with an experiential activities program. Courses, which lead to high school credit in English, math, art and the social sciences, convene in the morning on Monday through Thursday. Integrated learning and activities fill the afternoon hours, while Fridays are reserved for field trips and off-campus learning. Students spend one of the seven weeks of the session engaged in off-campus adventure instead of academics. Faculty schedule recreational and enrichment pursuits for evenings and weekends.

WOLFEBORO
THE SUMMER BOARDING SCHOOL
Res — Coed Ages 10-18

Wolfeboro, NH 03894. 93 Camp School Rd, PO Box 390. Tel: 603-569-3451. Fax: 603-569-4080.
www.wolfeboro.org   **E-mail:** school@wolfeboro.org
Edward A. Cooper, Head.
Grades 6-PG. Adm: Selective. Admitted: 25%. **Appl**—Fee $0. Due: Rolling.
Enr: 180. **Enr cap:** 180. Intl: 30%. Non-White: 20%. **Fac 35.** K-12 staff 35. **Staff:** Admin 6. Res 35.

Type of instruction: Adv Dev_Read Enrich Preview Rem_Eng Rem_Math Rem_Read Rev SAT/ACT_Prep Study_Skills Tut. **Courses:** Fr Lat Span Eng Environ_Sci ESL Expository_Writing Hist Math Sci Fine_Arts. **Avg class size:** 5. **Daily hours for:** Classes 5. Study 4. Rec 4. Homework. Tests. Grades. **High school credit:** 3.
Features: Aquatics Boating Canoe Fishing Hiking Kayak Baseball Basketball Lacrosse Soccer Softball Swim Tennis Volleyball Watersports Weight_Trng.
Fees 2011: Res $12,500 (+$1500), 6 wks. Aid 2010 (Need): $190,000.
Housing: Tents. Avg per room/unit: 2. **Swimming:** Lake. Campus facilities avail.
Est 1910. Nonprofit. **Ses:** 1. **Wks/ses:** 6. Operates June-Aug.

Wolfeboro combines individualized academic instruction in the mornings with recreational activities in the afternoons and on weekends. Students may take courses for credit, or they may review or preview work, or strengthen skills in core subjects. Particularly noteworthy among extracurriculars is the school's strong intramural sports program. Boys and girls may go on weekend excursions to nearby events and areas of interest, including professional baseball games, water and amusement parks, and movies.

NEW JERSEY

THE HUN SCHOOL OF PRINCETON
SUMMER ACADEMIC SESSION
Res — Coed Ages 13-17; Day — Coed 11-17

Princeton, NJ 08540. 176 Edgerstoune Rd. Tel: 609-921-7600. Fax: 609-921-0953.
www.hunschool.org　E-mail: summer@hunschool.org
Donna O'Sullivan, Dir.
Grades 6-12. Adm: Somewhat_selective. Admitted: 98%. **Appl**—Fee $0. Due: June. Rec.
Enr: 120. Enr cap: 150. Intl: 20%. **Fac 25.** K-12 staff 25. **Staff:** Admin 5. Couns 12.
Type of instruction: Adv Enrich Preview Rev ESL/TOEFL_Prep SAT/ACT_Prep. **Courses:** Econ Eng Marine_Bio/Stud Math Sci Amer_Stud Human_Rights Creative_Writing. **Avg class size:** 12. **Daily hours for:** Classes 5. Study 2. Rec 6. Homework. Tests. Grades. **High school credit:** 1/crse, total 1.
Features: Basketball Soccer Ultimate_Frisbee Volleyball.
Fees 2013: Res $5765 (+$25-200), 5 wks. Day $1335-2320 (+$25-200), 5 wks.
Housing: Dorms. Campus facilities avail.
Est 1984. Nonprofit. **Ses:** 1. **Wks/ses:** 5. Operates June-July.

The Hun School offers summer classes for credit, preview, review and enrichment. Credit-bearing courses are available in chemistry, algebra, geometry and pre-calculus. Enrichment options include SAT critical reading and SAT math preparation, creative writing, literature, math and science. Fitness training, games and off-campus trips are popular activities.

NEW JERSEY SCHOLARS PROGRAM
Res — Coed Ages 16-18

Lawrenceville, NJ 08648. c/o Lawrenceville School, PO Box 6008. Tel: 609-620-6106.
Fax: 609-620-6894.
www.newjerseyscholarsprogram.org　E-mail: njsp@lawrenceville.org
John P. Sauerman, Dir.
Grade 12. Adm: Very selective. Priority: Low-income. **Appl**—Fee $0. Due: Jan. Essays, rec, group interview.
Enr: 39. Enr cap: 39.
Type of instruction: Adv Enrich. **Courses:** Expository_Writing Public_Speak Drama Music. **Daily hours for:** Classes 4½. Homework.
Features: Swim.
Fees 2014: Free (in-state residents). Res 5 wks.
Housing: Dorms. **Swimming:** Pool. Campus facilities avail.

Nonprofit. **Ses:** 1. **Wks/ses:** 5. Operates June-July.

Limited to New Jersey residents, NJSP brings highly motivated rising seniors from diverse socioeconomic, ethnic and racial backgrounds to the Lawrenceville School campus for five weeks of college-level study. Program topics, which rotate biennially, are interdisciplinary in nature. Each day begins with a whole-group lecture, after which boys and girls attend morning and afternoon group seminars and engage in extensive reading assignments and research at museums and libraries. Students work closely with college faculty to produce a 10- to 15-page research paper, and they also contribute to an arts festival that is thematically related to the academic curriculum. Each pupil must be nominated by his or her guidance counselor.

NEW YORK

BARNARD COLLEGE
SUMMER IN THE CITY
Res and Day — Coed Ages 16-18

New York, NY 10027. Office of Pre-College Prgms, 3009 Broadway, Milbank 235. Tel: 212-854-8866. Fax: 212-854-8867.
www.barnard.edu/precollege   E-mail: pcp@barnard.edu
Ann Dachs, Dir.
Grades 11-12. Adm: Selective. **Appl**—Fee $50. Due: May. Transcript, essay, 2 recs.
Enr cap: 160. **Staff:** Admin 3. Res 22.
Type of instruction: Adv Enrich Undergrad. **Courses:** Architect Comp_Sci Hist Pol_Sci Psych Sci Anthro Sociol Women's_Stud Acting Creative_Writing Dance Film Music Theater. **Avg class size:** 15. **Daily hours for:** Classes 4. Study 2. Rec 3. Homework.
Fees 2014: Res $6450 (+$75-150), 1-4 wks. Day $4150 (+$75-150), 1-4 wks. Aid (Need).
Housing: Dorms. Avg per room/unit: 2.
Est 1984. Nonprofit. **Ses:** 2. **Wks/ses:** 1-4. Operates June-July.

Barnard offers four-week courses and weeklong minicourses in the liberal arts and the humanities. Four-week program participants attend morning and afternoon classes four days each week, with Wednesdays spent visiting professional or community service organizations or attending on-campus seminars. Evening and weekend pursuits include dance classes, movie nights, and trips to New York City landmarks and festivals.

COLUMBIA UNIVERSITY
SUMMER PROGRAM FOR HIGH SCHOOL STUDENTS
Res and Day — Coed Ages 14-18

New York, NY., 2970 Broadway
Contact (Year-round): Mail Code 4110, New York, NY 10027. Tel: 212-854-9889. Fax: 212-854-7077.
www.ce.columbia.edu/hs   E-mail: hsp@columbia.edu
Mark Blacher, Dir.
Grades 9-12. Adm: Selective. Admitted: 75%. Prereqs: GPA 3.0. **Appl**—Fee $75-150. Due: Apr. Transcript, 2 recommendations, essay.
Enr: 1000. **Enr cap:** 1500. Intl: 33%. **Fac** 80. **Staff:** Admin 10. Res 150.
Type of instruction: Adv Enrich Study_Skills Undergrad. **Courses:** Bus/Fin Comp_Sci Debate Econ Engineering Expository_Writing Govt Law Creative_Writing Drawing Filmmaking Media Photog Theater. **Avg class size:** 25. **Daily hours for:** Classes 4. Homework.
Travel: NY Europe Middle_East.
Features: Swim.
Fees 2014: Res $4506-9850 (+$985-1310), 3 wks. Day 3 wks.
Housing: Dorms. Avg per room/unit: 1. **Swimming:** Pool. Campus facilities avail.

Est 1987. Nonprofit. **Ses:** 2. **Wks/ses:** 3. Operates June-Aug.

The program enrolls high schoolers in two divisions, organized by grade level: one for students entering grades 9 and 10, the other for pupils entering grades 11 and 12. Participants in both sections follow a curriculum designed to meet the interests, talents and needs of college-bound students. The program includes time each day for independent study and tutorials, private meetings with instructors, extracurricular activities, and use of the university's libraries and other facilities. Although these noncredit courses do not culminate in letter grades, participants receive extensive performance evaluations throughout and at course's end.

HUMANITIES SPRING IN NEW YORK
Res and Day — Coed Ages 18 and up

New York, NY.
Contact (Year-round): Santa Maria di Lignano 2, Assisi, 06081 Italy. **Tel:** 011-39-075-802400. **Fax:** 011-39-075-802400.
www.humanitiesspring.com   E-mail: info@humanitiesspring.com
Jane R. Oliensis, Dir. Student contact: Alessia Montanucci.
Adm: FCFS. **Appl**—Fee $50. Due: Rolling.
Enr: 15. **Enr cap:** 15. **Intl:** 80%. **Fac 4.** Prof 1. Col/grad students 1. K-12 staff 1. Specialists 1. **Staff:** Admin 1. Couns 2.
Type of instruction: Enrich. **Courses:** Architect NYC_Hist Poetry Creative_Writing Photog Studio_Art. **Daily hours for:** Classes 4. Study 1. Rec 7½.
Features: Cooking Swim.
Fees 2012: Res $4250 **(+$500), 4½ wks. Day** $3500 **(+$100), 4½ wks.** Aid 2011 (Merit & Need): $5000.
Swimming: Pool. Campus facilities avail.
Est 2006. Nonprofit. **Ses:** 1. **Wks/ses:** 4½. Operates Aug.

From their home base at the 92nd Street YMHA, HSNY students learn about New York City through a combination of academics and firsthand exploration of related works of art and architecture. During four hours of class work each morning, participants take courses that examine the history, architecture and art of the city. Pupils spend the afternoon hours visiting such sites as City Hall, the Chrysler Building and the Empire State Building in the company of New York architects. Applicants need not have any background knowledge of art or architecture.

RENSSELAER POLYTECHNIC INSTITUTE
SUMMER@RENSSELAER
Res — Coed Ages 15-18

Troy, NY 12180. Academic Outreach Programs Office, 110 8th St. **Tel:** 518-276-8351. **Fax:** 518-276-8738.
http://summer.rpi.edu   E-mail: gunthm@rpi.edu
Student contact: Mike Gunther.
Grades 10-12. Adm: Somewhat_selective. **Appl**—Fee $0. Due: Rolling.
Type of instruction: Enrich Undergrad. **Courses:** Architect Bus/Fin Computers Engineering Med/Healthcare Sci.
Features: Aviation/Aero.
Fees 2011: Res $1400-3000, 1-2 wks.
Housing: Dorms.
Wks/ses: 1-2. Operates July-Aug.

Rensselaer conducts a range of residential, noncredit enrichment programs for high school students. Program sessions, which last for one or two weeks (depending upon the subject area), specialize in aerospace engineering, architecture, business, chemistry and medicine, computer game development and engineering. In addition to these high school residential options, RPI offers various commuter programs for elementary, middle school and high school pupils.

SKIDMORE COLLEGE
PRE-COLLEGE PROGRAM IN THE LIBERAL AND STUDIO ARTS
Res — Coed Ages 16-18; Day — Coed 15-18

Saratoga Springs, NY 12866. 815 N Broadway. Tel: 518-580-5590. Fax: 518-580-5548. www.skidmore.edu/precollege   E-mail: summerprecollege@skidmore.edu
Michelle Paquette, Dir.
Student contact: Mary Cogan, E-mail: mcogan@skidmore.edu.
Grades 9-12. Adm: Selective. Appl—Fee $40. Due: Rolling. Transcript, 2 recs, art samples.
Enr: 110. Fac 20. Prof 20. Staff: Admin 3.
Type of instruction: Adv Undergrad. Courses: Ger Ecol Environ_Sci Expository_Writing Hist Sci Ceramics Creative_Writing Drama Filmmaking Music Painting Studio_Art. Avg class size: 10. Daily hours for: Classes 4. Study 4. High school & college credit: 8.
Features: Swim.
Fees 2014: Res $1450-5680 (+$2260), 5 wks. Day $1450-5680, 5 wks. Aid (Merit & Need).
Housing: Dorms. Swimming: Pool.
Est 1978. Nonprofit. Ses: 1. Wks/ses: 5. Operates June-Aug.

Students who have completed sophomore, junior or senior year may earn college credits in a variety of foundation-level Skidmore College courses in the liberal arts and sciences. In addition, rising sophomores may apply as commuter students to take noncredit studio arts classes that carry much of the same demands as for-credit courses. Extracurricular activities include poetry and fiction readings, films, art lectures, cultural field trips, and activities for recreation and relaxation.

TELLURIDE ASSOCIATION SUMMER PROGRAM
Res — Coed Ages 17-18

Ithaca, NY. Cornell Univ.
Contact (Year-round): 217 West Ave, Ithaca, NY 14850. Tel: 607-273-5011. Fax: 607-272-2667.
http://tasp.tellurideassociation.org   E-mail: telluride@tellurideassociation.org
Ellen Baer, Admin Dir.
Grade 11. Adm: Very selective. Appl—Fee $0. Due: Jan. Essays, transcript, standardized test scores.
Enr: 16-18.
Type of instruction: Adv Enrich. Courses: Eng Sci Philos.
Fees 2014: Free. Res 6 wks.
Housing: Dorms.
Nonprofit. Ses: 2. Wks/ses: 6. Operates June-Aug.

See program description under Ann Arbor, MI.

UNITED STATES MILITARY ACADEMY
SUMMER LEADERS SEMINAR
Res — Coed Ages 17-18

West Point, NY 10996. Office of Adm, 606 Thayer Rd. Tel: 845-938-4041.
www.admissions.usma.edu   E-mail: admissions-info@usma.edu
Grade 11. Adm: Very_selective. Admitted: 30%. Prereqs: 1200. Appl—Due: Apr. Transcript, standardized test scores.
Enr: 500. Enr cap: 500.
Type of instruction: Enrich. Courses: Arabic Chin Leadership Math Sci.
Focus: Leadership. Features: Leadership.
Fees 2014: Res $400, 1 wk.
Housing: Dorms. Campus facilities avail.
Nonprofit. Ses: 2. Wks/ses: 1. Operates May-June.

Rising high school juniors from around the country preview college life during SLS. The selective weeklong program combines academic classes, military and physical fitness training, and intramural athletics.

NORTH CAROLINA

DUKE UNIVERSITY TALENT IDENTIFICATION PROGRAM
SUMMER STUDIES PROGRAMS
Res — Coed Ages 12-16

Davidson, NC. Davidson College.
Contact (Year-round): 1121 W Main St, Durham, NC 27701. **Tel:** 919-668-9100. **Fax:** 919-681-7921.
www.tip.duke.edu   E-mail: information@tip.duke.edu
Brian Cooper, Dir.
Grades 8-11. Adm: Selective. **Appl**—Fee $25. Due: Rolling.
Type of instruction: Adv Enrich. **Courses:** Architect Bus/Fin Debate Engineering Math Med/Healthcare Sci Writing/Journ Creative_Writing. **Avg class size:** 16. **Daily hours for:** Classes 7. Rec 3.
Fees 2014: Res $3675-3925, 3 wks. Aid (Need).
Housing: Dorms.
Est 1980. Nonprofit. **Ses:** 2. **Wks/ses:** 3. Operates June-Aug.

See program description under Lawrence, KS.

DUKE UNIVERSITY TALENT IDENTIFICATION PROGRAM
SUMMER STUDIES PROGRAMS
Res — Coed Ages 11-15

Boone, NC. Appalachian State Univ.
Contact (Year-round): 1121 W Main St, Durham, NC 27701. **Tel:** 919-668-9100. **Fax:** 919-681-7921.
www.tip.duke.edu   E-mail: information@tip.duke.edu
Brian Cooper, Dir.
Grades 7-10. Adm: Selective. **Appl**—Fee $25. Due: Rolling. SAT/ACT requirement, personal statement.
Type of instruction: Adv Enrich. **Courses:** Engineering Environ_Sci Expository_Writing Math Creative_Writing Filmmaking Theater. **Avg class size:** 16. **Daily hours for:** Classes 7. Rec 3.
Fees 2014: Res $3675-3925, 3 wks. Aid (Need).
Housing: Dorms.
Est 1980. Nonprofit. **Ses:** 2. **Wks/ses:** 3. Operates June-July.

See program description under Lawrence, KS.

OAK RIDGE MILITARY ACADEMY
ACADEMIC SUMMER SCHOOL
Res and Day — Coed Ages 11-17

Oak Ridge, NC 27310. 2317 Oak Ridge Rd, PO Box 498. Tel: 336-643-4131. **Fax:** 336-643-1797.
www.oakridgemilitary.com/summer-camps   E-mail: admissions@ormila.com
Student contact: Bob Lipke, **E-mail:** blipke@ormila.com.
Grades 7-12. Adm: FCFS. **Appl**—Due: Rolling.
Fac 15.
Type of instruction: Adv Enrich Preview Rem_Eng Rem_Math Rem_Read Rev Study_

Skills. **Courses:** Span ESL. **Avg class size:** 11. **Daily hours for:** Classes 4. Study 2. Rec 4. **High school credit:** 1.
Features: Canoe Hiking Leadership Milit_Trng Rappelling Scuba Survival_Trng Wilderness_Camp Baseball Basketball Soccer Swim Tennis Volleyball Watersports.
Fees 2013: Res $3900. Day $1950.
Housing: Dorms. **Swimming:** Lake Pool.
Nonprofit. **Ses:** 4. **Wks/ses:** 2½-5. Operates July-Aug.

This academic summer school enables students to develop academically while developing leadership and self-discipline skills. Pupils may earn high school credit in various subject areas. Three days per week and on weekends, participants take part in leadership training activities involving rappelling, confidence courses and athletics.

OHIO

THE GRAND RIVER SUMMER ACADEMY
Res — Boys Ages 14-17

Austinburg, OH 44010. 3042 College St. Tel: 440-275-2811. Fax: 440-275-1825.
www.grandriver.org E-mail: admissions@grandriver.org
Grades 9-12. Adm: FCFS. **Appl**—Due: Rolling.
Enr: 100. **Fac** 20. **Staff:** Admin 6. Couns 1. Special needs 1.
Type of instruction: SAT/ACT_Prep. **Courses:** Fr Span Eng ESL Expository_Writing Govt Hist Math Sci.
Features: Paintball Basketball Cross-country Swim Tennis Ultimate_Frisbee Volleyball Weight_Trng.
Fees 2013: Res $3800, 5 wks.
Housing: Dorms. **Swimming:** Lake.
Est 1990. Nonprofit. **Spons:** Grand River Academy. **Ses:** 1. **Wks/ses:** 5. Operates June-Aug.

Offering five- and seven-day boarding options, Grand River's summer program allows students to either work on an academic problem area or investigate a new subject. An ESL immersion program is available for international students. Study skills are an integral aspect of the program, and all pupils take part in a proctored study period for two hours daily. Students devote afternoons to activity blocks that include horseback riding, arts and crafts, recreational electives and a sports program, and Grand River also schedules excursions to area attractions.

WRIGHT STATE UNIVERSITY PRE-COLLEGE PROGRAMS
Res — Coed Ages 12-17; Day — Coed 5-14

Dayton, OH 45435. 3640 Colonel Glenn Hwy. Tel: 937-775-3135. Fax: 937-775-4883.
www.wright.edu/academics/precollege E-mail: precollege@wright.edu
Brenda I. Dewberry, Dir.
Grades K-12. Adm: FCFS. **Appl**—Fee $150. Due: Rolling.
Fac 20. **Staff:** Admin 4.
Type of instruction: Adv Enrich Study_Skills. **Courses:** Comp_Sci Engineering Forensic_Sci Math Sci Speech Art Creative_Writing Music Photog Studio_Art Theater. **Avg class size:** 17. **Daily hours for:** Classes 6. Study 2. Rec 2. Homework.
Features: Cooking Leadership Swim.
Fees 2013: Res $650, 1 wk. Day $125, 1 wk.
Housing: Dorms. **Swimming:** Pool. Campus facilities avail.
Est 1988. Nonprofit. **Wks/ses:** 1. Operates June-Aug.

Wright State offers precollege enrichment programs in a rotating selection of subject areas. Residential Camps (for students entering grades 6-9) and Institutes (grades 10-12) are weeklong programs exploring engineering, law, leadership, math, science, technology, the arts, anatomy and physiology, forensic science and creative writing. Each program incorporates lectures, hands-on projects, small-group discussions and program-specific field trips. Nonresidential enrichment courses accommodate pupils entering grades K-9.

OREGON

DELPHIAN SCHOOL
SUMMER AT DELPHI
Res — Coed Ages 8-18; Day — Coed 5-18

Sheridan, OR 97378. 20950 SW Rock Creek Rd. Tel: 503-843-3521, 800-626-6610.
Fax: 503-843-4158.
www.summeratdelphi.org   E-mail: summer@delphian.org
Donetta Phelps, Dir.
Grades K-12 (younger if qualified). Adm: FCFS. Appl—Fee $50. Due: Rolling.
Enr: 300. Enr cap: 300. Intl: 42%. Non-White: 63%. Fac 54. K-12 staff 54. Staff: Admin 45.
Type of instruction: Enrich Rem_Eng Rem_Math Rem_Read Rev ESL/TOEFL_Prep Study_Skills Tut. Courses: Fr Comm Computers Econ Eng Environ_Sci ESL Expository_Writing Hist Math Public_Speak Sci Ceramics Crafts Creative_Writing Drama Filmmaking Music Photog Studio_Art. Avg class size: 17. Daily hours for: Classes 5. Rec 5.
Features: Archery Hiking Riding Wilderness_Camp Yoga Basketball Soccer Softball Swim Tennis Volleyball.
Fees 2014: Res $6398-8982 (+$1300), 4 wks. Day $3274-4096 (+$990), 4 wks.
Housing: Dorms. Avg per room/unit: 3. Swimming: Lake Ocean Pool River Stream. Campus facilities avail.
Est 1976. Nonprofit. Ses: 2. Wks/ses: 4-6. Operates June-Aug.

Summer at Delphi blends academics, sports, challenging activities and weekend trips. Additionally, students may brush up on weak areas, get ahead in others, or take advantage of such curricular opportunities as computers, outdoor courses and special-interest projects. Delphi tailors each program to the individual pupil. One-on-one assistance is available, and individual progress speed is not related to that of the student's classmates. Those who have mastered the basics may proceed to advanced subjects or explore new areas. An ESL program serves boys and girls seeking to improve their English language skills.

SOUTHERN OREGON UNIVERSITY
ACADEMIA LATINA
Res — Coed Ages 12-14

Ashland, OR 97520. 1250 Siskiyou Blvd. Tel: 541-552-6326. Fax: 541-552-6047.
www.sou.edu/youth/latino/index.html   E-mail: jensen@sou.edu
Carol Jensen, Dir.
Grades 7-9. Adm: Somewhat_selective. Priority: URM. Prereqs: GPA 2.75. Appl—Fee $0.
Due: May. Transcript, 3 recs, 2 essays, signs of special interest.
Enr: 66.
Type of instruction: Enrich. Courses: Portuguese Col_Prep Expository_Writing Forensic_ Sci Math Med/Healthcare Humanities Creative_Writing Dance Drama Music Photog Studio_Art. Daily hours for: Classes 4½.
Fees 2014: Free. Res (+$75), 1 wk.
Housing: Dorms.
Est 1999. Nonprofit. Ses: 1. Wks/ses: 1. Operates Aug.

This weeklong academic program exposes young Latino students to the learning and career possibilities of college. Academia Latina integrates classes, field trips, cultural experiences and recreational activities. The daily schedule on Monday through Friday includes three one-

and-a-half-hour classes, plus special presentations. Course work draws from the disciplines of math, science, the humanities, social studies, cultural studies, and the fine and performing arts.

SOUTHERN OREGON UNIVERSITY SUMMER ACADEMY
Res — Coed Ages 10-13

Ashland, OR 97520. 1250 Siskiyou Blvd. Tel: 541-552-6326. Fax: 541-552-6047. www.sou.edu/youth/academy   E-mail: jensen@sou.edu
Carol Jensen, Dir.
Grades 5-8. Adm: Selective. Admitted: 95%. Prereqs: GPA 3.4. **Appl**—Fee $25. Due: Rolling. Transcript, achievement test scores, essay, 2 recs.
Enr: 150. **Enr cap:** 150. **Fac 25.** Prof 13. K-12 staff 12. **Staff:** Admin 7.
Type of instruction: Adv Enrich SAT/ACT_Prep Study_Skills. **Courses:** Comm Ecol Engineering Environ_Sci Forensic_Sci Writing/Journ Creative_Writing Filmmaking Fine_Arts Music Sculpt Theater. **Avg class size:** 15. **Daily hours for:** Classes 4. Study 1. Rec 3.
Features: Cooking Ropes_Crse Basketball Swim Volleyball.
Fees 2014: Res $750, 1 wk. Aid (Need).
Housing: Dorms. **Swimming:** Lake Pool. Campus facilities avail.
Est 1982. Nonprofit. **Ses: 2. Wks/ses: 1.** Operates June.

The academy offers talented students a balance of science, math, language, fine arts and social studies courses designed to provide stimulation and challenge. The daily schedule includes four one-hour classes, plus special presentations built around a theme. In addition to the boarding program for middle schoolers, the university conducts day sessions for elementary and high school students.

PENNSYLVANIA

INDIANA UNIVERSITY OF PENNSYLVANIA
ROBERT E. COOK HONORS COLLEGE
SUMMER HONORS PROGRAM FOR HIGH SCHOOL STUDENTS
Res — Coed Ages 16-18

Indiana, PA 15705. 290 Pratt Dr, 136 Whitmyre Hall. Tel: 724-357-4971, 800-487-9122. Fax: 724-357-3906.
www.iup.edu/honors/summer   E-mail: honors@iup.edu
Janet Goebel, Dir.
Grades 11-12 (younger if qualified). Adm: Selective. **Appl**—Due: Rolling. Transcript, essays, 2 teacher recs.
Enr: 150. **Enr cap:** 200. **Fac 15. Staff:** Admin 4. Couns 18.
Type of instruction: Adv Enrich. **Courses:** Eng Forensic_Sci Law Psych Sci Writing/Journ Music. **Avg class size:** 18. **Daily hours for:** Classes 6. Study 2. Rec 2.
Fees 2013: Res $300, 2 wks. Aid (Need).
Housing: Dorms.
Est 1995. Nonprofit. **Ses: 2. Wks/ses:** 1-2. Operates July.

Conducted at the Honors College of the Indiana University of Pennsylvania, the Summer Honors Program enables rising high school juniors and seniors (and particularly able rising sophomores) to live and study in a university setting. In the morning, students attend a specialized course in a discipline such as physics, journalism or forensic science. Afternoons are devoted to a core course in which boys and girls develop critical thinking skills through group discussions, writing and presentations. In this interdisciplinary core course, pupils further develop their critical-thinking skills in the process of analyzing arguments and participating in group discussions, writing assignments and group presentations.

SAINT VINCENT COLLEGE CHALLENGE PROGRAM
Res and Day — Coed Ages 11-17

Latrobe, PA 15650. 300 Fraser Purchase Rd. Tel: 724-805-2363.
www.stvincent.edu/challenge_home   E-mail: challenge@email.stvincent.edu
Donna Hupe & Kathy Beining, Dirs.
Grades 6-12. Adm: Selective. **Appl—Fee** $0. Due: Rolling. Rec.
Enr: 125. **Fac 18. Staff:** Admin 4. Couns 12.
Type of instruction: Adv Enrich Undergrad. **Courses:** Archaeol Comp_Sci Debate Hist Law Math Acting Dance Drama Media Music Painting Photog. **Avg class size:** 18. **Daily hours for:** Classes 6. Rec 6. **College credit:** 4.
Features: Adventure_Travel Canoe Caving Chess Conservation Cooking Hiking Kayak Outdoor_Ed Ropes_Crse Survival_Trng Swim.
Fees 2011: Res $635, 1 wk. Day $535, 1 wk. Aid (Merit).
Housing: Dorms. Avg per room/unit: 2. **Swimming:** Pool. Campus facilities avail.
Est 1985. Nonprofit. Roman Catholic. **Ses:** 1. **Wks/ses:** 1. Operates July.

Saint Vincent conducts two programs for gifted, creative or talented pupils: one serving children entering grades 6-8, the other enrolling students entering grades 9-12. Challenge enables boys and girls to explore interests or develop skills through daytime classes in such areas as history, the humanities and computers. Course work content during the junior and senior high weeks differs to accommodate the varying age and ability levels of participating students. Evening activities include dinner parties, theater visits, swimming and dancing.

SUMMER STUDY AND SUMMER ENRICHMENT AT PENN STATE
Res — Coed Ages 14-18

University Park, PA. Pennsylvania State Univ.
Contact (Year-round): 900 Walt Whitman Rd, Melville, NY 11747. Tel: 631-424-1000,
800-666-2556. Fax: 631-424-0567.
www.summerstudy.com   E-mail: info@summerstudy.com
William Cooperman, Exec Dir.
Grades 9-12. Adm: FCFS. **Appl—Fee** $95. Due: Apr. Transcript, test scores.
Enr: 900. **Fac** 70. **Staff:** Admin 7. Couns 80.
Type of instruction: Adv Enrich Preview Rem_Eng Rem_Math Rem_Read Rev SAT/ACT_Prep Study_Skills Tut. **Courses:** Fr Ger Ital Russ Span Archaeol Astron Bus/Fin Debate Environ_Sci ESL Expository_Writing Geol Govt Crafts Creative_Writing Dance Filmmaking Fine_Arts Media Music Painting Photog Theater. **Daily hours for:** Classes 2½. Study 1. Rec 4. **College credit.**
Features: Adventure_Travel Aquatics Boating Canoe Chess Climbing_Wall Community_Serv Hiking Kayak Mtn_Biking Sail Wilderness_Canoe Yoga Baseball Basketball Cross-country Field_Hockey Football Golf Gymnastics Ice_Hockey Lacrosse Roller_Hockey Soccer Softball Swim Tennis Track Volleyball Watersports Wrestling.
Fees 2013: Res $2799-6499, 2-6½ wks. Aid (Need).
Housing: Dorms. **Swimming:** Lake Pool.
Est 1989. Inc. **Spons:** Summer Study Programs. **Ses:** 8. **Wks/ses:** 2-6½. Operates June-Aug.

Summer Study allows students who have completed grade 10, 11 or 12 to take freshman-level courses for college credit while also experiencing university life. Each pupil enrolls in one or two college-credit classes, an enrichment offering and the Pathways to College guidance course. Shorter enrichment programs for pupils entering grades 10-12 enroll participants in two or three noncredit classes. Students in both programs may perform community service, enroll in SAT prep courses and visit nearby colleges on weekends. Two- and four-week enrichment programs serve students entering grade 9.

UNIVERSITY OF PENNSYLVANIA PRE-COLLEGE PROGRAM
Res — Coed Ages 16-18

Philadelphia, PA 19104. 3440 Market St, Ste 100. Tel: 215-749-6901. Fax: 215-573-2053.
www.sas.upenn.edu/summer   E-mail: summer@sas.upenn.edu
Grades 11-12 (younger if qualified). Adm: Selective. Appl—Fee $75. Due: Rolling.
Transcript, test scores, personal statement, rec.
Enr: 96. Enr cap: 200. Intl: 39%. Staff: Couns 30.
Type of instruction: Adv SAT/ACT_Prep Undergrad. Courses: Ital Archaeol Bus/Fin
Expository_Writing Govt Hist Intl_Relations Law Math Sci Writing/Journ. Avg class
size: 18. Homework. Tests. Grades. College credit: 3/crse, total 6.
Features: Leadership.
Fees 2011: Res $9799-12,599, 6 wks. Aid (Need).
Housing: Dorms. Campus facilities avail.
Nonprofit. Ses: 1. Wks/ses: 6. Operates July-Aug.

Rising high school juniors and seniors take either one or two University of Pennsylvania undergraduate courses for college credit through the Pre-College Program. Students enrolling in only one credit-bearing course also take a noncredit learning skills enrichment course; students taking two credit courses pay a higher tuition rate. Curricular offerings comprise introductory courses in the arts and sciences. Students are integrated into the university's regular summer courses and are subject to the same academic standards. Weekly workshops seek to bridge the gap between high school and college. Various social activities balance academics.

WYOMING SEMINARY COLLEGE PREP INSTITUTE
Res and Day — Coed Ages 14-18

Kingston, PA 18704. 201 N Sprague Ave. Tel: 570-270-2186. Fax: 570-270-2198.
www.wyomingseminary.org/summer
E-mail: summeratsem@wyomingseminary.org
Jason Thatcher, Dir.
Student contact: Gayle Sekel, E-mail: gsekel@wyomingseminary.org.
Grades 9-12. Adm: Somewhat selective. Appl—Fee $50. Due: Rolling. Transcript, 2
teacher recs.
Enr: 400. Fac 16. Prof 4. K-12 staff 12. Staff: Couns 20.
Type of instruction: Adv Dev_Read Enrich Preview Rem_Math Rev ESL/TOEFL_Prep.
Courses: ESL Expository_Writing Math Med/Healthcare Public_Speak Speech
Ceramics Crafts Creative_Writing Drama Fine_Arts Music Painting Photog Studio_Art.
Avg class size: 15. Daily hours for: Classes 4. Study 2. Rec 1. Homework. Tests.
Grades. High school credit.
Features: Aquatics Climbing_Wall Baseball Swim Tennis Weight_Trng Wrestling.
Fees 2013: Res $3000-7500, 4 wks. Day $675/crse, 4 wks. Aid (Need).
Housing: Dorms. Swimming: Pool. Campus facilities avail.
Est 1844. Nonprofit. Ses: 2. Wks/ses: 4. Operates June-July.

The College Prep Institute allows boys and girls to either explore academic interests in depth or preview upcoming courses. Boarding students attend morning and afternoon courses, and day students may enroll in one or both. Classes are available in the following areas: communications, the fine arts, history and government, and science and mathematics.

RHODE ISLAND

BROWN UNIVERSITY SCHOLAR ATHLETE PROGRAM
Res — Coed Ages 14-17; Day — Coed 15-17

Providence, RI 02912. Box T, 200 Dyer St. Fax: 401-863-3916.

www.brown.edu/scs/pre-college/scholar-athlete   E-mail: summer@brown.edu
Grades 9-12. **Adm:** Selective. **Prereqs:** GPA 3.0. **Appl**—Fee $45-90. **Due:** Rolling. Transcript, teacher rec.
Type of instruction: Enrich. **Courses:** Sci Writing/Journ Physiol. **Daily hours for:** Classes 3.
Features: Swim.
Fees 2011: Res $2505, 1 wk. Day $2002, 1 wk. Aid (Need).
Housing: Dorms. **Swimming:** Pool. Campus facilities avail.
Ses: 1. **Wks/ses:** 1. Operates June.

This unusual program combines enrollment in one course with athletic instruction in either tennis or swimming. Students spend three hours per day in one of the following classes: sportswriting, sport physiology, or biomechanics of sport and exercise. Boys and girls need not have advanced skills in the sport of choice. Planned cocurricular and social activities round out the program.

PORTSMOUTH ABBEY SUMMER SCHOOL PROGRAM
Res and Day — Coed Ages 12-17

Portsmouth, RI 02871. 285 Cory's Ln. Tel: 401-683-2000. Fax: 401-643-1397.
www.portsmouthabbey.org/page/summerprogram
E-mail: summer@portsmouthabbey.org
Tim Seeley, Dir.
Grades 7-11. **Adm:** Somewhat selective. **Appl**—Fee $55. Due: Rolling. Transcript, rec.
Enr: 90. **Fac** 18. **Staff:** Admin 2. Couns 6.
Type of instruction: Enrich Preview ESL/TOEFL_Prep Study_Skills. **Courses:** Lat Debate Econ Eng Environ_Sci ESL Expository_Writing Geol Hist Marine_Bio/Stud Math Public_Speak Relig_Stud Speech Writing/Journ Creative_Writing Drama Film Media Studio_Art. **Avg class size:** 7. **Daily hours for:** Classes 3. Study 2. Rec 3. Homework. Tests. Grades.
Features: Outdoor_Ed Rowing/Sculling Sail Basketball Extreme_Sports Golf Soccer Squash Swim Tennis.
Fees 2013: Res $6250 (+$300), 4 wks. Day $3600 (+$100), 4 wks. Aid (Need).
Housing: Dorms Houses. **Swimming:** Ocean. Campus facilities avail.
Est 1943. Nonprofit. Roman Catholic. **Ses:** 1. **Wks/ses:** 4. Operates June-July.

Portsmouth Abbey provides a variety of review and enrichment courses six days per week. Pupils, who attend three courses per class day, choose from options in history, politics and economics; English; faith and culture; and mathematics. Afternoon enrichment courses introduce students to landscape painting and environmental and marine sciences. A well-balanced recreational schedule supplements academics.

TENNESSEE

VANDERBILT UNIVERSITY SUMMER ACADEMY
Res — Coed Ages 13-17

Nashville, TN 37203. Peabody 506, 230 Appleton Pl. Tel: 615-322-8261. Fax: 615-322-3457.
www.pty.vanderbilt.edu/vsa.html   E-mail: pty.peabody@vanderbilt.edu
Tamra Stambaugh, Dir.
Grades 8-12. **Adm:** Very_selective. **Appl**—Fee $35. Transcript, essays, portfolio/qualifying test scores.
Type of instruction: Adv Enrich. **Courses:** Astron Engineering Law Math Med/Healthcare Relig_Stud Sci Creative_Writing Filmmaking. **Avg class size:** 14.
Features: Yoga Martial_Arts.
Fees 2014: Res $1250-3250, 1-3 wks. Aid (Need).

Housing: Dorms. Avg per room/unit: 2.
Ses: 3. **Wks/ses:** 1-3. Operates June-July.

VSA offers advanced curricula in math, science and the humanities to gifted students. Taught by Vanderbilt professors, lecturers and graduate students, courses integrate resources from research centers and laboratories. Games, movies, sports and off-campus outings complement academics. Weeklong programs accommodate rising eighth graders who have participated in talent searches, two-week sessions serve pupils entering grades 9 and 10, and three-week courses enroll students entering grades 11 and 12. Three-week Law School 101 and Med School 101 programs operate in conjunction with Vanderbilt's professional schools; admission to both is highly competitive and is distinct from admission into other VSA courses.

TEXAS

DUKE UNIVERSITY TALENT IDENTIFICATION PROGRAM
SUMMER STUDIES PROGRAMS
Res — Coed Ages 12-16

College Station, TX. Texas A&M Univ.
Contact (Year-round): 1121 W Main St, Durham, NC 27701. Tel: 919-668-9100. Fax: 919-681-7921.
www.tip.duke.edu   E-mail: information@tip.duke.edu
Brian Cooper, Dir.
Grades 8-11. Adm: Selective. **Appl**—Fee $25. Due: Rolling. Qualifying SAT/ACT scores, personal statement.
Type of instruction: Adv Enrich. **Courses:** Architect Debate Engineering Expository_ Writing Law Pol_Sci SciVeterinary_Med Web_Design Creative_Writing. **Avg class size:** 16. **Daily hours for:** Classes 7. Rec 3.
Fees 2014: Res $3675-3925, 3 wks. Aid (Need).
Housing: Dorms.
Est 1980. Nonprofit. **Ses:** 2. **Wks/ses:** 3. Operates June-Aug.

See program description under Lawrence, KS.

CAMP KIOWA
Res — Coed Ages 7-16

Denton, TX 76204. PO Box 425286.
Contact (Aug-May): 1505 Kittyhawk Dr, Little Elm, TX 75068.
Year-round Tel: 940-239-5126, Fax: 940-239-5043.
www.campkiowa.com   E-mail: campinfo@campkiowa.com
Brian Manhart & Jennifer Manhart, Dirs.
Grades 1-11. Adm: FCFS. **Appl**—Fee $0. Due: May.
Enr: 100. **Fac** 5. **Staff:** Admin 4. Couns 16.
Type of instruction: Enrich. **Courses:** Writing/Journ Robotics Rocketry Creative_Writing Dance Drama Fashion Photog Sculpt Woodworking.
Features: Aquatics Archery Chess Community_Serv Cooking Kayak Rock_Climb Yoga Baseball Basketball Football Golf Martial_Arts Soccer Softball Swim Tennis Volleyball.
Fees 2013: Res $795-3180, 1-4 wks. Aid (Need).
Housing: Dorms. **Swimming:** Pool.
Est 2004. Inc. **Ses:** 8. **Wks/ses:** 1. Operates June-July.

Camp Kiowa combines academic enrichment with traditional summer recreation. Campers select two morning academic courses and two afternoon workshops in arts and sports. Evening activities include bingo, dance, karaoke, bowling, miniature golf and sports. Tennis and golf lessons are available for an additional fee.

SOUTHERN METHODIST UNIVERSITY
GIFTED STUDENTS INSTITUTE SUMMER PROGRAMS
Res — Coed Ages 13-18

Dallas, TX 75275. PO Box 750383. Tel: 214-768-0123. Fax: 214-768-3147.
www.smu.edu/Simmons/CommunityEnrichment/GSI/StudentServices/TAG
E-mail: gifted@smu.edu
Grades 8-12. Adm: Selective. **Appl**—Fee $35. Due: Rolling. Transcript, essay, standardized test scores, 2 recs.
Type of instruction: Adv Enrich Undergrad. **Courses:** Comp_Sci Econ Eng Govt Law Math Pol_Sci Psych Sci Anthro Philos Rhetoric Film Theater. **Avg class size:** 14. **Daily hours for:** Classes 6. Study 2. Rec 4. Grades. **College credit:** 3/crse, total 6.
Features: Chess Swim.
Fees 2013: Res $3875. Aid (Need).
Housing: Dorms. Avg per room/unit: 2. **Swimming:** Pool.
Est 1979. Nonprofit. **Ses:** 2. **Wks/ses:** 3-5. Operates June-Aug.

SMU's Gifted Studies Institute conducts two programs for able boys and girls. Students entering grades 8-10 may enroll in the Talented and Gifted (TAG) program, which allows them to take two classes: one in the morning and one in the afternoon. Particularly strong pupils may earn college credit for the morning course. Rising high school juniors and seniors take two college-level courses in the College Experience program. Each participant selects a morning course from the regular summer school credit offerings, then engages in an in-depth, interdisciplinary afternoon seminar.

TELLURIDE ASSOCIATION SUMMER PROGRAM
Res — Coed Ages 16-17

Austin, TX. Univ of Texas.
Contact (Year-round): 217 West Ave, Ithaca, NY 14850. **Tel:** 607-273-5011. **Fax:** 607-272-2667.
http://tasp.tellurideassociation.org   E-mail: telluride@tellurideassociation.org
Ellen Baer, Admin Dir.
Grade 11. Adm: Very selective. **Appl**—Fee $0. Due: Jan. Essays, transcript, standardized test scores.
Enr: 16-18.
Type of instruction: Adv Enrich. **Courses:** Eng Sci Philos.
Fees 2014: Free. Res 6 wks.
Housing: Dorms.
Nonprofit. **Ses:** 3. **Wks/ses:** 6. Operates June-Aug.

See program description under Ann Arbor, MI.

TEXAS LUTHERAN UNIVERSITY
SUMMER SCHOLARS ACADEMY
Res and Day — Coed Ages 15-17

Seguin, TX 78155. 1000 W Court St. Tel: 830-372-8050, 800-771-8521. **Fax:** 830-372-8096.
www.tlu.edu/ssa   E-mail: ssa@tlu.edu
Chris Bollinger, Dir.
Grades 10-12. Adm: Selective. Admitted: 95%. **Appl**—Fee $75. Due: Rolling. Transcript, rec, PSAT results.
Enr: 31. **Enr cap:** 60. **Fac** 6. Prof 6. **Staff:** Admin 2. Res 5.
Type of instruction: Adv Undergrad. **Courses:** ASL Astron Expository_Writing Forensic_ Sci Sci Creative_Writing Film. **Avg class size:** 12. **Daily hours for:** Classes 5. Study 2. Homework. Tests. Grades. **College credit:** 2.
Features: Swim Tennis.

Fees 2013: Res $1400, 2 wks. Day $950, 2 wks. Aid 2011 (Need): $900.
Housing: Dorms. Avg per room/unit: 2. **Swimming:** Pool. Campus facilities avail.
Est 1998. Nonprofit. **Ses: 1. Wks/ses: 2.** Operates July.

This two-week program allows academically advanced high schoolers to take two university-level courses for college credit. TLU faculty and area educators teach the courses in a small-class setting that provides boys and girls with a preview of the college experience. Field trips, a group service project and evening recreational activities round out SSA's program. Applicants should rank in the top half of their class.

VIRGINIA

FERRUM COLLEGE SUMMER ENRICHMENT CAMP
Res — Coed Ages 9-13

Ferrum, VA 24088. PO Box 1000. Tel: 540-365-2121. Fax: 540-365-5589.
www.ferrum.edu/fcsec   E-mail: cphillips@ferrum.edu
Chip Phillips, Dir.
Grades 4-7. Adm: FCFS. **Appl**—Fee $0. Due: Rolling. Essay.
Enr cap: 120. **Fac** 14. **Staff:** Admin 6.
Type of instruction: Enrich. **Courses:** Span Eng Forensic_Sci Sci Web_Design Creative_ Writing Drama Drawing Media Photog. **Avg class size:** 14. **Daily hours for:** Classes 6½. Rec 1.
Features: Chess Climbing_Wall Cooking Farm Rappelling Ropes_Crse Basketball Soccer Softball Swim Tennis Volleyball.
Fees 2013: Res $725 (+$200), 1 wk.
Housing: Dorms. **Swimming:** Pool.
Est 1990. Nonprofit. **Spons:** Ferrum College. **Ses: 2. Wks/ses: 1.** Operates July.

Young students enrolled in FCSEC engage in four daily enrichment classes, as well as afternoon and evening activities. Applicants should have a successful school record and should be both academically motivated and well behaved in the classroom. Activities range from juggling to jazz and modern dance to yoga, and workshops are also available.

FISHBURNE MILITARY SCHOOL SUMMER SCHOOL
Res — Boys Ages 12-17

Waynesboro, VA 22980. 225 S Wayne Ave, PO Box 988. Tel: 540-946-7700, 800-946-7773. Fax: 540-946-7738.
www.fishburne.org   E-mail: admissions@fishburne.org
Cedrick Broadhurst, Dir.
Grades 7-12. Adm: FCFS. **Appl**—Fee $50. Due: Rolling.
Enr: 100. **Fac** 20.
Type of instruction: Adv Enrich Preview Rem_Eng Rem_Read Rev SAT/ACT_Prep Study_Skills Tut. **Courses:** Span Eng Govt Hist Leadership Sci. **Avg class size:** 12. **Daily hours for:** Classes 6. Study 3. Rec 4. **High school credit.**
Features: Aviation/Aero Leadership Milit_Trng Paintball Rappelling Ropes_Crse Basketball Football Golf Martial_Arts Soccer Swim Tennis Watersports.
Fees 2012: Res $3660-3890, 5 wks.
Housing: Dorms. Avg per room/unit: 2. **Swimming:** Pool.
Nonprofit. **Ses: 1. Wks/ses: 5.** Operates June-July.

Located in the Shenandoah Valley, this military program offers both new and repeat classes in English, math, science, social studies and leadership training (Army JROTC), as well as repeat courses in chemistry, Spanish and French. Afternoons are reserved for compulsory recreational activities, while weekends provide an opportunity for field trips to Busch Gardens, Kings Dominion and other nearby parks.

FORK UNION MILITARY ACADEMY SUMMER SCHOOL
Res and Day — Boys Ages 12-18

Fork Union, VA 23055. 4744 James Madison Hwy. Tel: 434-842-4205, 800-462-3862. Fax: 434-842-4312.
www.forkunion.com/summer   E-mail: admissions@fuma.org
Maj. John F. DeVault, Dir.
Grades 7-12. Adm: FCFS. **Appl**—Fee $100. Due: Rolling. Transcript, 2 recs.
Enr: 200. **Fac 25. Staff:** Admin 10.
Type of instruction: Adv Rev SAT/ACT_Prep Study_Skills. **Courses:** Span Eng ESL Govt Hist Leadership Math Sci. **Avg class size:** 14. **Daily hours for:** Classes 6. Study 2. Rec 2. **High school credit:** 2.
Features: Aquatics Community_Serv Fishing Leadership Baseball Basketball Cross-country Football Lacrosse Soccer Swim Weight_Trng Wrestling.
Fees 2013: Res $4100 (+$60), 4 wks. Day $2800 (+$60), 4 wks.
Housing: Dorms. **Swimming:** Pool. Campus facilities avail.
Nonprofit. Baptist. **Ses:** 1. **Wks/ses:** 4. Operates July.

Fork Union's nonmilitary summer program includes English composition and literature, math, history, SAT preparation and Spanish. With classes conducted six days per week, the session enables students to earn academic credit for new course work, correct deficiencies through repeat work and improve study habits. Enrichment field trips and athletic activities complement academics.

4 STAR ACADEMICS PROGRAMS
Res and Day — Coed Ages 12-18

Charlottesville, VA. Univ of Virginia.
Contact (Year-round): PO Box 3387, Falls Church, VA 22043. Tel: 432-202-1896.
www.4starcamps.com   E-mail: info@4starcamps.com
Patrick Kearns & Patti Popple, Camp Dirs.
Grades 7-12. Adm: FCFS. **Appl**—Due: Rolling.
Enr: 130. **Fac 20. Staff:** Admin 2.
Type of instruction: Adv Enrich SAT/ACT_Prep Study_Skills Tut. **Courses:** Architect Astron Bus/Fin Econ Environ_Sci ESL Expository_Writing Math Psych Public_Speak Writing/Journ Anat Civics Acting Creative_Writing Filmmaking Fine_Arts Photog Studio_ Art Theater. **Avg class size:** 8. **Daily hours for:** Classes 3. Study 1. Rec 5.
Features: Canoe Hiking Scuba Basketball Golf Soccer Swim Tennis Ultimate_Frisbee Volleyball.
Fees 2011: Res $1395-6495, 1-4 wks. Day $1095-5495, 1-4 wks.
Housing: Dorms. **Swimming:** Pool.
Est 1975. Inc. **Ses:** 10. **Wks/ses:** 2-4. Operates June-July.

Conducted on the University of Virginia campus, these programs combine morning academic course work with afternoon sports instruction and informal recreation. The Junior Program, serving rising seventh through ninth graders, allows children to choose two enrichment courses each weekday from a varied selection. Tutorials are available in math and writing for an additional fee. For students entering grades 10-12, the Senior Program blends enrichment courses with such offerings as reading comprehension and PSAT and SAT preparation. Other offerings include an ESL program and a fine arts program that features photography, studio art, cinematography and acting classes.

HARGRAVE MILITARY SCHOOL SUMMER SESSION
Res and Day — Boys Ages 13-18

Chatham, VA 24531. 200 Military Dr. Tel: 434-432-2481, 800-432-2480. Fax: 434-432-3129.
www.hargrave.edu/summer-school   E-mail: admissions@hargrave.edu

Jim Tung, Dir.
Grades 7-12. Adm: FCFS. **Appl**—Fee $75. Due: Rolling.
Fac 19. Staff: Couns 2.
Type of instruction: Adv Dev_Read Enrich Rem_Eng Rem_Math Rem_Read Rev SAT/
ACT_Prep Study_Skills. **Courses:** Span Col_Prep Eng ESL Govt Hist Leadership Math
Sci Robotics Art Creative_Writing Photog Studio_Art. **Avg class size:** 12. **Daily hours
for:** Classes 5. Study 3. Rec 1½. **High school credit:** 2.
Features: Aquatics Canoe Climbing_Wall Exploration Hiking Mountaineering Mtn_Trips
Rappelling Riflery Rock_Climb White-water_Raft Baseball Basketball Football Lacrosse
Swim Tennis.
Fees 2014: Res $4099-4499, 4 wks. Day $875-1100, 4 wks.
Housing: Dorms. **Swimming:** Pool.
Est 1926. Nonprofit. Baptist. **Ses:** 1. **Wks/ses:** 4. Operates June-July.

Hargrave offers remedial and advanced work in most academic subjects, including math,
English and science. SAT Prep, leadership principles and art are available as electives. In the
afternoon, students choose from a full complement of athletic activities led by the school's
postgraduate and varsity coaches. Boys wear summer school uniforms and attend compulsory
Christian services two times per week.

MASSANUTTEN MILITARY ACADEMY SUMMER SCHOOL
Res and Day — Coed Ages 12-18

**Woodstock, VA 22664. 614 S Main St. Tel: 540-459-2167, 877-466-6222. Fax: 540-459-
5421.**
www.militaryschool.com   E-mail: admissions@militaryschool.com
R. Craig Jones, Head.
Grades 7-12. Adm: Selective. Admitted: 60%. **Appl**—Fee $50. Due: Rolling. Transcript.
Enr cap: 200. Fac 15. Prof 3. K-12 staff 12. **Staff:** Admin 5. Couns 2.
Type of instruction: Rem_Eng Rem_Read ESL/TOEFL_Prep SAT/ACT_Prep Study_
Skills. **Courses:** Span Eng Govt Hist Math Sci Fine_Arts Music. **Avg class size:** 9.
Daily hours for: Classes 6. Study 2. Rec 2. **High school credit:** 2.
Features: Canoe Fishing Hiking Milit_Trng Riflery Scuba Baseball Basketball Equestrian
Football Soccer Tennis Wrestling.
Fees 2014: Res $1175-3799 (+$750), 5 wks. Day $750-1995 (+$750), 5 wks.
Housing: Dorms. Campus facilities avail.
Nonprofit. **Ses:** 1. **Wks/ses:** 5. Operates June-Aug.

Cadets in this program take at least two courses during the session; students may enroll in
one new course or two repeat courses. SAT preparation and study skills classes are among the
class offerings. A military structure characterizes the program.

OAK HILL ACADEMY SUMMER SESSION
Res and Day — Coed Ages 13-18

Mouth of Wilson, VA 24363. 2635 Oak Hill Rd. Tel: 276-579-2619. Fax: 276-579-4722.
www.oak-hill.net/page.cfm?p=489   E-mail: info@oak-hill.net
Michael D. Groves, Pres.
Grades 8-12. Adm: Selective. Admitted: 80%. **Appl**—Fee $50. Due: Rolling. Transcript,
rec, interview.
Enr: 60. Intl: 20%. Non-White: 22%. **Fac 9.** K-12 staff 9.
Type of instruction: Rem_Eng Rem_Math Study_Skills. **Courses:** Span Bus/Fin
Computers Eng Govt Hist Math Relig_Stud Sci Music Studio_Art. **Avg class size:**
10. **Daily hours for:** Classes 5. Study 2½. Rec 2½. Homework. Tests. Grades. **High
school credit:** 2.
Features: Canoe Hiking Paintball Riding Swim.
Fees 2013: Res $3900 (+$400), 5 wks.
Housing: Dorms. Avg per room/unit: 2. **Swimming:** Lake. Campus facilities avail.
Nonprofit. Baptist. **Ses:** 1. **Wks/ses:** 5. Operates June-July.

Oak Hill's summer program offers courses for enrichment and credit in English, math, social studies and science. An intramural sports program includes basketball, volleyball, softball, tennis and soccer. Students take canoeing and hiking trips and may participate in horseback riding for an additional fee.

WASHINGTON

WASHINGTON STATE UNIVERSITY
COUGAR QUEST
Res — Coed Ages 12-18

Pullman, WA 99164. 346 French Administration Bldg, PO Box 641035. Tel: 509-335-1235. Fax: 509-335-4455.
www.cougarquest.wsu.edu   E-mail: cougarquest@wsu.edu
Linda Schoepflin, Dir. Student contact: Jordan Keithly, E-mail: jkeithley@wsu.edu.
Grades 7-12. Adm: FCFS. Appl—Fee $0. Due: May.
Enr: 180. Enr cap: 260. Non-White: 25%. Fac 36. Prof 32. Col/grad students 4. Staff: Admin 4. Couns 28.
Type of instruction: Adv Enrich Study_Skills. Courses: Architect Astron Ecol Forensic_ Sci SciVeterinary_Med Writing/Journ Crafts Dance Drama Fine_Arts Music Photog Printmaking. Avg class size: 25. Daily hours for: Classes 6. Rec 3.
Features: Cooking Badminton Basketball Soccer Swim Track Volleyball.
Fees 2013: Res $650, 1 wk. Aid (Need).
Housing: Dorms. Swimming: Pool. Campus facilities avail.
Est 2001. Nonprofit. Ses: 2. Wks/ses: 1. Operates July.

Cougar Quest comprises two programs: one for boys and girls entering grades 7-9 and another for those entering grades 9-12 (students entering grade 9 may attend either session). Pupils choose three workshops from a variety of subjects, all of which are taught by university faculty. Workshops incorporate interactive activities and new technologies whenever possible. Social and recreational activities complement academic work.

WISCONSIN

WISCONSIN CENTER FOR ACADEMICALLY TALENTED YOUTH
SUMMER PROGRAMS
Res and Day — Coed Ages 8-18

Madison, WI 53706. Teacher Education Bldg, Ste 264, 225 N Mills St. Tel: 608-890-3260. Fax: 608-265-4309.
www.wcaty.org   E-mail: academy@wcatyhelp.education.wisc.edu
Rebecca Vonesh, Dir.
Grades 4-12 (younger if qualified). Adm: Selective. Appl—Fee $60. Due: May. Transcript, standardized test scores, writing sample, 2 recs.
Enr: 100-130. Enr cap: 140. Fac 9. Prof 2. Col/grad students 2. K-12 staff 5. Staff: Admin 4. Couns 9.
Type of instruction: Adv Enrich. Courses: Arabic Lat Russ Comp_Sci Eng Engineering Environ_Sci Writing/Journ Crafts Dance Filmmaking Fine_Arts Media Music Photog Studio_Art Theater. Avg class size: 12. Daily hours for: Classes 6. Study 1. Rec 5. Homework. Tests. Grades. High school credit: 1.
Features: Aquatics Community_Serv Conservation Cooking Exploration Hiking Outdoor_ Ed Peace/Cross-cultural Riding Badminton Basketball Football Golf Gymnastics Soccer Swim Tennis Ultimate_Frisbee Volleyball.

Fees 2014: Res $890-2490 (+$50-150), 1-3 wks. Day $550-1850 (+$50-150), 1-3 wks. Aid 2009 (Need): $75,000. **Housing:** Dorms. Avg per room/unit: 2-3. **Swimming:** Lake Pool. **Est 1991.** Nonprofit. **Ses:** 3. **Wks/ses:** 1-3. Operates June-Aug.

WCATY conducts summer programs for advanced students at the elementary, middle and high school levels. The weeklong Young Students Summer Program, held at Beloit College and serving children in grades 4-6, combines enrichment courses with an exposure to new disciplines. Students in grades 7 and 8 may enroll in the Summer Transitional Enrichment Program, which enables pupils to take one two-week course for enrichment or acceleration. The Accelerated Learning Program (grades 9-12) consists of an intensive three-week course for each student. ALP courses are equivalent to an honors-level high school class or a semester-long college course.

ACADEMIC PROGRAMS
ABROAD

Academic programs abroad are arranged alphabetically by country and name.

Academic Programs Abroad

ENGLAND

THE CAMBRIDGE PREP EXPERIENCE
Res — Coed Ages 14-15

Cambridge, England.
Contact (Year-round): Oxbridge Academic Prgms, 601 Cathedral Pky, Ste 7R, New York, NY 10025. **Tel:** 212-932-3049, 800-828-8349. **Fax:** 212-663-8169.
www.oxbridgeprograms.com **E-mail:** info@oxbridgeprograms.com
John J. Pendergast IV, Dir.
Student contact: Doug Herman, E-mail: doug@oxbridgeprograms.com.
Grades 9-10 (younger if qualified). Adm: Selective. **Appl**—Fee $0. Due: Rolling. Transcript, essay.
Enr: 150. **Intl:** 20%.
Type of instruction: Adv Enrich. **Courses:** Debate Eng Expository_Writing Forensic_Sci Law Med/Healthcare Speech Philos Zoology Creative_Writing Drama Fine_Arts Studio_Art Art_Hist. **Avg class size:** 14. **Daily hours for:** Classes 4. Homework. Grades.
Features: Yoga Basketball Cricket Soccer Ultimate_Frisbee.
Fees 2014: Res $7495, 3½ wks. Aid (Merit & Need).
Housing: Dorms.
Est 1994. Spons: Oxbridge Academic Programs. **Ses:** 1. **Wks/ses:** 3½. Operates July.

Course work emphasizes writing and communicational skills and classes take a hands-on approach in this program, which operates at Peterhouse College. Each student takes two courses, one as a major and one as a minor. Major courses convene six mornings per week and entail both homework and project and preparation time; minor courses meet three afternoons a week, with all work contained within the class session. Cultural excursions to dramatic performances, art galleries, museums and historical sites enrich the program.

THE CAMBRIDGE TRADITION
Res — Coed Ages 14-17

Cambridge, England. Cambridge Univ.
Contact (Year-round): c/o Oxbridge Academic Prgms, 601 Cathedral Pky, Ste 7R, New York, NY 10025. **Tel:** 212-932-3049, 800-828-8349. **Fax:** 212-663-8169.
www.oxbridgeprograms.com **E-mail:** info@oxbridgeprograms.com
Greg Gonzalez, Dir.
Grades 10-12. Adm: Selective. **Appl**—Fee $0. Due: Rolling. Transcript, essay.
Enr: 250. **Intl:** 20%.
Type of instruction: Adv Enrich. **Courses:** Lat Architect Astron Bus/Fin Debate Eng Forensic_Sci Hist Med/Healthcare Psych Relig_Stud Speech Sports_Med Zoology Creative_Writing Drama Studio_Art Art_Hist. **Avg class size:** 12. **Daily hours for:** Classes 4. Homework.
Intl program focus: Acad.
Fees 2014: Res $7795, 4 wks. Aid (Merit & Need).
Housing: Dorms.
Est 1999. Spons: Oxbridge Academic Programs. **Ses:** 1. **Wks/ses:** 4. Operates July-Aug.

This precollege program, conducted at Cambridge University, enables students to engage in academic study while also taking advantage of the area's cultural resources. Pupils take two courses during the session, one as a major and one as a minor. Major courses, which meet six mornings per week, include homework and require additional project and preparation time. Less intensive minor courses meet three afternoons weekly and demand no work outside the classroom.

OXFORD ADVANCED STUDIES PROGRAM
SUMMER COURSE
Res — Coed Ages 16-19

London, SE10 8NB England. 259 Greenwich High Rd. Tel: 44-2083-128060.
Fax: 44-2082-931199.
http://advancedstudiesprogram.com　E-mail: info@oasp.ac.uk
Ralph Dennison, Dir.
Student contact: Charles Duncan, E-mail: charles.duncan@otc.ac.uk.
Grades 11-PG. Adm: Selective. **Appl**—Fee $0. Due: May. Essay, rec, transcript.
Enr: 60. **Enr cap:** 80. Intl: 40%. **Fac 25. Staff:** Admin 4. Couns 8.
Type of instruction: Adv Tut. **Courses:** Fr Ger Ital Lat Russ Span Architect Bus/Fin Debate
Econ Eng Expository_Writing Govt Hist Law Psych Writing/Journ Creative_Writing Film
Fine_Arts Media Theater Poetry. **Avg class size:** 6. **Daily hours for:** Classes 2. Study
3. Rec 4. Homework. Grades. **High school credit:** 1/crse, total 3.
Intl program focus: Acad Lang.
Features: Baseball Basketball Gymnastics Soccer Swim Tennis Weight_Trng.
Fees 2014: Res £2800-5600 (+£900), 3½ wks.
Housing: Dorms. **Swimming:** Pool.
Est 1984. Nonprofit. **Spons:** Oxford Tutorial College. **Ses:** 1. **Wks/ses:** 3½. Operates July-
Aug.

OASP's summer program consists of four seminar hours plus one hourlong tutorial per week. Students choose two or three courses from a selection that includes art and architecture, literature, history, philosophy, economics, international relations, languages, sciences, mathematics and creative writing. While mornings are devoted to academic study, afternoons and evenings consist of cultural visits, social activities and sports. Optional workshops are offered in drama, creative writing, film production and debate.

THE OXFORD PREP EXPERIENCE
Res — Coed Ages 13-14

Oxford, England. Oxford Univ.
Contact (Year-round): c/o Oxbridge Academic Prgms, 601 Cathedral Pky, Ste 7R,
New York, NY 10025. Tel: 212-932-3049, 800-828-8349. Fax: 212-663-8169.
www.oxbridgeprograms.com　E-mail: info@oxbridgeprograms.com
John J. Pendergast IV, Dir.
Grades 8-9. Adm: Selective. **Appl**—Fee $0. Due: Rolling. Transcript, essay.
Enr: 150.
Type of instruction: Adv Enrich. **Courses:** Architect Debate Eng Expository_Writing
Hist Intl_Relations Law Med/Healthcare Pol_Sci Psych Speech Writing/Journ Philos
Shakespeare Creative_Writing Drama Studio_Art. Homework.
Intl program focus: Acad.
Features: Basketball.
Fees 2014: Res $7495, 3½ wks.
Housing: Dorms.
Est 2004. Spons: Oxbridge Academic Programs. **Ses:** 1. **Wks/ses:** 3½. Operates July.

This hands-on academic program takes place on the campus of Corpus Christi College at Oxford University. Students choose both a major and a minor course, with each class convening in a small group that is conducive to interactive learning. Cultural excursions to dramatic performances, art galleries, museums and historical sites enrich the program.

THE OXFORD TRADITION
Res — Coed Ages 14-17

Oxford, England.
Contact (Year-round): Oxbridge Academic Prgms, 601 Cathedral Pky, Ste 7R, New

York, NY 10025. **Tel:** 212-932-3049, 800-828-8349. **Fax:** 212-663-8169. **www.oxbridgeprograms.com** **E-mail: info@oxbridgeprograms.com** **Michael McKinley, Dir.**
Student contact: Doug Herman, E-mail: doug@oxbridgeprograms.com.
Grades 10-12. Adm: Selective. **Appl**—Fee $0. Due: Rolling. Transcript, essay.
Enr: 400. Intl: 20%.
Type of instruction: Adv. **Courses:** Lat Archaeol Architect Debate Eng Engineering Hist Intl_Relations Law Med/Healthcare Speech Writing/Journ Bioethics Philos Creative_ Writing Drama Film Music Photog Studio_Art Art_Hist. **Avg class size:** 14. **Daily hours for:** Classes 4.
Intl program focus: Acad.
Fees 2014: Res $7795, 4 wks.
Housing: Dorms.
Est 1985. Spons: Oxbridge Academic Programs. **Ses:** 1. **Wks/ses:** 4. Operates July-Aug.

Conducted at Oxford University, this precollege program provides a rigorous academic program in a small-class environment for students who have completed grades 10-12. Pupils take two courses during the session, one as a major and one as a minor. Major courses, which meet six mornings per week, include homework and require additional project and preparation time. Less intensive minor courses meet three afternoons weekly and demand no work outside the classroom. Faculty schedule frequent excursions to local cultural events.

SUMMERFUEL
THE OXFORD EXPERIENCE
Res — Coed Ages 15-18

Oxford, England. Oxford Univ.
Contact (Year-round): 375 W Broadway, Ste 200, New York, NY 10012.
Tel: 212-796-8340, 800-752-2250. **Fax:** 212-334-4934.
www.summerfuel.com **E-mail: oxford@asaprograms.com**
Paul Saville & Sarah Gudis, Dirs.
Grades 10-PG. Adm: Selective. **Appl**—Due: Rolling. Transcript, rec.
Enr: 200. **Staff:** Admin 5. Couns 23.
Type of instruction: Adv Enrich Rev SAT/ACT_Prep. **Courses:** Chin Fr Architect Bus/ Fin Expository_Writing Hist Intl_Relations Psych Public_Speak Speech Writing/Journ Anthro Ethics Shakespeare Acting Creative_Writing Film Fine_Arts Music Painting Photog Studio_Art Theater. **Avg class size:** 10. **Daily hours for:** Classes 4½. Study 2. Rec 4. **High school credit.**
Intl program focus: Acad.
Features: Soccer.
Fees 2014: Res $7995 (+airfare), 4 wks.
Housing: Dorms.
Est 1984. Inc. **Spons:** Academic Study Associates. **Ses:** 1. **Wks/ses:** 4. Operates July.

Participants in the Oxford Experience pursue a range of courses in the following areas: humanities and the arts, the natural sciences, the social sciences and SAT preparation. Conducted at Oxford University, England, the program consists of three-hour seminars each morning and two-hour afternoon seminars four times weekly. Students incur additional fees for certain courses.

TASIS ENGLAND SUMMER SCHOOL
Res — Coed Ages 10-18; Day — Coed 5-11

Thorpe, TW20 8TE Surrey, England. Coldharbour Ln. Tel: 44-1932-565252. **Fax:** 44-1932-564644.
Contact (Sept-May): c/o TASIS US Office, 112 S Royal St, Alexandria, VA 22314. Tel: 703-299-8150. **Fax:** 703-299-8157.
www.tasisengland.org **E-mail: uksummer@tasisengland.org**

Chris Tragas, Dir.
Grades K-12. Adm: FCFS. **Appl**—Fee $0. Due: Rolling.
Enr: 250. **Enr cap:** 250. Intl: 50%. Non-White: 50%. **Fac 25.** K-12 staff 25. **Staff:** Couns 10.
Type of instruction: Adv Enrich Rev SAT/ACT_Prep Study_Skills. **Courses:** Computers Math Writing/Journ Crafts Dance Filmmaking Music Photog Studio_Art Theater. **Avg class size:** 13. **Daily hours for:** Classes 4. Study 2. Rec 2. Homework. Grades. **High school credit:** 1.
Intl program focus: Acad Lang Culture.
Features: Boating Caving Climbing_Wall Riding Aerobics Basketball Golf Soccer Softball Swim Tennis Volleyball Water-skiing Watersports Weight_Trng.
Fees 2012: Res £3250-6300 (+airfare), 3-6 wks. Day £290 (+airfare), 1 wk. Aid (Need).
Housing: Dorms. Avg per room/unit: 4. **Swimming:** Pool. Campus facilities avail.
Est 1976. Nonprofit. **Spons:** TASIS Foundation. **Ses:** 14. **Wks/ses:** 3-6. Operates June-Aug.

TASIS England provides an array of academic and enrichment courses for native or highly proficient English speakers. Students may take classes in traditional subjects and in such areas as SAT review, Shakespearean theater, movie animation, art in London, photography, dance and music. Each afternoon, pupils engage in arts and crafts and play various sports. On weekends, boarding boys and girls embark on day and overnight trips to the English cities of London, Bath, Windsor, Oxford and Cambridge, as well as to Paris, France; Brussels, Belgium; Wales; and Edinburgh, Scotland.

FRANCE

AMERICAN UNIVERSITY OF PARIS SUMMER SESSIONS
Res — Coed Ages 18 and up

Paris, France. 6 rue du Colonel Combes. Tel: 33-1-40-62-07-20. Fax: 33-1-47-05-34-32.
www.aup.edu/summer   E-mail: summer@aup.edu
Joumana Hassan, Dir.
Grades PG-Col (younger if qualified). Adm: Somewhat selective. Admitted: 98%. **Appl**—Fee €50. Due: Rolling. Transcript.
Enr: 220. **Enr cap:** 250. Intl: 50%. Non-White: 50%. **Fac 40.** Prof 30. Col/grad students 10. **Staff:** Admin 5.
Type of instruction: Adv Enrich Undergrad. **Courses:** Architect Bus/Fin Comm Econ Eng Environ_Sci Expository_Writing Hist Math Pol_Sci Psych Art Film Painting Photog. **Avg class size:** 15. **Daily hours for:** Classes 3. Homework. Tests. Grades. **College credit:** 4-8/crse, total 8.
Intl program focus: Acad Lang Culture. Home stays avail.
Focus: Fr.
Fees 2014: Res €3848-7696 (+€675), 3-7 wks. Aid (Merit).
Housing: Dorms. Campus facilities avail.
Est 1962. Nonprofit. **Spons:** American University of Paris. **Ses:** 3. **Wks/ses:** 3-6. Operates June-July.

AUP's programs are open to both college students and those just finishing secondary school. Participants take college courses in art history, fine arts, business administration, literature, math, economics, philosophy, French and international politics. A separate French immersion program offers a home stay residential option.

EXCEL PARIS/PROVENCE
Res — Coed Ages 14-17

Paris, France.
Contact (Year-round): 345 Hickory Ridge Rd, Putney, VT 05346. Tel: 802-387-5000. Fax: 802-387-4276.

www.goputney.com   E-mail: karen@goputney.com
Karen Phillips, Dir.
Grades 9-12. Adm: FCFS. **Appl**—Due: Rolling.
Enr cap: 60. **Staff:** Admin 10.
Courses: Fr Architect Hist Intl_Relations Creative_Writing Drawing Fashion Painting Photog Art_Hist.
Intl program focus: Acad.
Features: Cooking.
Fees 2014: Res $5290, 2 wks.
Housing: Dorms.
Spons: Putney Student Travel. **Ses:** 1. **Wks/ses:** 2. Operates July.

Divided between central Paris and the university town of Aix-en-Provence, this Excel program provides students with field-based seminars that lead to an exploration of French history, art and culture. Pupils may choose either to refine their French language skills or to gain a deeper understanding of the country through course work that emphasizes France. Each student chooses one major course and one minor course; both meet throughout the program (three full days weekly for major classes and two full days per week for minor courses). Instructors make significant use of the cultural and historical opportunities presented by the two cities.

L'ACADEMIE DE PARIS
Res — Coed Ages 14-18

Paris, France.
Contact (Year-round): Oxbridge Academic Prgms, 601 Cathedral Pky, Ste 7R, New York, NY 10025. **Tel:** 212-932-3049, 800-828-8349. **Fax:** 212-663-8169.
www.oxbridgeprograms.com   **E-mail:** info@oxbridgeprograms.com
Heidi Kasevich, Dir.
Grades 9-12. Adm: Selective. **Appl**—Fee $0. Due: Rolling. Transcript, personal statement.
Enr: 190. **Fac** 18.
Type of instruction: Adv Enrich. **Courses:** Fr Architect Med/Healthcare Psych Existentialism Creative_Writing Film Photog Studio_Art Art_Hist. **Avg class size:** 14.
Daily hours for: Classes 4. Homework.
Intl program focus: Acad.
Fees 2014: Res $7795, 4 wks.
Housing: Dorms.
Est 1990. Spons: Oxbridge Academic Programs. **Ses:** 1. **Wks/ses:** 4. Operates July-Aug.

Conducted in the heart of the city, this precollege program provides a curriculum that introduces pupils to French culture and Parisian life, regardless of the subjects selected. Offerings include art history, medicine, literature, international law and photography. Students who have taken French previously may participate in immersion classes taught by native French speakers; however, pupils need have no prior knowledge of French to attend. Each student takes both an in-depth major course and a less intensive minor class.

SUMMER STUDY IN PARIS
Res — Coed Ages 14-17

Paris, France. The Sorbonne.
Contact (Year-round): 900 Walt Whitman Rd, Ste 103, Melville, NY 11747. **Tel:** 631-424-1000, 800-666-2556. **Fax:** 631-424-0567.
www.summerstudy.com/paris   **E-mail:** info@summerstudy.com
William Cooperman, Exec Dir.
Grades 9-12. Adm: Selective. **Appl**—Due: Rolling.
Enr: 300. **Fac** 25. **Staff:** Admin 7. Couns 20.
Type of instruction: Adv Enrich Preview Rev SAT/ACT_Prep. **Courses:** Fr Architect Bus/

Fin Expository_Writing Hist Creative_Writing Drawing Fashion Film Photog Art_Hist. **Daily hours for:** Classes 2½. Study 1. Rec 4. **College credit:** 3/crse, total 3. **Intl program focus:** Acad Lang Culture. **Features:** Basketball Soccer Swim Tennis. **Fees 2014: Res $6799-9299 (+airfare), 3-5 wks.** Aid (Need). **Housing:** Dorms. Avg per room/unit: 3-4. **Swimming:** Pool. **Est 1989.** Inc. **Spons:** Summer Study Programs. **Ses:** 2. **Wks/ses:** 3-5. Operates July-Aug.

Students interested in studying in France choose from two programs. During the five-week Summer Study program, pupils take either a college-credit French course or two noncredit enrichment classes. Boys and girls in the three-week program select two noncredit enrichment courses. Both programs provide an in-depth exploration of the city, athletic and other recreational activities, and weekend excursions. For an additional fee, students may embark on a weekend trip to London, England.

GREECE

HYPHENOLOGY EDUCATIONAL SUMMER PROGRAMS
Res — Coed Ages 14-18

Mytilene, 81 100 Greece. 88 El Venizelou. Tel: 202-470-0922. Fax: 30-2251-027916. **www.hyphenology.com   E-mail:** director@hyphenology.com **Cindy Camatsos, Dir.** **Grades 9-PG. Adm:** FCFS. **Appl**—Fee $0. Due: May. **Enr: 12. Enr cap:** 25. Intl: 25%. Non-White: 10%. **Fac 6.** Prof 6. **Staff:** Admin 2. Couns 6. **Type of instruction:** Adv Enrich SAT/ACT_Prep Tut. **Courses:** Greek Astron Bus/Fin Environ_Sci Expository_Writing Writing/Journ Creative_Writing Dance Theater. **Avg class size:** 4. **Daily hours for:** Classes 3. Study 1. Rec 4. Homework. Tests. Grades. **Intl program focus:** Acad Culture. **Features:** Adventure_Travel Community_Serv Exploration Fishing Hiking Sea_Cruises Swim Volleyball Watersports. **Fees 2010: Res €1900 (+airfare), 2 wks.** Aid 2008 (Merit & Need): €500. **Housing:** Hotels. Avg per room/unit: 2. **Swimming:** Ocean Pool. **Est 2004.** Inc. **Ses: 1. Wks/ses:** 2. Operates July.

Academically motivated students spend two weeks on the Greek island of Lesvos taking subjects outside the traditional high school curriculum. As a complement to class work, boys and girls perform community service in the area. Study of the Greek language is not a primary aim of the program (although Greek is available as a subject).

IRELAND

THE IRISH WAY
SUMMER STUDY ABROAD FOR HIGH SCHOOL STUDENTS
Res — Coed Ages 14-18

Dublin, Ireland. **Contact (Year-round): Irish American Cultural Inst, 1 Lackawanna Pl, Morristown, NJ 07960. Tel: 973-605-1991.** **www.iaci-usa.org/program_iw.htm   E-mail:** irishway@iaci-usa.org **Grades 10-PG. Adm:** FCFS. **Appl**—Due: Mar. **Enr:** 100. **Type of instruction:** Enrich. **Courses:** Irish_Hist Irish_Lit. Homework. **Intl program focus:** Acad Culture. **Travel:** Europe. **Fees 2011: Res $4950, 3 wks.** Aid (Need).

Housing: Dorms.
Est 1976. Nonprofit. **Spons:** Irish American Cultural Institute. **Ses:** 1. **Wks/ses:** 3. Operates June-July.

The Irish Way provides an introduction to Ireland's history and traditions. Destinations include the cities of Dublin, Waterford, Killarney and Galway, where students live in traditional Irish boarding schools. Irish secondary school teachers conduct structured sessions in Irish language, literature, history and culture. Supplementary field trips and city excursions enrich the program. Students work on a group research project and have time to explore local host communities on their own. Participants tour the west coast of Ireland at the end of the session.

UNIVERSITY COLLEGE DUBLIN
SUMMER HIGH SCHOOL PROGRAM
Res — Coed Ages 16-18

Dublin, Ireland.
Contact (Year-round): North American Office, 345 Park Ave, 17th Fl, New York, NY 10154. Tel: 212-308-2877. Fax: 212-308-2899.
www.ucd.ie   E-mail: northamerica@ucd.ie
Enda Carroll, Mgr. Student contact: Molly Dineen, E-mail: molly.dineen@ucd.ie.
Grades 11-12. Adm: Somewhat_selective. Prereqs: GPA 2.5. **Appl**—Fee $0. Due: May.
Enr cap: 50. **Fac 5.** Prof 3. Col/grad students 2. **Staff:** Admin 4. Res 4.
Type of instruction: Enrich Preview Undergrad. **Courses:** Irish ArchitectCultural_Stud Eng Hist Pol_Sci Relig_Stud Dance Filmmaking Music Photog Theater Art_Hist. **Daily hours for:** Classes 3. Study 1½. Rec 6. Homework.
Features: Climbing_Wall Hiking Mtn_Trips Outdoor_Ed Lacrosse Soccer Softball Swim.
Fees 2014: Res €1900 (+airfare), 2½ wks.
Housing: Apartments. Avg per room/unit: 4. **Swimming:** Pool.
Est 2012. Nonprofit. **Ses:** 1. **Wks/ses:** 2½. Operates July.

Rising high school juniors and seniors sample university life abroad while studying various aspects of Ireland's culture and history in this UCD program. A four-part lecture series provides a thorough examination of Irish history. In addition, students explore an array of other topics related to Ireland, among them literature, religion, architecture, emigration, art, music and the Irish language. Interactive workshops and social activities include Ceili dancing, an introduction to Gaelic football and hurling, and a photography competition. Field trips to local sites of interest complete the program.

ITALY

SUMMER DISCOVERY
Res — Coed Ages 16-18

Florence, Italy.
Contact (Year-round): 1326 Old Northern Blvd, Roslyn, NY 11576. Tel: 516-621-3939.
Fax: 516-625-3438.
www.summerdiscovery.com   E-mail: discovery@summerdiscovery.com
Bob Musiker, Exec Dir.
Grades 11-PG. Adm: FCFS. **Appl**—Fee $95. Due: Rolling.
Enr: 80. **Enr cap:** 100. **Staff:** Admin 3. Couns 5.
Type of instruction: Enrich SAT/ACT_Prep. **Courses:** Ital Hist Ceramics Crafts Dance Fashion Fine_Arts Media Painting Photog Sculpt Studio_Art. Grades. **College credit:** 4.
Intl program focus: Acad Lang Culture.
Features: Cooking Swim.
Fees 2014: Res $7199-8899 (+airfare), 3-4 wks.
Housing: Hotels Lodges. **Swimming:** Pool.
Est 2006. Inc. **Ses:** 1. **Wks/ses:** 4. Operates July.

Precollege programs for high school students are held on university campuses throughout the US and abroad. Boys and girls take a college-credit course and an enrichment course during their stay. Other aspects of the program include community service, excursions, travel, sports and recreational activities. See other Summer Discovery listings under Los Angeles, CA; Santa Barbara, CA; San Diego, CA; Ann Arbor, MI; Washington, DC; and Valencia, Spain.

JORDAN

COLUMBIA UNIVERSITY
CULTURE AND HISTORY: UNDERSTANDING THE ARAB WORLD
Res — Coed Ages 16-18

Manja, Jordan. King's Academy.
Contact (Year-round): 203 Lewisohn Hall, 2970 Broadway, Mail Code 4119, New York, NY 10027. Tel: 212-854-9666.
http://ce.columbia.edu/high-school/middle-east   E-mail: hsp@columbia.edu
Anna Swank, Dir.
Grades 11-PG. Adm: Selective. **Appl**—Fee $80. Due: Mar. Transcript, personal statement, 2 recs.
Enr: 25.
Type of instruction: Enrich. **Courses:** Eng Hist Intl_Relations Pol_Sci Relig_Stud Anthro. Homework. Tests.
Intl program focus: Acad Lang.
Fees 2014: Res $9850 (+$300), 4 wks.
Housing: Dorms.
Est 2009. Ses: 1. Wks/ses: 4. Operates July.

Rising high school juniors and seniors engage in precollege study at both Columbia University and King's Academy in Jordan, in the process gaining exposure to the diverse cultures and history evident in the Arab world. After a week of study at Columbia, students spend two weeks living, studying and traveling in Jordan. Participants then return to New York to complete research projects for presentation. Visits to religious and cultural landmarks in Jordan are integral to the program. In lieu of grades, pupils receive written evaluations from their instructors upon successful completion of the program.

SCOTLAND

UNIVERSITY OF ST ANDREWS
SCOTTISH STUDIES SUMMER PROGRAMME
Res — Coed Ages 16-18

St Andrews, KY16 9AX Fife, Scotland. St Katherine's W, 16 The Scores.
Tel: 44-1334-462147. Fax: 44-1334-463330.
www.st-andrews.ac.uk/study/non-degree/summer/programmes/scottish
E-mail: fjt2@st-andrews.ac.uk
Frances Trahar, Dir.
Grades 11-PG. Adm: Somewhat_selective. Admitted: 95%. **Appl**—Fee £15. Due: Rolling. 2 recs, standardized test results, personal statement.
Enr: 24. Enr cap: 40. Intl: 20%. Non-White: 10%. **Fac 15.** Prof 7. Col/grad students 5. Specialists 3. **Staff:** Admin 2. Couns 2.
Type of instruction: Adv. **Courses:** Archaeol Ecol Eng Govt Hist Pol_Sci Film Music Photog Theater Art_Hist. **Daily hours for:** Classes 3. Study 3. Rec 4. Homework. Tests. Grades. **High school credit:** 12.
Intl program focus: Acad Culture.

Features: Conservation Exploration Hiking Mtn_Trips Swim.
Fees 2014: Res £2800, 4 wks.
Housing: Dorms. Avg per room/unit: 1. **Swimming:** Ocean Pool. Campus facilities avail.
Est 1999. Ses: 1. **Wks/ses:** 4. Operates June-July.

This academic program for North American students, taught by St Andrews faculty, focuses on Scottish studies. Employing an approach that includes seminars and tutorials, the program covers a millennium of Scottish history and also incorporates Scottish literature, archaeology, art history, film and traditional music. Frequent field trips and excursions—as well as cultural visits to art galleries, concerts and the theater—enrich the program.

SPAIN

COLUMBIA UNIVERSITY
THE BARCELONA EXPERIENCE
Res — Coed Ages 16-18

Barcelona, Spain. Univ of Barcelona.
Contact (Year-round): 203 Lewisohn Hall, 2970 Broadway, Mail Code 4119, New York, NY 10027. Tel: 212-854-9666.
http://ce.columbia.edu/high-school/barcelona   E-mail: hsp@columbia.edu
Evelyn Tavarelli, Dir.
Grades 11-PG. Adm: Selective. **Appl**—Fee $80. Due: Mar. Transcript, 2 recs, personal statement.
Enr: 20.
Type of instruction: Enrich. **Courses:** Span Architect Hist Art. Homework. Tests.
Intl program focus: Acad Lang Culture.
Fees 2014: Res $9850 (+$900), 3 wks.
Housing: Dorms.
Ses: 1. **Wks/ses:** 3. Operates July.

A collaborative effort between Columbia and the University of Barcelona, this three-week enrichment program takes place at the Spanish university. Participants examine the history, the art and the urban development of Barcelona while also enriching their understanding of how European communities forge local, regional, national and international identities. A Spanish-language workshop (offered at all ability levels) supplements the three-course curriculum. Boys and girls devote two Fridays to enriching, program-related excursions. In lieu of grades, pupils receive written evaluations from their instructors upon successful completion of the program.

EXCEL MADRID/BARCELONA
Res — Coed Ages 14-18

Madrid, Spain.
Contact (Year-round): 345 Hickory Ridge Rd, Putney, VT 05346. Tel: 802-387-5000.
Fax: 802-387-4276.
www.goputney.com   E-mail: zufan@goputney.com
Patrick Noyes, Dir.
Grades 9-12. Adm: FCFS. **Appl**—Due: Rolling.
Enr cap: 40. **Staff:** Admin 7.
Type of instruction: Enrich. **Courses:** Span Architect Creative_Writing Drawing Painting Photog Art_Hist.
Intl program focus: Acad.
Features: Cooking.
Fees 2014: Res $4900, 2 wks.
Housing: Dorms.
Spons: Putney Student Travel. **Ses:** 1. **Wks/ses:** 2. Operates July.

Participants in this Excel program split their time between Madrid and Barcelona while learning about the artistic, cultural and historical traditions of Spain. Students enroll in one major course and one minor course each; major courses convene three full days per week, while minor courses meet two full days weekly. Major course options are intermediate or advanced Spanish, creative writing, drawing and painting, Spanish art history and digital photography. All classes have a significant field component. Excel schedules frequent weekend excursions to areas of interest.

LA ACADEMIA DE ESPANA
Res — Coed Ages 13-17

Barcelona, Spain.
Contact (Year-round): c/o Oxbridge Academic Prgms, 601 Cathedral Pky, Ste 7R, New York, NY 10025. **Tel:** 212-932-3049, 800-828-8349. **Fax:** 212-663-8169.
www.oxbridgeprograms.com/la-academia-de-espana
E-mail: info@oxbridgeprograms.com
Jorge Salas, Dir.
Student contact: Doug Herman, **E-mail:** doug@oxbridgeprograms.com.
Grades PG-12. Adm: Selective. **Appl**—Fee $0. **Due:** Rolling. Transcript, essay.
Intl: 80%.
Type of instruction: Enrich. **Courses:** Architect Bus/Fin Hist Pol_Sci Creative_Writing Studio_Art Art_Hist. **Avg class size:** 14. **Daily hours for:** Classes 4. Homework. Grades.
Intl program focus: Acad.
Focus: Span. **Features:** Golf Rugby Soccer Tennis Volleyball.
Fees 2014: Res $7645, 4 wks. Aid (Need).
Housing: Dorms.
Est 2006. Ses: 1. **Wks/ses:** 4. Operates July-Aug.

This academic program for students who have completed grades 9-12 features roughly 15 courses, with some employing English as the language of instruction and others using Spanish. Each pupil chooses a major and a minor class; the major course meets six times weekly, the minor three times. Certain offerings relate to Spanish culture, while others take a global perspective. Athletics, beach excursions, field trips to sites of historical interest, theater and concert outings, workshops and appearances by guest speakers complete the program.

LA ESCUELA PREPARATORIA DE BARCELONA
Res — Coed Ages 15-18

Barcelona, Spain.
Contact (Year-round): c/o Oxbridge Academic Prgms, 601 Cathedral Pky, Ste 7R, New York, NY 10025. **Tel:** 212-932-3049, 800-828-8349. **Fax:** 212-663-8169.
www.oxbridgeprograms.com   **E-mail:** info@oxbridgeprograms.com
Jorge Rodriguez, Dir.
Student contact: Doug Herman, **E-mail:** doug@oxbridgeprograms.com.
Grades 10-12. Adm: Selective. **Appl**—Fee $0. **Due:** Rolling. Transcript, essay.
Enr: 60. Intl: 20%.
Type of instruction: Enrich. **Courses:** Intl_Relations Marine_Bio/Stud Psych Creative_Writing Studio_Art Art_Hist. **Avg class size:** 14. **Daily hours for:** Classes 4. Homework. Grades.
Intl program focus: Acad.
Focus: Span. **Features:** Yoga Basketball Soccer Swim.
Fees 2014: Res $7695, 4 wks. Aid (Need).
Housing: Dorms. **Swimming:** Ocean Pool.
Est 2008. Ses: 1. **Wks/ses:** 4. Operates July-Aug.

Held at the university residence Collegi Major Sant Jordi, this enrichment program for high school sophomores, juniors and seniors combines English-medium courses in such areas as creative writing and marine biology with Spanish-medium culture and arts classes. Each student enrolls in a major course that meets six mornings a week and a minor subject that convenes three afternoons weekly. Athletics, beach excursions, field trips to sites of historical interest, theater and concert outings, workshops and appearances by guest speakers complete the program.

SWITZERLAND

ST. GEORGE'S SCHOOL SUMMER CAMPS
Res and Day — Coed Ages 12-16

Clarens, 1815 Montreux, Switzerland. Chemin de St Georges 19.
Tel: 41-21-964-34-11. Fax: 41-21-964-49-32.
http://st-georgescamp.ch   E-mail: summeraccount@stgeorges.ch
David Chapuis, Dir.
Adm: FCFS. **Appl**—Fee $0. Due: Rolling.
Type of instruction: Enrich. **Courses:** Chin Fr ESL.
Intl program focus: Acad Lang.
Features: Cooking Tennis Watersports.
Fees 2014: Res SwF5200-9360. Day SwF2970-5346.
Housing: Dorms.
Ses: 4. **Wks/ses:** 2. Operates June-July.

This academic program enables students to enroll in intensive French or English courses. International Baccalaureate preparation is a class option for those about to enter the two-year IB Diploma Program. Boys and girls ages 14 and up may receive introductory Mandarin instruction, while all pupils may take tennis lessons once or twice a week; both offerings incur an additional fee.

TASIS SUMMER PROGRAMS
Res and Day — Coed Ages 11-18

Montagnola-Lugano, Switzerland.
Contact (Year-round): c/o TASIS US Office, 112 S Royal St, Alexandria, VA 22314.
Tel: 703-299-8150, 800-442-6005. Fax: 703-299-8157.
www.tasis.com   E-mail: usadmissions@tasis.com
Jim Haley & Marc-Pierre Jansen, Dirs. Student contact: Gianna Kestenholtz.
Grades 6-12. Adm: Somewhat_selective. **Appl**—Fee $0. Due: Rolling. Rec.
Enr: 120-160. **Enr cap:** 120-160. Intl: 80%. **Fac 20.** Col/grad students 20. **Staff:** Admin 6. Couns 15.
Type of instruction: Enrich ESL/TOEFL_Prep. **Courses:** Fr Ital ESL Expository_Writing Crafts Painting Photog Musical_Theater. **Avg class size:** 12. **Daily hours for:** Classes 4. Study 1. Rec 4. Homework. Grades.
Intl program focus: Lang Culture. Home stays avail.
Features: Hiking Mtn_Biking Rock_Climb Sail Basketball Soccer Swim Tennis Volleyball.
Fees 2012: Res SwF5900-7300 (+airfare), 3-4 wks. Day SwF3600-4400 (+airfare), 3-4 wks.
Housing: Dorms. Avg per room/unit: 3. **Swimming:** Lake Pool.
Est 1955. Nonprofit. **Spons:** TASIS Foundation. **Ses:** 2. **Wks/ses:** 3-4. Operates June-Aug.

TASIS Middle School Program (ages 11-13) and TASIS Summer Program (ages 14-18) balance academic subjects with intensive recreational and athletic activities. Students choose one course of study from a selection that comprises French, Italian, English as a Second Language, the performing and visual arts, and photography. Language instruction emphasizes spoken fluency and includes frequent practice time in the school's language lab. Courses in the performing and arts combine class work with off-campus enrichment trips. Regular homework assignments and compulsory evening study hall reinforce classroom learning. Younger children (ages 4-10) may enroll in Le Chateau des Enfants (see separate listing).

ACADEMIC PROGRAMS FOR STUDENTS WITH LEARNING DISABILITIES

Academic programs for students with learning disabilites are arranged alphabetically by state and then alphabetically by program name within each state. An index beginning on page 15 lists programs by features, as shown in the Table of Contents.

·

Academic Programs for Students with Learning Disabilities

ARIZONA

OAK CREEK RANCH SCHOOL SUMMER SCHOOL
Res — Coed Ages 12-18

West Sedona, AZ 86340. PO Box 4329. Tel: 928-634-5571, 877-554-6277. Fax: 928-634-4915.
www.ocrs.com   E-mail: dwick@ocrs.com
David Wick, Jr., Head.
Grades 7-12. Adm: FCFS. Appl—Due: Rolling.
Enr cap: 60.
Type of instruction: Dev_Read Rem_Read. Courses: Span Comp_Sci Eng Hist Math Sci Govt/Econ Theater. Avg class size: 10. High school credit.
Conditions accepted: ADD ADHD.
Features: Archery Fishing Riding Riflery White-water_Raft Golf Soccer Swim Volleyball Weight_Trng.
Fees 2012: Res $4750, 4 wks.
Housing: Dorms. Swimming: Pool.
Est 1972. Ses: 3. Wks/ses: 4-8. Operates June-Aug.

OCRS' summer session specializes in helping academic underachievers and students with attentional disorders. The program features developmental and remedial reading, English, computer, history, economics and government, math and science. Among OCRS' extracurricular activities are excursions to Fossil Creek, Sunset Crater, Meteor Crater and various Sedona hiking destinations.

GEORGIA

BRANDON HALL SCHOOL SUMMER PROGRAM
Res — Boys Ages 11-18; Day — Coed 10-18

Atlanta, GA 30350. 1701 Brandon Hall Dr. Tel: 770-394-8177. Fax: 770-804-8821.
www.brandonhall.org   E-mail: admissions@brandonhall.org
Patricia Smith, Dir.
Grades 4-12. Adm: FCFS. Admitted: 98%. Appl—Fee $25. Due: Rolling. Transcript.
Enr: 40. Fac 20. Staff: Admin 8.
Type of instruction: Dev_Read Preview Rem_Eng Rem_Math Rem_Read Rev ESL/TOEFL_Prep SAT/ACT_Prep Study_Skills Tut. LD Services: Mainstream Placement_Testing. Courses: Span Environ_Sci ESL Expository_Writing Govt. Avg class size: 4.
Daily hours for: Classes 6. Study 2. Rec 4. High school credit: 1½.
Conditions accepted: ADD ADHD Dx LD.
Fees 2014: Res $1300-3900, 2-6 wks. Day $650-1950, 2-6 wks.
Housing: Dorms.
Est 1959. Nonprofit. Ses: 3. Wks/ses: 2-6. Operates June-July.

Brandon Hall primarily serves intelligent students who are not achieving to potential due to academic difficulties or a lack of motivation. The summer program offers remedial and enrichment courses for most academic subjects. Electives include ESL, SAT Prep and recreational sports. Girls may enroll in the day program only.

IOWA

ST. AMBROSE UNIVERSITY SUMMER TRANSITION PROGRAM
Res and Day — Coed Ages 16-18

Davenport, IA 52803. 518 W Locust St. Tel: 563-333-6275. Fax: 563-333-6243.
www.sau.edu/student_disability_services/services.html   E-mail: saddlerryanc@sau.edu
Ryan C. Saddler, Dir.
Grades 12-Col. Adm: FCFS. Admitted: 95%. Prereqs: GPA 1.9. SAT M/CR 600. **Appl—**
Fee $0. Due: Rolling.
Enr: 16. **Enr cap:** 16. Non-White: 1%. **Fac 1.** Prof 1. **Staff:** Admin 4. Couns 2. Res 1.
Type of instruction: Preview Rev Study_Skills Tut. **LD Services:** Mainstream. **Courses:**
Psych Sociol. **Avg class size:** 10. **Daily hours for:** Classes 2. Study 4. Rec 2.
Homework. Tests. Grades. **College credit:** 3/crse, total 3.
Conditions accepted: ADHD Asp LD.
Features: Basketball Tennis Volleyball.
Fees 2011: Res $3339, 4 wks. Day $2699, 4 wks.
Housing: Dorms. Avg per room/unit: 1. Campus facilities avail.
Est 1990. Nonprofit. **Ses: 1. Wks/ses: 4.** Operates June-July.

The Summer Transition Program helps students with learning disabilities, attention deficit disorder or Asperger's syndrome develop the skills necessary for a successful college career. Depending on the year, students enroll in one three-credit introductory course in either psychology or sociology. In small-group review sessions each morning, staff members assist students with writing assignments and test preparation. Afternoon study skills and tutoring sessions provide instruction in note taking, textbook reading, memorization and other study skills. Academic orientation and self-advocacy seminars, held twice weekly, help students access university and community resources and develop skills that will ease the transition to college life. Students live in residence halls, play recreational sports on campus and visit local attractions.

MASSACHUSETTS

CURRY COLLEGE COLLEGE SEARCH EAST
Res — Coed Ages 16-18

Milton, MA 02186. 1071 Blue Hill Ave. Tel: 617-333-2250. Fax: 617-333-2018.
www.curry.edu   E-mail: palsummerprograms@curry.edu
Janis Peters, Coord.
Grade 12. Adm: Selective. **Appl—**Fee $0. Due: May. Interview, test results, rec.
Enr cap: 14. **Fac 3.** Prof 3. **Staff:** Admin 1. Couns 3.
Avg class size: 14. **Daily hours for:** Classes 6. Study 2. Rec 4. Homework. **College credit:** 1.
Conditions accepted: ADD ADHD Dx LD.
Features: Swim.
Fees 2014: Res $3200, 1 wk.
Housing: Dorms. **Swimming:** Pool.
Est 1996. Nonprofit. **Ses: 2. Wks/ses: 1.** Operates June-July.

This precollege program serves rising high school seniors diagnosed with a language-based learning disability or an attentional disorder. Students develop strategies for studying and taking tests, reading comprehension, written communication, time management, active listening and taking notes. Instructors also help familiarize students with the college search process, Web-based resources and assistive technologies. Students take part in various informal and planned activities, among them a tour of Boston. Applicants should possess average to above-average cognitive ability.

EAGLE HILL SCHOOL SUMMER SESSION
Res — Coed Ages 10-16

Hardwick, MA 01037. 242 Old Petersham Rd, PO Box 116. Tel: 413-477-6000. Fax: 413-477-6837.
www.ehs1.org E-mail: admission@ehs1.org
Peter J. McDonald, Head.
Adm: FCFS. Prereqs: IQ 90. **Appl**—Due: Rolling.
Enr: 70. **Enr cap:** 70. **Staff:** Admin 12.
Type of instruction: Dev_Read Enrich Rem_Eng Rem_Math Rem_Read Rev Study_Skills Tut. **LD Services:** Placement_Testing. **Courses:** Fr Lat Russ Span Astron Eng Expository_Writing Hist Psych Poetry Creative_Writing Film Fine_Arts Studio_Art Woodworking. **Avg class size:** 5. **Daily hours for:** Classes 4. Rec 6.
Conditions accepted: ADD ADHD Dx LD NLD.
Features: Adventure_Travel Chess Cooking Fishing Hiking Mtn_Biking Outdoor_Ed Woodcraft Basketball Equestrian Football Soccer Swim Ultimate_Frisbee Volleyball Weight_Trng.
Fees 2012: Res $8332 (+$750), 5 wks.
Housing: Dorms. **Swimming:** Pool.
Est 1967. Nonprofit. Ses: 1. **Wks/ses:** 5. Operates July-Aug.

Enrolling children with such learning differences as language-based learning disability, nonverbal learning disability and attentional disorders, this program offers a structured curriculum designed to build a basic foundation of academic competence. Various electives are available, and extracurricular and outdoor activities complement the educational program.

RIVERVIEW SUMMER
Res and Day — Coed Ages 11-19

East Sandwich, MA 02537. 551 Rte 6A. Tel: 508-888-0489. Fax: 508-833-7001.
www.riverviewschool.org/summer E-mail: admissions@riverviewschool.org
Grades 5-PG. Adm: FCFS. Prereqs: IQ 70-100. **Appl**—Due: Rolling.
Enr: 70. **Fac 7. Staff:** Admin 4. Couns 12.
Type of instruction: Dev_Read Rem_Math Rem_Read. **Courses:** Eng Math Crafts Photog. **Avg class size:** 8. **Daily hours for:** Classes 4. Rec 5.
Conditions accepted: Dx LD Phys_Impair Speech & Lang TBI.
Features: Kayak Swim.
Fees 2014: Res $7880, 5 wks.
Housing: Dorms. **Swimming:** Pond Ocean Pool.
Est 1957. Nonprofit. Spons: Riverview School. **Ses:** 1. **Wks/ses:** 5. Operates July-Aug.

Riverview enrolls students with complex language, learning and cognitive disabilities and an IQ between 70 and 100. Applicants should not have any primary emotional or behavioral issues. Course work builds upon the student's individual skills while maintaining progress achieved during the previous school year. The program seeks to develop pupil competence and confidence in the academic, social and independent living areas.

NEW YORK

DUNNABECK AT KILDONAN
Res and Day — Coed Ages 8-16

Amenia, NY 12501. 425 Morse Hill Rd. Tel: 845-373-8111. Fax: 845-373-9793.
www.kildonan.org E-mail: admissions@kildonan.org
Beth Rainey, Adm.
Adm: FCFS. **Appl**—Fee $30. Due: Rolling.
Enr: 60. **Staff:** Admin 50.

Type of instruction: Rem_Eng Rem_Math Rem_Read Tut. **Courses:** Computers Expository_Writing Ceramics Crafts Media.
Conditions accepted: Dx.
Features: Aquatics Archery Boating Climbing_Wall Hiking Mountaineering Mtn_Biking Riding Rock_Climb Sail Woodcraft Equestrian Martial_Arts Swim Water-skiing Watersports.
Fees 2014: Res $10,000 (+$500), 6 wks. Day $5000-7500 (+$250), 6 wks.
Housing: Dorms. **Swimming:** Pool. Campus facilities avail.
Est 1955. Nonprofit. **Spons:** Kildonan School. **Ses:** 1. **Wks/ses:** 6. Operates June-Aug.

Dunnabeck specializes in assisting intelligent children who are underachieving or failing in their academic work because of dyslexia. Teachers use the Orton-Gillingham approach while combining work in reading, writing and spelling. All tutoring is done individually, with each student receiving an hourlong daily lesson. Boys and girls engage in such extracurricular pursuits as horseback riding, mountain biking, watersports and arts offerings.

TEXAS

CHARIS HILLS SUMMER CAMP
Res — Coed Ages 7-18

Sunset, TX 76270. 498 Faulkner Rd. Tel: 940-964-2145, 888-681-2173. Fax: 940-964-2147.
www.charishills.org   E-mail: info@charishills.org
Rand Southard, Dir.
Student contact: Colleen Southard, E-mail: colleen@charishills.org.
Grades 1-12. Adm: FCFS. **Appl**—Fee $0. Due: Rolling.
Enr: 50. **Enr cap:** 60. Intl: 2%. Non-White: 6%. **Fac 4.** Col/grad students 4. **Staff:** Admin 5. Couns 40.
Type of instruction: Dev_Read Rem_Eng Rem_Math Rem_Read Rev Tut. **LD Services:** Tut. **Courses:** Astron Lang Sci Writing/Journ Crafts Creative_Writing Dance Music Photog Theater. **Avg class size:** 7. **Daily hours for:** Classes 1. Rec 7.
Conditions accepted: ADD ADHD Asp Au Dx LD.
Features: Aquatics Archery Boating Canoe Climbing_Wall Conservation Exploration Fishing Hiking Kayak Rappelling Riding Riflery Rock_Climb Wilderness_Camp Woodcraft Baseball Basketball Football Golf Soccer Softball Swim Volleyball Weight_Trng Snorkeling.
Fees 2012: Res $1190-2380, 1-2 wks. Aid avail.
Housing: Cabins Houses. Avg per room/unit: 9. **Swimming:** Lake. Campus facilities avail.
Est 2006. Nonprofit. Nondenom Christian. **Ses:** 8. **Wks/ses:** 1-3. Operates June-Aug.

Combining academics and recreation, Charis Hills seeks to promote social, emotional and physical growth in children with learning differences. In a Christian setting, students receive individualized instruction in reading, writing and language skills. Recreational activities emphasize self-esteem development and the acquisition of lifelong skills in a noncompetitive environment.

ACADEMIC PROGRAMS—
SPECIALIZED

Specialized summer academic boarding programs are arranged alphabetically by name. Page 5 of the Table of Contents lists the subject areas presented, and an index beginning on page 103 lists the programs under each of those subjects. Programs offering a family session are indicated by "FAM" at the end of the age range in the index.

INDEX BY FOCUS

BUSINESS & FINANCE (CONT.)

COLLEGE PREPARATION

COMMUNICATIONS & JOURNALISM

COMPUTER SCIENCE

CULTURAL & GLOBAL STUDIES

DEBATE & PUBLIC SPEAKING

ECOLOGY & ENVIRONMENTAL SCIENCE

ECONOMICS

ENGINEERING

ENGLISH

ENGLISH AS A SECOND LANGUAGE

ESL (CONT.)

FORENSIC SCIENCE

GOVERNMENT & POLITICAL SCIENCE

INTERNATIONAL RELATIONS

LANGUAGE IMMERSION

Abbey Road Summer *(Res — Coed Ages 14-19)* **[CH]** ....West Hollywood, CA... 115
Fr Ital Span

Ceran Lingua *(Res — Coed Ages 9-18)* ....Los Angeles, CA... 133
Fr Ger Dutch

Language Liaison *(Res — Coed Ages 13-17)* ....Pacific Palisades, CA... 153
Fr Ger Ital Span

Choate-Abroad *(Res — Coed Ages 14-17)* ....Wallingford, CT... 134
Chin Fr Span

Ctr X-Cultural Study *(Res — Coed Ages 16-18)* **[CH]** ....Amherst, MA... 131
Span

EF Intl Lang Schools *(Res — Coed Ages 10 and up)* **[C]**.............Cambridge, MA... 144
Chin Fr Ger Ital Span

Concordia Language **[CH]**.. Moorhead, MN... 138
　(Res — Coed Ages 7-18; Day — Coed 6-11) Arabic Chin Fr Ger Ital Japan Russ Span

St John's Prep-Ger *(Res — Coed Ages 8-16)* .... Collegeville, MN... 171
Ger

Broadreach Global *(Res — Coed Ages 13-19)* **[CH]** ....Raleigh, NC... 127
Chin Fr Span

Marist Inst-Academic *(Res — Coed Ages 16-18)* **[C]**...............Poughkeepsie, NY... 156
Span

Andeo Intl Homestays *(Res — Coed Ages 14-18)* ....Portland, OR... 117
Fr Ger Span

AmeriSpan Abroad *(Res — Coed Ages 14-18)* .... Philadelphia, PA... 116
Fr Ger Ital Span

Academic Prgms Intl *(Res — Coed Ages 18 and up)* **[C]**.................... Austin, TX... 115
Fr Ital Span

Learning Prgms Intl *(Res — Coed Ages 15-18)* **[C]** .... Austin, TX... 156
Chin Span

Middlebury-Monterey *(Res — Coed Ages 13-17)* .... Middlebury, VT... 160
Arabic Chin Fr Ger Span

Putney Travel-Lang *(Res — Coed Ages 14-18)*................................. Putney, VT... 169
Fr Span

Canoe Island French *(Res — Coed Ages 9-16)* ....Orcas, WA... 129
Fr

Beloit Language Stud **[C]** .... Beloit, WI... 123
　(Res — Coed Ages 17 and up; Day — Coed 16 and up) Arabic Chin Japan Russ

Amer Intl Salzburg *(Res and Day — Coed Ages 10-19)* **[H]** ..Salzburg, AUSTRIA... 116
Ger

LANGUAGE IMMERSION (CONT.)

LAW
Marist Inst-Academic *(Res — Coed Ages 16-18)* **[C]**..............Poughkeepsie, NY... 156

LEADERSHIP
Econ for Leaders *(Res — Coed Ages 16-17)* ....Davis, CA... 146
US Coast Guard Acad *(Res — Coed Ages 16-18)* ....New London, CT... 185
Global Young Leaders *(Res — Coed Ages 15-18)* **[C]**................Washington, DC... 149
Ethics/Leadership *(Res — Coed Ages 16-18)* ....Washington, DC... 173
Brown Leadership *(Res and Day — Coed Ages 14-18)* ....Providence, RI... 127
UVA High Sch Leaders *(Res — Coed Ages 16-18)* **[C]** ....Charlottesville, VA... 201

MARINE SCIENCE & OCEANOGRAPHY
U of AK Research **[C]**...Fairbanks, AK... 186
   (Res — Coed Ages 13-18; Day — Coed 14-18)
Dauphin Island Lab *(Res — Coed Ages 10-17)* **[H]** ....Dauphin Island, AL... 140
Lawrence Hall of Sci *(Res — Coed Ages 14-18)*...........................Berkeley, CA... 154
SEACAMP *(Res — Coed Ages 12-18)* ....San Diego, CA... 175
Odyssey Expeditions *(Res — Coed Ages 13-25)* **[C]**.............. Tarpon Springs, FL... 164
Seacamp *(Res — Coed Ages 12-17)* ....Big Pine Key, FL... 174
UMiami-Scholar-Acad *(Res — Coed Ages 16-17)* **[CH]** ....Coral Gables, FL... 193
Shedd Aquarium HSMB *(Res — Coed Ages 15-18)*.........................Chicago, IL... 176
Earthwatch Teen Exp *(Res — Coed Ages 15-18)* ....Allston, MA... 141
Sea Education Assoc *(Res — Coed Ages 15-19)* **[C]** ....Woods Hole, MA... 174
Broadreach Global *(Res — Coed Ages 13-19)* **[CH]** ....Raleigh, NC... 127
TX A&M Sea Camp *(Res — Coed Ages 10-18+FAM)* ....Galveston, TX... 183
TX St Aquatic Sci *(Res and Day — Coed Ages 9-15)*..................San Marcos, TX... 184
Christchurch-Marine *(Res and Day — Coed Ages 8-15)*............ Christchurch, VA... 135
Broadreach Marine *(Res — Coed Ages 15-18)* **[CH]**.. San Salvadore, BAHAMAS... 127
Whale Camp..........................Grand Manan Island, New Brunswick, CANADA... 203
   (Res — Coed Ages 10-17+FAM)

MATH
U of AK Research **[C]** ....Fairbanks, AK... 186
   (Res — Coed Ages 13-18; Day — Coed 14-18)
AZ St Math-Sci *(Res — Coed Ages 15-18)* **[C]** ....Tempe, AZ... 118
COSMOS *(Res — Coed Ages 14-18)* ....Oakland, CA... 138
Stanford Math Camp *(Res — Coed Ages 15-17)*............................ Stanford, CA... 178

MATH (CONT.)

MEDICINE & HEALTHCARE

RELIGIOUS STUDIES

SCIENCE

SCIENCE (CONT.)

SPEECH

STUDY SKILLS

VETERINARY MEDICINE

Academic Programs—Specialized

ABBEY ROAD SUMMER PROGRAMS
Res — Coed Ages 14-19

West Hollywood, CA 90046. 8266 Fountain Ave, Ste #B. Tel: 323-656-6200, 888-462-2239.
www.goabbeyroad.com   E-mail: info@goabbeyroad.com
Arthur Kian, Dir.
Grades 9-12 (younger if qualified). Adm: FCFS. **Appl**—Fee $500 dpst. Due: Rolling.
Type of instruction: ESL/TOEFL_Prep SAT/ACT_Prep Tut. **Courses:** Creative_Writing Fine_Arts Photog. **Avg class size:** 9. **Daily hours for:** Classes 3½. Homework. Tests. Grades. **High school & college credit.**
Intl program focus: Acad Lang Culture. **Locations:** CA MA Canada Europe. Home stays avail.
Focus: Col_Prep Environ_Sci Fr Ital Span. **Features:** Aquatics Boating Cooking Exploration Kayak Soccer Swim Tennis Volleyball Watersports.
Fees 2014: Res $3995-7995 (+airfare), 2-4 wks. Aid (Merit).
Housing: Dorms. **Swimming:** Pool.
Inc. **Ses:** 16. **Wks/ses:** 2-4. Operates June-Aug.

Abbey Road conducts a number of summer programs in Europe designed to facilitate cross-cultural understanding and enrichment through cultural immersion, intensive language study, exposure to new academic subjects, travel opportunities and recreational pursuits. Pupils may study French in Aix-en-Provence, Antibes, Beaulieu, Cannes (which also features precollege work), Cassis and St-Laurent, France; Italian in Amalfi, Bologna (which also includes precollege work) and Florence, Italy; and Spanish in Cadiz and Sanlucar, Spain. A separate program enables boys and girls to travel from the Italian cities of Athens, Rome and Florence to a final destination of Paris, France. This cultural immersion program serves as a hands-on study of Western civilization. In addition to the European sessions, Abbey Road conducts a French-immersion program in Quebec, Canada, as well as two programs in the US for American students: a precollege enrichment and SAT preparation session in Boston, MA, and an environmental studies program in Santa Barbara, CA.

ACADEMIC PROGRAMS INTERNATIONAL
Res — Coed Ages 18 and up

Austin, TX 78746. 301 Camp Craft Rd, Ste 100. Tel: 512-600-8900, 800-844-4124. Fax: 512-600-8999.
www.apistudyabroad.com   E-mail: api@apistudyabroad.com
Jennifer Allen, Exec Dir.
Grade 12. Adm: FCFS. **Appl**—Fee $150.
Type of instruction: Preview. **College credit.**
Intl program focus: Lang Culture. **Locations:** Asia Europe Mexico/Central_America Middle_East South_America.
Focus: Fr Ital Span.
Fees 2010: Res $3800-12,750, 3-14 wks. Aid (Merit & Need).
Ses: 55. **Wks/ses:** 3-14. Operates May-Aug.

API provides travel, educational and cultural opportunities for American students in sixteen different countries. Certain language immersion programs bear college credit. In addition to language immersion, some programs enable students to choose from classes in the liberal and studio arts, the humanities, business, history and science.

AIGLON COLLEGE SUMMER SCHOOL
Res — Coed Ages 9-16

Chesieres-Villars, 1885 Switzerland. Ave Centrale. Tel: 41-24-496-6171. Fax: 41-24-496-6162.
www.aiglon.ch/vacation-courses/summer-school   **E-mail: vacationcourses@ aiglon.ch**
Adm: FCFS. **Appl**—Due: Rolling. Teacher rec.
Enr: 201. **Enr cap:** 204. **Fac 22. Staff:** Admin 2. Couns 68.
Type of instruction: Enrich. **Courses:** Circus_Skills Crafts Dance Music Painting. **Avg class size:** 10. **Daily hours for:** Classes 2½. Rec 5.
Intl program focus: Lang.
Focus: ESL Fr. **Features:** Archery Bicycle_Tours Canoe Climbing_Wall Cooking Hiking Kayak Mountaineering Mtn_Biking Mtn_Trips Outdoor_Ed Rappelling Rock_Climb Ropes_Crse Sail White-water_Raft Basketball Football Golf Ice_Hockey Softball Swim Tennis Volleyball Watersports.
Fees 2014: Res SwF4900-SwF7200 (+SwF300), 2-3 wks.
Housing: Dorms Lodges. **Swimming:** Lake Pool.
Est 1974. Nonprofit. **Ses:** 2. **Wks/ses:** 2-3. Operates July.

This British-style boarding school combines morning language instruction in Englishand French with afternoon sports and other activities. Lessons, which are offered at introductory, intermediate and advanced levels, place emphasis on both conversational and written skills development. Each student receives approximately 48 hours of language instruction during the session. Often adventurous in nature, activities make significant use of the school's surroundings. Staff schedule a camping trip and several cultural excursions.

AMERICAN INTERNATIONAL SCHOOL-SALZBURG SUMMER LANGUAGE PROGRAM
Res and Day — Coed Ages 10-19

Salzburg, 5020 Austria. c/o American International School-Salzburg, Moosstrasse 106. Tel: 43-662-824617. Fax: 43-662-824555.
www.ais-salzburg.at   E-mail: office@ais-salzburg.at
Paul McLean, Head.
Adm: FCFS. **Appl**—Fee $0. Due: Rolling.
Enr: 90. **Fac 7. Staff:** Admin 4. Couns 4.
Type of instruction: Rem_Eng Rem_Read. **Avg class size:** 10. **Daily hours for:** Classes 5. Study 2. Rec 5. **High school credit.**
Intl program focus: Lang.
Focus: ESL Ger. **Features:** Bicycle_Tours Climbing_Wall Hiking Mtn_Trips Sail White-water_Raft Basketball Swim Tennis Ping-Pong.
Fees 2013: Res €1700-4300, 2-6 wks. Day €1020-2580, 2-6 wks.
Housing: Dorms. Avg per room/unit: 2-4. **Swimming:** Lake Pool.
Est 1977. Nonprofit. **Ses:** 3. **Wks/ses:** 2-6. Operates July-Aug.

Pupils from around the world enroll in intensive German or English language immersion courses at AIS-Salzburg. Participants attend classes for five hours daily, then engage in cultural and athletic activities each afternoon. Weekends provide time for excursions to historically and culturally significant sites in Munich, Innsbruck and the nearby Alps.

AMERISPAN STUDY ABROAD TEENAGER STUDY ABROAD AND SUMMER CAMPS
Res — Coed Ages 14-18

Philadelphia, PA 19107. 1334 Walnut St, 6th Fl. Tel: 215-531-7917, 800-511-0179. Fax: 215-751-1986.
www.amerispan.com   E-mail: info@amerispan.com

John Slocum, Pres.
Adm: FCFS. **Appl**—Due: Rolling.
Type of instruction: Enrich. **Courses:** Fine_Arts Theater.
Intl program focus: Lang Culture. **Locations:** Canada Europe South_America. Home stays avail.
Focus: Fr Ger Ital Span. **Features:** Cooking Badminton Basketball Soccer Volleyball.
Fees 2014: Res $1395-3800 (+airfare), 1-4 wks.
Housing: Dorms Houses.
Est 1993. Inc. **Ses:** 31. **Wks/ses:** 1-4. Operates June-July.

AmeriSpan's immersion programs expose teenagers to foreign languages both in the classroom and the community. In addition to daily classroom study, students participate in organized sports and excursions or explore their surroundings independently. Three program options offer varying levels of schoolwork and supervision. Residential summer camps include dormitory living, structured activities and strict curfews. Students in the supervised programs live with host families with some supervision. Unsupervised programs allow mature 16- to 18-year-olds to participate in AmeriSpan's adult program with no curfews or organized activities.

ANDEO INTERNATIONAL HOMESTAYS
HIGH SCHOOL IMMERSION PROGRAMS
Res — Coed Ages 14-18

Portland, OR 97204. 620 SW 5th Ave, Ste 625. Tel: 503-274-1776, 800-274-6007. Fax: 503-274-9004.
www.andeo.org   E-mail: info@andeo.org
Melinda Samis, Dir. Student contact: Andrea Bailey, E-mail: andrea@andeo.org.
Adm: FCFS. **Appl**—Fee $0. Due: Rolling.
Staff: Admin 2.
Type of instruction: Enrich. **Courses:** Creative_Writing. **Avg class size:** 4. **Daily hours for:** Classes 4. Rec 4.
Intl program focus: Lang Culture. **Locations:** Asia Europe Mexico/Central_America South_America. Home stays avail.
Focus: Fr Ger Span. **Features:** Adventure_Travel.
Fees 2014: Res $1800-4300 (+airfare), 2-5 wks. Aid 2014: $100-1000.
Housing: Houses.
Est 1981. Inc. **Ses:** 8. **Wks/ses:** 2-5. Operates June-Aug.

Andeo's Immersion Programs, which operate in Spain, Costa Rica, Ecuador, France, Japan and China provide students with language-study opportunities and cultural connections. Course work takes place in an accredited university or a language institute whose curriculum conforms to university standards. Pupils study in one city to experience the local culture and live with a host family. The itinerary includes overnight excursions and day trips to sites of historical and cultural interest. Applicants must have two years of previous study in the target language.

ARIANA SUMMER COURSES
Res — Coed Ages 6-20

St Gallen, 9000 Switzerland. Hohenweg 60. Tel: 41-71-277-92-91. Fax: 41-71-277-72-53.
www.ariana.ch   E-mail: info@ariana.ch
Monika A. Schmid, Dir.
Adm: FCFS. **Appl**—Due: Rolling.
Enr cap: 12.
Locations: Europe.
Focus: ESL Fr Ger. **Features:** Bicycle_Tours Hiking Riding Equestrian Golf Soccer Swim Tennis Water-skiing.

Fees 2014: Res SwF1680-2310, 1 wk.
Housing: Dorms. Swimming: Lake Pool.
Est 1982. Ses: 4. Wks/ses: 4-7. Operates June-Aug.
Ariana offers summer language immersion programs in Seefeld, Austria, and at two Swiss locations: St. Gallen and Arosa. Students participate in three lessons daily and two hours of conversation per week in either French, German or ESL. The programs include various recreational activities, and Ariana schedules organized excursions to sites of historical and cultural interest.

ARIZONA STATE UNIVERSITY
CRONKITE SUMMER JOURNALISM INSTITUTE
Res — Coed Ages 15-18

Phoenix, AZ 85004. 555 N Central Ave, Ste 302. Tel: 480-965-5251.
http://cronkite.asu.edu/beyond/hs_inst.php   E-mail: cronkitesji@asu.edu
Anita F. Luera, Dir.
Grades 10-PG. Adm: Selective. **Appl**—Due: Mar. Transcript, rec, 3 writing samples (print prgm).
Type of instruction: Enrich.
Focus: Writing/Journ.
Fees 2014: Free. Res 2 wks.
Housing: Dorms.
Nonprofit. **Ses: 1. Wks/ses: 2.** Operates June.
Conducted by the Walter Cronkite School of Journalism and Mass Communication at ASU's downtown campus, the Summer Journalism Institute comprises two tracks: the Broadcast Institute and the Print Journalism Institute. Both institutes seek to prepare high schoolers for college journalism studies while letting them explore future career options in a college setting. The Broadcast Institute features classes on writing, reporting, videography and editing; the opportunity to anchor, report, write, produce and direct a newscast; chances to meet and converse with broadcast professionals; and visits to local radio and television stations. The Print Journalism Institute includes classes on writing, editing, layout, design and photojournalism; discussions with professional journalists who provide advice on media careers; production of a newspaper; and visits to Phoenix media outlets.

ARIZONA STATE UNIVERSITY
JOAQUIN BUSTOZ MATH-SCIENCE HONORS PROGRAM
Res — Coed Ages 15-18

Tempe, AZ 85287. PO Box 873901. Tel: 480-965-1690. Fax: 480-965-0333.
www.asu.edu/mshp   E-mail: mshp@asu.edu
Cynthia Barragan Romero, Coord.
Grades 10-PG. Adm: Selective. Priority: URM. Prereqs: GPA 3.25. **Appl**—Fee $0. Due: Feb. Transcript, personal statement, rec.
Type of instruction: Adv Tut Undergrad. **Daily hours for:** Classes 6. Homework. Tests. Grades. **College credit:** 3-4/crse, total 6.
Focus: Math Sci.
Fees 2014: Free (in-state residents). Res 5-8 wks.
Housing: Dorms.
Est 1985. Nonprofit. Ses: 3. Wks/ses: 5-8. Operates May-Aug.
MSHP provides opportunities for Arizona residents from backgrounds traditionally underrepresented in the fields of math and science to begin university-level instruction while still in high school. Two five-week sessions offer three college credits, and an eight-week course yields four credits. Pupils complete daily homework, take quizzes twice a week and take weekly tests. Faculty provide tutoring and problem-solving sessions in the evening, and

a variety of academic presentations and activities are scheduled during each session. High school graduates may enroll only if they are preparing for freshman year at Arizona State.

ASIAN AMERICAN JOURNALISTS ASSOCIATION
J CAMP
Res — Coed Ages 15-17

New Orleans, LA.
Contact (Year-round): 1182 Market St, Ste 320, San Francisco, CA 94102. Tel: 415-346-2051. Fax: 415-346-6343.
www.aaja.org/jcamp2014   E-mail: programs@aaja.org
Student contact: Nao Vang.
Grades 9-11. Adm: Very selective. Admitted: 10%. **Appl**—Fee $0. Due: Mar. Transcript, test scores, essays, rec.
Enr: 42.
Type of instruction: Enrich. **Courses:** Media Photog.
Focus: Writing/Journ.
Fees 2014: Free. Res 1 wk.
Housing: Dorms.
Est 2001. Ses: 1. **Wks/ses:** 1. Operates July-Aug.

Designed to confront the lack of diversity in journalism, J Camp assembles a multicultural group of high school students for six days of intensive journalism training. The curriculum consists of interactive workshops, hands-on projects, guest speakers and field trips. Students learn from experienced professional journalists and receive training in writing, photography, television broadcasting, online media and reporting. The program is not restricted to Asian-American students.

ASTROCAMP
Res — Coed Ages 8-17

Claremont, CA 91711. 232 Harrison Ave, PO Box 1360. Fax: 909-625-7305.
Contact (Sept-May): Fax: 909-625-9977.
Year-round Tel: 909-625-6194, 800-645-1423.
www.guideddiscoveries.org   E-mail: info@guideddiscoveries.org
Allan Tiso, Dir.
Adm: FCFS. **Appl**—Fee $0. Due: Rolling.
Fac 20. Staff: Admin 5.
Type of instruction: Enrich. **Courses:** Geol Crafts.
Focus: Astron. **Features:** Hiking Mountaineering Mtn_Biking Rock_Climb Ropes_Crse Swim Volleyball.
Fees 2014: Res $950-2100, 1-2 wks.
Housing: Dorms. **Swimming:** Pool.
Est 1990. Nonprofit. **Spons:** Guided Discoveries. **Ses:** 5. **Wks/ses:** 1-2. Operates June-July.

At AstroCamp, boys and girls learn about astronomy and space exploration while also taking part in wilderness camping activities. Campers explore a mystery planetary surface, use telescopes and microscopes, launch rockets, go rock climbing and spend a week camping in the mountains.

THE ATHENIAN SCHOOL
SUMMER ENGLISH LANGUAGE PROGRAM
Res — Coed Ages 12-17

Danville, CA 94506. 2100 Mt Diablo Scenic Blvd. Tel: 925-837-5375. Fax: 925-362-7227.

www.athenian.org/esl　E-mail: debra.ataman@athenian.org
Debra Ataman, Assoc Dir.
Adm: FCFS. **Appl**—Fee $0. Due: Rolling.
Fac 8. Staff: Admin 1. Couns 6.
Type of instruction: Enrich. **Courses:** Expository_Writing Lang Creative_Writing Music Theater. **Daily hours for:** Classes 3½. Study 1½. Rec 3½.
Focus: ESL. **Features:** Aquatics Basketball Swim Tennis Volleyball.
Fees 2014: Res $6150, 4 wks.
Housing: Dorms. Avg per room/unit: 1-2. **Swimming:** Pool.
Nonprofit. **Ses:** 1. **Wks/ses:** 4. Operates July-Aug.

Located on the school's 75-acre campus in the foothills of Mount Diablo, SELP aids international students with conversation, pronunciation, listening, reading, vocabulary, writing and grammar. Pupils with varying fluency levels may take part in this intensive session. The program incorporates field trips to cultural locations throughout the Bay Area. Athenian also schedules optional trips to Universal Studios and Magic Mountain.

AUBURN UNIVERSITY ARCHITECTURE CAMP
Res — Coed Ages 16-18

Auburn, AL 36849. Outreach Prgm Office, 301 O D Smith Hall. Tel: 334-844-5100. Fax: 334-844-3101.
www.auburn.edu/outreach/opce/summercamps　E-mail: james.birdsong@auburn.edu
Carla Bell, Coord.
Grades 11-12. Adm: FCFS. **Appl**—Due: Rolling.
Type of instruction: Enrich.
Focus: Architect.
Fees 2014: Res $645, 1 wk.
Housing: Dorms.
Nonprofit. **Ses:** 2. **Wks/ses:** 1. Operates June-July.

This intensive workshop for rising high school upperclassmen interested in architecture begins with basic design concepts and ends with an architectural design project. Hands-on exercises, technical demonstrations and professional guest speakers round out the program. Students have studio space and access to computers and may engage in various social and recreational activities.

AUBURN UNIVERSITY BUILDING CONSTRUCTION CAMP
Res — Coed Ages 14-18

Auburn, AL 36849. OPCE Summer Experience, 301 O D Smith Hall. Tel: 334-844-5100. Fax: 334-844-3101.
www.auburn.edu/outreach/opce/summerexperience/construction.htm　E-mail: james.birdsong@auburn.edu
James Birdsong, Coord.
Grades 9-12. Adm: FCFS. **Appl**—Fee $0. Due: Rolling.
Type of instruction: Enrich.
Focus: Architect.
Fees 2014: Res $645, 1 wk. Aid (Need).
Housing: Dorms.
Ses: 1. **Wks/ses:** 1. Operates June.

Students learn construction basics and how to integrate building design with site, climate, function and environmental considerations. Each day includes hands-on activities and instruction from Auburn faculty.

AUBURN UNIVERSITY
TEAMS AND INDIVIDUALS GUIDED
BY ENGINEERING RESOURCES
Res — Coed Ages 14-17

Auburn, AL 36849. OPCE Summer Experience, 301 O D Smith Hall. Tel: 334-844-5100. Fax: 334-844-3101.
www.eng.auburn.edu/outreach/k-12/eng-summer-camp.html   E-mail: james.birdsong@auburn.edu
James Birdsong, Coord.
Grades 9-12. Adm: FCFS. Appl—Due: Rolling.
Type of instruction: Enrich.
Focus: Engineering.
Fees 2014: Res $685, 1 wk.
Housing: Dorms.
Ses: 2. Wks/ses: 1. Operates June.

Auburn offers two sessions for students interested in engineering: one week for students entering grades 9 and 10, and another for those entering grades 11 and 12. The curriculum combines hands-on activities, workshops, tours and lectures. In addition, engineers and engineering students advise participants on the high school courses they should take before pursuing college study or a career in engineering.

AUBURN UNIVERSITY
WORLD AFFAIRS YOUTH SEMINAR
Res — Coed Ages 15-18

Auburn, AL 36849. Office of Professional & Continuing Ed, 301 O D Smith Hall. Tel: 334-844-5100. Fax: 334-844-3101.
www.auburn.edu/outreach/opce/summerexperience/wa.htm   E-mail: opce@auburn.edu
James Birdsong, Coord.
Grades 10-12. Adm: FCFS. Appl—Fee $0. Due: Rolling.
Type of instruction: Enrich.
Focus: Intl_Relations.
Fees 2014: Res $574, 1 wk.
Housing: Dorms.
Est 1987. Ses: 1. Wks/ses: 1. Operates July.

World Affairs aims to develop the participant's global perspective of current events and world issues. Students attend classes, listen to guest speakers and conduct research in preparation for debates within the framework of Model United Nations sessions. Boys and girls preview college life through extracurricular activities.

AWESOMEMATH SUMMER PROGRAM
Res — Coed Ages 12-17

Plano, TX 75025. 3425 Neiman Rd. Tel: 214-549-6146.
www.awesomemath.org   E-mail: tandreescu@gmail.com
Titu Andreescu, Dir.
Grades 7-12 (younger if qualified). Adm: Selective. Appl—Fee $50. Due: May. Adm test, 2 recs, personal statement.
Enr: 120. Fac 15. Prof 10. K-12 staff 5. Staff: Admin 2.
Type of instruction: Adv Enrich. Daily hours for: Classes 6. Study 1½. Rec 3.
Locations: CA NY.
Focus: Math.
Fees 2014: Res $3875, 3 wks. Day $2575. Aid (Need).
Housing: Dorms. Campus facilities avail.

Ses: 2. **Wks/ses:** 3. Operates June-Aug.

Held on the campuses of Cornell University and the University of California-Santa Cruz, ASMP enables gifted math pupils to hone their problem-solving skills while exploring advanced topics in detail. Many participants seek to improve their performance in national math contests. Taught by distinguished faculty and Olympiad coaches from the US and abroad, lectures focus on number theory, Euclidean geometry, algebraic inequalities and techniques, modular arithmetic and computational geometry. A 90-minute problem-solving seminar (with active student participation) follows each teaching session.

BALL STATE UNIVERSITY
COLLEGE OF ARCHITECTURE AND PLANNING
SUMMER WORKSHOP
Res — Coed Ages 16-17

Muncie, IN 47306. AB 104. Tel: 765-285-5859. Fax: 765-285-3726.
www.bsu.edu/cap/workshop   E-mail: cap@bsu.edu
Melanie Smith, Coord.
Grades 11-12. Adm: Selective. Prereqs: GPA 3.0. **Appl**—Fee $0. Due: Rolling.
Type of instruction: Enrich. **Daily hours for:** Classes 6.
Focus: Architect.
Fees 2014: Res $2100, 2 wks. Aid (Need).
Housing: Dorms. Avg per room/unit: 2. Campus facilities avail.
Nonprofit. **Ses:** 1. **Wks/ses:** 2. Operates July.

Ball State's CAP Summer Workshop provides rising high school juniors and seniors with an intensive immersion into environmental design and problem solving. Faculty lead a series of exercises intended to both challenge students and encourage creative expression. Boys and girls engage in six hours of daily studio time, then have some unscheduled blocks in the evening to experience college life. A field trip study tour that includes bus travel to a major metropolitan city enriches classroom instruction. During the tour, participants analyze and document cultural aspects of the city's design and planning.

BAYLOR UNIVERSITY
HIGH SCHOOL SUMMER SCIENCE RESEARCH PROGRAM
Res — Coed Ages 17-18

Waco, TX 76798. 1 Bear Pl, PO Box 97344. Tel: 254-710-4288. Fax: 254-710-3639.
www.baylor.edu/summerscience   E-mail: hsssrp@baylor.edu
Frank Mathis, Dir.
Grade 12. Adm: Very selective. Admitted: 10%. **Appl**—Due: Mar.
Enr: 10. **Enr cap:** 10. **Fac 10. Staff:** Admin 3.
Type of instruction: Adv. **Courses:** Astron Environ_Sci Geol Math. **Avg class size:** 1.
    Daily hours for: Classes 5½. Rec 2. **College credit:** 1.
Focus: Sci. **Features:** Swim.
Fees 2012: Res $500-700, 5 wks. Aid (Need).
Housing: Dorms. **Swimming:** Pool. Campus facilities avail.
Est 1991. Nonprofit. Baptist. **Ses:** 1. **Wks/ses:** 5. Operates July-Aug.

HSSSRP offers hands-on research experiences with Baylor University professors to rising high school seniors who are strong in science. Students use the latest research instruments, interpret data, participate in science and technology seminars, and engage in group recreational activities. Specific areas of study include astronomy, biochemistry, biology, chemistry, computer science, engineering, environmental studies, geology, mathematics, museum studies, neuroscience, nutrition, physics and psychology. Successful completion of the program results in one hour of college credit.

BELOIT COLLEGE
SUMMER INTENSIVE LANGUAGE PROGRAM
Res — Coed Ages 17 and up; Day — Coed 16 and up

Beloit, WI 53511. **Ctr for Language Studies, 700 College St. Tel: 608-363-2277, 800-356-0751. Fax: 608-363-7129.**
www.beloit.edu/cls   E-mail: cls@beloit.edu
Dan Perusich, Dir.
Grades 12-Col. Adm: Selective. **Appl**—Fee $25. Due: Rolling. Transcript, 2 recs.
Type of instruction: Adv Undergrad. **Avg class size:** 10. **Daily hours for:** Classes 5½. Study 4½. Homework. Tests. Grades. **College credit.**
Focus: ESL Arabic Chin Japan Russ. **Features:** Swim.
Fees 2014: Res $3847-7695, 4-8 wks. Aid (Merit).
Housing: Dorms. Avg per room/unit: 2. **Swimming:** Pool. Campus facilities avail.
Est 1983. Ses: 2. Wks/ses: 4-8. Operates June-Aug.

Advanced high school students complete course work in Arabic, Chinese, Japanese, Russian or English as a Second Language through Beloit's Center for Language Study. No prior experience is required in the target language. Students speak the language of instruction during all academic hours, and language groups eat lunch and dinner with program instructors. The four-week session is equivalent to one semester of language study; the eight-week session, a full year. Individualized tutorial sessions and weekly movie nights and cultural events round out the program.

THE BEMENT SCHOOL
ENGLISH LANGUAGE AND AMERICAN CULTURE PROGRAM
Res — Coed Ages 7-12

Deerfield, MA 01342. **94 Old Main St, PO Box 8. Tel: 413-475-3044. Fax: 413-774-7863.**
www.bement.org/elac   E-mail: summer@bement.org
Emily Lent, Dir.
Adm: FCFS. **Appl**—Fee $60. Due: Apr. Transcript, 1 Eng teacher rec, writing sample.
Enr cap: 20. **Intl:** 100%. **Non-White:** 90%. **Fac 4.** K-12 staff 4. **Staff:** Admin 3. Couns 4.
Type of instruction: Enrich Study_Skills. **Courses:** Lang Speech Writing/Journ Crafts Creative_Writing Dance Music Theater. **Avg class size:** 6. **Daily hours for:** Classes 4. Study 1½. Rec 4. Homework. Tests.
Focus: ESL. **Features:** Canoe Climbing_Wall Hiking Wilderness_Camp Basketball Soccer Softball Swim Ultimate_Frisbee.
Fees 2014: Res $4500 (+$250), 3½ wks.
Housing: Dorms. Avg per room/unit: 2. **Swimming:** Lake Pond Pool River. Campus facilities avail.
Nonprofit. **Ses:** 1. **Wks/ses:** 3½. Operates July-Aug.

Emphasizing speaking, listening, reading and writing proficiency, ELAC addresses speaking skills through interviewing, debate, oral presentation and group work. Students broaden vocabulary and analytical skills while reading various materials, and writing instruction focuses on sentence structure and paragraph construction. Teachers employ audio- and videotapes to improve listening abilities. Workshops assist children with SSAT and TOEFL preparation.

BENTLEY UNIVERSITY
WALL STREET 101
Res — Coed Ages 17-18

Waltham, MA 02452. **175 Forest St. Tel: 781-891-2664. Fax: 781-891-3476.**
www.bentley.edu/centers/trading-room/wall-street-101   E-mail: ga_wallstreet@bentley.edu

Amy Whittaker, Dir.
Grade 12. Adm: Selective. **Appl**—Fee $50. Due: Apr. Transcript, rec, standardized test scores, essay.
Type of instruction: Enrich.
Focus: Bus/Fin Econ.
Fees 2014: Res $699, 1 wk.
Nonprofit. **Ses:** 1. **Wks/ses:** 1. Operates June-Aug.

This enrichment program employs hands-on exercises to teach students about the stock market and the process of investment. Course work addresses various aspects of the financial industry and other business fields. Boys and girls get to experience the trading-room environment through simulated trading sessions. Pupils work in groups of five to construct a diversified portfolio of equity securities, then prepare a formal presentation detailing the rationale of their selections. Wall Street 101 also features trips to Boston investment firms and other area attractions.

BISHOP'S COLLEGE SCHOOL SUMMER LANGUAGE CAMP
Res and Day — Coed Ages 11-16

Sherbrooke, J1M 1Z8 Quebec, Canada. 80 Chemin Moulton Hill, PO Box 5001, Lennoxville. Tel: 819-566-0227. Fax: 819-822-8917.
www.bishopscollegeschool.com   E-mail: summer@bishopscollegeschool.com
Julie Lowry, Dir.
Grades 6-11. Adm: FCFS. **Appl**—Fee $0. Due: Rolling.
Enr: 185. **Fac** 20. **Staff:** Admin 4.
Avg class size: 12. **Daily hours for:** Classes 4½. Study 1. Rec 2.
Intl program focus: Lang.
Focus: ESL Fr. **Features:** Canoe Climbing_Wall Riding Basketball Soccer Softball Swim Tennis Ultimate_Frisbee.
Fees 2012: Res Can$3675 (+Can$100), 4 wks. **Day** Can$2300, 4 wks.
Housing: Dorms. **Swimming:** Lake Pool.
Est 1961. Ses: 1. **Wks/ses:** 4. Operates June-July.

BCS provides summer instruction for motivated students interested in gaining proficiency in French or English. Both programs offer instruction at beginning, intermediate and advanced levels. Each level includes oral and written work and offers a solid base for work in grammar and conversation. Supplementary study is required in the areas of reading, writing and comprehension. Pupils take placement exams at the beginning of the program, then frequent classroom tests thereafter.

BOSTON UNIVERSITY RESEARCH INTERNSHIP
IN SCIENCE AND ENGINEERING PROGRAM
Res and Day — Coed Ages 16-18

Boston, MA 02215. 755 Commonwealth Ave, Rm 105. Tel: 617-353-1378. Fax: 617-353-5532.
www.bu.edu/summer/high-school-programs/research-internship   E-mail: rise@bu.edu
Student contact: Matthew Cobb, E-mail: mcobb@bu.edu.
Grade 12 (younger if qualified). Adm: Very selective. **Prereqs:** GPA 3.89. SAT M/CR 1470; PSAT: 142 (Math). **Appl**—Due: Apr. Transcripts, standardized test scores, 2 recs.
Enr: 50. **Non-White:** 54%. **Staff:** Admin 2. Couns 9.
Type of instruction: Adv Enrich. **Courses:** Astron Engineering Med/Healthcare Psych.
Daily hours for: Classes 8.
Focus: Sci. **Features:** Swim.
Fees 2014: Res $6494-6694, 6 wks. **Day** $4220, 6 wks. Aid (Merit & Need).
Housing: Dorms. **Swimming:** Pool. Campus facilities avail.
Est 1978. Ses: 1. **Wks/ses:** 6. Operates June-Aug.

RISE allows academically motivated rising high school seniors to conduct university-level laboratory research, under the guidance of a Boston University faculty mentor, in one of the following areas: astronomy, biology, chemistry, engineering, medicine, physics or psychology. Pupils work on an ongoing research project in their chosen area, in the process developing technical and analytical skills and gaining insight into the scientific method. Each student prepares a poster for display at a session-closing scientific conference. Participants have been recognized by the Intel Science Talent Search and the Siemens Westinghouse Competition.

BRANDEIS UNIVERSITY GENESIS PROGRAM
Res — Coed Ages 15-17

Waltham, MA 02454. 415 South St, MS 085. Tel: 781-736-8416. Fax: 815-301-2874.
www.brandeis.edu/highschool/genesis   E-mail: highschool@brandeis.edu
Dvora Goodman, Dir.
Grades 10-12 (younger if qualified). Adm: Selective. **Appl**—Fee $40. Due: Mar. Transcript, 2 essays, teacher & parent references.
Enr: 76. Fac 10. Staff: Admin 4. Couns 15.
Type of instruction: Adv. **Courses:** Law Writing/Journ Creative_Writing Dance Fine_Arts Music. **Avg class size: 13. Daily hours for:** Classes 3.
Focus: Relig_Stud. **Features:** Community_Serv Cooking Peace/Cross-cultural Basketball Tennis.
Fees 2014: Res $5600 (+$160), 4½ wks. Aid (Need).
Housing: Dorms. Avg per room/unit: 2. Campus facilities avail.
Est 1997. Nonprofit. Jewish. **Ses:** 1. **Wks/ses:** 4½. Operates July-Aug.

Judaic studies, the arts and the humanities constitute this academic and religious program. Students with diverse educational experiences and varying degrees of experience with Judaism engage with scholars, artists, activists and experiential educators. Field trips and meetings with relevant professionals supplement hands-on seminars. Courses vary by year but include such subjects as journalism, law, technology and world religion. Afternoon and evening workshops provide direct experiences with Israeli foods, music, folk dancing and creative writing. Select participants may return to Genesis for a second summer to take a Brandeis undergraduate communications course for college credit.

BREBEUF CITY RESIDENTIAL PROGRAMME
Res — Coed Ages 11-17

Montreal, H34T 1W4 Quebec, Canada. 5625 Rue Decelle.
Contact (Sept-June): c/o CISS, 439 University Ave, Ste 2110, Toronto, M5G 1Y8 Ontario, Canada.
Year-round Tel: 416-646-5400, 866-258-4303. Fax: 416-646-5403.
www.cisscanada.com   E-mail: camps@cisscanada.com
Nick Florian, Dir.
Adm: FCFS. **Appl**—Due: Rolling.
Staff: Admin 4.
Courses: Art Crafts Dance Drawing Sculpt Visual_Arts. **Avg class size:** 15.
Intl program focus: Lang. **Locations:** MA Canada Europe.
Focus: ESL Fr. **Features:** Basketball Figure_Skating Ice_Hockey Soccer Tennis Volleyball Ping-Pong Billiards.
Housing: Dorms.
Est 2000. Spons: Canadian International Student Services. **Ses:** 10. **Wks/ses:** 2-5. Operates July-Aug.

Located on Mount Royal, this French and English immersion program combines 15 hours of weekly instruction in the target language with afternoon excursions and recreational programming. Placement testing on the session's first day enables pupils to study with others of a similar aptitude level. Students choose either French or English—or both if the length of stay is four or five weeks. Staff converse with participants in the language of study outside of the classroom to enhance the immersion experience. Each week, Brebeuf organizes full-day, half-day and evening cultural excursions around Montreal and elsewhere in Quebec.

BRILLANTMONT INTERNATIONAL SCHOOL SUMMER COURSE
Res — Coed Ages 10-16

Lausanne, 1005 Switzerland. 16 Ave Secretan. Tel: 41-21-310-04-00. Fax: 41-21-320-84-17.
www.brillantmont.ch   E-mail: summercourse@brillantmont.ch
Philippe Pasche, Dir.
Adm: FCFS. **Appl**—Due: Rolling.
Enr: 90. **Fac** 20. **Staff:** Admin 3.
Type of instruction: Enrich. **Avg class size:** 15. **Daily hours for:** Classes 4. Study 1. Rec 3.
Intl program focus: Lang Culture.
Focus: ESL Fr. **Features:** Bicycle_Tours Hiking Mtn_Trips Rock_Climb Badminton Basketball Cross-country Field_Hockey Rugby Soccer Swim Tennis Volleyball Water-skiing Watersports.
Fees 2014: Res SwF1850, 1 wk.
Housing: Houses. Avg per room/unit: 2. **Swimming:** Lake Pool.
Est 1982. Ses: 6. **Wks/ses:** 1. Operates July-Aug.

Morning French or English language courses at Brillantmont emphasize oral communication, with attention also paid to grammar, written expression and vocabulary. In the afternoon, boys and girls engage in a sports program featuring such activities as tennis, basketball, windsurfing and water-skiing. Evening pursuits include bowling, ice skating, in-line skating and trips to the discotheque. Sundays are reserved for daylong excursions devoted to rock climbing, glacier walking, rafting or museum visitation, among other options.

BRITISH INTERNATIONAL SCHOOL-PHUKET
ENGLISH SUMMER SCHOOL
Res — Coed Ages 8-15; Day — Coed 7-15

Phuket, 83000 Thailand. 59 Moo 2, Thepkrasattri Rd, Tambon Koh Kaew, Amphur Muang. Tel: 66-7633-5555. Fax: 66-7623-8728.
www.bisphuket.ac.th   E-mail: summer@bisphuket.ac.th
Patrick du Preez, Dir.
Student contact: Christophe I. Espouy, E-mail: cespouy@bisphuket.ac.th.
Grades 3-9 (younger if qualified). Adm: FCFS. **Appl**—Fee $0. Due: Rolling.
Enr: 150. **Enr cap:** 180. **Intl:** 98%. **Fac** 15. **Staff:** Admin 6. Res 19.
Type of instruction: Enrich Rem_Eng Rem_Read Tut. **Courses:** Debate Expository_ Writing Speech Crafts Creative_Writing Drama Music. **Avg class size:** 12. **Daily hours for:** Classes 3. Study 1½. Rec 3. Tests. Grades.
Intl program focus: Acad Lang Culture.
Focus: ESL. **Features:** Aquatics Boating Canoe Cruises Exploration Hiking Kayak Mtn_ Biking Paintball Rappelling Rock_Climb Sail Badminton Basketball Cricket Golf Rugby Soccer Softball Swim Tennis Volleyball Water-skiing Watersports Ping-Pong Snorkeling.
Fees 2014: Res Bt80,000 (+Bt5000), 4 wks. Day 4 wks.
Housing: Dorms Hotels Houses Lodges. Avg per room/unit: 4. **Swimming:** Ocean Pool River Stream. Campus facilities avail.
Est 1996. Inc. Ses: 1. **Wks/ses:** 4. Operates July.

Students in this program receive small-group ESL instruction for 18 hours each week from native English speakers, and also learn English informally through participation in such activities as land sports and watersports, music, art and drama. Excursions off campus, which provide further exposure to English conversation, include trips to national parks and local beaches.

BROADREACH GLOBAL SUMMER EDUCATIONAL ADVENTURES
Res — Coed Ages 13-19

Raleigh, NC 27603. 806 McCulloch St, Ste 102. Tel: 919-256-8200, 888-833-1907. Fax: 919-833-2129.
www.gobroadreach.com   E-mail: info@academictreks.com
Carlton Goldthwaite, Dir.
Grades 8-Col. Adm: FCFS. Appl—Fee $0. Due: Rolling.
Enr: 10-12. Enr cap: 10-12. Intl: 10%. Fac 3. Staff: Admin 5. Couns 3.
Type of instruction: Adv. Courses: Ecol. Avg class size: 11. Daily hours for: Classes 4. Study 1. Rec 3. Homework. Tests. Grades. High school & college credit: 2-3/crse, total 3.
Intl program focus: Lang Culture. Locations: Africa Asia Australia/New_Zealand Caribbean Europe Mexico/Central_America South_America. Home stays avail.
Focus: Environ_Sci Chin Fr Span Marine_Bio/Stud Community_Serv. Features: Adventure_Travel Caving Conservation Exploration Hiking Kayak Mountaineering Mtn_Trips Outdoor_Ed Peace/Cross-cultural Riding Sail Scuba Sea_Cruises Seamanship White-water_Raft Wilderness_Camp Wilderness_Canoe Swim.
Fees 2014: Res $3180-7180 (+airfare), 2-4 wks.
Housing: Dorms Hotels Tents. Swimming: Ocean River.
Est 1992. Inc. Ses: 3. Wks/ses: 2-4. Operates June-Aug.

This Broadreach program combines hands-on learning, adventure, service work, cultural immersion and international travel. Different Academic Treks focus on marine science, language immersion, cultural studies and community service. All trips include 10 to 55 hours of community service as a complement to students' academic work.

BROADREACH MARINE BIOLOGY ADVENTURE
Res — Coed Ages 15-18

San Salvadore, Bahamas.
Contact (Year-round): 806 McCulloch St, Ste 102, Raleigh, NC 27603. Tel: 919-256-8200, 888-833-1907. Fax: 919-833-2129.
www.gobroadreach.com   E-mail: questions@gobroadreach.com
Carlton Goldwaithe, Dir.
Grades 9-11. Adm: FCFS. Appl—Fee $0. Due: Rolling.
Enr: 10-14. Enr cap: 10-14. Intl: 10%. Fac 5. Staff: Admin 2. Couns 4.
Type of instruction: Adv. Courses: Ecol. Avg class size: 12. Daily hours for: Classes 4½. Study 1½. Rec 2. High school & college credit: 3/crse, total 3.
Intl program focus: Acad Culture.
Focus: Marine_Bio/Stud. Features: Community_Serv Conservation Exploration Hiking Kayak Peace/Cross-cultural Scuba Swim Water-skiing Watersports.
Fees 2014: Res $5580-6170 (+airfare), 3 wks.
Housing: Dorms Lodges. Swimming: Ocean.
Est 1992. Inc. Ses: 2. Wks/ses: 3. Operates June-Aug.

Young people in this Broadreach program investigate the marine world through intensive field studies, research and diving. Students learn hands-on while diving alongside professional marine biologists on underwater reefs. Field research, labs, dive training and seminars qualify program participants for academic credit.

BROWN UNIVERSITY LEADERSHIP INSTITUTE
Res and Day — Coed Ages 14-18

Providence, RI 02912. Box T, 42 Charlesfield St. Tel: 401-863-7900. Fax: 401-863-3916.
www.brown.edu/scs/pre-college/leadership   E-mail: summer@brown.edu
Robin Rose, Dir.

Grades 9-12. Adm: Selective. **Appl**—Fee $45-90. **Due:** Rolling. Transcript, teacher rec, essay.
Type of instruction: Enrich. **Courses:** Bus/Fin Film. **Daily hours for:** Classes 4½.
Focus: Leadership.
Fees 2014: Res $3924, 2 wks. Aid (Merit).
Housing: Dorms. Campus facilities avail.
Ses: 3. **Wks/ses:** 2. Operates June-Aug.

This program for high schoolers seeks to develop their leadership skills through enrollment in one course and participation in several evening programs in which current events and leadership issues are addressed. Class topics involve such issues as global engagement, the civil rights movement, conflict resolution, global health, social change, women and leadership, social entrepreneurship and documentary film for social change. During the session, boys and girls identify and analyze their personal learning styles, engage in group problem solving, and work on their public speaking and interpersonal communication skills.

BROWN UNIVERSITY SPARK PROGRAM
Res — Coed Ages 12-15

Providence, RI 02912. 42 Charlesfield St, Box T. Tel: 401-863-7900. Fax: 401-863-7908.
www.brown.edu/ce/pre-college/spark/index.php   E-mail: summer@brown.edu
Jennifer Aizenman, Dir.
Grades 6-8. Adm: Selective. **Appl**—Fee $45-90. **Due:** Rolling. Transcript, teacher rec, essay.
Type of instruction: Enrich. **Courses:** Anat Robotics. **Daily hours for:** Classes 4.
Focus: Ecol Environ_Sci Sci.
Fees 2014: Res $3924 (+$40-90), 1-2 wks.
Housing: Dorms. Avg per room/unit: 1-2.
Nonprofit. Ses: 3. **Wks/ses:** 1-2. Operates July.

Designed for middle schoolers who have demonstrated noteworthy ability in science, SPARK provides students with an intellectual examination of concepts and familiar topics. Boys and girls attend class for four hours each morning, then take part in lab sessions or embark on field trips on Tuesday and Thursday afternoons. While the main program lasts for one week, a special two-week program focuses on the ecology of Narragansett Bay. This noncompetitive program features no tests or grades. Extracurricular activities and social events balance academics.

C-TECH²
COMPUTERS AND TECHNOLOGY AT VIRGINIA TECH
Res — Girls Ages 16-18

Blacksburg, VA 24061. 215 Hancock Hall. Tel: 540-231-3973. Fax: 540-231-1831.
www.eng.vt.edu/ctech2   E-mail: ctech2@vt.edu
Susan Arnold Christian, Dir.
Grades 11-12. Adm: Somewhat selective. **Appl**—Due: Apr. Transcript, essay, 2 recs.
Type of instruction: Enrich. **Courses:** Comp_Sci.
Focus: Engineering Math. **Features:** Swim.
Fees 2014: Res $1500, 2 wks. Aid (Need).
Housing: Dorms. **Swimming:** Pool. Campus facilities avail.
Nonprofit. Spons: Virginia Polytechnic Institute. **Ses:** 1. **Wks/ses:** 2. Operates June-July.

The program aims to develop and sustain the interests of young women in engineering and the sciences. Hands-on activities demonstrate the real-world applications of engineering, math and science. Seminars provided by Virginia Tech offices cover college admissions, scholarships, financial aid and career services, and presentations by each department of the

College of Engineering explore academic and career possibilities within different engineering fields.

CALIFORNIA SCHOLASTIC PRESS ASSOCIATION JOURNALISM WORKSHOP
Res — Coed Ages 16-18

San Luis Obispo, CA. California State Polytechnic Univ.
Contact (Year-round): 384 Mira Mar Ave, Long Beach, CA 90814. Tel: 714-834-3784.
www.cspaworkshop.org
Grades 10-PG. Adm: Selective. **Appl**—Fee $0. Due: Apr. Essay, 3 writing samples.
Enr: 25. Enr cap: 25. Fac 23. Specialists 23. **Staff:** Couns 3.
Type of instruction: Enrich. **Courses:** Photog.
Focus: Writing/Journ.
Fees 2014: Res $1275-1400, 2 wks. Aid (Need).
Housing: Dorms.
Est 1951. Nonprofit. **Ses: 1. Wks/ses: 2.** Operates July.

Writing up to five stories each day, students enrolled in the Journalism Workshop gain in-depth knowledge of news, sports, feature and opinion writing; practice interviewing and learn research techniques; tour newspaper offices and television studios; and explore graphics, photography, blogging and social media. Instructors include reporters, editors, photographers, graphic designers and broadcasters from news outlets across California.

CANADA/USA MATHCAMP
Res — Coed Ages 13-18

Cambridge, MA 02139. 129 Hancock St. Fax: 888-371-4159.
www.mathcamp.org
Mira Bernstein, Exec Dir.
Adm: Selective. Admitted: 40%. **Appl**—Fee $20. Due: Apr. Qualifying quiz, 2 recs, personal statement.
Enr cap: 110-120.
Type of instruction: Adv Enrich. Homework.
Focus: Math. **Features:** Hiking Basketball Soccer Swim Tennis Ultimate_Frisbee Volleyball.
Fees 2014: Res $4000, 5 wks. Aid (Need).
Housing: Dorms. Avg per room/unit: 1-2. **Swimming:** Pool. Campus facilities avail.
Est 1993. Spons: Mathematics Foundation of America. **Ses: 1. Wks/ses: 5.** Operates July-Aug.

Held on a different college campus each year, this program of the Mathematics Foundation of America is an intensive session of advanced math work for motivated high schoolers. An enrichment program, Mathcamp addresses advanced and unusual topics in pure and applied math through various formats: faculty-taught courses lasting anywhere from a few days to five weeks, lectures and seminars conducted by distinguished guests, math contests and problem-solving sessions, and hands-on workshops and individual projects. While students spend some time each evening completing homework, there is also time for recreational pursuits.

CANOE ISLAND FRENCH CAMP
Res — Coed Ages 9-16

Orcas, WA 98280. PO Box 370. Tel: 360-468-2329. Fax: 360-468-3027.
www.canoeisland.org   E-mail: info@canoeisland.org
Connie H. Jones, Dir.
Adm: FCFS. **Appl**—Fee $0. Due: Rolling.
Enr: 30-46. Enr cap: 46. Intl: 10%. Non-White: 10%. **Fac 10.** Col/grad students 10. **Staff:** Admin 3.

Type of instruction: Enrich Tut. **Courses:** Ecol Geol Marine_Bio/Stud Crafts Fine_Arts Music Painting Theater. **Avg class size:** 8. **Daily hours for:** Classes 1½. Rec 5. Tests. **Focus:** Fr. **Features:** Aquatics Archery Boating Canoe Cooking Kayak Rappelling Rock_ Climb Sail Badminton Basketball Swim Tennis Volleyball Watersports. **Fees 2014: Res $1995-3378, 2-3 wks.** Aid 2011 (Need): $52,000. **Housing:** Tepees. Avg per room/unit: 5. **Swimming:** Pool. Campus facilities avail. **Est 1969.** Nonprofit. **Ses:** 4. **Wks/ses:** 2-3. Operates June-Aug.

Campers learn French language, customs and traditions while taking part in an individualized activities program that includes watersports and land sports, theatricals and crafts, overnight hikes and trips to other islands in the San Juans. Canoe Island schedules family camps over the Memorial Day and Labor Day weekends each year. None of the camp's programs have language prerequisites.

CARLETON COLLEGE SUMMER SCIENCE INSTITUTE
Res — Coed Ages 15-18

Northfield, MN 55057. Office of Summer Academic Prgms, 1 N College St. Tel: 507-222-4038, 866-767-2275. Fax: 507-222-4540. http://apps.carleton.edu/summer/science   E-mail: cssi@carleton.edu **Cam Davidson, Dir.** **Student contact:** Jeremy M. Updike, E-mail: jupdike@carleton.edu. **Grades 11-12. Adm:** Very_selective. Admitted: 27%. **Appl**—Fee $0. Due: Mar. Transcript, standardized test scores. **Enr:** 48. **Enr cap:** 48. Non-White: 30%. **Fac 4.** Prof 4. **Staff:** Admin 1. Res 8. **Type of instruction:** Adv Undergrad. **Avg class size:** 12. **Daily hours for:** Classes 8. Study 1. Rec 2. Homework. **College credit:** 3/crse, total 6. **Focus:** Sci. **Features:** Climbing_Wall Swim. **Fees 2014: Res $3350, 3 wks.** Aid 2011 (Merit & Need): $47,000. **Housing:** Dorms. Avg per room/unit: 2. **Swimming:** Pool. Campus facilities avail. **Est 2009.** Nonprofit. **Ses:** 1. **Wks/ses:** 3. Operates July-Aug.

CSSI enables rising high school juniors and seniors to engage in hands-on scientific research, in groups of 10 to 12 students each, alongside Carleton College faculty and undergraduate research assistants. During the three-week session, participants also rotate through three weeklong courses in such areas as neuroscience, genetics, chemistry and animal behavior. The collaborative guided research project culminates in a presentation at the CSSI Research Symposium at program's end.

CARLETON SUMMER QUANTITATIVE REASONING
Res — Coed Ages 15-18

Northfield, MN 55057. Office of Summer Prgms, 1 N College St. Tel: 507-222-4038, 866-767-2275. Fax: 507-222-4540. http://apps.carleton.edu/summer/sqri   E-mail: summer@carleton.edu **Al Montero, Dir.** **Student contact:** Jeremy M. Updike, E-mail: jupdike@carleton.edu. **Grades 11-12. Adm:** Selective. **Appl**—Fee $0. Due: Apr. Transcript, standardized test scores. **Enr cap:** 36. **Fac 3.** Prof 3. **Staff:** Admin 1. Res 5. **Type of instruction:** Adv Undergrad. **Courses:** Psych. **Avg class size:** 12. **Daily hours for:** Classes 6. Study 2. Rec 2. Homework. **College credit:** 3/crse, total 6. **Focus:** Intl_Relations Pol_Sci Psych. **Features:** Swim. **Fees 2014: Res $2895, 3 wks.** Aid (Merit & Need). **Housing:** Dorms. Avg per room/unit: 2. **Swimming:** Pool. Campus facilities avail. **Est 2012.** Nonprofit. **Spons:** Carleton College. **Ses:** 1. **Wks/ses:** 3. Operates July-Aug.

CSQR provides rising high school juniors and seniors with a substantial college-level experience as they see how social scientists think about the world, measure important variables of study, prepare research and present their findings. Participants undertake hands-on examination of theories and collaborate on the design and the execution of an original research project with peers and a faculty advisor. The program's structure helps students to understand major theories and concepts, as well as the manner in which social scientists study them. During the session, pupils use quantitative data to support written and oral arguments, learn to rigorously test hypotheses with statistical data, and gain experience in thinking through central problems and research questions while measuring relevant variables.

CDE NATIONAL DEBATE INSTITUTE SUMMER CAMPS
Res — Coed Ages 13-17

Albuquerque, NM. Univ of New Mexico.
Contact (Year-round): PO Box 1890, Taos, NM 87571. Tel: 575-751-0514, 866-247-3178. Fax: 575-751-9788.
www.cdedebate.com   E-mail: bennett@cdedebate.com
William H. Bennett, Chair.
Grades 8-12. Adm: FCFS. **Appl**—Fee $95. Due: May.
Enr: 70. **Fac 11. Staff:** Admin 4. Couns 9.
Type of instruction: Adv Enrich. **Avg class size:** 7. **Daily hours for:** Classes 8.
Focus: Debate Public_Speak. **Features:** Swim.
Fees 2014: Res $1325, 2 wks. Day $585, 2 wks. Aid 2007 (Need): $4200.
Housing: Dorms. **Swimming:** Pool.
Est 1979. Ses: 1. **Wks/ses:** 2. Operates July.

CDE operates several debate and public speaking camps on the campus of the University of New Mexico. Each camp features critiqued practice rounds, usually on three different topics. Some camp divisions are open to all age-eligible students; applicants to higher-level divisions must satisfy certain qualifications.

THE CENTER FOR CROSS-CULTURAL STUDY
HIGH SCHOOL SUMMER PROGRAM
Res — Coed Ages 16-18

Amherst, MA 01002. 446 Main St. Tel: 413-256-0011. Fax: 413-256-1968.
www.spanishstudies.org   E-mail: info@spanishstudies.org
Carmen Sales Delgado, Pepe Vives & Alfredo Brunori, Dirs.
Grades 11-12. Adm: Selective. **Appl**—Fee $0. Due: Apr.
Enr: 30. **Fac 11. Prof 11. Staff:** Admin 4. Couns 2.
Type of instruction: Undergrad. **Avg class size:** 12. **Daily hours for:** Classes 4. Study 2. Rec 3. Homework. Tests. Grades. **High school & college credit:** 4/crse, total 8.
Intl program focus: Acad Lang Culture. **Locations:** Europe South_America. Home stays avail.
Focus: Span.
Fees 2014: Res $3400-6900, 3½ wks.
Housing: Dorms Houses. Avg per room/unit: 2.
Est 1969. Inc. **Ses:** 2. **Wks/ses:** 3½. Operates June-July.

CC-CS summer terms in Alicante and Seville, Spain combine language immersion with daily cultural activities and guided weekend excursions. Boys and girls live with local families, thereby facilitating more efficient language acquisition. CC-CS offers language instruction at beginning, intermediate and advanced levels, and students enroll in other academic courses related to the host country and its culture. High school students take courses alongside undergraduates.

CENTRAL WISCONSIN ENVIRONMENTAL STATION
SUMMER PROGRAMS
Res — Coed Ages 7-17

Amherst Junction, WI 54407. 10186 County Rd MM. Tel: 715-824-2428. Fax: 715-824-3201.
www.uwsp.edu/cwes   E-mail: sjohnson@uwsp.edu
Scott D. Johnson, Dir.
Adm: FCFS. **Appl**—Due: Rolling.
Enr: 45. **Enr cap:** 55. **Fac 3. Staff:** Admin 4. Couns 9.
Type of instruction: Enrich. **Courses:** Ecol Sci Writing/Journ Crafts Music Studio_Art.
Focus: Environ_Sci. **Features:** Adventure_Travel Aquatics Archery Boating Canoe Climbing_Wall Conservation Exploration Fishing Hiking Kayak Outdoor_Ed Swim Volleyball.
Fees 2014: Res $275-475, 1 wk. Day $45. Aid avail.
Housing: Cabins Lodges. **Swimming:** Lake.
Est 1975. Nonprofit. **Spons:** University of Wisconsin-Stevens Point. **Ses:** 10. **Wks/ses:** 1. Operates June-July.

A field station of the College of Natural Resources at the University of Wisconsin-Stevens Point, CWES offers nature exploration on 300 acres of forests, wetlands, lakes and fields. Programs for younger campers combine nature study and traditional camp activities, while those for older boys and girls focus on outdoor skill development. Natural Resource Careers Camp (for students ages 15-18) enables campers to explore career opportunities while gaining field experience in natural resource management and environmental protection.

CENTRE INTERNATIONAL D'ANTIBES
Res — Coed Ages 14-17

Antibes, 06600 France. 38 Blvd d'Aguillon. Tel: 202-470-6659. Fax: 33-811-035-167.
www.cia-france.com   E-mail: info@cia-france.com
Alexandre Garcia, Prgm Dir.
Adm: FCFS. **Appl**—Fee $0. Due: Rolling.
Staff: Admin 12.
Type of instruction: Enrich. **Avg class size:** 15. **Daily hours for:** Classes 3.
Intl program focus: Lang. Home stays avail.
Focus: Fr. **Features:** Sail Soccer Swim Tennis Volleyball.
Fees 2014: Res €730 (+airfare), 1 wk.
Housing: Dorms. Avg per room/unit: 2. **Swimming:** Ocean.
Est 1985. Ses: 6. **Wks/ses:** 1. Operates June-Sept.

Located between Nice and Cannes on the Cote d'Azur and conducted at Le Chateau Junior School, the Centre's Antibes program offers both standard and intensive French instruction. Pupils take 20 language courses per week, each of which lasts 45 minutes. Students often reside with host families and have access to the area's many beaches.

CENTRO KOINE
Res and Day — Coed Ages 14 and up

Florence, 50122 Italy. Via de Pandolfini 27. Tel: 39-055-213881. Fax: 39-055-216949.
www.koinecenter.com   E-mail: info@koinecenter.com
Adm: FCFS. **Appl**—Due: Rolling.
Enr: 70. **Enr cap:** 100. **Fac 10. Staff:** Admin 5. Couns 3.
Type of instruction: Adv Dev_Read Study_Skills Tut. **Courses:** Bus/Fin Comm Drama Fine_Arts Photog Studio_Art. **Avg class size:** 8. **Daily hours for:** Classes 4. Study 2. Rec 2. **College credit.**
Intl program focus: Lang. Home stays avail.

Focus: Ital. **Features:** Bicycle_Tours Cooking Hiking Mtn_Biking Outdoor_Ed Riding Sail Scuba Cross-country Soccer Swim Tennis.
Fees 2014: Res €1600, 1-4 wks.
Housing: Hotels Houses Lodges. **Swimming:** Pool.
Est 1980. Nonprofit. **Wks/ses:** 1-4. Operates July.

At locations in two Italian cities—Florence and Lucca—the center offers two week Italian courses of varying ability levels. In addition to language course work, pupils choose from a selection of Italian culture classes.

CERAN LINGUA JUNIOR SUMMER PROGRAMS
Res — Coed Ages 9-18

Los Angeles, CA 90066. 3614 Wade St. Tel: 310-429-7406, 866-722-3726.
www.ceran.com/us   E-mail: info@ceran-us.com
Fabienne Carmanne, Dir.
Student contact: Charlotte Neve, E-mail: charlotte@ceran-us.com.
Adm: FCFS. Admitted: 80%. **Appl**—Due: Rolling.
Enr: 250. **Enr cap:** 250. Intl: 90%. Non-White: 10%. **Fac 35. Staff:** Admin 19. Couns 30.
Type of instruction: Adv Study_Skills Tut. **Courses:** Crafts. **Avg class size:** 8. **Daily hours for:** Classes 5. Study 2. Rec 5. Homework.
Intl program focus: Lang Culture. **Locations:** Europe.
Focus: ESL Fr Ger Dutch. **Features:** Bicycle_Tours Canoe Kayak Mtn_Biking Sail Aerobics Baseball Basketball Equestrian Fencing Golf Martial_Arts Rugby Swim Tennis Ultimate_Frisbee Volleyball Watersports.
Fees 2014: Res $1875-2521 (+airfare), 1 wk.
Housing: Dorms. Avg per room/unit: 2. **Swimming:** Pool. Campus facilities avail.
Est 1975. Inc. **Ses:** 8. **Wks/ses:** 1. Operates June-Aug.

Ceran Lingua's summer programs offer intensive language immersion in five languages and three countries. French, German, Dutch and English programs are available in Belgium, English in the United Kingdom and Spanish in Spain. Students develop language skills through participation in learning activities, sports, and cultural and social activities.

CHOATE ROSEMARY HALL ENGLISH LANGUAGE INSTITUTE
Res and Day — Coed Ages 12-18

Wallingford, CT 06492. 333 Christian St. Tel: 203-697-2365. Fax: 203-697-2519.
www.choate.edu/summerprograms   E-mail: choatesummer@choate.edu
Eera Sharma, Dir.
Grades 7-12. Adm: Selective. Admitted: 90%. **Appl**—Fee $75. Due: Rolling. Transcript, 3 recs, essay.
Enr: 50. Intl: 100%.
Type of instruction: Enrich ESL/TOEFL_Prep. **Courses:** Expository_Writing Public_ Speak Creative_Writing Dance Film Music. **Avg class size:** 11. **Daily hours for:** Classes 5½. Study 2. Rec 2. Homework. Tests.
Focus: ESL. **Features:** Yoga Aerobics Baseball Basketball Rugby Soccer Softball Swim Tennis Volleyball.
Fees 2014: Res $8725 (+$500), 5 wks. Day $6725 (+$500), 5 wks. Aid 2011 (Need): $300,000.
Housing: Dorms. **Swimming:** Pool. Campus facilities avail.
Nonprofit. **Ses:** 1. **Wks/ses:** 5. Operates June-July.

Serving nonnative speakers of English who have studied the language for at least three years in their home schools and who can converse in English, these intensive courses help students develop proficiency in standard English. Students develop ability in such language skills as writing, speaking, listening and reading, and they participate in minor courses, sports, meals, weekend dances and various social activities with students from the academic summer session. Integral components of this program are off-campus trips to various cities, museums and cultural events that supplement and relate to course work.

CHOATE ROSEMARY HALL
JOHN F. KENNEDY '35 INSTITUTE IN GOVERNMENT
Res and Day — Coed Ages 15-18

Wallingford, CT 06492. 333 Christian St. Tel: 203-697-2365. Fax: 203-697-2519.
www.choate.edu/summerprograms   **E-mail: choatesummer@choate.edu**
Eera Sharma, Dir.
Grades 10-12. Adm: Selective. Admitted: 90%. **Appl**—Fee $75. Due: Rolling. Transcript, essay, 3 recs, graded English paper.
Enr: 12. Enr cap: 12. Intl: 20%. Non-White: 20%.
Type of instruction: Enrich. **Courses:** Dance Drama Fine_Arts Music. **Avg class size:** 12. **Daily hours for:** Classes 5½. Study 2. Rec 2. Homework. Tests.
Focus: Govt Pol_Sci. **Features:** Yoga Aerobics Baseball Basketball Rugby Soccer Softball Swim Tennis Volleyball.
Fees 2014: Res $8050 (+$500), 5 wks. Day $6050 (+$500), 5 wks. Aid 2011 (Need): $300,000.
Housing: Dorms. Avg per room/unit: 2. **Swimming:** Pool. Campus facilities avail.
Est 1985. Nonprofit. **Ses:** 1. **Wks/ses:** 5. Operates June-July.

Institute students take courses that focus on the formation of political ideas, the foundation and workings of the American government, and specific current domestic and foreign issues. Pupils spend the fourth week in Washington, DC, meeting with statesmen, interest groups, and organizations that work on the domestic and foreign issues that were discussed earlier in the session. Boys and girls engage in athletic, extracurricular and social activities with students from Choate's other summer programs.

CHOATE ROSEMARY HALL
MATH/SCIENCE INSTITUTE FOR GIRLS
Res and Day — Girls Ages 12-14

Wallingford, CT 06492. 333 Christian St. Tel: 203-697-2365. Fax: 203-697-2519.
www.choate.edu/summerprograms   **E-mail: choatesummer@choate.edu**
Eera Sharma, Dir.
Grades 7-9. Adm: Selective. Admitted: 90%. **Appl**—Fee $75. Due: Rolling.
Enr: 18. Enr cap: 24. Intl: 40%. Non-White: 10%.
Type of instruction: Enrich. **Courses:** Dance Drama Fine_Arts Music. **Avg class size:** 12. **Daily hours for:** Classes 5½. Study 2. Rec 2. Homework. Tests.
Focus: Math Sci. **Features:** Yoga Aerobics Baseball Basketball Rugby Soccer Softball Swim Tennis Volleyball.
Fees 2014: Res $7575 (+$500), 5 wks. Day $5625 (+$500), 5 wks. Aid 2011 (Need): $300,000.
Housing: Dorms. Avg per room/unit: 2. **Swimming:** Pool. Campus facilities avail.
Nonprofit. **Ses:** 1. **Wks/ses:** 5. Operates June-July.

This intensive, five-week program enrolls middle school girls with a strong interest in math and science; advanced knowledge in these areas is not necessary. The institute seeks to build knowledge through hands-on projects, cooperative learning and team building; use of technology, including graphing calculators, computer spreadsheets, statistics software and word processors; research skill and technique instruction; and enriching field trips. The program culminates with an independent research project: Each student conducts library research on a topic of interest and formulates a scientific hypothesis, then designs and performs an experiment to test the hypothesis.

CHOATE ROSEMARY HALL
SUMMER STUDY ABROAD PROGRAMS
Res — Coed Ages 14-17

Wallingford, CT 06942. 333 Christian St. Tel: 203-697-2365. Fax: 203-697-2519.
www.choate.edu/summer/high-school-programs/summer-study-abroad E-mail:
choatesummer@choate.edu
Eera Sharma, Dir.
Grades 9-11. Adm: Selective. Admitted: 90%. **Appl**—Fee $60. Due: Rolling. Transcript, 2 recs.
Enr: 25. **Enr cap:** 25. Intl: 30%. Non-White: 25%.
Type of instruction: Enrich. Arabic **Avg class size:** 12. **Daily hours for:** Classes 4. Study 2. Rec 3. Homework. Tests.
Intl program focus: Acad Lang Culture. **Locations:** Asia Europe Middle_East South_America. Home stays avail.
Focus: Chin Fr Span.
Fees 2014: Res $6500-8300, 5 wks.
Housing: Dorms Hotels Houses.
Nonprofit. **Ses:** 5. **Wks/ses:** 5. Operates June-July.

Five-week programs in China, France, Ireland, Jordan and Spain, each beginning with a one- or two-day orientation at Choate, combine academic study with total immersion in the language and the culture. Each program features day trips and extended excursions to historical and cultural sites.

CHRISTCHURCH SCHOOL MARINE SCIENCE PROGRAMS
Res and Day — Coed Ages 8-15

Christchurch, VA 23031. 49 Seahorse Ln. Tel: 804-758-2306. Fax: 804-758-0721.
www.christchurchschool.org/marineadventurecamp E-mail: aporter@
christchurchschool.org
Amanda G. Porter, Dir.
Adm: FCFS. **Appl**—Fee $0. Due: Rolling.
Type of instruction: Enrich. **Courses:** Environ_Sci. **Avg class size:** 10.
Focus: Marine_Bio/Stud. **Features:** Boating Canoe Conservation Deep-sea Fishing Field_Ecol Fishing Hiking Swim Watersports.
Fees 2014: Res $850, 1 wk. Day $550, 1 wk.
Housing: Dorms Tents. **Swimming:** River.
Est 1984. Nonprofit. Ses: 2. **Wks/ses:** 1. Operates June-July.

Christchurch offers two age-based marine science programs. For campers ages 8-11, Chesapeake Critter Camp involves the weeklong exploration of creatures dwelling in and around the Rappahannock River and Chesapeake Bay watersheds. Children search for insect and animal life while on foot or in a boat. Older boys and girls (ages 12-15) engage in a hands-on examination of the wetlands of the Chesapeake Bay Watersheds. Campers gain a better understanding of the wetlands and their importance by walking, crawling and swimming through swamps, bogs, and fresh- and saltwater marshes.

CLEMSON UNIVERSITY SUMMER SCHOLARS
Res — Coed Ages 12-18

Clemson, SC 29634. 2039 Barre Hall. Tel: 864-656-5535. Fax: 864-656-1480.
www.clemson.edu/summer/summer-science E-mail: cusummerscholars@
clemson.edu
Grades 7-12. Adm: Selective. **Appl**—Fee $0. Due: May. Transcript, test scores, rec.
Type of instruction: Adv Enrich. **Courses:** Comp_Sci Forensic_Sci Math Psych.
Focus: Architect Engineering Math Sci. **Features:** Swim.
Fees 2009: Res $850-1900, 1-2 wks.

Housing: Dorms. Avg per room/unit: 2. **Swimming:** Pool.
Ses: 8. **Wks/ses:** 1-2. Operates June-Aug.

Summer Scholars features weeklong introductions to college subjects for middle and high school students, as well as two-week specialized courses for advanced high school students. Classes, which vary by year, draw from the disciplines of the life sciences, math, engineering, computer science and architecture. Evening and weekend activities include nature study hikes, small-group discussions with Clemson faculty, and career and educational guidance.

COLLEGE DU LEMAN SUMMER CAMPUS
Res — Coed Ages 8-18

Versoix, 1290 Geneva, Switzerland. 74 Rte de Sauverny, PO Box 156. Tel: 41-22-775-55-55. Fax: 41-22-775-55-59.
www.cdl.ch   E-mail: summercampus@cdl.ch
Francis A. Clivaz, Dir.
Grades 3-12. Adm: FCFS. **Appl**—Fee $0. Due: Rolling.
Enr: 300. **Fac 40. Staff:** Admin 20.
Type of instruction: Adv Dev_Read Enrich Preview Rem_Eng Rem_Math Rem_Read Rev. **Courses:** Circus_Skills. **Avg class size:** 12. **Daily hours for:** Classes 3. **High school credit:** 2.
Intl program focus: Lang.
Focus: ESL Fr. **Features:** Archery Bicycle_Tours Canoe Cooking Cruises Hiking Kayak Mtn_Trips Riding Sail Baseball Basketball Cross-country Equestrian Golf Gymnastics Lacrosse Martial_Arts Soccer Softball Swim Tennis Track Water-skiing Watersports.
Fees 2014: Res SwF6750-13,000, 3 wks.
Housing: Dorms. **Swimming:** Lake Pool.
Est 1960. Inc. Spons: Meritas. **Ses:** 2. **Wks/ses:** 3. Operates June-Aug.

College du Leman offers French and English language instruction at beginning through advanced levels. Pupils attend language courses each Monday through Saturday morning, with afternoons devoted to sports and arts-related activities. Summer Campus features excursions once a week to nearby places of interest.

COLLEGE OF THE ATLANTIC
ISLANDS THROUGH TIME
Res — Coed Ages 15-18

Bar Harbor, ME 04609. 105 Eden St. Tel: 207-288-5015, 800-597-9500. Fax: 207-288-4126.
www.coa.edu/islandsthroughtime.htm   E-mail: islandsthroughtime@coa.edu
Marie Stivers, Dir.
Grades 11-12. Adm: Selective. **Appl**—Fee $0. Due: May. Rec, essays.
Enr: 16. **Enr cap:** 16. **Fac 5. Prof 5. Staff:** Admin 2. Couns 4.
Type of instruction: Adv Preview. **Courses:** Hist Marine_Bio/Stud Oceanog Writing/Journ Filmmaking Media Music Photog. **Avg class size:** 10. **Daily hours for:** Classes 7. Study 2½. Rec 1½. **College credit:** 3.
Focus: Ecol. **Features:** Conservation Exploration Hiking Kayak Outdoor_Ed Sea_Cruises Seamanship Swim.
Fees 2014: Res $3550-3750, 2 wks. Aid (Need).
Housing: Dorms. Avg per room/unit: 1-2. **Swimming:** Ocean. Campus facilities avail.
Est 2007. Nonprofit. Ses: 1. **Wks/ses:** 2. Operates July-Aug.

Students enrolled in this intensive precollege program explore the relationship between humans and the environment. ITT begins with an introduction to the ecology, the history and the culture of the Maine coast, taught from an interdisciplinary perspective that incorporates marine biology, oceanography, anthropology and literature. Boys and girls conduct marine research at island field stations; learn the basics of navigation, steering and ship handling aboard a research vessel; examine the lives of coastal Maine residents; and work on their reading and writing skills with college faculty. At the conclusion of the program, pupils work in teams on multimedia presentations that detail their experiences.

COLLEGE OF THE ATLANTIC
RIVERS: A WILDERNESS ODYSSEY
Res — Coed Ages 16-18

Bar Harbor, ME 04609. 105 Eden St. Tel: 207-288-5015, 800-597-9500. Fax: 207-288-4126.
www.coa.edu/riversawildernessodyssey.htm   E-mail: islandsthroughtime@coa.edu
Marie Stivers, Dir.
Grades 11-12. Adm: Selective. **Appl**—Fee $0. Due: May. Rec, essays.
Enr: 8. **Enr cap:** 8. **Fac 3.** Prof 3. **Staff:** Admin 2. Couns 2.
Type of instruction: Adv Undergrad. **Courses:** Leadership Psych Creative_Writing Photog. **Daily hours for:** Classes 7. Study 2½. Rec 1½. **College credit:** 3.
Focus: Ecol. **Features:** Canoe Conservation Exploration Outdoor_Ed Wilderness_Camp Wilderness_Canoe Swim Watersports.
Fees 2014: Res $2900-3100, 2 wks. Aid (Merit).
Housing: Dorms. Avg per room/unit: 1-2. **Swimming:** River. Campus facilities avail.
Nonprofit. **Ses:** 1. **Wks/ses:** 2. Operates July-Aug.

This intensive program for rising high school juniors and seniors begins on the College of the Atlantic campus with an introduction to the history and policy of the northern Maine woods. Students learn about the natural history, literature, conservation and psychological aspects of wilderness and river systems through readings and discussion. Participants then explore Acadia National Park and canoe down the Allagash Wilderness Waterway. These expeditions serve as a laboratory to experience and investigate group dynamics in a wilderness setting while also examining leadership, authority and community. A group presentation at session's end enables students to share samples of their writings and photographs with program peers and professors and the public.

COLUMBIA INTERNATIONAL COLLEGE ESL SUMMER CAMP
Res — Coed Ages 9-19

Hamilton, L8S 4P3 Ontario, Canada. 1003 Main St W. Tel: 905-572-7883. Fax: 905-572-9332.
www.cic-totalcare.com/en/summer-camp.php   E-mail: columbia@cic-totalcare.com
Clement Chan, Exec Dir.
Grades 4-12. Adm: FCFS. **Appl**—Due: Rolling.
Enr: 500. Intl: 100%. Non-White: 95%. **Staff:** Admin 8. Couns 35.
Type of instruction: Enrich Rem_Eng. **Courses:** Computers Debate Sci Speech Crafts Creative_Writing Dance Music Painting Photog Theater. **Avg class size:** 18. **Daily hours for:** Classes 3.
Intl program focus: Lang Culture.
Focus: ESL. **Features:** Aquatics Archery Canoe Climbing_Wall Conservation Cooking Fishing Hiking Kayak Leadership Outdoor_Ed Peace/Cross-cultural Rock_Climb Ropes_Crse Survival_Trng White-water_Raft Wilderness_Camp Wilderness_Canoe Badminton Baseball Basketball Field_Hockey Football Golf Gymnastics Lacrosse Martial_Arts Soccer Swim Tennis Volleyball Watersports.
Fees 2012: Res Can$3050-4200 (+Can$245), 3-4 wks.
Housing: Dorms Houses. Avg per room/unit: 2-4. **Swimming:** Lake Pool.
Est 1995. **Ses:** 5. **Wks/ses:** 3-4. Operates July-Aug.

This English as a Second Language camp combines three hours of daily English lessons (at beginning through advanced levels) with recreational activities and cultural trips. Science and computers and technology courses, arts and crafts, and sports complement language instruction. CIC schedules cultural trips to historic and cultural sites on weekends. The four-week session, at Bark Lake, features leadership and team-building pursuits and outdoor recreational activities.

CONCORDIA LANGUAGE VILLAGES
Res — Coed Ages 7-18; Day — Coed 6-11

Moorhead, MN 56562. 901 S 8th St. Tel: 218-299-4544, 800-222-4750. Fax: 218-299-3807.
www.concordialanguagevillages.org   E-mail: clv@cord.edu
Christine Schulze, Exec Dir.
Student contact: Carl-Martin Nelson, E-mail: cnelson@cord.edu.
Grades 1-12 (younger if qualified). Adm: FCFS. **Appl**—Fee $40. Due: Rolling.
Staff: Admin 50.
Type of instruction: Adv Enrich. **Courses:** Environ_Sci ESL Crafts Dance Filmmaking Media Music Theater. **Daily hours for:** Classes 3. Homework. Tests. Grades. **High school & college credit:** 4.
Focus: Arabic Chin Fr Ger Ital Japan Russ Span Danish Finnish Korean Norwegian Portuguese Swedish. **Features:** Bicycle_Tours Canoe Chess Conservation Cooking Fishing Hiking Sail Wilderness_Camp Wilderness_Canoe Baseball Fencing Martial_ Arts Soccer Swim Volleyball.
Fees 2014: Res $835-4570, 1-4 wks. Day $159-695, 1 wk. Aid (Merit & Need).
Housing: Cabins Tents. Avg per room/unit: 10. **Swimming:** Lake.
Est 1961. Nonprofit. **Spons:** Concordia College (MN). **Ses:** 124. **Wks/ses:** 1-4. Operates June-Aug.

Concordia provides immersion programs in more than a dozen languages. Students are immersed in the language and the culture of their village. In addition to one- and two-week sessions, Concordia offers an intensive four-week program that enables those entering grades 9-12 to earn high school credit or rising juniors or seniors to earn college credit. Twice each summer, the separate villages come together for International Day to share dance, arts and crafts, songs and languages from around the world.

COSMOS
CALIFORNIA STATE SUMMER SCHOOL
FOR MATHEMATICS AND SCIENCE
Res — Coed Ages 14-18

Oakland, CA 94612. 300 Lakeside Dr, 7th Fl. Tel: 510-987-9711. Fax: 510-763-4704.
www.ucop.edu/cosmos   E-mail: cosmos@ucop.edu
Melina Duarte, Dir.
Grades 9-PG. Adm: Selective. Prereqs: GPA 3.5. **Appl**—Fee $30. Due: Mar. Transcript, math & sci teacher recs.
Enr cap: 160.
Type of instruction: Adv Enrich.
Focus: Math Sci. **Features:** Basketball Soccer Volleyball.
Fees 2014: Res $3100-9100, 4 wks. Aid (Need).
Housing: Dorms. Avg per room/unit: 2.
Nonprofit. **Ses:** 4. **Wks/ses:** 4. Operates June-Aug.

On University of California campuses in Davis, Irvine, San Diego and Santa Cruz, COSMOS enables advanced math and science students to engage themselves in an intensive academic experience that addresses topics not generally taught in high schools. Among these subject areas are astronomy, aerospace engineering, biomedical science, wetlands ecology, ocean science, robotics and game theory. Pupils enroll in two classes drawn from math and science, along with a science communication course. The program includes hands-on lab work, field activities, lectures and discussions, and students also complete a research project.

CROW CANYON ARCHAEOLOGICAL CENTER
SUMMER FIELD SCHOOL FOR TEENS
Res — Coed Ages 15-18

Cortez, CO 81321. 23390 Rd K. Tel: 970-564-4346, 800-422-8975. Fax: 970-565-4859.
www.crowcanyon.org E-mail: summercamp@crowcanyon.org
Deborah Gangloff, Dir. Student contact: Debra K. Miller.
Grades 10-PG. Adm: Somewhat selective. Admitted: 99%. Priority: URM. **Appl**—Due: Apr.
Enr cap: 20-30. Intl: 5%. Non-White: 18%. **Fac 3.** K-12 staff 3. **Staff:** Admin 3. Couns 3.
Type of instruction: Adv. **Avg class size:** 25. **Daily hours for:** Classes 8. Rec 4. **High school & college credit:** 2.
Focus: Archaeol. **Features:** Conservation Exploration Hiking Outdoor_Ed White-water_ Raft.
Fees 2014: Res $4750-4875, 1-3 wks. Aid 2010 (Need): $8650.
Housing: Dorms. Avg per room/unit: 3-6.
Est 1983. Nonprofit. **Ses:** 3. **Wks/ses:** 1-3. Operates June-July.

Students in this hands-on introduction to archaeology spend up to three weeks exploring the Mesa Verde region of southwestern Colorado. After studying the history of the Pueblo Indians, boys and girls join teams of professional archaeologists at a working excavation site and learn to sort and identify artifacts. Pupils gain knowledge about the culture and the lifestyles of the ancestral people through games, concerts, crafts and discussions. Scholarships are available to American Indian students, as well as to those from the Four Corners region.

CUB CREEK SCIENCE CAMP
Res — Coed Ages 7-17

Rolla, MO 65401. c/o Bear River Ranch, 16795 Hwy E. Tel: 573-458-2125. Fax: 573-458-2126.
www.bearriverranch.com E-mail: director@bearriverranch.com
Lori Martin, Dir.
Grades 2-12. Adm: FCFS. **Appl**—Fee $0. Due: Apr.
Enr cap: 168. Intl: 5%. Non-White: 10%. **Fac 50. Staff:** Admin 5.
Type of instruction: Enrich. **Courses:** Forensic_Sci Geol Botany Entomology Crafts Photog Pottery. **Avg class size:** 8. **Daily hours for:** Classes 5. Rec 9.
Focus: Med/Healthcare Sci Veterinary_Med. **Features:** Aquatics Archery Caving Conservation Cooking Exploration Farm Fishing Hiking Outdoor_Ed Survival_Trng Swim.
Fees 2014: Res $875-5100 (+$40-160), 1-6 wks.
Housing: Cabins. Avg per room/unit: 14. **Swimming:** Pond Pool.
Est 1993. Inc. **Ses:** 10. **Wks/ses:** 1-6. Operates June-Aug.

At this science camp, children live on a working farm alongside some 200 animals representing more than 100 species. Campers enroll in two classes from a course list that combines animal courses with science and arts offerings. The hands-on junior veterinarian program prepares children to care for various mammals, birds and reptiles. Boys and girls gain experience in using the scientific method of inquiry.

CULTURAL EXPERIENCES ABROAD SUMMER PROGRAMS
Res — Coed Ages 18 and up

Phoenix, AZ 85018. 2999 N 44th St, Ste 200. Tel: 480-557-7900, 800-266-4441. Fax: 480-557-7926.
www.ceastudyabroad.com E-mail: info@ceastudyabroad.com
Brian Boubek, Exec Dir.
Grades PG-Col. Adm: FCFS. Prereqs: GPA 2.5. **Appl**—Fee $95. Due: Rolling.
Type of instruction: Enrich. **Courses:** Bus/Fin Econ Environ_Sci Art Theater.

Intl program focus: Lang Culture. **Locations:** Africa Asia Europe Mexico/Central_America South_America.
Focus: Arabic Chin Fr Ger Ital Span Portuguese Czech. **Features:** Community_Serv.
Fees 2014: Res $3295-32,595, 1-8 wks.
Ses: 117. **Wks/ses:** 1-8. Operates June-Aug.

CEA offers study-abroad programs for recent high school graduates and college students in Argentina, Brazil, Chile, China, Costa Rica, the Czech Republic, England, France, Germany, ireland, Italy, South Africa and Spain. While language and cultural immersion is the most common course emphasis, certain sessions address other subjects, including healthcare, the environment, history and business.

DAUPHIN ISLAND SEA LAB
RESIDENTIAL SUMMER OPPORTUNITIES
Res — Coed Ages 10-17

Dauphin Island, AL 36528. 101 Bienville Blvd. Tel: 251-861-2141. Fax: 251-861-4646.
www.disl.org   **E-mail:** sejohnson@disl.org
Sally Brennan, Dir. Student contact: Sara E. Johnson.
Grades 5-12. Adm: Somewhat_selective. **Appl**—Fee $75. Due: Apr. HS: Transcript, 2 teacher recs, essay.
Enr: 15-30. **Enr cap:** 15-30. Non-White: 15%. **Fac 3.** K-12 staff 3. **Staff:** Admin 2. Couns 5.
Type of instruction: Enrich. **Courses:** Crafts. **Avg class size:** 18. Tests. **High school credit.**
Focus: Marine_Bio/Stud Oceanog Sci. **Features:** Fishing Basketball Soccer Swim Volleyball.
Fees 2014: Res $545-4557, 1-4 wks. Aid 2011 (Merit & Need): $7250.
Housing: Dorms. Avg per room/unit: 2. **Swimming:** Ocean Pool.
Ses: 4. **Wks/ses:** 1-4. Operates May-Aug.

Rising seventh through ninth graders may enroll in DISL's Gulf Island Journey, an enrichment program of hands-on marine science programming. Activities include a trawling expedition aboard Sea Lab's research vessel, exploration of the salt marshes of Dauphin Island, and beachcombing and bird watching on nearby Sand Island. A second program, High School Summer Course, is an accredited, four-week marine science class for rising 10th through 12th graders. During this four-week program, students conduct an intensive exploration of marine science through 150 hours of supervised academic activities in the form of lectures, laboratory work and field pursuits.

DILE CURSOS INTERNACIONALES DE ESPANOL
SPANISH COURSE FOR YOUNG PEOPLE
Res — Coed Ages 14-18

Salamanca, 37007 Spain. Plaza del Oeste 3. Tel: 34-923-282-446. Fax: 34-923-282-566.
www.dilecursos.com   **E-mail:** salamanca@dilecursos.com
Lourdes Prieto de los Mozos, Dir. Student contact: Susan Bernamont.
Adm: FCFS. **Appl**—Fee $0. Due: Rolling.
Enr cap: 64. **Fac 8. Staff:** Admin 3.
Type of instruction: Enrich Tut. **Courses:** Dance Drama Music. **Avg class size:** 5. **Daily hours for:** Classes 4. Study 1. Rec 5. Homework. Tests. Grades.
Intl program focus: Lang. Home stays avail.
Focus: Span. **Features:** Boating Cooking Mtn_Biking Riding Basketball Equestrian Football Golf Soccer Swim Tennis Volleyball.
Fees 2014: Res €270-1340 (+€65), 2-6 wks.
Housing: Dorms Houses. **Swimming:** Pool.
Est 2000. Ses: 4. **Wks/ses:** 2. Operates July-Sept.

Students receive 20 lessons each week in this language immersion program. Classes ranging from beginning to advanced focus on listening and reading comprehension, as well as speaking and writing skills. Additional program elements are grammar structure, text analysis and composition, and various group activities. Outside class, pupils take part in dance, music, boating, equestrian, sports, cooking and weekend excursions.

DUKE UNIVERSITY
ACTION SCIENCE CAMP FOR YOUNG WOMEN
Res and Day — Girls Ages 10-13

Durham, NC 27708. Continuing Stud, 201 Bishop's House, Box 90700. Tel: 919-684-6259, 866-338-3853. Fax: 919-681-8235.
www.learnmore.duke.edu/youth/action   E-mail: youth@duke.edu
Randee Haven-O'Donnell, Dir. Student contact: Thomas Patterson.
Grades 5-7. Adm: FCFS. Admitted: 100%. **Appl**—Fee $0. Due: Rolling.
Enr cap: 30. **Fac 4.** Col/grad students 1. K-12 staff 3. **Staff:** Admin 6. Couns 3.
Type of instruction: Enrich. **Courses:** Ecol Environ_Sci Crafts. **Daily hours for:** Classes 4. Rec 3.
Focus: Sci.
Fees 2014: Res $2495 (+$75), 2 wks. Day $1305 (+$75), 2 wks. Aid (Need).
Housing: Dorms. Avg per room/unit: 2.
Est 1991. Ses: 1. **Wks/ses:** 2. Operates June.

Action Science Camp promotes scientific discovery through work in laboratories and at field sites in the Duke University forest. Girls examine ecological and biological principles through explorations of terrestrial and aquatic life, chemical and physical properties of the environment, and the impact of human activities on ecosystems.

DUKE UNIVERSITY TALENT IDENTIFICATION PROGRAM
FIELD STUDIES AND INSTITUTES
Res — Coed Ages 15-18

Durham, NC 27701. 1121 W Main St. Tel: 919-668-9100. Fax: 919-681-7921.
http://tip.duke.edu/node/61   E-mail: information@tip.duke.edu
Nicki Charles, Dir.
Grades 10-PG. Adm: Selective. **Appl**—Fee $35. Due: Mar. Transcript, test scores, rec, resume, essay.
Enr cap: 16-20.
Type of instruction: Adv Enrich. **Courses:** Psych Genetics Creative_Writing Filmmaking.
Locations: CA FL NM Asia Canada Europe Mexico/Central_America.
Focus: Sci. **Features:** Leadership.
Fees 2014: Res $3650 (+airfare), 2 wks. Aid (Need).
Housing: Dorms Hotels.
Est 1980. Nonprofit. **Ses:** 18. **Wks/ses:** 2. Operates June-Aug.

With content similar to a college field course, each Duke TIP field study combines an array of activities that may include discussions, research projects, field work and presentations. Program destinations, which vary each summer, consist of both domestic and international locations. Field courses incorporate the surroundings to enrich the learning experience. Institutes, held on the Duke campus, enable boys and girls to preview college life as they study university-level material and attend college admissions workshops. Each field study or institute explores a distinct program focus.

EARTHWATCH TEEN EXPEDITIONS
Res — Coed Ages 15-18

Allston, MA 02134. 114 Western Ave. Tel: 978-461-0081. Fax: 978-461-2332.
http://earthwatch.org/expeditions   E-mail: info@earthwatch.org

Kate Quinn, Prgm Mgr. Student contact: Colleen Spivey.
Grades 10-PG. Adm: FCFS. **Appl**—Fee $0. Due: Rolling.
Enr: 9-16. **Intl:** 44%. **Fac 3. Prof 2.** K-12 staff 1. **Staff:** Admin 100.
Type of instruction: Enrich. **Courses:** Ecol Geol Sci. **Avg class size:** 8.
Intl program focus: Acad Culture. **Locations:** CO Africa Asia Canada Caribbean Europe
Mexico/Central_America South_America.
Focus: Archaeol Environ_Sci Marine_Bio/Stud. **Features:** Adventure_Travel Conservation
Exploration Hiking Mtn_Trips Peace/Cross-cultural Scuba Wilderness_Camp Swim.
Fees 2014: Res $1295-3725 (+airfare), 1-2 wks. Aid (Need).
Housing: Cabins Dorms Houses Lodges Tents. Avg per room/unit: 2-4. **Swimming:** Lake
Pond Ocean Pool River Stream.
Est 1970. Nonprofit. **Spons:** Earthwatch Institute. **Ses:** 15. **Wks/ses:** 1-2. Operates June-
Aug.

Earthwatch recruits high school volunteers to assist scientists on field research and conservation expeditions in the US and around the world. The organization sponsors scholars in every field of study, from archaeology to marine biology and zoology. Projects include whale and dolphin surveys, archaeological excavations, rain forest mapping, animal behavior research and climate change studies, among others. Participants need not possess any special skills, as training is provided. Teen teams include additional organized group activities, as well as presentations on research and career development.

EDUCATION UNLIMITED
COLLEGE ADMISSION PREP CAMPS
Res and Day — Coed Ages 14-17

Berkeley, CA. Univ of California-Berkeley.
Contact (Year-round): 1700 Shattuck Ave, Ste 305, Berkeley, CA 94709. **Tel:** 510-548-
6612. **Fax:** 510-548-0212.
www.educationunlimited.com   E-mail: campinfo@educationunlimited.com
Matthew Fraser, Exec Dir.
Grades 9-12. Adm: FCFS. **Appl**—Due: Rolling.
Enr: 75. **Fac 8. Staff:** Admin 8. Couns 7.
Type of instruction: Adv Enrich Preview Rev SAT/ACT_Prep Tut. **Courses:** Expository_
Writing. **Avg class size:** 11. **Daily hours for:** Classes 6. Study 3. Rec 5.
Locations: CA MA.
Focus: Col_Prep Study_Skills. **Features:** White-water_Raft Soccer Softball Swim
Volleyball.
Fees 2014: Res $3955-8125 (+$200), 1-3 wks. Day $3065, 1-3 wks. Aid (Need).
Housing: Dorms. **Swimming:** Pool.
Est 1993. Inc. **Ses:** 2. **Wks/ses:** 1-3. Operates June-Aug.

Education Unlimited conducts similar college preparation programs at California and Massachusetts universities. Prep Camp Excel, enrolling pupils entering grades 9 and 10, focuses on PSAT preparation, essay writing and study skills training. College Admission Prep Camp Intensive, accepting rising juniors and seniors, provides SAT preparation, college counseling and information about college admissions procedures. Students in CAPC Intensive develop their time-management and interviewing skills, in addition to working one-on-one with writing instructors on application essays. Boys and girls also take part in recreational activities and go on a half-day excursion. CAPC Intensive also features a white-water rafting excursion and a daylong tour of nearby colleges.

EDUCATION UNLIMITED COMPUTER CAMP
Res and Day — Coed Ages 9-17

Berkeley, CA 94709. 1700 Shattuck Ave, Ste 305. **Tel:** 510-548-6612. **Fax:** 510-548-
0212.
www.educationunlimited.com   E-mail: campinfo@educationunlimited.com

Matthew Fraser, Exec Dir.
Grades 4-12. Adm: FCFS. **Appl**—Fee $0. Due: Rolling.
Fac 1. Staff: Admin 8.
Type of instruction: Enrich. **Courses:** Filmmaking Media. **Avg class size:** 10. **Daily hours for:** Classes 6. Study 1. Rec 7.
Locations: CA.
Focus: Comp_Sci. **Features:** Baseball Basketball Soccer Swim Tennis Volleyball.
Fees 2014: Res $1450-2375 (+$50), 1 wk. Day 1 wk. Aid (Need).
Housing: Dorms. **Swimming:** Pool.
Est 1995. Inc. **Ses:** 4. **Wks/ses:** 1. Operates June-Aug.

Appropriate for young people of all ability levels, Education Unlimited offers hands-on training in computer applications at Stanford and the University of California-Berkeley. The program addresses both creative and practical computer skills, and exposes boys and girls to emerging technologies and software. Students, each of whom has a dedicated computer, choose among camps focusing on video production, Java programming and Web design. Campers with multiple interests may enroll for more than one week to gain experience in different areas. Young students in grades 4-6 take a survey course that introduces them to desktop publishing and Web design.

EDUCATION UNLIMITED PUBLIC SPEAKING INSTITUTE
Res — Coed Ages 9-17

Berkeley, CA 94709. 1700 Shattuck Ave, Ste 305. Tel: 510-548-6612. Fax: 510-548-0212.
www.educationunlimited.com   E-mail: campinfo@educationunlimited.com
Matthew Fraser, Exec Dir.
Grades 4-12. Adm: FCFS. **Appl**—Fee $0. Due: Rolling.
Staff: Admin 8.
Type of instruction: Enrich. **Courses:** Expository_Writing Govt Creative_Writing Theater.
Avg class size: 10. **Daily hours for:** Classes 7. Study 1. Rec 6.
Locations: CA MA RI.
Focus: Debate Public_Speak. **Features:** Baseball Basketball Soccer Swim.
Fees 2014: Res $1940-2585 (+$50), 1 wk. Day $1370-1940 (+$50), 1 wk. Aid (Need).
Housing: Dorms. **Swimming:** Pool.
Est 1995. Inc. **Ses:** 9. **Wks/ses:** 1. Operates June-Aug.

Held at Stanford, UCLA, Georgetown University, Brown University, Tufts University, University of California-San Diego and the University of California-Berkeley, PSI trains students in public speaking, rhetoric and logic through an interactive curriculum. A special weeklong program for high schoolers, the American Legal Experience, teaches speaking and communicational skills through a concentrated emphasis on the American judicial system. The institute's sizeable international enrollment lends itself to a rich cultural experience. Recreational activities and a half-day off-campus excursion complement class work.

EDUCATION UNLIMITED
SALLY RIDE SCIENCE CAMP
Res — Girls Ages 9-14; Day — Girls 4-9

Berkeley, CA 94709. 1700 Shattuck Ave, Ste 305. Tel: 510-548-6612. Fax: 510-548-0212.
www.sallyridecamps.com   E-mail: campinfo@educationunlimited.com
Rhonda McCoy, Dir.
Grades 4-9. Adm: FCFS. **Appl**—Due: Rolling.
Type of instruction: Enrich. **Courses:** Astron Engineering Marine_Bio/Stud Robotics.
Locations: CA MA.
Focus: Sci.
Fees 2014: Res $950-2095.

Housing: Dorms.
Wks/ses: ½-1½.

Conducted at five college campuses in California and one in Cambridge, MA, Sally Ride Science Camp enables girls to explore science, technology and engineering through such hands-on activities as the construction of rockets, robots and marine habitats. Each student chooses a science major that includes several small labs and a substantial culminating project. Four-day programs allow girls to choose between an introduction to marine science and an introduction to engineering; five- and seven-day sessions provide a choice between marine biology and astronomy; and the 10-day advanced program offers another two options: advanced marine science/marine ecology and robotics. Afternoon and evening enrichment activities take the form of workshops, experiments, guest speakers and recreational pursuits.

EF INTERNATIONAL LANGUAGE SCHOOLS
Res — Coed Ages 10 and up

Cambridge, MA 02141. 1 Education St. Tel: 617-619-1700, 800-992-1892. Fax: 617-619-1701.
www.ef.com/ils   E-mail: ils@ef.com
Adm: FCFS. **Appl**—Fee $0. Due: Rolling.
Type of instruction: Adv Enrich Preview Rev. **Avg class size:** 11. **Daily hours for:** Classes 3½. Study 1½. Rec 2½. **College credit:** 11.
Intl program focus: Lang Culture. **Locations:** Asia Europe Mexico/Central_America South_America. Home stays avail.
Focus: Chin Fr Ger Ital Span.
Fees 2014: Res $1060-8200 (+$150/wk), 2-10 wks.
Housing: Dorms.
Est 1965. Wks/ses: 2-10. Operates Year-round.

EF's year-round language immersion programs enable students to study French, Italian, Spanish, German or Chinese where it is natively spoken. Participants live either with a carefully chosen host family, on a university campus, or in an EF residence or apartment. In addition to language instruction, programming includes exam preparation, business classes and internships. Cultural activities and excursions round out the program.

EMAGINATION COMPUTER CAMPS
Res and Day — Coed Ages 8-17

Salem, NH 03079. 54 Stiles Rd, Ste 205. Tel: 781-933-8795, 877-248-0206. Fax: 781-497-9864.
www.computercamps.com   E-mail: camp@computercamps.com
Craig Whiting, Exec Dir. Student contact: Allison Fitzgerald.
Adm: FCFS. **Appl**—Fee $0. Due: Rolling.
Enr: 150-180. **Enr cap:** 200. **Intl:** 8%. **Non-White:** 15%. **Fac 20. Staff:** Admin 8. Res 20.
Courses: Drama. **Avg class size:** 8. **Daily hours for:** Classes 4½. Rec 1½.
Locations: CT GA IL MA PA.
Focus: Comp_Sci. **Features:** Swim Tennis.
Fees 2014: Res $1425-10,475, 1-8 wks. Day $825-7155, 1-8 wks. Aid (Need).
Housing: Dorms. **Swimming:** Pool.
Est 1982. Ses: 4. **Wks/ses:** 1-2. Operates June-Aug.

Campers interested in computers and technology choose from various workshop options that allow them to further develop their skills, explore computer programming and think creatively; workshops accommodate beginners through advanced students. Each student is assigned a computer for the duration of the session. Leadership opportunities are available to boys and girls entering grade 10 or above. Emagination conducts on- and off-campus recreational activities—available to both boarders and day pupils—each Saturday. Camps operate on four college campuses: Bentley University (Waltham, MA), Mercer University (Atlanta, GA), Lake Forest College (Lake Forest, IL) and Rosemont College (Rosemont, PA).

EMORY UNIVERSITY
YOUTH THEOLOGICAL INITIATIVE SUMMER ACADEMY
Res — Coed Ages 16-18

Atlanta, GA 30322. **Candler School of Theology, 1531 Dickey Dr. Tel: 404-712-9160. Fax: 404-727-2494.**
www.yti.emory.edu   E-mail: yti@emory.edu
Elizabeth Corrie, Dir. Student contact: Brenda Bennefield.
Grades 11-12. Adm: Selective. Admitted: 60%. Priority: Low-income. URM. Prereqs: GPA 3.0. **Appl**—Fee $0. Due: Mar. Transcript, 2 recs, 4 essays.
Enr: 39. **Enr cap:** 39. Intl: 10%. Non-White: 50%. **Fac 11.** Prof 4. Col/grad students 5. Specialists 2. **Staff:** Admin 3. Couns 11.
Type of instruction: Enrich. **Courses:** Ethics Crafts Creative_Writing Dance Drama Music Painting. **Daily hours for:** Classes 4. Study 2. Rec 6. Homework.
Focus: Relig_Stud. **Features:** Climbing_Wall Community_Serv Conservation Cooking Peace/Cross-cultural Basketball Soccer Swim Ultimate_Frisbee.
Fees 2011: Res $1300 (+$50-100), 3 wks. Aid 2009 (Need): $6875.
Housing: Dorms. Avg per room/unit: 2. **Swimming:** Pool. Campus facilities avail.
Est 1993. Nonprofit. United Methodist. **Ses:** 1. **Wks/ses:** 3. Operates July.

With the goal of cultivating public theologians, YTI provides students with an intensive examination of theological issues. Faculty encourage boys and girls to ponder theological questions; explore theological literature (including the Bible); engage, analyze and address global issues from Christian theological perspectives; and experience various ways of worshipping together as an ecumenical group, such as attending services with Christian congregations and other religious communities. Students typically leave the program with more defined educational and vocational plans in theology.

FAY SCHOOL ENGLISH IMMERSION SUMMER PROGRAM
Res — Coed Ages 10-15

Southborough, MA 01772. **48 Main St. Tel: 508-490-8371, 800-933-2925.**
www.fayschool.org   E-mail: summer@fayschool.org
Bob Rojee, Dir.
Grades 5-9. Adm: FCFS. **Appl**—Fee $100. Due: Rolling.
Enr: 60. **Enr cap:** 70. Intl: 100%. **Fac 14.** K-12 staff 14. **Staff:** Admin 4.
Type of instruction: Enrich Rem_Eng Rem_Math Rem_Read Study_Skills. **Courses:** Eng Hist Sci Crafts Dance Filmmaking Theater. **Avg class size:** 6. **Daily hours for:** Classes 3. Study 1½. Rec 4. Homework. Tests. Grades.
Focus: ESL. **Features:** Archery Climbing_Wall Cooking Fishing Outdoor_Ed Ropes_Crse Woodcraft Baseball Basketball Soccer Swim Tennis.
Fees 2014: Res $6500-9400 (+$500-800), 4-6 wks.
Housing: Dorms. **Swimming:** Pool. Campus facilities avail.
Est 1985. Nonprofit. **Ses:** 2. **Wks/ses:** 4-6. Operates June-Aug.

Fay's English Immersion Summer Program combines study of the language with opportunities for students to hone their skills during extracurricular activities. Beginners study English for three hours each morning, intermediate pupils for two hours and advanced boys and girls for one hour. Intermediate and advanced students fill out their mornings with elective course work in other subjects, for one hour and two hours, respectively. Participants gain an introduction to American culture as part of the curriculum.

THE FLORIDA FORENSIC INSTITUTE
Res and Day — Coed Ages 13-18

Cooper City, FL 33024. 10000 Stirling Rd, Ste 1.
www.ffi4n6.com
Howard S. Miller, Dir.
Adm: Somewhat_selective. Admitted: 90%. **Appl**—Fee $0. Due: May.
Enr: 225. **Enr cap:** 250. Intl: 5%. Non-White: 40%. **Fac 40.** Prof 2. Col/grad students 10.
   K-12 staff 8. Specialists 20. **Staff:** Admin 6. Couns 4.
Type of instruction: Adv. **Daily hours for:** Classes 8.
Focus: Debate. **Features:** Swim.
Fees 2014: Res $2250, 2 wks. Day $1395, 2 wks. Aid 2011 (Merit & Need): $15,000.
Housing: Hotels. Avg per room/unit: 1-4. **Swimming:** Pool.
Est 1981. Inc. **Ses:** 1. **Wks/ses:** 2. Operates July-Aug.

FFI conducts a specialized summer program for young debaters of all ability levels. During the two-week session, boys and girls attend comprehensive courses in congressional debate, public forum debate, Lincoln-Douglas debate, extemporaneous speaking and original oratory. A four-day program extension at the conclusion of the regular session enables interested pupils to further develop their forensic skills through one-on-one tutorials with field experts.

FOUNDATION FOR TEACHING ECONOMICS
ECONOMICS FOR LEADERS
Res — Coed Ages 16-17

Davis, CA 95616. 260 Russell Blvd, Ste B. Tel: 530-757-4630, 800-383-4335. Fax: 530-
   757-4636.
www.fte.org/student-programs/economics-for-leaders-program   E-mail:
information@fte.org
Debbie Henney, Dir.
Grade 12. Adm: Selective. Admitted: 32%. **Appl**—Fee $0. Due: Mar. Essay.
Enr: 30-50. **Enr cap:** 30-50. **Fac 3.** Prof 3. **Staff:** Admin 8.
Type of instruction: Enrich. **Daily hours for:** Classes 4. Study 2. Rec 3. Tests.
Locations: CA CO GA KS MA MI NY OH TN TX VA WA.
Focus: Econ Leadership. **Features:** Swim.
Fees 2014: Res $600-1400, 1 wk.
Housing: Dorms. **Swimming:** Pool.
Ses: 13. **Wks/ses:** 1. Operates June-Aug.

Conducted on college campuses across the country, EFL teaches students about responsible leadership and economic analysis. Morning economics seminars introduce basic free-market concepts through simulations and discussions of current national and international issues. Outdoor leadership exercises in the afternoons challenge student teams with physical and mental problems. Among evening activities are a simulated political election and recreational and social events.

THE GARCIA CENTER FOR POLYMERS
AT ENGINEERED INTERFACES
RESEARCH SCHOLAR PROGRAM
FOR HIGH SCHOOL STUDENTS
Res and Day — Coed Ages 16-18

Stony Brook, NY 11794. State Univ of New York, 216 Engineering Bldg. Tel: 631-632-
   6097. Fax: 631-632-5764.
http://polymer.matscieng.sunysb.edu/srprog.html   E-mail: lourdes.collazo@
stonybrook.edu
Student contact: Lourdes Collazo, E-mail: lourdes.collazo@sunysb.edu.
Grades 11-12. Adm: Very selective. Prereqs: GPA 3.8. **Appl**—Due: Feb. Transcript, 3 recs.

Enr: 25.
Type of instruction: Adv Enrich.
Focus: Sci.
Fees 2009: Res $2150 (+$75), 7 wks. Day $950 (+$75), 7 wks.
Housing: Dorms.
Ses: 1. Wks/ses: 7. Operates June-Aug.

Funded by the National Science Foundation as part of its Materials Research Science and Engineering Center programs, the Garcia Center invites high school upperclassmen to work on focused polymer science and technology research teams. Participants create independent projects with the guidance of Garcia faculty and graduate students. In addition to entering national competitions, young men and women are encouraged to publish articles in scientific journals and to present their results at national conferences. Program dates are flexible, and students may continue their research during the following academic year. Participants have been recognized by the Intel Science Talent Search and the Siemens Competition in Math, Science & Technology.

GEORGETOWN PREPARATORY SCHOOL
ENGLISH AS A SECOND LANGUAGE PROGRAM
Res and Day — Coed Ages 14-17

North Bethesda, MD 20852. 10900 Rockville Pike. Tel: 301-214-1249. Fax: 301-214-8600.
www.gprep.org/esl E-mail: rwhitman@gprep.org
Rosita A. Whitman, Dir.
Grades 9-12. Adm: FCFS. **Appl**—Fee $250. Due: Rolling.
Enr: 100. **Intl:** 90%. **Fac 8. Staff:** Admin 2. Couns 15.
Courses: Govt Speech Writing/Journ Creative_Writing Theater. **Avg class size:** 13. **Daily hours for:** Classes 4½. Study 2. Rec 3. Homework. Tests. Grades. **High school credit.**
Focus: ESL. **Features:** Baseball Basketball Golf Soccer Softball Swim Tennis Track.
Fees 2014: Res $7597 (+$50-70), 6 wks. Day $4365 (+$50-70), 6 wks. Aid (Merit & Need).
Housing: Dorms. **Swimming:** Pool. Campus facilities avail.
Nonprofit. Roman Catholic. **Ses: 1. Wks/ses: 6.** Operates June-Aug.

Georgetown Prep's ESL Program offers intensive audio-lingual training in English for young people of high school age with or without previous knowledge of English. Pupils receive four and a half hours of instruction each weekday, in addition to two hours of supervised homework daily. Supplementary course work is also available, as is a full schedule of recreational and social activities.

GEORGETOWN UNIVERSITY COLLEGE PREP PROGRAM
Res and Day — Coed Ages 15-18

Washington, DC 20057. Summer Prgms for High School Students, Box 571006. Tel: 202-687-7807. Fax: 202-687-8954.
http://summer.georgetown.edu E-mail: highschool@georgetown.edu
Susan Manion, Dir.
Grades 10-12. Adm: Selective. **Appl**—Fee $50. Due: Rolling. Transcript, rec, essay.
Enr: 49. **Staff:** Couns 12.
Type of instruction: Adv Rem_Eng Rem_Math SAT/ACT_Prep. **Courses:** Bus/Fin Computers Eng Expository_Writing Sci Speech Creative_Writing. **Daily hours for:** Classes 3. Study 3. Grades. **College credit.**
Focus: Col_Prep Study_Skills. **Features:** Basketball Cross-country Soccer Swim Tennis Track.
Fees 2014: Res $5339 (+$548), 3 wks. Day $4400-4675 (+$548), 3 wks. Aid (Need).
Housing: Dorms. **Swimming:** Pool River.
Ses: 1. Wks/ses: 3. Operates June-July.

Open to rising high school sophomores, juniors and seniors, this enrichment program helps improve students' English and math fundamentals while also preparing them for the SAT examinations and the college admissions process. Course work enables boys and girls to further develop their critical thinking, composition, writing, research and study skill, and SAT test-taking workshops and practice tests address all sections of the exams. Students also preview college life through shared meals, social events, and conversations with faculty and fellow pupils.

GEORGETOWN UNIVERSITY
FUNDAMENTALS OF BUSINESS
Res and Day — Coed Ages 15-18

Washington, DC 20007. Summer Programs for High School Students, 3307 M St NW, Ste 202. Tel: 202-687-8600. Fax: 202-687-8954.
http://scs.georgetown.edu/hoyas   E-mail: highschool@georgetown.edu
Thomas Cooke, Dir.
Grades 10-12. Adm: Selective. **Appl**—Fee $50. Due: May. Transcript, test scores, rec, essay.
Enr: 53. Enr cap: 60. Fac 2. Prof 2.
Type of instruction: Adv. **Courses:** Comm Law. **Daily hours for:** Classes 3. Study 3. **College credit: 3.**
Focus: Bus/Fin. **Features:** Swim.
Fees 2014: Res $5313 (+$1375), 5 wks. Day $4123 (+$1375), 5 wks.
Housing: Dorms. **Swimming:** Pool River.
Ses: 2. **Wks/ses:** 5. Operates July-Aug.

During this five-week program, students examine various aspects of business, including finance, marketing, accounting, management, communications, strategy, planning, organizational behavior and business law. Course work also addresses basic business concepts, language and organization. Boys and girls, who are treated as college students, earn three college credits upon completion of the program. Participants take one field trip to a local company to learn firsthand about a working business.

GEORGETOWN UNIVERSITY
INTERNATIONAL RELATIONS PROGRAM
FOR HIGH SCHOOL STUDENTS
Res — Coed Ages 15-18

Washington, DC 20057. Summer Prgms for High School Students, Box 571006. Tel: 202-687-8700. Fax: 202-687-8954.
http://summer.georgetown.edu   E-mail: scsspecialprograms@georgetown.edu
Anthony Clark Arend, Dir.
Grades 10-12. Adm: Selective. **Appl**—Fee $50. Due: Rolling. Transcript, rec, essay.
Enr: 233. Fac 13.
Type of instruction: Adv Enrich. **Courses:** Global_Stud. **Daily hours for:** Classes 3. Study 3.
Focus: Govt Intl_Relations Pol_Sci. **Features:** Swim.
Fees 2014: Res $2595, 1 wk. Aid (Need).
Housing: Dorms. **Swimming:** Pool River.
Nonprofit. **Ses:** 2. Operates June-July.

This eight-day program combines classroom lectures from Georgetown faculty and guest speakers with visits to organizations involved in foreign policy, small-group discussions of newsworthy topics and an international crisis simulation. Areas of study include diplomatic, economic and military instruments of foreign policy; international organizations; international law; competing ideologies in international order; self-determination; the environment; terrorism; civil war; weapons of mass destruction; problems in the developing world; and the future of the international system.

GLOBAL YOUNG LEADERS CONFERENCE
Res — Coed Ages 15-18

Washington, DC 20006. 1700 Pennsylvania Ave NW, Ste 400. Tel: 703-584-9373.
www.envisionexperience.com/explore-our-programs/global-young-leaders-
conference E-mail: gylc_adm@cylc.org
Marguerite C. Regan, Dir.
Adm: Selective. **Appl**—Due: Rolling.
Type of instruction: Enrich. **Courses:** Bus/Fin Econ Govt Law Pol_Sci. **College credit.**
Locations: DC NY Asia Europe.
Focus: Leadership.
Fees 2014: Res $2895-5890, 1½-2 wks. Aid (Need).
Est 1985. Spons: Congressional Youth Leadership Council. **Ses:** 9. **Wks/ses:** 1½-2.
Operates June-Aug.

This leadership development program allows high-achieving boys and girls to learn from successful businesspeople, policy officials, lobbyists, journalists, diplomats and academics in Washington, DC; New York City; Vienna, Prauge and Berlin, Europe; or Beijing, Hangshou and Shanghai, China. Among concepts addressed on a broad scale during the GYLC sessions are communications, diplomacy, law, human rights, peace, security, economics and the role of the United Nations. All students are provided with written materials intended to promote self-directed, experiential learning. The Congressional Youth Leadership Council, which sponsors GYLC, identifies and nominates suitable candidates.

GREAT BOOKS SUMMER PROGRAM
Res — Coed Ages 11-17

Fairfield, CT 06824. PO Box 743. Fax: 203-255-0675.
www.greatbookssummer.com E-mail: info@greatbookssummer.com
Peter Temes, Dir.
Grades 6-12. Adm: Selective. **Appl**—Fee $0. Due: May. Nomination.
Type of instruction: Adv Enrich. **Courses:** Expository_Writing Art Music Theater.
Locations: CA MA.
Focus: Eng.
Fees 2014: Res $1825-5535 (+$175-450), 1-4 wks. Aid (Need).
Housing: Dorms.
Est 2002. Ses: 8. **Wks/ses:** 1-4. Operates June-July.

With locations at Amherst College and Stanford University, participants learn how to read and analyze material at a college level; engage in active discussions; and develop their perceptual, critical-thinking and self-expression skills. Special guests, authors and educators join class discussions in each session. Sessions serve boys and girls in two age groups: the Intermediate Program (for children entering grades 6-8) and the Senior Program (for students entering grades 9-12).

GREEN RIVER PRESERVE
Res — Coed Ages 8-18

Cedar Mountain, NC 28718. 301 Green River Rd. Tel: 828-698-8828. Fax: 828-698-9201.
www.greenriverpreserve.org E-mail: info@greenriverpreserve.org
Case Kennedy, Dir.
Student contact: Missy Schenck, **E-mail:** missy@greenriverpreserve.org.
Grades 2-12. Adm: Somewhat selective. Admitted: 98%. **Appl**—Fee $0. Due: Rolling.
Teacher rec.
Enr cap: 104. Non-White: 2%. **Fac** 15. **Staff:** Admin 10. Couns 32.
Type of instruction: Enrich. **Courses:** Crafts Creative_Writing Drawing Music Painting
Theater Pottery. **Avg class size:** 9.

Focus: Environ_Sci. **Features:** Archery Canoe Chess Climbing_Wall Conservation Cooking Exploration Farm Fishing Hiking Mtn_Trips Outdoor_Ed Riflery Rock_Climb Ropes_Crse Survival_Trng Wilderness_Camp Woodcraft Fencing Swim Gardening.
Fees 2014: Res $1275-3980, 1-3 wks. Aid (Need).
Housing: Cabins Lodges. Avg per room/unit: 7. **Swimming:** Lake Pond River Stream.
Est 1987. Nonprofit. **Ses:** 5. **Wks/ses:** 1-3. Operates June-Aug.

A wildlife preserve, GRP offers bright naturalists a recreational camp that combines the hands-on field study of natural science with work in the creative arts. Features include instruction in ecology and nature, as well as hiking and camping on the Preserve's 3400 acres in the Blue Ridge Mountains.

HAMPSHIRE COLLEGE SUMMER STUDIES IN MATHEMATICS
Res — Coed Ages 16-18

Amherst, MA 01002. 893 West St. Tel: 413-559-5375. Fax: 413-559-5448.
www.hcssim.org   E-mail: sgoff@hampshire.edu
David C. Kelly, Dir.
Grades 11-12 (younger if qualified). Adm: Selective. **Appl**—Fee $0. Due: Rolling. Personal statement, rec, adm test.
Enr: 40-55. **Fac 10. Staff:** Admin 1.
Type of instruction: Adv Enrich. **Courses:** Comp_Sci. **Avg class size:** 17. **Daily hours for:** Classes 7.
Focus: Math. **Features:** Basketball Soccer Softball Swim Tennis Volleyball.
Fees 2014: Res $3417, 6 wks. Aid (Need).
Housing: Dorms. **Swimming:** Pool. Campus facilities avail.
Est 1971. Nonprofit. **Ses:** 1. **Wks/ses:** 6. Operates June-Aug.

Intelligent, highly motivated high schoolers work both individually and in small groups during this rigorous program. HCSSiM participants investigate concrete problems, seek patterns and generalizations, formulate conjectures in the language of mathematics and apply insight and experience to the creation of proofs. For the first three weeks, college professors lead workshops covering undergraduate-level content in number theory, combinatorics/graph theory, modern algebra and other topics from outside the usual secondary school and early college curricula. Students then select one maxi-course (covering a semester-long elective's worth of material) and two minicourses. Most faculty live on campus and join students for meals and recreational activities.

HARVARD UNIVERSITY GRADUATE SCHOOL OF DESIGN
CAREER DISCOVERY PROGRAM
Res and Day — Coed Ages 18 and up

Cambridge, MA 02138. 48 Quincy St, 422 Gund Hall. Tel: 617-495-5453. Fax: 617-495-8949.
www.gsd.harvard.edu/careerdiscovery   E-mail: discovery@gsd.harvard.edu
Jeffrey L. Klug, Dir.
Grades PG-Col. Adm: FCFS. **Appl**—Fee 40. Due: Apr. Transcript, essay, 2 recs.
Enr: 270. **Enr cap:** 300. **Fac 40. Staff:** Admin 4. Couns 3.
Type of instruction: Enrich Preview. **Avg class size:** 11. **Daily hours for:** Classes 7. Study 3. Rec 2.
Focus: Architect.
Fees 2014: Res $4350 (+$150), 6 wks. Day $3100 (+$150), 6 wks. Aid (Need).
Housing: Dorms.
Est 1973. Nonprofit. **Ses:** 1. **Wks/ses:** 6. Operates June-July.

Through Career Discovery, participants gain an introduction to the design professions by means of intense studio work, seminars and lectures, workshops and field trips. Students spend most of their time on short, intensive projects similar to first-year graduate school work in architecture, landscape architecture, urban planning or urban design concentrations. Other activities include career advising panel discusssions, field trips, office visits and drawing and computer workshops. Most participants are college students or professionals with no previous design training, although recent high school graduates make up a small percentage of attendees.

HOTCHKISS SCHOOL
SUMMER ENVIRONMENTAL SCIENCE PROGRAM
Res — Coed Ages 12-15

Lakeville, CT 06039. 11 Interlaken Rd, PO Box 800. Tel: 860-435-3173. Fax: 860-435-4413.
www.hotchkissportals.org   E-mail: summer@hotchkiss.org
Stephen C. McKibben, Dir. Student contact: Christiana Gurney Rawlings.
Grades 8-10 (younger if qualified). Adm: Selective. **Appl**—Fee $55. Due: Rolling. SSAT/TOEFL scores.
Enr: 32. Enr cap: 36. Intl: 50%. **Fac 7.**
Type of instruction: Enrich. **Courses:** Ecol Fine_Arts. **Avg class size:** 12. **Daily hours for:** Classes 8. Study 1. Rec 2.
Focus: Environ_Sci. **Features:** Caving Farm Skateboarding Street_Hockey Swim Tennis Ultimate_Frisbee Volleyball.
Fees 2014: Res $4450 (+$50-100), 3 wks. Aid (Merit & Need).
Housing: Dorms. **Swimming:** Lake Pool.
Est 2004. Nonprofit. Ses: 1. Wks/ses: 3. Operates June-July.

The Hotchkiss SES program emphasizes hands-on field research, data collection and analysis techniques. Boys and girls begin by studying the basic aquatic and terrestrial ecology of the surrounding lakes, streams, woods, fields and farmland. They then connect with working environmental scientists on field projects that range from invasive species monitoring to global climate change modeling. Students who return for a second summer analyze data and formulate strategies for solving environmental problems; in their third summer, SES participants intern with local environmental organizations. Sports and other recreational activities round out the program.

IXBALANQUE SPANISH SCHOOL
Res — Coed Ages 6 and up

Copan Ruinas, Honduras. Barrio el Centro. Tel: 504-651-4432. Fax: 504-651-4432.
www.ixbalanque.com   E-mail: ixbalanquehn@yahoo.com
Adm: FCFS. **Appl**—Fee $0. Due: Rolling.
Enr: 30.
Type of instruction: Enrich. **Daily hours for:** Classes 4.
Intl program focus: Lang Culture. Home stays avail.
Focus: Span. **Features:** Riding.
Fees 2014: Res $250, 1 wk.
Ses: 4. **Wks/ses:** 1. Operates June-July.

Participants in this program take Spanish classes while learning about the local customs of Honduras and the Mayan culture. The school maintains a one-to-one student-teacher ratio, thereby ensuring individualized instruction. Ixbalanque's campus is proximate to the Mayan ruin of Copan and its archeological structures and sculptures. Students reside with a local family.

JOHNS HOPKINS UNIVERSITY
ENGINEERING INNOVATION
Res — Coed Ages 16-18

Baltimore, MD 21218. 3400 N Charles St, 040 Shriver Hall. Tel: 410-516-6224, 866-493-0517. Fax: 410-516-0264.

http://engineering.jhu.edu/ei   E-mail: engineering-innovation@jhu.edu
Karen Borgsmiller, Dir.
Grades 11-PG. Adm: Selective. **Appl**—Fee $55. Due: Apr. Transcript, essay, math/sci teacher rec.
Type of instruction: Undergrad. **Avg class size:** 21. **College credit:** 3.
Focus: Engineering.
Fees 2014: Res $2300-3300, 4 wks. Day $2300-3300, 4 wks. Aid (Need).
Housing: Dorms.
Nonprofit. **Ses:** 1. **Wks/ses:** 4. Operates June-July.

Following a program developed by Johns Hopkins University, students apply their knowledge of math and science to hands-on projects and laboratory work pertaining to engineering. Boys and girls attend college-level lectures, test theories, solve problems and generate solutions. As a complement to classroom work, students also learn from practicing engineers about career possibilities, internships and educational opportunities within the field. In addition to the residential and day program at Johns Hopkins, Engineering Innovation operates comparable day sessions at locations across the country. Applicants should have spreadsheet knowledge, as well as experience with lab science, algebra II and trigonometry.

JUNIOR STATE OF AMERICA SUMMER SCHOOL
Res — Coed Ages 14-18

San Mateo, CA 94402. 800 S Claremont St, Ste 202. Tel: 650-347-1600, 800-334-5353.
Fax: 650-347-7200.
www.jsa.org/summer-programs/summer-school   E-mail: summerprograms@jsa.org
Grades 9-12. Adm: Selective. **Appl**—Fee $0. Due: Rolling. Transcript, essay, rec.
Enr: 275. **Fac 16. Prof** 16. **Staff:** Admin 5.
Type of instruction: Adv Enrich. **Courses:** Comm Econ Intl_Relations Media. **Avg class size:** 30. **Daily hours for:** Classes 6. Homework. Grades. **High school credit.**
Locations: CA DC NJ VA.
Focus: Govt Pol_Sci. **Features:** Leadership.
Fees 2014: Res $4850-5250, 3 wks. Aid 2011 (Merit & Need): $750,000.
Housing: Dorms.
Est 1941. Nonprofit. **Spons:** Junior Statesmen Foundation. **Ses:** 4. **Wks/ses:** 3. Operates June-July.

At the University of Virginia, Georgetown, Princeton and Stanford universities, high school students follow a curriculum that includes a systematic introduction to American government and politics, a speaker program and student debates on current issues. The collegiate academic environment stresses substantial reading, research and writing. Meeting six days each week, classes are equivalent to one-semester high school honors or Advanced Placement courses. AP exam preparation is offered in US government, comparative government, US history and macroeconomics. The Georgetown program includes a high-level speakers program that takes students around Washington, DC, to meet with political leaders.

KANSAS STATE UNIVERSITY
EXCITE! SUMMER WORKSHOP
Res — Girls Ages 13-18

Manhattan, KS 66502. Division of Continuing Ed, 1615 Anderson Ave. Tel: 785-532-3395. Fax: 785-532-2422.
www.k-state.edu/excite   E-mail: kawse@ksu.edu
Sara Heiman, Coord.
Grades 9-12. Adm: FCFS. **Appl**—Due: Rolling.
Enr: 70. **Fac 2. Staff:** Admin 3. Couns 2.
Type of instruction: Enrich. **Courses:** Game_Design Nanotech Robotics. **Avg class size:** 11.

Focus: Engineering Math Sci.
Fees 2014: Res $350, ½ wk.
Housing: Dorms. Avg per room/unit: 2.
Est 2002. Nonprofit. **Ses:** 1. **Wks/ses:** ½. Operates June.

The three-day EXCITE! program guides young women through topics in mathematics, science, technology and engineering. The workshop emphasizes hands-on activities and team problem solving as students learn about the engineering design process. Girls work closely with KSU faculty and undergraduates in choosing a specific track from such fields as architecture, aeronautics, nanotechnology, robotics and game design.

KENT STATE UNIVERSITY
YOUNG BUSINESS SCHOLARS
Res — Coed Ages 17-18

Kent, OH 44242 United States. PO Box 5190.
www.kent.edu/business/undergrad/young-business-scholars/index.cfm
Nicole Kotlan, Dir, Undergrad Progs.
Grade 12. Adm: Selective. **Appl**—Due: Apr.
Focus: Bus/Fin.
Fees 2014: Free (+150),
Est 2011. Spons: Kent State University. **Ses:** 1. **Wks/ses:** 1. Operates June-July.

The Young Business Scholars Program invites promising high school seniors to Kent State University for a week-long business administration immersion program. Each day, a different business discipline will be discussed, ranging from accounting to marketing and entrepreneurship. Students will reside on campus, attend business lectures, and participate in social activities, with the goal of creating a new business.

KETTERING UNIVERSITY
LIVES IMPROVE THROUGH ENGINEERING
Res — Girls Ages 16-17

Flint, MI 48504. 1700 W 3rd Ave. Tel: 810-762-9679, 800-955-4464.
www.kettering.edu/futurestudents/precollege/lite   E-mail: lite@kettering.edu
Deborah Stewart, Prgm Dir.
Grade 11. Adm: Selective. **Prereqs:** GPA 3.0. **Appl**—Fee $0. Due: Apr. Transcript, essay, rec.
Enr: 36. **Enr cap:** 36. **Fac 6.** Prof 6.
Type of instruction: Enrich.
Focus: Engineering. **Features:** Swim.
Fees 2014: Res $600, 2 wks. Aid (Need).
Housing: Dorms. **Swimming:** Pool. Campus facilities avail.
Ses: 1. **Wks/ses:** 2. Operates July.

LITE shows young women how engineers use math, science and technology to solve human problems. Conducted by Kettering faculty, classes and labs address biomechanics, biochemistry, engineering for a sustainable society and vehicle collision analysis. Field trips to engineering sites, social activities and athletics round out the program.

LANGUAGE LIAISON GLOBAL TEEN
Res — Coed Ages 13-17

Pacific Palisades, CA 90272. PO Box 1772. Tel: 310-454-1701, 800-284-4448. Fax: 310-454-1706.
www.globalteen.org   E-mail: learn@languageliaison.com
Nancy Forman, Dir.
Grades 8-12. Adm: FCFS. **Appl**—Due: Rolling.

Type of instruction: Enrich Study_Skills. **Avg class size:** 8. **Daily hours for:** Classes 3½. Rec 5.
Intl program focus: Lang. **Locations:** Canada Europe Mexico/Central_America South_ America. Home stays avail.
Focus: Fr Ger Ital Span. **Features:** Riding Sail Basketball Golf Surfing Swim Tennis Volleyball Water-skiing Watersports.
Fees 2011: Res $978-6526 (+$130-200), 1-4 wks.
Housing: Dorms Houses. **Swimming:** Lake Ocean Pool.
Est 1987. Inc. **Wks/ses:** 1-5. Operates June-Aug.

Designed specifically for high schoolers (although some courses accept younger pupils), Language Liaison offers language immersion in France, Ecuador, Germany, Canada, Austria, Italy, Costa Rica, Spain and Mexico. No prior study of the target language is required. Home stay with carefully selected families is an important element of the program.

THE LAWRENCE HALL OF SCIENCE
MARINE BIOLOGY RESEARCH CAMP
Res — Coed Ages 14-18

Berkeley, CA 94720. Univ of California-Berkeley, 1 Centennial Dr, Rm 5200. Tel: 510-642-5134. Fax: 510-643-0994.
www.lawrencehallofscience.org/summercamp   E-mail: lhsreg@berkeley.edu
Grades 9-12. Adm: FCFS. **Appl**—Fee $0. Due: Rolling.
Type of instruction: Adv Enrich. **Courses:** Crafts. **Daily hours for:** Classes 7. Study 2. Rec 2.
Focus: Marine_Bio/Stud. **Features:** Archery Exploration Hiking Mtn_Trips Outdoor_Ed Wilderness_Camp Swim Volleyball.
Fees 2014: Res $1040-1095, 1 wk. Aid (Need).
Housing: Dorms. **Swimming:** Lake Pool.
Est 1968. Nonprofit. **Spons:** University of California-Berkeley. **Ses:** 1. **Wks/ses:** 1. Operates Aug.

The Lawrence Hall of Science, the University of California-Berkeley's public science center, conducts a weeklong marine biology program at Bodega Marine Lab in Bodega Bay. High school students develop laboratory and field investigation skills as they examine the rocky tide pools, mudflats, estuaries, coastal dunes and sandy beaches surrounding the modern research station. Participants design their own research projects with guidance from LHS instructors and scientists. Boys and girls engage in supervised recreational activities each evening.

LE CHAPERON ROUGE
Res and Day — Coed Ages 6-16

Crans-sur-Sierre, 3963 Valais, Switzerland. Tel: 41-27-481-25-00. Fax: 41-27-481-25-02.
www.chaperonrouge.ch   E-mail: office@chaperonrouge.ch
Gabrielle Bagnoud, Dir.
Adm: FCFS. **Appl**—Fee $0. Due: Rolling.
Enr: 65. **Enr cap:** 65. **Staff:** Admin 2. Couns 2.
Type of instruction: Adv Enrich Rem_Eng Rev Study_Skills. **Courses:** Crafts Dance. **Avg class size:** 7. **Daily hours for:** Classes 3. Rec 7.
Intl program focus: Lang.
Focus: ESL Fr Ger Ital Span. **Features:** Archery Boating Climbing_Wall Fishing Hiking Mountaineering Mtn_Trips Paintball Riding Sail Badminton Basketball Equestrian Golf Gymnastics In-line_Skating Soccer Swim Tennis Volleyball Winter_Sports Ping-Pong.
Fees 2014: Res SwF3265-4570 (+SwF270-480), 2-3 wks. Day SwF2745-3670 (+SwF270-480), 2-3 wks.
Housing: Houses. Avg per room/unit: 8. **Swimming:** Pool.

Est 1954. Ses: 3. **Wks/ses:** 2-3. Operates June-Aug.

Students receive language lessons in French, German, Italian, Spanish or English for three to four hours each morning. Beginning, intermediate and advanced levels are available for all languages. Students may choose to study two languages during one session. Among afternoon and weekend recreational activities are crafts, horseback riding and sports.

LE CHATEAU DES ENFANTS
Res — Coed Ages 6-10; Day — Coed 4-10

Montagnola-Lugano, Switzerland.
Contact (Year-round): c/o TASIS US Office, 112 S Royal St, Alexandria, VA 22314.
Tel: 703-299-8150. **Fax:** 703-299-8157.
http://summer.tasis.com/page.cfm?p=299   **E-mail:** usadmissions@tasis.com
Betsy Newell, Dir.
Adm: FCFS. **Appl**—Due: Rolling.
Enr: 120. **Enr cap:** 120. **Fac** 10. **Staff:** Admin 3. Couns 15.
Type of instruction: Enrich. **Courses:** Crafts Drama. **Avg class size:** 8. **Daily hours for:** Classes 3. Rec 6.
Intl program focus: Lang.
Focus: ESL Fr Ital. **Features:** Basketball Soccer Swim.
Fees 2014: Res SwF5950-7400 (+airfare), 3-4 wks. **Day** SwF3050-3550 (+airfare), 3-4 wks.
Housing: Dorms Houses. **Swimming:** Lake Pool.
Est 1969. Nonprofit. **Spons:** TASIS Foundation. **Ses:** 2. **Wks/ses:** 3-4. Operates June-Aug.

This highly international camp combines French, Italian or English language instruction with an array of traditional recreational activities. Boys and girls take two daily lessons (in groups of four to six students) in the target language. Thematically designed lessons incorporate drama and singing periods as learning tools. Swimming, sports, and arts and crafts are all offered on a daily basis.

LEAD SUMMER BUSINESS INSTITUTE
Res — Coed Ages 17-18

Fort Washington, PA 19034. 500 Office Center Dr, Ste 400. Tel: 215-261-7001.
www.leadprogram.org   **E-mail:** apply@leadprogram.org
Grade 11. Adm: Selective. **Prereqs:** GPA 3.0. PSAT M/CR 100; SAT M/CR 1000; ACT 22.
Appl—Fee $50. Due: Feb. Transcript, essays, test scores, 2 recs.
Type of instruction: Enrich Undergrad. **Courses:** Comp_Sci Econ Ethics.
Locations: DC GA IL MI NC NH NY PA VA.
Focus: Bus/Fin.
Fees 2014: Res $1400-2800, 3-4 wks. Aid (Need).
Housing: Dorms.
Est 1980. Wks/ses: 3-4.

Well-regarded American business schools throughout the country host rising high school seniors for a program that features interactive classes and one-on-one sessions led by university professors and corporate executives. SBI's curriculum addresses aspects of marketing, accounting, finance, economics, computer science and ethics. During the session, students employ case studies to work through business problems, analyze business issues and gain insight into difficulties faced by major corporations. Boys and girls develop a deeper understanding of business ownership through field trips to local businesses, meetings with entrepreneurs and the formulation of business plans.

LEAD SUMMER ENGINEERING INSTITUTE
Res — Coed Ages 15-17

Fort Washington, PA 19118. 500 Office Center Dr, Ste 400. Tel: 215-261-7001. www.leadprogram.org E-mail: apply@leadprogram.org Grades 10-11. Adm: Selective. **Prereqs:** GPA 3.2. 1000. **Appl**—Fee $50. Due: Feb. 2 recs, 2 essays. **Enr cap:** 30. **Type of instruction:** Adv Enrich. **Courses:** Comp_Sci Math. **Locations:** CA GA MI VA. **Focus:** Engineering. **Fees 2014: Res $1750 (+$350), 3 wks.** Aid (Need). **Housing:** Dorms. **Est 2008. Ses:** 4. **Wks/ses:** 3. Operates July-Aug.

SEI provides hands-on learning for mathematically inclined rising high school juniors and seniors. At Villanova University, LEAD admits the same number of boys and girls into each of its sessions. Students gain an introduction to engineering instruction, computer programming, problem solving, and data analysis.

LEARNING PROGRAMS INTERNATIONAL
Res — Coed Ages 15-18

Austin, TX 78704. 1112 W Ben White Blvd. Tel: 512-474-1041, 800-259-4439. Fax: 512-275-0770. www.lpiabroad.com E-mail: hs@studiesabroad.com Ivan Lopez, Exec Dir. Grades 10-PG. Adm: Somewhat_selective. **Prereqs:** GPA 2.0. **Appl**—Fee $0. Due: Rolling. Transcript, teacher rec. **Enr:** 15-20. **Enr cap:** 45. **Fac 3. Prof 3. Staff:** Admin 10. Couns 3. **Type of instruction:** Undergrad. **Courses:** Art. **Avg class size:** 15. **Daily hours for:** Classes 4½. Study 1. Rec 1½. Homework. Tests. Grades. **College credit:** 8. **Intl program focus:** Lang Culture. **Locations:** Asia Europe Mexico/Central_America South_America. Home stays avail. **Focus:** Chin Span. **Features:** Canoe Caving Hiking Mtn_Biking Riding Ropes_Crse Swim. **Fees 2014: Res $2495-5795 (+airfare), 2-6 wks.** Aid 2011 (Merit & Need): $4500. **Housing:** Dorms Houses. Avg per room/unit: 2-3. **Swimming:** Ocean Pool River. Campus facilities avail. **Est 1989.** Inc. **Ses:** 22. **Wks/ses:** 2-6. Operates June-Aug.

Offering summer programs in China, Costa Rica, England, France, Ireland, Italy, Peru and Spain, LPI provides language instruction and cultural immersion for high school students at all levels of proficiency. Pupils take classes at accredited foreign universities while living in dorms or with host families. Staff at each location provide tutoring services and assistance with class and language performance. Students develop a working knowledge of foreign languages, earn transferable college credit, experience another culture and explore the region through excursions.

MARIST COLLEGE SUMMER INSTITUTES
Res — Coed Ages 16-18

Poughkeepsie, NY 12601. Office of Undergraduate Adm, 3399 North Rd. Tel: 845-575-3226. Fax: 845-575-3215. www.marist.edu/summerinstitutes E-mail: precollege@marist.edu Grades 11-12. Adm: Selective. **Appl**—Due: Rolling. Transcript, essay, rec. **Type of instruction:** Undergrad. **College credit:** 3/crse, total 3. **Locations:** Europe. **Focus:** Bus/Fin Environ_Sci Span Law. **Fees 2014: Res $3200, 2 wks.**

Housing: Dorms. Campus facilities avail.
Ses: 1. **Wks/ses:** 2. Operates July.

Students earn college credit and preview campus life through Marist's Summer Institutes in business, creative writing, criminal justice, digital movie making, environmental science, fashion design, fashion merch, game design, sports communications, and theatre performance. Programming combines several class sessions each day with study time, local excursions, daylong field trips and recreational activities. Location in Italy, the program focuses on areas in interior design, fashion, and studio art.

MAUR HILL-MOUNT ACADEMY SUMMER ESL PROGRAM
Res — Coed Ages 12-18

Atchison, KS 66002. 1000 Green St. Tel: 913-367-5482. Fax: 913-367-5096.
www.mh-ma.com   E-mail: admissions@mh-ma.com
Student contact: Deke Nolan, E-mail: dnolan@mh-ma.com.
Grades 7-12 (younger if qualified). Adm: Somewhat_selective. Admitted: 90%. **Appl—**
Fee $100. Due: Rolling. SLEP/TOEFL/ILETS score (if available).
Enr: 20. Intl: 100%. **Fac 3.** Specialists 3. **Staff:** Admin 3. Couns 3.
Type of instruction: ESL/TOEFL_Prep. **Avg class size:** 8. **Daily hours for:** Classes 6.
Study 1. Rec 1. Homework. Tests.
Focus: ESL. **Features:** Basketball Soccer Swim Volleyball.
Fees 2014: Res $4200 (+$300), 6 wks.
Housing: Dorms. Avg per room/unit: 2. **Swimming:** Pond Pool. Campus facilities avail.
Nonprofit. Roman Catholic. **Ses:** 1. **Wks/ses:** 6. Operates July-Aug.

This intensive English program serves foreign students who wish to learn English or improve proficiency. Classes are held six hours daily, five days a week. Each weekend, students take cultural trips to gain experience and utilize skills acquired in the classroom.

MCDANIEL COLLEGE FORENSIC SCIENCE CAMP
Res and Day — Coed Ages 14-18

Westminster, MD 21157. 2 College Hill. Tel: 410-857-2458.
www.mcdaniel.edu/6801.htm   E-mail: ssa@mcdaniel.edu
Jeffrey Marx
Grades 9-12. Adm: FCFS. **Appl—**Fee $0. Due: May.
Type of instruction: Undergrad. **College credit:** 3.
Focus: Forensic_Sci.
Fees 2014: Res $875, 1 wk. Day $500, 1 wk.
Housing: Dorms.
Nonprofit. **Ses:** 3. **Wks/ses:** 1. Operates June-July.

This weeklong session addresses such topics as crime scene investigation, blood analysis, fingerprinting, analysis of hair and fibers, DNA analysis and ballistics analysis. Discussions and field trip complement class work. Successful completion of the program results in one semester of college credit.

MICHIGAN DEBATE INSTITUTES
Res — Coed Ages 14-17

Ann Arbor, MI 48109. 2205 Michigan Union, 530 S State St. Tel: 734-763-5903. Fax:
734-763-5902.
www.michigandebate.com   E-mail: akall@umich.edu
Aaron Kall, Dir.
Grades 9-12. Adm: FCFS. **Appl—**Fee $60. Due: June.
Type of instruction: Enrich.
Focus: Debate.

Fees 2014: Res $2400-5200, 3-7 wks.
Housing: Dorms.
Est 1985. Nonprofit. **Ses:** 3. **Wks/ses:** 3-7. Operates June-July.

With a faculty consisting of well-regarded high school and college coaches and top-tier intercollegiate debaters, these programs teach basic and advanced debating techniques to high schoolers. The three-week Michigan National Debate Institute emphasizes the development of well-organized arguments in national policy debate areas. The four-week Michigan Classic policy debate workshop provides communication skills and theory instruction for students wishing to debate at an advanced level in the coming school year. Finally, the exclusive Seven Week Program, which enrolls rising juniors and seniors, combines rigorous debate instruction with the university's extensive research facilities.

MICHIGAN STATE UNIVERSITY
CSI FORENSIC SCIENCE PROGRAM
Res and Day — Coed Ages 12-15

East Lansing, MI 48824. 186 Bessey Hall. Tel: 517-432-2129. Fax: 517-353-6464.
www.gifted.msu.edu   E-mail: gifted@msu.edu
Kathee McDonald, Dir.
Grades 7-9. Adm: Somewhat_selective. Admitted: 95%. Prereqs: GPA 3.5. **Appl**—Fee $100. Due: May. Test scores, rec.
Enr cap: 20. Intl: 5%. Non-White: 5%. **Fac 13.** Prof 4. Col/grad students 5. Specialists 4.
Staff: Admin 3. Couns 2.
Type of instruction: Adv Enrich. **Daily hours for:** Classes 5. Study 2. Rec 3.
Focus: Forensic_Sci. **Features:** Aquatics Swim.
Fees 2014: Res $1500, 1 wk. Day $750. Aid (Need).
Housing: Cabins. Avg per room/unit: 2. **Swimming:** Pool. Campus facilities avail.
Est 2006. Nonprofit. **Ses:** 1. **Wks/ses:** 1. Operates June.

Program participants learn about the field of forensic science through lectures and hands-on laboratory experiences conducted by experts in the field. Instructors include pathologists, anthropologists, entomologists, police experts, FBI agents, and volunteers who work with rescue and cadaver dogs.

MICHIGAN STATE UNIVERSITY
HIGH SCHOOL HONORS SCIENCE, MATH
AND ENGINEERING PROGRAM
Res — Coed Ages 16-17

East Lansing, MI 48824. 319 Erickson Hall. Tel: 517-432-4854.
www.education.msu.edu/hshsp   E-mail: gailr@msu.edu
Gail Richmond, Dir.
Grade 12 (younger if qualified). Adm: Very selective. **Appl**—Due: Mar. Transcript, test scores, essay, 2 recs.
Enr: 24.
Type of instruction: Adv Enrich.
Focus: Engineering Math Sci.
Fees 2011: Res $3300, 7 wks.
Housing: Dorms.
Est 1958. Ses: 1. **Wks/ses:** 7. Operates June-Aug.

Conducted on Michigan State University's Arboretum campus, HSHSP allows rising high school seniors to research individually chosen areas of science, math or engineering using the university's laboratory and library facilities. Individual research is combined with group visits to university science facilities and guidance by faculty and doctoral candidates. Participants have been recognized by the Intel Science Talent Search and the Siemens Competition in Math, Science & Technology.

MICHIGAN STATE UNIVERSITY
SPARTAN DEBATE INSTITUTES
Res — Coed Ages 14-17

East Lansing, MI 48824. 479 West Circle Dr, Rm 10. Tel: 517-798-6269. Fax: 517-432-9667.
http://debate.msu.edu/debate/sdi   E-mail: debate@msu.edu
Greta Stahl, Dir.
Grades 9-11. Adm: Selective. Appl—Due: May.
Enr cap: 120-300. Fac 19.
Focus: Debate.
Fees 2014: Res $1450-3900, 2-5 wks. Aid (Need).
Housing: Dorms. Avg per room/unit: 2.
Est 1992. Ses: 4. Wks/ses: 2-5. Operates July-Aug.

The curriculum at SDI includes lectures, labs, library research and practice debates beginning as early as the second day of camp. Lab placements accommodate all skill levels, from a pre-novice section for pupils with no debate experience to one designed for those seeking to polish elite varsity skills. Two- and three-week sessions are first-come, first-served; admission is selective for the four-week session, which is followed by an optional, nine-day strategy forum.

MICHIGAN STATE UNIVERSITY
MATH, SCIENCE & TECHNOLOGY SUMMER PROGRAM
Res — Coed Ages 12-15

East Lansing, MI 48824. 219 S Harrison Rd, Rm 8. Tel: 517-432-2129. Fax: 517-432-9541.
www.gifted.msu.edu/programs/mst-math-science-technology   E-mail: gifted@msu.edu
Kathee McDonald, Dir.
Grades 7-10. Adm: Selective. Prereqs: SAT M 520, CR 520, M/CR 960; ACT 20. Appl—Fee $100. Due: May. Transcript, essay, rec, test results.
Enr cap: 135. Fac 18. Prof 9. K-12 staff 9. Staff: Admin 3.
Type of instruction: Adv Enrich. Courses: Astron Comp_Sci Genetics Nuclear_Astrophysics Physiol Creative_Writing Filmmaking Photog Visual_Arts. Avg class size: 17. Daily hours for: Classes 4. Study 2. Rec 3. Homework.
Focus: Engineering Math Sci. Features: Basketball Soccer Swim.
Fees 2014: Res $1800, 2 wks. Day $950. Aid (Need).
Housing: Dorms. Avg per room/unit: 2. Swimming: Pool. Campus facilities avail.
Nonprofit. Ses: 1. Wks/ses: 2. Operates July.

This two-week program for academically talented boys and girls emphasizes math, science and technology, as well as applications in those areas. MST at MSU attempts to challenge students without duplicating course work that is part of the traditional kindergarten through grade 12 curriculum. Pupils investigate problems that can be explored through a better understanding of math, science, engineering and technology; focus on an intensive area of study suited to interdisciplinary research in these subject areas; and become acquainted with possible career fields. In addition to meeting academic requirements, applicants must display evidence of potential in math, science or technology through past competition participation or involvement in extracurricular activities.

MICHIGAN TECHNOLOGICAL UNIVERSITY
ENGINEERING SCHOLARS PROGRAM
Res — Coed Ages 15-17

Houghton, MI 49931. 1400 Townsend Dr, 217 Administration Bldg. Tel: 906-487-2219, 888-773-2655. Fax: 906-487-1136.

www.syp.mtu.edu   E-mail: esp@mtu.edu
Jamie Lindquist, Coord.
Grades 10-12 (younger if qualified). Adm: Selective. Admitted: 80%. Priority: URM.
Appl—Fee $0. Due: Apr. Transcript, rec, essay.
Enr: 120-150. **Enr cap:** 150. Intl: 1%. Non-White: 60%. **Fac 20.** Prof 10. Col/grad students
10. **Staff:** Admin 7. Couns 50.
Type of instruction: Adv Enrich. **Courses:** Comp_Sci Math Sci Crafts. **Avg class size:**
12. **Daily hours for:** Classes 8. Rec 3.
Focus: Engineering. **Features:** Swim.
Fees 2014: Free. Res (+$295), 1 wk.
Housing: Dorms. **Swimming:** Lake Pool. Campus facilities avail.
Est 1973. Nonprofit. **Ses:** 1. **Wks/ses:** 1. Operates June-July.

MTU offers a weeklong summer engineering program for high school students. The Engineering Scholars Program enrolls boys and girls from minority or economically or educationally disadvantaged backgrounds, while Women in Engineering serves young women. Students explore careers in mechanical, environmental, electrical, chemical, civil, geological and material engineering, as well as such other disciplines as mathematics, technology, technical writing and computer science. The program features hands-on laboratory and field exercises, group projects, visits with engineering professionals, college and career planning advice, and recreational activities.

MIDDLEBURY-MONTEREY LANGUAGE ACADEMY
Res — Coed Ages 13-17

Middlebury, VT 05753. 152 Maple St. Tel: 802-443-2900, 888-216-0135. Fax: 802-443-3220.
http://mmla.middlebury.edu/learn-more   E-mail: mmla.info@middlebury.edu
Amy Kluber, Dir.
Grades 8-12. Adm: Selective. **Appl**—Fee $350 dpsit. Due: Rolling. Transcript, essay in
target language.
Type of instruction: Adv Enrich Undergrad. **Courses:** Crafts Media Music Photog. **Avg
class size:** 15.
Locations— CA OH PA VT.
Focus: Arabic Chin Fr Ger Span. **Features:** Swim.
Fees 2014: Res $5995-6295, 4 wks.
Housing: Dorms. **Swimming:** Pool.
Est 2008. Spons: Middlebury College/Monterey Institute of International Studies. **Wks/
ses:** 4. Operates June-July.

Middlebury Interactive Languages conducts four-week residential programs at Green Mountain College in Poultney, Vermont; Pomona College in Claremont, California; and Swarthmore College in Swarthmore, Pennsylvania. Students work on fluency and comprehension skills in Arabic, Chinese, French, German or Spanish each morning, then spend the rest of the day reinforcing their language skills during meals, field trips and recreational camp activities. MMLA groups pupils by ability level and houses them with others who are studying the same language. Weekend activities for boarders include field trips to local recreational and cultural attractions.

MISSOURI UNIVERSITY OF SCIENCE & TECHNOLOGY
JACKLING INTRODUCTION TO ENGINEERING
Res and Day — Coed Ages 16-18

**Rolla, MO 65409. Distance & Continuing Ed, 216 Centennial Hall, 300 W 12th St. Tel:
573-341-6222. Fax: 573-341-4992.**
https://futurestudents.mst.edu/summercamps/intro   E-mail: dce@mst.edu
Will Perkins, Dir.
Grades 11-12. Adm: FCFS. **Appl**—Due: Rolling.

Type of instruction: Enrich.
Focus: Engineering.
Fees 2014: Res $500, 1 wk. Day $420, 1 wk.
Housing: Dorms.
Ses: 3. **Wks/ses:** 1. Operates June-July.

This five-day introductory course helps students understand the relationship that mathematics and the sciences have to engineering. Rising high school juniors and seniors learn about engineering disciplines and work on hands-on projects. Laboratory and industry visits and evening student competitions complete the program.

MISSOURI UNIVERSITY OF SCIENCE & TECHNOLOGY
MINORITY INTRODUCTION TO TECHNOLOGY & ENGINEERING
Res — Coed Ages 15-18

Rolla, MO 65409. Center for Pre-College Prgms, 500 W 16th St, 212 Engineering Research Lab. Tel: 573-341-4228. Fax: 573-341-4890.
http://sdowp.mst.edu/outreachindex/mite   E-mail: precollege@mst.edu
Frank Mack, Coord.
Grades 11-12 (younger if qualified). Adm: Somewhat selective. Admitted: 90%. Priority: URM. **Appl**—Fee $0. Due: Apr. Transcript, rec.
Enr: 30. **Enr cap:** 30. Non-White: 100%. **Fac 15.** Prof 11. Col/grad students 4. **Staff:** Admin 1. Couns 5.
Type of instruction: Enrich Preview.
Focus: Engineering.
Fees 2014: Res $180 (+$50), 1 wk. Aid 2009 (Merit & Need): $1800.
Housing: Dorms. Campus facilities avail.
Ses: 2. **Wks/ses:** 1. Operates June.

African-American, Hispanic and Native American students preview college life while learning about engineering careers and the demands faced by professional engineers. Participants devote mornings listening to lectures on various engineering disciplines, then gain practical engineering experience during afternoon lab and industry visits. Orientation sessions address admissions procedures and requirements, scholarships and financial aid. Recreational and social activities, which include sports, bowling, dances and picnics, enable boys and girls to interact with current Missouri S&T undergraduates.

MISSOURI UNIVERSITY OF SCIENCE & TECHNOLOGY
NUCLEAR ENGINEERING CAMP
Res — Coed Ages 16-19

Rolla, MO 65409. Nuclear Engineering Dept, 222 Fulton Hall, 301 W 14th St. Tel: 573-341-4720. Fax: 573-341-4174.
http://nuclear.mst.edu   E-mail: nuclear@mst.edu
Grades 11-PG. Adm: Selective. **Appl**—Fee $0. Due: Rolling. Transcript, ACT/SAT scores, rec.
Enr: 30. **Enr cap:** 30.
Type of instruction: Enrich.
Focus: Engineering.
Fees 2014: Res $600, 1 wk.
Housing: Dorms.
Ses: 1. **Wks/ses:** 1. Operates July.

This weeklong introduction to nuclear engineering careers features tours of a nuclear reactor and nuclear power plant; focus groups on the nuclear fuel cycle, reactor operations and radiation reality; and experiments on natural radioactivity, reactor operations and reactor shielding.

MONTE VISTA CHRISTIAN SCHOOL
ESL SUMMER INTENSIVE LANGUAGE INSTITUTE
Res — Coed Ages 12-16

Watsonville, CA 95076. 2 School Way. Tel: 831-722-8178. Fax: 831-722-6003.
www.mvcs.org/495079.ihtml E-mail: admissions@mvcs.org
Kim Dawes, Dir. Student contact: Peter C. Gieseke, E-mail: petergieseke@mvcs.org.
Adm: FCFS. Admitted: 95%. Appl—Fee $0. Due: Rolling.
Enr: 24. Enr cap: 35. Intl: 100%. Fac 4. Staff: Admin 1. Couns 7.
Courses: Drama Fine_Arts Music. Avg class size: 8. Daily hours for: Classes 4½. Study
2. Rec 3. Homework. Tests.
Focus: ESL. Features: Cooking Swim.
Fees 2014: Res $6900 (+$200), 5 wks.
Housing: Dorms. Swimming: Pool. Campus facilities avail.
Est 1926. Nonprofit. Nondenom Christian. Ses: 1. Wks/ses: 5. Operates July-Aug.

Monte Vista helps students improve their English skills and learn more about American culture. Boys and girls receive language instruction at the beginning, intermediate and advanced levels. Evening and weekend leisure activities and trips provide further opportunities for pupils to develop their skills.

NASA/MORGAN STATE UNIVERSITY
SUMMER INSTITUTE OF ROBOTICS
Res — Coed Ages 15-18

Baltimore, MD 21251. School of Engineering, 1700 E Coldspring Ln. Tel: 301-286-0904.
www.nasa.gov/offices/education/programs
David Rosage, Dir.
Grades 10-12. Adm: Very selective. Admitted: 12%. Priority: URM.
Enr cap: 25. Intl: 12%.
Type of instruction: Adv Enrich. Courses: Public_Speak. Daily hours for: Classes 6½.
Study 1½.
Focus: Comp_Sci Engineering.
Fees 2014: Free. Res 4 wks.
Housing: Dorms.
Est 2006. Ses: 1. Wks/ses: 4.

Developed as a collaboration between the NASA Robotics Academy at Goddard Space Flight Center and the School of Engineering at Morgan State University, SIR aims to increase the knowledge and understanding of the concepts and principles of robotics for urban high school students. Instruction covers robotic theory and design, computer programming and presentation skills. Lab work allows students to put skills to use in weekly competitions. The program also features visits to corporations that specialize in robotics, as well as trips to nearby engineering organizations and agencies.

NATIONAL COMPUTER CAMPS
Res and Day — Coed Ages 8-18

Milford, CT 06460. 102 Shorefront. Tel: 203-710-5771. Fax: 313-557-1999.
www.nccamp.com E-mail: info@nccamp.com
Michael Zabinski, Exec Dir.
Grades 2-12. Adm: FCFS. Appl—Fee $0. Due: Rolling.
Enr: 75. Enr cap: 75. Fac 12.
Type of instruction: Enrich.
Locations: CT GA NY OH.
Focus: Comp_Sci Computers. Features: Basketball Soccer Swim Tennis.
Fees 2014: Res $1095, 1 wk. Day $895, 1 wk.

Housing: Dorms. **Swimming:** Pool.
Est 1977. Inc. **Ses:** 15. **Wks/ses:** 1. Operates June-Aug.

These camps operate at Fairfield University (Fairfield, CT), Oglethorpe University (Atlanta, GA) and John Caroroll University (Cleveland, OH). Small-group instruction is provided through workshops and lab sessions. NCC focuses on video game design, computer programming, digital video production, Web page design, and such software applications as animation, Flash and graphics. Campers may attend for one or more weeks; the continuous curriculum runs from beginning through highly advanced levels. An optional athletic program is available.

NATIONAL YOUTH SCIENCE CAMP
Res — Coed Ages 17-18

Bartow, WV.
Contact (Year-round): c/o Natl Youth Science Foundation, PO Box 3387, Charleston, WV 25333. **Tel:** 304-342-3326. **Fax:** 866-833-0875.
www.nysc.org E-mail: office@nysf.com
Andrew N. Blackwood, Dir.
Grade PG. Adm: Very selective. **Appl**—Due: Mar.
Enr: 100. **Enr cap:** 100.
Type of instruction: Adv Enrich.
Focus: Sci. **Features:** Caving Hiking Kayak Mtn_Biking Rock_Climb Ultimate_Frisbee.
Fees 2014: Free. Res 3½ wks.
Housing: Cabins.
Est 1963. Nonprofit. **Spons:** National Youth Science Foundation. **Ses:** 1. **Wks/ses:** 3½. Operates July.

The governor of each state helps appoint two newly graduated delegates to this free science camp each year. A roster of educators and researchers leads NYSC, which has three main academic components: 60- to 90-minute lectures that are delivered to the entire camp community; directed study, three 90-minute sessions that consist of roughly 10 students and a presenter and typically involve a larger project or trips to a specific ecological area or scientific facility; and seminars, which are sometimes led by delegates and which may be nonscientific and informal. An unusual aspect of NYSC's session is the well-developed outdoor program: Students engage in a variety of outdoor activities, including overnight backpacking and camping trips that range from short, nature-based hikes to more challenging backpacking treks along rough terrain.

NORTH CAROLINA STATE UNIVERSITY
SUMMER COLLEGE IN BIOTECHNOLOGY AND LIFE SCIENCES
Res and Day — Coed Ages 16-18

Raleigh, NC 27695. Campus Box 7642. **Tel:** 919-515-2614. **Fax:** 919-515-5266.
http://harvest.cals.ncsu.edu/academic/index.cfm?pageID=1975
E-mail: summer_college@ncsu.edu
William Edwards, Dir.
Grades 11-12 (younger if qualified). Adm: Selective. Prereqs: GPA 3.5. **Appl**—Fee $0. Due: May.
Enr: 54. **Fac 4. Staff:** Admin 1. Couns 10.
Type of instruction: Adv. **Avg class size:** 18. **Daily hours for:** Classes 6½. Homework. Tests. Grades. **College credit:** 3/crse, total 3.
Focus: Sci. **Features:** Swim.
Fees 2014: Res $1752-3330 (+$400), 4 wks. Day $1282, 4 wks.
Housing: Dorms. **Swimming:** Pool.
Est 2003. Nonprofit. **Ses:** 1. **Wks/ses:** 4. Operates July-Aug.

Designed for college-bound students with a strong interest in science, SCIBLS offers rigorous course work, hands-on laboratory experiences and a preview of college life. Tours of nearby research facilities and visits with industry professionals complement course offerings, which include molecular biology, biotechnology, microbiology and biochemistry. Boarders participate in group activities on weekends and are responsible for their own meals. Applicants have completed high school biology and chemistry classes.

NORTHWESTERN COLLEGE NEUROSCIENCE CAMP
Res — Coed Ages 16-18

Orange City, IA 51041. **Department of Biology, 101 7th St SW. Tel: 712-707-7006.**
www.nwciowa.edu/biology/neuroscience/camp **E-mail: redavis@nwciowa.edu**
Ralph Davis, Dir.
Grades 11-12. Adm: Selective. **Appl**—Due: Rolling. Rec.
Enr cap: 10.
Type of instruction: Enrich. **Daily hours for:** Classes 7.
Focus: Med/Healthcare Psych Sci.
Fees 2014: Res $650, 1 wk.
Housing: Apartments.
Ses: 2. **Wks/ses:** 1. Operates June.

Lectures, demonstrations and hands-on experiments introduce NNC students to the study of the brain and nervous system. Participants conduct electrophysiology and neuropharmacology experiments, dissect a sheep brain, use computer simulation to dissect a human brain and learn to record electrical activity. The week includes visits to a local hospital's active neuroscience laboratories and imaging and scanning facilities.

NORTHWESTERN UNIVERSITY
NATIONAL HIGH SCHOOL INSTITUTE
Res — Coed Ages 15-18

Evanston, IL 60208. 617 Noyes St. **Tel: 847-491-3026, 800-662-6474. Fax: 847-467-1057.**
www.northwestern.edu/nhsi **E-mail: nhsi@northwestern.edu**
Adam Joyce, Dir.
Grades 10-12. Adm: Selective. **Appl**—Fee $50. Transcript, PSAT scores, rec.
Enr cap: 30-80. Fac 22.
Type of instruction: Adv Enrich. **Courses:** Media Music. **Avg class size:** 15. **Daily hours for:** Classes 9. Study 2.
Focus: Debate Speech Writing/Journ. **Features:** Swim.
Fees 2014: Res $1150-7300, 4 wks. Aid (Merit & Need).
Housing: Dorms. **Swimming:** Lake.
Est 1931. Nonprofit. **Ses:** 2. **Wks/ses:** 4. Operates July-Aug.

Serving academically talented high school students, NHSI programs in speech and debate comprise classes, workshops, field trips, projects and lectures. The Debate Institute offers rigorous four- and five-week programs for rising sophomores, juniors and seniors, with an emphasis on incoming seniors. Students attending the Speech Division's four-week session train for competition in debate, interpretation, oratory and extemporaneous speaking. Group outings and social events balance class work. Northwestern also conducts workshops in film and video production, musical theater and theater arts (see separate listing for details).

ODYSSEY EXPEDITIONS
TROPICAL MARINE BIOLOGY VOYAGES
Res — Coed Ages 13-25

Tarpon Springs, FL 34689. 418 Shaddock St. **Tel: 352-400-4076, 800-929-7749. Fax: 815-642-1272.**

www.odysseyexpeditions.com E-mail: odyssey@usa.net
Jason Buchheim & Jon Buchheim, Dirs.
Grades 7-Col. Adm: FCFS. **Appl**—Fee $0. Due: Rolling.
Enr: 48. **Enr cap:** 48. Intl: 10%. Non-White: 5%. **Fac 14.** Col/grad students 6. Specialists
  8. **Staff:** Admin 3. Res 15.
Type of instruction: Enrich. **Courses:** Ecol Environ_Sci Photog. **Avg class size:** 10.
  Daily hours for: Classes 3. Study 3. Rec 3. Homework. Tests. **College credit:** 5.
Intl program focus: Acad. **Locations:** Caribbean.
Focus: Marine_Bio/Stud Oceanog. **Features:** Adventure_Travel Community_Serv
  Conservation Fishing Sail Scuba Seamanship Swim Water-skiing Watersports.
Fees 2014: Res $4690-5390, 2-4 wks.
Swimming: Ocean.
Est 1996. Inc. **Ses:** 11. **Wks/ses:** 2-4. Operates June-Aug.

Odyssey Expeditions conducts four marine biology voyages for capable swimmers. Discovery Voyages, which explores the British Virgin Islands, comprises scuba certification programs, sailing instruction, watersports, island exploration and more than 20 dives. The SEA program emphasizes marine biology research while also providing instruction in navigation and underwater photography. Advanced divers age 18 and up may enroll in Divemaster Challenge, which provides hands-on training for those considering a career in the field.

THE OHIO STATE UNIVERSITY
ROSS MATHEMATICS PROGRAM
Res — Coed Ages 14-18

Columbus, OH 43210. **Dept of Mathematics, 231 W 18th Ave. Tel:** 614-292-5101. **Fax:** 614-292-1479.
www.math.ohio-state.edu/ross E-mail: ross@math.osu.edu
Daniel Shapiro, Dir.
Grades 9-PG. Adm: Very selective. **Appl**—Due: Rolling. Transcript, teacher recs, essays.
Type of instruction: Adv Enrich Undergrad.
Focus: Math.
Fees 2014: Res $2700, 8 wks. Aid (Need).
Housing: Dorms.
Est 1957. Nonprofit. **Ses:** 1. **Wks/ses:** 8. Operates June-July.

A partnership between the university and the Clay Mathematics Institute, this intensive program enrolls precollege students who have displayed significant achievement in math. Participants explore concepts in number theory; work with mathematical ideas built from concrete observations and resulting in proofs of general patterns and abstract properties; and develop learning strategies for use in later scientific endeavors. On weekday mornings, students attend a number theory lecture and receive a problem set that leads to further exploration. Pupils also attend problem seminars given by experienced faculty members.

COLORADO SCHOOL OF MINES
SUMMER MULTICULTURAL ENGINEERING TRAINING PROGRAM
Res — Coed Ages 16-17

Golden, CO 80401. **1112 18th St. Tel:** 303-273-3286, 800-446-9488. **Fax:** 303-273-3760.
http://mep.mines.edu E-mail: mep@mines.edu
Louisa Duley, Asst Dir.
Grades 11-12. Adm: Selective. Priority: URM. **Appl**—Fee $0. Due: Apr. Transcript, 2 recs, essays.
Enr: 24. **Fac 8. Staff:** Res 6.
Type of instruction: Enrich. **Courses:** Comp_Sci Geol Math Sci. **Avg class size:** 24.
  Homework. Tests. Grades.
Focus: Engineering. **Features:** Swim.
Fees 2014: Free. Res (+$50), 3 wks.

Housing: Dorms. **Swimming:** Pool.
Est 1971. Nonprofit. **Ses:** 1. **Wks/ses:** 3. Operates June-July.

Designed for talented rising high school juniors and seniors with strong aptitude in math and science and a minority background, the SUMMET Program combines class work, hands-on projects, industry tours, athletic activities and social events. The curriculum, which consists of various math and science courses, addresses basic to advanced engineering concepts.

OPERATION ENTERPRISE
Res — Coed Ages 16-25

New York, NY 10019. c/o American Management Assoc, 1601 Broadway, 8th Fl. Tel:
212-586-8100, 800-634-4262. Fax: 212-903-8509.
www.amanet.org/advantage/operation-enterprise.aspx   E-mail:
operationenterprise@amanet.org
Marina Marmut, Dir.
Grades 11-Col. Adm: Selective. **Appl**—Due: Apr. Transcript, rec.
Enr: 25-30. **Enr cap:** 25-30. **Fac 10. Staff:** Admin 2. Couns 5.
Type of instruction: Adv Enrich. **Avg class size:** 25. **Daily hours for:** Classes 6. Study 1. Rec 3. **College credit:** 3.
Locations: GA NY TX.
Focus: Bus/Fin. **Features:** Leadership Swim.
Fees 2009: Res $1750, 1 wk. Aid (Need).
Housing: Dorms. **Swimming:** Pool.
Est 1963. Nonprofit. **Spons:** American Management Association. **Ses:** 4. **Wks/ses:** 1.
Operates June-Aug.

This management and leadership development program consists of high school and college divisions. High school programs operate at Emory University (Atlanta, GA), Columbia University (New York, NY) and the University of Texas-Austin. Senior executives and American Management Association faculty conduct highly interactive, practical workshops that focus upon the skills necessary for success in business. The core curriculum in each program addresses leadership, management, business writing, presentation skills, strategic planning and negotiation. Practice presentations (given to a board of directors) and a full-day management simulation complete the program.

OREGON MUSEUM OF SCIENCE AND INDUSTRY
SCIENCE CAMPS AND ADVENTURES
Res — Coed Ages 7-18

Portland, OR 97214. 1945 SE Water Ave. Tel: 503-797-4661. Fax: 503-239-7800.
www.omsi.edu/camps-classes   E-mail: register@omsi.edu
Travis Neumeyer, Dir.
Grades 3-PG. Adm: FCFS. **Appl**—Fee $0. Due: Rolling.
Enr: 35. **Enr cap:** 40. **Fac 4.** Specialists 4. **Staff:** Admin 6. Couns 30.
Courses: Archaeol Astron Ecol Environ_Sci Geol Marine_Bio/Stud. **Avg class size:** 12.
Daily hours for: Classes 6. Study 6. Rec 6.
Locations: CA ID OR UT WA.
Focus: Sci. **Features:** Canoe Climbing_Wall Conservation Exploration Hiking Mtn_Trips Survival_Trng White-water_Raft Wilderness_Camp Swim.
Fees 2014: Res $565-875, 1-2 wks. Aid 2008 (Need): $90,000.
Housing: Cabins Houses Lodges Tents Tepees. Avg per room/unit: 8. **Swimming:** Lake Pond Ocean River.
Est 1951. Nonprofit. **Ses:** 86. **Wks/ses:** 1-3. Operates June-Aug.

Numerous science-oriented outdoor education courses—ranging from high-adventure backpacking trips to residential camp programs—are available in various locations throughout the West. Programs for young people, organized according to age, serve campers ages 7-10, 10-12, 12-14 and 14-18.

OREGON STATE UNIVERSITY
SUMMER EXPERIENCE IN SCIENCE
AND ENGINEERING FOR YOUTH
Res — Coed Ages 15-18

Corvallis, OR 97331. **School of Chemical, Biological & Environmental Engineering, 103 Gleeson Hall. Tel: 541-737-4791. Fax: 541-737-4600.**
http://cbee.oregonstate.edu/sesey   E-mail: skip.rochefort@oregonstate.edu
Willie E. Rochefort, Dir.
Grades 10-12. Adm: Selective. Priority: URM. **Appl**—Due: May. Transcript, essay.
Type of instruction: Enrich.
Focus: Engineering Sci.
Fees 2014: Res $200, 1 wk. Aid (Need).
Housing: Dorms.
Est 1997. Ses: 1. **Wks/ses:** 1. Operates July.

Targeting high school girls and minorities traditionally underrepresented in science and engineering, SESEY places students in research groups from Oregon State University's departments of chemical engineering or bioengineering. Each pupil works with a faculty member and college student mentors on such projects as plastics recycling, biomedical polymers, materials processing, biomedical technology and waste remediation. The program also includes a trip to the Hatfield Marine Science Center, computer instruction and evening recreational programs.

PICKERING COLLEGE ESL SUMMER CAMP
Res — Coed Ages 12-18

Newmarket, L3Y 4X2 Ontario, Canada. **16945 Bayview Ave. Tel: 905-895-1700, 877-895-1700. Fax: 905-895-1306.**
www.pickeringcollege.on.ca   E-mail: eslsummer@pickeringcollege.on.ca
Claudia Chavez, Coord.
Grades 7-12. Adm: FCFS. **Appl**—Due: Apr.
Enr: 45. **Fac** 3. **Staff:** Admin 2. Couns 7.
Type of instruction: Enrich. **Courses:** Debate Expository_Writing Speech Crafts Creative_Writing Dance Drama. **Daily hours for:** Classes 5. Study ½. Rec 6.
Intl program focus: Acad Lang Culture.
Focus: ESL. **Features:** Aquatics Archery Canoe Climbing_Wall Rock_Climb Ropes_Crse Baseball Basketball Golf Soccer Softball Swim Ultimate_Frisbee Volleyball.
Fees 2014: Res Can$4000-5200 (+Can$200-300), 4 wks.
Housing: Dorms. Avg per room/unit: 2. **Swimming:** Pool. Campus facilities avail.
Est 1990. Nonprofit. **Ses:** 2. **Wks/ses:** 3-4. Operates June-Aug.

Serving boys and girls planning to study in an English-speaking school or intending to take English as an academic subject in the home country, this college English as a Second Language program combines daytime academics with evening and weekend activities. Off-campus excursions serve to further improve English skills. Although the session length is four weeks, students may enroll for eight weeks.

PURDUE UNIVERSITY ACCESS ENGINEERING
Res and Day — Girls Ages 6-12

West Lafayette, IN 47907. **701 W Stadium Ave. Tel: 765-494-3889. Fax: 765-496-1349.**
www.engineering.purdue.edu/wiep/programs   E-mail: wiep@purdue.edu
Sue Bayley, Prgm Coord. Student contact: Jennifer Groh, E-mail: jgroh@purdue.edu.
Grades K-8. Adm: Somewhat selective. Admitted: 90%. **Appl**—Fee $0. Due: Apr. Teacher rec.
Enr: 40. **Enr cap:** 40. Non-White: 30%. **Fac** 8. Prof 4. Col/grad students 4. **Staff:** Admin 3. Res 10.

Type of instruction: Preview. **Courses:** Crafts.
Focus: Engineering. **Features:** Swim.
Fees 2012: Res $400-450 (+$15-20), 1 wk. Aid 2010 (Need): $5000.
Housing: Dorms. Avg per room/unit: 2. **Swimming:** Pool.
Est 2000. Nonprofit. **Ses:** 3. **Wks/ses:** 1. Operates June-Aug.

Purdue's offers the Access Engineering program for young women in grades K-8with an interest in engineering as a potential career choice. Participants learn about various engineering disciplines, tour engineering laboratories and production facilities, and meet faculty and graduate pupils who are engaged in cutting-edge research.

PURDUE UNIVERSITY
SEMINAR FOR TOP ENGINEERING PROSPECTS
Res — Coed Ages 17-18

West Lafayette, IN 47907. College of Engineering Honors, 550 Stadium Mall Dr, Rm G293. Tel: 765-494-3976. Fax: 765-494-5819.
www.engineering.purdue.edu/Engr/InfoFor/Honors/STEP   E-mail: step@purdue. edu
Grade 12. Adm: Selective. **Appl**—Due: Rolling.
Type of instruction: Enrich.
Focus: Engineering.
Fees 2014: Res $860-910, 1 wk. Aid (Need).
Housing: Dorms.
Ses: 2. **Wks/ses:** 1. Operates July.

STEP enables rising high school seniors to explore various engineering disciplines and job functions. Tours, demonstrations, classroom experiences and projects teach students about engineering and offer a preview of college life. Students work on engineering problems using software packages such as Microsoft Excel.

THE PUTNEY SCHOOL
PROGRAM FOR INTERNATIONAL EDUCATION
Res — Coed Ages 14-17

Putney, VT 05346. Elm Lea Farm, 418 Houghton Brook Rd. Tel: 802-387-6297. Fax: 802-387-6216.
www.putneyschoolsummer.org   E-mail: summer@putneyschool.org
Thomas D. Howe, Dir.
Grades 9-12. Adm: FCFS. **Appl**—Fee $50. Due: Rolling.
Enr: 20. **Fac** 40. **Staff:** Admin 7. Couns 18.
Type of instruction: Courses: Dance Drawing Music Painting Sculpt Theater. **Avg class size:** 10. **Daily hours for:** Classes 6. Rec 2.
Focus: ESL. **Features:** Farm Hiking Basketball Equestrian Soccer Swim Volleyball.
Fees 2014: Res $4125-7525, 3-6 wks. Day $1535-2650. Aid (Need).
Housing: Dorms. **Swimming:** Pond.
Est 1987. Nonprofit. **Ses:** 2. **Wks/ses:** 3. Operates June-Aug.

PIE serves international students interested in improving their English language skills. Morning classes emphasize speaking and listening and incorporate work in writing, vocabulary and grammar. In the afternoon, students work on supervised group projects of their own design, embark on local trips or take part in outdoor activities with other Putney summer students. Regularly scheduled field trips to places of cultural interest are part of the program, as is a weekly full-day excursion to a larger city such as Montpelier, Burlington or Boston, MA.

PUTNEY STUDENT TRAVEL LANGUAGE LEARNING PROGRAMS
Res — Coed Ages 14-18

Putney, VT 05346. 345 Hickory Ridge Rd. Tel: 802-387-5885. Fax: 802-387-4276. www.goputney.com E-mail: info@goputney.com Peter Shumlin & Jeffrey Shumlin, Dirs.
Grades 9-PG. Adm: FCFS. **Appl**—Fee $0. Due: Rolling.
Enr: 14-22.
Intl program focus: Lang. **Locations:** Europe Mexico/Central_America South_America. Home stays avail.
Focus: Fr Span. **Features:** Adventure_Travel Bicycle_Tours Exploration Hiking Rock_ Climb Sail Watersports.
Fees 2014: Res $3390-9690, 2-5½ wks.
Est 1952. Ses: 8. **Wks/ses:** 4½-5½. Operates June-Aug.

PST's overseas language programs allow pupils to study French in France and Spanish in Spain, Argentina or Costa Rica. Programs combine carefully planned itineraries with an active language learning approach. Students move toward fluency by communicating with local people during the course of everyday activities, and participants must agree to speak only the target language during the course of the program.

RESEARCH SCIENCE INSTITUTE
Res — Coed Ages 13-18

Cambridge, MA. Massachusetts Inst of Technology.
Contact (Year-round): 8201 Greensboro Dr, Ste 215, McLean, VA 22102. Tel: 703-448-9062. Fax: 703-448-9068.
www.cee.org/programs/rsi E-mail: rsi@cee.org
Maite Ballestero, Dir.
Grade 12. Adm: Very selective. Prereqs: PSAT M/CR/W 220. **Appl**—Fee $50. Due: Jan. Transcript, standardized test results, 2 recs, essay.
Enr: 80. **Enr cap:** 80. **Fac** 5. **Staff:** Admin 9. Couns 6.
Type of instruction: Adv. **Avg class size:** 15. **Daily hours for:** Classes 6. Study 4. Rec 2. Homework.
Focus: Engineering Math Sci.
Fees 2014: Free. Res 6 wks.
Housing: Dorms.
Est 1984. Nonprofit. **Spons:** Center for Excellence in Education. **Ses:** 1. **Wks/ses:** 6. Operates June-Aug.

Held at the Massachusetts Institute of Technology, this tuition-free program combines on-campus course work with hands-on research experience. The first week of the program is dedicated to college-level classes in mathematics, science, engineering, computer skills and research techniques. Students spend the next four weeks conducting open-ended, relevant research projects at Boston-area colleges, universities, hospitals and corporate facilities, supervised by noted scientists and mathematicians. Students deliver their findings in conference-style oral and written presentations during the final week. Guest lectures, field trips around Boston and a weekend trip to the beach round out the program. Successful applicants should demonstrate superior achievement in math and science in the classroom and beyond. Exceptional students as young as 13 may apply if they have completed grade 11. Participants have been recognized by the Intel Science Talent Search; the Intel International Science and Engineering Fair; and the Siemens Competition in Math, Science & Technology.

ROBERT WOOD JOHNSON MEDICAL SCHOOL
SUMMER SCIENCE SCHOLARS ACADEMY
Res and Day — Coed Ages 17-18

**Piscataway, NJ 08854. Office of Special Academic Prgms, 675 Hoes Ln, Rm N-224.
Tel: 732-235-4558. Fax: 732-235-2121.
www.rwjms.umdnj.edu/education/sap/s3a.html**   **E-mail: summerprogram@umdnj.
edu
Grades 12-PG. Adm:** Very selective. Prereqs: GPA 3.5. **Appl**—Due: Mar. Transcript, rec,
essay.
Type of instruction: Adv Enrich SAT/ACT_Prep Study_Skills. **Courses:** Anat & Physiol.
Focus: Med/Healthcare Sci.
Fees: Day $3000, 4 wks.
Housing: Dorms.
Ses: 1. **Wks/ses:** 4. Operates June-July.

This program for high-achieving students interested in medicine focuses on exploring the human body through a series of lectures, organ laboratories and clinical experiences. Core courses address anatomy, physiology, biopharmaceuticals and research methods in health. The academy also includes seminars on science and health career planning, clinical skills, public health and patient-centered care. SSSA enrolls only those pupils who have previously attended a health or science summer program.

ROSE-HULMAN INSTITUTE OF TECHNOLOGY
OPERATION CATAPULT
Res — Coed Ages 16-18

**Terre Haute, IN 47803. 5500 Wabash Ave. Tel: 812-877-8893, 800-248-7448. Fax: 812-
877-8941.
www.rose-hulman.edu/catapult**   **E-mail: admissions@rose-hulman.edu**
Patsy Brackin, Dir. Student contact: Abby Croft, **E-mail:** abby.croft@rose-hulman.
edu.
Grade 12. Adm: Selective. **Appl**—Fee $0. Due: Rolling. Counselor rec, standardized test scores.
Enr: 102-116. **Enr cap:** 125. **Fac 9.** Prof 9. **Staff:** Admin 4. Couns 11.
Type of instruction: Adv. **College credit:** 2.
Focus: Engineering Math Sci. **Features:** Caving Outdoor_Ed Basketball Soccer Swim Ultimate_Frisbee Volleyball.
Fees 2014: Res $2500 (+$100-150), 2½ wks.
Housing: Dorms. Avg per room/unit: 2. **Swimming:** Pond Pool. Campus facilities avail.
Est 1965. Nonprofit. **Ses:** 2. **Wks/ses:** 2½. Operates June-July.

Operation Catapult exposes students to principles of engineering and applied science through group project work. Groups design and conduct experiments, collect and analyze data, reach conclusions and make recommendations for further study. Lectures, demonstrations and tours of industrial plants round out the program. Applicants must have taken three years of high school mathematics and at least one year of chemistry or physics. College credit for program completion is available to those pupils who later matriculate at RHIT.

ROXBURY LATIN SCHOOL
ADVANCED BIOTECHNOLOGY INSTITUTE
Res and Day — Coed Ages 14-18

**West Roxbury, MA 02132. 101 St Theresa Ave. Tel: 617-325-0547. Fax: 617-325-3585.
www.biotech-institute.org**   **E-mail: lmurphy3@post.harvard.edu**
Lawrence J. Murphy, Dir.
Grades 9-12 (younger if qualified). Adm: Selective. Admitted: 40%. **Appl**—Fee $0. Due:
Apr. Transcript, sci teacher rec, essay.

Enr: 20. **Enr cap:** 20. Intl: 20%. Non-White: 20%. **Fac 3.** K-12 staff 3. **Staff:** Couns 3.
Type of instruction: Adv Enrich. **Daily hours for:** Classes 7½. Study ½. Rec ½. Homework.
Focus: Sci. **Features:** Swim Volleyball.
Fees 2014: Res $3400, 3 wks.
Housing: Dorms. Avg per room/unit: 1-2. **Swimming:** Pool.
Est 2002. Ses: 1. **Wks/ses:** 3. Operates June-July.

ABI conducts an advanced lab-based curriculum in DNA and protein science for top-tier high school science students. During the session, boys and girls apply the scientific method while exploring such topics as genetic engineering, DNA fingerprinting, immunology, genetically modified foods and gene silencing. Enhancing the rigorous program are visits to biotechnology and pharmaceutical companies and a lab-based excursion to the Woods Hole Oceanographic Institution on Cape Cod.

RUTGERS YOUNG SCHOLARS PROGRAM
IN DISCRETE MATHEMATICS
Res — Coed Ages 15-17

Piscataway, NJ 08854. SERC Bldg, Rm 225, 118 Frelinghuysen Rd. Tel: 848-445-4065.
www.dimacs.rutgers.edu/ysp   E-mail: jemara@dimacs.rutgers.edu
Jean Mara, Dir.
Grades 10-12. Adm: Selective. **Appl**—Due: Rolling. Math problems, rec.
Enr: 30. **Enr cap:** 30.
Type of instruction: Adv Enrich.
Focus: Math.
Fees 2014: Res $3500, 4 wks. Aid (Need).
Housing: Dorms.
Est 1994. Nonprofit. **Spons:** Rutgers University. **Ses:** 1. **Wks/ses:** 4. Operates July-Aug.

This intensive program serves mathematically talented high schoolers who are considering careers in the mathematical sciences. Students gain an introduction to the growing area of discrete mathematics, in the process enhancing their problem-solving abilities by applying mathematical concepts to an array of problems. During the course of the four weeks, boys and girls also meet with professionals in the field who serve as mentors and help the student assess his or her suitability for a career in math. Instructional sessions, field trips, research projects, technology-based activities, career workshops, and informal evening and recreational activities are all part of the program.

SAINT JOHN'S PREPARATORY SCHOOL GERMAN CAMP
Res — Coed Ages 8-16

Collegeville, MN 56321. 1857 Watertower Rd, PO Box 4000. Tel: 320-363-3315, 800-525-7737. Fax: 320-363-3513.
www.sjprep.net   E-mail: admitprep@csbsju.edu
Jason Kirsch, Dir.
Adm: FCFS. **Appl**—Fee $0. Due: Rolling.
Enr cap: 75. **Staff:** Admin 2. Couns 8.
Type of instruction: Enrich.
Focus: Ger. **Features:** Canoe Fishing Hiking Swim.
Fees 2014: Res $400 (+$20), 1 wk.
Housing: Dorms. **Swimming:** Lake Pool. Campus facilities avail.
Est 1979. Nonprofit. Roman Catholic. **Ses:** 1. **Wks/ses:** 1. Operates June.

German Camp enables children to study the German language and learn about German and Austrian culture. Campers receive individualized attention and work closely with counselors and other children in small groups. Native speakers of German and teachers and students who have studied in German-speaking countries constitute the staff. Applicants need not possess any previous knowledge of German.

ST. OLAF COLLEGE
ENGINEERING AND PHYSICS CAMP FOR GIRLS
Res and Day — Girls Ages 14-17

Northfield, MN 55057. 1520 St Olaf Ave. Tel: 507-786-3042. Fax: 507-786-3690.
www.stolaf.edu/camps   E-mail: summer@stolaf.edu
Teresa Lebens, Dir.
Grades 9-12. Adm: FCFS. **Appl**—Fee $0. Due: Rolling.
Enr: 40. Enr cap: 40-48. Fac 10. Prof 1. Col/grad students 8. K-12 staff 1. **Staff:** Admin 1. Res 8.
Type of instruction: Enrich. **Avg class size:** 5.
Focus: Engineering Sci.
Fees 2014: Res $570, 1 wk. Day $520, 1 wk. Aid (Need).
Housing: Dorms.
Nonprofit. **Ses: 1. Wks/ses:** 1. Operates July.

High school girls learn physics and engineering principles and techniques as they construct their own Rube Goldberg machines during this weeklong camp. The hands-on building exercise forces students to account for various laws of physics to make their machines function as efficiently as possible. Girls put their completed machines on display for family, friends, faculty members and their fellow campers on the session's last day.

SALISBURY SUMMER SCHOOL
Res and Day — Coed Ages 12-18

Salisbury, CT 06068. 251 Canaan Rd. Tel: 860-435-5700. Fax: 860-435-5750.
www.salisburysummerschool.org   E-mail: admissions@salisburyschool.org
Peter Wood, Dir.
Grades 7-12. Adm: FCFS. **Appl**—Due: Rolling. Transcript, 2 recs, test scores.
Fac 33. Staff: Admin 1.
Type of instruction: Adv Dev_Read Enrich Preview Rem_Eng Rem_Math Rem_Read Rev ESL/TOEFL_Prep SAT/ACT_Prep Tut. **Courses:** ESL Crafts Creative_Writing. **Daily hours for:** Classes 5. Study 2. Rec 2.
Focus: Study_Skills. **Features:** Yoga Basketball Soccer Swim Tennis Ultimate_Frisbee Weight_Trng.
Fees 2014: Res $7365 (+$250), 5 wks. Day $6365 (+$250), 5 wks.
Housing: Dorms. **Swimming:** Lake.
Est 1946. Nonprofit. **Spons:** Salisbury School. **Ses: 1. Wks/ses:** 5. Operates July-Aug.

Salisbury immerses students in a curriculum and an academic environment designed to improve organizational and reading and writing skills. The program addresses reading comprehension, composition, spelling, vocabulary, word attack, speed-reading and study methods. Maintaining a small-class environment, Salisbury utilizes assessments in place of letter grades. Math review, creative writing, ESL and SAT preparation courses are also available as electives.

SANTA CLARA UNIVERSITY SUMMER ENGINEERING SEMINAR
Res — Coed Ages 16-18

Santa Clara, CA 95053. 500 El Camino Real. Tel: 408-554-4728.
www.scu.edu/engineering/about/ses.cfm   E-mail: summerengineeringseminar@scu.edu
Grades 11-12. Adm: Selective. **Appl**—Due: Mar. 2 essays, rec.
Type of instruction: Enrich.

Focus: Engineering.
Fees 2014: Free. Res 1 wk.
Housing: Dorms.
Est 1990. Ses: 2. **Wks/ses:** 1. Operates July-Aug.

This tuition-free seminar introduces rising high school juniors and seniors to college life as they explore career possibilities in engineering. Taught by Santa Clara faculty, courses examine such engineering disciplines environmental engineering, robotics, nanotechnology and bioengineering. Students perform independent projects as part of the curriculum. SES particularly encourages young women and members of other groups lacking prominent representation in the field of engineering to apply.

THE SCHOOL FOR ETHICS AND GLOBAL LEADERSHIP
Res — Coed Ages 16-18

Washington, DC 20036. 1528 18th St NW.
http://schoolforethics.org/admissions/summer-at-segl   **E-mail: summer@**
schoolforethics.org
Grades 11-12. Adm: Selective.
Focus: Global_Stud Leadership.
Fees 2014: Res $6950.
Wks/ses: 5. Operates June-Aug.

The School for Ethics and Global Leadership (SEGL) is a semester-long academic program for motivated high schoolers. The program selects students who have shown outstanding character, promise for leadership, and scholastic ability and provides them with a unique curriculum that emphasizes ethical thinking, leadership development, and international affairs.

THE SCHOOL FOR FIELD STUDIES
Res — Coed Ages 18-21

Beverly, MA 01915. 100 Cummings Ctr, Ste 534-G. Tel: 978-741-3544, 800-989-4418.
www.fieldstudies.org   **E-mail: admissions@fieldstudies.org**
James A. Cramer, Pres.
Student contact: Leslie Granese, E-mail: lgranese@fieldstudies.org.
Grades 12-Col. Adm: Selective. Prereqs: GPA 2.6. **Appl**—Fee $50. Due: Rolling.
Enr: 160.
Type of instruction: Adv. **Courses:** Ecol Marine_Bio/Stud. **Avg class size:** 23. **Daily hours for:** Classes 5. Study 3. Rec 2. **College credit:** 4.
Intl program focus: Acad. **Locations:** Africa Australia/New_Zealand Caribbean Mexico/Central_America.
Focus: Environ_Sci. **Features:** Adventure_Travel Aquatics Community_Serv Conservation Farm Hiking Peace/Cross-cultural Scuba Wilderness_Camp Swim.
Fees 2014: Res $5400-9425, 5-6 wks. Aid (Need).
Housing: Cabins Dorms. Avg per room/unit: 5. **Swimming:** Lake Ocean Pool.
Est 1980. Nonprofit. **Ses:** 5. **Wks/ses:** 5-6. Operates June-Aug.

This alternative school develops and sponsors field experiences for rising high school seniors and college students in remote wilderness areas around the world. The program helps train students to address environmental issues through scientific research and fieldwork. Scuba diving, hiking, gardening and snorkeling present opportunities for learning and exploration. Programs operate in Costa Rica, the Turks and Caicos Islands, Kenya, Tanzania, Bhutan, Australia and New Zealand.

SCIENCE CAMP WATONKA
Res — Boys Ages 7-15

Hawley, PA 18428. PO Box 127. Tel: 570-226-4779. Fax: 570-857-9653.

www.watonka.com   E-mail: mail@watonka.com
Donald Wacker, Dir.
Grades 1-11. Adm: FCFS.
Enr: 130. **Fac 26. Staff: Admin** 6. **Couns** 34.
Type of instruction: Adv Enrich Preview Rev. **Courses:** Astron Comp_Sci Ecol Environ_
Sci Geol Marine_Bio/Stud Electronics Robotics Crafts Media Photog. **Avg class size:**
10. **Daily hours for:** Classes 3. Rec 6.
Focus: Sci. **Features:** Archery Climbing_Wall Fishing Mtn_Biking Outdoor_Ed Riflery
Ropes_Crse Rowing/Sculling Woodcraft Badminton Basketball Soccer Softball Swim
Tennis Volleyball Watersports.
Fees 2014: Res $2600-7200, 2-8 wks.
Housing: Cabins. Avg per room/unit: 8. **Swimming:** Lake.
Est 1963. Inc. **Ses:** 10. **Wks/ses:** 2-8. Operates June-Aug.

Campers, who are grouped by age, interest and ability, spend half of each day receiving
laboratory instruction in two of the following sciences: chemistry, electronics, robotics,
computer science, biology, photography, rocketry, geology, astronomy, ecology, physics or
earth science. The remainder of the day is devoted to free choice from a range of activities.

SEA EDUCATION ASSOCIATION
HIGH SCHOOL SUMMER SEMINARS
Res — Coed Ages 15-19

Woods Hole, MA 02543. PO Box 6. Tel: 508-540-3954, 800-552-3633. Fax: 800-977-
8516.
www.sea.edu   E-mail: admission@sea.edu
Scott Branco, Actg Pres.
Grades 10-Col. Adm: Selective. **Appl**—Fee $25. Due: Rolling. Transcript, 2 essays,
teacher rec.
Enr cap: 30. **Fac** 10. Prof 10. **Staff: Admin** 6. Couns 5.
Type of instruction: Adv. **Courses:** Astron Ecol Environ_Sci Expository_Writing Geol.
Daily hours for: Classes 8. Study 4. Rec 4. **College credit:** 3.
Locations: CA MA ME.
Focus: Marine_Bio/Stud Oceanog. **Features:** Adventure_Travel Fishing Sail Sea_Cruises
Seamanship Swim.
Fees 2014: Res $4600, 3 wks. Aid (Need).
Housing: Cabins Dorms. Avg per room/unit: 8. **Swimming:** Ocean. Campus facilities avail.
Est 1971. Nonprofit. **Ses:** 2. **Wks/ses:** 3. Operates June-Aug.

SEA conducts two high school seminars for motivated high schoolers and recent graduates
interested in science, the sea and learning to sail through Science at SEA (Woods Hole).
Students commence each program with academic course work during a shore component in
which they live in a community setting and develop team-building and leadership skills. The
second half of each program takes place at sea, where boys and girls gain hands-on experience
on a modern sailing research vessel. While at sea, students collect scientific data, set and strike
sails, operate sophisticated equipment and help out in the ship's galley.

SEACAMP
Res — Coed Ages 12-17

Big Pine Key, FL 33043. 1300 Big Pine Ave. Tel: 305-872-2331, 877-732-2267. Fax:
305-872-2555.
www.seacamp.org   E-mail: info@seacamp.org
Grace Upshaw, Dir.
Grades 7-12. Adm: FCFS. **Appl**—Due: Rolling.
Enr: 160. **Enr cap:** 160. **Intl:** 20%. **Fac 18.** Col/grad students 18. **Staff:** Couns 30.
Type of instruction: Adv Enrich. **Courses:** Archaeol Astron Ecol Environ_Sci Expository_

Writing Geol Writing/Journ Crafts Creative_Writing Music. **Avg class size:** 10. **Daily hours for:** Classes 6.
Focus: Marine_Bio/Stud Scuba. **Features:** Aquatics Boating Canoe Exploration Fishing Kayak Sail Woodcraft Swim Volleyball Watersports.
Fees 2014: Res $4050 (+$425), 2½ wks.
Swimming: Ocean.
Est 1966. Nonprofit. **Ses:** 2. **Wks/ses:** 2½. Operates June-Aug.

This comprehensive marine science program offers teenagers an opportunity to explore the waters of the Florida Keys, both in the Atlantic Ocean and in the Gulf of Mexico. Seacamp offers certification courses in scuba diving to qualified campers. Snorkeling, sailing, windsurfing, kayaking, a camp newspaper, music and arts, and crafts are among the camp's other daily offerings.

SEACAMP
Res — Coed Ages 12-18

San Diego, CA 92109. 1380 Garnet Ave, PMB E6. Tel: 858-268-0919, 800-732-2267.
Fax: 858-268-0229.
www.seacamp.com E-mail: seacamp@seacamp.com
Phil Zerofski, Exec Dir.
Grades 7-12. Adm: FCFS. **Appl**—Fee $0. Due: Rolling.
Enr cap: 28-56. **Fac 11. Staff:** Admin 5.
Courses: Ecol Environ_Sci Sci Speech Photog.
Focus: Marine_Bio/Stud. **Features:** Adventure_Travel Aquatics Boating Kayak Scuba Sea_Cruises Swim.
Fees 2014: Res $860-1840 (+$75), 1 wk.
Housing: Dorms. **Swimming:** Ocean.
Est 1986. Inc. **Ses:** 9. **Wks/ses:** 1. Operates June-Aug.

SEACAMP provides marine science education in San Diego. Combining traditional classroom and laboratory teaching with hands-on experience, the program allows students to participate in a core curriculum of marine biology, marine mammals and behavior, marine ecology and physical oceanography. Students also explore career opportunities and educational programs in the marine sciences.

SEATTLE UNIVERSITY
ALBERS SCHOOL OF BUSINESS AND ECONOMICS
SUMMER BUSINESS INSTITUTE
Res — Coed Ages 16-17

Seattle, WA 98122. 901 12th Ave, PO Box 222000. Tel: 206-296-5700. Fax: 206-296-5795.
www.seattleu.edu/albers/programs/SBI E-mail: cmarino@seattleu.edu
Carl Marino, Prgm Dir.
Grade 12. Adm: Selective. Admitted: 60%. Priority: URM. Prereqs: GPA 3.0. **Appl**—Fee $0. Due: Apr. Personal statement, teacher/counselor rec.
Enr: 25. **Enr cap:** 26. Non-White: 100%. **Fac 8. Prof 8. Staff:** Admin 2. Couns 6.
Type of instruction: Enrich Preview. **Courses:** Econ Accounting Bus_Law Ethics Marketing. **Daily hours for:** Classes 6. Study 3. Rec 3. Homework.
Focus: Bus/Fin. **Features:** Badminton Basketball Swim Bowling.
Fees 2014: Res $50, 1 wk.
Housing: Dorms. Avg per room/unit: 2. **Swimming:** Pool.
Est 2003. Nonprofit. **Ses:** 1. **Wks/ses:** 1. Operates June.

SBI provides a preview of university life for African-American, Latino and Native American pupils with an interest in business. Hands-on seminars acquaint students with college course work in such business areas as economics, accounting, business law, ethics, finance, business administration, international business, management and marketing. Participants visit the corporate headquarters of program sponsors and meet with executives. The program also addresses the college selection and financial aid processes, and current Seattle University undergraduates are available for guidance.

SEATTLE UNIVERSITY JOURNALISM SUMMER WORKSHOP
Res — Coed Ages 15-18

Seattle, WA 98122. Communication Dept, Lynn Bldg, 901 12th Ave. Tel: 206-296-5300.
www.seattleu.edu/artsci/jsw   E-mail: tomasg@seattleu.edu
Tomas Guillen, Dir.
Grades 10-12. Adm: Selective. Appl—Due: Apr.
Enr: 15. Enr cap: 15.
Type of instruction: Enrich.
Focus: Writing/Journ.
Fees 2014: Free. Res 1 wk.
Housing: Dorms.
Ses: 1. Wks/ses: 1. Operates June.

This weeklong workshop enrolls talented high schoolers with an interest in journalism. Pupils receive intensive instruction and mentoring from professional journalists and college professors. Student work is published by major Seattle news organizations. Each year, the university awards two college scholarships to particularly strong workshop participants.

SHEDD AQUARIUM
HIGH SCHOOL MARINE BIOLOGY SUMMER PROGRAM
Res — Coed Ages 15-18

Chicago, IL 60605. 1200 S Lake Shore Dr. Tel: 312-692-3158.
www.sheddaquarium.org   E-mail: teens@sheddaquarium.org
Stephanie Bohr, Coord.
Grades 9-12. Adm: Selective. Appl—Due: Dec. Transcript, rec, swim test.
Enr: 30. Enr cap: 30. Fac 4.
Courses: Ecol Environ_Sci Sci.
Travel: Caribbean.
Focus: Marine_Bio/Stud. Features: Adventure_Travel Aquatics Boating Conservation Exploration Outdoor_Ed Sea_Cruises Seamanship Swim Snorkeling.
Fees 2008: Res $1600 (+$300), 3 wks. Aid (Need).
Swimming: Ocean Pool.
Est 1973. Nonprofit. Ses: 1. Wks/ses: 3. Operates July-Aug.

The aquarium's program offers students the opportunity to learn the fundamentals of marine biology and island ecology through lectures, field study and experimentation. Following an introduction at the Shedd Aquarium, participants spend six days living on a research vessel off the coast of the Bimini, Bahamas. Pupils spend the final week at the aquarium analyzing the data from the field. Students must make housing arrangements for their time in Chicago.

SILC INTERNATIONAL SUMMER CENTRES
Res — Coed Ages 13-17

Angouleme Cedex, 16022 France. 32 rempart de l'Est. Tel: 33-5-45-97-41-25. Fax: 33-5-45-94-20-63.
www.silc-in-france.com   E-mail: volodia.m@silc.fr
Adm: FCFS. Appl—Due: Rolling.
Enr cap: 8-15. Intl: 85%. Non-White: 30%. Staff: Admin 3. Couns 2.
Type of instruction: Enrich. Courses: Music Theater. Avg class size: 13. Daily hours for: Classes 3. Homework. Tests. Grades.

Intl program focus: Lang Culture. Home stays avail.
Focus: Fr. **Features:** Soccer.
Fees 2010: Res €314-1253 (+airfare), 1-4 wks.
Est 1965. Inc. **Ses:** 4. **Wks/ses:** 1-4. Operates June-Aug.

With locations in suburban Paris (Bretigny-sur-Orge) and the French Riviera (Biarritz), the Summer Centres feature 15 hours of weekly French language study. SILC accepts students at beginning, elementary, intermediate and advanced levels. Boys and girls reside with a host family, thereby hastening the pupil's language development.

SMITH COLLEGE
SUMMER SCIENCE AND ENGINEERING PROGRAM
Res — Girls Ages 13-18

Northampton, MA 01063. Center for Community Collaboration, Wright Hall. Tel: 413-585-3060. Fax: 413-585-3068.
www.smith.edu/ssep   E-mail: ccc@smith.edu
Sarah Craig, **Dir.**
Grades 9-12. Adm: Selective. **Appl**—Fee $0. Due: Rolling. Transcript, essay, teacher rec.
Enr: 100. **Non-White:** 50%. **Fac 14. Prof 14. Staff:** Admin 4.
Type of instruction: Adv Enrich. **Courses:** Astron Ecol Environ_Sci Expository_Writing Crafts Creative_Writing Dance Music Theater. **Avg class size:** 14. **Daily hours for:** Classes 5. Rec 5.
Focus: Engineering Med/Healthcare Sci. **Features:** Basketball Equestrian Swim Tennis Track Volleyball.
Fees 2014: Res $5500, 4 wks. Aid (Need).
Housing: Dorms. **Swimming:** Pool. Campus facilities avail.
Est 1990. Nonprofit. **Ses:** 1. **Wks/ses:** 4. Operates July-Aug.

Conducted by Smith College faculty, SSEP is a month-long enrichment program for talented high school girls with interests in science, engineering and medicine. During their stay, girls select two two-week research courses in such subjects as astronomy, biochemistry, biology, chemistry, engineering, women's health and writing. The program offers cooperative, hands-on investigations in engineering and the life and physical sciences. In their free time, students participate in organized sports, as well as in various recreational and cultural activities.

SOCIETY OF AMERICAN MILITARY ENGINEERS
ENGINEERING & CONSTRUCTION CAMPS
Res — Coed Ages 15-18

Bothell, WA 98012. 18421 38th Dr SE.
http://posts.same.org/camps   E-mail: camp.info@same.org
Kurt Ubbelohde, **Dir.**
Student contact: Erin Ingersoll, **E-mail:** erini@meetingvisions.net.
Grades 10-12. Adm: Selective. Prereqs: GPA 3.0. **Appl**—Due: Mar.
Type of instruction: Enrich.
Locations: CA CO MI.
Focus: Engineering. **Features:** Basketball Volleyball.
Fees 2009: Res $275, 1 wk.
Housing: Dorms.
Est 1999. Nonprofit. **Ses:** 3. **Wks/ses:** 1. Operates June-July.

Weeklong SAME camps provide students who excel in math, science and technical courses with opportunities to learn from professional engineers from the military and private sectors, develop practical skills and gain exposure to the service academies. Camps take place at three locations annually: the US Army Camp in Vicksburg, MS; the US Air Force Academy Camp in Colorado Springs, CO; and the US Navy Seabees Camp in Port Hueneme, CA.

SOTOGRANDE CAMPS
Res — Coed Ages 7-14; Day — Coed 3-14

Sotogrande, 11310 Cadiz, Spain. Apartado 15. Tel: 34-956-795-902. **Fax:** 34-956-794-816.
www.sotograndecamps.com   E-mail: info@sotograndecamps.com
Adm: FCFS. **Appl**—Fee $0. Due: Rolling.
Enr cap: 200. **Staff:** Admin 4.
Intl program focus: Lang.
Focus: ESL Span. **Features:** Golf Soccer Swim Tennis.
Fees 2014: Res €1675-2995, 2-4 wks. Day €670-1570, 2-4 wks.
Housing: Dorms. **Swimming:** Ocean Pool.
Est 1978. Spons: Sotogrande International School. **Ses:** 3. **Wks/ses:** 2-4. Operates June-July.

Conducted on the campus of Sotogrande International School, the camp combines intensive Spanish or English language instruction with professionally taught sports. During the session, campers concentrate on one of the following sports: tennis, soccer, golf or paddle tennis.

SOUTH CAROLINA STATE UNIVERSITY
SUMMER TRANSPORTATION INSTITUTE
Res — Coed Ages 14-17

Orangeburg, SC 29117. PO Box 8144. Tel: 803-516-4990.
www.nrc.scsu.edu   E-mail: jecutc@scsu.edu
Larrie B. Butler, Dir.
Grades 9-11. Adm: Selective. **Prereqs:** GPA 2.5. **Appl**—Fee $0. Due: May. Transcript, essays, standardized test scores, 2 recs.
Enr: 16. Non-White: 100%. **Fac** 6. **Staff:** Admin 2. Couns 2.
Type of instruction: Enrich SAT/ACT_Prep.
Focus: Engineering.
Fees 2014: Free (in-state residents). Res 4 wks.
Housing: Dorms.
Est 1993. Nonprofit. Ses: 1. **Wks/ses:** 4. Operates July.

STI exposes South Carolina high schoolers to career opportunities in transportation industries. Program topics include highway design, transportation of people and cargo, laws, regulations, safety and environmentalism. Among other activities are SAT prep courses, computer training, reading and writing enhancement skills and field trips.

STANFORD NATIONAL FORENSIC INSTITUTE
Res and Day — Coed Ages 14-18

Palo Alto, CA 94301. 555 Bryant St, Ste 599. Tel: 650-723-9086. **Fax:** 650-350-4345.
www.snfi.org   E-mail: info@snfi.org
Rich Boltizar, Exec Dir.
Grades 9-12. Adm: FCFS. **Appl**—Fee $0. Due: May.
Type of instruction: Enrich.
Focus: Debate.
Fees 2014: Res $1150-4850, 1-4 wks. Day $1395-1650, 1-4 wks.
Housing: Dorms. Avg per room/unit: 2.
Spons: Stanford University. **Ses:** 5. **Wks/ses:** 1-4. Operates July-Aug.

High school students choose from the following camps at SNFI: individual events, Lincoln-Douglas debate, parliamentary debate, policy debate and public forum debate. Those choosing the policy debate program have an accelerated camp option, and boys and girls in the policy, public forum and Lincoln-Douglas programs may enroll in a fourth week (other programs last one to three weeks). Programming balances lab time, practice rounds, mandatory lectures and electives.

STANFORD UNIVERSITY MATHEMATICS CAMP
Res — Coed Ages 15-17

Stanford, CA 94305. Math Dept, Bldg 380, 450 Serra Mall. Tel: 650-721-2947.
http://math.stanford.edu/sumac   E-mail: sumacinfo@stanford.edu
Rick Sommer, Dir.
Grades 11-12. Adm: Selective. Admitted: 33%. **Appl**—Transcript, standardized math tests, teacher recs.
Type of instruction: Enrich.
Focus: Math.
Fees 2014: Res $6150, 4 wks. Aid (Need).
Housing: Dorms. Campus facilities avail.
Est 1995. Nonprofit. **Ses: 1. Wks/ses: 4.** Operates July-Aug.

SUMaC enrolls motivated and mathematically motivated high school upperclassmen who are interested in exploring advanced math topics over the summer. The program includes the following: an intensive course in higher math, a guided research project allowing pupils to pursue a focused and course-related area of interest, a series of guest lectures, group problem solving and one-on-one tutoring, and social events and outings. Boys and girls have access to Stanford's athletic and library facilities.

CAMP START-UP
Res and Day — Coed Ages 14-18

Wilbraham, MA. Wilbraham & Monson Acad.
Contact (Year-round): 1209½ De La Vina St, Santa Barbara, CA 93103. Tel: 805-965-0475. Fax: 805-965-3148.
www.independentmeans.com   E-mail: info@independentmeans.com
Sarah Maine, Dir.
Adm: FCFS. **Appl**—Fee $0. Due: Rolling.
Enr cap: 30. Intl: 8%. Non-White: 45%. **Fac 7. Staff:** Admin 2. Res 7.
Type of instruction: Enrich. **Courses:** Leadership.
Travel: Europe.
Focus: Bus/Fin. **Features:** Basketball Swim Tennis.
Fees 2014: Res $4000, 1½ wks. Aid (Merit & Need).
Housing: Dorms. Avg per room/unit: 2. **Swimming:** Pool. Campus facilities avail.
Est 1994. Inc. **Spons:** Independent Means. **Ses: 1. Wks/ses:** 1½. Operates Aug.

Conducted at Wilbraham & Monson Academy, Camp Start-Up enables teenagers from around the world to learn about entrepreneurship, budgeting, saving and investing. Students work in groups to form mock start-ups, build business plans and create investment portfolios. They also meet local business leaders from successful companies on class field trips. Leadership skills training is an important aspect of each session. Boys and girls may engage in various recreational and athletic pursuits during their free time.

STONELEIGH-BURNHAM SCHOOL
A VOICE OF HER OWN
Res — Girls Ages 11-17

Greenfield, MA 01301. 574 Bernardston Rd. Tel: 413-774-2711. Fax: 413-772-2602.
www.sbschool.org/debatecamp   E-mail: summerprograms@sbschool.org
Paul Bassett, Dir.
Adm: FCFS. **Appl**—Fee $0. Due: Rolling.
Enr: 40. **Enr cap:** 40. **Fac 5. Staff:** Admin 3. Couns 5.
Type of instruction: Adv.
Focus: Debate Public_Speak. **Features:** Aquatics Swim Track.
Fees 2014: Res $600, 1 wk.
Housing: Dorms. **Swimming:** Pool.

Est 1982. Nonprofit. **Ses:** 2. **Wks/ses:** 1. Operates July-Aug.

A Voice of Her Own teaches lifetime speaking and debating skills to young women. Instruction includes interpretive reading, dramatic interpretation, impromptu speaking, persuasive speaking and various forms of debate. Girls devote mornings to preparing speeches or debate briefs, then spend afternoons polishing their delivery of the material. Participants deliver presentations to the assembled camp each evening.

SUMMER INSTITUTE FOR MATHEMATICS AT THE UNIVERSITY OF WASHINGTON
Res — Coed Ages 14-18

Seattle, WA 98195. Dept of Math, Box 354350. Tel: 206-543-1150. Fax: 206-543-0397.
www.math.washington.edu/~simuw   E-mail: simuw@math.washington.edu
Ron Irving, Exec Dir.
Grades 9-12 (younger if qualified). Adm: Selective. **Appl**—Fee $0. Due: Mar. Transcript, math problems, math teacher rec.
Enr: 24. **Enr cap:** 24.
Type of instruction: Adv Enrich.
Focus: Math.
Fees 2014: Free. **Res 6 wks.**
Housing: Dorms.
Nonprofit. **Ses:** 1. **Wks/ses:** 6. Operates June-Aug.

A select group of high school upperclassmen from Washington State, Oregon, Idaho, Alaska and British Columbia, Canada, who have completed at least three years of high school math may apply for this intensive program. Two instructors lead each of the three two-week blocks; during four of the five weekdays of the week, participants meet with one instructor in the morning, the other in the afternoon. These sessions combine work on math problems with some limited lecture time. On the fifth weekday, SIMUW schedules a special program in which a morning speaker discusses math's role in his or her line of work; in the afternoon, students will either listen to a second speaker or engage in a special activity or field trip related to math. Boys and girls embark on trips to local places of interest on Saturdays, then have Sundays available for group or individual activities.

SUPERCAMP
Res — Coed Ages 11-24

Oceanside, CA 92056. 1938 Avenida del Oro. Tel: 760-722-0072, 800-285-3276. Fax: 760-305-7770.
www.supercamp.com   E-mail: info@supercamp.com
Grades 6-Col. Adm: FCFS. **Appl**—Fee $0. Due: Rolling.
Enr: 100. **Enr cap:** 100. **Intl:** 5%. **Fac** 4. **Staff:** Admin 28.
Type of instruction: Dev_Read Enrich Preview Rev SAT/ACT_Prep. **Daily hours for:** Classes 10. Rec 2.
Locations: CA FL NC OH RI.
Focus: Study_Skills. **Features:** Rock_Climb Swim.
Fees 2014: Res $2495-3295, 1-1½ wks.
Housing: Dorms. **Swimming:** Pool.
Est 1982. Inc. **Ses:** 22. **Wks/ses:** 1-1½. Operates June-Aug.

SuperCamp's academic program focuses on improving learning skills. Middle school, high school and college-age programs are held on university campuses throughout the US. The curriculum addresses power reading, memory mastering, writing, problem solving, note taking and test taking. Students also take part in a life skills program.

SURVAL MONT-FLEURI SUMMER PROGRAM
Res — Girls Ages 11-16

Montreux, 1820 Switzerland. Rte de Glion 56. Tel: 41-21-966-16-16. Fax: 41-21-966-16-17.
www.surval.ch   E-mail: info@surval.ch
Jean-Pierre Fauquez, Dir.
Adm: Somewhat_selective. Admitted: 90%. **Appl**—Fee SwF450. Due: Rolling.
Enr: 75. **Enr cap:** 85. Intl: 75%. Non-White: 30%. **Fac 36. Staff:** Admin 7.
Type of instruction: Adv Rem_Eng Rem_Math Rem_Read SAT/ACT_Prep Tut. **Courses:** Bus/Fin Ceramics Crafts Dance Fine_Arts Music Painting Photog. **Avg class size:** 10. **Daily hours for:** Classes 6. Homework. Tests. Grades. **High school & college credit. Intl program focus:** Lang.
Focus: ESL Fr. **Features:** Bicycle_Tours Cooking Cruises Riding Aerobics Gymnastics Swim Tennis Water-skiing Watersports.
Fees 2011: Res SwF7500-12500 (+SwF1500), 3-5 wks.
Housing: Dorms. Avg per room/unit: 3. **Swimming:** Lake Pool. Campus facilities avail.
Est 1961. Ses: 3. **Wks/ses:** 3-5. Operates July-Aug.

Girls enrolled at Surval Mont-Fleuri study French or English intensively for four hours each weekday morning. A full- or half-day excursion is scheduled every Saturday. For an additional fee, students may enroll in cooking, pastry, ceramics, photography and etiquette classes, among others.

SUSQUEHANNA UNIVERSITY
LEADERSHIP INSTITUTE FOR ENTREPRENEURSHIP
Res — Coed Ages 15-17

Selinsgrove, PA 17870. c/o Office of Continuing Ed, 530 University Ave. Tel: 570-372-4235. Fax: 570-372-4021.
www.susqu.edu/life   E-mail: mischel@susqu.edu
Jayme Long, Coord.
Grades 10-12. Adm: Selective. **Appl**—Due: Rolling. Transcript, recs.
Type of instruction: Enrich. **Courses:** Leadership.
Focus: Bus/Fin.
Fees 2014: Res $795, 1 wk.
Housing: Dorms.
Nonprofit. **Ses:** 1. **Wks/ses:** 1. Operates July.

This hands-on introduction to entrepreneurship enables students in grades 10-12 to engage in a simulated experience as a business owner. Pupils learn about finance, banking, stocks and bonds, sales, advertising, global trade issues and the importance of effective collaboration. As owner of a theoretical business, each student acquires seed money, hires personnel, pays expenses, manages inventory, and sells his or her company. Faculty and staff from the university's Sigmund Weis School of Business conduct the program.

TASIS MIDDLE SCHOOL PROGRAM
Res and Day — Coed Ages 11-13

Montagnola-Lugano, Switzerland.
Contact (Year-round): 112 S Royal St, Alexandria, VA 22314. Tel: 703-299-8150. Fax: 703-299-8157.
www.tasis.com   E-mail: usadmissions@tasis.com
Marie-Josee Breton, Dir.
Adm: FCFS. **Appl**—Fee $0. Due: Rolling. Rec.
Enr: 130. **Enr cap:** 130. **Fac 15. Staff:** Admin 4.
Type of instruction: Enrich. **Courses:** Art Theater. **Avg class size:** 12. **Daily hours for:** Classes 3. Study 1. Rec 4.

Intl program focus: Lang Culture.
Focus: ESL Fr Ital. **Features:** Archery Hiking Mtn_Biking Riding Rock_Climb Basketball Soccer Swim Tennis Volleyball Water-skiing.
Fees 2012: Res SwF7300 (+airfare), 3-4 wks. Day SwF4400 (+airfare), 3-4 wks.
Housing: Dorms. **Swimming:** Lake Pool.
Est 1976. Nonprofit. **Spons:** TASIS Foundation. **Ses:** 2. **Wks/ses:** 3-4. Operates June-July.

Accepting students of all ability levels, MSP provides three hours each morning of intensive French or English instruction. While fluency is the primary goal, classes also emphasize grammar, vocabulary and written work; advanced pupils also study literature. Boys and girls devote two afternoons per week to artistic workshops or specialized sports, then choose from various activities on other class days. In addition, MSP schedules full-day excursions and special events on Sundays and Mondays.

TASIS SPANISH SUMMER PROGRAM
Res — Coed Ages 13-18

Sabanera, Puerto Rico. 11 Carr 693.
Contact (Year-round): 112 S Royal St, Alexandria, VA 22314. Tel: 787-796-0440.
www.tasis.com   E-mail: uksummer@tasisengland.org
Eva Snyders, Dir.
Grades 8-12. Adm: Somewhat_selective. Admitted: 99%. **Appl**—Fee $0. Due: Rolling. Rec.
Enr: 52. **Enr cap:** 52. **Fac 10. Staff:** Admin 4. Couns 7.
Avg class size: 12. **Daily hours for:** Classes 4. Homework. Tests. Grades. **High school credit:** 1/crse, total 1.
Intl program focus: Lang Culture. **Travel:** Mexico/Central_America.
Focus: Span. **Features:** Kayak Sail Golf Soccer Swim Tennis Track.
Fees 2011: Res €3700-4850, 3-4 wks.
Housing: Dorms. **Swimming:** Pool. Campus facilities avail.
Est 1991. Nonprofit. **Spons:** TASIS Foundation. **Ses:** 2. **Wks/ses:** 3-4. Operates July.

This language immersion program enables students who pass a final examination and fulfill all session requirements to earn high school credit in Spanish. Pupils receive extensive practice in listening, speaking, reading and writing, and they also learn about Spanish culture. TASIS accommodates Spanish speakers of all fluency levels.

TELLURIDE ASSOCIATION SOPHOMORE SEMINARS
Res — Coed Ages 16-17

Ithaca, NY 14850. 217 West Ave. Tel: 607-273-5011. Fax: 607-272-2667.
www.tass.tellurideassociation.org   E-mail: telluride@tellurideassociation.org
Ellen Baer, Admin Dir.
Grade 11. Adm: Very selective. Priority: URM. **Appl**—Fee $0. Due: Jan. Essays, transcript, rec, interview.
Enr: 36. **Enr cap:** 36. **Fac 8.** Prof 4. Col/grad students 4.
Type of instruction: Adv Enrich. **Courses:** Expository_Writing Public_Speak. **Daily hours for:** Classes 3. Homework.
Locations: IN MI.
Focus: African-Amer_Stud.
Fees 2014: Free. Res 6 wks.
Housing: Dorms.
Est 1993. Nonprofit. **Ses:** 2. **Wks/ses:** 6. Operates June-Aug.

TASS, held on two college campuses, is a free, six-week program in which rising juniors interested in African-American studies explore this area and other topics that address diversity in society. After convening for a three-hour seminar each weekday morning with two college professors, students spend the remainder of the day completing reading, writing and oral-presentation assignments with the assistance of college-age tutors; watching films related to their seminar topic; and attending guest lectures. Undergraduate student-tutors live in residence halls with TASS pupils, working with them on critical reading and writing skills. Outside the classroom, boys and girls have opportunities to attend cultural events and explore the host institution.

TETON SCIENCE SCHOOLS SUMMER YOUTH ADVENTURES
Res — Coed Ages 12-18; Day — Coed 3-18

Jackson, WY 83001. 700 Coyote Canyon Rd. Tel: 307-733-1313. Fax: 307-733-7560.
www.tetonscience.org   E-mail: info@tetonscience.org
April Landale, Dir.
Grades PS-12. Adm: FCFS. **Appl**—Due: Mar.
Enr cap: 24. **Staff:** Couns 3.
Courses: Environ_Sci Geol. **High school credit.**
Focus: Ecol Sci. **Features:** Canoe Conservation Exploration Fishing Hiking Mtn_Trips Wilderness_Camp.
Fees 2014: Res $898-1067, 1-4 wks. Day $263-800, 1-1½ wks. Aid (Need).
Housing: Cabins Lodges Tents. Avg per room/unit: 3.
Est 1967. Nonprofit. **Ses:** 51. **Wks/ses:** 1-4. Operates June-Sept.

Utilizing the Grand Teton National Park as an outdoor classroom, Teton Science Schools offers summer programming in the natural sciences, natural history and conservation. Students entering grades 11 and 12 and high school graduates enroll in a four-week course that leads to high school credit in field ecology. Participants identify and investigate plants and animals, study natural communities and learn about the foundations of geology. A three-week course in natural field history serves boys and girls entering grades 9-11. For junior high schoolers entering grades 7-9, TSS conducts a 10-day field ecology course. Backpacking and canoeing are elements of all programs.

TEXAS A&M UNIVERSITY-GALVESTON SEA CAMP
Res — Coed Ages 10-18

Galveston, TX 77553. PO Box 1675. Tel: 409-740-4525. Fax: 409-740-4894.
www.tamug.edu/seacamp   E-mail: seacamp@tamug.edu
Grades 5-12. Adm: FCFS. **Appl**—Due: Rolling.
Staff: Admin 4.
Type of instruction: Adv Enrich. **Courses:** Environ_Sci Photog.
Intl program focus: Culture. **Locations:** Canada.
Focus: Ecol Marine_Bio/Stud Oceanog. **Features:** Adventure_Travel Fishing Swim.
Fees 2014: Res $850-950, 1 wk.
Housing: Dorms. **Swimming:** Ocean Pool.
Est 1986. Nonprofit. **Ses:** 16. **Wks/ses:** 1. Operates June-Aug.

This weeklong, hands-on camp enables boys and girls to study marine and estuarine environments. Students have access to research vessels, oceanographic equipment and lab facilities as they learn about various aspects of marine science and ecology.

TEXAS ACADEMY OF MATHEMATICS AND SCIENCE
SUMMER MATH INSTITUTE
Res — Coed Ages 12-16

Denton, TX 76203. c/o Texas Acad of Mathematics and Science, 1155 Union Cr, #305309. Tel: 940-565-4369. Fax: 940-369-8796.
https://tams.unt.edu/academics/summer-math-institute   E-mail: wendy.boyd-brown@unt.edu
Wendy Boyd-Brown, Dir.

Grades 7-11. Adm: Selective. **Appl**—Due: Apr.
Staff: Res 5.
Daily hours for: Classes 6. Study 1.
Focus: Math.
Fees 2014: Res $2250, 3 wks. Aid (Need).
Housing: Dorms. Avg per room/unit: 2.
Ses: 1. **Wks/ses:** 3. Operates July.

SMI participants cover the equivalent of a year's worth of math material in one class during their three weeks at the academy. Students attend class for six hours on weekdays and three hours on Saturdays, and they must also attend a supervised study/tutorial session for an hour each Monday through Friday evening. At the end of the program, faculty formulate a final performance report for the pupil's school and his or her parents.

TEXAS STATE UNIVERSITY
AQUATIC SCIENCES ADVENTURE CAMP
Res and Day — Coed Ages 9-15

San Marcos, TX 78666. 248 Freeman Bldg. Tel: 512-245-2329. Fax: 512-245-2669.
www.eardc.txstate.edu/camp.html   E-mail: lg16@txstate.edu
Lendon Gilpin, Dir.
Grades 4-10. Adm: FCFS. **Appl**—Due: Rolling.
Enr: 26. **Enr cap:** 26. **Fac** 5. Prof 1. K-12 staff 4. **Staff: Res 4.**
Type of instruction: Adv Enrich. **Courses:** Environ_Sci. **Daily hours for:** Classes 4. Rec 4.
Focus: Marine_Bio/Stud. **Features:** Aquatics Fishing Scuba White-water_Raft Swim.
Fees 2014: Res $775, 1 wk. Day $150, ½ wk.
Housing: Dorms. Avg per room/unit: 2. **Swimming:** Pool River.
Est 1988. Ses: 10. **Wks/ses:** ½-1. Operates June-Aug.

TSU's Edwards Aquifer Research and Data Center guides this program, in which boys and girls study freshwater ecosystems in the Central Texas Hill Country. Mornings at the camp are devoted to educational activities related to water resources, aquatic biology and water chemistry, while afternoons include aquatic activities (such as tubing, scuba/snorkeling, rafting, fishing and swimming) that are intended to increase campers' appreciation of aquatic resources. Although two two-day commuter options are available, most sessions accommodate boarders only.

TEXAS STATE UNIVERSITY
MATHWORKS JUNIOR SUMMER MATH CAMP
Res — Coed Ages 11-13; Day — Coed 8-13

San Marcos, TX 78666. ASB South 110, 601 University Dr. Tel: 512-245-3439. Fax: 512-245-1469.
www.txstate.edu/mathworks   E-mail: mathworks@txstate.edu
Max L. Warshauer, Dir.
Grades 4-8 (younger if qualified). Adm: FCFS. **Appl**—Fee $0. Due: Apr. Math teacher rec.
Enr: 180-200. **Enr cap:** 200.
Type of instruction: Enrich. **Daily hours for:** Classes 4. Rec 1.
Focus: Math. **Features:** Basketball.
Fees: Day $345, 2 wks.
Housing: Dorms.
Est 1995. Ses: 1. **Wks/ses:** 2. Operates June.

Offered at five levels of instruction, the Junior Summer Math Camp ranges from a first-year program that introduces students to beginning concepts in algebra through play-acting and drama to a more advanced program in problem solving and discrete math.

TUFTS UNIVERSITY
ADVENTURES IN VETERINARY MEDICINE
Res — Coed Ages 15-18; Day — Coed 13-21

North Grafton, MA 01536. Cummings School of Veterinary Med, 200 Westboro Rd. Tel: 508-839-7962. Fax: 508-839-7952.
www.tufts.edu/vet/avm   E-mail: avm@tufts.edu
Grades 8-Col. Adm: Selective. **Appl**—Fee $40. Due: Rolling. Transcript, essay, 2 recs.
Enr: 20-40. **Enr cap:** 20-40. **Staff:** Admin 2. Couns 5.
Type of instruction: Enrich.
Focus: Veterinary_Med. **Features:** Swim.
Fees 2014: Res $3250 (+$100), 2 wks. Day $750, 1 wk. Aid 2006 (Need): $12,000.
Housing: Dorms. **Swimming:** Pool.
Est 1991. Nonprofit. **Ses:** 9. **Wks/ses:** 1-2. Operates Apr-Aug.

This academic career exploration program allows boys and girls to learn about veterinary school and consider alternatives within the veterinary profession. Students spend about half the day attending lecture-style classes, the other half involved in hands-on activities. AVM offers separate middle school (entering grades 8 and 9; day only), high school (entering grades 10-PG; boarding and day), and college (rising sophomores, juniors and seniors; day only) programs.

UNITED STATES COAST GUARD ACADEMY
ACADEMY INTRODUCTION MISSION
Res — Coed Ages 16-18

New London, CT 06320. 31 Mohegan Ave. Tel: 860-444-8500, 800-883-8724. Fax: 860-701-6700.
www.cga.edu/aim   E-mail: admissions@uscga.edu
Grades 11-12. Adm: Selective. Admitted: 37%. Priority: URM. **Appl**—Fee $0. Due: Apr. Transcript, essay, teacher rec.
Enr: 167. **Enr cap:** 167. Non-White: 16%. **Fac** 12. Prof 12. **Staff:** Admin 23. Couns 65.
Type of instruction: Enrich. **Daily hours for:** Classes 4.
Focus: Col_Prep Engineering Leadership. **Features:** Boating Milit_Trng Sail Seamanship Work Aerobics Baseball Basketball Cross-country Soccer Softball Swim Ultimate_ Frisbee Volleyball.
Fees 2014: Res $400, 1 wk. Aid 2009 (Need): $8750.
Housing: Dorms. Avg per room/unit: 2. **Swimming:** Pool.
Est 1955. Nonprofit. **Ses:** 3. **Wks/ses:** 1. Operates July.

AIM allows rising high school seniors to sample life at the US Coast Guard Academy while also completing an engineering project and engaging in military training. The physically demanding weeklong session approximates the undergraduate experience at the academy. Applicants must be in good health and physical condition and must not be colorblind, have asthma or have vision that is not correctable to 20/20. Roughly half of AIM graduates earn appointments to the academy.

UNITED STATES DEPARTMENT OF AGRICULTURE
AGDISCOVERY PROGRAM
Res — Coed Ages 12-17

Riverdale, MD 20737. APHIS, Office of the Admin, 4700 River Rd, Unit 92. Tel: 301-734-6312. Fax: 301-734-3698.
www.aphis.usda.gov/agdiscovery   E-mail: agdiscovery@aphis.usda.gov
Terry Henson, Coord.
Adm: Selective. **Appl**—Due: Apr. Essay, 3 recs.
Type of instruction: Enrich.
Locations: AL AR AZ DE FL GA HI IO KY MD MI NC SC.

Focus: Agriculture Environ_Sci Sci Veterinary_Med.
Fees 2014: Free. Res 2-3 wks.
Housing: Dorms.
Est 2002. Ses: 13. **Wks/ses:** 2-3. Operates June-July.

Hosted on approximately a dozen college campuses, AgDiscovery allows participants to preview college life while learning about careers in animal science, veterinary medicine, agribusiness and plant pathology from university professors, practicing veterinarians and government professionals. Students gain experience through hands-on labs, workshops, field trips, and other group and team-building activities. While one program enrolls boys and girls ages 12-16, all other programs accept applicants ages 14-17.

UNIVERSITY OF ALASKA-FAIRBANKS
ALASKA SUMMER RESEARCH ACADEMY
Res — Coed Ages 13-18; Day — Coed 14-18

Fairbanks, AK 99775. College of Natural Sci & Math, PO Box 755940. Tel: 907-474-7077. Fax: 907-474-5101.
www.uaf.edu/asra   E-mail: jdrake@gi.alaska.edu
Tiffany DeRuyter, Dir. Student contact: Kate Pendleton, E-mail: fnkp@uaf.edu.
Grades 8-12. Adm: Selective. **Appl**—Fee $50. Due: Rolling. Essay, 2 references.
Enr cap: 120.
College credit: 1.
Focus: Archaeol Astron Comp_Sci Engineering Marine_Bio/Stud Math Med/Healthcare Sci Creative_Writing Photog.
Fees 2014: Res $1200, 2 wks. Aid (Need).
Housing: Dorms.
Ses: 1. **Wks/ses:** 2. Operates July.

Emphasizing exploration and creativity, ASRA immerses students in a single subject for two weeks of intensive, hands-on research. Topics vary by year; past subjects have included archaeology, biomedicine, creative writing, earth and space science, earthquakes, engineering design, photography, fisheries, energy and climate change, physiology, marine biology, marine mammals, programming and robotics. Certain remote modules require participants to travel off-campus and stay at camp sites or research facilities.

UNIVERSITY OF ARIZONA ASTRONOMY CAMP
Res — Coed Ages 13-18

Tucson, AZ 85721. 933 N Cherry Ave. Tel: 520-621-4079, 800-232-8278. Fax: 520-621-9843.
www.astronomycamp.org   E-mail: dmccarthy@as.arizona.edu
Don McCarthy, Dir.
Grades 7-12 (younger if qualified). Adm: Somewhat_selective. Admitted: 95%. **Appl**—Fee $0. Due: Rolling. Essay, teacher rec.
Enr: 30. **Enr cap:** 30. Intl: 90%. Non-White: 10%. **Fac 9.** Prof 2. Col/grad students 7. **Staff:** Admin 3. Couns 10.
Type of instruction: Adv Enrich. **Courses:** Environ_Sci Geol Crafts. **Avg class size:** 30.
Focus: Astron. **Features:** Aviation/Aero Hiking.
Fees 2014: Res $600-975, 1 wk. Aid 2006 (Need): $4000.
Housing: Dorms.
Est 1988. Nonprofit. **Ses:** 2. **Wks/ses:** 1. Operates June.

An astronomy program that emphasizes hands-on learning, the camp has students operate research telescopes, keep nighttime hours, interact with scientists and interpret their own observations. Facilities at the Mount Lemmon site include several telescopes and direct imaging, solar imaging and spectroscopy equipment. Applicants need not possess any prior knowledge of astronomy.

UNIVERSITY OF ARIZONA
BUSINESS CAREERS AWARENESS PROGRAM
Res — Coed Ages 16-17

Tucson, AZ 85721. McClelland Hall 301, PO Box 210108. Tel: 520-621-3713. Fax: 520-621-3742.
www.accounting.eller.arizona.edu/bcap   E-mail: bcap@eller.arizona.edu
Katie Maxwell, Dir.
Grade 11. Adm: Somewhat selective. Priority: URM. **Appl**—Fee $0. Due: Mar. Transcript, 2 recs.
Enr cap: 30. **Fac 6.** Prof 6. **Staff:** Couns 7.
Type of instruction: Enrich.
Focus: Bus/Fin.
Fees 2014: Free. Res 1 wk.
Housing: Dorms. Avg per room/unit: 2.
Ses: 1. **Wks/ses:** 1. Operates June.

Sponsored by the University of Arizona and the accounting firm Ernst & Young, BCAP provides students from populations that are underrepresented in college accounting classes with an opportunity to explore the field. The program features introductory accounting, finance and economics classes; a case study competition; visits to local nonprofit organizations and corporations; and etiquette training for formal dining.

UNIVERSITY OF ARIZONA SUMMER ENGINEERING ACADEMY
Res — Coed Ages 14-18

Tucson, AZ 85721. Engineering Bldg, Rm 200, PO Box 210020. Tel: 520-621-6032. Fax: 520-621-9995.
www.engineering.arizona.edu/future   E-mail: gaxiola@engr.arizona.edu
Grades 9-12. Adm: Selective. **Appl**—Fee $10. Due: Apr. Transcript, rec.
Type of instruction: Enrich.
Focus: Engineering.
Fees 2014: Res $500, 1 wk.
Housing: Dorms.
Ses: 3. **Wks/ses:** 1. Operates June.

SEA serves as a weeklong investigation into engineering careers. Classroom sessions with university professors address topics ranging from the fundamentals of aerodynamics to materials used in engineering. Working in teams, students design aerodynamic cars and devices, then test their models in a specially built wind tunnel. During the program, participants learn to use three-dimensional computer-aided design software. The first session hosts rising freshmen and sophomores, while the second and third sessions enroll rising juniors and seniors.

UNIVERSITY OF CALIFORNIA-DAVIS
YOUNG SCHOLARS PROGRAM
Res — Coed Ages 16-17

Davis, CA 95616. School of Ed, 1 Shields Ave. Tel: 530-574-0289.
http://ysp.ucdavis.edu
J. Richard Pomeroy, Dir.
Grades 11-12. Adm: Selective. **Appl**—Due: Mar. Transcript, sci teacher rec, another rec.
Enr: 40. **Enr cap:** 40.
Type of instruction: Adv. Grades. **College credit:** 5.
Focus: Environ_Sci Sci.
Fees 2014: Res $6200, 6 wks. Aid (Need).
Housing: Dorms.
Ses: 1. **Wks/ses:** 6. Operates June-Aug.

This apprentice-level research opportunity for rising high school juniors and seniors involves extensive laboratory experience (85 percent of the session time). The program focuses on original research that includes experimental design, data collection, statistical analysis, and the communication of results through both written and oral means. YSP's six-week session features morning lectures, group study, educational excursions, seminars, and individual and group instruction time. Students complete research notebooks, write an article describing the research project and its conclusions, make a presentation of the individual project at a research symposium and present their research to pupils at the home high school.

UNIVERSITY OF CALIFORNIA-IRVINE
AMERICAN INDIAN SUMMER ACADEMY
Res — Coed Ages 14-18

Irvine, CA 92697. Center for Educational Partnerships, 407 Social Science Tower. Tel: 949-824-0291. Fax: 949-824-8219.
www.airp.uci.edu/aisa.php   E-mail: yleon@uci.edu
Yolanda Leon, Coord.
Grades 9-12. Adm: Selective. Prereqs: GPA 2.5. **Appl**—Fee $0. Due: Apr. Transcript, essay.
Type of instruction: Enrich.
Focus: Cultural_Stud.
Fees 2014: Free (in-state residents). Res 2 wks.
Housing: Dorms.
Ses: 1. **Wks/ses:** 1. Operates July.

Students interested in contributing to the American Indian community participate in interactive presentations from various UC-Irvine departments, cultural workshops and activities, field trips and social events. Group projects identify and address an important issue pertaining to the American Indian community, and boys and girls present their work at a closing symposium. AISA participants receive follow-up mentorship from university staff and students throughout their remaining high school years.

UNIVERSITY OF CALIFORNIA-LOS ANGELES
SCI/ART NANOLAB SUMMER INSTITUTE
Res and Day — Coed Ages 16-18

Los Angeles, CA 90095. California NanoSystems Inst, 570 Westwood Plaza. Tel: 310-983-1026. Fax: 310-825-9233.
http://artsci.ucla.edu/summer   E-mail: sciart@cnsi.ucla.edu
Adam Z. Stieg, Dir.
Grades 11-12 (younger if qualified). Adm: Selective. Admitted: 75%. **Appl**—Fee $0. Due: May. Essay, teacher/counselor rec.
Enr: 45. **Enr cap:** 45. Intl: 17%. Non-White: 40%. **Fac** 6. Col/grad students 6. **Staff:** Admin 3. Res 4.
Type of instruction: Adv Undergrad. **Courses:** Biotech Nanotech Web_Design Fine_ Arts Media Photog. **Avg class size:** 15. **Daily hours for:** Classes 8. Study 2. Rec 2. Homework. Grades. **College credit:** 4/crse, total 4.
Focus: Sci. **Features:** Swim.
Fees 2012: Res $2986 (+$200), 2 wks. Day $2050 (+$200), 2 wks.
Housing: Dorms. Avg per room/unit: 2. **Swimming:** Pool. Campus facilities avail.
Est 2008. Nonprofit. Ses: 1. **Wks/ses:** 2. Operates July-Aug.

Conducted at UCLA's California NanoSystems Institute, this rigorous precollege program is a joint venture between the institute and Design Media Arts at UCLA that enables high school juniors and seniors to examine the impact of new sciences (such as bio- and nanotechnology) on contemporary art and popular culture through the completion of a credit-bearing, pass-fail course. The two-week program comprises 80 hours of required lab time, lectures and discussions; 40 hours of field trip time; and daily written compositions that reflect upon lectures and the daily science topic. During the session, boys and girls further benefit from their interactions with undergraduate science students in two different programs: one dealing with design and media, the other with cutting-edge scientific research.

UNIVERSITY OF DELAWARE
FAME/UD SUMMER RESIDENTIAL PROGRAM
Res — Coed Ages 16-18

Newark, DE 19716. College of Engineering, 141 Dupont Hall. Tel: 302-831-6315. Fax: 302-831-7399.
www.engr.udel.edu/rise/fame/index.html   E-mail: mlbrown@udel.edu
Marianne T. Johnson, Dir. Student contact: Michele L. Brown.
Grades 11-12. Adm: Selective. Admitted: 65%. Priority: URM. Prereqs: GPA 3.0. Appl—Fee $0. Due: Apr. Transcript, essay, 2 recs.
Enr: 40. Enr cap: 40. Non-White: 98%. Fac 9. Prof 3. Col/grad students 2. K-12 staff 4. Staff: Admin 2. Couns 8.
Type of instruction: Enrich Undergrad. Courses: Eng. Avg class size: 11. Daily hours for: Classes 3½. Study 4½. Rec 3. Homework. Tests. Grades.
Focus: Engineering Math Sci.
Fees 2011: Res $100 (+$40-60), 4 wks.
Housing: Dorms. Avg per room/unit: 2.
Est 1980. Nonprofit. Ses: 1. Wks/ses: 4. Operates June-July.

Although students of all backgrounds may apply, this program for high school upperclassmen seeks to facilitate increased participation of African-American, Latino and Native American youth in engineering and other science professions. Course work, which is conducted in a demanding academic setting, consists of accelerated enrichment classes in math, science, English and engineering. Personal/professional development workshops, college selection advice, and information on engineering and other science professions complement academics. Participants should plan on attending all four weeks of the program; students go home each weekend.

UNIVERSITY OF EVANSVILLE OPTIONS
Res — Girls Ages 11-17

Evansville, IN 47722. 1800 Lincoln Ave. Tel: 812-488-2651, 800-423-8633. Fax: 812-488-2780.
http://options.evansville.edu   E-mail: tn2@evansville.edu
Phil Gerhart, Dir. Student contact: Tina Newman.
Grades 6-11. Adm: Somewhat_selective. Admitted: 95%. Appl—Fee $0. Due: Rolling. Transcript, essay.
Enr: 20. Enr cap: 20. Non-White: 30%. Fac 11. Prof 7. Col/grad students 4. Staff: Admin 3. Res 4.
Type of instruction: Enrich. Courses: Comp_Sci. Daily hours for: Classes 8. Rec 6.
Focus: Engineering. Features: Rock_Climb Swim Volleyball.
Fees 2014: Res $300-500, 1 wk. Aid (Need).
Housing: Dorms. Swimming: Pool. Campus facilities avail.
Est 1992. Nonprofit. Methodist. Ses: 2. Wks/ses: 1. Operates June.

Conducted by University of Evansville faculty and staff, UE Options consists of two sessions for girls interested in learning more about engineering as an area of potential future study. Middle school sessions enroll pupils about to enter grades 6-8, while the high school Options program accepts girls preparing for grades 9-11. Course work comprises short classes, plant tours to observe engineers and computer scientists at work, and recreational pursuits with participants and college student counselors. Options also acquaints students with career possibilities for individuals with a degree in engineering or computer science.

UNIVERSITY OF FLORIDA
STUDENT SCIENCE TRAINING PROGRAM
Res — Coed Ages 16-18

Gainesville, FL 32611. 334 Yon Hall, PO Box 112010. Tel: 352-392-2310. Fax: 352-392-2344.
www.cpet.ufl.edu/sstp   E-mail: sstp@cpet.ufl.edu
Christy Rodkin, Admin.
Grades 11-12. Adm: Selective. Appl—Due: Mar. Transcript, rec.
Enr: 88. Enr cap: 100. Fac 80. Staff: Admin 5. Couns 10.
Type of instruction: Adv. Courses: Archaeol Astron Computers Ecol Engineering Environ_Sci Geol Marine_Bio/Stud Med/Healthcare Speech. High school & college credit: 6.
Focus: Sci. Features: Social_Servs Work Basketball Swim Tennis Volleyball Racquetball.
Fees 2014: Res $4000 (+$100-200), 7 wks. Aid (Need).
Housing: Dorms. Avg per room/unit: 2. Swimming: Pool. Campus facilities avail.
Est 1959. Nonprofit. Ses: 1. Wks/ses: 7. Operates June-July.

SSTP introduces students to various disciplines of science, medicine and engineering to aid them in choosing career fields. Students spend more than two dozen hours a week participating in active projects with research professors in on-campus laboratories. Lectures, field trips and seminars supplement laboratory participation and class instruction. Topics assigned cover a broad area of scientific study; some students will do field research, some bench research and some computer research. Weekend activities include sports and social activities. Students may earn up to six college credits, and high school credit may be available to Florida students.

UNIVERSITY OF FLORIDA SUMMER JOURNALISM INSTITUTE
Res — Coed Ages 15-18

Gainesville, FL 32611. 2070 Weimer Hall, College of Journ & Communications, PO Box 118400. Tel: 941-661-0021.
www.jou.ufl.edu/sji   E-mail: sji@jou.ufl.edu
Grades 10-12. Adm: Selective. Appl—Due: Rolling. Advisor/prin rec.
Type of instruction: Enrich. Courses: Photog.
Focus: Writing/Journ.
Fees 2014: Res $695, 1 wk.
Housing: Dorms.
Nonprofit. Ses: 1. Wks/ses: 1. Operates June.

This six-day program offers specialized classes in writing, editing, photography, broadcasting and Web design. Guest speakers address such topics as communications law and the role of journalism in society. University of Florida faculty members, high school publications advisers and journalism graduate students serve as course instructors.

UNIVERSITY OF HOUSTON
MENTORING AND ENRICHMENT SEMINAR
IN ENGINEERING TRAINING
Res — Coed Ages 17-18

Houston, TX 77204. E301 Engineering Bldg 2. Tel: 713-743-4222. Fax: 713-743-4228.
www.egr.uh.edu/promes/camps   E-mail: promescamp@egr.uh.edu
Grade 12. Adm: Selective. Appl—Fee $0. Due: Apr. Transcript, test scores, essay, rec.
Enr: 100.
Type of instruction: Enrich.
Focus: Engineering.
Fees 2014: Res $300, 1 wk. Aid (Need).
Housing: Dorms.
Ses: 2. Wks/ses: 1. Operates June.

MESET introduces students to various disciplines of engineering. The project-based curriculum features a team competition in engineering design. Site visits to Houston-area engineering firms, panel discussions by working engineers and current engineering students, and activities at the campus sports and recreation center round out the program. Texas residents receive admissions priority, and MESET actively encourages young women and underrepresented minorities to apply.

UNIVERSITY OF ILLINOIS
COLLEGE OF AGRICULTURAL, CONSUMER AND ENVIRONMENTAL SCIENCES
RESEARCH APPRENTICE PROGRAM
Res — Coed Ages 13-18

Urbana, IL 61801. 123 Mumford Hall, 1301 W Gregory Dr. Tel: 217-333-3380. Fax: 217-244-6537.
www.summerprograms.aces.illinois.edu   E-mail: jthomps5@illinois.edu
Jesse Thompson, Coord.
Grades 9-12. Adm: Selective. Priority: Low-income. URM. Prereqs: GPA 3.0. **Appl**—Fee $25. Due: Mar. Transcript, 2 recs.
Enr: 85. **Enr cap:** 85. **Fac 5. Staff:** Admin 2.
Type of instruction: Adv Enrich Rev SAT/ACT_Prep. **Courses:** Engineering MathVeterinary_Med. **Avg class size:** 20. **Daily hours for:** Classes 4. Study 4. Rec 2. Homework.
Focus: Environ_Sci Sci. **Features:** Swim.
Fees 2014: Free. Res 2-7 wks.
Housing: Dorms. **Swimming:** Pool.
Est 1989. Nonprofit. Ses: 2. Wks/ses: 4-7. Operates June-Aug.

The tuition-free Research Apprentice Program provides career exploration opportunities for students in the top quarter of their class who represent underserved or economically disadvantaged groups. RAP I, a four-week session for students entering grades 9-10, explores career pathways in either food; human and environmental sciences; or children, families and education. Participants visit corporate facilities, attend seminars and minicourses and work in teams to solve problems. RAP II is an intensive, seven-week laboratory and academic program for previous RAP I students and others entering grade 11 who have an interest in food, agricultural and environmental sciences. Laboratory research topics include plant genetics, animal physiology, nutritional sciences, food chemistry and engineering, veterinary medicine, computer imaging and environmental studies.

UNIVERSITY OF ILLINOIS
GIRLS' ADVENTURES IN MATHEMATICS, ENGINEERING AND SCIENCE
Res — Girls Ages 14-18

Urbana, IL 61801. 206 Engineering Hall, 1308 W Green St. Tel: 217-244-3817. Fax: 217-244-4974.
http://engineering.illinois.edu/academics/undergraduate/communities/WIE/games.html
E-mail: engr-games@illinois.edu
Kris Ackerman, Dir.
Grades 9-12. Adm: Selective. **Appl**—Fee $0. Due: Apr. Transcript, teacher rec, personal statement.
Enr: 235. **Enr cap:** 250. **Non-White:** 40%. **Staff:** Admin 3.
Type of instruction: Adv. **Courses:** Math Robotics Crafts Dance Music. **Avg class size:** 18. **Daily hours for:** Classes 7. Rec 3.
Focus: Comp_Sci Engineering Sci. **Features:** Swim.
Fees 2014: Res $1050, 1 wk. Aid (Need).
Housing: Dorms. **Swimming:** Pool.

Est 1998. Nonprofit. Ses: 1. **Wks/ses:** 1. Operates July.

Conducted at the University of Illinois-Urbana, GAMES enables high school girls to explore science and engineering through demonstrations, classroom presentations, hands-on activities and meetings with professional women in relevant fields. The Structures program introduces girls entering grades 9 and 10 to civil engineering basics, and campers design and construct bridges, water towers or boats. Also serving girls entering grades 9 and 10, the robotics camp explores computer technology and hands-on robotic development. The bio-imaging program for girls entering grades 9-11 explores biomedical imaging, optics and image analysis. In the chemical engineering program, girls entering grades 9-11 learn about developing medical advances and alternative energy sources in University of Illinois laboratories. Three programs serve students entering grades 10-12: one focusing on aerospace engineering; another on electrical engineering; and a third on energy generation, conversion and efficiency.

UNIVERSITY OF KANSAS
JAYHAWK DEBATE INSTITUTE
Res — Coed Ages 15-18

Lawrence, KS 66045. Dept of Communication Stud, 1440 Jayhawk Blvd, 102 Bailey Hall. Tel: 785-864-9893. Fax: 785-864-5203.
www.ku.edu/~coms3/camp   E-mail: jayhawkdebateinstitute@gmail.com
Scott Harris, Dir.
Grades 10-12. Adm: Selective. **Appl**—Due: Rolling.
Enr cap: 64-96. **Fac** 7.
Type of instruction: Enrich.
Focus: Debate.
Fees 2014: Res $1700-2300, 2-3 wks. Day $1150-1400, 2-3 wks.
Housing: Dorms.
Ses: 2. **Wks/ses:** 2-3. Operates June-July.

JDI offers two-week intermediate and advanced and three-week advanced policy debate workshops. Programming includes topic lectures; classes in debate theory, case construction, strategy and refutation; research at the University of Kansas libraries; and practice debates and tournaments.

UNIVERSITY OF MARYLAND
DISCOVERING ENGINEERING
Res — Coed Ages 16-17

College Park, MD 20742. 1131 Glenn L Martin Hall. Tel: 301-405-0287. Fax: 301-314-9867.
www.engrscholarships.umd.edu/summer   E-mail: summerengr@umd.edu
Bruk Berhane, Dir.
Grades 11-12. Adm: Selective. **Appl**—Due: Apr. Transcript, rec, personal statement.
Enr: 30. **Enr cap:** 30.
Type of instruction: Enrich.
Focus: Engineering.
Fees 2014: Res $1000, 1 wk.
Housing: Dorms. Campus facilities avail.
Nonprofit. Ses: 2. **Wks/ses:** 1. Operates July.

Rising high school juniors and seniors with a strong interest in engineering, math, science or a combination thereof sample college living as they explore different engineering disciplines during this weeklong session. Programming consists of lab work and demonstrations, lectures, discussions, computer instruction and a team design project. Students visit each of the engineering majors to learn more about specific departments and their projects.

UNIVERSITY OF MASSACHUSETTS MEDICAL SCHOOL
HIGH SCHOOL HEALTH CAREERS PROGRAM
Res — Coed Ages 15-17

Worcester, MA 01655. Office of Outreach Prgms, S3-104, 55 Lake Ave N. Tel: 508-856-2707, 877-395-3149. Fax: 508-856-6540.
www.umassmed.edu/hshcp/index.aspx   E-mail: outreach.programs@umassmed.edu
Robert E. Layne, Dir.
Grades 10-11. Adm: Very selective. Priority: Low-income. URM. Appl—Fee $0. Due: Mar. Transcript, essay, 3 recs, interview.
Type of instruction: Enrich Study_Skills. Courses: Comp_Sci Eng Math Sci.
Focus: Med/Healthcare.
Fees 2014: Free (in-state residents). Res 4 wks.
Housing: Dorms.
Ses: 1. Wks/ses: 4. Operates June-July.

HSHCP exposes Massachusetts high schoolers from backgrounds lacking strong representation in medicine to healthcare professions and biomedical and biotechnology careers. Classroom sessions address language arts skills, math, science/biology and information technology. Students also take part in internships with physicians and other healthcare professionals. Seminars provide information about college application and financial aid procedures.

UNIVERSITY OF MIAMI SUMMER SCHOLAR PROGRAMS
Res — Coed Ages 16-17

Coral Gables, FL 33124. PO Box 248005. Tel: 305-284-4000. Fax: 305-284-6629.
www.miami.edu/ssp   E-mail: ssp@miami.edu
Grades 11-12. Adm: Selective. Prereqs: GPA 3.0. Appl—Fee $35. Due: May. Transcript, essay, rec.
Enr: 196. Fac 25. Staff: Admin 1.
Type of instruction: Adv. Courses: Sports_Admin Sports_Med. Avg class size: 18. Daily hours for: Classes 6. Study 3. Rec 2. High school & college credit: 3/crse, total 6.
Focus: Bus/Fin Engineering Forensic_Sci Intl_Relations Marine_Bio/Stud Med/Healthcare Writing/Journ. Features: Community_Serv Swim.
Fees 2014: Res $7295, 3 wks. Day $6168-6393.
Housing: Dorms. Swimming: Ocean Pool.
Est 1991. Nonprofit. Ses: 1. Wks/ses: 3. Operates June-July.

The programs, taught by university faculty, allow highly motivated rising high school juniors and seniors to pursue course work in the following areas: broadcast journalism, business, engineering, forensic investigation, health and medicine, international relations, marine science, sports administration and sports medicine. Guest speakers and visits to local sites relevant to the field of study supplement in-class work. Students earn three to six college credits, which are also accepted at many high schools. In addition to the disciplines mentioned above, the university conducts a program focusing on filmmaking (see separate listing for details).

UNIVERSITY OF MICHIGAN MEDICAL SCHOOL
SUMMER SCIENCE ACADEMY
Res — Coed Ages 14-16

Ann Arbor, MI 48109. 2919C Taubman Medical Library, 1135 Catherine St. Tel: 734-615-8185. Fax: 734-615-4828.
www.med.umich.edu/medschool/ssa   E-mail: oheiprecollegeprograms@umich.edu
Makeda Turner, Dir.

Grades 9-10. Adm: Selective. **Appl**—Fee $0. Due: Mar. Transcript, 2 recs, personal statement.
Enr: 50.
Type of instruction: Enrich. **Courses:** Expository_Writing Sci.
Focus: Med/Healthcare.
Fees 2014: Free. Res 2 wks.
Housing: Dorms.
Nonprofit. **Ses:** 1. **Wks/ses:** 2. Operates June.

Sponsored by the university's Diversity and Career Development Office, this enrichment program enables rising high school juniors and seniors from Michigan to preview medical school and college life. Current medical school and program alumni live in the dorms with SSA participants as they provide classroom tutoring, intellectual and social stimulation, one-on-one and small-group mentoring, and insight into college and medical school. During the day, pupils attend classes taught by experts in the field. Evening recreational pursuits include activities in the arts.

UNIVERSITY OF MICHIGAN
MICHIGAN MATH AND SCIENCE SCHOLARS
Res and Day — Coed Ages 15-17

Ann Arbor, MI 48109. 2074 East Hall, 530 Church St. Tel: 734-647-4466. Fax: 734-763-0937.
www.math.lsa.umich.edu/mmss   E-mail: mmss@umich.edu
Stephen DeBacker, Dir.
Grades 10-12. Adm: Selective. **Appl**—Fee $100. Due: Rolling. Transcript, rec, personal statement.
Type of instruction: Adv Enrich. **Courses:** Astron Ecol Environ_Sci Geol. **Avg class size:** 15.
Focus: Math Sci.
Fees 2014: Res $1850-3700 (+$100), 2-4 wks. Day $1100-2200 (+$100), 2-4 wks.
Housing: Dorms. Campus facilities avail.
Nonprofit. **Spons:** University of Michigan. **Ses:** 2. **Wks/ses:** 2. Operates June-July.

In classes of 15 students, MMSS exposes high schoolers to current developments and research in the sciences in a college setting. Each session features such course selections as astronomy; chemistry; ecology and evolutionary biology; geology; math, molecular, cellular and developmental biology; physics; environmental studies; and statistics. Students conduct research, work in computer labs and engage in fieldwork with their professors. Boys and girls take one course per session and may attend one or both two-week sessions.

UNIVERSITY OF MICHIGAN SUMMER ENGINEERING ACADEMY
Res — Coed Ages 15-18; Day — Coed 12-14

Ann Arbor, MI 48109. Center for Engineering Diversity & Outreach, 2121 Bonisteel Blvd, 153 Chrysler Ctr. Tel: 734-647-7120. Fax: 734-647-7011.
www.engin.umich.edu/diversity   E-mail: cedo-admin@umich.edu
Robert Scott
Grades 8-12. Adm: Selective. **Appl**—Fee $0. Due: Mar. Transcript, essay, 2 recs.
Enr: 30-60.
Type of instruction: Enrich Study_Skills. **Courses:** Math Sci.
Focus: Engineering.
Fees 2014: Res $100-300, 2 wks. Aid (Need).
Housing: Dorms. Avg per room/unit: 2.
Ses: 3. **Wks/ses:** 2. Operates June-Aug.

The university's summer precollege engineering offerings include the Summer Enrichment Program at the Michigan Engineering Zone, Michigan Introduction to Technology and Engineering (for rising sophomores and juniors) and the Summer College Engineering

Exposure Program (for rising seniors). SEP at MEZ is a commuter program educating rising eighth and ninth graders about applied engineering. MITE classes address math, engineering concepts, communication skills and study skills, while guidance workshops focus on college admissions and financial aid. SCEEP exposes students to various engineering departments and covers the skills required as one transitions from high school to college.

UNIVERSITY OF MISSISSIPPI
LOTT LEADERSHIP INSTITUTE FOR HIGH SCHOOL STUDENTS
Res — Coed Ages 17-18

University, MS 38677. PO Box 9. Tel: 662-915-6614. Fax: 662-915-6622.
http://lottinst.olemiss.edu/high-school-students/for-high-school-students E-mail: summercollege@olemis.edu
Cass Dodgen, Dir.
Grade 12. Adm: Selective. Prereqs: GPA 3.2. **Appl**—Fee $0. Due: Jan. Transcript, 2 recs. **Enr:** 20. **Enr cap:** 20.
Type of instruction: Adv. **Courses:** Leadership Public_Speak. **College credit:** 6.
Focus: Pol_Sci Leadership.
Fees 2014: Res $600, 5 wks.
Housing: Dorms.
Est 1990. Nonprofit. **Ses:** 2. **Wks/ses:** 5. Operates May-July.

Rising high school seniors who have been nominated by their high school principals. The program combines college course work in political science (for transferable college credit) with general college preparation. Participants have opportunities to meet college administrators, student leaders and community figures while engaged in current event debates, discussions and decision-making activities. The program concludes with a weeklong trip to Washington, DC, during which students observe the Federal Government, hear from national politicians and tour the Capitol.

UNIVERSITY OF NEW ORLEANS
THE GLORIES OF FRANCE
Res — Coed Ages 16-17

Montpellier, France.
Contact (Year-round): International Ed, 2000 Lakeshore Dr, New Orleans, LA 70148. Tel: 504-280-7455. Fax: 504-280-7317.
www.inst.uno.edu/france   E-mail: gofmc@uno.edu
Marie Kaposchyn, Dir.
Grades 11-12. Adm: Selective. **Appl**—Fee $150. Due: Mar.
Enr: 50. **Fac 10. Staff:** Admin 8. Couns 8.
College credit.
Travel: Europe.
Focus: Fr. **Features:** Swim.
Fees 2014: Res $4495 (+airfare), 5 wks. Aid (Merit & Need).
Housing: Dorms. Avg per room/unit: 1. **Swimming:** Pool.
Est 1973. Ses: 1. **Wks/ses:** 5. Operates July-Aug.

Four days per week, students spend mornings at this academic program taking college-level French courses or other classes (taught in English) relevant to their college studies. Ten proficiency tracks are available for French study. Leisure time and weekend activities include trips to Mediterranean beaches, an optional excursion to Barcelona, Spain, and recreational activities.

THE UNIVERSITY OF NORTHERN COLORADO
FRONTIERS OF SCIENCE INSTITUTE
Res — Coed Ages 15-18

Greeley, CO 80639. Campus Box 123. Tel: 970-351-2976. Fax: 970-351-1269.
www.mast.unco.edu/fsi   E-mail: lori.ball@unco.edu
Lori K. Ball, Prgm Admin.
Grades 11-12 (younger if qualified). Adm: Selective. Admitted: 62%. Prereqs: GPA 3.0.
Appl—Fee $0. Due: Apr. Transcript, 3 recs.
Enr: 23. Enr cap: 30. Intl: 10%. Non-White: 26%. Fac 7. Prof 2. Col/grad students 2. K-12
staff 2. Specialists 1. Staff: Admin 1. Couns 2.
Type of instruction: Adv. Courses: Astron Comp_Sci Engineering Environ_Sci Geol. Avg
class size: 13. Daily hours for: Classes 4. Rec 4. Grades. College credit: 4/crse,
total 4.
Focus: Sci. Features: Caving Hiking Ropes_Crse Wilderness_Camp Basketball Swim
Volleyball.
Fees 2014: Res $800-3400, 6 wks. Aid 2009 (Merit & Need): $61,600.
Housing: Dorms. Avg per room/unit: 2. Swimming: Pool. Campus facilities avail.
Est 1959. Nonprofit. Ses: 1. Wks/ses: 6. Operates June-July.

Selected for their overall academic acheivement and their interest in science, FSI participants engage in various aspects of science, technology, engineering and math through classroom and lab activity, field trips and industrial visits, and seminars conducted by academic and industry professionals. Although the curriculum varies year to year, instructors place particular emphasis on the relationships and interdependence among such math and science disciplines as biology, chemistry, physics, earth and space science, computer science and engineering. Most boys and girls work with a mentor on an in-depth scientific research project.

UNIVERSITY OF NOTRE DAME
INTRODUCTION TO ENGINEERING
Res — Coed Ages 17-18

Notre Dame, IN 46556. 384 Fitzpatrick Hall of Engineering. Tel: 574-631-6092. Fax:
574-631-9260.
http://iep.nd.edu   E-mail: iep@nd.edu
Ramzi K. Bualuan, Dir.
Grade 12 (younger if qualified). Adm: Selective. Admitted: 60%. Appl—Fee $0. Due:
Apr.
Enr: 65. Enr cap: 65. Fac 18. Prof 18. Staff: Admin 2. Res 15.
Type of instruction: Enrich Undergrad. Homework.
Focus: Engineering.
Fees 2014: Res $1850, 2 wks. Aid (Need).
Housing: Dorms. Campus facilities avail.
Nonprofit. Ses: 2. Wks/ses: 2. Operates June-July.

Designed for rising high school seniors, IEP provides students with an overview of the elements of engineering design and computer programming, a discussion of career opportunities in engineering, a chance to meet professional engineers and a preview of college life. In the morning, boys and girls attend two hourlong lectures, while afternoons provide time for hands-on computer sessions and work in the engineering learning center. Pupils write a report on each talk, learn concepts of design and implement them by building systems, and team up with fellow students to compose and deliver a presentation during the program's final week. Two plant trips to nearby engineering facilities complete the curriculum.

UNIVERSITY OF NOTRE DAME
SCHOOL OF ARCHITECTURE
CAREER DISCOVERY
Res — Coed Ages 16-18

Notre Dame, IN 46556. 110 Bond Hall. Tel: 574-631-2322. Fax: 574-631-8486.
http://architecture.nd.edu/academics/professional-development/career-discovery
E-mail: arch@nd.edu
Grades 11-12. Adm: FCFS. Appl—Due: Apr.
Type of instruction: Enrich.
Focus: Architect.
Fees 2014: Res $1900, 2 wks.
Housing: Dorms.
Ses: 1. Wks/ses: 2. Operates June.

Young men and women considering careers in architecture learn about both college-level study and the steps they can take in grades 11 and 12 to prepare themselves for a future in the field. Notre Dame professors and advanced university pupils teach architectural history, as well as the skills and responsibilities required in contemporary architectural practice. Design studios, architecture seminars and field trips to notable architectural sites enrich the program.

UNIVERSITY OF PENNSYLVANIA
LEADERSHIP IN THE BUSINESS WORLD
Res — Coed Ages 17-18

Philadelphia, PA 19104. G95 Jon M Huntsman Hall, 3730 Walnut St. Tel: 215-746-8765.
www.wharton.upenn.edu/academics/lbw.cfm   E-mail: lbw-inquiries@wharton.upenn.edu
Helene Elting, Dir.
Grade 12. Adm: Selective. Appl—Fee $75. Due: Mar. Transcript, 2 recs, standardized test results, essay.
Enr: 60. Enr cap: 60.
Type of instruction: Enrich.
Focus: Bus/Fin.
Fees 2014: Res $6595, 4 wks. Aid (Need).
Housing: Dorms.
Est 1999. Ses: 1. Wks/ses: 4. Operates July-Aug.

Sponsored by Penn's Wharton School of Business, LBW enrolls a select group of rising high school seniors who have an interest in the business world. Students engage in classroom discussions about leadership, business ethics, entrepreneurship, accounting, management and economics; attend lectures and presentations by Wharton faculty and guest speakers; visit business enterprises and converse with businesspeople in the areas of finance, entrepreneurship, entertainment, real estate and retail; work in teams to design, prepare and formulate a business plan for evaluation by a panel of venture capitalists; receive coaching on communicational and team-building skills from six upper-level Wharton undergraduates; and improve their leadership skills through collaborative teamwork.

UNIVERSITY OF PENNSYLVANIA
MANAGEMENT AND TECHNOLOGY SUMMER INSTITUTE
Res — Coed Ages 17-18

Philadelphia, PA 19104. 3537 Locust Walk, Ste 100. Tel: 215-898-4145.
www.upenn.edu/fisher/summer-mt   E-mail: mgtech@seas.upenn.edu
Jaime Davis, Coord.
Grade 12 (younger if qualified). Adm: Selective. Appl—Fee $75. Due: Apr. Transcript, 2 recs, standardized test results, essay.

Enr: 50. **Enr cap:** 50.
Type of instruction: Adv. **College credit.**
Focus: Bus/Fin Engineering.
Fees 2014: Res $6000 (+$225-375), 3 wks.
Housing: Dorms.
Ses: 1. **Wks/ses:** 3. Operates July-Aug.

This unusual credit-bearing program for rising high seniors (and a limited number of particularly capable rising juniors) addresses both technological concepts and management principles. College professors and successful entrepreneurs teach M&TSI's classes. Other aspects of the program are intensive team projects, activities focusing upon the principles and the practice of technological innovation, and field trips to companies and research and development facilities. In addition to gaining an introduction to core engineering and business disciplines, participants also learn about academic and career opportunities available in these two fields.

UNIVERSITY OF PENNSYLVANIA
PENN SUMMER SCIENCE ACADEMIES
Res and Day — Coed Ages 15-18

Philadelphia, PA 19104. 3440 Market St, Ste 100. Tel: 516-621-3939. Fax: 215-573-2053.
www.sas.upenn.edu/summer/programs/highschool   E-mail: hsprogs@sas.upenn.edu
Grades 10-12. Adm: Selective. Admitted: 57%. **Appl**—Fee $70. Due: May. Transcript, rec, essay, resume, standardized test scores.
Enr: 100. **Fac 3. Staff:** Couns 30.
Type of instruction: Adv Enrich. **Courses:** Physics. **Daily hours for:** Classes 7. Study 2. Rec 3.
Focus: Med/Healthcare Sci. **Features:** Swim.
Fees 2014: Res $7299-12299, 3-5½ wks. Day $6199, 3-5½ wks. Aid (Need).
Housing: Dorms. **Swimming:** Pool.
Est 1987. Nonprofit. **Ses:** 1. **Wks/ses:** 4. Operates July.

This intensive, noncredit science program comprises guided laboratory projects, seminars, faculty lectures, discussion groups, problem-solving sessions and field trips. University of Pennsylvania scientists and students provide all instruction. Participants choose a concentration in experimental physics or biomedical research, and the Monday through Friday programming varies according to the pupil's chosen concentration. Although some local day students attend PSSA, most boys and girls elect to board at the university.

UNIVERSITY OF ST ANDREWS
INTERNATIONAL SCIENCE SUMMER PROGRAMME
Res — Coed Ages 16-18

St Andrews, KY16 9AX Fife, Scotland. St Katharine's W, 16 The Scores. Tel: 44-1334-462147. Fax: 44-1334-463330.
www.st-andrews.ac.uk/admissions/ug/int/summerschools   E-mail: fjt2@st-andrews.ac.uk
Frances Trahar, Dir.
Grades 11-PG. Adm: Somewhat_selective. Prereqs: GPA 3.0. **Appl**—Fee £15. Due: Apr. 2 recs, standardized test results, personal statement.
Enr cap: 25. Intl: 20%. Non-White: 10%. **Fac 16.** Prof 8. Col/grad students 8. **Staff:** Admin 2. Couns 2.
Type of instruction: Adv. **Courses:** Ecol Math Geosci Music Photog Theater. **Daily hours for:** Classes 3. Study 3. Rec 4. Homework. Tests. Grades. **College credit:** 12.
Intl program focus: Acad.
Focus: Sci. **Features:** Conservation Exploration Hiking Mtn_Trips Swim.

Fees 2014: Res £3000 (+£200), 4 wks.
Housing: Dorms. Avg per room/unit: 1. **Swimming:** Ocean Pool. Campus facilities avail.
Est 2012. Ses: 1. Wks/ses: 4. Operates June-July.

This precollege program provides students with a college-level academic experience that focuses on various science disciplines, including biology, chemistry, ecology, physics and geoscience. Graduate students and full-time professors from the University of St Andrews serve as course instructors. Extensive field trips to sites of scientific interest enrich the curriculum. Cultural excursions and activities round out the program.

UNIVERSITY OF ST. THOMAS
THREESIXTY JOURNALISM SUMMER WORKSHOP
Res and Day — Coed Ages 14-18

St Paul, MN 55105. 2115 Summit Ave, Mail 5057. Tel: 651-962-5282.
www.threesixtyjournalism.org E-mail: info@threesixtyjournalism.org
Lynda McDonnell, Exec Dir.
Grades 8-12. Adm: Selective. Priority: Low-income. URM. **Appl**—Due: Apr. Transcript, rec, writing sample, essay.
Enr: 15. Enr cap: 15. Fac 4. Staff: Admin 3. Couns 3.
Type of instruction: Enrich. **Courses:** Media.
Focus: Writing/Journ. **Features:** Swim.
Fees 2014: Res $900, 2 wks. Day $200, 2 wks.
Housing: Dorms. **Swimming:** Pool.
Est 2001. Nonprofit. **Ses: 2. Wks/ses: 2.** Operates June-July.

Designed primarily for minority students with an interest in writing and reporting—especially those who work on high school newspapers or television production—this tuition-free program consists of writing and reporting courses, layout and design classes, visits to Twin Cities' newspapers and television stations, team production of special newspaper pages for publication in two area newspapers, and assignment of a professional reporter/writer as a mentor for each student. Writers, photographers, artists and editors employed by the Minneapolis *Star Tribune* and the St. Paul *Pioneer Press*; reporters, producers and photographers from local TV stations; and members of the St. Thomas journalism staff serve as faculty for the program. Particularly able pupils may earn a four-year scholarship to study journalism at the University of St. Thomas.

UNIVERSITY OF SOUTHERN CALIFORNIA
FRONTIERS OF ENERGY RESOURCES SUMMER CAMP
Res — Coed Ages 16-18

Los Angeles, CA 90089. Ctr for Interactive Smart Oilfield Technologies, 3710 S McClintock Ave, RTH 311. Tel: 213-740-1076. Fax: 213-740-1077.
http://cisoft.usc.edu/uscchevron-summercamp/summer-camp-2013
E-mail: cisoft@vsoe.usc.edu
Student contact: Juli Legat.
Grade 12. Adm: Selective. **Appl**—Due: Apr. Transcript, teacher rec.
Enr: 23.
Type of instruction: Adv Enrich.
Focus: Sci. **Features:** Swim.
Fees 2014: Free. Res 1 wk.
Housing: Dorms. **Swimming:** Pool.
Est 2009. Ses: 1. Wks/ses: 1. Operates June.

This USC program offers a preparatory, interactive training program that focuses on various energy resources, among them fossil fuels, solar power, bio-fuels, wind power, nuclear energy and information technologies for energy-efficient operations. Students develop problem-solving techniques and team-building skills while living in residence halls and previewing the college experience.

UNIVERSITY OF TEXAS-ARLINGTON
ENGINEERING AND COMPUTER SCIENCE SUMMER CAMPS
Res — Coed Ages 12-15; Day — Coed 11-16

Arlington, TX 76019. College of Engineering, PO Box 19014. Tel: 817-272-1295. Fax: 817-272-1296.
www.uta.edu/engineering/summercamps   E-mail: engineeringoutreach@uta.edu
J. Carter M. Tiernan, Dir. Student contact: Ashley Bigley, E-mail: ashleyb@uta.edu.
Grades 6-11. Adm: Selective. Admitted: 90%. **Appl**—Fee $0. Due: Apr. Transcript, teacher rec.
Enr: 50. **Enr cap:** 50. Intl: 5%. Non-White: 45%. **Fac 15.** Prof 12. Col/grad students 3. **Staff:** Admin 3. Couns 2.
Type of instruction: Enrich. **Courses:** Math Sci.
Focus: Comp_Sci Engineering. **Features:** Aviation/Aero Basketball Soccer.
Fees 2014: Res $250-375, 1 wk. Aid 2009 (Need): $7600.
Housing: Dorms. Avg per room/unit: 2.
Est 1994. Nonprofit. Ses: 5. Wks/ses: 1. Operates June-Aug.

Weeklong day and residential camps expose middle and high school students to various engineering disciplines (aerospace, biomedical, civil and environmental, computer science, electrical, materials science and mechanical), as well as related topics in chemistry and physics. Professors and graduate and undergraduate students lead lectures, hands-on exercises and special presentations. Field trips to local businesses introduce students to engineering careers.

UNIVERSITY OF THE SOUTH
BRIDGE PROGRAM IN MATH AND SCIENCE
Res — Coed Ages 17-18

Sewanee, TN 37383. 735 University Ave. Tel: 931-598-1997. Fax: 931-598-1864.
www.sewanee.edu/bridgeprogram   E-mail: bridgepr@sewanee.edu
Catalina Jordan Alvarez, Dir.
Grade 12. Adm: Selective. Admitted: 40%. Priority: URM. **Appl**—Fee $0. Due: Mar. Transcript, standardized test scores, 2 recs.
Enr: 20. **Enr cap:** 20. Non-White: 90%. **Fac 3.** Prof 3. **Staff:** Admin 2. Couns 5.
Type of instruction: Adv Enrich Undergrad. **Courses:** Astron Comp_Sci. **Daily hours for:** Classes 5. Study 2. Rec 5. Homework.
Focus: Math Sci. **Features:** Canoe Caving Climbing_Wall Hiking Mtn_Trips Ropes_Crse Basketball Golf Soccer Swim Tennis Track Ultimate_Frisbee Weight_Trng.
Fees 2014: Free. Res 3 wks.
Housing: Dorms. Avg per room/unit: 2. **Swimming:** Lake Pool. Campus facilities avail.
Est 1999. Nonprofit. Ses: 1. Wks/ses: 3. Operates June-July.

This intensive precollege program enrolls rising seniors who have displayed high achievement in math and science, particularly those students of ethnic groups lacking prominent representation in these fields of study. University faculty members teach calculus and research-based science classes in astronomy and computer science. Current Sewanee undergraduates assist the professors and serve as mentors to Bridge Program participants. Students need pay only for their trip to campus, as the university covers all program expenses.

UNIVERSITY OF VIRGINIA INTRODUCTION TO ENGINEERING
Res — Coed Ages 16-18

Charlottesville, VA 22904. 351 McCormick Rd, PO Box 400255. Tel: 434-924-0614.

www.seas.virginia.edu/diversity/pre_college/ite.php   E-mail: eng-cde@virginia.edu
Carolyn Vallas, Dir.
Grades 11-12. Adm: Selective. Prereqs: GPA 3.0. **Appl**—Due: Apr. Essay, transcript, standardized test scores.
Staff: Couns 4.
Type of instruction: Enrich.
Focus: Engineering.
Fees 2014: Res $650, 1 wk. Aid (Need).
Housing: Dorms.
Est 1987. Nonprofit. **Ses:** 1. **Wks/ses:** 1. Operates June.

ITE features daily introductory engineering classes, seminars on college admissions and financial aid, demonstrations, hands-on experiments, and departmental and university tours. Instructors devote special attention to the concerns of groups typically underrepresented in engineering fields.

UNIVERSITY OF VIRGINIA
SORENSEN INSTITUTE FOR POLITICAL LEADERSHIP
HIGH SCHOOL LEADERS PROGRAM
Res — Coed Ages 16-18

Charlottesville, VA 22904. PO Box 400206. Tel: 434-243-2470. Fax: 434-982-5536.
www.sorenseninstitute.org/programs/hslp   E-mail: april.auger@virginia.edu
Lauren Gilbert, Dir.
Grades 11-PG (younger if qualified). Adm: Selective. Admitted: 50%. **Appl**—Fee $0. Due: Mar. Transcript, reference, essay, interview.
Enr: 32. **Enr cap:** 35. **Fac** 2. Prof 2. **Staff:** Admin 5. Couns 3.
Type of instruction: Enrich. **Daily hours for:** Classes 7. Study 2. Rec 1. Homework. Grades. **College credit:** 3.
Focus: Govt Leadership Pol_Sci. **Features:** Ropes_Crse.
Fees 2014: Res $1800, 2 wks. Aid (Need).
Housing: Dorms. Avg per room/unit: 4.
Est 2003. Nonprofit. **Ses:** 1. **Wks/ses:** 2. Operates July.

HSLP participants, who must be either state residents or out-of-state pupils studying in Virginia, engage in substantive public policy debates and interact with political and business leaders. Classroom instruction focuses on local- and state-government structures and processes, major policy issues and advocacy tools. Students work in groups on a culminating project in which they develop policy proposals and reports for presentation to a group of government and business professionals. Guest speakers include a range of elected officials, business and nonprofit leaders, academics, lobbyists and government employees.

UNIVERSITY OF WISCONSIN-MADISON
ENGINEERING SUMMER PROGRAM
Res — Coed Ages 16-17

Madison, WI 53706. 1150 Engineering Hall, 1415 Engineering Dr. Tel: 608-263-5367. Fax: 608-262-6400.
www.engr.wisc.edu/current/coe-dao-engineering-summer-program-esp.html
E-mail: bcnunez@engr.wisc.edu
Grades 11-12. Adm: Very selective. Priority: URM. Prereqs: GPA 3.0. **Appl**—Fee $0. Due: Apr. Transcript, math & sci teacher recs, essay.
Type of instruction: Enrich Undergrad. **Courses:** Math Sci.
Focus: Engineering.
Fees 2014: Free. Res 6 wks.
Housing: Dorms.
Nonprofit. **Ses:** 1. **Wks/ses:** 6. Operates June-Aug.

Designed for rising high school juniors and seniors from groups traditionally underrepresented in science, technology, math and engineering (including females), ESP addresses math, engineering, science and technical communications. This free, structured program promotes further understanding of the field of engineering and its disciplines through industry site visits, cultural enrichment activities and faculty mentoring. Students sample a university environment and learn the importance of early college preparation.

UTAH BUSINESS WEEK
Res — Coed Ages 15-16

Logan, UT. Utah State Univ.
Contact (Year-round): c/o Workers Compensation Fund, 392 E 6400 S, Salt Lake City, UT 84107. **Tel:** 801-288-8340, 800-446-2667. **Fax:** 801-284-8984.
www.utahbusinessweek.org   **E-mail:** ubw@utahbusinessweek.org
Grades 10-11. Adm: Selective. **Appl—Due:** May. Rec, essay.
Type of instruction: Enrich.
Focus: Bus/Fin.
Fees 2014: Res $100, 1 wk. Aid (Need).
Housing: Dorms. Avg per room/unit: 2.
Nonprofit. **Ses:** 1. **Wks/ses:** 1. Operates July-Aug.

Conducted at Utah State University, UBW gives rising high school sophomores and juniors a taste of college life while educating them about all aspects of business and preparing them for a future business career. Students develop leadership and teamwork skills through a program that includes speakers, tours of local companies, simulations and team-building exercises. Volunteers from the Utah business community organize and completely run the program.

VANDERBILT UNIVERSITY PRE-COLLEGE PAVE
Res and Day — Coed Ages 16-18

Nashville, TN 37235. 2301 Vanderbilt Pl, VU Sta B 351736. Tel: 615-322-7827. Fax:
615-322-3297.
http://pave.vanderbilt.edu   **E-mail: pave@vanderbilt.edu**
John Veillette, Dir.
Grades 12-PG. Adm: Selective. **Appl—Due:** Apr. Transcript, recs, standardized test scores.
Enr: 175. **Enr cap:** 175. **Intl:** 30%.
Type of instruction: Adv Enrich Undergrad. **Daily hours for:** Classes 6. Study 2½.
Focus: Engineering Med/Healthcare Sci.
Fees 2014: Res $6200, 5 wks. Day $4475, 5 wks.
Housing: Dorms.
Est 1990. Nonprofit. **Ses:** 1. **Wks/ses:** 6. Operates June-July.

PAVE seeks to strengthen the academic skills of students planning to enter a college engineering, pre-medicine/healthcare, science or technology program. Rising high school seniors expecting to take Advanced Placement or honors math or science courses stand to benefit, and the five-week session may also help pupils improve their ACT, AP, SAT or TOEFL scores. The program addresses problem-solving, technical writing, computer application and laboratory skills through experimentation. Participants also gain an introduction to college life.

VICTORY BRIEFS INSTITUTE
Res and Day — Coed Ages 13-18

Los Angeles, CA 90049. 925 N Norman Pl. Tel: 310-472-6364. Fax: 208-248-9801.
http://victorybriefs.com   **E-mail: help@victorybriefs.com**
Mike Bietz, Dir.
Grades 8-12. Adm: FCFS. **Appl—Due:** Rolling.
Type of instruction: Enrich.

Focus: Debate.
Fees 2014: Res $1500-3450, 2-3 wks. Day $900-1900, 2-3 wks. Aid (Need).
Housing: Dorms. Avg per room/unit: 2.
Est 2003. Ses: 2. **Wks/ses:** 2-3. Operates July-Aug.

VBI offers two- and three-week sessions on the campuses of the University of California-Los Angeles and Loyola Marymount University. The curriculum includes lectures, smaller seminars, demonstration and practice rounds, informal discussions and one-on-one sessions with coaches. The institute places students in lab groups of 12 to 15 based upon area of focus and experience level. A novice lab serves boys and girls with no previous Lincoln-Douglas experience. High school debate coaches and former invitational and national tournament champions serve as VBI instructors.

WASHINGTON UNIVERSITY
ARCHITECTURE DISCOVERY PROGRAM
Res — Coed Ages 17-18

St Louis, MO 63130. Campus Box 1031, 1 Brookings Dr. Tel: 314-935-8652. Fax: 314-935-6462.
www.samfoxschool.wustl.edu/summer/adp   E-mail: wardenburg@samfox.wustl.edu
Student contact: Elizabeth Roeleveld, E-mail: eroeleveld@samfox.wustl.edu.
Grade 12. Adm: Selective. **Appl**—Fee $35. Due: May.
Enr: 60. Enr cap: 60. Fac 4. Col/grad students 4. **Staff:** Admin 2. Res 4.
Type of instruction: Undergrad. **Avg class size:** 12. **College credit:** 1/crse, total 3.
Focus: Architect.
Fees 2014: Res $2947 (+$250), 2 wks.
Housing: Dorms. Campus facilities avail.
Ses: 1. **Wks/ses:** 2. Operates July.

Conducted by Washington University's Sam Fox School of Design & Visual Arts, this introduction to architecture for rising seniors focuses on creative design and environmental sustainability. Morning activities include field trips to construction sites, visits to architecture firms, lectures and drawing sessions. Afternoons provide time for work in the studio, where students initiate and develop an architectural design for a final review.

WHALE CAMP
Res — Coed Ages 10-17

Grand Manan Island, New Brunswick, Canada.
Contact (Year-round): PO Box 63, Cheney, PA 19319. Tel: 610-399-1463, 888-549-4253. Fax: 610-399-4482.
www.whalecamp.com   E-mail: info@whalecamp.com
Dennis Bowen, Dir.
Grades 5-12. Adm: FCFS. **Appl**—Fee $0. Due: Rolling.
Enr cap: 36-38. Fac 11. Staff: Admin 3. Couns 9.
Type of instruction: Enrich. **Courses:** Ecol Geol Creative_Writing Fine_Arts Photog.
Focus: Environ_Sci Marine_Bio/Stud Oceanog. **Features:** Adventure_Travel Aquatics Boating Conservation Exploration Hiking Kayak Outdoor_Ed Sail Sea_Cruises Seamanship Field_Hockey Roller_Hockey Soccer Swim Ultimate_Frisbee Volleyball Watersports.
Fees 2014: Res $1395-4995, 1-3 wks.
Housing: Dorms. **Swimming:** Lake Ocean.
Est 1983. Inc. **Ses:** 22. **Wks/ses:** 1-3. Operates June-Aug.

Students in this marine science program sail aboard the program's schooner while learning about the geology of Canada's Bay of Fundy region, the bay's marine life and the land-based life of Grand Manan Island. Aspects of the program include whale tracking, whale research, study of marine mammals and birds, ocean life photography, sailing, sea kayaking, hiking and sea navigation. Students utilize professional marine science and oceanography equipment.

WHITMAN NATIONAL DEBATE INSTITUTE
Res and Day — Coed Ages 13-19

Walla Walla, WA 99362. Whitman College, Dept of Rhetoric. Tel: 509-527-5499. Fax: 509-527-4959.
www.whitman.edu/academics/whitman-debate   E-mail: debate@whitman.edu
Jim Hanson, Dir.
Grades 8-12 (younger if qualified). Adm: FCFS. **Appl**—Fee $0. Due: May.
Enr: 126. Non-White: 20%. **Fac 30.** Col/grad students 30. **Staff:** Admin 4. Couns 3.
Type of instruction: Adv Enrich. **Avg class size:** 8. **Daily hours for:** Classes 10. Rec 3. Homework.
Focus: Debate. **Features:** Basketball.
Fees 2014: Res $800-2200, 1-3 wks. Aid 2011 (Merit & Need): $14,000.
Housing: Dorms. Avg per room/unit: 2.
Est 2000. Nonprofit. **Spons:** Whitman College. **Ses:** 5. **Wks/ses:** 1-3. Operates July-Aug.

WNDI conducts two- and three-week policy and Lincoln-Douglas debate camps, as well as a weeklong public forum debate session. The first part of the policy debate camp consists of lectures, examples, drills and lab work for affirmative cases, disadvantages, counterplans, kritiks and topicality arguments; the second part features independent research projects, practice and tournament debates, and advanced theory lectures. During the first part of the Lincoln-Douglas camp, the focus is on case construction and value argumentation in both traditional and mainly contemporary styles, along with lab work and practice debates and drills on current Lincoln-Douglas topics. The final week provides time for in-depth topic exploration, extensive work on delivery and presentation, discussion of additional philosophies and value conflict issues, and a round-robin competition. The public forum camp begins with an emphasis on core argument and delivery skills and the development of case and argument preparation. Public forum students engage in frequent practice debates and attend lectures on domestic and international policy.

WINCHENDON SCHOOL SUMMER SEMESTER ENGLISH IMMERSION PROGRAM
Res — Coed Ages 13-18

Winchendon, MA 01475. 172 Ash St. Tel: 978-297-4476, 800-622-1119. Fax: 978-297-0911.
www.winchendon.org   E-mail: admissions@winchendon.org
Elliot Harvey, Dir.
Grades 8-12. Adm: FCFS. **Appl**—Fee $0. Due: June.
Type of instruction: SAT/ACT_Prep Study_Skills. **Courses:** Drawing Painting. **Avg class size:** 7. **High school credit.**
Focus: ESL. **Features:** Badminton Baseball Basketball Golf Soccer Swim Tennis.
Fees 2014: Res $3600-6500 (+$100-150), 3-6 wks.
Housing: Dorms. **Swimming:** Pool. Campus facilities avail.
Est 1973. Nonprofit. **Ses:** 1. **Wks/ses:** 6. Operates July-Aug.

Featuring intensive, structured instruction in and out of the classroom, Summer Semester helps students wishing to improve their English proficiency through a combination of English immersion, classroom study and experiential learning. Boys and girls choose from four levels of ESL instruction: beginning, intermediate, advanced and transition (a bridge course to mainstream English). Faculty devote the entire school day to English instruction in a variety of contexts. Classes seek to develop vocabulary, reading comprehension, oral and written communicational skills, and subject-specific terminology. Experiential education takes the form of afternoon excursions, lectures and student interviews of local citizens.

WYOMING SEMINARY
ENGLISH AS A SECOND LANGUAGE INSTITUTE
Res — Coed Ages 13-18

Kingston, PA 18704. 201 N Sprague Ave. Tel: 570-270-2186. Fax: 570-270-2198.
www.wyomingseminary.org/summer E-mail: summeratsem@wyomingseminary.org
Gayle Sekel, Dir.
Grades 9-12. Adm: FCFS. **Appl**—Fee $100. Due: Rolling. Transcript, 2 recs.
Intl: 100%. **Fac 12.** K-12 staff 12. **Staff:** Couns 20.
Type of instruction: Preview Rev. **Courses:** Crafts Drama Painting. **Daily hours for:** Classes 4. Study 2. Rec 1. Homework. Tests. Grades. **High school credit.**
Travel: ME.
Focus: ESL. **Features:** Climbing_Wall Basketball Swim Weight_Trng.
Fees 2014: Res $2850-7500 (+$450), 2-6 wks.
Housing: Dorms. **Swimming:** Pool. Campus facilities avail.
Est 1988. Nonprofit. **Ses:** 3. **Wks/ses:** 4-5. Operates July-Aug.

The ESL Institute provides an introduction to boarding school life for students who have had some exposure to the English language. Wyoming Seminary groups boys and girls by ability level in a program that addresses listening, speaking, reading and writing skills. Advanced students read short stories and novels, then write objective, critical essays. Activities include sports, fine arts courses and performing arts ensembles. Dances, movies, and day trips to historic and metropolitan areas enrich the weekend schedule. Participants enrolled in the second session may continue on for a fifth week in August that features a four-night experiential camping trip through Maine.

YALE YOUNG GLOBAL SCHOLARS PROGRAM
Res — Coed Ages 15-18

New Haven, CT 06511. Yale Young Global Scholars Program, 393 Prospect St. Tel: 203-436-4097. Fax: 203-436-2395.
http://globalscholars.yale.edu E-mail: global.scholars@yale.edu
Minh A. Luong, Dir.
Grades 10-PG. Adm: Very selective. **Appl**—Fee $50. Due: May. Transcript, essay, 2 recs.
Enr: 46. **Enr cap:** 60. **Fac 11. Staff:** Admin 5.
Type of instruction: Adv Enrich. **Courses:** Bus/Fin Econ Hist Public_Speak.
Focus: Intl_Relations.
Fees 2014: Res $5000, 3 wks. Aid (Need).
Housing: Dorms. Campus facilities avail.
Nonprofit. **Ses:** 3. **Wks/ses:** 2. Operates July-Aug.

Global Scholars combines college-level academic study in applied ethics, business, economics, history, international relations, law, politics and public policy with strategic leadership and advocacy skills instruction. The program features morning lectures by Yale faculty, afternoon seminars on grand strategy, and mentoring sessions with distinguished alumni and rising professionals. Evening training sessions address the areas of public speaking and debate, writing, networking, social and professional etiquette, study skills and time management.

MUSIC AND ARTS
PROGRAMS

Music and arts programs are arranged alphabetically by name. Page 6 of the Table of Contents lists the subject areas presented, and an index beginning on page 209 lists the programs under each of those subjects. Programs offering a family session are indicated by "FAM" at the end of the age range in the index.

INDEX BY FOCUS

CREATIVE WRITING (CONT.)

DANCE

DRAMA

DRAWING

FASHION

FILM

FILMMAKING

FINE ARTS

MEDIA

MUSIC

MUSIC (CONT.)

MUSIC TECHNOLOGY

PAINTING

PHOTOGRAPHY

SCULPTURE

STUDIO ART

THEATER

Music and Arts Programs

ACADEMY OF ART UNIVERSITY
PRE-COLLEGE SUMMER ART EXPERIENCE
Res and Day — Coed Ages 15-18

San Francisco, CA 94105. 79 New Montgomery St. Tel: 415-274-2200, 800-544-2787.
www.academyart.edu/degrees/summer_artexperience.html
E-mail: experience@academyart.edu
Grades 10-PG. **Adm:** FCFS. **Appl**—Fee $525. Due: Rolling.
Type of instruction: Enrich. **Courses:** Animation Fashion Filmmaking Photog Sculpt.
Focus: Studio_Art.
Housing: Dorms.
Ses: 1. **Wks/ses:** 6. Operates June-Aug.

Students in this intensive precollege program take up to four arts classes during the course of the session. Courses, which meet twice a week for two hours and 50 minutes per class, provide boys and girls with an exposure to college life and also help them determine if art and design is a suitable area for future study. Chaperoned recreational, cultural and community-oriented activities supplement course work.

THE AILEY SCHOOL SUMMER INTENSIVE PROGRAMS
Res — Coed Ages 15-25; Day — Coed 11-15

New York, NY 10019. 405 W 55th St. Tel: 212-405-9000. Fax: 212-405-9001.
www.theaileyschool.edu   E-mail: admissions@alvinailey.org
Student contact: JoAnne Ruggeri.
Adm: Selective. **Appl**—Due: Rolling. Live audition or DVD recording & photos.
Type of instruction: Enrich.
Focus: Dance.
Fees 2014: Res $2675-2895, 5-6 wks. Day $2235-2430, 5-6 wks.
Housing: Dorms.
Ses: 2. **Wks/ses:** 5-6. Operates June-Aug.

The Ailey School offers a six-week Professional Division Summer Intensive for dancers ages 16-25 and a five-week Junior Division program for those ages 12-15 (only 15-year-olds may attend as boarding students). Students take 12 to 15 technique classes weekly from the school's core curriculum, including daily ballet classes and Horton- or Graham-based modern classes five to six times a week. Additional instruction addresses jazz, tap, hip-hop, Dunham, barre a terre, yoga, body conditioning and two levels of pointe. Guest choreographers conduct repertory workshops. Boarding students live in Fordham University housing. Three years of prior ballet training is a prerequisite.

ALPHA SCIENCE FICTION/FANTASY/HORROR
WORKSHOP FOR YOUNG WRITERS
Res — Coed Ages 14-19

Greensburg, PA. Univ of Pittsburgh-Greensburg.
Contact (Year-round): PO Box 3681, Pittsburgh, PA 15230. Tel: 412-344-0456.
www.alpha.spellcaster.org
Diane Turnshek, Dir.
Adm: Very selective. **Admitted:** 25%. **Appl**—Fee $10. Due: Mar. 2000- to 6000-word genre piece.
Enr: 20. **Enr cap:** 20. **Fac 4.** Specialists 4. **Staff:** Admin 2. Couns 10.
Type of instruction: Enrich. **Daily hours for:** Classes 4. Study 4. Homework.
Focus: Creative_Writing.

Fees 2014: Res $2100, 1½ wks. Aid (Merit & Need).
Housing: Dorms. Avg per room/unit: 1. Campus facilities avail.
Est 2002. Nonprofit. **Ses:** 1. **Wks/ses:** 1½. Operates July.

Alpha seeks talented young writers who have a strong interest in one of the following genres: science fiction, fantasy, or horror. Topics covered in lectures and writing studios include character creation, plot, conflict and tension, dialogue, pace and structure. Working with professional authors, participants brainstorm on story ideas, compose first drafts, receive feedback and rewrite their pieces. Students also deliver public readings and learn about submitting manuscripts for publication.

AMERICAN BOYCHOIR SCHOOL
CAMP ALBEMARLE
Res — Boys Ages 9-14; Day — Boys 7-14

Princeton, NJ 08540. 75 Mapleton Rd. Tel: 609-924-5858. Fax: 609-924-5812.
www.americanboychoir.org/summer/index.php#CA
E-mail: rellsworth@americanboychoir.org
Rob D'Avanzo, Dir. Student contact: Roberta Griffith Ellsworth.
Grades 2-9. Adm: FCFS. **Appl**—Due: Rolling.
Enr: 75-100. Non-White: 20%. **Fac 4.** K-12 staff 4. **Staff:** Admin 3. Couns 8.
Courses: Crafts. **Avg class size:** 10. **Daily hours for:** Classes 3. Rec 7.
Focus: Music. **Features:** Basketball Soccer Softball Swim Volleyball.
Fees 2013: Res $5750-7250 (+$35), 2 wks. Day 2 wks.
Housing: Dorms. **Swimming:** Pool. Campus facilities avail.
Est 1941. Inc. **Ses:** 2. **Wks/ses:** 2. Operates July.

This American Boychoir School music camp accepts any child, with or without previous training. Choral singing and musicianship training classes are at the core of the program. Albemarle balances its musical curriculum with an active, compulsory recreational sports program designed to address both social and motor skills. Daily supervised swimming is a noteworthy aspect of the recreational program.

AMERICAN BOYCHOIR SCHOOL EXPERIENCE CAMP
Res and Day — Boys Ages 8-12

Princeton, NJ 08540. 75 Mapleton Rd. Tel: 609-924-5858. Fax: 609-924-5812.
www.americanboychoir.org/summer   E-mail: admissions@americanboychoir.org
Fernando Malvar-Ruiz, Dir.
**Student contact: Roberta Griffith Ellsworth, E-mail: rellsworth@americanboychoir.
org.**
Adm: Selective. **Appl**—Fee $0. Due: Rolling. Audition.
Enr: 29. **Enr cap:** 40. **Fac 6.** Prof 1. Col/grad students 3. K-12 staff 2. **Staff:** Admin 3.
Type of instruction: Enrich. **Courses:** Crafts Music_Theory. **Daily hours for:** Classes 4.
Rec 4.
Focus: Music. **Features:** Aquatics Swim.
Fees 2014: Res $675, 1 wk. Day 1 wk.
Housing: Dorms. **Swimming:** Pool. Campus facilities avail.
Est 2009. Nonprofit. **Ses:** 1. **Wks/ses:** 1. Operates June-July.

This choral music camp enrolls young boys with or without previous training. Boys further develop their vocal skills in small-group instruction classes, while also improving their music theory skills in sight reading and ear training by following the Kodaly Method. Traditional recreational activities round out the program. Candidates for admission should have unchanged voices and must also pass an audition.

AMERICAN UNIVERSITY
DISCOVER THE WORLD OF COMMUNICATION
Res — Coed Ages 15-18; Day — Coed 13-18

Washington, DC 20016. School of Communication, 4400 Massachusetts Ave NW. Tel: 202-885-2098. Fax: 202-885-2019. www.audiscover.org E-mail: audiscover@gmail.com Sarah Menke-Fish, Dir. Grades 9-PG. Adm: FCFS. **Appl**—Fee $0. Due: Rolling. **Enr:** 250. **Enr cap:** 250. Intl: 10%. Non-White: 20%. **Fac 20.** Prof 15. Col/grad students 2. Specialists 3. **Staff:** Admin 3. Couns 15. **Type of instruction:** Adv Enrich Undergrad. **Courses:** Speech Writing/Journ Sportswriting Web_Design Screenwriting. **Avg class size:** 12. **Daily hours for:** Classes 6. Study 1. Rec 3. Homework. **College credit:** 1-2/crse. **Intl program focus:** Acad Culture. **Locations:** Mexico/Central_America. **Focus:** Comm Acting Animation Film Filmmaking Media Photog. **Features:** Aquatics Baseball Basketball Soccer Swim. **Fees 2014: Res $700-2400, 2-4 wks.** Aid 2011 (Need): $5000. **Housing:** Dorms. **Swimming:** Pool. Campus facilities avail. Nonprofit. **Ses:** 2. **Wks/ses:** 2. Operates June-July.

High schoolers taking part in this program have access to the resources of American University and its school of communication. Students focus upon fiction or documentary filmmaking, acting and directing, public speaking, photography, broadcast journalism or animation. In addition to the Washington, DC, program, the program includes a Costa Rica option that incorporates environmental filmmaking, Spanish-language immersion and community service.

APPLE HILL CENTER FOR CHAMBER MUSIC
SUMMER CHAMBER MUSIC WORKSHOP
Res — Coed Ages 12 and up

Sullivan, NH 03445. PO Box 217. Tel: 603-847-3371. Fax: 603-847-9734. www.applehill.org E-mail: music@applehill.org Lenny Matczynski, Dir. Adm: FCFS. **Appl**—Fee $75. Due: Apr. CD/DVD/digital placement recording. **Enr:** 60. **Enr cap:** 60. Intl: 20%. **Fac 10.** Specialists 10. **Staff:** Admin 2. Couns 11. Res 10. **Courses:** Dance. **Daily hours for:** Classes 3. Study 1-2. Rec 3. **Focus:** Music. **Features:** Hiking Soccer Swim Bowling Ping-Pong. **Fees 2014: Res $1700-3200 (+$10-40), 1½-3 wks.** Aid (Need). **Housing:** Cabins. Avg per room/unit: 4-6. **Swimming:** Pond. Campus facilities avail. **Est 1971.** Nonprofit. **Ses:** 5. **Wks/ses:** 1½. Operates June-Aug.

Apple Hill conducts short sessions for musicians at many different skill levels who are placed in two ensembles, according to ability. Each ensemble rehearses daily. Both informal and structured sight-reading sessions of chamber works are offered. In the student concerts that close each session, all groups perform for an audience of fellow participants, faculty, family and friends.

ASPEN MUSIC FESTIVAL AND SCHOOL
Res — Coed Ages 15 and up; Day — Coed 8 and up

Aspen, CO 81611. 225 Music School Rd. Tel: 970-925-3254. Fax: 970-925-3802. www.aspenmusicfestival.com E-mail: school@aspenmusic.org Alan Fletcher, Pres. Adm: Selective. **Appl**—Fee $25-100. Due: Jan. CD/DVD recordings. **Enr:** 625. **Fac 140.** **Focus:** Music.

Fees 2014: Res $4400-7100 (+$600), 4-8 wks.
Housing: Dorms. Avg per room/unit: 2-3.
Est 1949. Nonprofit. Ses: 3. **Wks/ses:** 4-8. Operates June-Aug.

Aspen Music School, designed for students of college age or older, enrolls a limited number of exceptionally talented younger students who possess outstanding maturity, strong musical talent and serious professional intent. The students, in conjunction with members of the artist/ faculty and guests, present the Aspen Music Festival concurrent with the school term. Younger students generally participate in orchestras and chamber ensembles.

ATHENS CENTRE SUMMER WORKSHOPS
Res — Coed Ages 16 and up

Athens, 116 36 Greece. 48 Archimidous St. Tel: 30-210-7012-268. Fax: 30-210-7018-603.
www.athenscentre.gr　E-mail: info@athenscentre.gr
Rosemary C. Donnelly, Dir.
Grades 12-Col. Adm: FCFS. **Appl**—Fee €250. Due: Rolling.
Enr: 40. **Enr cap:** 50. **Intl:** 70%. **Non-White:** 2%. **Fac 5.** Prof 5. **Staff:** Admin 7. Couns 2.
Type of instruction: Adv. **Courses:** Greek Poetry. **Avg class size:** 10. **Daily hours for:** Classes 4. Grades. **College credit:** 6.
Intl program focus: Acad.
Focus: Fine_Arts Theater. **Features:** Bicycle_Tours Hiking Swim.
Fees 2014: Res €690-2060 (+€500), 3 wks.
Housing: Apartments. Avg per room/unit: 2. **Swimming:** Ocean.
Est 1969. Nonprofit. Ses: 2. **Wks/ses:** 1-3. Operates June-July.

The Centre operates separate arts and poetry summer workshops in Athens. The poetry seminar focuses on the writing and appreciation of poetry. Students read and discuss Homer's Odyssey and an array of poems from contemporary and modern Greek and Anglophone authors. The arts workshop concentrates on creating images of island life through drawing, painting and mixed media.

AUBURN UNIVERSITY MUSICAL THEATRE CAMP
Res — Coed Ages 14-18

Auburn, AL 36849. Office of Professional & Continuing Ed, 301 O D Smith Hall. Tel: 334-844-5100. Fax: 334-844-3101.
www.auburn.edu/outreach/opce/summerexperience/musicaltheatre.htm
E-mail: james.birdsong@auburn.edu
James Birdsong, Coord.
Grades 9-12. Adm: FCFS. **Appl**—Fee $0. Due: Rolling.
Type of instruction: Enrich. **Courses:** Dance Music.
Focus: Theater.
Fees 2014: Res $635, 1 wk.
Housing: Dorms.
Ses: 1. **Wks/ses:** 1. Operates June-July.

This weeklong workshop features classes in acting, dance, singing and musical theater history. Instructors include music and theater professionals from Auburn's faculty.

BOSTON UNIVERSITY ACADEMY OF MEDIA PRODUCTION
Res — Coed Ages 16-18

Boston, MA 02215. College of Communication, 640 Commonwealth Ave. Tel: 617-353-5015, 800-992-6514. Fax: 617-353-3405.
www.academyofmediaproduction.com　E-mail: chriscav@bu.edu
Grades 11-12. Adm: Selective. **Appl**—Fee $25. Due: May. Transcript, essay, rec.

Enr: 60. Fac 17. Staff: Admin 2. Couns 2.
Type of instruction: Enrich. Avg class size: 15. Daily hours for: Classes 6.
Focus: Filmmaking Media. Features: Swim.
Fees 2014: Res $4950 (+$400), 4 wks.
Housing: Dorms. Swimming: Pond Ocean Pool.
Est 1987. Nonprofit. Ses: 1. Wks/ses: 4. Operates July-Aug.

Students interested in television, film, and radio production and programming choose three AMP workshops from the following options: film, field video production, studio television, editing, and radio for broadcast and the Web. Each workshop consists of eight classes. Participants create and deliver original programs and attend weekly seminars in directing, producing or screenwriting that include group discussion, role playing, project work and critiques. Guest lectures and site visits round out the program.

BOSTON UNIVERSITY THEATRE INSTITUTE
Res and Day — Coed Ages 16-18

Boston, MA 02215. 855 Commonwealth Ave, Rm 470. Tel: 617-353-3390. Fax: 617-353-4363.
www.bu.edu/cfa/busti   E-mail: theatre@bu.edu
Emily Ranii, Dir.
Grades 11-12. Adm: Selective. Appl—Fee 65. Due: Apr. Resume, essay, 2 recs.
Enr: 70. Enr cap: 70. Fac 6. Staff: Admin 3. Res 6.
Type of instruction: Adv. Avg class size: 15. Daily hours for: Classes 10. Study 1. Rec 2. College credit: 4.
Focus: Acting Theater.
Fees 2014: Res $5678-5836, 5 wks. Day 5 wks.
Housing: Dorms.
Est 1980. Nonprofit. Ses: 1. Wks/ses: 5. Operates June-Aug.

The institute features intensive professional training in acting (improvisation, monologue work and scene study), dramatic literature, movement for actors and singing with a faculty of working artists. Instruction also addresses script analysis, character development and playwriting. A master class in Shakespeare performance is also offered. Workshops offered throughout the summer introduce students to an array of subjects. Each student is cast in a performance project that rehearses throughout the five weeks.

BOSTON UNIVERSITY VISUAL ARTS SUMMER INSTITUTE
Res and Day — Coed Ages 14-17

Boston, MA 02215. College of Fine Arts, 855 Commonwealth Ave, Rm 552. Tel: 617-353-3371. Fax: 617-353-7217.
www.bu.edu/cfa/vasi   E-mail: visuarts@bu.edu
Jeanette Guillemin & Alana Silva, Dirs.
Grades 9-12 (younger if qualified). Adm: Selective. Admitted: 75%. Appl—Fee $75. Due: Apr. Art samples, essay, rec.
Enr cap: 25. Intl: 20%. Non-White: 10%. Fac 8. Prof 4. Col/grad students 4. Staff: Admin 2. Couns 3.
Type of instruction: Undergrad. Courses: Photog Bookmaking Printmaking Silkscreen. Daily hours for: Classes 6. Study 4. Rec 4. Homework. Grades. College credit: 3/crse, total 3.
Focus: Drawing Painting Sculpt Studio_Art. Features: Climbing_Wall Swim.
Fees 2014: Res $4616-4749 (+$150), 4 wks. Day $3100 (+$150), 4 wks. Aid 2011 (Merit & Need): $1000.
Housing: Dorms. Avg per room/unit: 2. Swimming: Pool. Campus facilities avail.
Est 2005. Nonprofit. Ses: 1. Wks/ses: 4. Operates June-July.

The institute enables high school students interested in art to gain skills in drawing, painting, printmaking and sculpture while living on the campus of Boston University. Boys and girls also learn about art through museum trips and attendance at master classes taught by professional artists. Successful completion of the four-week program results in the credit equivalent of one college course.

BRANDEIS UNIVERSITY BIMA PROGRAM
Res — Coed Ages 15-18

Waltham, MA 02454. 415 South St, MS 065. Tel: 781-736-8416. Fax: 815-301-2874.
www.brandeis.edu/highschool   E-mail: highschool@brandeis.edu
Rachel Happel, Dir.
Grades 10-12. Adm: Selective. **Appl**—Fee $40. Due: Mar. Arts sample, essays, 2 recs.
Enr: 95. **Fac 10.** Specialists 10. **Staff:** Admin 6. Couns 12.
Type of instruction: Enrich. **Courses:** Relig_Stud. **Avg class size:** 13.
Focus: Creative_Writing Dance Music Studio_Art Theater.
Fees 2014: Res $6000, 4 wks. Aid (Need).
Housing: Dorms. Avg per room/unit: 2. Campus facilities avail.
Est 2004. Nonprofit. Jewish. **Ses:** 1. **Wks/ses:** 4. Operates July-Aug.

BIMA participants hone their artistic skills while exploring Jewish traditions and Jewish identity. The program addresses six core areas of artistic study: filmmaking, music (instrumental or vocal), visual arts, creative writing, theater and dance. Boys and girls develop techniques and collaborate artistically with other participants. In addition, students choose from a range of workshops pertaining to various media. Other activities include concerts, performances and exhibitions at cultural institutions. The community celebrates Shabbat, and Kosher dining is observed at all meals.

BRANT LAKE DANCE CENTRE
Res — Girls Ages 12-16

Brant Lake, NY 12815. 7586 State Rte 8. Tel: 518-494-2406. Fax: 518-494-7372.
www.blcdance.com   E-mail: dance@brantlake.com
Lynn Brown, Dir.
Grades 7-11. Adm: FCFS. **Appl**—Fee $0. Due: Apr.
Enr: 60. **Fac 4. Staff:** Admin 10. Couns 12.
Type of instruction: Enrich. **Courses:** Crafts Drama Drawing Painting Photog Sculpt.
Daily hours for: Classes 5.
Focus: Dance. **Features:** Aquatics Canoe Climbing_Wall Sail Golf Swim Tennis Water-skiing Watersports.
Fees 2014: Res $7000, 4½ wks.
Housing: Cabins. **Swimming:** Lake.
Ses: 1. **Wks/ses:** 4½. Operates June-July.

Located in the Adirondack Mountains, Brant Lake provides professional instruction at all levels of dance. Advanced dancers may take up to five hourlong classes daily, while others round out their schedules with various recreational camping pursuits. One evening each week, the group attends a ballet performance, a rock concert or a play, while other evenings are usually spent in shared social activities with the affiliated Brant Lake Camp for boys.

BREVARD MUSIC CENTER
Res — Coed Ages 14-29

Brevard, NC 28712. 349 Andante Ln, PO Box 312. Tel: 828-862-2100. Fax: 828-884-2036.
www.brevardmusic.org   E-mail: bmcadmissions@brevardmusic.org
Keith Lockhart, Dir.
Student contact: Dorothy Knowles, E-mail: dknowles@brevardmusic.org.

Grades 9-Col. Adm: Very selective. Admitted: 23%. **Appl**—Fee $65. Due: Mar. Recorded audition.
Enr: 410. **Enr cap:** 410. Intl: 3%. Non-White: 10%. **Fac 65.** Prof 63. Specialists 2. **Staff: Admin** 15.
Type of instruction: Adv.
Focus: Music. **Features:** Soccer Swim.
Fees 2014: Res $3350-5950 (+$200), 6 wks. Aid 2011 (Merit & Need): $1,020,000.
Housing: Cabins. Avg per room/unit: 16. **Swimming:** Lake.
Est 1936. Nonprofit. **Ses:** 1. **Wks/ses:** 6. Operates June-Aug.

Conducting high school and college divisions, BMC provides an intensive program in music study and practice. Brevard offers five courses of study: orchestral studies, piano, composition, voice for high schoolers and opera for college students. During the course of the session, young musicians participate in more than 80 public performances, many of which feature renowned guest artists. While most students attend for six or seven weeks, pianists and high school singers may enroll for either three or six weeks.

BROADWAY THEATRE PROJECT
Res — Coed Ages 16 and up

Tampa, FL. Univ of South Florida.
Contact (Year-round): 2780 E Fowler Ave, Ste 106, Tampa, FL 33612. **Toll-free: 888-874-1764.**
www.broadwaytheatreproject.com   **E-mail:** broadwaytp@aol.com
Debra McWaters, Exec Dir.
Grades 10-Col. Adm: Selective. **Appl**—Fee $35. Due: Mar. Live/DVD audition, rec.
Enr cap: 200. **Fac 50. Staff:** Admin 12. Couns 7.
Courses: Dance Fine_Arts Music.
Focus: Theater. **Features:** Swim.
Fees 2014: Res $3500 (+$50), 3 wks. Aid (Need).
Housing: Hotels. **Swimming:** Pool.
Est 1991. Nonprofit. **Ses:** 1. **Wks/ses:** 3. Operates July-Aug.

Conducted at the University of South Florida, BTP enables high school and college students who have prior musical theater training to study intensively with professional artists and educators in theater, film and television. Pupils attend classes in acting, dance, voice and writing, with emphasis placed on the collaborative process and the collective creation of art. The program also includes specialty classes in stage combat, Broadway repertory and auditioning, as well as private vocal and acting lessons. Participants spend evenings rehearsing for a final performance at the Tampa Bay Performing Arts Center.

BROWN UNIVERSITY
THEATREBRIDGE
Res — Coed Ages 16-18

Providence, RI 02912. Box T, 42 Charlesfield St. Tel: 401-863-7900. Fax: 401-863-3916.
www.brown.edu/scs/pre-college/theatrebridge   **E-mail:** summer@brown.edu
Mark Cohen, Dir.
Grades 10-11. Adm: Selective. **Appl**—Fee $45-90. Due: Rolling. Transcript, teacher rec, video interview.
Type of instruction: Enrich. **Courses:** Creative_Writing.
Focus: Acting Theater.
Fees 2014: Res $7875, 6 wks. Aid (Need).
Housing: Dorms. Campus facilities avail.
Ses: 1. **Wks/ses:** 6. Operates June-July.

This intensive precollege theater program provides promising actors and actresses with an opportunity to hone their acting, directing and writing skills as they work under the guidance of established theater professionals. Classes, which meet six days a week, address text, improvisation and movement. Students spend the majority of their evening and weekend hours rehearsing and preparing for class. TheatreBridge culminates in a free public performance on the final afternoon.

CALIFORNIA COLLEGE OF THE ARTS PRE-COLLEGE PROGRAM
Res and Day — Coed Ages 15-18

Oakland, CA 94618. Office of Extended Ed, 5212 Broadway. Tel: 510-594-3638. Fax: 510-594-3771.
www.cca.edu/precollege   E-mail: precollege@cca.edu
Jane Brady, Coord.
Grades 10-PG. Adm: Selective. **Appl**—Fee $75. Due: Mar.
Enr: 250. Intl: 3%. **Fac 25. Prof 25. Staff:** Admin 6.
Type of instruction: Adv Enrich Undergrad. **Courses:** Architect. **Avg class size:** 12. **Daily hours for:** Classes 6. Homework. Grades. **College credit:** 3/crse, total 3.
Focus: Animation Creative_Writing Drawing Fashion Filmmaking Painting Photog Sculpt.
Fees 2014: Res $2970 (+$290), 4 wks. Aid 2007 (Merit & Need): $95,000.
Housing: Dorms. Avg per room/unit: 2-3. Campus facilities avail.
Est 1986. Nonprofit. **Ses:** 1. **Wks/ses:** 4. Operates June-July.

CCA's Pre-College Program enables high schoolers to earn three college credits while studying art, architecture, design or creative writing in an art school setting. As an immersion program, Pre-College requires students to attend class each morning and afternoon, then develop work outside of class time. In CCA's Bay Area setting, pupils sample college life as they develop portfolio pieces. Special activities, evening workshops and field trips enrich the program.

CALIFORNIA STATE SUMMER SCHOOL FOR THE ARTS
Res — Coed Ages 14-18

Sacramento, CA 95812. c/o California Inst of the Arts, PO Box 1077. Tel: 916-229-5160. Fax: 916-229-5170.
www.csssa.org   E-mail: application@csssa.org
Student contact: Neil Brilliante, E-mail: application@innerspark.us.
Grades 9-12. Adm: Very selective. Admitted: 45%. **Appl**—Fee $20. Due: Feb. Recorded audition, portfolio, screening, 2 teacher recs.
Enr: 520. **Enr cap:** 520. Intl: 1%. Non-White: 49%. **Fac 129.** Prof 58. Col/grad students 20. Specialists 51. **Staff:** Admin 10. Couns 18.
Courses: Digital_Arts. **Avg class size:** 16. **Daily hours for:** Classes 7. Study 4. **College credit:** 3.
Focus: Animation Creative_Writing Dance Film Music Theater. **Features:** Basketball Swim Tennis.
Fees 2014: Res $1550-5000 (+$60-325), 4 wks. Aid 2008 (Need): $218,000.
Housing: Dorms. **Swimming:** Pool. Campus facilities avail.
Est 1985. Nonprofit. **Ses:** 1. **Wks/ses:** 4. Operates July-Aug.

A rigorous preprofessional training program for talented high schoolers interested in a career in the arts or entertainment, CSSSA offers course work in seven disciplines: animation, dance, theater, music, creative writing, the visual arts and film/video. Admission is highly competitive, with all boys and girls having to audition, complete specific artistic assignments and submit teacher recommendations; priority is given to California residents, although a limited number of out-of-state and international students enroll each year. Participants may earn three units of California State University elective credit upon completion of the program. Scholarships are available to California residents only.

CAZADERO MUSIC CAMP
Res — Coed Ages 10-18

Cazadero, CA.
Contact (Year-round): PO Box 7908, Berkeley, CA 94707. Tel: 510-527-7500. Fax: 510-527-2790.
www.cazadero.org   E-mail: execdir@cazadero.org
Jim Mazzaferro, Dir. Student contact: Emily Brockman, E-mail: emily@cazadero.org.
Grades 5-12. Adm: Selective. **Appl**—Fee $40. Due: Rolling. Music teacher rec.
Enr: 120. **Enr cap:** 160. **Fac** 40. **Staff:** Admin 4.
Courses: Crafts Dance Theater.
Focus: Music. **Features:** Hiking Basketball Swim Volleyball.
Fees 2014: Res $755-1650 (+$40), 1-2 wks. Aid (Merit & Need).
Housing: Cabins Dorms Tents. **Swimming:** Pool.
Est 1957. Nonprofit. **Ses:** 6. **Wks/ses:** 1-2. Operates June-Aug.

Located in an old-growth redwood grove in the Russian River Valley of Sonoma County, Cazadero provides music instruction for young people and families. Students in grades 5-8 who have at least a year of prior musical training may enroll in the Young Musicians session; campers take classes in technique and music theory while also playing in an ensemble. The middle school session (grades 6-8), for which two years of primary instrument instruction is a prerequisite, encourages further development of ensemble skills through participation in chamber groups, orchestra, symphonic band and campwide chorus. A more challenging program is in place for junior high students (grades 7-9), while accomplished players with at least four years of musical training refine their skills during the high school session (grades 9-12).

CENTAURI SUMMER ARTS CAMP
Res and Day — Coed Ages 8-18

Wellandport, L0R 2J0 Ontario, Canada. RR 3.
Contact (Sept-June): 85 Humbercrest Blvd, Toronto, M6S 4L2 Ontario, Canada.
Year-round Tel: 416-766-7124, Fax: 647-494-8840.
www.centauriartscamp.com   E-mail: info@centauriartscamp.com
Julie Hartley & Craig Hartley, Dirs.
Adm: FCFS. **Appl**—Fee $0. Due: Rolling.
Enr: 145. **Enr cap:** 145. **Fac** 10. **Prof** 10. **Staff:** Admin 5. Couns 26.
Type of instruction: Adv Enrich. **Courses:** Crafts Drama Filmmaking Music Studio_Art.
Avg class size: 16. **Daily hours for:** Classes 4.
Focus: Creative_Writing Dance Film Fine_Arts Media Music Painting Photog Sculpt Theater. **Features:** Baseball Basketball Football Soccer Swim Volleyball.
Fees 2014: Res Can$975-1725, 1-2 wks. Day Can$480-1150, 1-2 wks. Aid 2006 (Need): Can$2500.
Housing: Dorms. **Swimming:** Pool.
Est 1994. Inc. **Ses:** 4. **Wks/ses:** 1-2. Operates July-Aug.

Trained professionals instruct campers in theater, dance, art, photography, musical theater, film and writing. Campers receive instruction in the art form of their choice in the morning, then take part in recreational activities each afternoon.

CENTER FOR CREATIVE YOUTH
Res — Coed Ages 14-18

Middletown, CT 06459. c/o Wesleyan Univ. Tel: 860-757-6391. Fax: 860-757-6377.
Contact (Aug-May): 111 Charter Oak Ave, Hartford, CT 06106. Tel: 860-757-6391. Fax: 860-757-6377.
www.crec.org/ccy   E-mail: ccy@crec.org
Nancy Wolfe, Dir.

Grades 10-12. Adm: Somewhat selective. Admitted: 85%. **Appl**—Fee $35. Due: Mar. Personal statement, 2 recs.
Enr: 170. **Fac 10. Staff:** Admin 2. Couns 23.
Courses: Musical_Theater. **Daily hours for:** Classes 5½. **High school credit:** 1½.
Focus: Creative_Writing Dance Filmmaking Music Photog Studio_Art Theater. **Features:** Swim.
Fees 2014: Res $3600 (+$100), 5 wks. Aid (Merit & Need).
Housing: Dorms. **Swimming:** Pool.
Est 1977. Nonprofit. **Ses:** 1. **Wks/ses:** 5. Operates June-July.

Conducted at Wesleyan University, CCY enrolls students who are talented in music, creative writing, theater, visual arts, dance, photography, filmmaking and technical theater. Students participate in intensive daily sessions in areas of interest and attend interdisciplinary classes. The program also includes leadership training opportunities.

CHAUTAUQUA SUMMER SCHOOLS OF FINE & PERFORMING ARTS
Res — Coed Ages 16-28

Chautauqua, NY 14722. 1 Ames Ave, PO Box 1098. Tel: 716-357-6233. Fax: 716-357-9014.
www.ciweb.org/school-of-art   E-mail: art@ciweb.org
Don Kimes, Dir.
Student contact: Sarah R. Malinoski-Umberger, E-mail: smalinoski@ciweb.org.
Adm: Very_selective. Admitted: 10%. **Appl**—Fee $50. Due: Apr. 20 images of recent work.
Enr cap: 40. **Fac 50. Staff:** Admin 100. Couns 10.
Type of instruction: Adv. **College credit:** 3.
Focus: Ceramics Dance Drawing Fine_Arts Music Painting Sculpt Theater. **Features:** Golf Swim Tennis Weight_Trng.
Fees 2014: Res $2425-4220, 7 wks. Aid 2009 (Merit & Need): $500,000.
Housing: Dorms. Avg per room/unit: 2. **Swimming:** Lake Pool. Campus facilities avail.
Nonprofit. **Spons:** Chautauqua Institution. **Ses:** 1. **Wks/ses:** 7. Operates June-Aug.

Chautauqua's summer programs offer serious preprofessional study in the fine and performing arts. Various formal and informal courses, particularly in music, the arts, theater and dance, are offered. In addition, the school conducts special studies courses and workshops, as well as courses carrying university credit. Recreational activities supplement class work.

CHOATE ROSEMARY HALL
DOCUMENTARY FILMMAKING
Res — Coed Ages 14-18

Wallingford, CT 06492. 333 Christian St. Tel: 203-697-2365. Fax: 203-697-2519.
www.choate.edu/summerprograms   E-mail: choatesummer@choate.edu
Eera Sharma, Dir.
Grades 9-12. Adm: Selective. Admitted: 90%. **Appl**—Fee $75. Due: Rolling. Transcript, 3 recs, optional CD/DVD of work.
Enr: 12. **Intl:** 5%. **Non-White:** 5%.
Type of instruction: Enrich. **Courses:** Dance Drama Fine_Arts Music. **Avg class size:** 12. **Daily hours for:** Classes 5½. Study 2. Rec 2. Homework.
Focus: Filmmaking. **Features:** Yoga Aerobics Baseball Basketball Rugby Soccer Softball Swim Track Volleyball.
Fees 2014: Res $3175 (+$200), 2 wks. Day $2325 (+$200), 2 wks. Aid 2011 (Need): $300,000.
Housing: Dorms. Avg per room/unit: 2. **Swimming:** Pool. Campus facilities avail.
Nonprofit. **Ses:** 1. **Wks/ses:** 2. Operates June-July.

During the first week of this introductory documentary filmmaking program, high schoolers attend screenings of landmark films and iconic moving images. Students develop critical skills for reading and appreciating screen-based communication during the week. The second week, which includes a shooting and editing practicum, culminates in the creation of a documentary short film or a personal video essay. Guest presenters enrich the program during both weeks.

CHOATE ROSEMARY HALL THEATER ARTS INSTITUTE
Res — Coed Ages 12-18

Wallingford, CT 06492. 333 Christian St. Tel: 203-697-2365. Fax: 203-697-2519.
www.choate.edu/summerprograms   E-mail: choatesummer@choate.edu
Eera Sharma, Dir.
Grades 7-12. Adm: Selective. Admitted: 90%. **Appl**—Fee $75. Due: Rolling. Transcript, 3 recs, performance CD/DVD, personal statement.
Enr: 24. **Intl:** 10%. **Non-White:** 10%.
Type of instruction: Enrich. **Courses:** Dance Fine_Arts Music. **Avg class size:** 12. **Daily hours for:** Classes 5. Rec 2.
Focus: Theater. **Features:** Yoga Aerobics Baseball Basketball Rugby Soccer Swim Tennis Volleyball.
Fees 2014: Res $5750 (+$400), 4 wks. Day $4250 (+$400), 4 wks. Aid 2011 (Need): $300,000.
Housing: Dorms. Avg per room/unit: 2. **Swimming:** Pool. Campus facilities avail. Nonprofit. **Ses:** 1. **Wks/ses:** 4. Operates June-July.

In this immersive, four-week theater program, boys and girls of all ability levels study vocal performance; develop dance skills in tap, ballet, modern and jazz styles; and learn classical and modern acting techniques. A New York City trip during the second full weekend of the institute enables students and faculty to attend Broadway and off-Broadway shows, museums and other cultural venues. Field trips to evening performances are also part of the program. Participants collaborate on an original theater piece and musical revue.

CHOATE ROSEMARY HALL WRITING WORKSHOPS
Res — Coed Ages 12-18; Day — Coed 11-18

Wallingford, CT 06492. 333 Christian St. Tel: 203-697-2365. Fax: 203-697-2519.
www.choate.edu/summerprograms   E-mail: choatesummer@choate.edu
Eera Sharma, Dir.
Grades 6-12. Adm: Selective. Admitted: 90%. **Appl**—Fee $60. Due: Rolling. Transcript, essay, 3 recs, 2 graded English papers.
Enr: 50. **Intl:** 30%. **Non-White:** 25%.
Type of instruction: Enrich. **Courses:** Expository_Writing Dance Drama Fine_Arts Music. **Avg class size:** 12. **Daily hours for:** Classes 5½. Study 2. Rec 2. Homework.
Focus: Creative_Writing. **Features:** Yoga Aerobics Baseball Basketball Rugby Soccer Softball Swim Tennis Volleyball.
Fees 2014: Res $3175 (+$200), 2 wks. Day $2325 (+$200), 2 wks. Aid 2011 (Need): $300,000.
Housing: Dorms. Avg per room/unit: 2. **Swimming:** Pool. Campus facilities avail. Nonprofit. **Ses:** 2. **Wks/ses:** 2. Operates June-July.

This intensive writing course serves students interested in exploring, improving and gaining confidence in their writing skills. Working with the teacher either individually or in small groups, pupils learn the importance of including detail and description in their creative writing and evidence and support in their analytical pieces. Boys and girls experiment with different kinds of writing, such as personal narrative, dialogue, poetry, short stories and thesis papers. Students play sports on weekday afternoons and engage in on- and off-campus social activities on weekends. Rising sixth graders attend as day pupils.

DENISON UNIVERSITY
JONATHAN R. REYNOLDS YOUNG WRITERS WORKSHOP
Res — Coed Ages 16-18

Granville, OH 43023. English Dept, Box 810. Tel: 740-587-6207, 800-336-4766. Fax: 740-587-5680.
http://reynolds.denison.edu   E-mail: reynoldswriting@denison.edu
Margot Singer, Dir.
Grades 11-PG. Adm: Selective. Admitted: 50%. **Appl**—Fee $25. Due: Mar. Rec, creative writing sample.
Enr: 30. **Enr cap:** 36. Intl: 1%. Non-White: 16%. **Fac 3.** Prof 3. **Staff:** Admin 1. Couns 5.
Type of instruction: Enrich Undergrad. **Courses:** Creative_Nonfiction Fiction Poetry.
Focus: Creative_Writing. **Features:** Swim.
Fees 2014: Res $1300, 1 wk. Aid 2010 (Need): $18,100.
Housing: Dorms. **Swimming:** Lake Pool. Campus facilities avail.
Est 1994. Nonprofit. **Ses:** 1. **Wks/ses:** 1. Operates June.

Workshop participants choose a primary area of focus—poetry, fiction or creative nonfiction—for the duration of the eight-day session. Small, intensive groups of 10 or fewer students meet daily, and boys and girls also engage in one-on-one conferences with faculty members. Structured writing time is built into the program. In addition, pupils attend workshops with visiting writers and gain exposure to other genres through cross-writing sessions.

DUKE UNIVERSITY CREATIVE WRITERS' WORKSHOP
Res — Coed Ages 15-16

Durham, NC 27708. Continuing Stud, 201 Bishop's House, Box 90700. Tel: 919-684-6259. Fax: 919-681-8235.
www.learnmore.duke.edu/youth/creativewriter   E-mail: youth@duke.edu
Grades 10-11. Adm: Selective. **Appl**—Due: Rolling.
Type of instruction: Enrich.
Focus: Creative_Writing.
Fees 2014: Res $2465, 2 wks. Day $1485, 2 wks.
Housing: Dorms.
Ses: 1. **Wks/ses:** 2. Operates July.

Similar to a college creative writing course, the CWW has each student design and pursue a writing project with advisory help from a primary instructor. Course faculty are practicing writers with advanced degrees in their craft. Writing time takes up most of the day, with feedback and constructive criticism being important aspects of the program. Prospective applicants should have significant creative writing experience and should be interested in developing and refining their writing for a particular genre.

DUKE UNIVERSITY YOUNG WRITERS' CAMP
Res and Day — Coed Ages 11-16

Durham, NC 27708. Continuing Stud, 201 Bishop's House, Box 90700. Tel: 919-684-6259. Fax: 919-681-8235.
www.learnmore.duke.edu/youth/youngwriter   E-mail: youth@duke.edu
Thomas Patterson, Dir.
Grades 6-11. Adm: Selective. **Appl**—Due: Rolling.
Type of instruction: Enrich.
Focus: Creative_Writing.
Fees 2014: Res $2295, 2 wks. Day $1095-1425, 2 wks.
Housing: Dorms.
Ses: 3. **Wks/ses:** 2. Operates June-July.

Middle school and high school students enrolled in this Duke program explore different creative writing genres, among them short fiction, poetry, journalism and playwriting.

Professional writers and educators lead the program, and local guest speakers are also featured. A daily readers' forum enables pupils to share their work with peers.

EDUCATION UNLIMITED CALIFORNIA ACTORS WORKSHOP
Res — Coed Ages 14-17

Palo Alto, CA. Stanford Univ.
Contact (Year-round): 1700 Shattuck Ave, Ste 305, Berkeley, CA 94709. Tel: 510-548-6612. Fax: 510-548-0212.
www.educationunlimited.com/camp/13
E-mail: campinfo@educationunlimited.com
Matthew Fraser, Exec Dir.
Grades 9-12. Adm: FCFS. Appl—Fee $0. Due: Rolling. Personal statement.
Enr cap: 15-40. Fac 3. Staff: Admin 8.
Type of instruction: Enrich. Avg class size: 10. Daily hours for: Classes 6. Rec 5.
Focus: Acting Theater. Features: Swim.
Fees 2014: Res $4195 (+$50-150), 2 wks. Day $3555 (+$50-150), 2 wks. Aid (Need).
Housing: Dorms. Swimming: Pool.
Est 1999. Inc. Ses: 1. Wks/ses: 2. Operates July.

This studio theater program, held on the campus of Stanford University, focuses on developing various skills integral to a young actor's success. Students enroll in morning core courses and choose from a variety of specialized afternoon electives. The core curriculum focuses on combining creative intuition with concrete technical skills, and electives may include solo performance, musical theater and stand-up comedy.

EDUCATION UNLIMITED EMERGING WRITERS INSTITUTE
Res and Day — Coed Ages 15-18

Berkeley, CA 94709. 1700 Shattuck Ave, Ste 305. Tel: 510-548-6612. Fax: 510-548-0212.
www.educationunlimited.com   E-mail: campinfo@educationunlimited.com
Matthew Fraser, Exec Dir.
Grades 10-12. Adm: Selective. Appl—Due: Rolling.
Staff: Admin 8.
Type of instruction: Adv Enrich. Avg class size: 10. Daily hours for: Classes 7. Study 1. Rec 6.
Locations: CA.
Focus: Creative_Writing. Features: Swim.
Fees 2014: Res $4350 (+$50), 2 wks. Day $3695, 2 wks. Aid (Need).
Housing: Dorms. Swimming: Pool.
Est 2007. Inc. Ses: 2. Wks/ses: 2. Operates June-Aug.

Held at Stanford University and the University of California-Berkeley, the Emerging Writers Institute seeks to develop students' imaginative writing across the literary genres of fiction, nonfiction, playwriting and poetry. Daily writing workshops, one-on-one instructor evaluations, group editing sessions and creative presentations of student work focus upon both the technical and the artistic aspects of writing. Participants benefit from the literary culture of Berkeley and the Bay Area.

EMERSON COLLEGE
ARTS & COMMUNICATION PRE-COLLEGE PROGRAM
Res and Day — Coed Ages 14-18

Boston, MA 02116. Dept of Professional Stud & Special Prgms, 120 Boylston St. Tel: 617-824-2800. Fax: 617-824-8158.

www.emerson.edu/academics/professional-studies/programs-high-school-students
E-mail: precollege@emerson.edu
Tori Weston, Dir.
Grades 10-12. Adm: Somewhat selective. Admitted: 90%. **Appl**—Fee $0. Due: Rolling.
Essay, resume, writing samples.
Non-White: 10%. **Fac 20.** Prof 16. Col/grad students 4. **Staff:** Admin 6. Couns 3.
Type of instruction: Enrich Undergrad. **Courses:** Media. **Daily hours for:** Classes 8.
Homework. **College credit:** 4.
Focus: Pol_Sci Writing/Journ Acting Creative_Writing Filmmaking Theater. **Features:**
Ultimate_Frisbee.
Fees 2014: Res $3070, 5 wks. Day $1895, 5 wks.
Housing: Dorms. Campus facilities avail.
Ses: 1. **Wks/ses:** 5. Operates July-Aug.

Rising seniors and exceptional rising juniors may earn college credit through courses in political communication, advocacy, leadership, college writing, film production and film writing. Emerson also offers noncredit summer programs in creative writing, studio television and filmmaking (open to boys and girls entering grades 9-12); stage design (entering grades 10-12) and acting and musical theater (entering grades 11 and 12). Hands-on workshops and projects help students develop skills knowledge, and professors provide feedback on participants' work.

ENCORE! BAND CAMP
Res — Coed Ages 11-15

Milledgeville, GA. Georgia College & State Univ.
Contact (Year-round): 1240 Lakehaven Pky, McDonough, GA 30253. Tel: 678-643-7766. Fax: 770-914-2161.
www.encoremusiccamps.com   E-mail: info@EncoreBandCamp.com
Kreg Biffle & William Kilgore, Dirs.
Grades 6-10 (younger if qualified). Adm: FCFS. **Appl**—Fee $50. Due: June.
Enr: 150-220. **Enr cap:** 250. **Fac 20.** K-12 staff 20. **Staff:** Couns 20.
Type of instruction: Enrich. **Daily hours for:** Classes 6. Rec 4.
Focus: Music. **Features:** Swim.
Fees 2014: Res $435-510, 1 wk. Aid avail.
Housing: Dorms. Avg per room/unit: 2. **Swimming:** Pool. Campus facilities avail.
Est 1984. Inc. **Ses:** 1. **Wks/ses:** 1. Operates July.

Conducted at Georgia College and State University, Band Camp features rehearsals, master classes and performances. During the course of the weeklong session, students develop their technique for future auditioning success. Various social and recreational activities round out the program.

CAMP ENCORE/CODA
Res and Day — Coed Ages 9-18

Sweden, ME 04040. 50 Encore/Coda Ln. Tel: 207-647-3947.
Contact (Sept-May): 32 Grassmere Rd, Brookline, MA 02167. Tel: 617-325-1541.
Year-round Fax: 207-647-3259.
www.encore-coda.com   E-mail: jamie@encore-coda.com
Jamie Saltman & Ellen Donohue-Saltman, Dirs.
Grades 4-12. Adm: FCFS. **Appl**—Fee $0. Due: Rolling.
Enr: 140. **Enr cap:** 140. **Fac 60. Staff:** Admin 5.
Courses: Crafts Theater.
Focus: Music. **Features:** Aquatics Canoe Kayak Sail Badminton Basketball Soccer
Softball Swim Tennis Volleyball.
Fees 2014: Res $4050-7500, 3-6½ wks. Day 3-6½ wks. Aid (Need).
Housing: Cabins. **Swimming:** Lake.

Est 1950. Ses: 3. Wks/ses: 3-6½. Operates June-Aug.

Encore/Coda offers a summer of music and sports. Musical instruction includes symphony orchestra, jazz band, chamber groups, private instrumental lessons, musical theater, voice and guitar. Waterfront activities and team sports complete the program.

EPISCOPAL HIGH SCHOOL YOUNG WRITERS WORKSHOP
Res and Day — Coed Ages 13-15

Alexandria, VA 22302. 1200 N Quaker Ln. Tel: 703-933-4043.
www.episcopalhighschool.org E-mail: dcw@episcopalhighschool.org
Damian Walsh, Dir.
Grades 7-9. Adm: FCFS. **Appl**—Due: Rolling.
Type of instruction: Enrich. **Courses:** Public_Speak. Homework.
Focus: Expository_Writing Creative_Writing.
Fees 2014: Res $750, 1 wk. Day $600, 1 wk.
Housing: Dorms.
Nonprofit. Episcopal. **Ses:** 2. **Wks/ses:** 1. Operates July.

The Young Writers Workshop offers intensive instruction in written communication skills while providing multiple opportunities for students to practice public speaking. The course focuses on three major types of writing—creative, persuasive and analytical—by devoting a full day to the specific techniques of each genre. Participants present their work to peers in a concluding poetry reading/storytelling event. Activities outside the classroom include guest speakers and a field writing experience at the Botanical Gardens in Washington, DC.

FRIENDS MUSIC CAMP
Res — Coed Ages 10-18

Barnesville, OH 43713. c/o Olney Friends School, 61830 Sandy Ridge Rd. Tel: 740-425-3655.
Contact (Aug-June): PO Box 59311, Chicago, IL 60659. Tel: 773-573-9181.
Year-round Fax: 937-767-2254.
www.friendsmusiccamp.org E-mail: friendsmusiccamp@gmail.com
Drea Gallaga & Nicholas Hutchinson, Dirs.
Grades 5-12. Adm: FCFS. **Appl**—Fee $100. Due: Rolling. 2 recs.
Enr: 75. Intl: 2%. Non-White: 3%. **Fac 20. Staff:** Admin 3. Couns 6.
Courses: Dance Theater. **Daily hours for:** Classes 6. Study 1. Rec 2.
Focus: Music. **Features:** Swim.
Fees 2014: Res $1460-2110 (+$30-50), 2-4 wks. Aid 2009 (Need): $22,000.
Housing: Dorms. **Swimming:** Pool.
Est 1980. Nonprofit. Religious Society of Friends. **Ses:** 2. **Wks/ses:** 2-4. Operates July-Aug.

Held at Olney Friends School, FMC conducts a varied music program in a Quaker setting. Each camper receives instruction on the instrument of his or her choice and participates in ensemble lessons, chorus, swimming and sports. While older boys and girls attend for four weeks, 10- and 11-year-olds enroll in a two-week session. Participants should arrive at the camp with at least one year of previous study.

GLICKMAN-POPKIN BASSOON CAMP
Res — Coed Ages 18 and up

Little Switzerland, NC.
Contact (Year-round): 717 S Marshall St, Ste 103, Winston-Salem, NC 27101. Tel: 336-602-5159. Fax: 336-777-8254.
www.bassooncamp.com E-mail: amber@bassooncamp.com
Jim Poe

Adm: FCFS.
Enr: 100. **Fac 5. Staff:** Admin 2.
Focus: Music.
Fees 2014: Res $750, 1½ wks.
Housing: Lodges. Avg per room/unit: 2.
Est 1977. Nonprofit. **Ses:** 1. **Wks/ses:** 1½. Operates May-June.

The camp offers master classes in performance practices, reed making and repertoire. Performers of all skill levels are welcome to attend. Guest artists, lectures and instrument repair complement instruction.

HARAND CAMP
Res — Coed Ages 7-18

Kenosha, WI 53140. c/o Carthage College, 2001 Alford Park Dr. Tel: 262-551-2140.
Fax: 262-551-2142.
Contact (Aug-May): 1569 Sherman Ave, Ste 201A, Evanston, IL 60201. Tel: 847-864-1500. Fax: 847-864-1588.
www.harandcamp.com   E-mail: harandcamp@gmail.com
Sulie Harand, Janice Gaffin Lovell, Nora Gaffin Shore & Judy Friedman Mooney, Dirs.
Grades 3-12. Adm: FCFS. **Appl**—Fee $0. Due: Mar.
Enr: 200. **Fac 15. Staff:** Admin 9. Couns 33.
Courses: Speech Acting Circus_Skills Crafts Creative_Writing Dance Fine_Arts Media Music.
Focus: Theater. **Features:** Basketball Cheerleading Martial_Arts Soccer Swim Volleyball.
Fees 2014: Res $1050-5399, 1-6 wks. Aid (Need).
Housing: Dorms. **Swimming:** Pool.
Est 1955. Inc. **Ses:** 4. **Wks/ses:** 1-6. Operates June-Aug.

Integral to this musical theater/performing arts program, which is conducted on the campus of Carthage College, are daily acting, singing and dance classes. Classes are coordinated with musical theater productions that boys and girls deliver at the end of each session. Sports, electives and other activities round out the program.

HARDING UNIVERSITY SUMMER HONOR CHOIR
Res — Coed Ages 15-18

Searcy, AR 72149. Box 10877. Tel: 501-279-4311. Fax: 501-279-4086.
www.harding.edu/honorchoir   E-mail: music@harding.edu
Cliff Ganus, Dir.
Grades 10-PG (younger if qualified). Adm: FCFS. **Appl**—Fee $0. Due: Rolling. Choral director's rec.
Enr: 62. **Enr cap:** 70. Non-White: 5%. **Fac 7.** Prof 5. K-12 staff 2. **Staff:** Admin 1. Couns 4.
Avg class size: 14. **Daily hours for:** Classes 7. Rec 1. Grades. **College credit:** 1/crse, total 1.
Focus: Music.
Fees 2014: Res $395, 1 wk. Aid 2009 (Merit): $6000.
Housing: Dorms. Avg per room/unit: 2.
Est 2003. Nondenom Christian. **Ses:** 1. **Wks/ses:** 1. Operates July.

Students have a college-level music experience at a Christian liberal arts university through Summer Choir. In daily classes, choristers develop their music-reading and vocal skills and presentation, then rehearse in preparation for a final concert. Special performances, events, devotionals and recreational activities are also part of the program. Boys and girls earn one hour of college credit upon completion of the program.

HEIFETZ INTERNATIONAL MUSIC INSTITUTE
Res — Coed Ages 14-25

Staunton, VA. Mary Baldwin College.
Contact (Year-round): PO Box 6443, Ellicott City, MD 21042. Tel: 410-480-8007. Fax: 410-480-8010.
www.heifetzinstitute.org E-mail: office@heifetzinstitute.org
Daniel Heifetz, Pres.
Student contact: Patrick Locklin, E-mail: patrick@heifetzinstitute.org.
Adm: Very selective. Admitted: 35%. **Appl**—Fee $95. Due: Jan. Live or recorded audition.
Enr: 62. **Enr cap:** 75. Intl: 40%. **Fac 40.** Prof 40. **Staff:** Admin 14. Couns 5.
Type of instruction: Adv. **Courses:** Public_Speak Dance Drama. **Avg class size: 8. Daily hours for:** Classes 1. Study 5.
Focus: Music. **Features:** Swim.
Fees 2014: Res $5600, 6 wks. Aid 2011 (Merit & Need): $150,000.
Housing: Dorms. **Swimming:** Pool River.
Est 1996. Nonprofit. **Ses:** 1. **Wks/ses:** 6. Operates June-Aug.

Serving advanced students of violin, viola, cello and piano, Heifetz seeks to develop the expressive potential of every performer while encouraging technical growth. In addition to twice-weekly private lessons and five hours of daily practice time, participants take a series of afternoon classes in public speaking, voice, drama, movement and freedom of expression. The schedule incorporates three weekly performance opportunities, a celebrity concert series and guest artists.

INTERLOCHEN SUMMER ARTS CAMP
Res — Coed Ages 7-18

Interlochen, MI 49643. PO Box 199. Tel: 231-276-7472, 800-681-5912. Fax: 231-276-7464.
www.camp.interlochen.org E-mail: admission@interlochen.org
Jeffrey S. Kimpton, Pres.
Grades 3-12. Adm: Selective. Admitted: 85%. **Appl**—Due: Feb. Varying audition/portfolio requirements.
Enr: 2500. **Fac 247. Staff:** Admin 205. Couns 208.
Type of instruction: Enrich. **Courses:** Ceramics Crafts Media Painting Photog Sculpt.
Daily hours for: Classes 6. Study 4. Rec 2.
Focus: Creative_Writing Dance Filmmaking Music Theater. **Features:** Aquatics Boating Canoe Exploration Fishing Hiking Outdoor_Ed Ropes_Crse Sail Swim Watersports.
Fees 2014: Res $1075-8355, 1-6 wks. Aid (Merit & Need).
Housing: Cabins Lodges. **Swimming:** Lake. Campus facilities avail.
Est 1928. Nonprofit. **Ses:** 7. **Wks/ses:** 1-6. Operates June-Aug.

Interlochen offers intensive study of the arts—music, visual arts, dance, creative writing, motion picture arts and theater—from beginning through advanced levels. Students choose from junior (entering grades 4-7), intermediate (entering grades 7-10) and high school (entering grade 10 through recent high school graduates) divisions. Many of the programs for younger children do not require an audition, but the more challenging and competitive intermediate and high school programs often necessitate an audition. Private lessons are available at an additional fee in all band and orchestra instruments, piano, organ, voice and classical guitar. A diverse recreational program, including watersports, is available.

JACOB'S PILLOW DANCE FESTIVAL AND SCHOOL
Res — Coed Ages 16 and up

Becket, MA 01223. 358 George Carter Rd. Tel: 413-243-9919. Fax: 413-243-4744.
www.jacobspillow.org E-mail: info@jacobspillow.org
J. R. Glover, Dir.

Adm: Selective. **Appl**—Fee $25-50. Due: Mar. Audition, personal statement, resume.
Enr: 25. **Enr cap:** 25. **Fac 30.**
Type of instruction: Adv. **College credit.**
Focus: Dance. **Features:** Swim.
Fees 2014: Res $1500-2250, 2-3 wks. Aid (Merit & Need).
Housing: Cabins. Avg per room/unit: 20. **Swimming:** Lake.
Est 1933. Nonprofit. **Ses:** 4. **Wks/ses:** 2-3. Operates June-Aug.

Advanced students, professionals and teachers may enroll in this school of dance. Ballet, modern, culturally specific, choreographic, jazz/musical theater and community dance courses are offered. An intern/apprentice program provides on-the-job training in arts management and technical production. Pupils may earn undergraduate college credit.

JUILLIARD SCHOOL SUMMER DANCE INTENSIVE
Res — Coed Ages 15-17

**New York, NY 10023. Office of Adm, 60 Lincoln Center Plz. Tel: 212-799-5000. Fax:
212-769-6420.**
**www.juilliard.edu/youth-adult-programs/summer-programs
summer-dance-intensive E-mail: summerdance@juilliard.edu**
Grades 10-12. Adm: Selective. **Appl**—Fee $40. Due: Jan. Video/DVD/live audition, ballet teacher rec.
Enr: 44. **Enr cap:** 44.
Type of instruction: Adv Enrich.
Focus: Dance.
Fees 2014: Res $2630, 3 wks. Day $1435, 3 wks. Aid (Merit & Need).
Housing: Dorms.
Ses: 1. **Wks/ses:** 3. Operates July-Aug.

Rising high school sophomores, juniors and seniors who are advanced ballet dancers may apply to this precollege program; females should be en pointe. Each day begins in one of Juilliard's studios with a ballet technique class, followed by pointe, men's or classical partnering classes. After lunch, students take a modern dance class, then contemporary partnering, ballroom and music. Dancers supplement daily technique classes with evening rehearsals of new choreography and repertoire. Students perform the resulting pieces on the session's final day as part of a production that includes ballroom and music class presentations.

JUILLIARD SCHOOL SUMMER PERCUSSION SEMINAR
Res — Coed Ages 15-17

**New York, NY 10023. Office of Adm, 60 Lincoln Center Plz. Tel: 212-799-5000. Fax:
212-769-6420.**
**www.juilliard.edu/youth-adult-programs/summer-programs
summer-percussion-seminar E-mail: jgramley@umich.edu**
Joseph Gramley, Dir.
Grades 10-12. Adm: Selective. **Appl**—Fee $50. Due: Feb. Audition recording, rec.
Type of instruction: Enrich.
Focus: Music.
Fees 2014: Res $1765, 2 wks.
Housing: Dorms.
Ses: 1. **Wks/ses:** 2. Operates July.

Advanced high school percussionists entering grades 10-12 may enroll in this intensive program. Students engage in hands-on study of all major percussive instruments: two- and four-mallet keyboard, snare drum, timpani and orchestral accessories. In addition, participants gain an introduction to world hand drums, percussion chamber music, and both solo- and multi-percussion repertoire. Programming combines master classes, clinics, lectures, rehearsals and performances. Private lessons are also part of the program.

LEBANON VALLEY COLLEGE SUMMER MUSIC CAMP
Res and Day — Coed Ages 14-17

Annville, PA 17003. 101 N College Ave. Tel: 717-867-6293. Fax: 717-867-6390.
www.lvc.edu/music-camp   E-mail: mixonmusic@rcn.com
Joe Mixon, Dir.
Grades 9-12 (younger if qualified). Adm: FCFS. Admitted: 100%. **Appl**—Fee $0. Due:
Rolling.
Enr: 100. **Enr cap:** 100. Intl: 2%. **Fac 12.** Prof 12. **Staff:** Admin 1. Couns 10.
Type of instruction: Enrich. **Daily hours for:** Classes 6. Study 1. Rec 1.
Focus: Music. **Features:** Baseball Basketball Swim Tennis.
Fees 2014: Res $595 (+$22), 1 wk. Day $295-395 (+$22), 1 wk.
Housing: Dorms. **Swimming:** Pool. Campus facilities avail.
Est 1987. Nonprofit. **Ses:** 1. **Wks/ses:** 1. Operates July.

Students choose their own programs from a selection of seminars, ensembles and private instruction. Academic electives such as music theory, jazz improvisation and music technology, as well as performance opportunities, are available. Pupils may take half-hour private lessons for an additional fee.

LIM COLLEGE SUMMER FASHION LAB
Res — Coed Ages 15-17

New York, NY 10022. 12 E 53rd St. Tel: 646-388-8421. Fax: 212-750-3479.
www.limcollege.edu/academics/3495.aspx   E-mail: fashionlab@limcollege.edu
Jennifer Bullis, Coord.
Grades 10-12. Adm: FCFS. **Appl**—Fee $25. Due: Rolling.
Enr: 260. Intl: 8%.
Type of instruction: Undergrad. **Avg class size:** 20. **Daily hours for:** Classes 7½.
College credit: 1/crse, total 3.
Focus: Fashion.
Fees 2014: Res $225-890 (+$10-35/crse), 1-4 wks. Aid avail.
Housing: Dorms. Avg per room/unit: 2-3. Campus facilities avail.
Ses: 1. **Wks/ses:** 1-4. Operates July-Aug.

Summer Fashion Lab's series of weeklong courses allows participants to explore various career opportunities in the fashion business. Students may enroll in one course in the morning session, one course in the afternoon session or both, for a total of up to eight courses over four weeks. Course offerings cover fashion buying, event planning, photography, fashion magazines, fashion show production, styling, marketing, Photoshop, social media and visual merchandising. Boarders live in a LIM College dormitory and participate in organized evening activities.

LITCHFIELD JAZZ CAMP
Res and Day — Coed Ages 13 and up

Litchfield, CT 06759. PO Box 69. Tel: 860-361-6285. Fax: 860-361-6288.
www.litchfieldjazzfest.com/jazz-camp   E-mail: info@litchfieldjazzfest.com
Don Braden, Dir.
Student contact: Karen Hussey, **E-mail:** karenh@litchfieldjazzfest.com.
Adm: FCFS. **Appl**—Fee $50. Due: Rolling.
Enr: 100-150. **Enr cap:** 150. Intl: 2%. Non-White: 33%. **Fac 30.** Specialists 30. **Staff:**
Admin 4.
Avg class size: 10. **Daily hours for:** Classes 8. Rec 2.
Focus: Music.
Fees 2014: Res $1380-5490, 1-5 wks. Day $970-4180, 1-4 wks. Aid 2011 (Need):
$100,000.
Housing: Dorms.

Est 1996. Nonprofit. **Spons:** Litchfield Performing Arts. **Ses:** 5. **Wks/ses:** 1. Operates July-Aug.

Boys and girls of all ability levels study with an internationally recognized faculty of jazz musicians at the camp. Students perform in combos at the appropriate skill level, both at the school and on the Jazz Festival stage. Faculty guide students through classes in performance, improvisation, jazz history, rhythm and percussion, music theory, composition, recording and the business of music, among others. Instructors teach voice, piano, guitar, bass, drums, Latin rhythms, saxophones, clarinet, flute, trumpet, trombone and violin. Private instruction is available for an additional fee.

LONG LAKE CAMP FOR THE ARTS
Res — Coed Ages 10-16

Long Lake, NY 12847. 83 Long Lake Camp Way. Tel: 518-624-4831. Fax: 518-624-6003.
Contact (Sept-June): 199 Washington Ave, Dobbs Ferry, NY 10522. Tel: 914-693-7111. Fax: 914-693-7684.
Year-round Toll-free: 800-767-7111.
www.longlakecamp.com   E-mail: marc@longlakecamp.com
Marc Katz, Susan Katz & Geoffrey Burnett, Dirs.
Grades 5-11. Adm: FCFS. Admitted: 100%. **Appl**—Fee $0. Due: Rolling.
Enr: 235. **Enr cap:** 250. Intl: 10%. Non-White: 12%. **Fac 140. Staff:** Admin 4.
Courses: Ecol Environ_Sci Expository_Writing Speech Writing/Journ Ceramics Crafts Creative_Writing Photog Sculpt.
Focus: Circus_Skills Dance Filmmaking Fine_Arts Music Painting Theater. **Features:** Archery Canoe Hiking Mountaineering Mtn_Trips Riding Sail Seamanship Wilderness_ Camp Woodcraft Baseball Basketball Equestrian Field_Hockey Football Golf Gymnastics Martial_Arts Soccer Swim Tennis Volleyball Water-skiing Watersports.
Fees 2014: Res $5600-9650 (+$20-375), 3-6 wks. Aid 2009 (Need): $100,000.
Housing: Cabins Houses. Avg per room/unit: 10. **Swimming:** Lake.
Est 1969. Inc. **Ses:** 5. **Wks/ses:** 3-6. Operates June-Aug.

Long Lake's activities include theater; orchestra; chorus; ballet, modern and folk dance; jazz ensembles; rock 'n' roll bands; guitar and folk singing; and choreography. Participants deliver full-scale performances on campus and in surrounding communities. An arts and crafts program includes painting, silver, sculpture, ceramics, photography, weaving, printing, computer science and creative writing. Horseback riding, waterfront activities, an overnight canoe trip and sports complete the camp's offerings.

LUZERNE MUSIC CENTER
Res — Coed Ages 11-18

Lake Luzerne, NY 12846. PO Box 39, 203 Lake Tour Rd.
Contact (Oct-May): 899 S College Mall Rd, Ste 353, Bloomington, IN 47401.
Year-round Tel: 518-696-2771, Fax: 518-615-1226.
www.luzernemusic.org   E-mail: info@luzernemusic.org
Elizabeth Pitcairn, Pres.
Grades 6-12 (younger if qualified). Adm: Selective. Admitted: 75%. **Appl**—Fee $50. Due: Rolling. Teacher rec, performance recording/audition.
Enr: 85. **Enr cap:** 100. Intl: 5%. Non-White: 25%. **Fac 30.** Prof 10. Col/grad students 5. Specialists 15. **Staff:** Admin 3. Couns 18.
Type of instruction: Adv. **Avg class size:** 6. **Daily hours for:** Classes 5. Study 2. Rec 2.
Focus: Music. **Features:** Boating Canoe Chess Hiking Peace/Cross-cultural Sail White-water_Raft Wilderness_Canoe Baseball Basketball Cross-country Soccer Softball Swim Tennis Ultimate_Frisbee.
Fees 2014: Res $2299-7790, 2-8 wks. Aid 2011 (Merit & Need): $120,000.
Housing: Cabins Lodges. Avg per room/unit: 5. **Swimming:** Lake.

Est 1980. Nonprofit. **Ses:** 4. **Wks/ses:** 2-8. Operates June-Aug.

Luzerne offers instruction in orchestra, chamber music, piano, woodwinds, brass, percussion, jazz, conducting, vocal studies, and theory and composition, and students perform in concerts each week. Recreational and waterfront programs include tennis, baseball, hiking, swimming, sailing and canoeing. The program is divided into a junior session (ages 11-14) and a senior session (ages 15-18).

MAINE ARTS CAMP
Res — Coed Ages 8-15

Unity, ME 04988. c/o Unity College, 90 Quaker Hill Rd.
Contact (Sept-June): PO Box 812076, Boca Raton, FL 33481.
Year-round Tel: 561-865-4330, Fax: 561-865-0855.
www.maineartscamp.com   E-mail: info@maineartscamp.com
Rick Mades, Dir.
Grades 3-10. Adm: FCFS. **Appl**—Fee $0. Due: Rolling.
Enr cap: 115. Intl: 5%. Non-White: 5%. **Fac 35.** Col/grad students 20. K-12 staff 15. **Staff:** Admin 2. Couns 30.
Type of instruction: Enrich. **Courses:** Comp_Sci Robotics Creative_Writing Music. **Avg class size:** 8. **Daily hours for:** Classes 3. Rec 5.
Focus: Acting Ceramics Dance Drawing Filmmaking Painting Photog Sculpt Theater. **Features:** Archery Canoe Chess Cooking Hiking Kayak Mtn_Biking Ultimate_Frisbee Gardening Rocketry.
Fees 2014: Res $1250-5300, 2-4 wks.
Housing: Dorms. Campus facilities avail.
Est 2005. Inc. Ses: 3. **Wks/ses:** 2-4. Operates July-Aug.

Conducted at Unity College, this general arts camp allows each student to create an individual program of activities. Individual sports, robotics and kayaking and canoeing supplement instruction in the visual and performing arts. Trips to Lake St. George and Peaks Kenny State Parks complete the program.

THE MARIE WALSH SHARPE ART FOUNDATION
SUMMER SEMINAR
Res — Coed Ages 17-18

Colorado Springs, CO. Colorado College.
Contact (Year-round): 725 N Tejon St, Colorado Springs, CO 80903. Tel: 719-635-3220. Fax: 719-635-3018.
www.sharpeartfdn.org   E-mail: office@sharpeartfdn.org
Kimberly M. Taylor, Dir.
Grade 11. Adm: Selective. **Appl**—Fee $0. Due: Apr. Art teacher rec, artwork, personal statement.
Enr: 20. **Enr cap:** 20. **Fac 2. Staff:** Admin 3. Couns 5.
Type of instruction: Adv Enrich. **Avg class size:** 20.
Focus: Drawing Fine_Arts Painting.
Fees 2014: Free. Res 2 wks.
Housing: Dorms. Avg per room/unit: 1-2. Campus facilities avail.
Est 1987. Nonprofit. Ses: 3. **Wks/ses:** 2. Operates June-July.

Held on the campus of Colorado College, this art institute offers intensive visual arts instruction for rising high school juniors who are artistically gifted. Students experience college-level drawing and painting courses in a group setting, with artists-in-residence serving as instructors. The development of a portfolio, small-group discussions with artists and sessions concerning careers in art are other program features. Scholarship funding covers full tuition, room and board, and related expenses.

MARIST COLLEGE SUMMER INSTITUTES
Res — Coed Ages 16-18

Poughkeepsie, NY 12601. Office of Undergraduate Adm, 3399 North Rd. Tel: 845-575-3226. Fax: 845-575-3215.
www.marist.edu/summerinstitutes   E-mail: precollege@marist.edu
Grades 11-12. Adm: Selective. **Appl**—Due: Rolling. Transcript, essay, rec.
Type of instruction: Undergrad. **College credit:** 3/crse, total 3.
Locations: Europe.
Focus: Fashion Studio_Art Theater.
Fees 2014: Res $3950, 2 wks.
Housing: Dorms. Campus facilities avail.
Ses: 1. **Wks/ses:** 2. Operates July.

Students earn college credit and preview campus life through Marist's Summer Institutes in interior design, studio art and fashion. Programming combines several class sessions each day with study time, local excursions, daylong field trips and recreational activities. New York institute focuses on other academic areas.

MARROWSTONE MUSIC FESTIVAL
Res and Day — Coed Ages 14-25

Bellingham, WA. Western Washington Univ.
Contact (Year-round): 11065 5th Ave NE, Ste A, Seattle, WA 98125. Tel: 206-362-2300. Fax: 206-361-9254.
http://marrowstone.syso.org/ms/index.html   E-mail: marrowstone@syso.org
Dan Petersen, Exec Dir.
Adm: Selective. **Appl**—Fee $65. Due: Apr. Audition CD, teacher rec.
Enr: 200. Fac 20. Staff: Admin 7. Couns 12.
Type of instruction: Adv. **College credit.**
Focus: Music. **Features:** Swim.
Fees 2014: Res $2570, 2 wks. Day $2050, 2 wks. Aid (Merit & Need).
Housing: Dorms. **Swimming:** Lake Pool.
Est 1943. Nonprofit. **Spons:** Seattle Youth Symphony Orchestras. **Ses:** 1. **Wks/ses:** 2. Operates July-Aug.

Marrowstone offers students a program of intense musical study. A diverse group of artist faculty guide students in a curriculum that includes master classes, chamber music coaching, orchestra and section rehearsals. These elements culminate in orchestral and chamber performances. Students may apply for college credit for chamber music, orchestra and elective course work.

MARYLAND INSTITUTE COLLEGE OF ART
BALTIMORE PRE-COLLEGE STUDIO RESIDENCY PROGRAM
Res — Coed Ages 16-17

Baltimore, MD 21217. 1300 W Mt Royal Ave. Tel: 410-225-2219. Fax: 410-225-2229.
www.mica.edu/programs/cs/precollege   E-mail: precollege@mica.edu
Grades 11-12. Adm: Selective. **Appl**—Fee $50. Due: Apr. Transcript, portfolio, rec, personal statement.
Enr: 250. Enr cap: 250.
Type of instruction: Undergrad. **Courses:** Architect Animation Painting Photog Sculpt Video. **College credit:** 3.
Focus: Studio_Art.
Fees 2014: Res $4500, 4 wks.
Housing: Dorms. Avg per room/unit: 1-2.
Est 1994. Ses: 1. **Wks/ses:** 4. Operates June-July.

Participants in MICA's intensive, four-week program earn three college credits for completion of a core class and a workshop. Students choose from 11 core classes and 12 workshops in such disciplines as figure painting, graphic design, sculpture, black and white photography, digital photography, 3-D gaming and animation, illustration, fiber, architecture and video. Enrollment in a class entitled critical methods of studying art completed the academic experience. Field trips to Washington, DC, and New York City to explore contemporary art and noteworthy historical pieces at galleries and museums enrich the program.

MEXART SUMMER TEEN PROGRAM
Res — Coed Ages 13-18

San Miguel de Allende, Mexico.
Contact (Year-round): 9902 Crystal Ct, Ste 107, BC-2323, Laredo, TX 78045. **Tel: 202-391-0004. Fax: 52-415-152-8900.**
www.gomexart.com   E-mail: carly@gomexart.com
Carly Cross, Dir.
Grades 8-12. Adm: FCFS. **Appl—Fee** $0. Due: Rolling. Essay.
Enr: 20. Enr cap: 20. Fac 16. Staff: Admin 2. Couns 4.
Type of instruction: Adv Enrich Preview Rev Tut. **Courses:** Span Crafts Fine_Arts Photog. **Daily hours for:** Classes 7. Study 1½. Rec 3.
Intl program focus: Acad Lang Culture. Home stays avail.
Focus: Dance Studio_Art. **Features:** Community_Serv Peace/Cross-cultural.
Fees 2014: Res $4100 (+$200), 4 wks.
Housing: Dorms.
Est 1999. Inc. **Ses: 3. Wks/ses: 4.** Operates July-Aug.

MexArt participants take daily Spanish classes with either art or dance courses. Art students choose one focus area and one or two electives from the following selections: painting, drawing, ceramics, photography, printmaking, color and design, welding and silver jewelry. Those in the dance program choose from jazz, hip-hop, modern and ballet in the morning session, and salsa, flamenco and improvisation in the afternoon. Dance students also teach dance to local children as a community service project.

NEW ENGLAND MUSIC CAMP
Res — Coed Ages 11-18

Sidney, ME 04330. 8 Goldenrod Rd. Tel: 207-465-3025. Fax: 207-465-9831.
Contact (Sept-May): 47 Cedar Grove Ter, Essex, CT 06426. **Tel:** 860-767-6530. **Fax:** 860-767-6548.
http://nemusiccamp.com   E-mail: registrar@nemusiccamp.com
John Wiggin & Kim Wiggin, Dirs.
Grades 5-12. Adm: Somewhat selective. Admitted: 98%. **Appl—**Due: Rolling. 2 recs, audition recording.
Enr: 195. Fac 40. Staff: Admin 10.
Type of instruction: Adv. **Courses:** Dance Theater. **Daily hours for:** Classes 4. Study 1. Rec 2.
Focus: Music. **Features:** Aquatics Archery Boating Canoe Fishing Hiking Mountaineering Sail Basketball Cross-country Golf Martial_Arts Soccer Softball Swim Tennis Volleyball.
Fees 2014: Res $3850-7250, 3-7 wks. Aid avail.
Housing: Cabins Dorms. **Swimming:** Lake.
Est 1937. Nonprofit. **Ses: 3. Wks/ses:** 3-7. Operates June-Aug.

NEMC offers a program of music and recreation on Lake Messalonskee. Musical activities include bands, choirs, orchestras, stage and jazz bands, a brass choir and ensembles. Class work and two private lessons are conducted weekly. A full range of social and recreational activities rounds out the program. Campers must be able to read music.

NEW ENGLAND SCHOOL OF COMMUNICATIONS
MAINE MEDIA CAMP
Res and Day — Coed Ages 15-17

Bangor, ME 04401. 1 College Cir. Tel: 207-941-7176, 888-877-1876. Fax: 207-947-3987.
www.nescom.edu/mediacamp   E-mail: info@nescom.edu
Mark F. Nason, Dir.
Grades 10-12. Adm: FCFS. **Appl**—Fee $25. Due: Rolling.
Enr cap: 40. **Fac 8. Staff:** Couns 3.
Type of instruction: Enrich.
Focus: Comm Writing/Journ Media Music_Tech. **Features:** Swim.
Fees 2014: Res $625, 1 wk. Day $400, 1 wk. Aid 2007 (Need): $1500.
Housing: Dorms. **Swimming:** Pool. Campus facilities avail.
Est 1989. Ses: 1. **Wks/ses:** 1. Operates Aug.

Maine Media Camp introduces participants to career opportunities in such media fields as audio engineering, digital photography, journalism, marketing communications, radio broadcasting and video production. The curriculum comprises lectures, labs, hands-on instruction, professional speakers, and tours of local television and radio stations.

NEW YORK MILITARY ACADEMY
NEW TRADITIONS JAZZ PROGRAM
Res and Day — Coed Ages 13-18

Cornwall-on-Hudson, NY 12520. 78 Academy Ave. Tel: 845-534-3710, 888-275-6962. Fax: 845-534-7699.
www.nyma.org   E-mail: admissions@nyma.org
Jason Furman, Dir. Student contact: Alisa Southwell, E-mail: asouthwell@nyma.org.
Grades 8-12. Adm: Very_selective. **Appl**—Fee $200. Due: June.
Enr cap: 20.
Avg class size: 5.
Focus: Music. **Features:** Swim.
Fees 2014: Res $2500, 2 wks. Day $1500-2000, 2 wks.
Housing: Dorms. **Swimming:** Pool.
Est 2011. Ses: 1. **Wks/ses:** 2. Operates July-Aug.

Advanced middle school instrumentalists join high school musicians of all ability levels in this two-week program that focuses on jazz study and performance (in solo and small-group settings). The curriculum addresses three main areas: bebop and post bop, modal music, and avant-garde and ethereal styles. Private lessons and classes on improvisation, music theory and listening reinforce small-group playing. Ensembles perform weekly in a forum setting, and the program culminates in a final performance. Students may also participate in master classes and attend concerts with faculty and guest artists.

NEW YORK UNIVERSITY
SUMMER INSTITUTE OF MUSIC PRODUCTION TECHNOLOGY
Res — Coed Ages 16-18

New York, NY 10012. 35 W 4th St, Ste 1077. Tel: 212-998-5141. Fax: 212-995-4043.
www.steinhardt.nyu.edu/music/technology   E-mail: roginska@nyu.edu
Kenneth J. Peacock, Dir. Student contact: Agnieszka Roginska.
Grades 11-12 (younger if qualified). Adm: Very selective. Admitted: 30%. Priority: URM.
Appl—Fee $50. Due: Apr. Short essays, optional work samples.
Enr cap: 24. **Intl:** 10%. Non-White: 15%. **Fac 8.** Prof 8. **Staff:** Admin 2. Couns 2.
Type of instruction: Enrich Undergrad. **Courses:** Media. **Daily hours for:** Classes 7. Rec 4.
Focus: Music_Tech.

Fees 2014: Res $3418, 2 wks. Aid 2009 (Need): $4000.
Housing: Dorms. Avg per room/unit: 2-3.
Nonprofit. **Ses:** 1. **Wks/ses:** 2. Operates July.

Through class lectures, labs and individualized studio time, students learn the fundamentals of music technology and audio engineering. The curriculum covers music studio formation; signal representation and synthesis; MIDI and sequencing; sound recording in analog and digital, single and multitrack; and editing, mixing and postproduction. Participants learn to use ProTools and Reason software and work in small groups on a project of their choice, with assistance from graduate students. Other activities include trips to recording and postproduction studios, concerts and audio installations, Broadway shows, tours of New York City and evenings with experts in the music technology field.

NORTHWESTERN UNIVERSITY
NATIONAL HIGH SCHOOL INSTITUTE
Res — Coed Ages 17-18

Evanston, IL 60208. 617 Noyes St. Tel: 847-491-3026, 800-662-6474. Fax: 847-467-1057.
www.northwestern.edu/nhsi   E-mail: nhsi@northwestern.edu
Ruth Bistrow, Coord.
Grade 12. Adm: Selective. **Appl**—Fee $35. Due: Apr. Transcript, PSAT scores.
Enr: 850. **Enr cap:** 850. **Fac** 100.
Type of instruction: Adv Enrich. **Courses:** Music. **Avg class size:** 15. **Daily hours for:** Classes 9. Study 2.
Focus: Acting Filmmaking Theater. **Features:** Swim.
Fees 2014: Res $1150-7300, 4-7 wks. Aid (Need).
Housing: Dorms. **Swimming:** Lake.
Est 1931. Nonprofit. **Ses:** 8. **Wks/ses:** 1-6. Operates June-Aug.

Serving artistically inclined rising high school seniors, the institute offers college-level study and experience in film and video production (including concentrations in acting, production, animation and screenwriting), musical theater and theater arts. NHSI's academic program comprises classes, workshops, field trips, projects and lectures. Group outings and social events balance class work. Workshops are also available in speech and debate (see separate listing for details).

OBERLIN CONSERVATORY OF MUSIC SUMMER PROGRAMS
Res — Coed Ages 16-18

Oberlin, OH 44074. Oberlin Univ, 77 W College St. Tel: 440-775-8044. Fax: 440-775-8942.
http://new.oberlin.edu/conservatory/summer   E-mail: anna.hoffmann@oberlin.edu
Anna Hoffmann, Admin.
Grades 10-12. Adm: Selective. **Appl**—Fee $50. Due: Apr. DVD audition, repertoire list, rec.
Type of instruction: Enrich.
Focus: Music.
Fees 2012: Res $730-1175, 1-2 wks. Aid (Need).
Housing: Dorms Hotels.
Spons: Oberlin University. **Ses:** 3. **Wks/ses:** 1-2. Operates June-July.

Oberlin offers three programs to high school pupils considering a college major in music. Students in the Summer Academy for High School Organists attend five days of private lessons and master classes and have access to 17 practice organs. The weeklong Sonic Arts Workshop, which focuses on the composition of original electroacoustic music, addresses digital-audio editing and manipulation, real-time performance techniques, sampling and production using Macintosh-based software. The nine-day Vocal Academy for High School Students features master classes on performance practice, diction, style, phrasing and textual communication, in addition to private lessons and evening workshops on audition techniques. Each participant performs at a final concert.

OKLAHOMA SUMMER ARTS INSTITUTE
Res — Coed Ages 14-19

Norman, OK 73072. 2600 Van Buren St, Ste 2606. Tel: 405-321-9000. Fax: 405-321-9001.
www.oaiquartz.org　**E-mail:** oai@oaiquartz.org
Emily Claude, Dir.
Grades 9-PG. Adm: Very selective. Admitted: 19%. **Appl**—Fee $20. Due: Feb. Audition, 2 recs.
Enr: 270. **Enr cap:** 270. **Fac 35.**
Type of instruction: Enrich. **Daily hours for:** Classes 6.
Focus: Acting Creative_Writing Dance Drawing Filmmaking Music Painting Photog Studio_Art. **Features:** Hiking.
Fees 2014: Free (in-state residents). Res (+$250), 2 wks.
Housing: Cabins Dorms.
Ses: 1. **Wks/ses:** 2. Operates June.

Hosted by Quartz Mountain Arts and Conference Center at a state park, this highly competitive, intensive academy serves motivated Oklahoma high schoolers. Students receive professional training in such disciplines as acting, creative writing, ballet, modern dance, orchestra, chorus, drawing and painting, photography, and film and video. Boys and girls gain exposure to various art forms and learning experiences and attend or participate in performances, gallery openings, poetry readings and ballroom dance classes. All participants attend on full scholarship, aside from a processing fee.

OTIS COLLEGE OF ART AND DESIGN
SUMMER OF ART
Res and Day — Coed Ages 15 and up

Los Angeles, CA 90045. 9045 Lincoln Blvd. Tel: 310-665-6864, 800-527-6847. Fax: 310-665-6854.
www.otis.edu/soa　**E-mail:** soa@otis.edu
Kathleen Masselink, Prgm Mgr.
Adm: FCFS. **Appl**—Fee $0. Due: Rolling.
Enr cap: 20. **Fac 30. Staff:** Admin 2.
Type of instruction: Adv Enrich Preview. **Courses:** Architect Anime Graphic_Design Product_Design Toy_Design. **Daily hours for:** Classes 6. Homework. Grades. **College credit:** 3.
Focus: Architect Animation Ceramics Drawing.
Fees 2011: Res $4391 (+$200-400), 4 wks. Day $1355-2575 (+$200-400), 4 wks. Aid (Merit & Need).
Housing: Apartments Dorms. Avg per room/unit: 3.
Est 1918. Nonprofit. Ses: 1. **Wks/ses:** 4. Operates July-Aug.

During this four-week precollege program, students engage in both foundation courses and hands-on studio classes in a chosen area of concentration. Concentration courses meet three times a week for six hours, while the one participant's one selected foundation class convenes twice a week for six hours. Areas of concentration are as follows: animation, architecture/landscape/interiors, ceramics, digital media, fashion design, graphic design, illustration, painting, photography, printmaking/urban art, toy design, web design, drawing/composition and art/design/culture. The three foundation choices are beginning drawing, intermediate drawing and life drawing.

PACIFIC MUSIC CAMP
Res and Day — Coed Ages 12-18

Stockton, CA 95211. Univ of the Pacific, Conservatory of Music, 3601 Pacific Ave. Tel: 209-946-2416.
www.pacific.edu/conservatory   E-mail: musiccamp@pacific.edu
Steve Perdicaris, Dir.
Grades 5-12. Adm: FCFS. **Appl**—Fee $0. Due: Rolling. Audition (piano camp).
Enr: 450. **Fac** 60. **Staff:** Admin 6. Couns 16.
Focus: Music. **Features:** Swim.
Fees 2014: Res $695-820, 1 wk. Day $595-720, 1 wk.
Housing: Dorms. Avg per room/unit: 2. **Swimming:** Pool.
Est 1946. Nonprofit. **Spons:** University of the Pacific. **Ses:** 3. **Wks/ses:** 1. Operates June-July.

In addition to separate camps for junior high and high school students interested in joining a band, orchestra or choir, Pacific offers a jazz camp for pupils entering grades 8-12 and a piano camp for those entering grades 9-12. Two years of prior study of the subject instrument are compulsory, and piano camp applicants must submit an audition tape. Private lessons are available for an additional fee.

PACIFIC NORTHWEST COLLEGE OF ART
PRE-COLLEGE SUMMER STUDIOS
Res and Day — Coed Ages 14-18

Portland, OR 97209. 1241 NW Johnson St. Tel: 503-821-8967. Fax: 503-226-3587.
www.pnca.edu/programs/ce/c/precollege   E-mail: precollege@pnca.edu
Sara Kaltwasser, Coord.
Adm: FCFS. **Appl**—Fee $0. Due: Rolling. Transcript, personal statement, rec, portfolio.
Fac 4. Prof 3. Specialists 1. **Staff:** Couns 1.
Type of instruction: Undergrad. **Courses:** Art_Hist Illustration. **Daily hours for:** Classes 6. **College credit:** 3.
Focus: Crafts Fine_Arts Painting.
Fees 2014: Res $1150-2850 (+$45-90), 1-2 wks. Day $650-1300 (+$45-90), 1-2 wks. Aid (Merit).
Housing: Dorms.
Ses: 2. **Wks/ses:** 1-2. Operates July-Aug.

Pre-College Studios begins with a week of foundation courses in figure drawing and modeling, perspective drawing and composition, surface and color design, space design and time-based arts. Students then focus on one specialized studio in either three-dimensional design, design and illustration, or painting. As a complement to studio work, boys and girls participate in group discussions, visit working artists in their studios, take trips to museums and galleries, and view films and slide shows. The program concludes with a public gallery exhibition. Participants reside at Concordia University.

PERRY-MANSFIELD PERFORMING ARTS CAMP
Res — Coed Ages 10-24; Day — Coed 8-24

Steamboat Springs, CO 80487. 40755 Routt County Rd 36. Tel: 970-879-7125, 800-430-2787. Fax: 970-879-5823.
www.perry-mansfield.org   E-mail: info@perry-mansfield.org
Joan Lazarus, Exec Dir.
Grades 3-Col. Adm: Selective. **Appl**—Fee $0-50. Due: Apr. Video audition/writing sample, 3 recs (certain programs).
Enr: 450.
Courses: Fine_Arts Musical_Theater. **Avg class size:** 12. **Daily hours for:** Classes 5. **College credit.**

Focus: Creative_Writing Dance Music Theater. **Features:** Equestrian.
Fees 2014: Res $2700-5250, 2-6 wks. Day $500, 1-6 wks.
Housing: Cabins Dorms.
Est 1913. Nonprofit. **Ses:** 7. **Wks/ses:** 1-6. Operates June-Aug.

Boys and girls at Perry-Mansfield's various performing arts camps receive daily instruction in the areas of dance, theater, musical theater, music, art and creative writing. Older students take a minimum of four classes daily and participate in evening rehearsals six days a week. These rehearsals conclude with theater, dance and musical productions. Younger campers gain an introduction to the performing arts while also participating in such activities as hiking, swimming, horseback riding and field trips.

PORTSMOUTH ACADEMY OF PERFORMING ARTS CAMP
Res — Coed Ages 8-17

Raymond, ME.
Contact (Year-round): c/o Seacoast Repertory Theatre, 125 Bow St, Portsmouth, NH 03801. Tel: 603-433-4793. Fax: 603-431-7818.
www.papacamp.org   E-mail: miles@seacoastrep.org
Miles Burns, Dir.
Adm: Selective. **Appl**—Fee $0. Due: June.
Enr: 100.
Focus: Acting Dance Music Theater. **Features:** Hiking Swim.
Fees 2011: Res $1295, 2 wks.
Housing: Cabins. **Swimming:** Lake.
Est 1989. Nonprofit. **Spons:** Seacoast Repertory Theatre. **Ses:** 1. **Wks/ses:** 2. Operates Aug.

A program of the Seacoast Repertory Theatre, PAPA Camp allows boys and girls to choose their own programs of study from a curriculum that includes acting, singing, dance, poetry and storytelling. All campers participate in the following core classes: drama workshop, choral singing and dance. Traditional camp activities such as swimming, boating, canoeing, tennis and hiking are also available.

PRATT INSTITUTE PRECOLLEGE PROGRAM
Res and Day — Coed Ages 16-18

Brooklyn, NY 11205. Ctr for Continuing & Professional Stud, 200 Willoughby Ave. Tel: 718-636-3453. Fax: 718-399-4410.
www.pratt.edu/precollege   E-mail: preco@pratt.edu
Elizabeth Kisseleff, Coord.
Grades 11-PG. Adm: FCFS. **Appl**—Fee $40. Due: Apr. Rec.
Enr cap: 400. **Fac** 60. **Staff:** Admin 6.
Type of instruction: Undergrad. **Courses:** Architect Art_Hist. **Avg class size:** 15. **Daily hours for:** Classes 7. Homework. Grades. **College credit:** 4.
Focus: Creative_Writing Drawing Fashion Film Fine_Arts Media Painting Photog Sculpt Studio_Art.
Fees 2014: Res $4904 (+$300), 4 wks. Day $3298 (+$300), 4 wks. Aid (Merit & Need).
Housing: Dorms. Avg per room/unit: 2. Campus facilities avail.
Nonprofit. **Ses:** 1. **Wks/ses:** 4. Operates July-Aug.

This intensive, college-level program covers the fine arts, design, architecture, fashion, creative writing, sculpture and photography. The structured curriculum includes a credit-bearing foundation course that explores drawing, color and design, or writing; a second credit-bearing course in a elective area of choice; and noncredit, pass-fail art history and portfolio development courses. Most courses are taught by Pratt's faculty architects, artists and designers, with the assistance of guest lecturers and critics.

PRINCETON BALLET SCHOOL SUMMER INTENSIVE WORKSHOP
Res — Coed Ages 14-21; Day — Coed 13-21

Princeton, NJ 08540. 301 N Harrison St. Tel: 609-921-7758. Fax: 609-921-3249.
www.arballet.org   E-mail: pbsandarb@aol.com
Mary Pat Robertson, Dir. Student contact: Carol Bellis, E-mail: cbellis@arballet.org.
Adm: Very selective. Admitted: 60%. **Appl**—Fee $25-35. Due: Rolling. Live/DVD audition.
Enr: 100. **Enr cap:** 100. Intl: 15%. Non-White: 15%. **Fac 10.** Specialists 10. **Staff:** Admin 7. Couns 5.
Type of instruction: Adv. **Avg class size:** 20. **Daily hours for:** Classes 8. Rec 5.
Focus: Dance. **Features:** Swim.
Fees 2014: Res $5250 (+$100), 5 wks. Day $2500 (+$100), 5 wks. Aid 2009 (Merit): $15,000.
Housing: Dorms. Avg per room/unit: 2. **Swimming:** Pool.
Est 1980. Nonprofit. **Spons:** American Repertory Ballet. **Ses: 1. Wks/ses: 5.** Operates June-July.

Students enrolled in this preprofessional program receive three hours of ballet instruction daily. Additional classes are offered in pointe and partnering as well as in modern and jazz dance. PBS also schedules choreography workshops, lectures and rehearsals for a final performance. Faculty are former professional dancers with major US companies. The program is open to advanced and advanced intermediate students by in-person or recorded audition.

THE PUTNEY SCHOOL CREATIVE WRITING WORKSHOPS
Res and Day — Coed Ages 14-17

Putney, VT 05346. Elm Lea Farm, 418 Houghton Brook Rd. Tel: 802-387-6297. Fax: 802-387-6216.
http://summer.putneyschool.org/creative-writing
E-mail: summer@putneyschool.org
Thomas D. Howe, Dir.
Grades 9-12. Adm: Selective. **Appl**—Fee $50. Due: Rolling. Rec, 2-3 writing samples.
Enr: 15. **Fac 4. Staff:** Admin 3. Couns 17.
Type of instruction: Enrich. **Courses:** Dance Filmmaking Fine_Arts Music Photog Theater Playwriting. **Avg class size:** 15. **Daily hours for:** Classes 6. Rec 2.
Focus: Creative_Writing. **Features:** Farm Hiking Riding Soccer Swim Volleyball.
Fees 2014: Res $4125-7525 (+$100-150), 1-2 wks. Day $1535-2650, 1-2 wks. Aid (Merit & Need).
Housing: Dorms. **Swimming:** Pond.
Est 1987. Nonprofit. **Ses: 4. Wks/ses: 2.** Operates June-Aug.

This enrichment program enables participants to explore all aspects of writing. Types of writing addressed include essay composition, nature writing, poetry, journal writing, fiction, memoir writing and creative nonfiction. Roundtable seminars, free writing time, one-on-one instruction, group editing, and presentations and class readings by guest writers help pupils further develop their writing skills. Boys and girls may read selections from new work each week during programwide open-reading sessions, and students produce a literary magazine at program's end.

THE PUTNEY SCHOOL
VISUAL AND PERFORMING ARTS WORKSHOPS
Res and Day — Coed Ages 14-17

Putney, VT 05346. Elm Lea Farm, 418 Houghton Brook Rd. Tel: 802-387-6297. Fax: 802-387-6216.
www.putneyschool.org/summer   E-mail: summer@putneyschool.org
Thomas D. Howe, Dir.
Grades 9-12. Adm: Selective. **Appl**—Fee $50. Due: Rolling. Rec.
Enr: 120. **Enr cap:** 130. Intl: 12%. Non-White: 20%. **Fac 40. Staff:** Admin 4. Couns 21.

Type of instruction: Enrich. **Courses:** Filmmaking Media Painting Sculpt. **Avg class size:** 8. **Daily hours for:** Classes 6. Rec 2.
Focus: Ceramics Creative_Writing Dance Fine_Arts Music Photog Theater. **Features:** Canoe Farm Hiking Riding Woodcraft Basketball Equestrian Soccer Swim Ultimate_ Frisbee Volleyball.
Fees 2014: Res $4125-7525 (+$50), 3-6 wks. Day $1535-2650 (+$45), 3-6 wks. Aid (Need).
Housing: Dorms. **Swimming:** Pond.
Est 1987. Nonprofit. **Ses:** 2. **Wks/ses:** 3. Operates June-Aug.

Designed for students displaying serious interest in the visual or performing arts, these workshops encompass the following: animation, audio art, ceramics, chamber music, dance, drawing, filmmaking, glass arts, metalwork and jewelry, music composition, painting, photography, printmaking, sculpture, songwriting, theater, vocal ensemble, wearable art, and weaving and fiber arts. Pupils choose two workshops during the session, one in the morning and one in the afternoon. The program features meetings with local artists and field trips to galleries and museums, and Putney schedules student exhibits and performances on closing day.

RHODE ISLAND SCHOOL OF DESIGN PRE-COLLEGE PROGRAM
Res and Day — Coed Ages 16-18

Providence, RI 02903. Continuing Ed, 2 College St. Tel: 401-454-6200, 800-364-7473. Fax: 401-454-6218.
www.risd.edu/precollege   E-mail: cemail@risd.edu
Joy McLaughlin, Coord.
Grades 11-12. Adm: Somewhat selective. **Appl**—Fee $0. Due: Apr. Essay, rec.
Enr cap: 250. Intl: 20%. Non-White: 35%. **Fac 75. Staff:** Admin 8. Couns 25.
Type of instruction: Adv Enrich. **Courses:** Furniture_Design Game_Design Illustration Interior_Design Jewelry Printmaking Web_Design. **Avg class size:** 15. **Daily hours for:** Classes 6. Study 2. Rec 2. Homework. Grades.
Focus: Architect Animation Ceramics Drawing Fashion Film Filmmaking Painting Photog Sculpt.
Fees 2014: Res $7617 (+$800), 6 wks. Day $5025 (+$800), 6 wks. Aid (Merit & Need).
Housing: Dorms.
Est 1970. Nonprofit. **Ses:** 1. **Wks/ses:** 6. Operates June-Aug.

The program provides a preprofessional introduction to the visual arts for rising high school juniors and seniors. Students choose from 21 major course offerings (meeting for two full days each week) in addition to foundation courses in drawing, design and critical studies. Studio work, evening workshops and extracurricular activities complement classroom instruction.

RUTGERS UNIVERSITY SUMMER ACTING CONSERVATORY
Res — Coed Ages 14-18

New Brunswick, NJ 08901. Theater Arts Dept, 2 Chapel Dr, Douglass College. Tel: 732-932-9891. Fax: 732-932-1409.
www.masongross.rutgers.edu/content/rutgers-summer-acting-conservatory
E-mail: mjones3@rci.rutgers.edu
Marshall Jones III, Dir.
Grades 10-12. Adm: Very selective. **Appl**—Fee $50. Due: Rolling. Essay, resume, rec, video/live audition.
Enr: 36.
Type of instruction: Adv. **Courses:** Musical_Theater. **College credit:** 3.
Focus: Acting.
Fees 2014: Res $4950, 4 wks. Day $3950. Aid (Need).
Housing: Dorms.
Est 2003. Ses: 1. **Wks/ses:** 4. Operates June-July.

Working theater professionals teach RSAC's daily classes in acting, movement and voice/ speech. Evenings feature master classes, special seminars and workshops conducted by visiting actors, producers, writers and other professionals. Field trips to three Broadway shows and other cultural institutions round out the program. A musical theater track, limited to about 12 students, places equal emphasis on acting, singing and dancing.

ST. OLAF COLLEGE MUSIC CAMP
Res and Day — Coed Ages 15-18

Northfield, MN 55057. 1520 St Olaf Ave. Tel: 507-786-3042, 800-726-6523. Fax: 507-786-3690.
www.stolaf.edu/camps   E-mail: summer@stolaf.edu**Teresa Lebens, Dir.**
Grades 10-PG (younger if qualified). Adm: FCFS. **Appl**—Fee $0. Due: Rolling.
Enr: 200. **Enr cap: 200. Fac 35.** Prof 25. Col/grad students 10.
Focus: Music.
Fees 2014: Res $610, 1 wk.
Housing: Dorms.
Est 1970. Nonprofit. **Ses: 1. Wks/ses:** 1. Operates June.

All campers at St. Olaf participate in a band, choir or orchestra, and involvement in a second large ensemble is possible. In addition, there are opportunities for solo and small-ensemble performance. Tuition includes two private lessons on an instrument or in voice.

ST. OLAF COLLEGE SUMMER PIANO ACADEMY
Res and Day — Coed Ages 14-18

Northfield, MN 55057. 1520 St Olaf Ave. Tel: 507-786-3042, 800-726-6523. Fax: 507-786-3690.
www.stolaf.edu/camps   E-mail: summer@stolaf.edu
Kent McWilliams, Dir. Student contact: Teresa Lebens, **E-mail: lebens@stolaf.edu.**
Grades 9-PG (younger if qualified). Adm: Selective. Admitted: 75%. **Appl**—Fee $0. Due: Apr. Audition tape: 2 pieces of contrasting styles.
Enr: 20. **Enr cap: 20. Fac 5.** Prof 3. Col/grad students 2. **Staff:** Admin 3. Res 2.
Type of instruction: Adv. **Avg class size:** 10.
Focus: Music.
Fees 2014: Res $700, 1 wk. Day $700, 1 wk.
Housing: Dorms.
Nonprofit. **Ses: 1. Wks/ses:** 1. Operates June.

Accomplished high school piano players work closely with St. Olaf's piano faculty in private lessons, master classes, chamber ensembles and enrichment classes. The daily schedule includes classes and rehearsals, elective recreation, and performances by St. Olaf faculty and student counselors. Applicants must furnish a 10-minute audition tape that comprises two pieces of contrasting styles.

ST. OLAF COLLEGE THEATRE CAMP
Res — Coed Ages 13-17

Northfield, MN 55057. 1520 St Olaf Ave. Tel: 507-786-3042, 800-726-6523. Fax: 507-786-3690.
www.stolaf.edu/camps   E-mail: summer@stolaf.edu
Todd Edwards & Mishia B. Edwards, Dirs.
Student contact: Teresa Lebens, E-mail: lebens@stolaf.edu.
Adm: FCFS. **Appl**—Fee $0. Due: Rolling.
Enr cap: 55. Fac 6. Prof 2. Col/grad students 4. **Staff:** Admin 1. Couns 6.
Focus: Theater.
Fees 2014: Res $515-875, 1 wk.

Housing: Dorms.
Nonprofit. **Ses:** 1. **Wks/ses:** 1. Operates June.

Serving aspiring thespians who may or may not have prior acting experience, the camp addresses all facets of theater through classes and rehearsals. Program topics include movement, vocal expression, playwriting, character development, basic stage combat, auditioning techniques, theater production and musical theater. A master class option enrolls students who have attended at least one previous session of the program. All participants take part in a session-closing theatrical production.

SAN FRANCISCO ART INSTITUTE PRECOLLEGE PROGRAM
Res and Day — Coed Ages 16-18

San Francisco, CA 94133. 800 Chestnut St. Tel: 415-749-4554. Fax: 415-351-3516.
www.sfai.edu/precollege   E-mail: precollege@sfai.edu
Tammy Ko Robinson, Dir.
Grades 11-PG. Adm: Selective. **Appl**—Fee $65. Due: May. Portfolio (5-8 samples), rec, essay.
Type of instruction: Adv. **Courses:** Animation Creative_Writing Drawing Film Painting Photog Art_Hist. **Daily hours for:** Classes 6. Grades. **College credit:** 1-2/crse, total 5.
Focus: Studio_Art.
Fees 2014: Res $5000 (+$50), 5 wks. Day $3000 (+$50-300), 5 wks. Aid (Need).
Housing: Dorms. Avg per room/unit: 2.
Nonprofit. **Ses:** 1. **Wks/ses:** 5. Operates June-July.

Designed for aspiring artists who have completed grade 10 but have not yet started college, this credit-bearing program provides a preview of art school life as it exposes students to the broad range of techniques, concepts and debates that constitute the contemporary art scene. Programming combines interdisciplinary thinking with studio practice. In addition to a required art history seminary, boys and girls select two core studio courses (each of which meets for three hours per day) that replicate an introductory course of study and offer an experience comparable to that of first-year bachelor of fine arts pupils at SFAI.

SARAH LAWRENCE COLLEGE
PRE-COLLEGE PROGRAMS FOR HIGH SCHOOL STUDENTS
Res and Day — Coed Ages 15-18

Bronxville, NY 10708. Office of Special Prgms, 1 Mead Way. Tel: 914-395-2205. Fax: 914-395-2608.
www.sarahlawrence.edu/highschool
E-mail: specialprograms@sarahlawrence.edu
Sheelagh Lynch, Coord.
Grades 10-12. Adm: FCFS. **Appl**—Fee $50. Due: Rolling.
Type of instruction: Enrich. **Courses:** Hist. Homework.
Focus: Animation Creative_Writing Dance Filmmaking Theater.
Fees 2014: Res $3140-6650, 4-5 wks. Day $725, 4 wks.
Housing: Dorms. Avg per room/unit: 1.
Ses: 4. **Wks/ses:** 4-5. Operates June-Aug.

Sarah Lawrence's noncredit summer offerings include a three-week creative writing program; a five-week course in filmmaking (in partnership with the International Film Institute of New York); a three-week musical theater program; and a three-week session that examines the literature, history, filmmaking and science of New York City. Students in all courses meet at least twice with faculty in one-on-one conferences to discuss their personal motivations and interests. Evening and weekend pursuits include film viewings; karaoke nights and other social events; and visits to New York City museums, parks and concerts.

SAVANNAH COLLEGE OF ART AND DESIGN PROGRAMS FOR HIGH SCHOOL STUDENTS
Res — Coed Ages 15-18

Savannah, GA 31402. **SCAD Summer Seminars, PO Box 2072. Tel: 912-525-5100, 800-869-7223. Fax: 912-525-5986.**
www.scad.edu/admission/summer_programs   E-mail: savannahsss@scad.edu
Grades 10-12. Adm: FCFS. **Appl**—Due: Rolling.
Type of instruction: Adv Undergrad. **College credit.**
Focus: Fashion Studio_Art.
Fees 2014: Res $1100. Day $900.
Housing: Dorms.
Nonprofit. **Wks/ses:** 1-4. Operates June-July.

SCAD conducts two residential arts programs for high schoolers. Rising Star, which serves rising seniors, enables students to enroll in two college-level classes while also building or enhancing their visual arts portfolios. Successful completion of the session results in college credit for use at SCAD or another institution. Field trips and excursions to area parks and attractions enrich the program. For pupils entering grades 10-12, the Summer Seminars program consists of weeklong educational workshops in Savannah and Atlanta.

THE SCHOOL OF AMERICAN BALLET SUMMER COURSE
Res and Day — Coed Ages 12-18

New York, NY 10023. 70 Lincoln Center Plz. Tel: 212-769-6600. Fax: 212-769-4897.
www.sab.org/summercourse
Peter Martins, Dir.
Adm: Selective. **Appl**—Fee $35. Due: Feb. Live audition.
Enr cap: 200. **Fac 13.**
Focus: Dance.
Fees 2014: Res $5274 (+$225), 5 wks. Day $2560 (+$225), 5 wks.
Housing: Dorms. Avg per room/unit: 2-3.
Ses: 1. **Wks/ses:** 5. Operates July-Aug.

Conducted on SAB's self-contained campus in Lincoln Center, Summer Course has dancers of all ability levels take two daily classes in ballet technique, variations, pointe, character or adagio. Pilates instruction, weight training and other seminars are also part of the program. Participants view performances by the New York City Ballet and other major companies. Recreational and social activities include games, movies, and visits to New York City landmarks, museums and Broadway shows. SAB sometimes invites a few particularly talented dancers to continue their studies at the school's winter term.

SCHOOL OF CINEMA AND PERFORMING ARTS SUMMER CAMPS
Res and Day — Coed Ages 13-18

New York, NY 10013. Tribeca Film Ctr, 375 Greenwich St. Tel: 212-941-4057, 800-718-2787. Fax: 646-536-8725.
www.socapa.org   E-mail: arts@socapa.org
Jamie Yerkes, Dir.
Adm: FCFS. **Appl**—Fee $0. Due: Rolling. Transcript.
Enr: 80. **Intl:** 30%. **Fac 10.** Prof 8. Col/grad students 2. **Staff:** Admin 10. Couns 15.
Type of instruction: Undergrad. **Avg class size:** 16. **Daily hours for:** Classes 7. Grades.
    College credit: 3/crse, total 3.
Locations: CA NY VT.
Focus: Acting Dance Filmmaking Media Photog Theater. **Features:** Hiking Kayak Swim.
Fees 2014: Res $1740-4740, 1-3 wks. Day $995-3995, 1-3 wks. Aid 2011 (Need): $20,000.
Housing: Dorms. Avg per room/unit: 2. **Swimming:** Lake Pool River.
Est 1998. Inc. **Ses:** 22. **Wks/ses:** 2-3. Operates June-Aug.

With locations on five college and prep school campuses—Occidental College in Los Angeles, CA; Pace University in Manahattan, NY; New York University in Brooklyn, NY; and Champlain College in Burlington, VT—SOCAPA conducts distinct programs in filmmaking and advanced filmmaking, film acting, photography and dance. Schedules for all programs include in-class instruction on Mondays, Tuesdays and Wednesdays, then on-location direction, photography or performance on Thursdays and Fridays. Saturdays are devoted to organized off-campus excursions and group dinners.

SCHOOL OF VISUAL ARTS SUMMER PRE-COLLEGE PROGRAM
Res and Day — Coed Ages 16-18

New York, NY 10010. 209 E 23rd St. Tel: 212-595-2100. Fax: 212-592-2116.
www.sva.edu/special-programs/pre-college-program
E-mail: admissions@sva.edu
Grades 10-12. Adm: FCFS. **Appl**—Due: Rolling.
Enr: 400.
Type of instruction: Undergrad. **Courses:** Advertising Graphic_Design Interior_Design Screenwriting. **Avg class size:** 20. **Daily hours for:** Classes 6. Rec 3. **College credit:** 3/crse, total 3.
Focus: Animation Drawing Filmmaking Painting Photog Sculpt.
Fees 2014: Res $1400 (+$75-160), 3 wks. Day $2300 (+$75-300), 3 wks. Aid (Merit & Need).
Housing: Dorms. Avg per room/unit: 2.
Ses: 1. **Wks/ses:** 3. Operates July-Aug.

The Pre-College Summer Program mimics a fast-paced foundation year experience in the New York art scene. Pre-College students are immersed in their chosen field of study through lectures on art history, theory, and the use of media and material. The program is further enhanced with a comprehensive list of supervised activities that takes full advantage of the social and cultural life of New York City. Participants must have a serious attitude toward making artwork as their primary focus during the program. The summer program is open to all students who will be enrolled in high school. Students will receive three college credits for the successful completion of the summer program.

CAMP SHAKESPEARE
Res and Day — Coed Ages 16 and up

Cedar City, UT 84720. c/o Utah Shakespearean Festival, 351 W Center St.
Contact (Winter): c/o California State Univ, Dept of English, 9001 Stockdale Hwy, Bakersfield, CA 93311.
Year-round Tel: 661-654-3038, Fax: 661-654-2063.
www.csub.edu/campshakespeare   E-mail: mflachmann@csub.edu
Michael Flachmann, Dir.
Grades 11-Col. Adm: FCFS. **Appl**—Due: Rolling.
Enr: 90. **Fac** 20. **Staff:** Admin 2.
Type of instruction: Preview. **College credit:** 3.
Focus: Theater. **Features:** Swim.
Fees 2014: Res $1610, ½-1 wks.
Housing: Dorms. **Swimming:** Pool.
Ses: 1. **Wks/ses:** ½-1. Operates July-Aug.

Participants in this theater program may earn three semesters of college credit. Daily classes feature lectures and discussions led by actors, directors, designers, stage technicians and scholars. Tuition includes tickets to each play performed at the Utah Shakespearean Festival.

SIGNATURE MUSIC CAMP
Res — Coed Ages 12-17

Ithaca, NY. Ithaca College.
Contact (Year-round): 509 W Fayette St, Delavan Center, Syracuse, NY 13204. Tel: 315-478-7840. Fax: 315-478-0962.
www.signaturemusic.org   E-mail: contact@signaturemusic.org
Richard W. Ford, Exec Dir.
Grades 7-12. Adm: Somewhat selective. Admitted: 95%. Priority: Low-income. URM. **Appl**—Fee $0. Due: Rolling. 2 teacher recs.
Enr: 85. **Enr cap:** 100. Intl: 3%. Non-White: 10%. **Fac 16.** Prof 3. Col/grad students 8. K-12 staff 5. **Staff:** Admin 4. Res 30.
Type of instruction: Adv Enrich. **Avg class size:** 10. **Daily hours for:** Classes 6. Rec 4.
Focus: Music. **Features:** Swim.
Fees 2014: Res $975-1950, 2 wks. Aid 2009 (Need): $20,000.
Housing: Dorms. Avg per room/unit: 2. **Swimming:** Pool.
Est 1993. Nonprofit. **Ses: 1. Wks/ses:** 2. Operates June-July.

Students in this instructional program at Ithaca College choose from jazz, vocal/piano, and band/choir programs. Sight singing, jazz ensemble, show choir, concert band, jazz and film music history, improvisation and master classes are offered to all students. Swimming, game nights and other recreational activities are part of the program, as are recitals and cabaret.

SOUTH CAROLINA GOVERNOR'S SCHOOL FOR THE ARTS AND HUMANITIES SUMMER PROGRAMS
Res — Coed Ages 12-18

Greenville, SC 29601. 15 University St. Tel: 864-282-3844. Fax: 864-282-3712.
www.scgsah.org   E-mail: admissions@scgsah.state.sc.us
Anna King, Dir.
Grades 7-12. Adm: Selective. Prereqs: GPA 2.5. **Appl**—Fee $25. Due: Jan. Work samples/audition, interview, transcript, 2 teacher recs.
Type of instruction: Enrich. **Daily hours for:** Classes 6. Rec 2. Homework.
Focus: Creative_Writing Dance Drama Music Studio_Art.
Fees 2014: Res $950-2100 (+$50), 2-5 wks. Aid (Need).
Housing: Dorms. Avg per room/unit: 2. Campus facilities avail.
Ses: 3. **Wks/ses:** 2-5. Operates June-July.

Governor's School summer students receive intensive arts training from practicing artists. Limited to South Carolina residents, the two-week Discovery (for rising ninth graders) and Academy (for rising 10th graders) programs focus upon creative writing, drama, visual arts, and vocal or instrumental music. The curriculum incorporates studio work, self-directed studies, performances, field trips, lectures and presentations by faculty and guest artists. The five-week Summer Dance program, open to students around the world entering grades 7-12, offers complex exercise training in both classical ballet and modern dance. Participants in all programs may showcase their work in end-of-session recitals, readings and presentations.

SOUTHERN ILLINOIS UNIVERSITY YOUNG WRITERS WORKSHOP
Res and Day — Coed Ages 15-18

Carbondale, IL 62901. Div of Continuing Ed, MC 6705, Washington Sq C. Tel: 618-453-2121.
http://cola.siu.edu/english/graduate/internships/young-writers-workshop.php
E-mail: aljoseph@siu.edu
Allison Joseph, Dir.
Grades 10-12. Adm: FCFS. **Appl**—Due: Rolling. Writing sample.
Enr: 30. **Enr cap:** 30.

Type of instruction: Enrich.
Focus: Creative_Writing.
Fees 2013: Res $350, 1 wk. Day 1 wk.
Housing: Dorms.
Est 1999. Ses: 1. Wks/ses: 1. Operates June.

This five-day program consists of daily poetry and prose classes, readings shared by faculty and participants, and panels on special writing topics. Workshops help students generate new story and poem ideas, and hourlong minisessions offer an introduction to various creative writing topics. Graduate students and creative writing faculty at SIU constitute YWW's faculty.

STAGEDOOR MANOR
Res — Coed Ages 10-18

Loch Sheldrake, NY 12759. 116 Karmel Rd. Tel: 845-434-4290.
Contact (Sept-May): 8 Wingate Rd, Lexington, MA 02421. Tel: 540-337-7619.
Year-round Toll-free: 888-782-4388, Fax: 845-434-3779.
www.stagedoormanor.com　E-mail: info2014@stagedoormanor.com
Cynthia Samuelson, Dir.
Adm: FCFS. **Appl**—Fee $0. Due: Rolling.
Enr: 240. **Fac 150. Staff:** Admin 10.
Courses: Dance Media Music.
Focus: Acting Theater. **Features:** Soccer Swim Tennis Volleyball.
Fees 2014: Res $5395, 3-6 wks.
Housing: Dorms. **Swimming:** Pool.
Est 1976. Inc. Ses: 3. Wks/ses: 3-6. Operates June-Aug.

Stagedoor's program consists of daily class work in acting, musical comedy, dance, modeling, television acting, voice, directing, stagecraft and costuming. Stagedoor provides specialized programs for younger campers and college-level courses for high school students. Boys and girls perform at the camp's theaters and at major resort hotels.

STANFORD JAZZ WORKSHOP JAZZ CAMP
Res and Day — Coed Ages 12-17

Stanford, CA 94309. PO Box 20454. Tel: 650-736-0324. Fax: 650-856-4155.
www.stanfordjazz.org　E-mail: registrar@stanfordjazz.org
Jim Nadel, Dir. Student contact: Janel Thysen.
Adm: FCFS. **Appl**—Fee $25. Due: Rolling.
Enr: 200. **Enr cap:** 200. **Fac 55. Staff:** Admin 6. Couns 12.
Type of instruction: Enrich. **Avg class size:** 6. **Daily hours for:** Classes 8. Study 1½. Rec 1½.
Focus: Music. **Features:** Swim.
Fees 2014: Res $2120, 1-2 wks. Day $850 (+$60), 1 wk. Aid 2011 (Need): $110,000.
Housing: Dorms. Avg per room/unit: 2. **Swimming:** Pool.
Est 1972. Nonprofit. Spons: Stanford University. **Ses:** 2. **Wks/ses:** 1. Operates July-Aug.

Serving students from beginning to advanced skill levels, Jazz Camp is open to players of all instruments (including violin, viola and cello), and to vocalists as well. Campers play with other young people while learning from a faculty composed of well-known professional jazz musicians and educators. The curriculum comprises jazz ensemble playing, master classes, private lessons and performances, as well as theory, musicianship and jazz history courses. In addition to daily class sessions and rehearsals, participants attend jam sessions and Stanford Jazz Festival evening concerts to enhance their training and experience.

STONELEIGH-BURNHAM SCHOOL
SORVINO DANCE INTENSIVE
Res — Girls Ages 11-17

Greenfield, MA 01301. 574 Bernardston Rd. Tel: 413-774-2711. Fax: 413-772-2602.
www.sbschool.org/default.aspx?relid=607553
E-mail: summerprograms@sbschool.org
Ann Sorvino, Dir.
Adm: FCFS. Appl—Due: Rolling.
Enr: 24. Enr cap: 24. Staff: Admin 3. Couns 3.
Focus: Dance. Features: Aquatics Swim.
Fees 2014: Res $800, 1 wk.
Housing: Dorms. Swimming: Pool.
Est 1997. Nonprofit. Ses: 2. Wks/ses: 1. Operates June-July.

Girls enrolled in the program work on their dancing skills in an intensive and noncompetitive environment. Experienced teachers offer instruction in modern dance, ballet and jazz techniques. Special repertory, improvisation and choreography sessions are also available. Applicants must display a serious interest in dance but need not audition.

SUMMER SONATINA INTERNATIONAL PIANO CAMP
Res — Coed Ages 7-16

Bennington, VT 05201. 5 Catamount Ln. Tel: 802-442-9197. Fax: 802-447-3175.
www.sonatina.com E-mail: piano@sonatina.com
Polly van der Linde, Dir.
Student contact: Andrea Lindhardt, E-mail: andrea@sonatina.com.
Adm: FCFS. Appl—Fee $0. Due: Rolling.
Enr: 150. Enr cap: 170. Intl: 10%. Non-White: 10%. Fac 6. Prof 4. Col/grad students 2.
Staff: Admin 2. Couns 10.
Type of instruction: Adv Enrich Rev Study_Skills Tut. Courses: Crafts. Avg class size: 42. Daily hours for: Classes 1. Study 3. Rec 2½.
Focus: Music. Features: Cooking Hiking Kayak Soccer Swim Volleyball Croquet.
Fees 2014: Res $1050, 1 wk.
Housing: Houses. Swimming: Lake Pool. Campus facilities avail.
Est 1969. Inc. Ses: 5. Wks/ses: 1. Operates June-July.

Summer Sonatina, located in the historic Vermont mansion of the van der Linde family, offers a piano program for beginning through advanced performers. Students live with the family and share in household duties while receiving three to five private lessons weekly and classes in sight-reading, chorus, music theory and composition. Pupils attend performances at Tanglewood and the Saratoga Performing Arts Center once a week.

TENNESSEE GOVERNOR'S SCHOOL FOR THE ARTS
Res — Coed Ages 15-17

Murfreesboro, TN 37132. Middle Tennessee State Univ, 1301 E Main St, Box 38. Tel: 615-898-2223. Fax: 615-898-2326.
www.gsfta.com E-mail: gjrobins@mtsu.edu
Raphael B. Bundage, Dir. Student contact: Glenna Robinson.
Grades 10-11. Adm: Very selective. Appl—Fee $0. Due: Nov. Transcript, 2 recs, audition.
Enr: 230. Enr cap: 230.
Type of instruction: Enrich. Courses: Ceramics Drawing Painting Sculpt. College credit: 3.
Focus: Dance Filmmaking Music Studio_Art Theater.
Fees 2014: Free (in-state residents). Res 4 wks.
Housing: Dorms.
Est 1984. Ses: 1. Wks/ses: 4. Operates June.

Professional visual and performing artists lead these intensive programs for Tennessee residents in visual arts, dance, filmmaking, theater and music. Visual arts media include clay, drawing, painting, sculpture, printmaking, computer imagery, photography and video. The dance program covers ballet and pointe technique, modern and jazz. Filmmakers produce a five- to 10-minute narrative. Music students choose from orchestra, wind, chorale, piano and guitar ensembles. The theater program develops both technical and performance skills. All boys and girls attend nightly demonstrations, slide shows, films and lectures.

TEXAS ARTS PROJECT
Res — Coed Ages 8-18

Austin, TX 78746. c/o St Stephen's Episcopal School, 6500 St Stephen's Dr. Tel: 512-553-6276. Fax: 512-327-1311.
www.texasartsproject.com   E-mail: info@texasartsproject.com
Ginger Morris, Dir.
Grades 1-12. Adm: Somewhat_selective. Admitted: 90%. **Appl**—Fee $0. Due: Rolling. Video/portfolio submission for advanced program.
Enr: 58. **Enr cap:** 75. **Intl:** 2%. Non-White: 15%. **Fac 30.** Prof 3. Col/grad students 10. K-12 staff 5. Specialists 12. **Staff:** Admin 2. Couns 10.
Courses: Classical_Guitar Musical_Theater. **Avg class size:** 10. **Daily hours for:** Classes 8. Study 2. Rec 2.
Focus: Acting Dance Filmmaking Music Theater. **Features:** Swim.
Fees 2014: Res $875-3075, 1-4 wks. Aid 2010 (Merit & Need): $20,000.
Housing: Dorms. Avg per room/unit: 4. **Swimming:** Lake Pool. Campus facilities avail.
Est 2001. Nonprofit. **Spons:** St. Stephen's Episcopal School. **Ses:** 3. **Wks/ses:** 1-4. Operates June-July.

Conducted at St. Stephen's Episcopal School, TAP is a summer training program for young artists interested in developing their skills in musical theater, dance, acting, filmmaking and technical theater. The program consists of classes, private lessons, master classes with visiting artists, theater outings and seminars. The junior session (for children ages 8-12) lasts for one week, while the main session (ages 13-18) runs for three weeks. All sessions culminate in a production on the final day that enables campers to display their talents.

UNIVERSITY OF CALIFORNIA-LOS ANGELES
ACTING AND PERFORMANCE INSTITUTE
Res and Day — Coed Ages 14-18

Los Angeles, CA 90095. Summer Sessions & Special Prgms, 1331 Murphy Hall. Tel: 310-267-4836. Fax: 310-825-3383.
www.summer.ucla.edu/institutes/acting&performance/overview.htm
E-mail: institutes@summer.ucla.edu
Patricia Harter, Dir.
Grades 9-12. Adm: Selective. **Appl**—Due: Rolling. Rec.
Type of instruction: Adv. **College credit:** 2.
Focus: Acting Theater.
Fees 2014: Res $3043-3293.
Housing: Dorms. Avg per room/unit: 2.
Nonprofit. **Ses:** 1. **Wks/ses:** 6. Operates June-Aug.

High school students with a serious interest in theater gain exposure at UCLA to the training and discipline required for participation in a university theater program or a career in the performing arts. Boys and girls attend morning performance classes addressing acting fundamentals, movement and improvisation, and scene. A performance workshop in the afternoon offers practical experience in the rehearsal and performance process. Under the guidance of an instructor, students take part in all aspects of the creative process: conceptualizing, writing and transforming ideas into dramatic action. A collaborative project leads to a session-closing performance for invited guests.

UNIVERSITY OF CALIFORNIA-LOS ANGELES
SUMMER DANCE-THEATER INTENSIVE
Res — Coed Ages 16-18

Los Angeles, CA 90095. Summer Sessions & Special Prgms, 1331 Murphy Hall. Tel: 310-267-4836.
www.summer.ucla.edu/institutes/dance/overview.htm
E-mail: institutes@summer.ucla.edu
Kevin Kane, Dir.
Grades 11-PG. **Adm:** Selective. **Appl**—Due: Rolling. Rec.
Type of instruction: Adv. **Courses:** Music. **College credit:** 2.
Focus: Dance Theater.
Fees 2014: Res $1966, 1 wk.
Housing: Dorms. Avg per room/unit: 2.
Nonprofit. **Ses:** 1. **Wks/ses:** 1. Operates June.

This eight-day program for advanced high schoolers combines the disciplines of dance, theater, music and social activism. The program is particularly suited to those interested in exploring the ways in which art can raise awareness and consciousness pertaining to various socially relevant themes. Students engage in daily movement classes, ensemble physical theater, and improvisation and composition. The Dance-Theatre Intensive is noncompetitive and does not involve any conservatory-style dancing. Parents and friends may attend the session-closing collaborative performance.

UNIVERSITY OF IOWA YOUNG WRITERS' STUDIO
Res — Coed Ages 16-18

Iowa City, IA 52242. The University of Iowa, 250 CEF. Tel: 319-335-4209. Fax: 319-335-4743.
http://iowayoungwritersstudio.org   E-mail: iyws@uiowa.edu
Stephen Lovely, Dir.
Grades 11-PG (younger if qualified). **Adm:** Very selective. **Appl**—Fee $0. Due: Feb. Creative writing sample, transcript, teacher rec, essay.
Enr: 60. **Enr cap:** 60.
Type of instruction: Enrich. **Avg class size:** 12.
Focus: Creative_Writing.
Fees 2014: Res $2000, 2 wks. Aid (Need).
Housing: Dorms.
Nonprofit. **Ses:** 2. **Wks/ses:** 2. Operates June-July.

Participants in this college program for high school students focus upon a single course of study for the duration of this two-week program. Options are poetry, fiction and creative writing (a survey course that comprises fiction, poetry and creative nonfiction). Each course includes both a seminar and a workshop; the same instructor teaches both. Seminars provide participants with a broad range of readings, while workshops enable boys and girls to work on their writing with the benefit of constructive criticism from fellow students and the instructor.

UNIVERSITY OF KANSAS
MIDWESTERN MUSIC ACADEMY
Res — Coed Ages 11-18; Day — Coed 7-18

Lawrence, KS 66045. 460 Murphy Hall, 1530 Naismith Dr. Tel: 785-864-9751. Fax: 785-864-5866.
www.musicacademy.ku.edu   E-mail: musiccamp@ku.edu
Dan Gailey, Dir.
Grades 6-PG. **Adm:** FCFS. **Appl**—Fee $0.
Enr: 400. **Staff:** Admin 30. Couns 23.
Courses: Computers.

Focus: Music.
Fees 2014: Res $540-665, 1 wk. **Day** $140-420, 1 wk. Aid (Merit).
Est 1936. **Nonprofit. Ses:** 7. **Wks/ses:** 1. Operates June-July.

Midwestern Music Academy's offers four weeklong summer programs, all taught by University of Kansas faculty and guest artists. Jayhawk Junior Musicians camp is open to students in grades 3-6 who are seeking learning experiences within music. Junior High Music Camp, open to band and choir students entering grades 6-9 and orchestra students entering grades 6-8, offers instruction through master classes, rehearsals and electives. Programs for students completing grades 8-12 include the String Institute; the Wind, Brass and Percussion Institute; and the Jazz Workshop.

UNIVERSITY OF MASSACHUSETTS-AMHERST
JUNIPER INSTITUTE FOR YOUNG WRITERS
Res and Day — Coed Ages 15-18

Amherst, MA 01003. c/o University Conference Services, 918 Campus Ctr, 1 Campus Center Way. Tel: 413-545-5503. Fax: 413-545-3880.
www.umass.edu/juniperyoungwriters
E-mail: juniperyoungwriters@hfa.umass.edu
Jennifer Jacobson, Dir.
Grades 11-PG (younger if qualified). Adm: Selective. Admitted: 50%. **Appl**—Fee $25. Due: Rolling. Creative writing sample, rec, personal statement.
Enr: 72. **Enr cap:** 72. Intl: 2%. Non-White: 20%. **Fac 10.** Col/grad students 10. **Staff:** Admin 3. Couns 7.
Courses: Crafts Theater. **Avg class size:** 12. **Daily hours for:** Classes 4½. Study 1½. Rec 3½. Homework. **College credit:** 2/crse, total 2.
Focus: Creative_Writing.
Fees 2014: Res $1300, 1 wk. Aid 2011 (Merit & Need): $2775.
Housing: Dorms. Avg per room/unit: 2.
Est 2005. Nonprofit. Ses: 1. **Wks/ses:** 1. Operates June.

Hosted by the University of Massachusetts' MFA Program for Poets and Writers, this intensive, weeklong program combines creative writing workshops, studio courses and readings. Daily workshops in poetry and fiction form the core of the session. Participants work with Juniper faculty and a core group of their peers to generate new work, revise work in progress and form a community of writers designed to foster shared feedback. Question and answer sessions with faculty and writers-in-residence enable students to explore the creative process and the writing life. Noted authors and poets deliver evening readings.

UNIVERSITY OF MIAMI SUMMER SCHOLAR PROGRAMS
Res — Coed Ages 15-17

Coral Gables, FL 33124. PO Box 248005. Tel: 305-284-5078. Fax: 305-284-6629.
www.miami.edu/ssp   E-mail: ssp@miami.edu
Grades 10-11. Adm: Selective. Prereqs: GPA 3.0. **Appl**—Fee $35. Due: May. Transcript, rec, essay.
Enr: 196. **Fac 25. Staff:** Admin 1.
Avg class size: 18. **Daily hours for:** Classes 6. Study 3. Rec 2. **High school & college credit:** 3/crse, total 6.
Focus: Filmmaking. **Features:** Community_Serv Swim.
Fees 2014: Res $7295, 3 wks. **Day** $6168-6393.
Housing: Dorms. **Swimming:** Ocean Pool.
Est 1991. Nonprofit. Ses: 1. **Wks/ses:** 3. Operates June-July.

SSP, taught by university faculty, allows highly motivated rising high school juniors and seniors to pursue course work in filmmaking. Guest speakers and visits to local sites relevant to the field of study supplement in-class work. Students earn three to six college credits, which are also accepted at many high schools. In addition to filmmaking, the university conducts programs focusing on broadcast journalism, business, engineering, forensic investigation, health and medicine, international relations, marine science, sports medicine and sports administration (see separate listing for details).

UNIVERSITY OF ST ANDREWS
CREATIVE WRITING SUMMER PROGRAMME
Res — Coed Ages 16-18

St Andrews, KY16 9AX Fife, Scotland. St Katharine's W, 16 The Scores. Tel: 44-1334-462147. Fax: 44-1334-463330.
www.st-andrews.ac.uk/admissions/ug/int/summerschools
E-mail: fjt2@st-andrews.ac.uk
Frances Trahar, Dir.
Grades 11-PG. Adm: Selective. Admitted: 90%. Prereqs: GPA 3.0. Appl—Fee £15. Due: Apr. Creative writing sample (4 poems or piece of short fiction), 2 recs, standardized test results, personal statement.
Enr cap: 25. Intl: 20%. Non-White: 10%. Fac 12. Prof 1. Col/grad students 4. Specialists 7. Staff: Admin 2. Couns 2.
Type of instruction: Adv. Courses: Fine_Arts Music Photog Theater. Daily hours for: Classes 4. Study 3. Rec 3. Homework. Grades. College credit: 12.
Intl program focus: Acad Culture.
Focus: Writing/Journ Creative_Writing. Features: Conservation Exploration Hiking Mtn_ Trips Swim.
Fees 2014: Res £2800 (+£200), 4 wks.
Housing: Dorms. Avg per room/unit: 1. Swimming: Ocean Pool. Campus facilities avail.
Est 2003. Ses: 1. Wks/ses: 4. Operates June-July.

Aspiring young fiction writers and poets who have completed grades 10-12 take a series of master classes and workshops with noted Scottish writers and poets. Skills addressed include editing, analysis and oral presentation. Frequent field trips and excursions—in addition to cultural visits to art galleries, concerts and the theater—enrich the program.

THE UNIVERSITY OF THE ARTS
PRE-COLLEGE SUMMER INSTITUTE
Res and Day — Coed Ages 16-18

Philadelphia, PA 19102. 320 S Broad St. Tel: 215-717-6430, 800-616-2787. Fax: 215-717-6538.
http://cs.uarts.edu/precollege   E-mail: precollege@uarts.edu
Rosi Dispensa, Dir.
Grades 11-12 (younger if qualified). Adm: Selective. Admitted: 85%. Prereqs: GPA 2.0. Appl—Fee 50. Due: May. Transcript, teacher rec, portfolio/audition, essay.
Enr: 250. Enr cap: 350. Fac 150. Staff: Admin 8.
Type of instruction: Undergrad. Avg class size: 12. Daily hours for: Classes 8. College credit: 3/crse, total 3.
Focus: Acting Dance Media Music Photog Studio_Art Theater.
Fees 2014: Res $4720 (+$150-600), 2-4 wks. Day $3440 (+$150-600), 2 wks. Aid (Need).
Housing: Apartments Dorms. Avg per room/unit: 2-4.
Est 1900. Nonprofit. Ses: 2. Wks/ses: 2-4. Operates July-Aug.

The Pre-College Summer Institute offers talented high school students the opportunity to study the visual and performing arts. Course offerings in performing arts include acting, musical theater, dance and jazz performance, while art and media offerings include animation, Web design, photography, painting, printmaking, sculpture, graphic design, film, industrial design, illustration, mixed media, jewelry, fibers and ceramics.

UNIVERSITY OF VIRGINIA YOUNG WRITERS WORKSHOP
Res — Coed Ages 13-17

Charlottesville, VA 22904. c/o The Curry School, PO Box 400273. Tel: 434-924-0836.
http://theyoungwriters.org   E-mail: writers@virginia.edu
Margo Figgins, Dir.
Grades 9-12. Adm: Selective. Appl—Due: Mar. Writing samples, rec.
Type of instruction: Enrich.
Focus: Creative_Writing.
Fees 2014: Res $1650-2650, 2-3 wks. Aid (Need).
Housing: Dorms.
Est 1982. Ses: 2. Wks/ses: 2-3. Operates June-July.

UVA conducts two annual sessions for aspiring writers: a two-week program for those new to study within a specific genre, and a three-week program for writers who wish to deepen their understanding and mastery of a specific genre. Both sessions feature intensive workshops, labs, readings, conferences with instructors, independent writing time, and opportunities for publication and performance. Intensive workshops employed in the three-week program focus upon songwriting, poetry, screen- and playwriting, fiction and creative nonfiction.

WALNUT HILL SUMMER WRITING PROGRAM
Res — Coed Ages 13-17

Natick, MA 01760. 12 Highland St. Tel: 508-650-5020. Fax: 508-653-9593.
www.walnuthillarts.org   E-mail: admissions@walnuthillarts.org
Margaret Funkhouser, Dir.
Adm: Selective. Appl—Fee $30. Due: May. Essay, Eng teacher/guidance counselor rec.
Fac 6. Staff: Admin 1.
Type of instruction: Enrich. Courses: Poetry.
Focus: Creative_Writing. Features: Swim.
Fees 2014: Res $3060, 3 wks. Aid (Need).
Housing: Dorms. Swimming: Pool.
Inc. Ses: 1. Wks/ses: 3. Operates June-July.

Students enrolled in this intensive, multigenre writing program develop their skills through workshops in poetry and fiction. Students work individually in collaborative projects and meet with faculty one-on-one. Published authors visit campus to teach master classes and give readings of their work. Excursions to local museums and literary landmarks

WASHINGTON UNIVERSITY
PORTFOLIO PLUS
Res and Day — Coed Ages 16-18

St Louis, MO 63130. 1 Brookings Dr, Campus Box 1031. Tel: 314-935-8652. Fax: 314-935-6462.
www.samfoxschool.wustl.edu/summer/portplus   E-mail: lee@samfox.wustl.edu
Belinda Lee, Dir.
Student contact: Elisabeth Roeleveld, E-mail: eroeleveld@samefox.wustl.edu.
Grades 11-12. Adm: Somewhat_selective. Admitted: 80%. Appl—Fee $35. Due: May.
Transcript, rec, personal statement.
Enr cap: 45. Fac 9. Prof 6. Col/grad students 3. Staff: Admin 2. Res 3.
Type of instruction: Undergrad. Courses: Drawing Fashion Painting Printmaking. Avg class size: 15. Daily hours for: Classes 6. College credit: 6.
Focus: Studio_Art. Features: Swim.
Fees 2014: Res $4377 (+$200), 5 wks.
Housing: Dorms. Avg per room/unit: 2. Swimming: Pool. Campus facilities avail.
Est 2004. Ses: 1. Wks/ses: 5. Operates July.

This five-week introduction to the study and practice of making art is open to rising high school juniors and seniors. All participants take a morning art foundations course, then choose from afternoon electives in digital photography, fashion design, painting and printmaking/book arts. Outside of class, students embark on organized trips to museums and visit artist studios. Successful completion of the program yields six college credits.

WESTMINSTER CHOIR COLLEGE SUMMER PROGRAMS
Res and Day — Coed Ages 11-18

Princeton, NJ 08540. 101 Walnut Ln. Tel: 609-924-7416. Fax: 609-921-6187.
www.rider.edu/academics/colleges-schools/wca/woce/summer-camps
E-mail: woce@rider.edu
Scott R. Hoerl, Exec Dir.
Grades 6-PG. Adm: Somewhat_selective. **Appl**—Fee $50. Due: Rolling. DVD audition for certain programs.
Type of instruction: Adv Enrich. **Courses:** Theater.
Focus: Music.
Fees 2014: Res $995-1850, 1-2 wks. Day $795. Aid (Need).
Housing: Dorms. Avg per room/unit: 2.
Est 1926. Nonprofit. **Spons:** Rider University. **Ses:** 14. **Wks/ses:** 1-2. Operates June-Aug.

Part of Rider University, Westminster Choir College conducts summer music programs for middle school and high school students. Classes are available in choral studies, piano, organ, voice, music education, composition and musical theater, among others. The program includes private and group lessons, concerts, recitals and on-campus recreational activities.

CAMP WINNARAINBOW
Res — Coed Ages 7-14

Laytonville, CA 95454. PO Box 1359. Tel: 707-984-6507. Fax: 707-984-8087.
Contact (Sept-May): 1301 Henry St, Berkeley, CA 94709. Tel: 510-525-4304. Fax: 510-528-8775.
www.campwinnarainbow.org   E-mail: arainbow@mcn.org
Jahanara Romney & Wavy Gravy, Dirs.
Adm: FCFS. **Appl**—Due: Rolling.
Enr: 150. **Enr cap:** 150. **Fac 10. Staff:** Admin 4. Couns 34.
Courses: Crafts. **Daily hours for:** Classes 2. Rec 3.
Focus: Circus_Skills Dance Music Theater. **Features:** Peace/Cross-cultural Basketball Gymnastics Swim.
Fees 2014: Res $850-7090 (+$20), 1-9 wks. Aid 2008 (Need): $154,000.
Housing: Tepees. Avg per room/unit: 9. **Swimming:** Lake.
Est 1972. Nonprofit. **Ses:** 5. **Wks/ses:** 1-9. Operates June-Aug.

The camp focuses on performing arts and circus skills. Activities and classes include acting and play production; clowning, mime, juggling, falling and stilt walking; unicycling; tightrope; trapeze; cloud swing and Spanish web; gymnastics; music; dance; arts and crafts; mask making; magic; martial arts; swimming; team sports; nature walks; poetry; songwriting; capoeira; and hip-hop and salsa dancing.

YOUNG ACTORS CAMP
Res — Coed Ages 8-19

Azusa, CA. Azusa Pacific Univ.
Contact (Year-round): 689 W Foothill Blvd, Ste A, Claremont, CA 91711. Tel: 909-982-8059. Fax: 909-482-2011.
www.youngactorscamp.com   E-mail: request@youngactorscamp.com
Nichelle Rodriguez, Dir.

Adm: Selective. Admitted: 25%. **Appl**—Fee $0. Due: Apr. Phone interview, nomination (Casting Call prgm).
Enr: 200. Intl: 60%. Non-White: 20%. **Fac 20.** Prof 4. Col/grad students 12. Specialists 4.
Staff: Admin 4. Couns 20.
Type of instruction: Undergrad. **Courses:** Media Theater. **Avg class size:** 12. **Daily hours for:** Classes 6. Study 1. Rec 4. **College credit:** 4/crse, total 4.
Focus: Acting.
Fees 2014: Res $1790-7870, 1-5 wks.
Housing: Dorms. Campus facilities avail.
Est 2000. Inc. **Spons:** Inspire Me Corporation. **Ses: 5. Wks/ses:** 1-4. Operates June-July.

Children and adolescents who wish to improve their acting skills attend sessions at Azusa Pacific University. The Acting Camp enrolls boys and girls ages 8-18 with or without acting experience into a program that features an on-camera commercial workshop, an exploration of acting terms and techniques, on-camera screen study, improvisational games and memory skills training. Campers of the same age with at least a year of acting experience may enroll in the Pre-Professional Program, where they learn extensively about the film and television industries. Boys and girls ages 12-17 who are serious about pursuing a career in film or television—and who can furnish a referral from an acting teacher, director or out-of-state agent—may apply for the Casting Call program; this is an invitation-only session, and a phone interview is required.

YOUNG ARTISTS' WORKSHOPS
Res — Coed Ages 14-18

Rockport, ME 04856. 70 Camden St. Tel: 207-236-8581, 877-577-7700. Fax: 207-236-2558.
www.mainemedia.edu/workshops/young-artists   E-mail: info@mainemedia.edu
Charles Altschul, Exec Dir.
Adm: Somewhat_selective. Admitted: 95%. **Appl**—Fee $55. Due: Rolling. Portfolio required for advanced classes.
Enr: 16. **Enr cap:** 16. **Fac 1.** Specialists 1. **Staff:** Couns 4.
Courses: Animation.
Focus: Acting Animation Filmmaking Media Photog. **Features:** Hiking Swim.
Fees 2014: Res $1495-2895, 1-2 wks. Aid (Merit & Need).
Housing: Dorms. **Swimming:** Lake Ocean.
Est 1973. Nonprofit. **Spons:** Maine Media Workshops/Maine Media College. **Ses: 34.**
Wks/ses: 1-2. Operates June-Aug.

Artistically talented high schoolers enrolled in this Maine Media Workshops summer program spend their time studying and exploring a potential career field in one of the following areas: photography, filmmaking and video, multimedia, documentary, acting or digital media. Instructors, who are drawn from industry professionals and experienced educators, each receive classroom support from a teaching assistant. Students spend weekends on class field trips, at work in labs or editing suites, or engaged in recreational pursuits along the coast of Maine.

YOUNG MUSICIANS & ARTISTS
Res — Coed Ages 10-18

Salem, OR. Willamette Univ.
Contact (Year-round): PO Box 13277, Portland, OR 97213. Tel: 503-281-9528. Fax: 888-793-2583.
www.ymainc.org   E-mail: info@ymainc.org
Peter Markgraf, Pres.
Grades 5-PG. Adm: FCFS. **Appl**—Fee $0. Due: Apr.
Enr: 110. **Enr cap:** 140. Non-White: 18%. **Fac 30. Staff:** Admin 10. Couns 20.

Type of instruction: Adv Enrich. **Avg class size:** 8. **Daily hours for:** Classes 5. Study 1. Rec 3.
Focus: Creative_Writing Dance Music Painting Photog Studio_Art Theater. **Features:** Badminton Soccer Softball Tennis Volleyball.
Fees 2014: Res $1700 (+$25), 2 wks. Aid 2011 (Need): $58,000.
Housing: Dorms. Avg per room/unit: 2.
Est 1965. Nonprofit. **Ses:** 2. **Wks/ses:** 2. Operates June-July.

Held at Willamette University, YMA offers a range of arts programs that encompasses instrumental music, theater, musical theater, choir, piano, dance, digital photography, creative writing and the visual arts. Students select a major area of study, then also enroll in an elective class. Classes meet Monday through Saturday, with boys and girls spending four hours daily attending class in their majors, 45 minutes in the elective class and 30 minutes in an orientation class. Supervised recreational activities round out the day.

YOUTH THEATRE OF NEW JERSEY
SUMMER THEATRE INSTITUTE-NEW YORK CITY
Res — Coed Ages 10-19

New York, NY. Juilliard School.
Contact (Year-round): 23 Tomahawk Trl, Sparta, NJ 07871. Tel: 201-415-5329.
www.youththeatreinstitutes.org E-mail: sti.triplethreatstudios.nyc@gmail.com
Allyn Sitjar, Dir.
Adm: Selective. **Appl**—Fee $75. Due: Rolling. Live/DVD audition.
Enr: 30. Intl: 10%. Non-White: 25%. **Fac 10.** Prof 5. Specialists 5. **Staff:** Admin 3. Couns 3.
Courses: Dance Music Directing Mime Musical_Theater Playwriting. **Avg class size:** 15.
Daily hours for: Classes 10.
Focus: Acting Theater.
Fees 2013: Res $3600, 4 wks. Aid 2009 (Merit): $800.
Housing: Dorms. Avg per room/unit: 2.
Est 1989. Nonprofit. **Ses:** 1. **Wks/ses:** 4. Operates June-July.

Summer Theatre Institute-NYC offers intensive training with professional artists in a variety of theater techniques. Instruction combines core classes with specialized training in acting, musical theater, playwriting and directing. The session culminates in an original production that is a result of work at the institute. Professional theater teaching artists—many of whom teach at area colleges—serve as program instructors. Students live in Juilliard School dormitories and train at studios in the city's theater district.

TRAVEL
PROGRAMS

Travel programs are arranged alphabetically by name. An index beginning on page 266 lists the world regions to which participants travel. Programs offering a family session are indicated by "FAM" at the end of the age range in the index.

INDEX BY DESTINATION

MEXICO & CENTRAL AMERICA

MIDDLE EAST

SOUTH AMERICA

USA

Travel Programs

AMERICAN TRAILS WEST
Res — Coed Ages 12-17

Great Neck, NY 11021. 92 Middle Neck Rd. Tel: 516-487-2800, 800-645-6260. Fax: 516-487-2855.
www.atwteentours.com   E-mail: info@atwteentours.com
Howard Fox, Pres.
Grades 7-12. Adm: FCFS. Appl due: Rolling. Enr: 43.
Intl program focus: Culture. Travel: AK AZ CA CO FL GA HI MA MT NM NY PA SC SD UT VA WA WY Canada Europe.
Features: Hiking Mtn_Biking White-water_Raft Swim Water-skiing.
Fees 2012: Res $2595-10,495, 2-5 wks.
Housing: Dorms Hotels Tents. Swimming: Lake Ocean Pool.
Est 1965. Inc. Ses: 22. Wks/ses: 2-5. Operates June-Aug.

Diversified itineraries give participants a comprehensive view of the Continental US, Canada, Alaska, Hawaii and Europe. Trips offer accommodations of camping, college dorms, hotels or a combination thereof. Participants are grouped by age, and ATW maintains a favorable camper-staff ratio.

BOLD EARTH TEEN ADVENTURES
Res — Coed Ages 11-18

Golden, CO 80401. 2308 Fossil Trace Dr. Tel: 303-526-0806. Fax: 303-531-2717.
www.boldearth.com   E-mail: info@boldearth.com
Sean Kuprevich, Dir.
Grades 7-12. Adm: FCFS. Appl due: Rolling. Enr: 12-16. Staff: Admin 5. Couns 70.
Avg class size: 5. Daily hours for: Classes 4. Rec 7.
Intl program focus: Lang Culture. Travel: AK AZ CA CO HI OR UT WA Africa Asia Europe Mexico/Central_America South_America. Home stays avail.
Features: Environ_Sci Crafts Adventure_Travel Bicycle_Tours Boating Canoe Caving Community_Serv Conservation Cooking Exploration Hiking Kayak Mountaineering Mtn_Biking Mtn_Trips Outdoor_Ed Rappelling Riding Rock_Climb Ropes_Crse Sail Scuba Seamanship White-water_Raft Wilderness_Camp Yoga Equestrian Surfing Swim Water-skiing Watersports Winter_Sports.
Fees 2014: Res $2488-6788 (+airfare), 2-4 wks. Aid 2011 (Need): $25,000.
Housing: Cabins Hotels Lodges Tents. Avg per room/unit: 2-4. Swimming: Lake Pond Ocean Pool River Stream.
Est 1976. Inc. Ses: 24. Wks/ses: 2-4. Operates June-Aug. ACA.

Offering roughly two dozen programs around the world, Bold Earth conducts adventure travel camps that focus on travel, outdoor activities, service learning and Spanish-language immersion. Domestic programs operate in Alaska, Hawaii, and the American West, Northwest and Southwest, while international destinations include Europe, Central and South America, Asia and Africa.

COSTA RICA RAINFOREST OUTWARD BOUND SCHOOL SUMMER ADVENTURES
Res — Coed Ages 17 and up

San Jose, 02050 Costa Rica. PO Box 1817-2050, San Pedro. Fax: 866-374-2483.
www.crrobs.org   E-mail: enrollment@crrobs.org
James Rowe, Exec Dir.
Adm: FCFS. Appl due: Rolling. Fac 2. Staff: Admin 10.

Avg class size: 10. **Daily hours for:** Classes 2. Rec 6. **High school & college credit:** 3/crse, total 9.
Intl program focus: Acad Lang Culture. **Travel:** Mexico/Central_America. Home stays avail.
Focus: Adventure_Travel. **Features:** Ecol Environ_Sci Crafts Canoe Climbing_Wall Community_Serv Conservation Exploration Hiking Kayak Mountaineering Mtn_Trips Rappelling Rock_Climb Sail Scuba White-water_Raft Wilderness_Camp Wilderness_Canoe Surfing Swim Water-skiing.
Fees 2012: Res $2600-5600, 1½-4 wks.
Housing: Cabins Dorms Lodges Tents. Avg per room/unit: 2. **Swimming:** Ocean River.
Est 1997. Nonprofit. **Ses:** 18. **Wks/ses:** 1½-4. Operates June-Aug.

CRROBS offers various adventure-oriented summer programs, some of which integrate Spanish language immersion. Students learn through an interactive teaching style focusing on language supplements, verbal communication and cultural immersion. Adventure options include rainforest hikes, white-water rafting and sea kayaking, surfing at various beaches and exploration of the country's volcano region.

THE EXPERIMENT IN INTERNATIONAL LIVING
Res — Coed Ages 14-18

Brattleboro, VT 05302. 1 Kipling Rd, PO Box 676. Tel: 802-257-7751, 800-345-2929.
Fax: 802-258-3428.
www.experimentinternational.org   E-mail: experiment@worldlearning.org
Heather Beard, Assoc Dir of Adm.
Grades 9-12. Adm: FCFS. **Appl due:** Apr.
Intl program focus: Lang Culture. **Travel:** AZ NM Africa Asia Europe Mexico/Central_America South_America. Home stays avail.
Features: Ecol Lang Marine_Bio/Stud Relig_Stud Sci Dance Filmmaking Fine_Arts Music Painting Photog Theater Adventure_Travel Bicycle_Tours Community_Serv Conservation Cooking Exploration Hiking Mtn_Trips Peace/Cross-cultural Riding White-water_Raft Wilderness_Camp Soccer.
Fees 2014: Res $4200-6900 (+airfare), 3-5 wks. Aid (Need).
Housing: Dorms Hotels Houses Lodges Tents. Avg per room/unit: 2.
Est 1932. Nonprofit. **Ses:** 31. **Wks/ses:** 3-5. Operates June-Aug.

EIL conducts summer abroad programs in Argentina, Botswana, Brazil, China, Costa Rica, Ecuador, France, Germany, Italy, Japan, Korea, Mexico, Mongolia, Morocco, Nicaragua and Cuba, Peru, South Africa, Spain, Tanzania and Thailand.. All programs include home stay with a local host family and a cross-cultural orientation component. Depending on the program chosen, travel, language study, community service, peace studies, the arts or ecology may be featured. Emphasis throughout is on in-depth immersion into a foreign culture. Prior language training is a prerequisite for certain programs.

INTERNATIONAL SUMMER CAMP MONTANA
Res — Coed Ages 8-17

Crans-Montana, 3963 Switzerland. 43 Rte de La Moubra, CP 369. Tel: 41-27-486-86-86. Fax: 41-27-486-86-87.
www.campmontana.ch   E-mail: info@campmontana.ch
Philippe Studer & Erwin Mathieu, Dirs.
Adm: FCFS. **Appl due:** Apr. **Enr cap:** 380. **Staff:** Admin 6. Couns 100.
Type of instruction: Enrich. **Avg class size:** 8. **Daily hours for:** Classes 1. Rec 7.
Intl program focus: Lang Culture. **Travel:** Europe.
Features: ESL Circus_Skills Crafts Drama Photog Archery Chess Climbing_Wall Hiking Mtn_Biking Riding Yoga Aerobics Baseball Basketball Cricket Equestrian Fencing Football Golf Gymnastics Soccer Softball Swim Tennis Volleyball Watersports.
Fees 2014: Res SwF6700 (+SwF200-500), 3 wks.

Housing: Dorms. Avg per room/unit: 4. **Swimming:** Pool.
Est 1961. Ses: 3. **Wks/ses:** 3. Operates June-Aug.

Located in the Swiss Alps, this program is an American-style recreational camp with European traditions in sports and education. Excursions, hikes, swimming, tennis, horseback riding, gymnastics and crafts are among the camp's activities. An optional language program enables boys and girls to study English, French or Spanish as a foreign language. Native speakers conduct these lessons, which occur five times a week.

MACHANEH BONIM IN ISRAEL
Res — Coed Ages 15-16

New York, NY 10011. 114 W 26th St, Ste 1004. Tel: 212-255-1796. Fax: 212-929-3459.
www.habonimdror.org/chaverim/mbi   E-mail: programs@habonimdror.org
Zoey Green, Prgm Dir.
Grade 11. Adm: FCFS. **Appl due:** Feb. **Staff:** Admin 9. Couns 12.
Intl program focus: Culture. **Travel:** Middle_East.
Features: Ecol Govt Lang Relig_Stud Dance Media Theater Exploration Hiking Kayak Peace/Cross-cultural Rappelling Swim.
Fees 2014: Res $7200 (+$200), 5 wks.
Swimming: Lake Pond Ocean Pool.
Est 1935. Nonprofit. Orthodox Jewish. **Ses:** 1. **Wks/ses:** 5. Operates July-Aug.

Habonim Dror, the progressive Labor Zionist Youth Movement, emphasizes peer-led activities that foster Zionist identities through education about Zionism, Judaism and cooperative community building. The MBI program, for those who have completed grade 10, provides the opportunity for participants to tour the sites and cities of Israel and experience a kibbutz. The program focuses on peace building, coexistence and current events and may include such activities as hiking, kayaking and rappelling.

NFTY IN ISRAEL
Res — Coed Ages 15-18

New York, NY 10017. c/o Union for Reform Judaism, 633 3rd Ave, 7th Fl. Tel: 212-452-6517. Fax: 212-650-4199.
www.nftyisrael.org   E-mail: nftytravel@urj.org
Laurence Jacobs, Coord.
Grades 10-12. Adm: FCFS. **Appl due:** May. **Enr:** 500. **Staff:** Admin 5. Couns 60.
High school credit: 3. Accred: Middle States Association of Colleges and Schools.
Intl program focus: Lang Culture. **Travel:** Europe Middle_East.
Features: Archaeol Ecol Environ_Sci Geol Govt Lang Dance Music Photog Theater Adventure_Travel Aquatics Bicycle_Tours Boating Canoe Caving Climbing_Wall Community_Serv Conservation Cooking Cruises Exploration Hiking Kayak Milit_Trng Mountaineering Mtn_Biking Mtn_Trips Outdoor_Ed Peace/Cross-cultural Rappelling Rock_Climb Ropes_Crse Survival_Trng Wilderness_Camp Swim Watersports.
Fees 2014: Res $7945-9595 (+$400), 4-6 wks.
Housing: Hotels Tents. **Swimming:** Lake Ocean Pool.
Est 1964. Nonprofit. **Spons:** Union for Reform Judaism. Jewish. **Ses:** 4. **Wks/ses:** 4-6. Operates June-Aug.

NFTY conducts high school summer programs in Israel that combine touring with a special activity: camping and hiking, taking part in an archaeological dig, performing social service work or studying Hebrew. The L'Dor V'Dor program option begins with a week spent exploring European Jewish heritage in Prague, Czech Republic, and Krakow, Poland, before students arrive in Israel.

OVERLAND
Res — Coed Ages 10-18

Williamstown, MA 01267. 63 Spring St, PO Box 31. Tel: 413-458-9672. Fax: 413-458-5208.
www.overlandsummers.com   E-mail: info@overlandsummers.com
Tom Costley, Dir.
Grades 5-PG. Adm: FCFS. **Appl due:** Rolling. **Enr:** 12. **Enr cap:** 12. **Fac 3. Staff:** Admin 15. Couns 150.
Type of instruction: Enrich. **Daily hours for:** Classes 4.
Intl program focus: Lang Culture. **Travel:** AK AL AR AZ CA CO GA HI KS MA ME MI NH NM OK OR VT WA Africa Canada Caribbean Europe Mexico/Central_America South_America. Home stays avail.
Features: Expository_Writing Creative_Writing Adventure_Travel Bicycle_Tours Boating Community_Serv Conservation Exploration Farm Hiking Kayak Mountaineering Mtn_Trips Outdoor_Ed Peace/Cross-cultural Rappelling Rock_Climb Ropes_Crse Scuba White-water_Raft Wilderness_Camp Swim.
Fees 2012: Res $1495-6995, 1-6 wks. Aid 2010 (Merit & Need): $65,000.
Housing: Apartments Dorms Tents. **Swimming:** Lake Pond Ocean Pool River.
Est 1984. Inc. **Ses:** 150. **Wks/ses:** 1-6. Operates June-Aug.

Overland provides small-group travel throughout the United States, Europe, Central and South America, and Africa. Points of emphasis for the tours include hiking, bicycling, community service work, writing and language study abroad.

PEOPLE TO PEOPLE STUDENT AMBASSADOR PROGRAM
Res — Coed Ages 11-19

Spokane, WA 99224. Dwight D Eisenhower Bldg, 1956 Ambassador Way. Tel: 509-568-7000, 800-669-7882. Fax: 509-568-7050.
www.studentambassadors.org   E-mail: info@peopletopeople.com
Mary Eisenhower, Pres.
Grades 6-PG. Adm: Selective.
College credit: 12.
Intl program focus: Culture. **Travel:** CA CO DC FL MT Africa Asia Australia/New_Zealand Canada Europe. Home stays avail.
Features: Bus/Fin Govt Fine_Arts Canoe Climbing_Wall Community_Serv Conservation Cruises Hiking Peace/Cross-cultural Rappelling Baseball Basketball Golf Soccer Softball Swim Tennis Volleyball.
Fees 2014: Res $4500-7999.
Swimming: Lake Ocean River.
Est 1963. Inc. **Wks/ses:** 1-3.

Student delegations gain balanced exposure to a variety of nations in a specific region and a comprehensive overview of economic, political and cultural factors through such activities as special briefings, visits to factories and schools, meetings at international organizations, attendance at cultural performances and home stays with selected families.

REIN TEEN TOURS
Res — Coed Ages 12-18

Wayne, NJ 07470. 30 Galesi Dr. Tel: 973-785-1113, 800-831-1313. Fax: 973-785-4268.
www.reinteentours.com   E-mail: info@reinteentours.com
Norman Rein, Dir.
Adm: FCFS. **Appl due:** Rolling. **Staff:** Admin 20. Couns 100.
Intl program focus: Culture. **Travel:** AK AZ CA CO DC FL HI MA ME MI MN MT NC NH NV NY OH OR PA SC SD UT VA WA WI WY Canada Europe.
Features: Circus_Skills Adventure_Travel Canoe Community_Serv Cruises Exploration

Ropes_Crse White-water_Raft Wilderness_Camp Basketball Swim Tennis Volleyball Watersports.
Fees 2012: Res $2495-9799, 2-6 wks.
Housing: Dorms Tents. **Swimming:** Ocean Pool.
Est 1985. Inc. **Ses:** 40. **Wks/ses:** 2-6. Operates June-Aug.

Rein conducts tours of varying lengths in the United States, Canada and Europe. Teens stay in hotels, campgrounds and university dorms in cities and national parks. Activities include hiking in national parks, summer snow skiing, surfing, jet boating, jeep tours and sand buggy trips and theme park visits. Boys and girls may also engage in sports and other traditional recreational camping pursuits. Two California tours focus on community service.

TRAVEL FOR TEENS
Res — Coed Ages 13-18

Wayne, PA 19087. 900 W Valley Rd, Ste 300. Tel: 484-654-1032, 888-457-4534. Fax: 484-654-1041.
www.travelforteens.com   E-mail: info@travelforteens.com
Patricia Maloney, Pres.
Grades 8-PG. Adm: FCFS. **Appl due:** Rolling.
Intl program focus: Lang Culture. **Travel:** Africa Asia Australia/New_Zealand Europe Mexico/Central_America.
Features: Fine_Arts Photog Adventure_Travel Bicycle_Tours Community_Serv Cooking Exploration Hiking Peace/Cross-cultural Scuba Swim.
Fees 2014: Res $2385-5985 (+airfare), 1½-3 wks.
Housing: Hotels. **Swimming:** Ocean Pool.
Est 2003. Ses: 29. **Wks/ses:** 1½-3. Operates June-Aug.

Travel for Teens offers language study, community service and cultural exploration trips at a variety of destinations. Participants in language programs attend French or Spanish classes in the morning and apply their lessons in afternoon and evening activities. Nonlanguage programs typically emphasize community service, backpacking, photography or adventure. In all programs, boys and girls immerse themselves in the host culture.

WEISSMAN TEEN TOURS
Res — Coed Ages 13-17

Ardsley, NY 10502. 517 Almena Ave. Tel: 914-693-7575, 800-942-8005. Fax: 914-693-4807.
www.weissmantours.com   E-mail: wtt@cloud9.net
Eugene Weissman & Ronee Weissman, Dirs.
Grades 8-12. Adm: Somewhat_selective. Admitted: 90%. **Appl due:** Rolling. **Enr cap:** 120. **Staff:** Couns 16.
Intl program focus: Culture. **Travel:** AZ CA CO HI MT NV UT WA WY Canada Europe Mexico/Central_America.
Features: Adventure_Travel Aquatics Boating Climbing_Wall Community_Serv Cruises Hiking Kayak Mountaineering Mtn_Biking Rock_Climb Scuba Sea_Cruises White-water_Raft Aerobics Golf Swim Tennis Volleyball Water-skiing Watersports Winter_Sports Parasailing.
Fees 2014: Res $5399-11899 (+airfare), 2-6 wks.
Housing: Hotels Lodges. Avg per room/unit: 3. **Swimming:** Lake Ocean Pool.
Est 1974. Inc. **Ses:** 9. **Wks/ses:** 3-5. Operates June-Aug.

Teen tours enable participants to explore the natural beauty of the western US (including Hawaii), Canada and Europe, while also learning more about a region's history, culture and people. Planned activities include sightseeing, a full social and athletic program, theater excursions and concerts. Domestic and Canadian tours serve students ages 13-17, while European tours accommodate those ages 14-17.

WHERE THERE BE DRAGONS SUMMER YOUTH PROGRAMS
Res — Coed Ages 15 and up

Boulder, CO 80301. 3200 Carbon Pl, Ste 102. Tel: 303-413-0822, 800-982-9203. Fax: 303-413-0857.
www.wheretherebedragons.com   E-mail: info@wheretherebedragons.com
Simon Hart, Dir.
Adm: FCFS. **Appl due:** Rolling. **Enr:** 12. **Enr cap:** 12. **Staff:** Admin 12. Couns 60.
Intl program focus: Lang Culture. **Travel:** Africa Asia Mexico/Central_America Middle_ East South_America. Home stays avail.
Features: Bus/Fin Expository_Writing Govt Fine_Arts Adventure_Travel Community_Serv Conservation Exploration Hiking Mountaineering Mtn_Trips Outdoor_Ed Pack_Train Peace/Cross-cultural Social_Servs Wilderness_Camp.
Fees 2014: Res $6280-7985 (+airfare), 4-6 wks. Aid (Need).
Housing: Houses Lodges Tents.
Est 1993. Inc. **Ses:** 23. **Wks/ses:** 4-6. Operates June-Aug.

Dragons offers small-group learning adventures throughout the developing world. Programs involve one or more of the following: community service, language learning, the study of religion philosophy, and home stays. Summer sessions operate in China, Tibet, North India, Laos, Thailand, Cambodia, Burma, Indonesia, Brazil, Guatemala, Peru, Bolivia, Senegal, Morocco, Rwanda and Jordan/Syria. In addition to its summer options, Dragons conducts gap-year semester programs.

WINDSOR MOUNTAIN STUDENT TRAVEL
Res — Coed Ages 7-16

Windsor, NH 03244. 1 World Way. Tel: 603-478-3166, 800-862-7760. Fax: 603-478-5260.
www.windsormountain.org   E-mail: mail@windsormountain.org
Jake Labovitz, Dir.
Grades 5-10. Adm: FCFS. **Appl due:** Rolling. **Enr:** 103. **Fac 8. Staff:** Admin 10. Couns 75.
Type of instruction: Adv Rem_Eng Tut. **Daily hours for:** Classes 3. Rec 2. **High school & college credit:** 1.
Intl program focus: Lang Culture. **Travel:** MA ME NH PR VT Africa Asia Caribbean Mexico/Central_America. Home stays avail.
Focus: Fr Span. **Features:** ESL Writing/Journ Circus_Skills Crafts Creative_Writing Dance Filmmaking Fine_Arts Music Painting Photog Theater Adventure_Travel Aquatics Archery Boating Canoe Caving Climbing_Wall Community_Serv Conservation Cooking Exploration Fishing Hiking Kayak Mountaineering Mtn_Biking Mtn_Trips Outdoor_Ed Pack_Train Peace/Cross-cultural Ranch Rappelling Riding Rock_Climb Ropes_Crse Sail Scuba Social_Servs White-water_Raft Wilderness_Camp Wilderness_Canoe Woodcraft Work Yoga Basketball Cricket Football Gymnastics Martial_Arts Rugby Soccer Softball Swim Tennis Ultimate_Frisbee Volleyball Watersports.
Fees 2014: Res $2495-7795, 2-4 wks. Aid (Need).
Housing: Cabins Dorms Houses Lodges Tents. Avg per room/unit: 6. **Swimming:** Lake Pond River.
Est 1961. Inc. **Ses:** 12. **Wks/ses:** 2-4. Operates June-Aug.

Windsor Mountain conducts small-group educational travel adventures for students having completed grades 7-12. Destinations include the Caribbean, Peru, Puerto Rico, Ecuador, France, Puerto Rico, southern Africa, Montana, New Orleans and the West Coast. Programs focus on adventure and wilderness, language and culture, the environment, world change, community service and traveling theater.

YOUTH FOR UNDERSTANDING
INTERNATIONAL EXCHANGE SUMMER PROGRAMS
Res — Coed Ages 15-18

Bethesda, MD 20817. 6400 Goldsboro Rd, Ste 100. **Tel: 240-235-2100, 800-833-6243. Fax: 240-235-2104.**
www.yfu-usa.org   E-mail: admissions@yfu.org
Grades 9-PG. Adm: Somewhat selective. **Appl due:** Apr. **Staff:** Admin 2. Couns 3. High school & college credit.
Intl program focus: Acad Lang Culture. **Travel:** Africa Asia Australia/New_Zealand Europe Middle_East South_America. Home stays avail.
Focus: Chin Fr Japan Span Adventure_Travel. **Features:** Community_Serv Peace/Cross-cultural.
Fees 2014: Res $6995-11,495 (+$250-375), 4-6 wks. Aid (Merit & Need). **Est 1951.** Nonprofit. **Ses:** 25. **Wks/ses:** 4-6. Operates June-Aug.

YFU's summer sessions allow students to live in and experience another culture while participating in intensive language study, journey or discovery programs. Not all programs are academic in nature, but many of them have a significant classroom component. Students at all locations embark on trips and engage in recreational activities while living with a host family.

SPECIAL-NEEDS PROGRAMS

Special-needs programs are arranged alphabetically by name. Page 7 of the Table of Contents lists the conditions addressed, and an index beginning on page 279 lists the programs under each of those conditions. Programs offering a family session are indicated by "FAM" at the end of the age range in the index. A Key to Conditions Accepted on page 297 presents the abbreviations used in this chapter.

INDEX BY CONDITION ACCEPTED

DEAFNESS (CONT.)

Camp Little Giant *(Res — Coed Ages 8 and up; Day — Coed 7 and up)*....... Carbondale, IL.... 328
Therapies: *Rec*

Camp Red Leaf *(Res — Coed Ages 9 and up)* ....Ingleside, IL.... 337
Therapies: *Music Rec*

Deaf Children's Camp *(Res — Coed Ages 4-16)*.. Milford, IN.... 309

Clarke Schools *(Res and Day — Coed Ages 9-14)*.............................. Northampton, MA.... 306

4-H Camp Howe *(Res — Coed Ages 7-16; Day — Coed 7-13)* ....Goshen, MA.... 316

Lions Camp Merrick *(Res — Coed Ages 6-16+FAM)* ....Nanjemoy, MD.... 327

Camp Courage *(Res — Coed Ages 7 and up+FAM)*................................. Maple Lake, MN.... 304
Therapies: *Speech*

Courage North *(Res — Coed Ages 7-17)*...Lake George, MN.... 308

Camp Friendship-MN *(Res and Day — Coed Ages 5 and up)* ....Annandale, MN.... 317

Easter Seals NE *(Res — Coed Ages 6 and up+FAM)* .... Fremont, NE.... 313
Therapies: *Rec*

Camp Allen *(Res and Day — Coed Ages 6 and up)*....................................... Bedford, NH.... 299

Easter Seals Sno-Mo *(Res — Coed Ages 11-21)* ....Gilmanton Iron Works, NH.... 311

Camp Nova *(Res — Coed Ages 12-28)* ....Branchville, NJ.... 334

Clover Patch Camp *(Res — Coed Ages 5 and up; Day — Coed 5-18)*.............Glenville, NY.... 307
Therapies: *Art Music Rec Occup*

Explore Your Future *(Res — Coed Ages 16-18)*.. Rochester, NY.... 316

Camp Mark Seven *(Res — Coed Ages 9-16+FAM)*...................................Old Forge, NY.... 329

Sunshine Camp *(Res — Coed Ages 7-21)*Rush, NY 341

Camp Echoing Hills *(Res — Coed Ages 7 and up+FAM)* .... Warsaw, OH.... 314

Meadowood Springs *(Res — Coed Ages 6-16; Day — Coed 5-11)* ....Weston, OR.... 329
Therapies: *Speech*

Beacon Lodge Camp *(Res — Coed Ages 6-18+FAM)* ....Mount Union, PA.... 300
Therapies: *Art Music Rec*

Variety Camp *(Res — Coed Ages 7-17; Day — Coed 5-21)* ....Worcester, PA.... 343
Therapies: *Rec Phys Speech Occup*

Camp Summit-TX *(Res — Coed Ages 6 and up)* ....Argyle, TX.... 340

Texas Lions Camp *(Res and Day — Coed Ages 7-16)* ....Kerrville, TX.... 342
Therapies: *Music Rec*

Camp Kostopulos *(Res — Coed Ages 7 and up+FAM)*........................... Salt Lake City, UT.... 325
Therapies: *Rec*

Camp Holiday Trails *(Res — Coed Ages 5-17+FAM)* ....Charlottesville, VA.... 321

DIABETES

DIABETES (CONT.)

EMOTIONAL DISTURBANCES

HIV/AIDS

INTELLECTUAL DISABILITIES

LEARNING DISABILITIES

Camp ASCCA *(Res — Coed Ages 6 and up+FAM)* .... Jacksons Gap, AL 300
Therapies: *Music Rec*

Easter Seals Harmon *(Res — Coed Ages 8 and up)* .... Boulder Creek, CA 311

Camp Krem *(Res — Coed Ages 5 and up)* .... Boulder Creek, CA 326

Breckenridge Outdoor *(Res — Coed Ages 8-25)* .... Breckenridge, CO 303
Therapies: *Art Music Rec Phys Occup*

Colorado Lions Camp *(Res — Coed Ages 8 and up)* .... Woodland Park, CO 307
Therapies: *Rec Psych*

Easter Seals Challng *(Res — Coed Ages 6 and up)* .... Sorrento, FL 311

Albrecht Acres *(Res — Coed Ages 2 and up)* .... Sherrill, IA 299

Camp Courageous-Iowa *(Res — Coed Ages 3-21)* .... Monticello, IA 309

East Seals-Sunnyside *(Res — Coed Ages 4 and up; Day — Coed 4-17)* .... Des Moines, IA 312

Camp Little Giant *(Res — Coed Ages 8 and up; Day — Coed 7 and up)* .... Carbondale, IL 328
Therapies: *Rec*

Camp Red Leaf *(Res — Coed Ages 9 and up)* .... Ingleside, IL 337
Therapies: *Music Rec*

Jameson Camp *(Res — Coed Ages 7-17)* .... Indianapolis, IN 323

4-H Camp Howe *(Res — Coed Ages 7-16; Day — Coed 7-13)* .... Goshen, MA 316

Camp Mitton *(Res — Coed Ages 7-13)* .... Brewster, MA 330

Fowler Ctr *(Res — Coed Ages 6-26; Day — Coed 6-20)* .... Mayville, MI 317

Camp Buckskin *(Res — Coed Ages 6-18)* .... Ely, MN 304

Camp Courage *(Res — Coed Ages 7 and up+FAM)* .... Maple Lake, MN 304
Therapies: *Speech*

Camp Friendship-MN *(Res and Day — Coed Ages 5 and up)* .... Annandale, MN 317

Camp New Hope *(Res — Coed Ages 6 and up)* .... McGregor, MN 332

Talisman Summer Camp *(Res — Coed Ages 8-21+FAM)* .... Zirconia, NC 342

Easter Seals NE *(Res — Coed Ages 6 and up+FAM)* .... Fremont, NE 313
Therapies: *Rec*

Camp Allen *(Res and Day — Coed Ages 6 and up)* .... Bedford, NH 299

Easter Seals Sno-Mo *(Res — Coed Ages 11-21)* .... Gilmanton Iron Works, NH 311

Camp Merry Heart *(Res and Day — Coed Ages 5 and up)* .... Hackettstown, NJ 330

Camp Nova *(Res — Coed Ages 12-28)* .... Branchville, NJ 334

Clover Patch Camp *(Res — Coed Ages 5 and up; Day — Coed 5-18)* .... Glenville, NY 307
Therapies: *Art Music Rec Occup*

ORTHOPEDIC/NEUROLOGICAL DISORDERS

ORTHO/NEURO (CONT.)

Texas Lions Camp *(Res and Day — Coed Ages 7-16)* ....Kerrville, TX 342
Therapies: *Music Rec*

Camp Kostopulos *(Res — Coed Ages 7 and up+FAM)* .... Salt Lake City, UT 325
Therapies: *Rec*

Easter Seals UCP *(Res — Coed Ages 7 and up+FAM)* .... New Castle, VA 313
Therapies: *Rec Speech Occup*

Camp Holiday Trails *(Res — Coed Ages 5-17+FAM)* ....Charlottesville, VA 321

Camp Virginia Jaycee ....Blue Ridge, VA 344
　　(Res — Coed Ages 7 and up; Day — Coed 5 and up)

Camp Thorpe *(Res — Coed Ages 10-20)* ....Goshen, VT 342

Stand By Me-Vaughn *(Res — Coed Ages 7 and up+FAM)* .... Vaughn, WA 340

Wawbeek *(Res — Coed Ages 7 and up)* .... Wisconsin Dells, WI 312
Therapies: *Rec*

Special Touch *(Res — Coed Ages 10 and up+FAM)* .... Waupaca, WI 339
Therapies: *Art Music Rec Phys*

Wisconsin Badger *(Res — Coed Ages 3-21)* .... Prairie du Chien, WI 346

OTHER CONDITIONS

MDA Summer Camp *(Res — Coed Ages 6-17)* .... Tucson, AZ 331

Dream Street Camps *(Res — Coed Ages 4-24)* .... Beverly Hills, CA 310

Easter Seals Harmon *(Res — Coed Ages 8 and up)* .... Boulder Creek, CA 311

Camp Esperanza *(Res — Coed Ages 8-17)* .... Big Bear Lake, CA 315

Colorado Lions Camp *(Res — Coed Ages 8 and up)* .... Woodland Park, CO 307
Therapies: *Rec Psych*

Rocky Mountain Vill *(Res — Coed Ages 6 and up)* ....Empire, CO 337

Camp Thunderbird *(Res — Coed Ages 8 and up)* ....Apopka, FL 343

Camp Courageous-Iowa *(Res — Coed Ages 3-21)* ....Monticello, IA 309

Camp Little Giant *(Res — Coed Ages 8 and up; Day — Coed 7 and up)* .... Carbondale, IL 328
Therapies: *Rec*

Camp Oakhurst *(Res — Coed Ages 6-21)* .... Oakhurst, NJ 335
Therapies: *Art Music Rec Phys*

Summit Camp & Travel *(Res — Coed Ages 8-19)* ....Honesdale, PA 340

Marbridge *(Res — Coed Ages 16-30)* ....Manchaca, TX 329
Therapies: *Art Music Rec Phys Occup*

PDD (CONT.)

Stand By Me-Vaughn *(Res — Coed Ages 7 and up+FAM)* ....Vaughn, WA.... 340

Wawbeek *(Res — Coed Ages 7 and up)* .... Wisconsin Dells, WI.... 312
Therapies: *Rec*

Special Touch *(Res — Coed Ages 10 and up+FAM)* ....Waupaca, WI.... 339
Therapies: *Art Music Rec Phys*

Wisconsin Badger *(Res — Coed Ages 3-21)*.. Prairie du Chien, WI.... 346

Camp Kodiak *(Res — Coed Ages 6-18)* ....McKellar, Ontario, CANADA.... 324
Therapies: *Art Music Rec*

SPEECH AND LANGUAGE DISORDERS

Camp ASCCA *(Res — Coed Ages 6 and up+FAM)* ....Jacksons Gap, AL.... 300
Therapies: *Music Rec*

Breckenridge Outdoor *(Res — Coed Ages 8-25)*.....................................Breckenridge, CO.... 303
Therapies: *Art Music Rec Phys Occup*

Talking with Tech *(Res — Coed Ages 6-21)* ....Empire, CO.... 305
Therapies: *Speech*

Easter Seals Challng *(Res — Coed Ages 6 and up)* ....Sorrento, FL.... 311

Albrecht Acres *(Res — Coed Ages 2 and up)* ....Sherrill, IA.... 299

Camp Courageous-Iowa *(Res — Coed Ages 3-21)* ....Monticello, IA.... 309

East Seals-Sunnyside *(Res — Coed Ages 4 and up; Day — Coed 4-17)* .... Des Moines, IA.... 312

Camp Little Giant *(Res — Coed Ages 8 and up; Day — Coed 7 and up)* .... Carbondale, IL.... 328
Therapies: *Rec*

Camp Red Leaf *(Res — Coed Ages 9 and up)* ....Ingleside, IL.... 337
Therapies: *Music Rec*

4-H Camp Howe *(Res — Coed Ages 7-16; Day — Coed 7-13)* ....Goshen, MA.... 316

Fowler Ctr *(Res — Coed Ages 6-26; Day — Coed 6-20)* .... Mayville, MI.... 317

Camp Courage *(Res — Coed Ages 7 and up+FAM)* .... Maple Lake, MN.... 304
Therapies: *Speech*

Camp Friendship-MN *(Res and Day — Coed Ages 5 and up)* .... Annandale, MN.... 317

Easter Seals NE *(Res — Coed Ages 6 and up+FAM)* .... Fremont, NE.... 313
Therapies: *Rec*

Camp Allen *(Res and Day — Coed Ages 6 and up)*.. Bedford, NH.... 299

Easter Seals Sno-Mo *(Res — Coed Ages 11-21)* ....Gilmanton Iron Works, NH.... 311

Camp Nova *(Res — Coed Ages 12-28)*..Branchville, NJ.... 334

Clover Patch Camp *(Res — Coed Ages 5 and up; Day — Coed 5-18)*.............Glenville, NY.... 307
Therapies: *Art Music Rec Occup*

SPEECH AND LANGUAGE (CONT.)

VISUAL IMPAIRMENTS

Enchanted Hills Camp *(Res — Coed Ages 5 and up+FAM)* ....Napa, CA.... 315

Breckenridge Outdoor *(Res — Coed Ages 8-25)*....................................Breckenridge, CO.... 303
Therapies: *Art Music Rec Phys Occup*

Colorado Lions Camp *(Res — Coed Ages 8 and up)* .... Woodland Park, CO.... 307
Therapies: *Rec Psych*

Easter Seals Challng *(Res — Coed Ages 6 and up)* ....Sorrento, FL.... 311

Albrecht Acres *(Res — Coed Ages 2 and up)* ....Sherrill, IA.... 299

Camp Courageous-Iowa *(Res — Coed Ages 3-21)* ....Monticello, IA.... 309

East Seals-Sunnyside *(Res — Coed Ages 4 and up; Day — Coed 4-17)* .... Des Moines, IA.... 312

Camp Little Giant *(Res — Coed Ages 8 and up; Day — Coed 7 and up)*....... Carbondale, IL.... 328
Therapies: *Rec*

Camp Red Leaf *(Res — Coed Ages 9 and up)* ....Ingleside, IL.... 337
Therapies: *Music Rec*

Carroll Center Blind *(Res — Coed Ages 15-21)*... Newton, MA.... 305

4-H Camp Howe *(Res — Coed Ages 7-16; Day — Coed 7-13)* ....Goshen, MA.... 316

Lions Camp Merrick *(Res — Coed Ages 6-16+FAM)* ....Nanjemoy, MD.... 327

Fowler Ctr *(Res — Coed Ages 6-26; Day — Coed 6-20)* ....Mayville, MI.... 317

Camp Courage *(Res — Coed Ages 7 and up+FAM)* .... Maple Lake, MN.... 304
Therapies: *Speech*

Camp Friendship-MN *(Res and Day — Coed Ages 5 and up)* .... Annandale, MN.... 317

Easter Seals NE *(Res — Coed Ages 6 and up+FAM)* .... Fremont, NE.... 313
Therapies: *Rec*

Natl Blind Children *(Res — Coed Ages 9-65)* .... Lincoln, NE.... 331

Camp Allen *(Res and Day — Coed Ages 6 and up)*.. Bedford, NH.... 299

Easter Seals Sno-Mo *(Res — Coed Ages 11-21)* ....Gilmanton Iron Works, NH.... 311

Camp Nova *(Res — Coed Ages 12-28)*..Branchville, NJ.... 334

Clover Patch Camp *(Res — Coed Ages 5 and up; Day — Coed 5-18)*.............Glenville, NY.... 307
Therapies: *Art Music Rec Occup*

Double H Ranch *(Res — Coed Ages 6-16)*... Lake Luzerne, NY.... 310
Therapies: *Art Music Rec Phys Speech Psych*

Sunshine Camp *(Res — Coed Ages 7-21)* ....Rush, NY.... 341

Highbrook Lodge *(Res — Coed Ages 8-18+FAM)* ....Cleveland, OH.... 306

Camp Echoing Hills *(Res — Coed Ages 7 and up+FAM)* .... Warsaw, OH.... 314

Beacon Lodge Camp *(Res — Coed Ages 6-18+FAM)* ....Mount Union, PA.... 300
Therapies: *Art Music Rec*

VISUAL IMPAIRMENTS (CONT.)

Variety Camp *(Res — Coed Ages 7-17; Day — Coed 5-21)* ....Worcester, PA 343
Therapies: *Rec Phys Speech Occup*

Mid-South Arc Camp *(Res — Coed Ages 8 and up)* ....Memphis, TN 330

Camp Summit-TX *(Res — Coed Ages 6 and up)* ....Argyle, TX 340

Texas Lions Camp *(Res and Day — Coed Ages 7-16)* ....Kerrville, TX 342
Therapies: *Music Rec*

Camp Kostopulos *(Res — Coed Ages 7 and up+FAM)* ....Salt Lake City, UT 325
Therapies: *Rec*

Easter Seals UCP *(Res — Coed Ages 7 and up+FAM)* ....New Castle, VA 313
Therapies: *Rec Speech Occup*

Camp Holiday Trails *(Res — Coed Ages 5-17+FAM)* ....Charlottesville, VA 321

Stand By Me-Vaughn *(Res — Coed Ages 7 and up+FAM)* ....Vaughn, WA 340

Special Touch *(Res — Coed Ages 10 and up+FAM)* ....Waupaca, WI 339
Therapies: *Art Music Rec Phys*

Wisconsin Badger *(Res — Coed Ages 3-21)* ....Prairie du Chien, WI 346

Wisconsin Lions Camp *(Res — Coed Ages 6-17)* ....Rosholt, WI 346

WEIGHT LOSS

Camp La Jolla *(Res — Coed Ages 10-17)* ....La Jolla, CA 326

Wellspring-CA *(Res — Coed Ages 14-19)* ....Reedley, CA 344
Therapies: *Art Rec Psych*

New Image-Vanguard *(Res — Coed Ages 7-19)* ....Lake Wales, FL 333

Camp Kingsmont *(Res — Coed Ages 9-18)* ....Amherst, MA 324

Camp Jump Start *(Res — Coed Ages 9-17)* ....Imperial, MO 323

Wellspring Adventure *(Res — Coed Ages 11-18)* ....Durham, NC 345
Therapies: *Art Rec Psych*

Camp Pennbrook *(Res — Girls Ages 8-21)* ....Pennington, NJ 336

Camp Shane *(Res — Boys Ages 7-19, Girls 7-25)* ....Ferndale, NY 339

Wellspring NY *(Res — Girls Ages 11-24)* ....Paul Smiths, NY 345

New Image-Pocono *(Res — Coed Ages 7-19)* ....Reeders, PA 333

Camp Sweeney *(Res — Coed Ages 5-18+FAM)* ....Gainesville, TX 341
Therapies: *Art Music Rec Phys Psych Occup*

Camp Holiday Trails *(Res — Coed Ages 5-17+FAM)* ....Charlottesville, VA 321

KEY TO CONDITIONS ACCEPTED

ADD	Attention Deficit Disorder	**HI**	Hearing Impairment
ADHD	Attention Deficit Hyperactivity Disorder	**ID**	Intellectual Disabilities
		IP	Infantile Paralysis
AN	Anorexia Nervosa	**LD**	Learning Disabilities
Anx	Anxiety Disorders	**Ll**	Leukemia
Ap	Aphasia	**MD**	Muscular Dystrophy
APD	Auditory Processing Disorders	**Mood**	Mood Disorder
Apr	Apraxia	**MS**	Multiple Sclerosis
Ar	Arthritis	**Nf**	Neurofibromatosis
As	Asthma	**NLD**	Nonverbal Learning Disorders
Asp	Asperger's Syndrome	**OCD**	Obsessive–Compulsive Disorder
Au	Autism	**ODD**	Oppositional Defiant Disorder
B/VI	Blindness/Visual Impairment	**ON**	Orthopedic/Neurological Disorders
Bu	Bulimia		
C	Cardiac Disorder	**PDD**	Pervasive Developmental Disorder
CD	Conduct Disorder		
CF	Cystic Fibrosis	**Psy**	Psychosis
CLP	Cleft Lip/Cleft Palate	**PTSD**	Posttraumatic Stress Disorder
CP	Cerebral Palsy	**PW**	Prader–Willi Syndrome
D	Deafness	**S**	Speech Impairments
DB	Deaf-Blindness	**SA**	Sexually Abused
Db	Diabetes	**SB**	Spina Bifida
Dc	Dyscalculia	**SC**	Sickle Cell Anemia
Dg	Dysgraphia	**SO**	Sex Offender
Dlx	Dyslexia	**SP**	School Phobia
Dpx	Dyspraxia	**Subst**	Substance Abuse
DS	Down Syndrome	**Sz**	Schizophrenia
ED	Emotional Disturbances	**TBI**	Traumatic Brain Injury
Ep	Epilepsy	**TS**	Tourette's Syndrome
Hemo	Hemophilia		

Special-Needs Programs

AGASSIZ VILLAGE
Res — Coed Ages 8-17

Poland, ME 04274. 71 Agassiz Village Ln. Tel: 207-998-4340. Fax: 207-998-5043.
Contact (Sept-June): 238 Bedford St, Ste 8, Lexington, MA 02420. Tel: 781-860-0200.
Fax: 781-860-0352.
www.agassizvillage.org   E-mail: tsemeta@agassizvillage.org
Thomas Semeta, Dir.
Adm: FCFS. Appl due: Rolling. Enr: 100.
Conditions accepted: Phys_Impair.
Features: Crafts Dance Drama Music Photog Aquatics Archery Boating Canoe Fishing
Hiking Kayak Ropes_Crse Sail Scuba Wilderness_Camp Wilderness_Canoe Baseball
Basketball Lacrosse Soccer Softball Swim Tennis Watersports.
Fees 2014: Res $175-750, 1-2 wks. Aid (Need).
Housing: Cabins. Swimming: Lake.
Est 1935. Nonprofit. Wks/ses: 1-2. Operates July-Aug. ACA.

Serving boys and girls with physical special needs, the Village offers traditional waterfront
activities, sports, camp craft, nature studies, arts and crafts, drama and music. A wilderness
tripping program for campers ages 13 and 14 seeks to develop leadership skills on hiking and
canoeing excursions.

CAMP ALBRECHT ACRES OF THE MIDWEST
Res — Coed Ages 2 and up

Sherrill, IA 52073. 14837 Sherrill Rd, PO Box 50. Tel: 563-552-1771. Fax: 563-552-
2732.
www.albrechtacres.org   E-mail: info@albrechtacres.org
Deborah L. Rahe, Exec Dir.
Adm: FCFS. Appl due: Rolling. Enr cap: 72. Staff: Admin 2. Couns 35.
Conditions accepted: ADD ADHD As Asp Au C CP D Diabetes Dx ED Ep ID LD PDD
Phys_Impair Speech & Lang TBI Visual_Impair.
Features: Crafts Dance Drama Music Aquatics Fishing Hiking Swim.
Fees 2014: Res $540, 1 wk.
Housing: Cabins Lodges Tepees. Avg per room/unit: 10. Swimming: Pool.
Est 1975. Nonprofit. Ses: 8. Wks/ses: 1. Operates June-Aug. ACA.

This camp for children and adults with mental or physical special needs offers daily classes
in art, music and drama, and nature study. Activities include swimming, fishing, camping,
sing-alongs and hiking. Special programs serve those with severe or profound disabilities.

CAMP ALLEN
Res and Day — Coed Ages 6 and up

Bedford, NH 03110. 56 Camp Allen Rd. Tel: 603-622-8471. Fax: 603-626-4295.
www.campallennh.org   E-mail: deb@campallennh.org
Michael Constance, Dir.
Adm: FCFS. Appl due: Rolling. Enr: 65. Staff: Admin 3. Couns 40. Special needs 2.
Conditions accepted: ADD ADHD Asp Au CP D Diabetes Ep ID LD Phys_Impair Speech
& Lang Visual_Impair.
Features: Crafts Dance Music Theater Aquatics Fishing Hiking Basketball Swim.
Fees 2014: Res $775-1550 (+$275), 1 wk. Day $400, 1 wk.
Housing: Cabins Dorms Tents Tepees. Swimming: Pool.
Est 1931. Nonprofit. Ses: 17. Wks/ses: 1. Operates June-Aug. ACA.

Accepting children and adults with disabilities, this camp adjusts activities to camper ability. Projects include arts and crafts, nature, aquatics, games, special events, evening programs and field trips.

CAMP ASCCA
Res — Coed Ages 6 and up

Jacksons Gap, AL 36861. 5278 Camp ASCCA Dr, PO Box 21. Tel: 256-825-9226, 800-843-2267. Fax: 256-825-8332.
www.campascca.org   E-mail: info@campascca.org
Matt Rickman, Dir.
Adm: Selective. **Appl due:** Rolling. **Enr cap:** 100. **Staff:** Admin 7. Couns 40. Special needs 3.
Conditions accepted: As Asp Au CP Diabetes Ep ID LD Phys_Impair Speech & Lang TBI Visual_Impair. **Therapy:** Music Rec.
Features: Environ_Sci Crafts Filmmaking Music Aquatics Archery Boating Canoe Climbing_Wall Farm Fishing Outdoor_Ed Rappelling Riding Riflery Ropes_Crse Scuba Badminton Basketball Equestrian Golf Softball Swim Tennis Volleyball Water-skiing Watersports.
Fees 2014: Res $695, 1 wk. Aid 2007 (Need): $300,000.
Housing: Cabins Lodges. Avg per room/unit: 10. **Swimming:** Lake Pool.
Est 1976. Nonprofit. **Spons:** Alabama Easter Seal Society. **Ses:** 8. **Wks/ses:** 1. Operates June-Aug. ACA.

This large camp offers traditional camping activities to children and adults with disabilities. Outdoor adventure, aquatics and outdoor education are among more than 20 recreational and educational activities. While campers from out of state pay a set weekly fee, Alabama residents may receive camperships.

AUSTINE GREEN MOUNTAIN LIONS CAMP
Res — Coed Ages 6-18; Day — Coed 3-5

Brattleboro, VT 05301. 209 Austine Dr. Tel: 802-258-9513. Fax: 802-254-3921.
www.vcdhh.org   E-mail: camp@vcdhh.org
Clint Woosley, Dir.
Grades K-12. Adm: FCFS. **Appl due:** May. **Enr:** 35. **Staff:** Admin 3. Couns 8.
LD Services: Acad_Instruction Tut.
Conditions accepted: D.
Features: Ecol Environ_Sci Crafts Creative_Writing Theater Aquatics Canoe Conservation Fishing Hiking Rappelling Rock_Climb Ropes_Crse Survival_Trng Wilderness_Camp Wilderness_Canoe Swim.
Fees 2014: Res $395-750, 2 wks. Day $395, 1 wk. Aid (Need).
Housing: Cabins Tents. Avg per room/unit: 8. **Swimming:** Lake Pond Pool River.
Est 1992. Nonprofit. **Ses:** 4. **Wks/ses:** 1-2. Operates June-July.

A collaboration between the Vermont Lions Club and Austine School for the Deaf, the camp serves children who are deaf or hard of hearing and their siblings. Counselors teach American Sign Language and other strategies for effective communication. Sessions, which serve children ages 3-5 (commuters only), 6-12 and 13-18, involve various age-appropriate recreational activities, as well as such special events as a fishing contest, hot-air balloon rides and field trips.

BEACON LODGE CAMP
Res — Coed Ages 6-18

Mount Union, PA 17066. 114 SR 103 S. Tel: 814-542-2511. Fax: 814-542-7437.
www.beaconlodge.com   E-mail: beaconlodgecamp@verizon.net

Ellen Miller, Dir.
Adm: FCFS. **Appl due:** Rolling. **Enr:** 6-23. **Enr cap:** 72. **Staff:** Admin 5. Couns 23. Special needs 2.
Conditions accepted: ADD ADHD As Asp Au CP D Diabetes Dx ED Ep ID LD PDD Phys_Impair Speech & Lang TBI Visual_Impair. **Therapy:** Art Music Rec.
Features: Crafts Dance Music Theater Aquatics Archery Canoe Climbing_Wall Community_Serv Cooking Exploration Fishing Hiking Kayak Rappelling Riflery Rock_Climb Ropes_Crse Wilderness_Camp Woodcraft Yoga Aerobics Basketball Swim.
Fees 2012: Res $450-550 (+$75), 1-1½ wks. Aid (Need).
Housing: Cabins Dorms Lodges. Avg per room/unit: 6. **Swimming:** Pond Pool River.
Est 1948. Nonprofit. **Spons:** Pennsylvania Lions. **Ses:** 7. **Wks/ses:** 1-1½. Operates June-Aug.

The summer camping program provides recreation and rehabilitation for children and adults (in separate sessions) with various special needs. Activities include swimming, arts and crafts, bowling, archery/riflery, a climbing wall and a zip line, among other pursuits. Boys and girls also go on an overnight camping trip.

BEARSKIN MEADOW CAMP
Res and Day — Coed Ages 7-13

Kings Canyon National Park, CA.
Contact (Year-round): c/o Diabetic Youth Foundation, 5167 Clayton Rd, Ste F, Concord, CA 94521. **Tel:** 925-680-4994. **Fax:** 925-680-4863.
www.dyf.org **E-mail:** info@dyf.org
Jennifer Goerzen, Dir.
Adm: FCFS. **Appl due:** Rolling. **Staff:** Admin 8. Couns 50. Special needs 48.
Conditions accepted: Diabetes.
Features: Crafts Dance Fine_Arts Music Photog Theater Adventure_Travel Aquatics Archery Conservation Fishing Hiking Mountaineering Mtn_Trips Wilderness_Camp Baseball Basketball Football Soccer Softball Swim.
Fees 2014: Res $1843, 1-1½ wks.
Swimming: Pool.
Est 1938. Nonprofit. **Spons:** Diabetic Youth Foundation. **Ses:** 3. **Wks/ses:** 1-1½. Operates June-July. ACA.

Bearskin Meadow enables young children, adolescents and families affected by diabetes to develop self-reliance and partake of camping experiences, while also receiving support and learning to better manage the disease. Activities include traditional recreational pursuits, backpacking, campfires and dances. Family camps enable a child with diabetes to attend with one or both parents.

CAMP BLOOMFIELD
Res — Coed Ages 3-25

Malibu, CA.
Contact (Year-round): c/o Junior Blind of America, 5300 Angeles Vista Blvd, Los Angeles, CA 90043. **Tel:** 323-295-4555, 800-352-2290. **Fax:** 323-296-0424.
www.juniorblind.org/site/camp-bloomfield **E-mail:** info@juniorblind.org
Shirley Manning, Dir.
Grades 2-PG. Adm: FCFS. **Appl due:** Rolling. **Staff:** Admin 4. Couns 40. Special needs 2.
Conditions accepted: Phys_Impair Visual_Impair.
Features: Art Crafts Dance Music Theater Aquatics Archery Fishing Hiking Kayak Riding Ropes_Crse Equestrian Martial_Arts Swim Track.
Fees 2009: Res $25, 1 wk.
Housing: Cabins Lodges. **Swimming:** Ocean Pool.
Est 1958. Nonprofit. **Spons:** Junior Blind of America. **Ses:** 6. **Wks/ses:** 1-2. Operates June-Aug. ACA.

Serving those with visual impairments, Bloomfield offers specialized sessions for children and young adults. Activities include traditional recreational pursuits, campfires, riding and beach trips.

CAMP BOLD EAGLE
Res — Coed Ages 6-13

Holton, MI.
Contact (Year-round): c/o Hemophilia Foundation of Michigan, 1921 W Michigan Ave, Ypsilanti, MI 48197. Tel: 734-544-0015, 800-482-3041. Fax: 734-544-0095.
www.pioneertrails.net/camps/boldeaglecamp.html   E-mail: hfm@hfmich.org
Tim Wicks, Coord.
Grades 1-8. Adm: FCFS. Appl due: May. Enr: 100.
Conditions accepted: Blood.
Features: Crafts Archery Boating Canoe Fishing Hiking Baseball Basketball Soccer Softball Swim.
Fees 2009: Res $500, 1 wk. Aid (Need).
Housing: Cabins. Avg per room/unit: 6. **Swimming:** Lake.
Est 1969. Nonprofit. **Spons:** Hemophilia Foundation of Michigan. **Ses:** 2. **Wks/ses:** 1. Operates July.

Located on the shores of Big Blue Lake, this camp for young people with hereditary bleeding disorders combines traditional summer recreation with bleeding disorders education. Archery, arts and crafts, water activities and nature exploration are particularly popular. Campers are encouraged to self-infuse their own factor while at camp.

CAMP BON COEUR
Res — Coed Ages 7-16

Eunice, LA 70535. 1202 Academy Rd.
Contact (Aug-June): 405 W Main St, Lafayette, LA 70501.
Year-round Tel: 337-233-8437, Fax: 337-233-4160.
www.heartcamp.com   E-mail: info@heartcamp.com
Susannah Craig, Dir.
Adm: FCFS. Appl due: May. Enr: 50. Staff: Admin 2. Couns 8. Special needs 10.
Conditions accepted: C.
Features: Crafts Drama Fine_Arts Media Music Aquatics Archery Canoe Conservation Outdoor_Ed Riding Baseball Basketball Street_Hockey Swim.
Fees 2013: Res $1500 (+$40-60), 2 wks. Aid 2006 (Need): $40,000.
Housing: Dorms. **Swimming:** Pool.
Est 1985. Nonprofit. **Ses:** 2. **Wks/ses:** 2. Operates July. ACA.

Bon Coeur serves children with heart defects. Campers learn more about their heart conditions in class and participate in typical summer camp activities, among them sports, swimming, canoeing, horseback riding and art.

CAMP BREATHE EASY
Res — Coed Ages 7-13

Rutledge, GA.
Contact (Year-round): c/o Camp Twin Lakes, 600 Means St, Ste 110, Atlanta, GA 30318. Tel: 404-231-9887. Fax: 404-577-8854.
www.campbreatheeasy.com   E-mail: camp@lungga.org
Annie Garrett, Dir.
Adm: FCFS. Appl due: Apr. Enr: 200. Staff: Admin 2. Couns 100. Special needs 5.
Conditions accepted: As.
Features: Crafts Music Photog Archery Bicycle_Tours Canoe Climbing_Wall Community_

Serv Cooking Fishing Kayak Mtn_Biking Rappelling Ropes_Crse Survival_Trng Wilderness_Camp Baseball Basketball Golf Softball Swim Tennis Volleyball.
Fees 2014: Res $275, 1 wk. Aid (Need).
Housing: Cabins. **Swimming:** Pool.
Nonprofit. **Spons:** American Lung Association—Southeast Region. **Ses:** 1. **Wks/ses:** 1. Operates June-July.

This camp for children with asthma offers such traditional camping activities as survival training, canoeing, biking, tennis, baseball, basketball, volleyball and swimming. Campers learn strategies for best coping with the disease.

BRECKENRIDGE OUTDOOR EDUCATION CENTER SUMMER CAMPS
Res — Coed Ages 8-25

Breckenridge, CO 80424. PO Box 697. Tel: 970-453-6422, 800-383-2632. Fax: 970-453-4676.
www.boec.org   E-mail: boec@boec.org
Bruce Fitch, Exec Dir.
Adm: FCFS. **Appl due:** Rolling. **Enr cap:** 6-10. **Staff:** Admin 10.
Conditions accepted: ADD ADHD Asp Au Cancer CP D Diabetes Dx ED Ep ID LD Phys_ Impair Speech & Lang TBI Visual_Impair. **Therapy:** Art Music Occup Phys Rec.
Features: Crafts Adventure_Travel Canoe Climbing_Wall Cooking Exploration Hiking Kayak Mountaineering Rock_Climb Ropes_Crse Survival_Trng White-water_Raft Wilderness_Camp Wilderness_Canoe Equestrian.
Fees 2010: Res $500-900 (+$100), 1 wk. Aid (Merit & Need).
Housing: Cabins Lodges Tepees.
Est 1976. Nonprofit. **Ses:** 4. **Wks/ses:** 1. Operates June-Aug.

BOEC conducts four weeklong summer programs for at-risk groups and individuals with physical or mental disabilities or serious illnesses: Camp Big Tree (for campers ages 12-16 who have sensory processing disorders), Wilderness Camp (ages 16-25; developmental disabilities), Junior Adventures Camp (ages 8-14; developmental and processing disorders) and Visually Impaired Wilderness Camp (ages 15-19). BOEC programs accommodate boys and girls of all ability levels and include such mountain and river activities as canoeing, rafting, rock climbing, teamwork and leadership development, ropes courses, hiking, backpacking and camping.

CAMP BUCK
Res — Coed Ages 7-17

Portola, CA.
Contact (Year-round): 1005 Terminal Way, Ste 170, Reno, NV 89502. Tel: 775-856-3839, 800-379-3839. Fax: 775-348-7591.
www.diabetesnv.org/camps/camp-buck   E-mail: camp@diabetesnv.org
Sarah Gleich, Dir.
Adm: FCFS. **Appl due:** Rolling. **Staff:** Admin 4. Couns 30. Special needs 15.
Conditions accepted: Diabetes.
Features: Ecol Environ_Sci Crafts Dance Drama Music Painting Archery Boating Canoe Climbing_Wall Community_Serv Cooking Fishing Hiking Kayak Rock_Climb Ropes_ Crse Yoga Aerobics Baseball Basketball Field_Hockey Football Soccer Softball Street_ Hockey Swim Ultimate_Frisbee Volleyball Watersports.
Fees 2014: Res $650-900, 1 wk. Aid (Need).
Housing: Cabins. **Swimming:** Lake Pool Stream.
Est 1988. Nonprofit. **Ses:** 1. **Wks/ses:** 1. Operates Aug.

In an outdoor, recreational setting, the camp helps children with Type 1 diabetes better understand and control the condition. Staff promote nutritional awareness as an essential component of diabetes management. Activities include music, art, dance, aquatic sports and riding.

CAMP BUCKSKIN
Res — Coed Ages 6-18

Ely, MN 55731. PO Box 389. Fax: 218-365-2880.
Contact (Sept-May): 4124 Quebec Ave N, Ste 300, Minneapolis, MN 55427. Fax: 763-208-8668.
Year-round Tel: 763-432-9177.
www.campbuckskin.com   E-mail: info@campbuckskin.com
Thomas R. Bauer, Dir.
Grades K-12. Adm: FCFS. **Appl due:** Rolling. **Enr:** 100. **Staff:** Admin 11. Couns 45. Special needs 3.
LD Services: Acad_Instruction Tut.
Conditions accepted: ADD ADHD Asp Dx LD PDD.
Features: Ecol Environ_Sci Expository_Writing Crafts Creative_Writing Music Aquatics Archery Canoe Conservation Fishing Hiking Outdoor_Ed Riflery Wilderness_Camp Wilderness_Canoe Woodcraft Aerobics Basketball Cricket Football Rugby Soccer Softball Swim Ultimate_Frisbee Volleyball Watersports.
Fees 2014: Res $4235-4665 (+$60), 4½ wks.
Housing: Cabins Tents. Avg per room/unit: 9. **Swimming:** Lake.
Est 1959. Inc. **Ses:** 2. **Wks/ses:** 4½. Operates June-Aug. ACA.

The typical camper at Buckskin has an attentional disorder, a learning disability or Asperger's syndrome and, as a result, has experienced social-skill difficulties, diminished academic success and self-esteem issues. Regularly scheduled activities include canoeing, swimming, nature studies, arts and crafts, archery, riflery and reading, in addition to electives and field trips. A formalized social skills program addresses such areas as interpersonal communication, problem solving, initiative and task completion.

CAMP COURAGE
Res — Coed Ages 7 and up

Maple Lake, MN 55358. 8046 83rd St NW. Tel: 320-963-3121, 866-520-0504. Fax: 320-963-3698.
www.couragecenter.org/camp   E-mail: camping@couragecenter.org
Tom Fogarty, Dir.
Adm: FCFS. **Appl due:** Rolling. **Enr:** 700. **Staff:** Admin 10. Couns 90. Special needs 11.
Conditions accepted: As Asp Au Blood Cancer CP D Ep LD Phys_Impair Speech & Lang TBI Visual_Impair. **Therapy:** Speech.
Features: Computers Ecol Environ_Sci Crafts Media Photog Aquatics Bicycle_Tours Canoe Farm Riding Sail Wilderness_Camp Swim.
Fees 2012: Res $500-950, ½-1 wks. Aid (Need).
Housing: Cabins. Avg per room/unit: 20. **Swimming:** Lake Pool.
Est 1955. Nonprofit. **Spons:** Courage Center. **Ses:** 19. **Wks/ses:** ½-1. Operates June-Aug. ACA.

Courage Center conducts recreational summer programming for young people with various special needs at the 305-acre Camp Courage site, located approximately 50 miles west of the Twin Cities. A teen session serves boys and girls with a physical disability or a visual impairment, while a leadership week offers intensive leadership and life skills training for teens with a physical disability or a sensory impairment. A specialty week accommodates campers ages 7-14 who have a communication disorder. Also available is a half-week sampler session for first-time overnight campers.

CARROLL CENTER FOR THE BLIND
YOUTH IN TRANSITION PROGRAM
Res — Coed Ages 15-21

Newton, MA 02458. 770 Centre St. Tel: 617-969-6200, 800-852-3131. Fax: 617-969-6204.
www.carroll.org   E-mail: intake@carroll.org
Karen Ross, Dir.
Adm: FCFS. Admitted: 90%. **Appl due:** Rolling. **Enr:** 40. **Staff:** Special needs 12.
LD Services: Acad_Instruction Tut.
Conditions accepted: Visual_Impair.
Features: Crafts Drama Music Photog Canoe Climbing_Wall Cooking Sail Social_Servs Work Fencing Swim.
Fees 2009: Res $7400, 5 wks.
Housing: Dorms. **Swimming:** Pool.
Est 1966. Nonprofit. **Ses:** 2. **Wks/ses:** 5. Operates June-Aug.

Youth in Transition assists teens and young adults who are blind or visually impaired in developing life skills and independence. Tutoring and instruction are available in personal management, mobility and communications. Counseling is also offered individually or in peer groups. Recreational and social activities include field trips, canoeing, sailing and dances. The center also provides academic tutoring and conducts work experience and computer training programs.

CHAMP CAMP
Res — Coed Ages 6-18

Martinsville, IN.
Contact (Year-round): 212 W 10th St, Ste B-210, Indianapolis, IN 46202. Tel: 317-679-1860. Fax: 317-245-2291.
www.champcamp.org   E-mail: admin@champcamp.org
Jennifer Kobylarz, Exec Dir.
Grades 1-12. Adm: FCFS. **Appl due:** Apr. **Staff:** Couns 100. Special needs 75.
Conditions accepted: As.
Features: Crafts Music Aquatics Boating Canoe Climbing_Wall Conservation Fishing Riding Rock_Climb Wilderness_Camp Woodcraft Equestrian Swim.
Fees 2014: Res $250, 1 wk. Aid (Need).
Housing: Cabins. **Swimming:** Pool.
Est 1991. Nonprofit. **Ses:** 1. **Wks/ses:** 1. Operates June. ACA.

Children and adolescents with tracheostomies and those who require respiratory assistance (including the use of ventilators) may enroll in this program. Crafts, music, climbing, canoeing, boating, fishing and games are among the activities. Most counselors are medical professionals.

CHILDREN'S HOSPITAL OF DENVER
TALKING WITH TECHNOLOGY CAMP
Res — Coed Ages 6-21

Empire, CO.
Contact (Year-round): 13123 E 16th Ave, Aurora, CO 80045. Tel: 720-777-6024. Fax: 720-777-7169.
www.thechildrenshospital.org/conditions/speech/camp
E-mail: lich.kim@tchden.org
Christy Schneller, Coord.
Adm: FCFS. **Appl due:** Apr. **Enr:** 38. **Staff:** Admin 3. Couns 25. Res 25. Special needs 40.
Conditions accepted: Au CP ID Speech & Lang. **Therapy:** Speech.

Features: Computers Crafts Dance Drama Media Music Photog Aquatics Farm Fishing Hiking Riding Ropes_Crse Equestrian Golf Swim.
Fees 2007: Res $2124 (+$30), 1 wk. Aid (Need).
Housing: Cabins. Avg per room/unit: 20. **Swimming:** Pool.
Est 1985. Ses: 1. **Wks/ses:** 1. Operates July.

This intensive, weeklong program serves young people who use augmentative and alternative communication devices as their primary means of expression. TWT provides individualized instruction in system use and also teaches campers new uses of vocabulary. The improvement of social skills is another program goal, as boys and girls learn to interact more effectively with adults and other children. Traditional camp activities round out the program. Scholarship assistance (through the Scottish Rite Foundation) is available to Colorado residents only.

CLARKE SCHOOLS FOR HEARING AND SPEECH
SUMMER ADVENTURE
Res and Day — Coed Ages 9-14

Northampton, MA 01060. 47 Round Hill Rd. Tel: 413-584-3450. Fax: 413-584-8273.
www.clarkeschools.org   E-mail: info@clarkeschools.org
Martha A. deHahn, Coord.
Adm: FCFS. **Appl due:** Rolling. **Enr:** 30. **Enr cap:** 30. **Staff:** Admin 2.
LD Services: Acad_Instruction.
Conditions accepted: D.
Features: Computers Speech Writing/Journ Crafts Music Exploration Hiking Outdoor_Ed Swim.
Fees 2014: Res $1295 (+$75), 2 wks. Day $725 (+$75), 2 wks. Aid (Merit & Need).
Housing: Dorms. Avg per room/unit: 2. **Swimming:** Pool.
Est 1982. Nonprofit. **Ses:** 1. **Wks/ses:** 2. Operates July.

Summer Adventure provides an enriched academic experience for children with hearing loss, as well as an opportunity for boys and girls to interact socially with others who have hearing loss. Masters-level trained teachers of the deaf maintain an auditory/oral environment for the campers. Various enrichment and recreational activities take place during the day, while evenings provide children with the opportunity to relax and get to know one another. A number of off-site field trips augment the program, including a daylong trip during the weekend.

CLEVELAND SIGHT CENTER
HIGHBROOK LODGE
Res — Coed Ages 8-18

Cleveland, OH 44106. 1909 E 101st St, PO Box 1988. Tel: 216-791-8118. Fax: 216-791-1101.
www.clevelandsightcenter.org/highbrooklodge.aspx
E-mail: camp@clevelandsightcenter.org
Bob Kochmit, Mgr.
Adm: FCFS. **Appl due:** Rolling. **Enr:** 45. **Enr cap:** 45. **Staff:** Admin 4. Couns 20.
LD Services: Tut.
Conditions accepted: Visual_Impair.
Features: Bus/Fin Computers Ecol Crafts Creative_Writing Dance Music Theater Aquatics Archery Climbing_Wall Exploration Riding Ropes_Crse Sail Social_Servs Wilderness_Camp Baseball Swim Watersports.
Fees 2011: Res $480-540 (+$20), 1 wk. Aid 2006 (Need): $60,000.
Housing: Cabins Lodges Tents. Avg per room/unit: 40. **Swimming:** Pond Pool.
Est 1928. Nonprofit. **Ses:** 4. **Wks/ses:** 1. Operates June-Aug. ACA.

Sponsored by the Cleveland Sight Center, Highbrook Lodge offers academics and recreation for individuals with visual impairments who may also have other disabilities. Camp life includes tutoring, music, art, dance, aquatic sports, trips and riding. Various adult and family programs are available.

CLOVER PATCH CAMP
Res — Coed Ages 5 and up; Day — Coed 5-18

Glenville, NY 12302. 55 Helping Hand Ln. Tel: 518-384-3081. Fax: 518-384-3001.
www.cloverpatchcamp.org E-mail: cloverpatchcamp@cfdsny.org
Laura Taylor, Dir.
Adm: FCFS. **Appl due:** Rolling. **Enr:** 24. **Enr cap:** 24. **Staff:** Admin 3. Couns 18. Res 23. Special needs 5.
Conditions accepted: ADD ADHD Asp Au CP D Diabetes Dx ED Ep ID LD PDD Phys_ Impair Speech & Lang TBI Visual_Impair. **Therapy:** Art Music Occup Rec.
Features: Environ_Sci Sci Crafts Dance Music Painting Theater Aquatics Hiking Baseball Basketball Golf Soccer Softball Swim Volleyball Watersports.
Fees 2014: Res $1300, 1 wk. Day $625-780, 1 wk. Aid 2009 (Need): $84,000.
Housing: Cabins. Avg per room/unit: 8. **Swimming:** Pool.
Est 1965. Nonprofit. **Spons:** Center for Disability Services. **Ses:** 11. **Wks/ses:** 1. Operates June-July. ACA.

Clover Patch provides a program of swimming, arts and crafts, music, drama and outdoor living skills for children and adults with various special needs, including mental retardation, physical handicaps, cerebral palsy and seizure disorders. Individuals with extreme behavioral disorders are not accepted. Medical approval and screening precedes admittance.

CAMP COLORADO
Res — Coed Ages 8-17

Woodland Park, CO.
Contact (Year-round): c/o American Diabetes Assoc, 2480 W 26th Ave, Ste 120B, Denver, CO 80211. Tel: 720-855-1102, 800-676-4065. Fax: 720-855-1302.
www.diabetes.org/adacampcolorado E-mail: emfay@diabetes.org
Emily Fay, Dir.
Adm: FCFS. **Appl due:** May. **Enr:** 260. **Enr cap:** 260. **Staff:** Admin 5. Couns 75. Special needs 15.
Conditions accepted: Diabetes.
Features: Crafts Aquatics Archery Canoe Climbing_Wall Fishing Hiking Kayak Mtn_Biking Mtn_Trips Rappelling Riflery Rock_Climb Ropes_Crse White-water_Raft Wilderness_ Camp Basketball Equestrian Swim Volleyball Watersports.
Fees 2014: Res $560-650, 1 wk. Aid 2007 (Need): $25,000.
Housing: Cabins Tents. Avg per room/unit: 7. **Swimming:** Lake.
Nonprofit. **Spons:** American Diabetes Association. **Ses:** 1. **Wks/ses:** 1. Operates June-July.

Children at the camp, which is held at Eagle Lake Camp in the Pike National Forest, participate in a camping program while learning diabetes management. Staff address diabetic lifestyle issues through discussion of nutrition, exercise, emotional well-being and glucose control. Two programs operate each summer: a traditional recreational camp and a teen camp that combines recreational activities with adventure pursuits.

COLORADO LIONS CAMP
Res — Coed Ages 8 and up

Woodland Park, CO 80866. PO Box 9043. Tel: 719-687-2087. Fax: 719-687-7435.
www.coloradolionscamp.org E-mail: jpierie@coloradolionscamp.org
James Pierie, Exec Dir.
Adm: FCFS. **Appl due:** Rolling. **Enr:** 40-45. **Staff:** Admin 3. Couns 22. Special needs 2.

Conditions accepted: ADD ADHD Asp Au D ID Phys_Impair Visual_Impair DS. **Therapy:** Psych Rec.
Features: Astron Crafts Dance Music Theater Aquatics Fishing Hiking Mtn_Biking Outdoor_Ed Ropes_Crse Badminton Baseball Basketball Softball Swim Volleyball.
Fees 2014: Res $500, 1 wk. Aid 2011 (Need): $70,000.
Housing: Dorms Tepees. **Swimming:** Pool.
Est 1969. Nonprofit. **Spons:** Lions Clubs Colorado. **Ses:** 10. **Wks/ses:** 1. Operates June-Aug.

A project of Lions Clubs throughout the state of Colorado, the camp provides mountain camping experiences and outdoor adventures for blind, deaf, mentally limited and physically impaired populations. Campers participate in backpacking, swimming, riding, hiking, fishing, overnight camping, outdoor cooking, hayrides, nature study, and arts and crafts.

CAMP CONRAD-CHINNOCK
Res — Coed Ages 7-16

Angelus Oaks, CA 92305. 4700 Jenks Lake Rd E. Tel: 909-794-6712. Fax: 909-752-5354.
Contact (Sept-June): c/o Diabetes Camping & Educational Services, 12045 E Waterfront Dr, Playa Vista, CA 90094. Tel: 310-751-3057. Fax: 888-800-4010.
Year-round Toll-free: 888-800-4010.
www.diabetescamping.org   E-mail: rosie.dubois@diabetescamping.org
Rosie DuBois, Exec Dir.
Adm: FCFS. **Appl due:** Rolling. **Enr:** 95. **Enr cap:** 110. **Staff:** Admin 6. Couns 12. Special needs 20.
Conditions accepted: Diabetes.
Features: Astron Ecol Crafts Drama Aquatics Archery Canoe Caving Climbing_Wall Exploration Fishing Hiking Mountaineering Mtn_Biking Rappelling Riflery Rock_Climb Ropes_Crse Basketball Swim.
Fees 2014: Res $216-791 (+$30), 1 wk. Aid 2010 (Need): $18,000.
Housing: Cabins. Avg per room/unit: 10. **Swimming:** Pool.
Est 1957. Nonprofit. **Spons:** Diabetes Camping and Educational Services. **Ses:** 6. **Wks/ses:** 1. Operates June-Aug. ACA.

The camp provides recreational, social and educational opportunities for youth with insulin-dependent diabetes. Campers acquire diabetes self-management skills while participating in many traditional camping activities. Programming combines cabin-group activities with free-choice periods. Younger children spend most of their time with cabin mates, while older campers exercise a greater degree of control over their schedules.

COURAGE NORTH
Res — Coed Ages 7-17

Lake George, MN 56458. PO Box 1626. Tel: 218-266-3658. Fax: 218-266-3458.
Contact (Winter): c/o Courage Ctr, 3915 Golden Valley Rd, Golden Valley, MN 55422. Tel: 763-520-0520. Fax: 763-520-0577.
Year-round Toll-free: 888-276-3631.
http://truefriends.org   E-mail: couragecamps@couragecenter.org
Jan Malcolm, CEO.
Adm: FCFS. **Appl due:** Rolling.
Conditions accepted: D.
Focus: Basketball. **Features:** Crafts Photog Adventure_Travel Archery Boating Canoe Hiking Kayak Sail Soccer Swim Tennis Watersports.
Fees 2014: Res $780-1560, 1 wk.
Housing: Cabins. **Swimming:** Lake.
Est 1972. Nonprofit. **Spons:** Courage Center. **Ses:** 1. **Wks/ses:** 1. Operates Aug. ACA.

Operated by True Friends, Courage North is a traditional summer camp for children and adolescents who are deaf or hard of hearing. A sliding fee scale is available. Popular pursuits include watersports and other water activities, digital photography, and arts and crafts. The camp also seeks to help boys and girls gain independence and develop social and leadership skills. An optional canoeing trip (offered for an additional fee) runs for five days at the conclusion of the regular session.

CAMP COURAGEOUS
Res — Coed Ages 15 and up; Day — Coed 7-21

Whitehouse, OH 43571. 12701 Waterville-Swanton Rd. Tel: 419-875-6828. Fax: 419-875-5598.
www.campcourageous.com   E-mail: camping@campcourageous.com
Chelsea Banas, Dir.
Adm: FCFS. **Appl due:** Rolling. **Enr:** 200. **Staff:** Admin 3. Couns 20.
Conditions accepted: ADD ADHD Asp ID LD Phys_Impair. **Therapy:** Art Rec.
Features: Crafts Dance Music Aquatics Hiking Wilderness_Camp Baseball Basketball Swim.
Fees 2014: Res $750, 1 wk. Day $300, 1 wk.
Housing: Dorms. **Swimming:** Pool.
Est 1963. Nonprofit. **Ses:** 9. **Wks/ses:** 1. Operates June-Aug. ACA.

Courageous provides residential camping for children and adults with mental retardation and developmental disabilities. Core program activities are aquatics, arts and crafts, sports, outdoor recreation and leisure skills, nature and weather studies, drama, cookouts and campfires. The camp's facilities and grounds are wheelchair accessible.

CAMP COURAGEOUS OF IOWA SUMMER YOUTH WEEKS
Res — Coed Ages 3-21

Monticello, IA 52310. 12007 190th St, PO Box 418. Tel: 319-465-5916. Fax: 319-465-5919.
www.campcourageous.org   E-mail: info@campcourageous.org
Stephen Fasnacht
Adm: FCFS. **Appl due:** Jan. **Enr:** 45-80. **Enr cap:** 80. **Staff:** Admin 4. Couns 40. Res 55.
Conditions accepted: As Asp Au CP Ep ID LD PDD Phys_Impair Speech & Lang TBI Visual_Impair MD MS.
Features: Crafts Fine_Arts Adventure_Travel Aquatics Archery Canoe Caving Climbing_ Wall Farm Fishing Hiking Outdoor_Ed Rappelling Riding Rock_Climb Ropes_Crse Basketball Swim.
Fees 2014: Res $475, 1 wk. Aid (Need).
Housing: Cabins Dorms Houses Tents Tepees. Avg per room/unit: 8. **Swimming:** Pool.
Est 1972. Nonprofit. **Ses:** 12. **Wks/ses:** 1. Operates May-Aug. ACA.

This year-round recreational and respite care facility for children and adults with special needs conducts weeklong summer camps for young people. Offerings include traditional outdoor activities, arts and crafts, and adventure pursuits. Persons served range from those with mental, physical or multiple disabilities to those with Asperger's syndrome or brain injury.

DEAF CHILDREN'S CAMP
Res — Coed Ages 4-16

Milford, IN.
Contact (Year-round): 100 W 86th St, Indianapolis, IN 46260. Tel: 317-846-3404. Fax: 317-844-1034.
www.indeafcamps.org   E-mail: deafcamp@hotmail.com
Phil Harden, Dir.
Adm: FCFS. **Appl due:** Rolling. **Enr cap:** 180. **Staff:** Admin 4. Couns 90. Special needs 3.

Conditions accepted: D.
Features: Sci Crafts Drama Music Painting Aquatics Archery Boating Canoe Climbing_ Wall Fishing Kayak Ropes_Crse Sail Basketball Golf Soccer Swim Ultimate_Frisbee Volleyball Watersports.
Fees 2014: Res $300, 1 wk. Aid 2012 (Need): $12,775.
Housing: Cabins Dorms Lodges Tents. Avg per room/unit: 10. **Swimming:** Lake.
Est 1973. Nonprofit. **Ses:** 1. **Wks/ses:** 1. Operates July.

The camp serves children who are deaf or hard of hearing. Both speaking and signing campers participate in such activities as swimming, canoeing, crafts, hiking, games, fishing and sports. A CIT program serves boys and girls ages 17 and 18.

THE DOUBLE H RANCH
Res — Coed Ages 6-16

Lake Luzerne, NY 12846. 97 Hidden Valley Rd. Tel: 518-696-5676. Fax: 518-696-4528.
www.doublehranch.org   **E-mail: theranch@doublehranch.org**
Jacqueline Royael, Dir.
Adm: FCFS. **Appl due:** Rolling. **Enr:** 105. **Enr cap:** 126. **Staff:** Admin 22. Couns 50. Res 10. Special needs 30.
Conditions accepted: Blood Cancer CP HIV/AIDS Phys_Impair TBI Visual_Impair.
Therapy: Art Music Phys Psych Rec Speech.
Features: Crafts Creative_Writing Dance Drama Music Aquatics Archery Boating Conservation Exploration Fishing Hiking Riding Ropes_Crse Wilderness_Camp Woodcraft Baseball Basketball Equestrian Football Swim Tennis.
Fees 2014: Free. Res 1 wk.
Housing: Cabins. **Swimming:** Lake Pool.
Est 1993. Nonprofit. **Spons:** Hole in the Wall Gang Association. **Ses:** 8. **Wks/ses:** 1. Operates June-Aug. ACA.

The camp provides recreation and education for children with cancer, serious blood disorders and neuromuscular impairments. The schedule of activities includes swimming, fishing, boating, riding, conservation practices, camping, nature walks, arts and crafts, music and theater. Weekly scheduled trips allow campers to go white-water rafting and to local amusement and water parks.

DREAM STREET FOUNDATION SUMMER CAMPS
Res — Coed Ages 4-24

Beverly Hills, CA 90212. 324 S Beverly Dr, Ste 500. Tel: 424-248-0696.
www.dreamstreetfoundation.org   **E-mail: dreamstreetca@gmail.com**
Patty Grubman, Dir.
Adm: FCFS. **Appl due:** Apr. **Enr:** 140. **Enr cap:** 140. **Staff:** Admin 6. Couns 125. Special needs 18.
Locations: AR AZ CA MI NJ.
Conditions accepted: Blood Cancer C Ep HIV/AIDS CF.
Features: Circus_Skills Crafts Dance Music Aquatics Archery Climbing_Wall Hiking Riding Ropes_Crse Survival_Trng Woodcraft Basketball Gymnastics Swim.
Fees 2014: Free. Res 1 wk.
Housing: Cabins Dorms Lodges. Avg per room/unit: 6. **Swimming:** Pool.
Est 1989. Nonprofit. **Ses:** 3. **Wks/ses:** 1. Operates July-Aug.

Dream Street sponsors cost-free camps across the country for children with such chronic and life-threatening illnesses as cancer, AIDS and blood disorders. At the camps, boys and girls take part in activities from which they would typically be excluded due to their illnesses. Offerings include arts and crafts, sports, dance, drama, music, aquatics and hiking.

EASTER SEALS CAMP CHALLENGE
Res — Coed Ages 6 and up

Sorrento, FL 32776. 31600 Camp Challenge Rd. Tel: 352-383-4711. **Fax:** 352-383-0744.
www.easterseals.com/florida E-mail: camp@fl.easterseals.com
Michael Archbold, Dir.
Adm: FCFS. **Appl due:** Rolling. **Enr cap:** 70. **Staff:** Couns 20.
Conditions accepted: ADD ADHD Asp Au CP D ID LD PDD Phys_Impair Speech & Lang TBI Visual_Impair.
Features: Crafts Dance Drama Music Painting Archery Climbing_Wall Farm Hiking Paintball Rappelling Ropes_Crse Baseball Basketball Field_Hockey Football Golf Soccer Softball Swim Ultimate_Frisbee Volleyball.
Fees 2012: Res $900-2700, 1-2 wks. Aid (Need).
Housing: Cabins Dorms. Avg per room/unit: 12-18. **Swimming:** Pool.
Est 1961. Nonprofit. **Spons:** Easter Seals Florida. **Ses:** 4. **Wks/ses:** 1-2. Operates June-July. ACA.

Camp Challenge, Florida's Easter Seal camp, addresses the needs of individuals with physical or cognitive disabilities. The camp provides specific activities for children, adolescents and adults, including aquatic sports, arts and crafts, socials, skits, nature study and a challenge course. Children accepted to the camp must not be aggressive towards themselves or others.

EASTER SEALS CAMP HARMON
Res — Coed Ages 8 and up

Boulder Creek, CA 95006. 16403 Hwy 9. Tel: 831-338-3383.
Contact (Sept-May): c/o Easter Seals Central California, 9010 Soquel Dr, Aptos, CA 95003. Tel: 831-684-2166.
Year-round Fax: 831-684-1018.
www.campharmon.org E-mail: campharmon@es-cc.org
Scott Webb, Dir.
Adm: FCFS. **Appl due:** Rolling. **Enr:** 75. **Enr cap:** 80. **Staff:** Admin 3. Couns 30. Res 10.
Conditions accepted: ADD ADHD Asp Au CP D ID LD Phys_Impair TBI DS.
Features: Computers Crafts Dance Drama Aquatics Archery Hiking Baseball Basketball Equestrian Golf Swim Track Volleyball.
Fees 2012: Res $726, 1 wk. Aid (Need).
Housing: Cabins Lodges. Avg per room/unit: 9. **Swimming:** Pool.
Est 1964. Nonprofit. **Spons:** Easter Seals Central California. **Ses:** 7. **Wks/ses:** 1. Operates June-July. ACA.

Each session at the camp accommodates a specific age group and works with individuals with developmental or physical disabilities or both. Campers engage in a variety of activities, enabling them to explore new interests while also participating in favorite pursuits. Harmon maintains the camper-staff ratio at 2:1.

EASTER SEALS CAMP SNO-MO
Res — Coed Ages 11-21

Gilmanton Iron Works, NH 03837. 260 Griswold Ln. Tel: 603-364-5818. **Fax:** 603-364-0230.
Contact (Sept-Apr): 200 Zachary Rd, Bldg B, Manchester, NH 03109. Tel: 603-206-6733. **Fax:** 603-669-9413.
www.eastersealsnh.org E-mail: rkelly@eastersealsnh.org
Robert E. Kelly, Dir.
Adm: FCFS. Admitted: 95%. **Appl due:** Rolling. **Staff:** Admin 1. Couns 12.
Conditions accepted: ADHD Asp Au CP D ED Ep ID LD Phys_Impair Speech & Lang TBI Visual_Impair.

Features: Ecol Crafts Dance Fine_Arts Music Aquatics Archery Boating Canoe Exploration Fishing Kayak Mountaineering Riflery Ropes_Crse Sail Baseball Soccer Swim Volleyball. **Fees 2012: Res $640-1280 (+$150-300), 1-2 wks.** Aid (Need). **Housing:** Lodges Tents. Avg per room/unit: 15. **Swimming:** Lake. **Est 1972.** Nonprofit. **Spons:** Easter Seals New Hampshire/New Hampshire Snowmobile Association. **Ses: 7. Wks/ses:** 1-2. Operates June-Aug.

This coeducational camp integrates campers with disabilities and able-bodied Boy Scouts. Campers are involved in developing their schedules of activities for the week. In addition to the usual recreational activities, the program includes animal shows and woodworking. Sno-Mo is equipped to accommodate campers with special medical and nutritional needs.

EASTER SEALS CAMP SUNNYSIDE
Res — Coed Ages 4 and up; Day — Coed 4-17

Des Moines, IA 50313. 401 NE 66th Ave. Tel: 515-289-1933. Fax: 515-289-1281.
www.eastersealsia.org   E-mail: kanderson@eastersealsia.org
Adm: FCFS. **Appl due:** Rolling. **Staff:** Admin 10. Couns 75.
Conditions accepted: Asp Au Cancer C CP D Diabetes ED Ep HIV/AIDS ID LD Phys_ Impair Speech & Lang TBI Visual_Impair.
Features: Crafts Fine_Arts Music Aquatics Archery Boating Canoe Climbing_Wall Fishing Hiking Riding Social_Servs Weight_Loss Swim.
Fees 2011: Res $575, 1 wk. Aid 2007 (Need): $70,000.
Housing: Cabins Tents. **Swimming:** Lake Pool.
Est 1961. Nonprofit. **Spons:** Easter Seals of Iowa. **Ses: 8. Wks/ses:** 1. Operates June-Aug. ACA.

Camp Sunnyside offers a full recreational program for children and adults with disabilities. In addition to its summer programming, Easter Seals of Iowa conducts weekend respite camps and winter break and spring break residential programs.

EASTER SEALS CAMP WAWBEEK
Res — Coed Ages 7 and up

Wisconsin Dells, WI.
Contact (Year-round): c/o Easter Seals Wisconsin, 101 Nob Hill Rd, Ste 301, Madison, WI 53713. Tel: 608-277-8288, 800-422-2324. Fax: 608-277-8333.
www.eastersealswisconsin.com   E-mail: camp@eastersealswisconsin.com
Carissa Miller, Dir.
Adm: FCFS. **Appl due:** Rolling. **Staff:** Admin 5. Couns 90. Special needs 3.
Conditions accepted: ADD ADHD As Asp Au CP ED Ep ID LD PDD Phys_Impair Speech & Lang TBI. **Therapy:** Rec.
Features: Crafts Drama Music Aquatics Archery Canoe Climbing_Wall Cooking Fishing Hiking Riflery Ropes_Crse Baseball Basketball Soccer Softball Swim.
Fees 2013: Res $761-1102 (+$100), 1-2 wks.
Housing: Cabins. **Swimming:** Pool.
Est 1938. Nonprofit. **Spons:** Easter Seals Wisconsin. **Ses: 6. Wks/ses:** 1-2. Operates June-July. ACA.

This recreational program for individuals with physical, cognitive, emotional and behavioral disabilities enables parents and caregivers to receive a break from caring for their loved one. Held on a 400-acre, wooded site, Wawbeek features sports, arts and crafts, trail rides, nature hikes, singing, storytelling, campfires and many other traditional recreational pursuits. A one-to-one camper to counselor ratio enables staff to assist with activities and address the specific needs of the camper. A separate session serves teens and young adults with Asperger's syndrome or high-functioning autism.

EASTER SEALS CAMPING PROGRAM
Res — Coed Ages 8-14

West Poland, ME.
Contact (Year-round): c/o Easter Seals Massachusetts, 484 Main St, 6th Fl, Worcester, MA 01608. **Tel:** 508-751-6410, 800-244-2756. **Fax:** 508-751-6444.
www.eastersealsma.org **E-mail:** camp@eastersealsma.org
Colleen Flanagan, Mgr.
Adm: FCFS. **Appl due:** Rolling. **Enr:** 30. **Enr cap:** 30.
Locations: CT ME.
Conditions accepted: Au CP Phys_Impair.
Features: Crafts Dance Music Theater Adventure_Travel Aquatics Archery Boating Canoe Farm Fishing Hiking Ropes_Crse Sail Wilderness_Camp Woodcraft Baseball Basketball Gymnastics Softball Swim Tennis Watersports.
Fees 2011: Res $2700-3100, 1-2 wks. Aid (Need).
Housing: Cabins. **Swimming:** Lake Pond Pool.
Est 1965. Nonprofit. **Spons:** Easter Seals Massachusetts. **Ses:** 2. **Wks/ses:** 1-2. Operates Aug.

Held at Agassiz Village in Maine, the program provide traditional camping activities for children with physical disabilities. Significant financial assistance is available, with fees determined along a sliding scale according to family income.

CAMP EASTER SEALS NEBRASKA
Res — Coed Ages 6 and up

Fremont, NE.
Contact (Year-round): c/o Easter Seals Nebraska, 638 N 109th Plz, Omaha, NE 68154. **Tel:** 402-345-2200, 800-650-9880. **Fax:** 402-345-2500.
www.easterseals.com/ne/our-programs/camping-recreation/camps.html
E-mail: tlewis@ne.easterseals.com
Lily Sughroue, Coord.
Adm: FCFS. **Appl due:** Apr. **Enr:** 25. **Enr cap:** 28. **Staff:** Admin 2. Couns 20. Special needs 3.
Conditions accepted: ADD ADHD Asp Au C CP D Diabetes Dx ED Ep ID LD PDD Phys_ Impair Speech & Lang TBI Visual_Impair. **Therapy:** Rec.
Features: Astron Ecol Crafts Creative_Writing Dance Music Painting Theater Aquatics Archery Boating Canoe Climbing_Wall Cooking Fishing Hiking Kayak Mountaineering Rappelling Riding Riflery Ropes_Crse Wilderness_Camp Woodcraft Work Baseball Basketball Equestrian Football Golf Gymnastics Rugby Soccer Softball Swim Tennis Track Watersports.
Fees 2014: Res $900 (+$25), 1 wk. Aid 2006 (Need): $13,000.
Housing: Cabins. Avg per room/unit: 8. **Swimming:** Pool.
Est 1968. Nonprofit. **Ses:** 6. **Wks/ses:** 1. Operates June-July.

This recreational camp serves children and adults with all types of physical and developmental disabilities. Activities include swimming, arts and crafts, music, canoeing, fishing, camp outs, cookouts, nature hikes and a ropes course.

CAMP EASTER SEALS UCP
Res — Coed Ages 7 and up

New Castle, VA 24127. 900 Camp Easter Seals Rd. **Tel:** 540-864-5750. **Fax:** 540-864-6797.
Contact (Sept-May): 201 E Main St, Salem, VA 24153. **Tel:** 540-777-7325. **Fax:** 540-777-2194.
www.campeastersealsucp.com **E-mail:** camp@eastersealsucp.com
Alex Barge, Dir.
Adm: FCFS. **Appl due:** Rolling. **Enr:** 63. **Staff:** Admin 3. Couns 40. Special needs 8.

Conditions accepted: ADD ADHD Asp Au CP Ep ID LD PDD Phys_Impair Speech & Lang TBI Visual_Impair. **Therapy:** Occup Rec Speech.
Features: Crafts Drama Music Aquatics Archery Canoe Climbing_Wall Fishing Hiking Peace/Cross-cultural Riding Riflery Basketball Softball Swim.
Fees 2011: Res $750-3575, 1-4 wks. Aid (Need).
Housing: Cabins. Avg per room/unit: 14-20. **Swimming:** Pool.
Est 1957. Nonprofit. **Spons:** Easter Seals UCP North Carolina & Virginia. **Ses: 6. Wks/ses:** 1-2. Operates June-July. ACA.

Easter Seals UCP provides recreational therapy, activities, sports and nature study for campers with cognitive or physical disabilities. An adventure camp features hiking, exploration and camping.

CAMP ECHOING HILLS
Res — Coed Ages 7 and up

Warsaw, OH 43844. 36272 County Rd 79. Tel: 740-327-2311, 800-419-6513. Fax: 740-327-2333.
www.campechoinghills.org   E-mail: info@ehvi.org
Emily Smith, Dir.
Adm: FCFS. **Appl due:** Apr. **Enr:** 84. **Staff:** Admin 3. Couns 30. Special needs 3.
Conditions accepted: ADD ADHD Au CP D Ep ID LD Phys_Impair Speech & Lang TBI Visual_Impair.
Features: Crafts Aquatics Archery Canoe Fishing Hiking Ropes_Crse Swim.
Fees 2012: Res $650-1000, 1 wk.
Housing: Cabins. Avg per room/unit: 15. **Swimming:** Pool.
Est 1966. Nonprofit. Nondenom Christian. **Ses: 8. Wks/ses:** 1. Operates June-Aug. ACA.

A Christian camp for individuals with developmental disabilities, Echoing Hills seeks to bring healthy social, physical and spiritual development to its members. Swimming, hayrides, cookouts, music and art are all part of the summer plan for campers.

CAMP EDEN WOOD
Res — Coed Ages 5 and up; Day — Coed 5-21

Eden Prairie, MN 55346. 6350 Indian Chief Rd.
Contact (Sept-May): 10509 108th St NW, Annandale, MN 55302.
Year-round Tel: 952-852-0101, 800-450-8376. Fax: 952-852-0123.
http://truefriends.org   E-mail: info@friendshipventures.org
Laurie Tschetter, Exec Dir.
Adm: FCFS. **Appl due:** Rolling. **Enr:** 35. **Staff:** Admin 2. Couns 15.
Conditions accepted: Asp Au CP ID Phys_Impair.
Features: Crafts Dance Music Aquatics Archery Boating Canoe Climbing_Wall Cooking Fishing Ropes_Crse Basketball Golf Swim Volleyball.
Fees 2014: Res $780-1860, 1 wk. Day $276-690, 1 wk.
Housing: Cabins Dorms. **Swimming:** Lake Pool.
Est 1958. Nonprofit. **Spons:** Friendship Ventures. **Ses: 24. Wks/ses:** 1. Operates June-Aug. ACA.

Eden Wood is open to children and adults with developmental disabilities. Traditional and specialty sessions are adapted to the age and ability level of the camper. Eden Wood schedules day and evening excursions out of camp.

CAMP EDI
THE GLORIA HIRSCH CAMP FOR CHILDREN WITH DIABETES
Res — Coed Ages 9-17

Fredericktown, MO.

Contact (Year-round): c/o American Diabetes Association, 425 S Woods Mill Rd, Ste 110, Town and Country, MO 63017. Tel: 314-822-5490, 888-342-2383. Fax: 314-576-0002.
www.diabetes.org   E-mail: aholmesbownes@diabetes.org
Andrea Holmes-Bownes, Dir.
Adm: FCFS. Appl due: Rolling. Enr: 128. Enr cap: 128. Staff: Admin 3. Couns 39. Special needs 40.
Locations: AK AR AZ CA CO FL IL IN KS LA MI MO NC ND NH NM NY OH PA TN TX WA WI.
Conditions accepted: Diabetes.
Features: Ecol Environ_Sci Crafts Aquatics Archery Boating Canoe Conservation Exploration Fishing Hiking Kayak Outdoor_Ed Weight_Loss Woodcraft Basketball Football Soccer Softball Swim Tennis Ultimate_Frisbee Volleyball.
Fees 2014: Res $850, 1 wk. Aid 2011 (Merit & Need): $20,000.
Housing: Cabins Dorms. Avg per room/unit: 8. Swimming: Lake.
Est 1952. Nonprofit. Spons: American Diabetes Association. Ses: 2. Wks/ses: 1. Operates June.

Camp EDI (Exercise-Diet-Insulin) provides an opportunity for children with diabetes to learn to manage their disease more independently. Camping activities include games, swimming, canoeing, crafts, hiking, sports and wellness classes.

ENCHANTED HILLS CAMP
Res — Coed Ages 5 and up

Napa, CA 94558. 3410 Mt Veeder Rd. Tel: 707-224-4023. Fax: 707-224-5435.
Contact (Sept-May): c/o LightHouse for the Blind, 214 Van Ness Ave, San Francisco, CA 94102. Tel: 415-431-1481. Fax: 415-863-7568.
www.lighthouse-sf.org   E-mail: ehc@lighthouse-sf.org
Tony Fletcher, Dir.
Adm: FCFS. Admitted: 90%. Appl due: Rolling. Enr: 60. Enr cap: 60. Staff: Admin 4. Couns 21. Res 6. Special needs 3.
Conditions accepted: Visual_Impair.
Features: Environ_Sci Crafts Dance Music Theater Aquatics Cooking Hiking Riding Yoga Swim.
Fees 2014: Res $60-600, ½-1½ wks. Aid 2009 (Need): $150,000.
Housing: Cabins Dorms Houses. Swimming: Pool.
Est 1958. Nonprofit. Spons: LightHouse for the Blind. Ses: 9. Wks/ses: ½-1½. Operates June-Aug. ACA.

Enchanted Hills offers a traditional camping experience for children and adult campers with blindness, visual impairments, deafness and blindness, or multiple disabilities. The program includes activities in swimming, sports, horseback riding, hiking, dancing, drama, music and crafts.

CAMP ESPERANZA
Res — Coed Ages 8-17

Big Bear Lake, CA.
Contact (Year-round): c/o Arthritis Foundation, Southern California Chapter, 800 W 6th St, Ste 1250, Los Angeles, CA 90017. Tel: 323-954-5750, 800-954-2873. Fax: 323-954-5790.
www.arthritis.org/california/campesperanzadetailsteen
E-mail: jziegler@arthritis.org
Jennifer Ziegler, Dir.
Adm: FCFS. Admitted: 98%. Appl due: Rolling. Enr: 115. Staff: Admin 3. Couns 70. Special needs 9.
Conditions accepted: Phys_Impair Ar.

Features: Astron Crafts Music Aquatics Archery Canoe Climbing_Wall Rappelling Riding Rock_Climb Ropes_Crse Basketball Equestrian Swim Volleyball.
Fees 2014: Free. Res (+$25), 1 wk.
Housing: Cabins Lodges. Avg per room/unit: 3-16. **Swimming:** Pool.
Est 1985. Nonprofit. **Spons:** Arthritis Foundation—Southern California Chapter. **Ses:** 2.
Wks/ses: 1. Operates July-Aug.

Providing a five-day recreational program, the camp serves children with either juvenile arthritis or a rheumatic disease such as lupus or scleroderma. Activities include riding, swimming, arts and crafts, a ropes course and campfires. Families pay a nominal registration fee only.

EXPLORE YOUR FUTURE
Res — Coed Ages 16-18

Rochester, NY 14623. 52 Lomb Memorial Dr. Tel: 585-475-6700. Fax: 585-475-2696.
www.ntid.rit.edu/camps/eyf E-mail: eyfinfo@rit.edu
Grades 11-12. Adm: Selective. **Appl due:** Apr. **Enr:** 140. **Fac 20. Staff:** Admin 4. Couns 12.
Avg class size: 11.
Conditions accepted: D.
Features: Bus/Fin Comp_Sci Engineering Sci Studio_Art Baseball Swim.
Fees 2014: Res $700, 1 wk. Aid (Need).
Housing: Dorms. **Swimming:** Pool.
Est 1985. Spons: Rochester Institute of Technology/National Technical Institute for the Deaf. **Ses:** 2. **Wks/ses:** 1. Operates July.

This program at Rochester Institute of Technology, conducted in conjunction with the National Technical Institute for the Deaf, enrolls rising high school juniors and seniors who are deaf or hard of hearing. Campers experience college life by participating in various academic and social activities. Career awareness activities are offered in business, computer science, engineering, science and visual communications.

FLORIDA DIABETES CAMP
Res — Coed Ages 6-18

Gainesville, FL 32604. University Sta, PO Box 14136. Tel: 352-334-1321. Fax: 352-334-1326.
www.floridadiabetescamp.org E-mail: fccyd@floridadiabetescamp.org
Gary Cornwell, Dir.
Adm: FCFS. **Appl due:** Rolling. **Enr:** 67. **Staff:** Admin 3. Couns 120. Special needs 50.
Conditions accepted: Diabetes.
Features: Crafts Aquatics Bicycle_Tours Canoe Exploration Hiking Sail Baseball Basketball Football Golf Soccer Swim Tennis Volleyball Watersports.
Fees 2011: Res $450-575, 1 wk.
Housing: Cabins. Avg per room/unit: 12. **Swimming:** Lake Pool.
Est 1962. Nonprofit. **Ses:** 6. **Wks/ses:** 1. Operates June-Aug. ACA.

The camp provides summer programs for insulin-dependent children with Type 1 diabetes. Sessions include family retreats, a teen cycling camp, a teen sports camp and traditional residential programs.

4-H CAMP HOWE
Res — Coed Ages 7-16; Day — Coed 7-13

Goshen, MA 01032. PO Box 326. Tel: 413-549-3969. Fax: 413-577-0760.
www.camphowe.com E-mail: office@camphowe.com
Heidi Gutekenst, Dir.

Adm: FCFS. **Admitted:** 95%. **Appl due:** Rolling. **Enr:** 110. **Staff:** Admin 8. Couns 32. Res 40.
Conditions accepted: ADD ADHD As Asp Au CP D Diabetes Dx Ep ID LD Phys_Impair Speech & Lang TBI Visual_Impair.
Features: Ecol Environ_Sci Crafts Dance Theater Aquatics Archery Boating Canoe Climbing_Wall Conservation Cooking Exploration Farm Fishing Hiking Kayak Outdoor_ Ed Rappelling Riflery Rock_Climb Ropes_Crse Sail White-water_Raft Basketball Cricket Swim.
Fees 2014: Res $485-1320, 1-2 wks. Day $320-460, 1 wk. Aid (Need).
Housing: Cabins. Avg per room/unit: 9. **Swimming:** Lake.
Est 1928. Nonprofit. **Ses:** 7. **Wks/ses:** 1-2. Operates June-Aug. ACA.

Located on a 52-acre tract of state forestland in the foothills of the Berkshire Mountains, Camp Howe offers an array of traditional recreational pursuits to both nondisabled and special-needs children. Among the camp's activities are a challenge course, wall and rock climbing, skeet shooting, and farm and leadership programs. Campers ages 7-20 with various physical special needs may enroll in the ECHO Program, which promotes a greater degree of independence, encourages social integration within the camp and teaches leisure skills.

THE FOWLER CENTER FOR OUTDOOR LEARNING
RESIDENTIAL SUMMER CAMP
Res — Coed Ages 6-26; Day — Coed 6-20

Mayville, MI 48744. 2315 Harmon Lake Rd. Tel: 989-673-2050. Fax: 989-673-6355.
www.thefowlercenter.org   E-mail: info@thefowlercenter.org
Kyle L. Middleton, Exec Dir.
Adm: FCFS. **Appl due:** Mar. **Enr:** 80-90. **Enr cap:** 90. **Staff:** Admin 8. Couns 40.
Conditions accepted: Asp Au CP ED Ep HIV/AIDS ID LD Phys_Impair Speech & Lang TBI Visual_Impair.
Features: Crafts Adventure_Travel Aquatics Archery Boating Canoe Climbing_Wall Fishing Hiking Rock_Climb Ropes_Crse Wilderness_Camp Baseball Basketball Equestrian Swim Volleyball.
Fees 2014: Res $600-1115, 1 wk. Day $150, 1 wk. Aid 2009 (Need): $20,000.
Housing: Cabins. Avg per room/unit: 16. **Swimming:** Lake.
Est 1957. Nonprofit. **Spons:** Fowler Center. **Ses:** 5. **Wks/ses:** 1. Operates July-Aug.

The camp serves persons with multiple special needs, including intellectual disabilities, autism and emotional disturbances. Those with associated physical disabilities, such as spina bifida, muscular dystrophy, cystic fibrosis, multiple sclerosis, cerebral palsy, Down syndrome, epilepsy and HIV/AIDS, as well as individuals with problems arising from closed head injuries, may also attend. Activities include boating, picnics, dances, nature study, field trips, a challenge course, equestrianism and archery.

CAMP FRIENDSHIP
Res and Day — Coed Ages 5 and up

Annandale, MN 55302. c/o Friendship Ventures, 10509 108th St NW. Tel: 952-852-0101, 800-450-8376. Fax: 952-852-0123.
http://truefriends.org   E-mail: fv@friendshipventures.org
Laurie Tschetter, Exec Dir.
Adm: FCFS. **Appl due:** Rolling. **Enr cap:** 30-135.
Conditions accepted: ADD ADHD Asp Au CP D Diabetes Dx ED Ep ID LD PDD Phys_ Impair Speech & Lang Visual_Impair.
Features: Crafts Dance Music Aquatics Archery Boating Canoe Climbing_Wall Community_ Serv Cooking Exploration Farm Hiking Mtn_Biking Mtn_Trips Rock_Climb Ropes_Crse Equestrian Swim.
Fees 2014: Res $468-1560, 1 wk. Day $276-690, 1 wk. Aid (Need).
Housing: Cabins. Avg per room/unit: 8. **Swimming:** Lake Pool.

Est 1964. Nonprofit. **Spons:** Friendship Ventures. **Ses:** 62. **Wks/ses:** 1. Operates June-Aug. ACA.

The camp serves children and adults who have developmental or physical disabilities or both. Traditional recreational activities are adapted to the age and ability level of the camper, and participants choose either a general session or a special-interest camp.

GALES CREEK CAMP
Res — Coed Ages 8-17

Tigard, OR 97223. 7110 SW Fir Loop, Ste 170. Tel: 503-968-2267. Fax: 503-443-2313.
www.galescreekcamp.org   E-mail: cheryl@galescreekcamp.org
Cheryl Sheppard, Exec Dir.
Grades 3-12. Adm: FCFS. **Appl due:** Rolling. **Staff:** Admin 2. Couns 12.
LD Services: Acad_Instruction.
Conditions accepted: Diabetes.
Features: Crafts Aquatics Conservation Hiking Badminton Baseball Basketball Field_ Hockey Football Soccer Softball Swim Tennis Volleyball Watersports Ping-Pong.
Fees 2014: Res $375 (+$20), 1 wk.
Housing: Dorms. **Swimming:** Pool.
Est 1953. Nonprofit. **Ses:** 8. **Wks/ses:** 1. Operates June-Aug. ACA.

Young people with diabetes receive training and participate in recreational activities suited to their needs. Campers participate in swimming, hiking, fishing, field trips, crafts and games, and various sports.

CAMP GOOD DAYS AND SPECIAL TIMES
Res — Coed Ages 8-17; Day — Coed 4-7

Branchport, NY 14418. 58 W Lake Rd. Tel: 315-595-2779. Fax: 315-595-6153.
Contact (Oct-May): 1332 Pittsford-Mendon Rd, PO Box 665, Mendon, NY 14506. Tel: 585-624-5555. Fax: 585-624-5799.
Year-round Toll-free: 800-785-2135.
www.campgooddays.org   E-mail: info@campgooddays.org
Wendy Bleier-Mervis, Exec Dir.
Adm: FCFS. **Appl due:** Rolling. **Staff:** Admin 10. Special needs 10.
Conditions accepted: Blood Cancer HIV/AIDS. **Therapy:** Art Psych.
Features: Crafts Drama Music Aquatics Archery Boating Canoe Climbing_Wall Community_Serv Fishing Hiking Peace/Cross-cultural Rock_Climb Ropes_Crse Scuba Social_Servs Woodcraft Baseball Basketball Golf Soccer Softball Swim Tennis Volleyball Watersports.
Fees 2014: Free. Res 1 wk. Day 1 wk.
Housing: Cabins Dorms. **Swimming:** Lake Pool.
Est 1979. Nonprofit. **Ses:** 13. **Wks/ses:** 1. Operates June-Sept. ACA.

The camp provides a full recreational program for children and families affected by cancer, AIDS, sickle cell anemia or violence. Activities include crafts, music, drama, canoeing, scuba diving, hiking, swimming and land sports.

CAMP GRANADA
Res — Coed Ages 8-16

Monticello, IL. 4-H Memorial Campground, 499 Old Timber Rd.
Contact (Year-round): c/o American Diabetes Assoc, 2501 Chatham Rd, Ste 210, Springfield, IL 62704. Tel: 217-875-9011, 888-342-2383. Fax: 217-875-6849.
www.diabetes.org/adacampgranada   E-mail: kdarneille@diabetes.org
Kate Darneille, Dir.

Adm: FCFS. **Appl due:** Rolling. **Enr:** 141. **Enr cap:** 141. **Staff:** Admin 4. Couns 57. Special needs 21.
LD Services: Acad_Instruction.
Conditions accepted: Diabetes.
Features: Crafts Aquatics Archery Canoe Climbing_Wall Fishing Hiking Ropes_Crse Softball Swim Volleyball.
Fees 2014: Res $550, 1 wk. Aid 2007 (Need): $36,000.
Housing: Cabins. **Swimming:** Lake.
Est 1979. Nonprofit. **Ses:** 1. **Wks/ses:** 1. Operates July.

At Granada, campers with diabetes learn to better manage their condition in a recreational setting. Volleyball, softball, canoeing, swimming, archery, and arts and crafts are among the camp's activities.

CAMP HAMWI
Res — Coed Ages 7-17

Danville, OH.
Contact (Year-round): c/o Central Ohio Diabetes Assoc, 1100 Dennison Ave, Columbus, OH 43201. Tel: 614-884-4400, 800-422-7946. Fax: 614-884-4484.
www.diabetesohio.org   E-mail: coda@diabetesohio.org
Darlene Honigford, Dir.
Grades 2-12. Adm: FCFS. **Appl due:** Rolling. **Enr:** 80. **Enr cap:** 80. **Staff:** Admin 6. Couns 72. Special needs 20.
Conditions accepted: Diabetes.
Features: Crafts Theater Aquatics Archery Canoe Fishing Hiking Rappelling Riding Ropes_Crse Wilderness_Camp Baseball Basketball Equestrian Football Soccer Swim Ultimate_Frisbee Volleyball.
Fees 2012: Res $410, 1 wk. Aid 2011 (Need): $28,683.
Housing: Cabins. Avg per room/unit: 8. **Swimming:** Pool.
Est 1967. Nonprofit. **Spons:** Central Ohio Diabetes Association. **Ses:** 2. **Wks/ses:** 1. Operates July-Aug. ACA.

Hamwi offers children and young adults with diabetes a combination of diabetes education and traditional camping activities. Art, dance, watersports, riding, archery, canoeing and rappelling are among the camp's most popular activities.

CAMP HAPPY DAYS
Res — Coed Ages 4-18

Charleston, SC 29407. 1622 Ashley Hall Rd. Tel: 843-571-4336. Fax: 843-571-4394.
www.camphappydays.org   E-mail: teresa@camphappydays.com
Teresa Bishop, Prgm Dir.
Grades K-12. Adm: FCFS. **Appl due:** Rolling. **Enr:** 160. **Enr cap:** 200. **Staff:** Admin 4. Couns 100.
Conditions accepted: Cancer. **Therapy:** Rec.
Features: Circus_Skills Crafts Dance Aquatics Boating Canoe Climbing_Wall Fishing Kayak Rappelling Riding Ropes_Crse Baseball Basketball Football Golf Swim.
Fees 2014: Free. Res 1 wk.
Housing: Lodges. Avg per room/unit: 12. **Swimming:** Lake.
Est 1982. Nonprofit. **Ses:** 1. **Wks/ses:** 1. Operates June-July.

Happy Days offers a traditional camp experience to children diagnosed with cancer and their siblings. The waterfront program features swimming, boating, tubing, fishing and a waterslide. Other popular activities are woodworking, arts and crafts, painting, sewing, baking, ceramics, a climbing wall, a high-ropes adventure course and team-building games.

CAMP HASC
Res — Coed Ages 3 and up; Day — Coed 3-21

Parksville, NY 12768. 361 Parksville Rd. Tel: 845-292-6821. Fax: 845-292-9492.
Contact (Sept-June): 5902 14th Ave, Brooklyn, NY 11219. Tel: 718-686-5930. Fax:
718-686-5935.
www.camphasc.org   E-mail: info@camphasc.org
Shmiel Kahn, Dir.
Adm: FCFS. Appl due: Feb. Enr: 300. Staff: Admin 10. Couns 225. Special needs 35.
LD Services: Acad_Instruction Mainstream.
Conditions accepted: Au CP Ep ID LD Phys_Impair Speech & Lang. **Therapy:** Art Music
Occup Phys Psych Rec Speech.
Features: Crafts Dance Drama Music Aquatics Baseball Basketball Gymnastics Softball
Swim Volleyball.
Fees 2012: Res $6500-7500 (+$450), 7 wks. Aid 2008 (Need): $130,000.
Housing: Cabins. Avg per room/unit: 12. **Swimming:** Pool.
Est 1972. Nonprofit. **Spons:** Hebrew Academy for Special Children. Jewish. **Ses:** 1. **Wks/**
ses: 7. Operates July-Aug.

Serving children and adults with mental retardation, the program provides academic
instruction, remedial reading, music, art, dance, aquatic sports and trips. Speech therapy,
occupational therapy, physical education and rehabilitation counseling are available.

CAMP HERTKO HOLLOW
Res — Coed Ages 6-18

Boone, IA. Tel: 515-897-9009. Fax: 352-259-4776.
101 Locust St, Des Moines, IA 50309. Tel: 515-471-8547. Fax: 515-288-2531.
Year-round Toll-free: 888-437-8652.
www.camphertkohollow.com   E-mail: camphertkohollow@aol.com
Vivian Murray, Dir.
Grades 1-PG. Adm: FCFS. Admitted: 100%. **Appl due:** Rolling. **Enr:** 200. **Enr cap:** 200.
Staff: Admin 3. Couns 35. Res 70. Special needs 30.
Conditions accepted: Diabetes.
Features: Crafts Aquatics Archery Canoe Climbing_Wall Hiking Riding Ropes_Crse
Basketball Equestrian Swim.
Fees 2014: Res $1100, 1 wk. Aid (Need).
Housing: Cabins. Avg per room/unit: 10. **Swimming:** Pool.
Est 1968. Nonprofit. **Ses:** 2. **Wks/ses:** 1. Operates June-July. ACA.

Activities at this camp for boys and girls with diabetes include horseback riding, swimming,
athletics, canoeing, rappelling, crafts, high and low ropes courses, archery, riflery, a zip line
and a climbing wall. Healthcare professionals and counselors provide diabetes education and
help campers gain independence. Hertko Hollow schedules the following special events: a
carnival, a talent contest, a dance and overnight trips.

CAMP HICKORY HILL
Res — Coed Ages 7-17

Columbia, MO 65205. PO Box 1942. Tel: 573-445-9146. Fax: 573-884-4609.
www.camphickoryhill.com   E-mail: camphickoryhill@gmail.com
Jessica La Mantia Bernhardt, Dir.
Adm: FCFS. Appl due: Rolling. Enr: 75. Staff: Admin 2. Couns 12. Special needs 4.
Conditions accepted: Diabetes.
Features: Crafts Aquatics Archery Boating Canoe Caving Fishing Hiking Rappelling Riflery
Ropes_Crse Basketball Soccer Softball Swim Tennis Volleyball.
Fees 2011: Res $1200, 1 wk.
Housing: Cabins. Avg per room/unit: 7. **Swimming:** Pool.
Est 1975. Nonprofit. **Ses:** 3. **Wks/ses:** 1. Operates July. ACA.

Campers at Hickory Hill learn more about diabetes and how to better manage it. The educational program includes one hour of formal classroom training per day in such subjects as insulin administration, insulin reactions, glucose monitoring, diet, complications and the emotional aspects of living with diabetes. In addition to learning more about their disease, campers take part in various recreational pursuits. Camp costs are determined along a sliding scale according to family income.

CAMP HO MITA KODA
Res — Coed Ages 6-15

Newbury, OH 44065. 14040 Auburn Rd. Tel: 440-564-5125.
Contact (Aug-May): c/o Diabetes Partnership of Cleveland, 3601 S Green Rd, Ste 100, Cleveland, OH 44122. Tel: 216-591-0800.
Year-round Fax: 216-591-0320.
www.diabetespartnership.org/CampHoMitaKoda
E-mail: camp@diabetespartnership.org
Cheri Collier, Dir.
Adm: FCFS. **Appl due:** Rolling. **Enr:** 64. **Staff:** Admin 10. Couns 16.
Conditions accepted: Diabetes.
Features: Sci Crafts Dance Music Theater Aquatics Archery Bicycle_Tours Boating Canoe Climbing_Wall Fishing Hiking Riding Ropes_Crse Survival_Trng Weight_Loss Baseball Basketball Equestrian Field_Hockey Football Softball Swim Tennis Volleyball Watersports.
Fees 2014: Res $750-1500, ½-2 wks.
Housing: Cabins. Avg per room/unit: 8. **Swimming:** Lake Pool.
Est 1929. Nonprofit. **Spons:** Diabetes Partnership of Cleveland. **Ses:** 5. **Wks/ses:** ½-2. Operates June-July. ACA.

Insulin-dependent children with Type 1 diabetes take part in music, art, and recreational and aquatic sports at Ho Mita Koda. The camp is open to any child with diabetes who is able to function in a normal summer camp setting. In addition to the main residential camp, Ho Mita Koda conducts a one-day mini-camp for children ages 4-10 and their siblings and parents.

CAMP HOLIDAY TRAILS
Res — Coed Ages 5-17

Charlottesville, VA 22903. 400 Holiday Trails Ln. Tel: 434-977-3781. Fax: 434-977-8814.
www.campholidaytrails.org **E-mail: campisgood@campholidaytrails.org**
Tina LaRoche, Exec Dir.
Grades K-12. Adm: FCFS. **Appl due:** Rolling. **Enr:** 60. **Enr cap:** 60. **Staff:** Admin 5. Couns 24. Res 27. Special needs 8.
Conditions accepted: As Blood Cancer C CP D Diabetes Ep HIV/AIDS Visual_Impair.
Focus: Health/Weight_Reduct. **Features:** Environ_Sci Sci Crafts Dance Drama Music Photog Aquatics Archery Canoe Climbing_Wall Community_Serv Conservation Cooking Fishing Hiking Kayak Outdoor_Ed Rappelling Riding Ropes_Crse Basketball Equestrian Football Lacrosse Soccer Swim Tennis Volleyball.
Fees 2014: Res $125, 1-2 wks. Aid 2009 (Need): $89,000.
Housing: Cabins. Avg per room/unit: 6. **Swimming:** Pool.
Est 1973. Nonprofit. **Ses:** 5. **Wks/ses:** 1-2. Operates June-Aug. ACA.

Located in the foothills of the Blue Ridge Mountains, near the University of Virginia and its medical center, the camp brings together children with special medical needs and chronic illnesses. One- and two-week sessions feature a full program of sports and therapeutic and educational activities. Family weekend camps and a weeklong family camp are available.

CAMP HONOR
Res — Coed Ages 8-17

Payson, AZ.
Contact (Year-round): c/o Hemophilia Assoc, 826 North 5th Ave, Phoenix, AZ 85003.
Tel: 602-955-3947. **Fax:** 602-955-1962.
www.arizonahemophilia.org/camp-programs   **E-mail:** info@hemophiliaz.org
Andy Blackledge, Dir.
Adm: FCFS. **Appl due:** Rolling. **Enr cap:** 126. **Staff:** Admin 20. Couns 60.
Conditions accepted: Blood HIV/AIDS.
Features: Circus_Skills Crafts Aquatics Archery Canoe Outdoor_Ed Paintball Basketball Skateboarding Swim.
Fees 2014: Res $35, 1 wk. Aid (Need).
Housing: Cabins. **Swimming:** Lake Pool.
Est 1994. Nonprofit. **Spons:** Hemophilia Association. **Ses:** 1. **Wks/ses:** 1. Operates June. ACA.

Camp HONOR (Hemophiliacs Overcoming New Obstacles Resourcefully) provides a traditional summer camp experience for children with such blood disorders as hemophilia, von Willebrand's disease and thrombophilia, as well as boys and girls who have been diagnosed with HIV/AIDS. Activities include swimming, canoeing, sports, archery and arts and crafts. Siblings may also enroll in the camp.

CAMP HORIZONS
Res — Coed Ages 8-39

South Windham, CT 06266. 127 Babcock Hill Rd.
Contact (Winter): PO Box 323, South Windham, CT 06266.
Year-round Tel: 860-456-1032, **Fax:** 860-456-4721.
www.horizonsct.org   **E-mail:** cmcnaboe@horizonsct.org
Scott Lambeck, Dir.
Adm: FCFS. **Appl due:** Rolling. **Enr:** 130. **Enr cap:** 130. **Staff:** Admin 16. Couns 75.
Conditions accepted: Au ID PDD.
Features: Crafts Dance Music Theater Aquatics Boating Exploration Fishing Riding Woodcraft Badminton Basketball Equestrian Golf Soccer Swim Tennis Volleyball Weight_Trng.
Fees 2012: Res $2372-8790, 2-8 wks.
Housing: Cabins. Avg per room/unit: 12. **Swimming:** Pool.
Est 1979. Nonprofit. **Ses:** 4. **Wks/ses:** 2-8. Operates June-Aug. ACA.

Horizons serves children and adults with developmental disabilities. Prominent offerings include horseback riding, aquatics, crafts, fitness activities and nature study. Pottery, boating, language arts, drama and vocational training are also available.

CAMP HUNTINGTON
Res — Coed Ages 6-21

High Falls, NY 12440. 56 Bruceville Rd, PO Box 37. Tel: 845-687-7840, 855-707-2267.
Fax: 845-853-1172.
www.camphuntington.com
Michael Bednarz, Exec Dir.
Adm: FCFS. **Appl due:** Rolling.
LD Services: Acad_Instruction.
Conditions accepted: ADD ADHD Asp Au ID LD PDD.
Features: Computers Art Crafts Drama Filmmaking Music Outdoor_Ed Riding Ropes_Crse Badminton Baseball Basketball Soccer Tennis Volleyball Handball Ping-Pong.
Fees 2014: Res $2150, 3 wks.
Housing: Cabins.
Est 1961. Ses: 3. **Wks/ses:** 3. Operates June-Aug. ACA.

Camp Huntington serves children and young adults with learning disabilities, neurological impairments, attentional disorders or mild to moderate developmental disabilities. A comprehensive schedule of recreational and educational activities includes work training for eligible teenagers and young adults.

CAMP INDEPENDENCE
Res — Coed Ages 8-18

Rutledge, GA.
Contact (Year-round): c/o National Kidney Foundation of Georgia, 2951 Flowers Rd S, Ste 211, Atlanta, GA 30341. **Tel:** 770-452-1539, 800-633-2339. **Fax:** 770-452-7564.
www.choa.org/campindependence **E-mail:** danielle.hall@kidney.org
Stephanie Oprea, Dir.
Adm: FCFS. **Appl due:** May.
Conditions accepted: Phys_Impair.
Features: Crafts Drama Aquatics Archery Bicycle_Tours Boating Canoe Climbing_Wall Fishing Mtn_Biking Riding Ropes_Crse Basketball Softball Swim Tennis.
Fees 2014: Free (in-state residents). Res 1 wk.
Housing: Cabins. **Swimming:** Pool.
Est 1973. Nonprofit. **Spons:** National Kidney Foundation of Georgia. **Ses:** 1. **Wks/ses:** 1. Operates July-Aug.

Held at the Camp Twin Lakes facility in Georgia, Camp Independence serves children who have been diagnosed with kidney disease, are on dialysis, or have had a kidney, heart, lung or liver transplant. The program is free for Georgia and Alabama residents. Activities include swimming, music, computers, art, dance and sports.

JAMESON CAMP
Res — Coed Ages 7-17

Indianapolis, IN 46231. 2001 Bridgeport Rd, PO Box 31156. **Tel:** 317-241-2661. **Fax:** 317-241-2760.
www.jamesoncamp.org **E-mail:** registrar@jamesoncamp.org
Tim Nowak, Prgm Dir.
Grades 1-12. Adm: FCFS. **Appl due:** Rolling. **Enr:** 75. **Enr cap:** 80. **Staff:** Admin 9. Couns 34. Special needs 1.
Conditions accepted: ADD ADHD As Asp Diabetes ED HIV/AIDS LD.
Features: Writing/Journ Crafts Dance Drama Aquatics Archery Climbing_Wall Community_ Serv Cooking Fishing Hiking Ropes_Crse Wilderness_Camp Basketball Soccer Swim Volleyball.
Fees 2014: Res $80-525, 1 wk.
Housing: Cabins. Avg per room/unit: 8. **Swimming:** Pool.
Est 1928. Nonprofit. **Ses:** 7. **Wks/ses:** 1. Operates June-July. ACA.

Serving children who may have minor social, emotional and behavioral challenges, Jameson also enrolls those who have been impacted by HIV or AIDS. Campers choose from a host of traditional summer activities. All fees are determined along a sliding scale according to family income.

CAMP JUMP START
Res — Coed Ages 9-17

Imperial, MO 63052. 3602 Lions Den Rd. **Tel:** 636-287-5004.
www.campjumpstart.com **E-mail:** contact@campjumpstart.com
Jean Huelsing, Dir.
Grades 6-12. Adm: FCFS. **Appl due:** Rolling. **Enr:** 120.

Focus: Health/Weight_Reduct. **Features:** Crafts Dance Drama Aquatics Bicycle_Tours Canoe Caving Conservation Fishing Hiking Mtn_Biking Rappelling Riding Rock_Climb Ropes_Crse Aerobics Baseball Basketball Equestrian Field_Hockey Football Martial_ Arts Soccer Softball Swim Volleyball Watersports.
Fees 2014: Res $3995-7295, 4-8 wks.
Housing: Cabins. Avg per room/unit: 10. **Swimming:** Lake Pool.
Est 2003. Ses: 3. **Wks/ses:** 4-8. Operates June-Aug. ACA.

This weight-loss camp emphasizes self-discipline and the development of an improved self-image as part of the camper's lifestyle adjustment. Boys and girls participate in fitness activities, behavior modification and nutrition education while eating balanced, portion-controlled meals. A self-defense program seeks to increase campers' confidence and self-esteem. Other activities include caving, rock climbing, mountain biking and talent shows.

CAMP KINGSMONT
Res — Coed Ages 9-18

Amherst, MA 01002. 893 West St. Tel: 413-835-5689.
Contact (Sept-May): 1638 1st Pl, McLean, VA 22101. Tel: 703-288-0047.
Year-round Toll-free: 877-348-2267, Fax: 703-288-0075.
www.campkingsmont.com   E-mail: info@campkingsmont.com
Danny Heisler, Dir.
Grades 4-12. Adm: FCFS. Admitted: 95%. **Appl due:** Rolling. **Enr:** 250. **Enr cap:** 350.
Staff: Admin 4. Couns 55. Res 59. Special needs 6.
LD Services: Tut.
Focus: Health/Weight_Reduct. **Features:** Crafts Music Theater Aquatics Archery Bicycle_Tours Cooking Hiking Mtn_Biking Mtn_Trips Paintball Riding Ropes_Crse White-water_Raft Aerobics Badminton Baseball Basketball Field_Hockey Football Golf Lacrosse Soccer Softball Street_Hockey Swim Tennis Track Ultimate_Frisbee Volleyball Watersports Weight_Trng.
Fees 2013: Res $2495-7995, 2-8 wks. Aid 2009 (Need): $100,000.
Housing: Dorms. Avg per room/unit: 2-3. **Swimming:** Lake Pool.
Est 1971. Nonprofit. **Ses:** 28. **Wks/ses:** 2-8. Operates June-Aug. ACA.

Kingsmont offers campers a specialized health and fitness program designed for weight reduction. Boys and girls take cooking and nutrition classes, and the camp emphasizes behavior modification as a means to improve eating habits and lead a more active lifestyle. A full range of traditional activities includes arts and crafts, individual and team sports, riding, canoeing, hiking and bicycling. Campers with diabetes and other weight-related conditions may enroll.

CAMP KODIAK
Res — Coed Ages 6-18

McKellar, P0G 1C0 Ontario, Canada. Gen Delivery. Tel: 705-389-1910. Fax: 705-389-1911.
Contact (Sept-June): 4069 Pheasant Run, Mississauga, L5L 2C2 Ontario, Canada. Tel: 905-569-7595. Fax: 905-569-6045.
Year-round Toll-free: 877-569-7595.
www.campkodiak.com   E-mail: info@campkodiak.com
David Stoch, Dir.
Adm: FCFS. **Appl due:** Rolling. **Enr:** 234. **Enr cap:** 234. **Staff:** Admin 35. Couns 90.
Special needs 6.
LD Services: Acad_Instruction Tut.
Conditions accepted: ADD ADHD Asp Dx LD Speech & Lang. **Therapy:** Art Music Rec.
Features: Computers Environ_Sci Expository_Writing Crafts Creative_Writing Dance Drama Filmmaking Fine_Arts Music Painting Photog Pottery Aquatics Archery Boating Canoe Chess Climbing_Wall Conservation Cooking Fishing Hiking Kayak Outdoor_Ed Rappelling Riding Rock_Climb Ropes_Crse Sail Survival_Trng Aerobics Badminton Baseball Basketball Cross-country Equestrian Football Golf Gymnastics Martial_Arts

Soccer Softball Swim Tennis Ultimate_Frisbee Volleyball Water-skiing Watersports Weight_Trng Wrestling Rocketry. **Fees 2014: Res $4275-8675, 3-7 wks. Housing:** Cabins. Avg per room/unit: 9. **Swimming:** Lake. **Est 1991.** Inc. **Ses:** 3. **Wks/ses:** 3-7. Operates June-Aug.

On a 425-acre site northeast of Parry Sound, Kodiak offers recreational camping activities, a social skills program and academic tutoring for children with learning disabilities, attentional disorders and Asperger's syndrome. Each morning, campers engage in one hour of enrichment course work or receive an hour of individual or small-group academic tutoring. The remainder of the day, boys and girls participate in traditional camping activities.

CAMP KORELITZ
Res — Coed Ages 8-15

Hamilton, OH.
Contact (Year-round): 4555 Lake Forest Dr, Ste 396, Cincinnati, OH 45242. Tel: 513-759-9330. Fax: 513-421-2203.
www.diabetes.org/adacampkorelitz **E-mail: ecrosby@diabetes.org**
Erin Crosby, Dir.
Adm: FCFS. **Appl due:** June. **Enr:** 150. **Enr cap:** 160. **Staff:** Admin 1. Couns 35. Res 75. Special needs 30.
Conditions accepted: Diabetes.
Features: Crafts Dance Aquatics Archery Bicycle_Tours Canoe Climbing_Wall Fishing Hiking Mtn_Biking Outdoor_Ed Rock_Climb Ropes_Crse Wilderness_Camp Woodcraft Baseball Basketball Field_Hockey Football Lacrosse Soccer Softball Street_Hockey Swim Ultimate_Frisbee Volleyball Watersports.
Fees 2014: Res $550-575, 1 wk. Aid 2011 (Need): $30,000.
Housing: Cabins. Avg per room/unit: 10. **Swimming:** Pool.
Est 1978. Nonprofit. **Spons:** American Diabetes Association. **Ses:** 1. **Wks/ses:** 1. Operates Aug.

Korelitz offers diabetes management instruction (for both Type 1 and Type 2 diabetes), as well as nature study and ecology. Other activities include team sports, waterfront games, campfires, arts and crafts, drama and archery.

CAMP KOSTOPULOS
Res — Coed Ages 7 and up

Salt Lake City, UT 84108. 2500 Emigration Canyon. Tel: 801-582-0700. Fax: 801-583-5176.
www.campk.org **E-mail: information@campk.org**
Michael Divricean, Dir.
Adm: FCFS. Admitted: 100%. **Appl due:** Rolling. **Enr:** 50. **Enr cap:** 50. **Staff:** Admin 6. Couns 30. Special needs 3.
Travel: UT WY.
Conditions accepted: ADD ADHD Asp Au CP D ED Ep ID LD Phys_Impair Speech & Lang TBI Visual_Impair OCD. **Therapy:** Rec.
Features: Crafts Dance Drama Music Adventure_Travel Aquatics Canoe Climbing_Wall Fishing Hiking Mtn_Trips Ropes_Crse Social_Servs Wilderness_Camp Equestrian Swim.
Fees 2014: Res $425, 1 wk. Aid (Need).
Housing: Cabins Lodges Tents Tepees. **Swimming:** Pool.
Est 1958. Nonprofit. **Ses:** 11. **Wks/ses:** 1. Operates June-Aug. ACA.

Kostopulos offers recreational opportunities for special-needs individuals of all ages and all ability levels. Activities include music, riding, nature study, arts and crafts, swimming, fishing, canoeing and hiking. In addition, Kostopulos conducts trips to Jackson Hole, WY, and to Yellowstone, Arches and Zion national parks.

CAMP KREM
Res — Coed Ages 5 and up

Boulder Creek, CA.
Contact (Year-round): 4610 Whitesands Ct, El Sobrante, CA 94803. Tel: 510-222-6662. Fax: 510-223-3046.
www.campingunlimited.com   E-mail: campkrem@gmail.com
Mary Farfaglia, Exec Dir.
Adm: FCFS. **Appl due:** Rolling. **Enr cap:** 85. **Staff:** Admin 18. Couns 55. Special needs 5.
Conditions accepted: ADD ADHD Asp Au CP ED ID LD Phys_Impair TBI.
Features: Crafts Dance Drama Fine_Arts Music Painting Adventure_Travel Aquatics Canoe Community_Serv Cooking Exploration Hiking Outdoor_Ed Sail White-water_ Raft Wilderness_Camp Woodcraft Work Badminton Baseball Basketball Soccer Softball Swim Volleyball Watersports.
Fees 2014: Res $700-1400, 1-2 wks. Aid (Need).
Housing: Cabins Tents. Avg per room/unit: 7. **Swimming:** Pool.
Est 1957. Nonprofit. **Spons:** Camping Unlimited. **Ses:** 6. **Wks/ses:** 1-2. Operates June-Aug. ACA.

Camp Krem offers various free-choice programs for children and adults with disabilities. Activities include daily swimming, hiking, field trips, arts and crafts, music, drama, backpacking, independent living skills, talent shows and theme-based events. Outdoor adventure and travel programs enable campers to experience challenges and develop more independence.

CAMP LA JOLLA
Res — Coed Ages 10-17

La Jolla, CA.
Contact (Year-round): 176 C Ave, Coronado, CA 92118. Tel: 619-435-7990, 800-825-8746. Fax: 619-435-8188.
www.camplajolla.com   E-mail: camp@camplajolla.com
Judith Wood, Exec Dir.
Grades 5-12. Adm: FCFS. **Appl due:** Rolling. **Enr:** 250. **Staff:** Admin 10. Couns 60.
Focus: Health/Weight_Reduct. **Features:** Crafts Dance Aquatics Climbing_Wall Cooking Hiking Kayak Mtn_Biking Rock_Climb Yoga Aerobics Basketball Football Martial_Arts Soccer Softball Swim Tennis Ultimate_Frisbee Volleyball Watersports Weight_Trng.
Fees 2014: Res $7500-13,250 (+$200), 3-8 wks.
Housing: Dorms. **Swimming:** Ocean Pool.
Est 1979. Inc. **Ses:** 6. **Wks/ses:** 2-8. Operates June-July. ACA.

This weight-loss and fitness camp combines a focus on healthy lifestyle changes with classes in nutrition and behavior modification. La Jolla also provides a 10-month follow-up program for its campers. Separate programs serve preteens, teens, boys and young adults.

CAMP LAUREL
Res and Day — Coed Ages 6-17

Pasadena, CA 91105. 75 S Grand Ave. Tel: 626-683-0800. Fax: 626-683-0890.
www.laurel-foundation.org   E-mail: info@laurel-foundation.org
Margot Anderson, Exec Dir.
Adm: FCFS. **Appl due:** Rolling. **Enr:** 90. **Enr cap:** 90. **Staff:** Admin 4. Couns 200. Special needs 10.
Conditions accepted: HIV/AIDS. **Therapy:** Art Psych Rec.
Features: Ecol Environ_Sci Writing/Journ Crafts Creative_Writing Music Photog Theater Adventure_Travel Aquatics Archery Canoe Climbing_Wall Conservation Hiking Kayak Mtn_Biking Outdoor_Ed Riding Rock_Climb Ropes_Crse Survival_Trng Wilderness_ Camp Baseball Basketball Soccer Softball Swim Volleyball Watersports.
Fees 2014: Free. Res 1 wk. Day 1 wk.

Housing: Cabins. **Swimming:** Lake Pool.
Est 1993. Nonprofit. **Ses:** 2. **Wks/ses:** 1. Operates July. ACA.

Children living with HIV or AIDS choose from traditional, adventure and leadership challenge programs at the camp. Neither overnight nor day campers incur a fee for attendance. Activities focus upon the camper's mental, physical, social and spiritual development.

CAMP LEE MAR
Res — Coed Ages 7-21

Lackawaxen, PA 18435. 450 Rte 590. Tel: 570-685-7188. Fax: 570-685-7590.
Contact (Sept-May): 805 Redgate Rd, Dresher, PA 19025. Tel: 215-658-1708. Fax: 215-658-1710.
www.leemar.com   E-mail: gtour400@aol.com
Lee Morrone, Dir.
Adm: FCFS. **Appl due:** Rolling. **Enr:** 160. **Fac 25. Staff:** Admin 15. Couns 70.
Conditions accepted: ADD ADHD Asp ID LD Speech & Lang.
Features: Speech Crafts Dance Music Work Basketball Football Swim Tennis.
Fees 2014: Res $10,100, 7 wks.
Housing: Cabins. **Swimming:** Pool.
Est 1953. Inc. **Ses:** 1. **Wks/ses:** 7. Operates June-Aug. ACA.

Children with mild to moderate developmental disabilities engage in academics, speech and language therapies, vocational training and recreation at Lee Mar. The academic program focuses on skill development in the areas of communication, reading and math. Activities include waterfront activities, tennis, calisthenics and perceptual-motor training.

LIONS CAMP MERRICK
Res — Coed Ages 6-16

Nanjemoy, MD 20662. 3650 Rick Hamilton Pl, PO Box 56. Tel: 301-870-5858. Fax: 301-246-9108.
Contact (Oct-May): 3050 Crain Hwy, Ste 202, PO Box 375, Waldorf, MD 20604. Tel: 301-645-5616. Fax: 301-374-2282.
www.lionscampmerrick.org   E-mail: campofficelcm@aol.com
Heidi Fick, Dir.
Adm: FCFS. Admitted: 99%. **Appl due:** Rolling. **Enr:** 85. **Enr cap:** 90. **Staff:** Admin 2. Couns 30. Res 1.
Conditions accepted: D Diabetes Visual_Impair.
Features: Crafts Dance Drama Aquatics Archery Canoe Climbing_Wall Community_ Serv Fishing Hiking Ropes_Crse Baseball Basketball Football Soccer Softball Swim Volleyball.
Fees 2014: Res $850-2400 (+$5), 1 wk. Aid 2009 (Need): $42,002.
Housing: Cabins Houses. Avg per room/unit: 12. **Swimming:** Pool.
Est 1980. Nonprofit. **Ses:** 7. **Wks/ses:** 1. Operates June-Sept. ACA.

This recreational camp offers separate programs for children who are deaf or hard-of-hearing, children who are blind and children who have diabetes. A complete waterfront program features swimming and canoeing, and other activities include a climbing wall, a high and low ropes course, sports, arts and crafts, and various outdoor pursuits.

LIONS CAMP TATIYEE
Res — Coed Ages 7 and up

Mesa, AZ 85216. PO Box 6910. Tel: 480-380-4254.
www.arizonalionscamp.org   E-mail: info@arizonalionscamp.org
Pamela Swanson, Exec Dir.
Adm: FCFS. **Enr cap:** 600.

Conditions accepted: CP D ID Phys_Impair Visual_Impair.
Features: Sci Crafts Dance Archery Cooking Fishing Rock_Climb Swim.
Fees 2014: Free. Res 1 wk.
Swimming: Pool.
Est 1961. Ses: 8. Wks/ses: 1. Operates June-Aug. ACA.

Sponsored by the Lions of Arizona, Lions Camp Tatiyee serves children and adults with physical handicaps, including those with cerebral palsy or visual or hearing impairments. Separate sessions serve adults, young adults, children and individuals with hearing impairments. Activities include arts and crafts, swimming, sports, games, camp outs, talent shows and movies.

CAMP LITTLE GIANT
Res — Coed Ages 8 and up; Day — Coed 7 and up

Carbondale, IL 62901. c/o Touch of Nature Environmental Ctr, Southern Illinois Univ, Mail Code 6888. Tel: 618-453-1121. Fax: 618-453-1188.
www.ton.siu.edu/programs/summer_camps/camp-little-giant/index.html
E-mail: tonec@siu.edu
Vicki Lang-Mendenhall, Dir.
Adm: FCFS. **Appl due:** Rolling. **Enr:** 80. **Enr cap:** 80. **Staff:** Admin 5. Couns 28. Special needs 1.
Conditions accepted: ADD ADHD Asp Au CP D Diabetes Dx ED Ep ID LD Phys_Impair Speech & Lang TBI Visual_Impair MD. **Therapy:** Rec.
Features: Ecol Environ_Sci Speech Crafts Dance Drama Music Painting Aquatics Boating Fishing Hiking Outdoor_Ed Riding Baseball Basketball Equestrian Softball Swim Volleyball.
Fees 2011: Res $500-2100, 1-2 wks. Aid 2011 (Need): $12,000.
Housing: Cabins. Avg per room/unit: 3-8. **Swimming:** Lake.
Est 1952. Nonprofit. **Spons:** Southern Illinois University. **Ses:** 8. **Wks/ses:** 1-2. Operates June-Aug. ACA.

Little Giant accepts children and adults with physical, developmental, cognitive and social disabilities. Swimming, arts and crafts, hayrides, special events, horseback riding, boating, games and sports are among the activities offered.

CAMP LITTLE RED DOOR
Res — Coed Ages 8-18

Martinsville, IN.
Contact (Year-round): c/o Little Red Door Cancer Agency, 1801 N Meridian St, Indianapolis, IN 46202. Tel: 317-925-5595. Fax: 317-925-5597.
www.littlereddoor.org   E-mail: mail@littlereddoor.org
Fred Duncan, Dir.
Adm: FCFS. **Appl due:** Rolling. **Enr:** 96. **Enr cap:** 96. **Staff:** Admin 10. Couns 50. Res 10. Special needs 5.
Conditions accepted: Cancer. **Therapy:** Rec.
Features: Crafts Aquatics Archery Canoe Climbing_Wall Community_Serv Conservation Exploration Hiking Outdoor_Ed Rappelling Riding Ropes_Crse Survival_Trng Wilderness_Camp Wilderness_Canoe Equestrian Swim.
Fees 2011: Res $25, 1 wk. Aid (Need).
Housing: Cabins Tents. Avg per room/unit: 10. **Swimming:** Lake Pool.
Est 1981. Nonprofit. **Spons:** Little Red Door Cancer Agency. **Ses:** 1. **Wks/ses:** 1. Operates July.

Camp Little Red Door serves children with cancer and, space permitting, one sibling per camper. All campers must have received or be receiving treatment in the state of Indiana. Older campers participate in the leadership program and mentor younger children. Activities include hiking, swimming, horseback riding, canoeing, archery, challenge course, and arts and crafts.

MARBRIDGE SUMMER CAMP
Res — Coed Ages 16-30

Manchaca, TX 78652. PO Box 2250. Tel: 512-282-1144. Fax: 512-282-3723.
www.marbridge.org/enrichment/summer-camp.php   E-mail: info@marbridge.org
Barbara Bush, Dir.
Adm: FCFS. **Appl due:** Apr. **Enr cap:** 223. **Staff:** Admin 1. Couns 6. Special needs 3.
LD Services: Acad_Instruction.
Conditions accepted: Asp Au CP ID LD PDD Speech & Lang TBI DS. **Therapy:** Art Music Occup Phys Rec.
Features: Crafts Dance Music Aquatics Hiking Ranch Riding Baseball Basketball Equestrian Softball Swim.
Fees 2014: Res $665 (+$10-20), 1 wk.
Housing: Cabins Houses. Avg per room/unit: 8. **Swimming:** Pool.
Est 1999. Nonprofit. **Ses:** 98. **Wks/ses:** 1. Operates June-Aug.

Located on a 300-acre ranch near Austin, Marbridge offers a varied recreational program to campers with a developmental disability or a cognitive challenge. Activities are adapted to meet campers' interest, skill and age levels and positively reinforce the progress that each person makes in problem solving, interpersonal communications, self-assurance and independent living tasks. Out-of-camp day trips, horseback riding, swimming and a low ropes course are part of the program. All applicants must be ambulatory.

CAMP MARK SEVEN
Res — Coed Ages 9-16

Old Forge, NY 13420. 144 Mohawk Hotel Rd. Tel: 315-357-6089. Fax: 315-357-6403.
Contact (Sept-May): PO Box 45, Boyds, MD 20841. Tel: 240-575-2073. Fax: 301-663-6174.
Year-round Toll-free: 866-572-9102.
www.campmark7.org   E-mail: deafdir@campmark7.org
David Staehle, Dir.
Adm: FCFS. **Appl due:** Rolling. **Enr:** 72. **Enr cap:** 74. **Staff:** Admin 10. Couns 16. Res 50.
Conditions accepted: D.
Features: Crafts Painting Theater Aquatics Boating Canoe Hiking Mtn_Trips Sail White-water_Raft Wilderness_Camp Wilderness_Canoe Basketball Equestrian Soccer Swim Tennis Volleyball Water-skiing Watersports.
Fees 2014: Res $400-1150, 1-2 wks. Aid (Need).
Housing: Lodges. Avg per room/unit: 2-6. **Swimming:** Lake.
Est 1981. Nonprofit. **Spons:** Mark Seven Deaf Foundation. Roman Catholic. **Ses:** 2. **Wks/ses:** 1-2. Operates July-Aug. ACA.

This intensive American Sign Language program facilitates learning with classroom instruction, recreational activities and a deaf culture. Classifiers, discourse, storytelling, pragmatics, semantics, nonmanual grammar and linguistics of ASL are all part of the program. CM7 boys and girls engage in an array of traditional camp activities.

MEADOWOOD SPRINGS SPEECH AND HEARING CAMP
Res — Coed Ages 6-16; Day — Coed 5-11

Weston, OR.
Contact (Year-round): 316 SE Emigrant Ave, PO Box 1025, Pendleton, OR 97801.
Tel: 541-276-2752. Fax: 541-276-7227.
www.meadowoodsprings.org   E-mail: info@meadowoodsprings.org
Adm: FCFS. **Appl due:** May. **Enr:** 60. **Staff:** Admin 2. Couns 50.
Conditions accepted: D LD Speech & Lang. **Therapy:** Speech.
Features: Crafts Canoe Soccer Swim Volleyball.
Fees 2012: Res $1500, 1 wk. Day $350, ½ wk.
Housing: Cabins Dorms Lodges. **Swimming:** Pool.

Est 1964. Nonprofit. **Ses:** 3. **Wks/ses:** ½-1. Operates July.

Designed to help young people with diagnosed speech, hearing or language difficulties, Meadowood offers campers a full range of recreational and clinical activities, including swimming, canoeing, fishing, camp outs, nature hikes, and arts and crafts. Boys and girls typically improve their communicational skills during the course of the camp.

CAMP MERRY HEART
Res and Day — Coed Ages 5 and up

Hackettstown, NJ 07840. 21 O'Brien Rd. Tel: 908-852-3896. Fax: 908-852-9263.
www.eastersealsnj.org   E-mail: camp@nj.easterseals.com
Todd Thompson, Dir.
Adm: FCFS.
Conditions accepted: ID LD Phys_Impair.
Features: Crafts Dance Music Aquatics Canoe Climbing_Wall Fishing Kayak Ropes_Crse Basketball Soccer Swim.
Fees 2011: Res $1100-2150, 1-2 wks. Aid (Need).
Housing: Cabins. **Swimming:** Pool.
Est 1949. Nonprofit. **Spons:** Easter Seals New Jersey. **Wks/ses:** 1-2. Operates Year-round.

New Jersey children and adults with developmental and physical challenges and learning disabilities follow an organized program of music, arts and crafts, a ropes course, swimming, boating and nature study.

MID-SOUTH ARC SUMMER CAMP
Res — Coed Ages 8 and up

Memphis, TN 38111. 3485 Poplar Ave, Ste 210. Tel: 901-327-2473. Fax: 901-327-2687.
www.thearcmidsouth.org/familyservices.htm   E-mail: info@thearcmidsouth.org
Michelle Alexander, Coord.
Adm: FCFS. **Appl due:** Rolling. **Enr:** 30. **Staff:** Couns 17.
Conditions accepted: As Au CP ED ID LD Phys_Impair Speech & Lang TBI Visual_Impair.
Features: Crafts Dance Fine_Arts Music Baseball Basketball Football Golf Swim Volleyball.
Fees 2011: Res $400, 1 wk. Aid (Need).
Housing: Cabins. **Swimming:** Pool.
Est 1967. Nonprofit. **Ses:** 2. **Wks/ses:** 1. Operates July.

The camp enables individuals with developmental disabilities to develop socially, physically and emotionally. Activities include arts and crafts, hiking, music, games, dancing, swimming, fishing, socializing, special guests, celebrity entertainment and campfires.

CAMP MITTON
Res — Coed Ages 7-13

Brewster, MA 02631. 46 Featherbed Ln. Tel: 508-385-0951. Fax: 508-385-0953.
Contact (Sept-May): 119 Myrtle St, Duxbury, MA 02332. Tel: 781-834-2700. Fax: 781-834-2701.
Year-round Toll-free: 888-543-7284.
www.crossroads4kids.org   E-mail: registrar@crossroads4kids.org
Lisa Bower & Michael Clancy, Co-Dirs.
Adm: FCFS. **Appl due:** Apr. **Enr:** 192. **Enr cap:** 192. **Staff:** Admin 5. Couns 30. Special needs 1.
Conditions accepted: ADD ADHD ED.
Features: Computers Ecol Environ_Sci Crafts Creative_Writing Dance Drama Fine_Arts Music Aquatics Canoe Exploration Hiking Mtn_Trips Rock_Climb Baseball Basketball Football Soccer Softball Swim Volleyball.

Fees 2014: Res $490-700, 2-3 wks.
Housing: Cabins. **Swimming:** Lake.
Est 1936. Nonprofit. **Spons:** Crossroads for Kids. **Ses:** 3. **Wks/ses:** 2-3. Operates June-Aug. ACA.

This Crossroads for Kids program serves children from Cape Cod and Greater Boston who have experienced or are still experiencing crisis situations in the form of homelessness, abuse or neglect. Mitton's small, structured program helps boys and girls better cope with their situations by combining anger and behavior management instruction with noncompetitive camp activities.

MUSCULAR DYSTROPHY ASSOCIATION SUMMER CAMP
Res — Coed Ages 6-17

Tucson, AZ 85718. 3300 E Sunrise Dr. Tel: 520-529-2000, 800-572-1717. Fax: 520-529-5300.
http://mda.org/summer-camp   E-mail: healthcareservices@mdausa.org
Jodi Wolff, Dir.
Adm: FCFS. **Appl due:** Rolling.
Locations: AK AL AR AZ CA CO CT DC DE FL GA HI IO ID IL IN KS KY LA MA MD ME MI MN MO MI MT NC NE NH NJ NM NV NY OH OK OR PA PR RI SC SD TN TX UT VA VT WA WI WV WY.
Conditions accepted: MD.
Features: Crafts Archery Boating Fishing Riding Soccer Softball Swim.
Fees 2014: Free. Res 1 wk.
Swimming: Pool.
Est 1955. Nonprofit. **Ses:** 80. **Wks/ses:** 1. Operates June-Aug.

A nationwide network of approximately 80 MDA-sponsored summer camp sessions offers a wide range of programs for young people with neuromuscular diseases. Activities, designed for children who have limited mobility or who use wheelchairs and geared to the abilities of campers, range from outdoor sports such as swimming, boating, baseball and horseback riding to less physically demanding programs like arts and crafts and talent shows. At most camps, counselors work one-on-one with campers on a 24-hour basis.

NATIONAL CAMPS FOR BLIND CHILDREN
Res — Coed Ages 9-65

Lincoln, NE 68506. PO Box 6097. Tel: 402-488-0981. Fax: 402-488-7582.
www.blindcamp.org   E-mail: info@christianrecord.org
Peggy Hansen, Dir.
Adm: FCFS. **Appl due:** Rolling.
Locations: AR CA CO FL ID IN MI TN Canada.
Conditions accepted: Visual_Impair.
Features: Marine_Bio/Stud Crafts Archery Bicycle_Tours Canoe Climbing_Wall Hiking Rappelling Rock_Climb Ropes_Crse Sail Sea_Cruises Woodcraft Baseball Basketball Equestrian Golf Softball Swim Water-skiing Watersports.
Fees 2014: Free. Res 1 wk.
Housing: Cabins Dorms. Avg per room/unit: 4. **Swimming:** Lake Pool.
Est 1967. Nonprofit. **Spons:** Christian Record Services. Seventh-day Adventist. **Ses:** 13. **Wks/ses:** 1. Operates June-Aug.

Christian Record Services operates programs throughout the country and in Canada for legally blind individuals. Activities include archery, beeper baseball, beeper basketball, watersports, tandem bicycling, crafts, hiking, rock climbing and horseback riding. Attendees must be able to take care of their personal needs. Campers attend free of charge, although they pay a nominal processing fee.

CAMP NEEDLEPOINT
Res — Coed Ages 8-16; Day — Coed 5-9

Hudson, WI.
Contact (Year-round): c/o American Diabetes Assoc, 5100 Gamble Dr, Ste 394, St Louis Park, MN 55416. **Tel:** 763-593-5333, 888-342-2383. **Fax:** 952-582-9000.
www.diabetes.org/adacampneedlepoint   **E-mail:** rbarnett@diabetes.org
Becky Barnett, Dir.
Adm: FCFS. **Appl due:** Rolling. **Enr:** 425. **Staff:** Admin 2. Couns 60. Special needs 2.
Conditions accepted: Diabetes.
Features: Crafts Archery Boating Canoe Climbing_Wall Kayak Riding Rock_Climb Ropes_ Crse Sail Wilderness_Camp Wilderness_Canoe Basketball Equestrian Soccer Swim Tennis Ultimate_Frisbee Volleyball.
Fees 2014: Res $375-1175, ½-1 **wks.** Aid 2007 (Need): $75,000.
Housing: Cabins Tents. Avg per room/unit: 9. **Swimming:** River.
Est 1957. Nonprofit. **Spons:** American Diabetes Association. **Ses:** 3. **Wks/ses:** ½-1. Operates Aug.

Sponsored by the American Diabetes Association, this camp for children living with diabetes offers a varied recreational program. Activities include swimming, sailing, rock climbing and athletics, among others. Needlepoint also schedules two- and three-night wilderness canoeing trips.

CAMP NEJEDA
Res — Coed Ages 7-16

Stillwater, NJ 07875. 910 Saddleback Rd, PO Box 156. Tel: 973-383-2611. Fax: 973-383-9891.
www.campnejeda.org   **E-mail:** information@campnejeda.org
Jim Daschbach, Dir.
Adm: FCFS. **Appl due:** Rolling. **Enr:** 80. **Enr cap:** 80. **Staff:** Admin 3. Couns 45.
Conditions accepted: Diabetes.
Features: Aquatics Archery Bicycle_Tours Boating Canoe Fishing Hiking Kayak Mtn_ Biking Ropes_Crse Sail Baseball Basketball Soccer Softball Swim Tennis Volleyball.
Fees 2014: Res $950-1850 (+$25), 1-2 **wks.** Aid 2009 (Need): $110,000.
Housing: Cabins Tepees. Avg per room/unit: 8. **Swimming:** Pond Pool.
Est 1958. Nonprofit. **Ses:** 4. **Wks/ses:** 1-2. Operates June-Aug. ACA.

Serving children with Type 1 diabetes, Nejeda provides an active and safe camping experience that helps them learn about and understand their disorder. Activities include boating, swimming, fishing, archery, sports, nature lore and crafts, as well as camping skills instruction.

CAMP NEW HOPE
Res — Coed Ages 6 and up

McGregor, MN 55760. 53035 Lake Ave.
Contact (Sept-May): c/o Friendship Ventures, 10509 108th St NW, Annandale, MN 55302.
Year-round Tel: 952-852-0101, 800-450-8376. **Fax:** 952-852-0123.
www.friendshipventures.org   **E-mail:** info@friendshipventures.org
Laurie Tschetter, Exec Dir.
Adm: FCFS. **Appl due:** Rolling. **Enr:** 30. **Enr cap:** 30. **Staff:** Admin 3. Couns 20.
Conditions accepted: ADD ADHD Au ID Phys_Impair.
Features: Crafts Dance Music Theater Aquatics Canoe Fishing Hiking Social_Servs Wilderness_Camp Basketball Softball Swim Volleyball.
Fees 2012: Res $1299-1559, 1 **wk.** Aid (Need).
Housing: Cabins. Avg per room/unit: 10. **Swimming:** Lake.

Est 1968. Nonprofit. **Spons:** Friendship Ventures. **Ses:** 6. **Wks/ses:** 1. Operates July-Aug. ACA.

New Hope provides recreational and educational services for youth and adults with developmental and physical disabilities. Activities include arts and crafts, music, swimming, boating, fishing and nature study.

NEW IMAGE CAMP POCONO TRAILS
Res — Coed Ages 7-19

Reeders, PA.
Contact (Year-round): PO Box 417, Norwood, NJ 07648. Tel: 201-750-1557, 800-365-0556. Fax: 201-750-1558.
www.newimagecamp.com   E-mail: tsparber@aol.com
Tony Sparber & Dale Sparber, Dirs.
Adm: FCFS. **Appl due:** Rolling.
Focus: Health/Weight_Reduct. **Features:** Dance Drama Aquatics Archery Climbing_Wall Hiking Riding Ropes_Crse Basketball Football Golf Ice_Hockey Soccer Softball Swim Tennis Track Volleyball Water-skiing Weight_Trng.
Fees 2014: Res $2690-6390 (+$200), 1½-7½ wks.
Housing: Cabins. **Swimming:** Lake Pool.
Est 1991. Inc. **Ses:** 11. **Wks/ses:** 1½-7½. Operates June-Aug. ACA.

Combining exercise, recreation and nutrition consultation, the camp helps boys and girls lose two to four pounds per week in a noncompetitive setting. The program does not include pills, drugs or food supplements, instead focusing on healthy eating habits and lifestyle changes. Campers who have vegetarian, Kosher or other special dietary requirements are accommodated. See the separate New Image listing under Lake Wales, FL.

NEW IMAGE CAMP VANGUARD
Res — Coed Ages 7-19

Lake Wales, FL.
Contact (Year-round): PO Box 417, Norwood, NJ 07648. Tel: 201-750-1557, 800-365-0556. Fax: 201-750-1558.
www.newimagecamp.com   E-mail: tsparber@aol.com
Maxine Spadaro, Dir.
Adm: FCFS. **Appl due:** Rolling.
Focus: Health/Weight_Reduct. **Features:** Crafts Dance Theater Mtn_Biking Paintball Ropes_Crse Yoga Cheerleading Football Soccer Softball Swim Ultimate_Frisbee Volleyball Weight_Trng.
Fees 2014: Res $3650-8090, 2-6 wks.
Housing: Dorms. **Swimming:** Pool.
Est 1991. Inc. **Ses:** 8. **Wks/ses:** 2-6. Operates June-Aug. ACA.

See program description under Reeders, PA.

NEW JERSEY CAMP JAYCEE
Res — Coed Ages 7 and up

Effort, PA 18330. 232 Ziegler Rd. Tel: 570-629-3291. Fax: 570-620-9851.
Contact (Sept-May): 985 Livingston Ave, North Brunswick, NJ 08902. Tel: 732-246-2525. Fax: 732-214-1834.
www.campjaycee.org   E-mail: info@campjaycee.org
Jason Brakeman, Dir.
Adm: FCFS. **Appl due:** Rolling. **Enr cap:** 200. **Staff:** Admin 2. Couns 80. Res 80.
Conditions accepted: ID.

Features: Environ_Sci Crafts Dance Music Canoe Baseball Basketball Soccer Softball Swim Tennis Volleyball.
Fees 2014: Res $750, 1 wk. Day 1 wk.
Housing: Cabins. Avg per room/unit: 8. **Swimming:** Lake Pond.
Est 1975. Nonprofit. **Spons:** New Jersey Jaycees/Arc of New Jersey. **Ses:** 8. **Wks/ses:** 1. Operates June-Aug. ACA.

This camp for children and adults with mental retardation is a collaborative effort of the New Jersey Jaycees and the Arc of New Jersey. Activities at the 185-acre Pocono Mountains camp include arts and crafts, games, sports, music, nature study, camp craft, aquatics, drama, dance and self-help skills. Prospective campers must be toilet trained and self-feeding, and they must not be severely emotionally disturbed.

CAMP NORTHWOOD
Res — Coed Ages 8-18

Remsen, NY 13438. 132 State Rte 365. Tel: 315-831-3621. Fax: 315-831-5867.
www.nwood.com   E-mail: northwoodprograms@hotmail.com
Gordon W. Felt, Dir.
Grades 5-12. Adm: Somewhat selective. **Appl due:** Rolling. **Enr:** 140. **Staff:** Admin 18. Couns 82. Special needs 12.
Type of instruction: Rem_Math Rem_Read Rev. **LD Services:** Acad_Instruction.
Conditions accepted: ADD ADHD Asp Dx LD PDD.
Features: Crafts Creative_Writing Dance Theater Aquatics Archery Canoe Chess Cooking Hiking Sail Wilderness_Camp Badminton Basketball Soccer Softball Swim Tennis Volleyball Water-skiing Watersports.
Fees 2014: Res $10,200-10,400, 7 wks.
Housing: Cabins. Avg per room/unit: 6. **Swimming:** Lake.
Est 1976. Inc. **Ses:** 1. **Wks/ses:** 7. Operates July-Aug. ACA.

Northwood's special-needs program serves learning-challenged and high-functioning autistic children. Campers take part in traditional camping activities while receiving the extra support and structure they require. Children develop self-esteem and social skills through participation in daily academics and an array of activities, and staff also provide formalized social skills instruction.

CAMP NOVA
Res — Coed Ages 12-28

Branchville, NJ.
Contact (Year-round): c/o Epilepsy Foundation of New Jersey, 1 AAA Dr, Ste 203, Trenton, NJ 08691. **Toll-free: 800-336-5843. Fax: 609-392-5621.**
www.efnj.com/what-we-offer/programs/camp-nova   E-mail: jandolora@efnj.com
Jenna, Dir.
Adm: FCFS. **Appl due:** Mar. **Enr:** 50. **Staff:** Admin 2. Couns 30.
Conditions accepted: ADD ADHD Asp Au CP D Ep ID LD PDD Phys_Impair Speech & Lang Visual_Impair.
Features: Acting Crafts Dance Archery Boating Fishing Yoga Basketball Martial_Arts Swim.
Fees 2005: Res $975-1075, 1 wk.
Housing: Cabins Lodges. **Swimming:** Lake Pool.
Est 1989. Nonprofit. **Spons:** Epilepsy Foundation of New Jersey. **Ses:** 1. **Wks/ses:** 1. Operates Aug.

Nova serves boys and girls with epilepsy and other developmental disabilities. Activities range from swimming to yoga. The camp cannot accept medically fragile individuals or those with severe behavioral problems.

CAMP NUHOP
Res — Coed Ages 6-18

Perrysville, OH 44864. Township Rd 2916. Tel: 419-938-7151. Fax: 419-938-7151.
Contact (Sept-May): 404 Hillcrest Dr, Ashland, OH 44805. Tel: 419-289-2227. Fax: 419-289-2227.
www.campnuhop.org E-mail: info@campnuhop.org
Trevor Dunlap, Exec Dir.
Grades 1-12. Adm: FCFS. **Appl due:** Rolling. **Enr:** 80. **Staff:** Admin 6. Couns 30.
Conditions accepted: ADD ADHD Au ED LD Speech & Lang.
Features: Adventure_Travel Aquatics Archery Bicycle_Tours Canoe Climbing_Wall Exploration Hiking Rock_Climb Ropes_Crse Sail Wilderness_Camp Swim.
Fees 2011: Res $745-2000, 1-2 wks. Aid (Need).
Housing: Cabins. **Swimming:** Lake Pool.
Est 1974. Nonprofit. **Ses:** 6. **Wks/ses:** 1-2. Operates June-Aug.

Serving children with learning, behavioral and attentional disorders, Nuhop offers 20 camps, from which a camper may choose exploration, wilderness, acclimatization, bicycling, backpacking, athletic skills, leadership, canoeing, discovery, arts, science or adventure. Daily activities incorporate basic academic concepts, problem solving and socialization skills, and the camp focuses on self-esteem building and behavior management techniques.

CAMP OAKHURST
Res — Coed Ages 6-21

Oakhurst, NJ 07755. 111 Monmouth Rd. Tel: 732-531-0215. Fax: 732-531-0292.
Contact (Sept-May): 1140 Broadway, Ste 903, New York, NY 10001. Tel: 212-533-4020. Fax: 212-533-4023.
www.campoakhurst.com E-mail: info@campoakhurst.com
Charles Sutherland, Dir.
Adm: FCFS. **Appl due:** Rolling. **Enr:** 90. **Staff:** Admin 7. Couns 45. Special needs 2.
LD Services: Acad_Instruction.
Conditions accepted: CP Phys_Impair TBI MD ON SB. **Therapy:** Art Music Phys Rec.
Features: Writing/Journ Crafts Creative_Writing Media Music Theater Aquatics Cooking Baseball Basketball Football Soccer Swim Volleyball.
Fees 2009: Res $750, 1 wk. Aid (Need).
Housing: Cabins. Avg per room/unit: 12. **Swimming:** Pool.
Est 1906. Nonprofit. **Ses:** 4. **Wks/ses:** 2. Operates June-Aug. ACA.

Oakhurst accepts children and young adults who have physical special needs. The daily program includes activities such as swimming, adaptive sports, arts, crafts, drama, music, dance, cooking, photography and nature programs. Special events and social outings to beaches, boardwalks and other areas of interest supplement the program.

CAMP OKIZU
Res — Coed Ages 6-17

Berry Creek, CA.
Contact (Year-round): c/o Okizu Foundation, 16 Digital Dr, Ste 130, Novato, CA 94949. Tel: 415-382-9083. Fax: 415-382-8384.
www.okizu.org E-mail: info@okizu.org
Suzanne B. Randall, Dir.
Adm: FCFS. **Appl due:** Rolling. **Staff:** Admin 15. Couns 40.
Conditions accepted: Cancer.
Features: Crafts Archery Fishing Hiking Ropes_Crse Social_Servs Basketball Swim Volleyball Watersports.
Fees 2014: Free. Res 1 wk.
Housing: Cabins Lodges. **Swimming:** Lake.

Est 1982. Nonprofit. **Spons:** Okizu Foundation. **Ses:** 3. **Wks/ses:** 1. Operates June-Aug. ACA.

Affiliated with the American Cancer Society, Okizu serves children who have or who once had cancer and their siblings. Activities include swimming, boating, fishing, archery, arts and crafts, and nature study.

ONE STEP AT A TIME CAMP
Res — Coed Ages 7-19

Williams Bay, WI 53191. 300 Conference Point Rd.
Contact (Winter): c/o Children's Oncology Services, 213 W Institute Pl, Ste 511, Chicago, IL 60610.
Year-round Tel: 312-924-4220, Fax: 312-440-8897.
www.onestepcamp.org   E-mail: jeff@onestepcamp.org
Maria T. Bernal, Dir.
Grades 2-12. Adm: FCFS. **Appl due:** Rolling. **Enr:** 250. **Enr cap:** 250. **Staff:** Admin 20. Couns 100. Special needs 23.
Conditions accepted: Cancer.
Features: Crafts Drama Filmmaking Riding Rock_Climb Sail Scuba Equestrian Golf Swim Volleyball Watersports.
Fees 2012: Res $100, 1 wk.
Housing: Cabins Dorms Tents. **Swimming:** Lake.
Est 1978. Nonprofit. **Spons:** Children's Oncology Services. **Ses:** 2. **Wks/ses:** 1. Operates July.

The camp serves boys and girls from Illinois, northern Indiana and Wisconsin who have cancer or leukemia. Any child well enough to enjoy the camp experience may attend, whether or not he or she is currently undergoing therapy. Programs progress from traditional recreational sessions for young children to more specialized sessions for older campers.

CAMP PENNBROOK
Res — Girls Ages 8-21

Pennington, NJ. Pennington School, 112 W Delaware Ave.
Contact (Year-round): PO Box 5, Leonia, NJ 07605. Tel: 212-354-2267, 800-442-7366.
www.camppennbrook.com   E-mail: info@camppennbrook.com
Flip Shulman, Exec Dir.
Adm: FCFS. **Appl due:** Rolling. **Staff:** Admin 8. Couns 20. Special needs 1.
Focus: Health/Weight_Reduct. **Features:** Crafts Dance Drama Aquatics Hiking Riding Basketball Soccer Swim Tennis Track Volleyball Watersports.
Fees 2014: Res $2250-8750 (+$25-250), 2-8 wks.
Housing: Dorms. **Swimming:** Pool.
Est 1993. Inc. **Ses:** 6. **Wks/ses:** 2-8. Operates June-Aug. ACA.

Campers at Pennbrook focus on the fundamentals of healthy eating. By combining proper nutrition with recreational activities, the program promotes a healthy approach to weight loss that parents can easily reinforce. Each camper meets with a food advisor upon arrival to review her goals and objectives. She has another private session before going home to review a personalized menu planner and discuss issues and concerns about maintaining weight loss after camp. A combination of recreational activities, specialty programs, events and trips completes the program.

PINE TREE CAMP
Res — Coed Ages 8-19; Day — Coed 5-12

Rome, ME 04963. 114 Pine Tree Camp Rd. Tel: 207-397-2141. Fax: 207-397-5324.
Contact (Oct-Apr): c/o Pine Tree Society, 149 Front St, PO Box 518, Bath, ME 04530.

Tel: 207-443-3341. **Fax:** 207-443-1070.
www.pinetreesociety.org/camp.asp   **E-mail:** ptcamp@pinetreesociety.org
Dawn Willard-Robinson, Prgm Dir.
Adm: FCFS. **Appl due:** Rolling. **Enr:** 100. **Fac** 70.
Conditions accepted: CP Ep ID Phys_Impair TBI.
Features: Art Crafts Drama Music Painting Photog Pottery Woodworking Archery Boating Fishing Hiking Kayak Baseball Basketball Soccer Street_Hockey Swim.
Fees 2014: Res $1900, 1 wk. Day $150, 1 wk. Aid (Need).
Swimming: Pond.
Est 1945. Nonprofit. **Spons:** Pine Tree Society. **Ses:** 7. **Wks/ses:** 1. Operates July-Aug. ACA.

Pine Tree accepts children with physical and developmental disabilities. Campers take part in activities such as swimming, basketball, crafts, music, drama, theater, canoeing and equestrian. No camper is denied acceptance due to an inability to pay, and fees may be determined along a sliding scale according to family income. Pine Tree operates a separate summer program for special-needs adults.

CAMP RED LEAF
Res — Coed Ages 9 and up

Ingleside, IL 60041. 26710 W Nippersink Rd. Tel: 847-740-5010. Fax: 847-740-5014.
www.jcys.org/locations/ingleside/camp-red-leaf   **E-mail:** enewport@jcys.org
Erin Newport, Dir.
Adm: FCFS. **Appl due:** Rolling. **Staff:** Admin 2. Couns 27. Special needs 1.
Conditions accepted: ADD ADHD Asp Au CP D Dx Ep ID LD PDD Phys_Impair Speech & Lang TBI Visual_Impair. **Therapy:** Music Rec.
Features: Crafts Music Theater Adventure_Travel Aquatics Archery Boating Canoe Climbing_Wall Fishing Hiking Ropes_Crse Sail Baseball Basketball Soccer Softball Swim Tennis Volleyball Watersports.
Fees 2014: Res $550-620, 1 wk. Aid (Need).
Housing: Lodges. Avg per room/unit: 35. **Swimming:** Lake Pool.
Est 1911. Nonprofit. **Spons:** Jewish Council for Youth Services. Jewish. **Ses:** 8. **Wks/ses:** 1. Operates June-Aug.

Affiliated with the Jewish Council for Youth Services, Red Leaf provides camping and training programs for young people and adults with mild to moderate developmental disabilities. Activities include crafts, music, boating and canoeing, fishing, hiking, nature study and sports.

ROCKY MOUNTAIN VILLAGE
Res — Coed Ages 6 and up

Empire, CO 80438. PO Box 115. Tel: 303-569-2333. Fax: 303-569-3857.
www.co.easterseals.com   **E-mail:** campinfo@eastersealscolorado.org
Adm: FCFS. **Appl due:** Apr.
Conditions accepted: Au Blood ID Phys_Impair TBI MD.
Features: Media Climbing_Wall Fishing Riding Basketball Softball Swim Tennis Gardening.
Fees 2014: Res $825, 1 wk. Aid (Need).
Swimming: Pool.
Est 1951. Spons: Colorado Easter Seal Society. **Ses:** 9. **Wks/ses:** 1. Operates May-Aug.

Operated by the Colorado Easter Seal Society, the camp conducts sessions for children and adults with developmental and physical disabilities, as well as specialty programs for those with hemophilia and autism. Activities include horseback riding, swimming, fishing and hiking, as well as wilderness camping and outdoor education.

CAMP RONALD MCDONALD FOR GOOD TIMES
Res — Coed Ages 9-18

Mountain Center, CA 92561. 56400 Apple Canyon Rd, PO Box 35. Tel: 951-659-4609. Fax: 951-659-4710.
Contact (Winter): 1250 Lyman Pl, Los Angeles, CA 90029. Tel: 310-268-8488. Fax: 310-473-3338.
Year-round Toll-free: 800-625-7295.
www.campronaldmcdonald.org   E-mail: dot@campronaldmcdonald.org
Chad Edwards, Dir.
Adm: FCFS. **Appl due:** Rolling. **Enr:** 100. **Staff:** Admin 3. Couns 50. Special needs 3.
Conditions accepted: Cancer.
Features: Crafts Dance Media Music Photog Theater Archery Cooking Fishing Hiking Riding Ropes_Crse Swim.
Fees 2014: Free. **Res** 1 wk.
Housing: Cabins. **Swimming:** Pool.
Est 1982. Nonprofit. **Ses:** 5. **Wks/ses:** 1. Operates June-Aug. ACA.

The camp serves children who have (or who once had) cancer and their families. Distinct sessions serve patients ages 9-15 and their siblings and patients ages 16-18 and their siblings. Activities include swimming, riding, nature study, hiking, sports, drama, dancing, photography, arts and crafts, a ropes course and a radio station.

SERTOMA CAMP ENDEAVOR
Res — Coed Ages 6-17

Dundee, FL 33838. 1301 Camp Endeavor Blvd, PO Box 910. Tel: 863-439-1300.
www.sertomacampendeavor.net   E-mail: campendeavor@verizon.net
George Boyd, Dir.
Adm: FCFS. **Appl due:** Rolling. **Enr:** 60. **Enr cap:** 96. **Staff:** Admin 1. Couns 8. Special needs 16.
Conditions accepted: D.
Features: Crafts Drama Archery Boating Canoe Climbing_Wall Fishing Hiking Mtn_Biking Outdoor_Ed Rappelling Riding Ropes_Crse Baseball Basketball Football Golf Swim Team_Handball Volleyball Watersports.
Fees 2007: Res $500 (+$20), 1 wk.
Housing: Cabins. Avg per room/unit: 16. **Swimming:** Lake.
Est 1976. Nonprofit. **Ses:** 2. **Wks/ses:** 1. Operates July.

Camp Endeavor provides a traditional camp experience for children who are deaf or hard of hearing. Wilderness education includes nature hikes and wildlife identification, while the performing arts program features dance, drama, storytelling, songs, and arts and crafts. Swimming, canoeing, water skiing and tubing are some of the pursuits in the aquatics program. Many counselors at Endeavor have hearing impairments.

CAMP SETEBAID
Res — Coed Ages 8-17

Shickshinny, PA.
Contact (Year-round): c/o Setebaid Services, PO Box 196, Winfield, PA 17889. Tel: 570-524-9090, 866-738-3224. Fax: 570-523-0769.
www.setebaidservices.org   E-mail: info@setebaidservices.org
Mark Moyer, Exec Dir.
Adm: FCFS. **Appl due:** Rolling. **Enr cap:** 100. **Staff:** Admin 10. Couns 70. Special needs 10.
Conditions accepted: Diabetes.
Features: Environ_Sci Writing/Journ Crafts Dance Music Photog Theater Aquatics Archery Bicycle_Tours Boating Canoe Climbing_Wall Hiking Ropes_Crse Wilderness_Camp Baseball Basketball Martial_Arts Soccer Softball Street_Hockey Swim Volleyball.

Fees 2010: Res $880, 1 wk. Aid 2009 (Need): $80,000.
Housing: Cabins Tents. Avg per room/unit: 4-12. **Swimming:** Pool.
Est 1978. Nonprofit. **Spons:** Setebaid Services. **Ses:** 5. **Wks/ses:** 1. Operates July-Aug.
ACA.

This recreational camping experience serves children with diabetes. Setebaid Services provides campers with professional assistance in developing diabetes management skills. Healthcare professionals, including physicians, nurses and dieticians, are on site at all times.

CAMP SHANE
Res — Boys Ages 7-19, Girls 7-25

Ferndale, NY 12734. 302 Harris Rd. Tel: 845-292-4644. Fax: 845-292-8636.
Contact (Sept-May): 134 Teatown Rd, Croton-on-Hudson, NY 10520. Tel: 914-271-4141. Fax: 914-271-2103.
www.campshane.com   E-mail: office@campshane.com
David Ettenberg, Dir.
Grades 3-12. Adm: FCFS. **Appl due:** Rolling. **Enr:** 797.
Focus: Health/Weight_Reduct. **Features:** Crafts Dance Fine_Arts Music Theater Bicycle_ Tours Boating Canoe Climbing_Wall Cooking Mtn_Biking Riding Ropes_Crse Scuba Wilderness_Camp Woodcraft Aerobics Baseball Basketball Equestrian Soccer Softball Swim Tennis Volleyball Water-skiing Weight_Trng.
Fees 2014: Res $2900-7500, 3-9 wks.
Housing: Cabins. **Swimming:** Lake Pool.
Est 1968. Ses: 5. **Wks/ses:** 3-9. Operates June-Aug.

This weight-reduction camp places particular emphasis on diet and nutrition. Classes in basic nutrition show boys and girls how to enjoy meals while losing weight through portion control and food substitutions. The traditional camp setting includes sports and creative activities. In addition to the regular camp, Shane offers a separate program for young women ages 18-25.

SPECIAL TOUCH MINISTRY SUMMER GET AWAY
Res — Coed Ages 10 and up

Waupaca, WI 54981. PO Box 25. Tel: 715-258-2713. Fax: 715-258-2777.
www.specialtouch.org   E-mail: centralprocessing@specialtouch.org
Debbie Chivers, Coord.
Adm: FCFS. **Appl due:** Rolling.
Locations: AR FL GA IL KY MA MI NC OK WI.
Conditions accepted: Asp Au CP D Ep ID LD Phys_Impair Speech & Lang TBI Visual_ Impair. **Therapy:** Art Music Phys Rec.
Features: Relig_Stud Crafts Music Painting Theater Aquatics Archery Boating Climbing_ Wall Fishing Hiking Outdoor_Ed Paintball Rappelling Ropes_Crse Aerobics Baseball Basketball Equestrian Soccer Softball Swim Volleyball Watersports.
Fees 2014: Res $290-699, 1 wk. Aid (Need).
Housing: Cabins Dorms Houses Lodges. Avg per room/unit: 4. **Swimming:** Lake Pool.
Est 1982. Nonprofit. Nondenom Christian. **Ses:** 9. **Wks/ses:** 1. Operates May-Sept.

Special Touch provides Christian camping experiences nationwide for people with intellectual or physical special needs and their families. Individuals with intellectual disabilities enter a program geared to their understanding and participation levels. Participants with physical special needs take part in a separate program that provides Bible teaching, tailored to the spiritual issues they face, as well as recreation, entertainment and fellowship. Activities vary by location.

CAMP STAND BY ME
Res — Coed Ages 7 and up

Vaughn, WA 98394. 17809 S Vaughn Rd KPN, PO Box 289. Tel: 253-884-2722. Fax: 253-884-0200.
www.wa.easterseals.com   E-mail: camp@wa.easterseals.com
Ellen Stone, Dir.
Adm: FCFS. **Enr:** 288.
Conditions accepted: ADD ADHD Au CP D Diabetes Dx Ep ID LD Phys_Impair Speech & Lang TBI Visual_Impair.
Features: Crafts Aquatics Archery Boating Fishing Hiking Riding Swim.
Fees 2014: Res $850-1125, 1 wk.
Housing: Cabins. Avg per room/unit: 8. **Swimming:** Pool.
Est 1975. Nonprofit. **Spons:** Easter Seals Washington. **Ses:** 9. **Wks/ses:** 1. Operates June-Aug. ACA.

Aquatics, arts and crafts, and riding are among the activities available at this camp for those with physical, mental, sensory or developmental special needs.

CAMP SUMMIT
Res — Coed Ages 6 and up

Argyle, TX 76226. 921 Copper Canyon Rd.
Contact (Sept-Apr): 17210 Campbell Rd, Ste 180-W, Dallas, TX 75252.
Year-round Tel: 972-484-8900, Fax: 972-620-1945.
www.campsummittx.org   E-mail: camp@campsummittx.org
Lisa J. Braziel, Dir.
Adm: FCFS. **Appl due:** Rolling. **Enr:** 80. **Staff:** Admin 10. Couns 60.
Conditions accepted: Asp Au CP D Ep ID LD Phys_Impair TBI Visual_Impair.
Features: Crafts Dance Music Theater Aquatics Hiking Riding Ropes_Crse Swim.
Fees 2014: Res $1400, 1 wk. Aid (Need).
Housing: Cabins. Avg per room/unit: 8. **Swimming:** Pool.
Est 1993. Nonprofit. **Ses:** 11. **Wks/ses:** 1. Operates May-Aug. ACA.

Various outdoor programs, including swimming, horseback riding, camp outs, a ropes course and handicrafts, are available for individuals with physical disabilities, developmental delays, or visual or hearing impairments.

SUMMIT CAMP & TRAVEL
Res — Coed Ages 8-19

Honesdale, PA 18431. 168 Duck Harbor Rd. Tel: 570-253-4381. Fax: 570-253-2937.
Contact (Sept-June): 322 Rte 46 W, Ste 210, Parsippany, NJ 07054. Tel: 973-732-3230. Fax: 973-732-3226.
Year-round Toll-free: 800-323-9908.
www.summitcamp.com   E-mail: info@summitcamp.com
Eugene Bell, Dir.
Adm: FCFS. **Appl due:** Rolling. **Enr:** 300. **Enr cap:** 300.
LD Services: Acad_Instruction.
Travel: AZ HI Canada Mexico/Central_America Middle_East.
Conditions accepted: ADD ADHD Asp Dx ED LD PDD Speech & Lang Mood NLD OCD TS.
Features: Computers Sci Crafts Dance Drama Music Adventure_Travel Aquatics Bicycle_Tours Canoe Climbing_Wall Hiking Kayak Mtn_Biking Ropes_Crse Sail Woodcraft Baseball Basketball Field_Hockey Gymnastics Martial_Arts Soccer Softball Swim Tennis Volleyball.
Fees 2014: Res $4395-8000, 2-3 wks.
Housing: Cabins. Avg per room/unit: 9. **Swimming:** Lake Pool.
Est 1969. Inc. **Ses:** 7. **Wks/ses:** 2-3. Operates June-Aug. ACA.

This therapeutic camp for boys and girls with various special needs provides waterfront and land sports; enrichment programs in nature study, overnight hiking, arts and crafts, dramatics, music, shop, home economics, creative movement and ceramics; academic remediation; videography; computers; and social programs. Older teens may take part in a work camp program that integrates young adult education with work experience while stressing life and social skills. A travel program offers campers ages 15-19 travel tours to the following destinations: Arizona and Hawaii, Israel, Canada and Costa Rica.

SUNSHINE CAMP
Res — Coed Ages 7-21

Rush, NY. Tel: 585-533-2080.
Contact (Year-round): c/o Rochester Rotary Club, 180 Linden Oaks, Ste 200, Rochester, NY 14625. Tel: 585-546-7435.
Year-round Fax: 585-546-8675.
www.sunshinecampus.org   E-mail: kelly@rochesterrotary.org
Tracy Dreisbach, Exec Dir.
Adm: FCFS. **Appl due:** May. **Enr:** 120. **Enr cap:** 130. **Staff:** Admin 6. Couns 75.
Conditions accepted: ADD ADHD As Asp Au Blood C CP D Diabetes Ep HIV/AIDS PDD Phys_Impair Speech & Lang TBI Visual_Impair.
Features: Ecol Crafts Music Theater Aquatics Archery Boating Canoe Climbing_Wall Fishing Outdoor_Ed Rock_Climb Ropes_Crse Wilderness_Camp Yoga Baseball Basketball Football Soccer Softball Swim Volleyball.
Fees 2014: Free (in-state residents). Res 1 wk.
Housing: Cabins. Avg per room/unit: 20. **Swimming:** Pool.
Est 1922. Nonprofit. **Spons:** Rochester Rotary Club. **Ses:** 2. **Wks/ses:** 1. Operates July.

The camp serves children and young adults with physical disabilities from the Greater Rochester area in a residential camping program. The cost-free program features a variety of traditional camp activities and sports.

CAMP SWEENEY
Res — Coed Ages 5-18

Gainesville, TX 76241. PO Box 918. Tel: 940-665-2011. Fax: 940-665-9467.
www.campsweeney.org   E-mail: info@campsweeney.org
Ernie M. Fernandez, Dir.
Grades K-12. Adm: FCFS. **Appl due:** Rolling. **Enr:** 245. **Enr cap:** 245. **Staff:** Admin 10. Couns 48. Special needs 16.
Conditions accepted: Diabetes. **Therapy:** Art Music Occup Phys Psych Rec.
Focus: Health/Weight_Reduct. **Features:** Computers Writing/Journ Crafts Dance Filmmaking Media Music Painting Photog Theater Aquatics Archery Boating Canoe Climbing_Wall Exploration Fishing Hiking Kayak Paintball Rappelling Riflery Rock_ Climb Ropes_Crse Aerobics Baseball Basketball Cross-country Field_Hockey Football Golf Gymnastics Lacrosse Roller_Hockey Skateboarding Soccer Softball Swim Tennis Ultimate_Frisbee Volleyball Water-skiing Watersports Weight_Trng.
Fees 2014: Res $3000, 3 wks. Aid 2008 (Need): $750,000.
Housing: Cabins Lodges. **Swimming:** Lake Pool.
Est 1950. Nonprofit. **Spons:** Southwestern Diabetic Foundation. **Ses:** 3. **Wks/ses:** 3. Operates June-Aug.

The only camp in Texas designed specifically to teach diabetes management skills to children with Type 1 or Type 2 diabetes, Camp Sweeney helps children with the disease learn how to live a near-normal lifestyle and to avoid the debilitating effects of their endocrine disorder. Lifestyle modification (appropriate dietary choices and regular exercise) is at the heart of the program. Campers learn how and when to give themselves insulin injections.

TALISMAN SUMMER CAMP
Res — Coed Ages 8-21

Zirconia, NC 28790. 64 Gap Creek Rd. Tel: 828-697-6313, 855-588-8254. Fax: 828-697-6249.
www.talismancamps.com   E-mail: summer@talismancamps.com
Linda Tatsapaugh, Exec Dir.
Adm: FCFS. **Appl due:** Rolling. **Enr:** 85. **Enr cap:** 100. **Staff:** Admin 7. Couns 45. Special needs 2.
LD Services: Acad_Instruction.
Conditions accepted: ADD ADHD Asp Au ED LD.
Features: Crafts Adventure_Travel Canoe Hiking Kayak Mountaineering Mtn_Trips Rock_Climb Ropes_Crse Sail White-water_Raft Wilderness_Camp Wilderness_Canoe Swim.
Fees 2014: Res $1500-4085, 2-3 wks.
Housing: Cabins Tents. Avg per room/unit: 8. **Swimming:** Lake Pond Pool Stream.
Est 1980. Spons: Aspen Education Group. **Ses:** 6. **Wks/ses:** 2-3. Operates June-Aug. ACA.

Talisman offers an adventure program of hiking, camping, white-water rafting, rock climbing and canoeing for young people with attentional disorders, learning disabilities, autism and Asperger's syndrome. Focused on social skills development, personal regulation and self-esteem, the camp is open to physically nonaggressive children with an IQ of 85 or above.

TEXAS LIONS CAMP
Res and Day — Coed Ages 7-16

Kerrville, TX 78029. PO Box 290247. Tel: 830-896-8500. Fax: 830-896-3666.
www.lionscamp.com   E-mail: tlc@lionscamp.com
Stephen S. Mabry, Exec Dir.
Adm: FCFS. **Appl due:** Rolling. **Staff:** Admin 18. Couns 140.
Conditions accepted: As C CP D Diabetes Ep Phys_Impair Visual_Impair. **Therapy:** Music Rec.
Features: Crafts Archery Boating Baseball Equestrian Golf Softball Swim Volleyball.
Fees 2014: Free. Res 1 wk. Day ½ wk.
Housing: Cabins. **Swimming:** Pond Pool.
Est 1949. Nonprofit. **Ses:** 9. **Wks/ses:** ½-1. Operates June-Aug. ACA.

TLC conducts distinct recreational camp sessions for Texas children with either physical disabilities or diabetes. Swimming, boating, music, sports, ropes courses, horseback riding, photography, arts and crafts, archery and nature studies are among the available activities. The half-week day camp serves children with physical disabilities only.

CAMP THORPE
Res — Coed Ages 10-20

Goshen, VT 05733. 680 Capen Hill Rd. Tel: 802-247-6611.
www.campthorpe.org   E-mail: cthorpe@sover.net
Lyle P. Jepson, Dir.
Adm: FCFS. **Appl due:** Rolling. **Enr:** 180. **Staff:** Admin 2. Couns 18.
Conditions accepted: Au CP Ep ID LD Phys_Impair Speech & Lang.
Features: Crafts Music Theater Boating Fishing Hiking Basketball Swim Tennis.
Fees 2014: Res $650-750, 1-2 wks. Aid (Need).
Housing: Cabins. **Swimming:** Pool.
Est 1927. Nonprofit. **Ses:** 4. **Wks/ses:** 1-2. Operates June-Aug.

The camp serves campers with such physical and mental challenges as cerebral palsy, intellectual disabilities, spina bifida, epilepsy, muscular dystrophy, emotional difficulties and abuse histories. Activities include swimming, boating, fishing, farm animal care, art, music, theater, dances, games and sports.

CAMP THUNDERBIRD
Res — Coed Ages 8 and up

Apopka, FL 32712. 909 E Welch Rd.
Contact (Winter): c/o Quest, PO Box 531125, Orlando, FL 32853.
Year-round Tel: 407-889-8088, Fax: 407-889-8072.
www.questinc.org/camp.html E-mail: rcage@questinc.org
Rob Cage, Dir.
Adm: FCFS. **Appl due:** Rolling. **Enr:** 500.
Conditions accepted: Au CP ID DS.
Features: Art Crafts Theater Canoe Fishing Ropes_Crse Swim.
Fees 2012: Res $675-1300, 1-2 wks.
Housing: Cabins. **Swimming:** Pool.
Est 1969. Nonprofit. **Spons:** Quest. **Ses:** 8. **Wks/ses:** 1-2. Operates June-Aug. ACA.

This camp for children and adults with physical and behavioral challenges offers a traditional camping experience that emphasizes daily living and social skills. Campers, who must be ambulatory, choose from six- and 12-day sessions. Activities include swimming, canoeing, nature study, drama, arts and crafts, sports, games and a ropes course.

TRIANGLE D CAMP FOR CHILDREN WITH DIABETES
Res — Coed Ages 9-13

Ingleside, IL. YMCA Camp Duncan, 32405 N Hwy 12.
Contact (Year-round): c/o American Diabetes Assoc, 55 E Monroe St, Ste 3420, Chicago, IL 60603. Tel: 312-346-1805. Fax: 312-346-5342.
www.diabetes.org/in-my-community/diabetes-camp/camps/triangle-d.html
E-mail: msullivan@diabetes.org
Mary Sullivan, Dir.
Grades 3-8. Adm: FCFS. **Appl due:** Rolling. **Enr:** 140. **Staff:** Admin 2. Special needs 40.
Conditions accepted: Diabetes.
Features: Crafts Aquatics Archery Canoe Climbing_Wall Basketball Soccer Softball Swim Volleyball.
Fees 2014: Res $820-920, 1 wk. Aid 2006 (Need): $10,000.
Housing: Cabins. **Swimming:** Pool.
Est 1944. Nonprofit. **Spons:** American Diabetes Association. **Ses:** 1. **Wks/ses:** 1. Operates July.

Triangle D's program for children with diabetes combines self-care education and recreation. Campers learn to be responsible for their diabetes management. Many traditional summer camp activities are available.

VARIETY CAMP
Res — Coed Ages 7-17; Day — Coed 5-21

Worcester, PA 19490. 2950 Potshop Rd, PO Box 609. Tel: 610-584-4366. Fax: 610-584-5586.
www.varietyphila.org E-mail: angusmurray@varietyphila.org
Samantha Friedman, Mng Dir.
Adm: FCFS. **Appl due:** Rolling. **Enr:** 230. **Staff:** Admin 10. Couns 120. Res 40. Special needs 4.
LD Services: Acad_Instruction.
Conditions accepted: ADD ADHD As Asp Au C CP D Dx Ep ID LD PDD Phys_Impair Speech & Lang TBI Visual_Impair. **Therapy:** Occup Phys Rec Speech.
Features: Computers Ecol Environ_Sci Sci Ceramics Crafts Dance Music Theater

Aquatics Canoe Cooking Farm Fishing Hiking Outdoor_Ed Scuba Baseball Basketball Golf Soccer Swim Tennis. **Fees 2014: Res $750 (+$20), 1 wk. Day $375 (+$25), 1 wk.** Aid 2010 (Need): $11,000. **Housing:** Cabins. Avg per room/unit: 10. **Swimming:** Pool. **Est 1949.** Nonprofit. **Spons:** Variety: The Children's Charity. **Ses:** 8. **Wks/ses:** 1. Operates June-Aug.

Variety conducts traditional camping sessions for children with physical or developmental disabilities. The overnight camp serves boys and girls with physical disabilities, while the day camp enrolls campers with developmental disabilities. Specialty programs focus upon adapted aquatics, wheelchair basketball, dance, music and scuba diving.

CAMP VIRGINIA JAYCEE
Res — Coed Ages 7 and up; Day — Coed 5 and up

Blue Ridge, VA 24064. 2494 Camp Jaycee Rd, PO Box 648. Tel: 540-947-2972, 800-865-0092.
www.campvajc.org   E-mail: info@campvajc.org
Dana Zyrowski, Dir.
Adm: FCFS. **Appl due:** Rolling. **Staff:** Admin 7. Couns 50.
Conditions accepted: Au CP Ep ID TBI DS PW.
Features: Crafts Dance Drama Music Aquatics Boating Climbing_Wall Fishing Hiking Baseball Basketball Equestrian Golf Soccer Softball Swim Tennis Volleyball.
Fees 2014: Res $725-775 (+$150), 1 wk. Day $250, 1 wk. Aid (Need).
Housing: Cabins. Avg per room/unit: 16. **Swimming:** Pool.
Est 1971. Nonprofit. **Ses:** 9. **Wks/ses:** 1. Operates June-July. ACA.

Virginia Jaycee provides outdoor education and traditional camping experiences for children and adults with mental retardation and, in some cases, other special needs. Campers engage in an array of traditional recreational pursuits during the day, then take part in such activities as dances, hayrides, vespers, talent shows, scavenger hunts, puppet shows, singing and campfires in the evening.

WELLSPRING ACADEMY OF CALIFORNIA SUMMER SESSION
Res — Coed Ages 14-19

Reedley, CA 93654. 42675 Rd 44.
http://treatment.psychologytoday.com/rms/name/Wellspring+Academy_Reedley_California_90778
Michaela Clinton, Exec Dir.
Adm: FCFS. **Appl due:** Rolling. **Enr:** 120. **Enr cap:** 120. **Fac 10. Staff:** Admin 15. Couns 30.
Type of instruction: Rem_Eng Rem_Math Rem_Read Study_Skills Tut. **LD Services:** Acad_Instruction Tut. **Avg class size:** 8. **Daily hours for:** Classes 5. Study 1. Rec 6. High school credit.
Therapy: Art Psych Rec.
Focus: Health/Weight_Reduct. **Features:** Bus/Fin Expository_Writing Govt Lang Crafts Creative_Writing Photog Theater Aquatics Bicycle_Tours Canoe Cooking Hiking Kayak Mountaineering Mtn_Biking Mtn_Trips Paintball Riding Rock_Climb Social_Servs White-water_Raft Wilderness_Camp Baseball Basketball Cross-country Equestrian Field_Hockey Football Golf Soccer Softball Swim Tennis Volleyball Watersports.
Fees 2012: Res $13,450-18,500, 10-13 wks.
Housing: Dorms. **Swimming:** Pool River.
Est 2004. Inc. **Spons:** Wellspring Academies. **Ses:** 2. **Wks/ses:** 10-13. Operates June-Aug. ACA.

Wellspring, which enrolls boys and girls who have had weight problems for two years or more and who are at least 30 pounds overweight, combines intensive diet and activity management with an emphasis on behavioral change. Instructors attempt to permanently change thinking and behavior regarding diet and physical activity. A classroom component includes compulsory nutrition and culinary arts course work and traditional academics; all students select two core classes that lead to transferable high school credit.

WELLSPRING ADVENTURE CAMP NORTH CAROLINA
Res — Coed Ages 11-18

Durham, NC 27705. Wellspring at Structure House, 3017 Pickett Rd.
Contact (Winter): c/o Wellspring Camps, 42675 Road 44, Reedley, CA 93654.
Year-round Tel: 866-786-3029, Fax: 559-638-2685.
http://treatment.psychologytoday.com/rms/name/Wellspring+Academy_Reedley_California_90778
Jessie Dean, Dir.
Grades 6-11. Adm: FCFS. **Appl due:** Rolling. **Enr:** 60. **Staff:** Admin 5. Couns 20.
LD Services: Acad_Instruction.
Therapy: Art Psych Rec.
Focus: Health/Weight_Reduct. **Features:** Crafts Adventure_Travel Bicycle_Tours Boating Canoe Caving Climbing_Wall Cooking Exploration Hiking Kayak Mountaineering Mtn_Biking Mtn_Trips Rappelling Rock_Climb Ropes_Crse Survival_Trng White-water_Raft Wilderness_Camp Wilderness_Canoe Baseball Field_Hockey Soccer Softball Swim Volleyball Watersports.
Fees 2012: Res $5345-12,495 (+$500), 3-12 wks.
Housing: Cabins Tents. Avg per room/unit: 10. **Swimming:** Pool Stream.
Est 2004. Inc. **Spons:** Wellspring Weight Loss Programs. **Ses:** 25. **Wks/ses:** 3-12.
Operates June-Aug.

Wellspring Adventure Camp is designed to help boys and girls lose weight, develop healthy habits and improve self-esteem. The camp offers beginning instruction in white-water rafting, rock climbing and rappelling. Wellspring's clinical program combines cognitive behavioral therapy, dietary changes and physical activity. Writing exercises and educational seminars complete the program. Applicants must be at least 20 pounds overweight and must have been attempting to lose weight for at least a year.

WELLSPRING NEW YORK
Res — Girls Ages 11-24

Paul Smiths, NY. Paul Smith's College.
Contact (Year-round): c/o Wellspring Camps, 42675 Road 44, Reedley, CA 93654.
Tel: 559-638-4570, 866-364-0808. Fax: 559-638-2685.
www.wellspringcamps.com/newyork   E-mail: ksomma@wellspringcamps.com
Kimberly Mueller, Dir.
Grades 9-Col. Adm: FCFS. **Appl due:** Rolling. **Enr:** 100. **Staff:** Admin 7. Couns 30.
Focus: Health/Weight_Reduct. **Features:** Crafts Dance Drama Fine_Arts Photog Aquatics Archery Bicycle_Tours Boating Canoe Climbing_Wall Exploration Fishing Hiking Mountaineering Mtn_Biking Mtn_Trips Rappelling Rock_Climb Ropes_Crse White-water_Raft Baseball Basketball Cross-country Field_Hockey Football Golf Lacrosse Soccer Softball Swim Tennis Volleyball Watersports Wrestling.
Fees 2014: Res $6400-11,750, 3-9 wks.
Housing: Dorms. **Swimming:** Lake Pool.
Est 2004. Inc. **Spons:** Wellspring Weight Loss Programs. **Ses:** 3. **Wks/ses:** 3-9. Operates June-Aug.

Wellspring New York's clinical weight-loss program focuses on behavioral change as a way of sustaining healthy living. Sessions use methods such as stimulus control, decision counseling, rational emotive therapy, relapse prevention training, positive focusing and stress management. Educational seminars and poetry workshops are also featured. Professional chefs conduct sessions on healthy foods preparation. Applicants must be at least 20 pounds overweight and must have been attempting to lose weight for at least a year.

CAMP WING/DUXBURY STOCKADE
Res — Coed Ages 7-14

Duxbury, MA 02332. 742 Keene St. Tel: 781-837-4279. Fax: 781-837-3892.
Contact (Sept-May): c/o Crossroads for Kids, 119 Myrtle St, Duxbury, MA 02332. Tel: 781-834-2700. Fax: 781-834-2701.
Year-round Toll-free: 888-543-7284.
www.crossroads4kids.org   E-mail: info@crossroads4kids.org
Benjamin Palmer, Dir.
Adm: FCFS. **Appl due:** Apr. **Enr:** 320. **Staff:** Admin 8. Couns 87. Special needs 1.
Conditions accepted: ED. **Therapy:** Art Music.
Features: Computers Crafts Creative_Writing Dance Drama Fine_Arts Aquatics Archery Boating Canoe Exploration Farm Hiking Sail Baseball Basketball Football Soccer Swim Volleyball Watersports.
Fees 2014: Res $1160-1655, 2-3 wks.
Housing: Cabins. **Swimming:** Lake Pool.
Est 1936. Nonprofit. **Ses:** 3. **Wks/ses:** 2-3. Operates June-Aug. ACA.

The camp offers a variety of activities designed to help emotionally and behaviorally at-risk youth build their self-esteem. Boys and girls engage in a wide range of traditional summer recreational pursuits.

WISCONSIN BADGER CAMP
Res — Coed Ages 3-21

Prairie du Chien, WI 53821. 11815 Munz Ln. Tel: 608-988-4558. Fax: 608-988-4586.
Contact (Sept-May): PO Box 723, Platteville, WI 53818. Tel: 608-348-9689. Fax: 608-348-9737.
www.badgercamp.org   E-mail: wiscbadgercamp@centurytel.net
Brent Bowers, Exec Dir.
Adm: FCFS. **Appl due:** Rolling. **Enr:** 104. **Enr cap:** 104. **Staff:** Admin 5. Couns 40. Special needs 3.
Conditions accepted: ADD ADHD Asp Au CP D ED Ep ID LD Phys_Impair Speech & Lang TBI Visual_Impair.
Features: Crafts Drama Music Aquatics Archery Canoe Fishing Hiking Riding Woodcraft Baseball Basketball Equestrian Soccer Softball Swim Volleyball.
Fees 2014: Res $700-1400, 1-2 wks. Aid 2010 (Need): $273,125.
Housing: Cabins Dorms Lodges. **Swimming:** Pool.
Est 1966. Nonprofit. **Ses:** 8. **Wks/ses:** 1-2. Operates June-Aug. ACA.

This camp for children and adults with developmental disabilities offers creative programs and a host of activities: swimming, camping, hiking, fishing, nature studies, arts and crafts, an animal farm, dances, a talent show, Olympic-style games, cookouts, campfires and theme weeks. A tripping program features horseback riding and a trek down the Mississippi River, among other options.

WISCONSIN LIONS CAMP
Res — Coed Ages 6-17

Rosholt, WI 54473. 3834 County Rd A. Tel: 715-677-4761. Fax: 715-677-3297.
www.wisconsinlionscamp.com E-mail: info@wisconsinlionscamp.com
Adm: FCFS. **Appl due:** Mar. **Enr:** 150. **Enr cap:** 150. **Staff:** Admin 7. Couns 28. Res 55.
Special needs 1.
Conditions accepted: D Diabetes ID Visual_Impair.
Features: Crafts Aquatics Archery Boating Canoe Climbing_Wall Fishing Hiking Kayak Ropes_Crse Sail Basketball Field_Hockey Soccer Swim Volleyball.
Fees 2014: Free. Res 1 wk.
Housing: Cabins. Avg per room/unit: 7. **Swimming:** Lake.
Est 1956. Nonprofit. **Ses:** 12. **Wks/ses:** 1. Operates June-Aug. ACA.

WLC offers separate camping sessions for children with visual, hearing or mild cognitive disabilities, and children with diabetes. All programs are offered free of charge to Wisconsin residents; nonresidents are admitted on a space-available basis after the deadline and pay a minimal fee. Typical camp activities include swimming, canoeing, sailing, boating, kayaking, fishing, archery, crafts, nature programs, sports and games. Older campers take canoeing and backpacking trips.

PROGRAM NAME INDEX

PROGRAM NAME INDEX

Program names are referenced by page number. Note that program names beginning with "Camp" are alphabetized under the next significant word in the Index.